Classical
Techniques and
Contemporary
Arguments

Classical Techniques and Contemporary Arguments

Elizabeth A. Stolarek
Ferris State University

Larry R. Juchartz
Mott Community College

PEARSON
Longman

New York San Francisco Boston
London Toronto Sydney Tokyo Singapore Madrid
Mexico City Munich Paris Cape Town Hong Kong Montreal

Publisher: Joseph Opiela
Senior Marketing Manager: Sandra McGuire
Production Manager: Denise Phillip
Project Coordination, Text Design, and Electronic Page Makeup: Electronic Publishing
    Services Inc., NYC
Cover Design/Manager: John Callahan
Cover Images: © PhotoDisc
Photo Researcher: Anita Dickhuth
Manufacturing Manager: Mary Fischer
Printer and Binder: R. R. Donnelley and Sons
Cover Printer: Phoenix Color Corporation

For permission to use copyrighted material, grateful acknowledgment is made to the
following copyright holders: Page 220: "Crush with Eyeliner" by William Thomas Berry,
Peter Lawrence Buck, Michael E. Mills, and John Michael Stipe. ©1994 Night Garden
Music (BMI). All rights on behalf of Night Garden Music (BMI) administered by Warner-
Tamerlane Publishing Corp. (BMI). All Rights Reserved. Used by Permission. Alfred
Publishing Co., Inc. Miami, Florida 33014; Page 222: "Thingmaker" by Scott Putesky.
© Dinger and Ollie Music. All rights reserved. Used by permission; Page 225: "Wherever I
May Roam," words and music by James Hetfield and Lars Ulrich. © 1991 Creeping Death
Music. Reprinted with permission; Page 226: "Damage, Inc.," words and music by James
Hetfield, Lars Ulrich, Kirk Hammett, and Cliff Burton. © 1986 Creeping Death Music.
Reprinted with permission.

Library of Congress Cataloging-in-Publication Data
Stolarek, Elizabeth A.
    Classical techniques and contemporary arguments / Elizabeth A. Stolarek ; Larry R. Juchartz.
        p. cm. — (Hardscrabble books)
    Includes index.
    ISBN 0-321-22718-2
    1. College readers.   2. English language—Rhetoric—Problems, exercises, etc.   3. Persua-
sion (Rhetoric)—Problems, exercises, etc.   4. Report writing—Problems, exercises, etc.
5. Critical thinking—Problems, exercises, etc.   I. Juchartz, Larry R.   II. Title.   III. Series.
PE1431.S76 2006
808'.0427—dc22

                                                                            2006002936

Please visit us at http://www.ablongman.com

ISBN 0-321-22718-2

2 3 4 5 6 7 8 9 10—DOC—09 08 07

With thanks to John Mellon, for Thad and Becky—and to Larry

For my students, with thanks to my family—and to Betty

Brief Contents

Detailed Contents

Preface for Instructors

The title of *Classical Techniques and Contemporary Arguments* makes clear our focus and purpose for this text, but our reasoning behind the project stems from many factors. English teachers and students have arrived at an age when the term "rhetoric"— the foundation of the "classical techniques" upon which we focus here—has in large part slipped into a two- and four-year political cycle of misuse, coming to mean "deception" if not outright lies to many Americans when they hear or see it used by various media sources (including the late-night TV comedians from whom millions of increasingly jaded citizens receive their news). This situation, coupled with a general climate of softened convictions in which many college students have learned from their previous schooling experience to write "informative" papers presenting both the "pro" and the "con" of a given issue, while avoiding any references to self or taking a side, leaves rhetoric standing somewhere in the shadows as something still practiced by many but examined by few. The contemporary arguments currently made by rhetoric's primary practitioners—advertisers, speechwriters, and (we hope) teachers—hold the key to a treasure box that remains locked to many of the people who are continually exposed to rhetoric's many nuanced workings. But as former teacher and current slam poet Taylor Mali has said, "It is not enough these days to simply question authority; you have to speak with it, too."

Of course, providing this key so that authority may be clearly and logically engaged is a goal for all writing textbooks, classes, and teachers. What's more, many students with a grasp of theory will come to see, in their college courses, how their "informative" and neutral papers in years past were actually argumentative in nature, and how a politician's shifting message, depending on the region or forum from which the message is delivered, is not lying to but rather *reading* the audience. Still, a central problem remains: If a high school paper's ultimate argument is only that its writer has informed the reader about Topic X in a suitably neutral fashion (per the audience/teacher's instructions), and if a politician's many campaign pledges ultimately are intended to gather votes rather than to express strong and genuine convictions (contrary to the audience/citizen's hopes), then what is the point of knowing what the classical techniques of rhetoric are and how they work? By these examples, rhetoric can appear to be primarily a manifestation of power applied and power obeyed—and of an authority that in certain political contexts will simply refuse to entertain questions. This is all the more reason, perhaps, for a society to become more disinterested in, and detached from, the endless rhetorical engagements taking place within its culture.

Thus, a renewed emphasis on classical rhetorical techniques, offering an immersion in some of rhetoric's rich history, its changing definitions and applications, and its continuing uses as not just an "art of persuasion" but as a way of thinking about and seeing reality, seems particularly useful at a time when families, schools, governmental systems, the natural environment, and relationships with the world community are all in transition and the stream of information about those changes can become overwhelming without a way to process it clearly. In this, *Classical Techniques and Contemporary Arguments* is at its core a guide to the thorough interrogation of issues through applications of the composing process that begin, and end, with "thinking critically"—a term that we have come to see as "thinking *rhetorically*"—an ability that remains one of the key factors for students' success both in and beyond school.

Our main challenge in assembling this book has been to avoid mapping out a single, tightly defined semester in rhetoric and composition, with sixteen weekly "units" all built upon the ones before. Rather, we have strived to offer our readers a wealth of material that is infinitely flexible according to instructors' professional preferences and their students' growing confidence levels and demonstrated abilities with the material. We do not assume that the main sections of this book should or will necessarily be followed chronologically, although such a syllabus would certainly work. We do not expect instructors to cover every section, assign every writing exercise, or explore every rhetorical concept in the same depth with students, although a rigorous and ambitious two-semester sequence would likely be able to do just that. Some instructors will want to spend weeks on each writing assignment, with plenty of reading and discussion as the writing's context; other instructors will prefer a faster pace with more papers and fewer readings, perhaps geared toward a final writing portfolio. We believe that because of *Classical Techniques and Contemporary Arguments*'s flexible structure and abundant content, any instructional preference and teaching methodology can be accommodated by this primary text.

As an introduction to rhetoric itself, *Classical Techniques and Contemporary Arguments* is built with the same flexibility in mind, combined with an approach to the subject matter that is direct without being simplistic. Given our intended audience of undergraduate students who may not have encountered many of the histories, principles, and methods covered by the text, we have endeavored to provide instructors with a book that engages their students by linking contemporary issues of varying complexity to rhetorical concepts of manageable scope and depth. One example of this is Chapter 6, in which we invite students to consider the notion of "selling out" in contemporary music. In order to sell out, an artist must have betrayed some genuine or authentic state of musicianship. And while many instructors may be familiar with a wide range of scholarship that has explored—and debunked—notions of "authenticity," *students* do not have that same familiarity with the same theories. For students, "sellouts" are very real people to be found not just in music, but in many other spheres of influence, ranging from the family dining room to the corporate board room and beyond.

Successful pedagogy is focused on both the presentation and the reception of ideas in students' terms from students' lives. Rhetoric can be a dead elephant in the writing classroom, or it can be a vibrant, living thing with a history reaching back to real people who struggled to make sense of the day's issues in the same ways that students and their teachers struggle today. In our quest to make rhetoric the latter rather than the former, we have tried whenever possible to address it in a fast-paced, accessible style unencumbered by the historical minutiae that may delight and infuriate us as professors at a professional conference, but which could easily overwhelm and alienate students in what many colleges see as an undergraduate "service course" called composition. However, we have also tried to infuse the discussions with energy sufficient to spark curiosity for students intending to major in a communication-related field or to take advanced coursework in such an area.

Toward this end, *Classical Techniques and Contemporary Arguments* stresses that the so-called "rhetorical modes" are not—as other texts often artificially present them—separate writing and/or thinking strategies; rather, they are choices to be *examined* so that they can later be *applied,* in combination, when writing about issues in a way that creates a fully developed composition employing numerous strategies appealing to an audience's interaction with the message. Too often, composition courses are merely sites for the steady production of disconnected and insignificant "papers"—cause/effect for Paper 1, compare/contrast for Paper 2, and so on—when in fact discursive modes have the most value when their *interconnectedness* and their *continual* availability as writing/communicating strategies are made clear. Accordingly, the model essays and articles in *Classical Techniques and Contemporary Arguments* are issue-oriented rather than "mode"-based, and they have been selected to pose compelling yet arguable positions to specific audiences. Each chapter also provides a comprehensive introduction to students wherein they receive an explanation of specific argument styles in terms of their uses within rhetorical/discursive practice. Additionally, the prose models in *Classical Techniques and Contemporary Arguments* are followed by explication focused on the rhetorical elements of the piece and on ways students can borrow the same strategies for application in their own arguments and critical interrogations. Finally, by including explanations of such rhetorical concepts as "dialectic," "appeals," "commonplaces," and "ideologies" as context toward enhanced student understanding of how rhetoric functions within argument, this book will help students understand argument as being much more than simply "having an opinion."

Because our text is admittedly different from many of the "rhetorics" (textbooks) currently available for composition, we are also aware that some readers may search without success for clear signs of a specific genre: Is *Classical Techniques and Contemporary Arguments* a classic how-to for argumentation, a guide to prose modeling, a primer in dialectic? The book is a hybrid of each of these, and more. For instructors who revel in argument and its intellectual rigors, we have included a great deal of discussion, along with many readings and prose models, of that form of discourse. For instructors who would like their students to focus intently on the choices, strategies, and techniques writers have available, we have included many sections on prose modeling. For dialecticians, we have tried to address the ever-lowering levels of students' critical thinking ability decried by many college teachers and workplace professionals. As a symptom of postmodernity, many current composition texts tend to ignore dialectic—the search for truth accomplished through structured dialogue. Many may argue the relevance of dialectic in a pluralistic society, and while we agree that there is much to be praised in postmodern perspectives on "truth," we nonetheless see dialectic as an important factor in the process of developing argumentative skills. Yet we serve that statement with a caveat: Proper instruction in dialectic is intended to teach students not *what* to think, but rather *how* to think. One of the major accomplishments students can gain from a writing course is an enhanced ability to view their own written ideas and the ideas of others in a critical fashion. By learning to think dialectically about the subject at hand, they can read closely the arguments of others, identify and label the strong aspects of that discourse, analyze an argument in terms of its rhetorical construction and functions, and then apply all of these rhetorical skills to their own writing—and to the formation of their own positions on issues.

In addition to our belief in the powers of dialectic, much of our research and pedagogical experimentation through the years has focused on another technique of classical rhetoric commonly ignored in current composition texts: Prose-modeling. In keeping with the classical sequence of instruction in rhetoric proposed by Cicero, Quintilian, and others, we begin our text with a chapter on imitation. We are convinced that this skill can be incorporated into the writing classroom to help students become skilled and confident writers by developing their metacognitive skills as they attempt to compose in discursive forms that are unfamiliar to them. Expert writers are more likely to behave in a self-conscious and self-critical manner while composing, and contrary to a commonly held opinion that prose-modeling inhibits the creative process, we have seen in our classrooms and our research how prose-modeling facilitates such metacognitive responses while also facilitating creativity.

We have long sought a textbook that incorporates discussion of rhetoric, dialectic, and the prose-modeling process in a way that engages student interest and invites them to participate actively in classroom pedagogy, while also inviting instructional decisions on the ways that the text can best be applied. We have written *Classical Techniques and Contemporary Arguments* to address this need. Thus, in designing *Classical Techniques and Contemporary Arguments,* we have intentionally included options and opportunities for instructional autonomy. For example, we discuss deductive argument only after completely discussing inductive, thus accommodating instructors' preferences for either a straightforward inductive or a more comprehensive approach. Most useful and practical applications here are intentionally left "open" this way, rather than fixed. We suspect this comes from our own tendency, as teachers, to "change up" on our methodologies from one year or semester to the next, in the interests of preventing boredom and routine from infecting our pedagogy, our classrooms, and worst of all, our students. Realistically, though, it is not feasible to also change textbooks incessantly—there is a certain comfort and accompanying confidence that comes with knowing a book well and using it long. Yet many textbooks do not offer enough flexibility to allow instructors to follow differing sequences or applications; to choose, modify, or disregard writing assignments; or to select or ignore readings depending upon the length of a semester or the makeup of a class. With *Classical Techniques and Contemporary Arguments,* we have tried to make up for these shortcomings by offering more material than one semester's worth of writing instruction can realistically handle, while also hoping to keep the surplus of materials from being a waste of students' money or a burden in their backpacks.

Acknowledgments

This preface would not be complete without the acknowledgment of many without whose help and support *Classical Techniques and Contemporary Arguments* would never have come about.

We thank our colleagues at Mott Community College who assisted us in preparing the supplemental materials for this text: Christy Rishoi, Kim Owens, Karen Janness, and Connie Johnston.

For support and extraordinary assistance, we thank the following from the College of Arts and Sciences at Ferris State University: Matt Klein, Reinhold Hill, Roxanne Cullen, Gayle Driggers, and Deb Vance.

For editorial assistance throughout the process of preparing the book, we especially thank Joseph Opiela, Brandon Hight, Susan Kunchandy, and Rebecca Gilpin at Longman and Lisa Kinne at Electronic Publishing Services Inc.

For guiding us through the intricacies and challenges of the permissions process, we thank Wesley Hall.

We thank our reviewers, whose insights and suggestions were invaluable in directing our course: Gail Chesson, Wake Technical Community College; Susan Fanetti, Southern Illinois University; Mary French, University of Texas at Arlington; Ruth Gerik, University of Texas at Arlington; Robert C. Gowdy, University of Mississippi; Andrea Kaitany, Grand Valley State University; Erin E. Kelly, Nazareth College; Jill A. Lahnstein, Cape Fear Community College; and Susie Crowson, Del Mar College.

Elizabeth A. Stolarek
Ferris State University

Larry R. Juchartz
Mott Community College

Preface for Students

The first bit of good news about this preface is that it's not very long. The second is that we're not going to tell you what you already know about writing and verbal communication: That these are vital "skills" for "success" in college and the workplace that will make you feel "empowered" when you know how to use them in an "effective" way.

Instead, let's talk about all of those "scare quotes" in the previous paragraph—this piece of paper's equivalent to putting two hands in the air and curling the second and third fingers twice while saying a word or phrase. Have you ever thought about the *rhetoric* that people are using when they wrap a word with those markers? When you see a scare-quoted word on the page, or when you see someone's fingers wrap it in the air, you know this is the equivalent of inserting the words, "so-called," before it. And when something is "so-called," then it's subject to debate. A set of scare quotes is shorthand for an otherwise lengthy explanation. If you write, *Recently, the college decided to stop sending paper transcripts and to post all grades to a "convenient" and "time-saving" Web portal,* your readers will understand immediately that you disagree with the two marked concepts.

With those two sets of scare quotes, you've set up reader expectations. They know that you intend to challenge the concepts. And when you follow that sentence with another—"Of course, this assumes that the Web server will never crash, that everyone has access to a fast cable modem, and that most students remember their passwords"—you fulfill those expectations. By identifying the assumptions that your school has made, you've made your position clear on the potential problems with technology. In terms of traditional composition, you've *introduced* an idea, *developed* it with *support,* and identified a clearly implied *thesis* for your argument. But in terms of rhetoric, you've set an idea (the school's recent decision) before your readers, given them a moment between sentences to consider their own opinions about the idea ("That's a good decision," or "That decision could cause problems"), and then delivered your own opinion as a point of reference for theirs. Now the readers evaluate the idea anew, fully engaging with you out of pleasure ("Yes—it's good to see someone challenging technology") or surprise ("What? How can technology be a negative thing?").

The pleased readers will likely sit back and enjoy the rest of the ride through your argument as you continue making it. And wouldn't it be great if this were always the case? But there are others, those who have been surprised, have already started to formulate their *counterarguments* and *objections.* Worse still, they're objecting on a point-by-point basis:

- The school has a triple-backup server configuration. Servers will fail only if the whole city's electricity goes out. That's a rare event.
- Fast modems are available from any campus building—and even off-campus, the Web pages containing student grades have been designed with only a few graphics so they will load quickly.
- Students who forget their passwords can click on a "Forgotten Password" link, and the information will be e-mailed to them within minutes.

You might start to feel overwhelmed now, as if a tank has rolled down the street to crush the slingshot you held up. If so, a small revision in thinking can make a huge difference. Instead of having written earlier, "*Worse* still, they're objecting on a point-by-point basis," we could have written, "*Better* still . . . ." By looking at argument as a challenge rather than a task, it stops being work to complete and becomes an opportunity to enjoy. You *anticipate,* and then *refute,* those objections while also finding *common ground* with any aspects of the readers' opposition that make good sense to you. For good measure, you even throw in a little bit of *expert testimony* to back up your rebuttal to the counterargument.

So jump in:

- It's good that the school had the foresight to install a triple-backup system before moving all grades to an online-only basis. (Now let's just hope that no bad storms blow through and knock out the city's power.)
- *However,* when it comes to fast-loading pages, the number of graphics a page contains is only a small part of the picture. As Microsoft Corporation's Web site explains, "factors may reduce either the transmission speed or the number of times that you successfully obtain the highest speed connection. For example, old lines, or lines that are subject to interference, might reduce transmission speeds."
- *Furthermore,* depending on how many spam filters and virus checkers are set up between the school's server and the student's home Internet provider, a password reminder could arrive hours, not minutes, after it's requested.
- *Therefore,* although cost savings for the college are important, the school should at least make paper transcripts an option for students who prefer them to electronic versions.

Do you still see your idea as merely a slingshot going up against a tank? Not likely. And to think, all of this came from two sets of scare quotes—and the rhetoric behind them.

The whole process you've seen unfold is just part of what we mean by *rhetoric,* and by using this book, you'll not only learn more about what that is, but also be able to use it in a deliberate, considered way as an essential part of your composing process. Yes, communication skills are, in fact, vital for success in college and the workplace, but *Classical Techniques and Contemporary Arguments* will encourage you to challenge even the common definitions of "success." Is success just attaining an entry-level corporate position and being able to buy the material trappings that announce the attainment? Most commercial interests wouldn't mind a bit if you used that rather hollow definition. Is success a school transcript (paper or electronic) showing a cumulative grade point average above 2.0 at graduation, or is it the act of graduating?

With this book, we'd like to argue that success is the ability to analyze the meaning of "success." And rhetoric is a key tool in getting there.

Real, good writing happens by applying rhetorical techniques in complex combination and addressing issues in a fully developed message that invites readers' interaction with what they're reading. And remember, that's just the first stage of the process. All writing instructors know that there are far more rules about writing than the average writer can remember easily, especially when there's only a sixteen-week semester in which to learn them. But often, the rules that worry students most are the ones about *editing:* Don't use fragments, don't use comma splices, don't write sentences that are all the same length and kind, don't misspell, don't forget to indent. (These are just a few of the more basic editing concerns, of course.)

But what we propose in this book is that you let the editing go until the last stage of the writing process, after all of the *content* of the communication is as detailed, supported, and fully *voiced* as you can make it by applying what you learn about rhetoric. (After all, if you take time to correct the spelling and grammar in two paragraphs that you ultimately delete from the paper, haven't you wasted valuable time?)

The many writing samples in this book will show you not only how writers write about argumentative issues, but also how they *think* about these issues through the act of writing. By focusing on structures of the writing as well as the strategies for examining the topics as you compose, we're confident that you will come away with an enhanced capacity for arguing—and communicating—in the new century.

Elizabeth A. Stolarek
Ferris State University

Larry R. Juchartz
Mott Community College

Section I

Tools for Argumentative Writing

CHAPTER I

Recognizing Situation and Strategy

"I like your paper; it's really good."

This is a comment we've heard thousands of times over the years in our classrooms as we've observed peer-group feedback sessions, where students distribute copies of their drafts and read their papers aloud to the group. Unfortunately, we sometimes hear another statement added to it: "I don't want to read mine now. It stinks."

If that sounds like something you've ever said or thought about your own writing, then this chapter will help to turn your dissatisfaction into confidence. And even if you're already a confident writer who generally receives positive comments about your drafts, you'll gain an enhanced understanding of what makes your writing have an impact on readers. Long ago, early teachers of **rhetoric** had their students begin their educations in the rhetorical arts by analyzing—and then imitating—speeches that were particularly moving and memorable. By memorizing a speech and imitating its oration, those students learned styles of message delivery for specific occasions, such as funerals, legal appeals, and political causes.

Defining Rhetoric

Rhetoric: the art of effective communication. The study of rhetoric examines all elements that are necessary to make communication persuasive to a reader or listener.

Although imitation was criticized in the twentieth century by a few composition theorists who claimed that imitating someone else's writing inspired no originality or creativity, our experience as both teachers and writers has shown how imitation is an important—even crucial—stepping stone on the way to composing confident, well-crafted, and fully original writing. For this reason, we begin this text as those early rhetoricians began their instruction—with a twenty-first century version of the same imitation process learned by those students long ago, but applied to writing.

To begin, think of a good piece of writing as something that can be read and followed almost like a set of blueprints in construction, or a schematic in electronics. Blueprints and schematics are basically forms to be followed: here's where the roof ties in with the outer wall; here's where the yellow wire connects to the circuit board. With sample writings, in addition to looking for the areas where authors have placed their papers' various features, you can also take note of the deliberately chosen ways—or *strategies*—in which the authors place those features. In determining the best strategies, writers are being rhetorical, and by studying the structure of a model closely, you can gain a new approach to and understanding of the many intricate features of writing and rhetoric.

For example, if the sample paper's statement of central focus (often referred to as a *thesis* in composition) appears in the beginning of the third paragraph, following two paragraphs of introduction to the general subject matter, then you realize that the thesis can appear in the same place if your own paper also requires a longer introduction. Many writers go through extreme contortions to pack both an introduction to a paper's subject matter and the paper's specific thesis into one brief opening paragraph. This may have met the writing requirements of earlier grades, but it usually presents a problem for readers of more mature papers, who expect to see issues developed much more fully. And meeting readers' expectations is a key aspect of good writing.

But writers also need to examine the structure of the paper carefully. What *kind* of introduction is in the model? Does it tell a personal story? Does it ask questions? Does it set out a case study—a short description of something that happened to a particular group in a particular place? Whatever that introduction does as its main strategy is what you can do in setting up your own main focus or thesis.

Using Imitation to Recognize Situation and Strategy: What Stephen King Can Tell Us

One writer whose choices and strategies have been extremely successful is Stephen King, the famous author of dozens of best-selling novels. Because King has been interviewed thousands of times about his characters, plots, settings, and techniques for frightening readers, when we had an opportunity to speak with him we used the time to discuss writing in general. Early in the conversation, the topic turned to the overall quality of the writing appearing in published fiction, a subject that in turn led to a discussion of imitation writing.

King: If you look at American pop-cult fiction, you see a lot of people who are just all over the map as far as their diction goes. But when you look at British pop-cult fiction, the diction is perfect—because all of those [writers] had Latin in school. In

---

Reprinted by permission of Stephen King.

Latin, you learn where everything goes, what everything means, and how to build a sentence. It's like teaching a mason how to build a perfect wall: here's where the bricks go, here's where the mortar goes. So once you learn those basics, you can do anything you want to do.

CTCA: We're reminded of an article you wrote for the *Writer's Handbook,* about a basketball game you reviewed back in high school. You'd already polished your syntax and diction, but then someone got you to trim the extra fat from your sentences.

King: Exactly. He was an editor at the local weekly paper. It was a sidebar piece about a basketball game where a guy had broken a record, and the editor clipped off all of my purple prose. He just said, "This is junk"—and he was right. It's like when a guy comes up to you and says, "Hey, you've got a ping under the hood of your literary car, so let's take up the hood and fix it."

CTCA: Our own writing styles have been influenced by reading people like you and a variety of other major authors, and at times the effect is that, after reading a novel by a particular writer, the next thing we write sounds just like that. Does this ever happen to you?

King: Sure. It's something that happens to a lot of writers, and I'm one of them. I'm like milk in the refrigerator; I take the flavor of whatever I'm next to.

CTCA: Several composition teachers and theorists promote the use of close imitation as a way for students to enhance their writing abilities. We've assigned it to our students, and while not everyone can stay as close to the original structure as expected, they come up with some really fine ideas.

King: It's like learning haiku. The form is so iron-clad: syllable for syllable, line for line. It's like pouring gelatin into a rabbit mold, isn't it? You're always going to get a rabbit. Of course, the main artist is the one who made the mold, but as an exercise for writers, that kind of imitation is great.

Studying the Structure, Getting a Sense

In the 1800s, a young slave named Frederick Douglass, who would go on to be remembered as one of the greatest orators of his century, taught himself to read and write through a number of ingenious ways. One of those ways, involving considerable risk to Douglass's safety, is described in his *Narrative of the Life of Fredrick Douglass:*

> . . . My little Master Thomas had gone to school and learned how to write, and had written over a number of copy-books. These had been brought home and shown to some of our near neighbors, and then laid aside. My mistress used to go to class meeting at the Wilk Street meeting house every Monday afternoon and leave me to take care of the house. When left thus, I used to spend the time in writing in the spaces left in Master Thomas's copy-book, copying what he had written. I continued to do this until I could write a hand very similar to that of Master Thomas. Thus, after a long, tedious effort for years, I finally succeeded in learning how to write.

In doing this, Douglass was performing the most basic form of imitation—paying careful attention to forms provided by someone else and crafting his own skills and knowledge while imitating those forms.

More recently, on the ABC television show *Whose Line Is It, Anyway?*, a recurring musical segment asked the show's regular performers to sing about a random topic announced by the audience. The songs were improvised on the spot, making them enough of a challenge for the performers already, but then the show's host, Drew Carey, added that the song should be sung in a particular *style* (country, Broadway musical, and hip-hop were favorites). The performers, all comedians, were not trained singers and had never specialized in any of these styles, yet they knew instantly what kind of rhythm, vocabulary, and vocal inflections to employ for the assigned skits because they had heard musicians singing in these styles. The *Whose Line* regulars were imitating what they'd heard.

As a college student you have more than just words and sounds to use as models; you have whole ideas that can come to you by looking carefully at the style and content of other writers' texts. Here, for instance, is a letter we received from a music magazine's billing department regarding a subscription that was still two months from expiring:

Dear Subscriber,
     That's right, it's serious, and we're down to the wire here. We made a deal. You haven't come through on your end yet.
     You won't feel good about stiffing us, will you? It's not something your friends will think you're cool for, is it?
     No, indeed. Those days are over. Integrity is in now. Ripping off is tacky. So you're forcing us to say:
     IF WE DON'T RECEIVE YOUR PAYMENT, WE WILL BE FORCED TO SUSPEND YOUR SUBSCRIPTION. NO MORE COPIES UNTIL YOU PAY.

Sincerely,
C. T. Rogers, Billing Manager
P.S. Bruce Springsteen pays *his* bills.
P.P.S. Needless to say, if you have already sent in payment, please disregard this letter and accept our thanks.

As we read the letter, we noticed several things: its very short sentences; its attempt to sound "cool" and unbusinesslike with phrasing like "down to the wire," "come through," "stiffing us," and "ripping off"; and its use of a second postscript to prevent causing any offense. But because that postscript came so late in the letter—*after* we had already been accused of "stiffing" and "ripping off" the magazine—it was not effective. We were already offended, and so we composed a response using the same overall tone, style, and structure of the letter to which we were replying:

Dear Mr/s. Rogers,
     Nice try. You thought your letter would be effective, and it was. But not in the way you thought.

Stiff you? Never. Our current subscription is good for two more months, and we saw no need to rush payment for an extension that hadn't begun yet.

Indeed, money's tight these days. Paying for something too far in advance is silly. So you've forced us to respond:

WHEN YOU SEND SARCASTIC LETTERS TO SUBSCRIBERS, YOU MAKE THEM ANGRY. OUR FIRST REACTION WAS TO TELL YOU TO CANCEL THE SUBSCRIPTION, BUT WE'D ALREADY SENT A CHECK TO YOU FIVE DAYS EARLIER. SO DUMP THE WISE-GUY APPROACH. IT DOESN'T WORK.

Sincerely,
Your Loyal Subscribers
P.S. We pay our bills, too. Just like Bruce Springsteen.
P.P.S. Of course, if you've already sent an apology, please disregard this letter and accept our forgiveness.

When you perform an imitation exercise such as the one above, you engage in a process that one composition teacher, Cheryl Glenn, has described as "becom[ing] increasingly sophisticated . . . some of the steps in the process are identical to those stressed in writing classes: attending to the rhetorical situation, following conventions, building a persuasive argument." Adapting to a model text's structure and ideas can strongly influence the creative process as well, as shown in this comparison of the following passages:

> **Original:** The only way to know if you're experiencing true love or not is to test for it. Will a woman who "loves" her new hair style weep in agony if it gets undone in the rain? Will a man who "loves" cigars sob uncontrollably if his cigar goes out and won't re-light? Will my parents cry if the band goes on strike in the middle of a waltz? Maybe. They really love to dance.
>
> **Student Imitation 1:** The best way to find out if you have a real friendship is to answer these questions: Is your friend never around when you need him? Does he tell others your personal and private thoughts? Does your friend keep making jokes about you even when he knows that they hurt you?
>
> **Student Imitation 2:** Courage is personal. Will the world come to a stop if I can't find the courage to jump out of the barn loft into the hay? No. But will I feel better and stronger if I do? Yes. So it comes to this: Jump and take a chance on getting hurt, or stay put and never know what flying feels like.

Let's take a moment to examine the key similarities between the original passage and the two imitations. (Note the terms in italics here; they're your keys to success when you perform your own analysis.) *Structurally*, all of the passages rely on the use of questions—although each author has chosen to use those questions in a different way. *Visually*, each of the three passages is roughly the same length and contains a similar word count. *Thematically*, each of the passages tries to define an abstract term—love, friendship, courage—through concrete examples. And *stylistically*, each of the passages takes on a warm, personal tone that engages the reader through the use of *I* or *you*.

> **LOOKING CRITICALLY** What are the differing effects of the ways in which each of the three writers above has used questions to define what love, friendship, and courage are—and are not?

Student Writing: Imitation

When asked to comment about the role imitation can play in their overall writing process, our students have offered the following reactions. Notice how the emphasis is on the *thinking* aspect of the larger composing process, rather than on the mechanics of writing itself:

- While doing this imitation, I noticed several things about the writing. It employs a lot of descriptive words, and the sentences are often very complex. Sometimes one adjective relates to many different things in the sentence, so I had to be really careful about the words I chose.

- It makes you think more about how to structure your sentences.

- Writing this way was like stepping out of my skin and into another writer's. I was really impressed by what I'd written, and all I had to do was imitate the form. But don't get me wrong—I had to do some intense thinking for this assignment!

- I had to use my imagination to create a different setting for the story I wanted to tell. Looking at the original author's style helped me to see where I could write in a more vivid and precise way for my readers.

- I wrote sentences I never even knew existed. I've never written such elaborate idea connections before, or used so many descriptive words. And this is the first time I've ever used dashes to emphasize an idea. Now I finally know how they work!

Having seen earlier how a brief paragraph can be imitated, take a look now at a full-length work attributed* to Chief Seattle, a nineteenth-century Suquamish (Duwamish) Indian. Following the reading are comments offered by students who have used this text as the basis for imitation writing.

Chief Seattle's Letter to President Pierce, 1855

We know that the white man does not understand our ways. One portion of the land is the same to him as the next, for he is a stranger who comes

---

*The authenticity of Seattle's letter has been questioned. See "Thus Spoke Chief Seattle: The Story of An Undocumented Speech" by Jerry L. Clark in *Prologue* magazine, U.S. National Archives & Records Administration, Spring 1985, Vol. 18, No. 1.

in the night and takes from the land whatever he needs. The earth is not his brother, but his enemy, and when he has conquered it, he moves on. He leaves his father's graves, and his children's birthright is forgotten. The sight of your cities pains the eyes of the red man. But perhaps it is because the red man is a savage and does not understand.

There is no quiet place in the white man's cities. No place to hear the leaves of spring or the rustle of insects' wings. But perhaps because I am a savage and do not understand, the clatter only seems to insult the ears. The Indian prefers the soft sound of the wind darting over the face of the pond, the smell of the wind itself cleansed by a midday rain, or scented with the *piñon* pine. The air is precious to the red man. For all things share the same breath—the beasts, the trees, the man. Like a man dying for many days, he is numb to the stench.

What is man without the beasts? If all the beasts were gone, men would die from great loneliness of spirit, for whatever happens to the beasts also happens to man. All things are connected. Whatever befalls the earth befalls the sons of the earth.

It matters little where we pass the rest of our days; they are not many. A few more hours, a few more winters, and none of the children of the great tribes that once lived on this earth, or that roamed in small bands in the woods, will be left to mourn the graves of a people once as powerful and hopeful as yours.

5   The whites, too, shall pass—perhaps sooner than other tribes. Continue to contaminate your bed, and you will one night suffocate in your own waste. When the buffalo are all slaughtered, the wild horses all tamed, the secret corners of the forest heavy with the scent of many men, and the view of the ripe hills blotted by talking [telegraph] wires, where is the thicket? Gone. Where is the eagle? Gone. And what is it to say goodbye to the swift and the hunt, the end of living and the beginning of survival? We might understand if we knew what it was that the white man dreams, what he describes to his children on the long winter nights, what visions he burns into their minds, so they will wish for tomorrow. But we are savages. The white man's dreams are hidden from us.

Students who have imitated Chief Seattle's letter have offered a variety of responses to the assignment. Through their responses, you'll notice that imitation not only offers you the same choices provided by any writing assignment, but it also goes further by providing inspiration and direction that can sometimes be slower to appear in a typical writing situation.

- This writer's sentences were much shorter than ones I typically use, but he was clear and specific in his word choice. To get this paper done, I typed out the original article, triple-spaced it, and wrote my imitation between the lines. This helped me to stay close to the original author's sentence structure. Before doing this assignment I thought I could only write in one style, but I noticed that the form of the original text was very good and different from mine as I imitated it.

- Imitation—I didn't like the sound of that word! I liked writing in my own, self-important way. At least that's how I felt when the assignment began, but then I was surprised when the imitation took a path all its own! The original article had a sorrowful feel to it; an Indian was pleading for his land. As I wrote, I seemed to be pleading for more understanding through my narration of my actions. What happened is that by imitating Chief Seattle, I discovered something about myself. It's nice to realize that I don't have to be limited in my writing by self-imposed restrictions!

- The way Chief Seattle wrote about white men reminded me of the way I'd heard a friend talk about her boyfriend, the way I'm sure every woman has felt toward a man at least once in her life. As I wrote my paper, instead of humbling myself, like Seattle did, I turned it around and made the woman better than the man.

- At first I was torn between imitating the original author's style and trying to incorporate my own ideas. But Chief Seattle's letter stirred feelings in me, and I wanted to write an imitation that would show my empathy for the Indians and serve as a sign of rebellion. So I chose to write about how it feels to be disabled. I didn't want to write a depressing piece, though, so I tried to write about living with hope and how that hope can help to make disabled people like me feel whole.

- I found Seattle's style very emotional and effective. Every person in my workshop group who chose to imitate Seattle had the same feeling from reading it. It gave a sad, depressing feeling, so I ran with that. Then I happened to watch an episode of Oprah Winfrey's show that dealt with obesity, so being overweight became the theme of my paper when I wrote my imitation.

From her perception of the original text's feeling and her stroke of good luck in finding more inspiration for a topic from Oprah Winfrey, this last student's imitation turned out to be a powerful statement on the superficiality that can plague modern culture. Here is the text of her imitation:

```
           Hidden (An Imitation of Chief Seattle)
                         by Phyllis
      I know that plastic surgery will not change my
insecurities. One blemish on the outside is the same as one on
the inside, and I am the same as anyone who comes with an
imperfection so I cover my appearance whenever I can. My body is
not my pride, but my embarrassment, and all of my best qualities
are hidden. One glimpse of myself in the mirror crushes every
```

hope I had. And this in turn reinforces my low self-esteem and lack of optimism.

I am never content in my body or mind. I have no strength to stand up for myself and show what I feel inside. Because of my weak self-image and deep pessimism, fighting to stand out just makes me feel more weak. The beautiful have lovely soft skin and their clothes wrap around their bodies perfectly, whether a shapely red dress that a size-two woman wears or a trimly tailored suit that a man models. Their appearance is crucial for their mental health. But I share that same problem—my body, its image, its style. Like a teenaged girl suffering from an eating disorder, I am obsessed with my appearance.

What's the problem if a person carries a little more weight? If everyone were a little larger, no one would feel unattractive, because how would we criticize someone else when we look the same? The insults we heap on others affect all of us eventually.

If it's not dangerous, then it doesn't matter how much extra weight we carry; weight is only a number. A little less dessert, a little more exercise, and the pounds will gradually wear away. But that will not mend my suffering heart, nor ease the pain I feel as I walk among thinner people, for it can only change my *outside*—which is only a cover for my true beauty and personality.

The thin, too, will die—maybe even sooner than I will. Continue to discriminate against others, and their children will not learn to respect others either. When every large person's self-image is poor, all of the insults grow stronger, the weak and unattractive are shunned even more, and our view of the future is bleeding with scornful sores, then where is the love? Dead. Where is the kindness? Dead. And what happens when people hurt one another because of appearance? The end of connection and the beginning of cruelty. I might feel differently if I ever knew what it felt like to be thin, what it feels like to be popular, so that I too could feel pride. But I am overweight. My true beauty and personality remain hidden inside.

Of course, not everyone enjoys or appreciates imitation writing as much as these students have, and possibilities for topics, tone, and other writing strategies can sometimes elude even the most determined writer. Even so, notice how one student was able to use her frustration over a topic that *wouldn't* fit the form to arrive at a unique topic that *did* fit perfectly:

> This is officially the toughest assignment I've ever had! I racked my brain for days and I wasn't writing what I wanted to say. What I originally wanted to write would not fit into the form that I was trying to imitate. Finally I got so frustrated that I turned this letter from a sad Indian to President Pierce into an angry student writing about teachers who oppress students with assignments like this one.

TECHNIQUES FOR WRITERS 1-a

Imitating the Classics

The following are excerpts of the writing of five well-known authors. Choose one excerpt to imitate, substituting different subject matter. In your imitation, strive to reproduce the feel of the author's writing—his or her way with language. The names of the authors and titles of their works follow the excerpts.

1. He was systematic, but to say he thought and acted like a machine would be to misunderstand the nature of his thought. It was not like pistons and wheels and gears all moving at once, massive and coordinated. The image of a laser beam comes to mind instead; a single pencil of light of such terrific energy in such extreme concentration it can be shot at the moon and its reflection seen back on earth. Phaedrus did not try to use his brilliance for general illumination. He sought one specific distant target and aimed for it and hit it. And that was all. General illumination of that target he hit now seems to be left for me.

2. Anything that happens after this party breaks up is nothing. Everything is now. It's like war. Everyone is handsome, shining just thinking about other people's blood. As though the red wash flying from veins not theirs is facial makeup patented for its glow. Inspiriting. Glamorous. Afterward there will be some chatter and recapitulation of what went on; nothing though like the action itself and the beat that pumps the heart. In war or at a party everyone is wily, intriguing; goals are set and altered; alliances rearranged. Partners and rivals devastated; new pairings triumphant. The knockout possibilities knock Dorcas out because here—with grown-ups and as in war—people play for keeps.

3. My nerves vibrated to those low-spoken words as they had never vibrated to thunder—my blood felt their subtle violence as it had

never felt frost or fire; but I was collected, and in no danger of swooning. I looked at Mr. Rochester; I made him look at me. His whole face was colourless rock; his eye was both spark and flint. He disavowed nothing: he seemed as if he would defy all things. Without speaking, without smiling, without seeming to recognize in me a human being, he only twined my waist with his arm and riveted me to his side.

4. "What should we drink?" the girl asked. She had taken off her hat and put it on the table.

"It's pretty hot," the man said.

"Let's drink beer."

"Dos cervezas," the man said into the curtain.

"Big ones?" a woman asked from the doorway.

"Yes. Two big ones."

The woman brought two glasses of beer and two felt pads. She put the felt pads and the beer glasses on the table and looked at the man and the girl. The girl was looking off at the line of hills. They were white in the sun and the country was brown and dry.

5. No doubt I grew *very* pale;—but I talked more fluently, and with a heightened voice. Yet the sound increased—and what could I do? It was *a low, dull, quick sound—much such a sound as a watch makes when enveloped in cotton.* I gasped for breath—and yet the officers heard it not. I talked more quickly—more vehemently; but the noise steadily increased. I arose and argued about trifles, in a high key and with violent gesticulations, but the noise steadily increased. Why *would* they not be gone? I paced the floor to and fro with heavy strides, as if excited to fury by the observation of the men—but the noise steadily increased. Oh God! What *could* I do? I foamed—I raved—I swore! I swung the chair upon which I had been sitting, and grated it upon the boards, but the noise arose over all and continually increased. It grew louder—louder—*louder*! And still the men chatted pleasantly, and smiled. Was it possible they heard not? Almighty God!—no, no! They heard!—they suspected!—they *knew*!—they were making a mockery of my horror!—this I thought, and this I think. But any thing was better than this agony! Any thing was more tolerable than this derision! I could bear those hypocritical smiles no longer! I felt that I must scream or die!—and now—again!—hark! louder! louder! louder! louder!—

1. Robert M. Pirsig, *Zen and the Art of Motorcycle Maintenance*
2. Toni Morrison, *Jazz*
3. Charlotte Brontë, *Jane Eyre*
4. Ernest Hemingway, "Hills Like White Elephants"
5. Edgar Allan Poe, "The Tell-Tale Heart"

Student Writing: Using the Nuts and Bolts of Close Imitation

Now that you have a good understanding of what imitation is, it's time to dig deeper into the actual process of imitating a piece of writing. Have a careful look at the following full-length essay by one student, Jehlen, and the imitation of that essay that follows it by another student, Matt. Try to absorb not only the writing style of Jehlen's original, but also the feeling of sadness and emptiness it conveys in describing a dying neighborhood. Then notice how Matt's imitation of the piece manages to convert this feeling into one of excitement and action while describing a concert.

Student Essay: *Silence*

by Jehlen

On the gravel shore of the canal, at the far end of a vacant lot on the southwest side of town where a cement factory once stood, a ten year old boy sits smoking a Kool and fishing for steelheads with his dog. The sun beats down mercilessly from a cloudless sky, its heat that much more intense since there is only the faintest whisper of a cooling breeze. The boy wipes his sweating brow with the back of his hand as his dog moves a few yards away to climb down the riverbank and drink from the stagnant canal.

"No, pooch," the boy warns, "that stuff's bad. Come away."

But the animal pays no attention.

"Get sick and die then," the boy says, shrugging. "Stupid dog."

A few hundred yards behind them, across Lincoln Avenue, the giant holding pools of the city's wastewater treatment plant offer their contents to be baked by the afternoon sun, and the overwhelming stench that results rises only so high before being trapped by the still air and held in nauseating limbo above this decaying area.

Once a thriving ethnic community made up primarily of Polish and Hungarian immigrants, filled with taverns and corner groceries to serve the thousands of workers from several different factories originally in its midst, this now mostly African-American and Hispanic neighborhood is dying a slow, painful death following the closure of the Darley Street Assembly plant—the only remaining area industry—last December.

Already, the railroad sidings behind the deserted manufacturing facility have become overgrown with weeds. On the front steps of a badly-leaning frame house across the tracks, an elderly man sits with a battered guitar on his lap, looking out at the broken factory windows and mumbling the lyrics of an obscure blues song in a low, sandpapery voice.

"How you doing, Charlie?" a neighbor woman asks in passing.

The man nods his head in acknowledgment, but his song goes on uninterrupted. It is Saturday afternoon, and at a time when this street was for so many years busy with factory workers heading toward the Springtown Inn on Wayford or the 747 Lounge on Darley, there is now only silence. It is so quiet that the man's singing is audible almost two blocks from his house, blocked out only once when a rusty pickup truck clatters past.

Around the corner from the old man's street, the steel-reinforced display window of Taczek's Market offers a glimpse of owner Joe Taczek sitting on a stool behind the meat counter, patiently waiting for a customer to come through the door. With any luck, he will make three or four sales before the day is through.

Across from the little store, a teenaged boy sits in a tattered lawn chair on the front lawn of his house, holding a hand-lettered sign that reads "CAR WASH $1.99." At his feet are a green garden hose, neatly coiled, and a cigar box filled with pennies for change. But both remain unused because there is no passing traffic to take advantage of his offer.

Two doors down from the boy's house is a red brick church building, the words *Assemblios de Dios* stenciled in black across its peeling wooden doors. All of the stained-glass windows, including what must have been a magnificent round one in the bell tower, have been smashed by vandals. The roof is bare of shingles in several spots, exposing the rotting ceiling beams, which moved the city to condemn the building in February.

On the corner opposite the church, a gang of teenaged boys, all of them wearing identical red sweatbands around their foreheads, gathers in front of an abandoned Salvation Army store. One of them takes a can of red Rust-Oleum spray paint from his back pocket and quickly scrawls the words "Almighty Scratch—Die Proud" in foot-high letters across one of the boarded-up windows.

"This lets them Johnny Trash boys know we're still around," the artist says, stepping back to assess his work.

"Never shoulda come over from the suburbs in the first place," one of his friends agrees, gesturing toward the neighboring city less than a mile away. The boys exchange high fives and the group moves on.

Across the street, the young fisherman on the canal leading to the offending suburb gathers his cigarettes and fishing gear and heads for home, his dog following close at his heels. They have caught nothing.

An aging white Pontiac cruises past the boy as he prepares to cross the street, its windows down and radio blaring. For just a moment the street is filled with the pounding bass and wailing guitar of a popular rock song, but then the car is gone just as quickly as it appeared and the neighborhood is quiet once again.

But this is not the peaceful silence of suburbia, where children ride tricycles in their driveways and neighbors exchange small talk across back fences. This is the silence of businesses abandoned by their customers and of churches abandoned by their parishioners. This is a silence brought on by deserted factories and empty houses, and by the locked doors and drawn curtains of those who cannot leave. It is a silence as audible as the music from a solitary passing automobile, as thick as the rancid air that clings like a shroud to the neighborhood rooftops.

This is the silence of dying.

* * *

Student Imitation: *Good Living*
by Matt

On the sticky floor of the Grand Theater, in the middle of town where student life has thrived for decades, a young man stands absorbing the atmosphere and waiting for the band. The spotlights shine brightly from the beams above, their glare intense because they are the only lights on. The young man stands on his tiptoes, his calves stretched, and the band walks onto the stage a few rows away to play its songs and entertain the crowd.

"All right, yeah!" the young man yells. "You guys are great! Let's go!"

But the band checks its sound equipment instead.

"Come on, start the show!" the young man yells urgently. "That's why I'm here!"

A few blocks away, across the main street, several dozen people sit in an outdoor cafe drinking espresso royale, and the overwhelming aroma of coffee beans wafts down the street to draw even more people to this part of the city.

Once just a sleepy little college town made up of mostly student residents, with not much to offer as far as entertainment for those students, this city is now a bustling place with industries that have thrived and prospered year after year, helped along by an international food company that has made its central office here.

Every year, new buildings go up at the company's headquarters. At the door of a posh clothing store in a mall not far from the site, a woman stands with a huge shopping bag in her hand, looking across the street into other store windows and wondering how much more she can spend on frivolous but fun things.

"May I help you, ma'am?" a shopkeeper asks her.

The woman shakes her head in answer, and her shopping goes on uninterrupted.

It is a Saturday afternoon, and at a time when the streets so many years ago were empty of shoppers to buy things at Urban Outfitters or The Buckle, now there is only commotion. The street is so busy that the woman's daydreaming is short-lived, her thoughts broken when someone bumps into her.

Around the corner from where she stands, the plate glass display window of Dunham's offers a glimpse of a salesperson frantically trying to help in the shoe department, hurrying from one customer to another. If things ever slow down he will get to take his lunch break.

Across from the store, a middle-aged man stands behind his gleaming chrome hot dog cart at the main intersection, holding an umbrella that protects him from the sun. In front of him is a line of hungry customers, all waiting patiently, and the shadow cast by the big umbrella. The shadow seems to droop at the edges, maybe because the sun's heat seems almost heavy.

Two doors down from the hot dog cart is a brand new storefront, the words "Hot Topic" hanging on a neon sign in the front window. All of the store's decorations, including a very expensive smoked-glass window, are spotlessly clean. The ceiling, instead of the usual white tile, is open to the rafters, exposing the black-painted rafters over the store set to open next week.

On the opposite corner, a group of college students, all of them carrying backpacks, gathers in front of a store selling new and used books. One of the students picks up a tattered book sitting on a table in front of the store and reads the title—*I'm Okay, You're Okay*—with great glee to his companions.

"Good to know we're all in good shape," the reader says, stepping back to judge the reaction of the others.

"We were never in bad shape to start with," one of his friends says, lifting the thumb of one hand in a gesture of contentment. He and the others exchange smiles and the group moves on.

Across the street, the young man in the theater emerges into the sunlight and walks to his apartment while talking to some friends, his girlfriend at his side. They have all enjoyed the afternoon concert.

A shiny red Volkswagen Beetle zooms past them as they prepare to cross the street. The car's sunroof is open and its CD player blasting. For a few seconds the street fills with the mellow voice and uptempo beat of a Snoop Dogg song, and although the car is gone just as quickly as it appeared, the street remains noisy.

But this is not the hedonistic sight that some would expect from a college town where students used to smoke marijuana openly on the street and noisy protests took place on the campus lawns. This is a scene of bustling downtown activity and new businesses

growing. This is a scene of happy and contented people, and its
background music is provided by the loud radios and CD players of
cars driving by. It is a day as clean as that passing red car, as
sweet as the aroma of that coffee brewing down the street.

    It is a good day to be alive.

As part of this assignment, students were asked to re-read their imitations and
then comment on them, and here is what Matt wrote about his:

> I found that in imitating the "Silence" piece I was forced to vary my word choice, just
> as the original author does. Also, I hardly ever use adjectives and adverbs in my writing,
> and using them so heavily made me realize that my writing must seem awfully plain. It
> was really strange to put together a seven-line, one-sentence paragraph; normally, I would
> cut that passage up into three or four sentences—and of course leave out the descriptive
> language. I know that most people enjoy reading things that pack lots of description and
> emotion, and I'm glad that this imitation let me write something that at least comes close
> to doing that.

Another member of Matt's critique group, Michelle, offered a similar reaction
to her own imitation:

> I've been writing in the same basic style for as long as I can remember. There aren't any
> words to describe my writing style—it just sort of exists. This assignment was a great
> challenge for me, and a challenge worth accepting. Granted, it took me a long time to
> complete the paper, but it was time well spent. When reading the completed draft of
> what I'd written, I felt a great sense of accomplishment. I've written something in a style
> of writing I like a lot, and in time, with more practice, I'd like to adopt some of that style
> as my own.

Looking Closely: A Line-By-Line Conversion of *Silence* to *A Quiet Athlete*

Before you try your own hand at imitation, it will be helpful to spend a few minutes
seeing how all of the writers whose work you've seen so far approached the task. As
we've stressed so far, essentially you want to absorb the overall tone, style, and structure of the text you choose to imitate, and at this point we'll look most closely at the
latter feature, *structure*.

    While some students are fortunate to have had a comprehensive introduction
to the parts of speech in earlier grades, and they may even have been asked to complete "syntax trees" as part of a linguistics-based English course, most often these
things are left to more advanced, college-level courses. Even so, it's possible to
determine what's going on in a sentence without being able to name the specific

grammatical components of that sentence, and this will be our approach here. (An analysis of the grammatical components of the first part of "Silence" appears in Appendix 3.)

In the text titled "Silence" that you read earlier, you saw how *description* played a significant role in the original writer's approach to the topic of a dying neighborhood. Indeed, the opening sentence alone provides readers with a great deal of description:

> On the gravel shore of the canal, at the far end of a vacant lot on the southwest side of town where a cement factory once stood, a ten year old boy sits smoking a Kool and fishing for steelheads with his dog.

Thus the opening sentence breaks down into seven parts:

1	On the gravel shore of the canal,	(location)
2	at the far end of a vacant lot	(specific location)
3	on the southwest side of town	(general location)
4	where a cement factory once stood,	(previous location)
5	a ten year old boy	(person)
6	sits smoking a Kool	(first action)
7	and fishing for steelheads with his dog.	(second action)

For our imitation, as Matt did earlier, we'll use Jehlen's description of an *empty* setting to write about a pre-game NBA team warm-up at a downtown arena. Bright lights, thousands of fans streaming through the gates, and the din of endless excited conversations become the setting for a description of a young athlete eagerly talking with his admirers. In this case, you'll notice that our imitation is fairly loose, using *some* of the original text's parts but not all of them:

On the gravel shore of the canal,   (location)

On the polished wooden floor of The Palace,

at the far end of a vacant lot on the southwest side
of town   (specific location)

on the outskirts of Auburn Hills

where a cement factory once stood,   (previous location)

where once were mostly farms and fields,

a ten-year-old boy   (person)

the newest member of the team

sits smoking a Kool   (first action)

> **stands holding a basketball**

and fishing for steelheads with his dog.   (second action)

> **and signing autographs for his fans.**

With the opening sentence completed, our description of the scene has begun nicely and the rest of the setting awaits description. Looking closely at the original text again, we resume the scene:

The sun

> **The sound of rock music**

beats down mercilessly

> **blares into the arena loudly**

from a cloudless sky,

> **from the overhead speakers,**

its heat that much more intense

> **its beat even more pounding**

since there is only the faintest whisper of a cooling breeze.

> **because the arena is only half-filled with tonight's crowd.**

The boy wipes his sweating brow with the back of his hand

> **The rookie spins the basketball on the finger of his right hand,**

as his dog moves a few yards away

> **and his young fans move even closer**

to climb down the riverbank and drink from the stagnant canal.

> **to watch and commit this fancy move to memory.**

Let's step back now to see what we've written so far as a full paragraph, going a couple of lines further into the imitation by adding some dialog in the process:

On the gravel shore of the canal, at the far end of a vacant lot on the southwest side of town where a cement factory once stood, a ten year old boy sits smoking a Kool and fishing for steelheads with his dog. The sun beats down mercilessly from a cloudless sky, its heat that much more intense since there is only the faintest whisper of a cooling breeze. The boy wipes his sweating brow with the back of his hand as his dog moves a few yards away to climb down the riverbank and drink from the stagnant canal.

"No, pooch," the boy warns, "that stuff's bad. Come away."

But the animal pays no attention.

"Get sick and die then," the boy says, shrugging. "Stupid dog."

On the polished wooden floor of The Palace, on the outskirts of Auburn Hills where once were mostly farms and fields, the newest member of the team stands holding a basketball and signing autographs for his fans. The sound of rock music blares loudly into the arena from the overhead speakers, its beat even more incessant since the place is only half-filled with tonight's crowd. The rookie spins the basketball on the finger of his right hand, and his young fans move even closer to watch and commit the fancy move to memory.

"It's easy," the rookie says. "Just give it a good spin. Nothing to it."

The kids look at him like he's God.

"I hope you all cheer real loud tonight," the athlete says, smiling. "We need the win."

When you imitate a model text, you'll find yourself paying a great deal more attention than usual to aspects of writing such as word choice and arrangement, punctuation, and paragraph structure, all of which go far in creating a rewarding reading experience for your **audience**.

Determining what kinds of readers constitute your audience and choosing an appropriate tone and style for your message to them is vital for creating a message that succeeds rhetorically; therefore, the next chapter focuses on developing your awareness of audience and your options in responding to that awareness.

TECHNIQUES FOR WRITERS 1-b
Close Imitation

Option A

Write your own close imitation of "Silence" (pp. 14–16), following the example of the student imitation process explained on pp. 20–22.

Option B

Write a close imitation of a selection in the Point/Counterpoint readings on pp. 47–62 of Chapter 2, letting the style influence your writing. With your imitation, include a one-page description of the challenges and successes you encountered during the writing process.

Option C

Study the structure and style of a reading you've enjoyed and write a one-page informal analysis of the methods the author used to create a compelling text.

Option D

Look through the pages of a novel, story, or essay (including newspaper/magazine columns) by a writer whose style you appreciate until you find a passage of reasonable length to imitate. Photocopy the passage to turn in with your imitation, the topic of which can be influenced by, or independent of, the original piece's content.

Identifying the Elements of Argumentative Writing

Harnessing the Power to Persuade

Imagine:

You're ten years old and it's a beautiful June morning—too beautiful a day to spend in school. You look longingly at your new skateboard as you hear your parents knocking on your closed bedroom door, informing you that the school bus will be arriving any minute. You reply that your studies are suffering from a lack of fresh air and physical activity; after all, even the ancient Greeks recognized the relationship between a sound mind and a sound body (you saw that on an ad for a local health club). Your parents offer to call the school and explain that you won't be attending classes.

Or:

It's late on a Tuesday night, and you are conquering whole new worlds on your Game Boy. Your parents, upset with the D you received last marking period in high school algebra, strongly suggest you put down the video game and do some homework. You explain to them that this game not only develops hand-eye coordination, but also strengthens your *eye-hand* coordination, an ability you will definitely need in your future career as a brain surgeon. Your parents ask if there is a newer, perhaps better game available, and they volunteer to pick it up at the electronics store on their way home from work.

© Jef Mallett/Dist. By United Feature Syndicate, Inc.

Or perhaps:

You've found the car of your dreams, but it's beyond your budget, even after nearly two hours of negotiation with the sales staff. You explain that you need this car to get to your college classes, and that a productive, successful society can be sustained only if its population is educated. The salesperson goes to the back room to consult the manager, returning to offer you the car at your price.

If these examples sound farfetched, that's because they're meant to be. But consider some genuine historical examples:

In 1415, King Henry V of England faces a decisive battle with a French force that outnumbers his five to one. In his camp at Agincourt, Henry addresses the British generals and troops, assuring them that he would not desire more soldiers; after all, they would only diminish the glory of each man fighting the coming battle. In fact, he asserts (in language provided by Shakespeare) that Englishmen who are now peacefully sleeping in their beds "shall think themselves accursed they were not here." The English soundly defeat the French and Henry marries the French Princess Katharine, securing the thrones of both England and France for his son, Henry VI.

Or:

By the early twentieth century the people of India, a British colony since 1858, long for independence and some relief from their poverty under British rule. Mahatma Gandhi, recognizing the overpowering economic and military strength of England, urges his people to oppose their oppressors not by waging battle, but through passive resistance, using such methods as boycotts, strikes, and fasting. In 1947, yielding to Gandhi's moral and ethical stance—and to the overwhelming support his movement gains from the Indian people and the world community—England grants India independence.

It's obvious from these examples that the power to persuade can alter the course of history, often for the better. But consider this example:

Discouraged by their losses in World War I and by growing economic difficulties, the people of Germany elect Adolf Hitler chancellor in 1933. Hitler's confident and charismatic speeches invigorate the German people and restore their pride, but also arouse latent German anti-Semitism and militarism. Hitler's invasion of Poland in 1939 sparks World War II, and by the end of the war in 1946, sixty million are dead and three continents devastated.

Would the British have defeated the French at Agincourt without the words of Henry V? Would India have achieved its independence without Gandhi? Would World War II have occurred without Adolf Hitler? We will never know. But what we do know is that Henry V, Gandhi, and Hitler all shared one skill: they were experts in rhetoric, the art of persuasion.

Defining Rhetoric

Perhaps no word in the English language has fallen on such hard times as the word *rhetoric*. Few people can define it, and its usage is limited mostly to negative phrases such as "campaign rhetoric," "advertising rhetoric," and "rhetorical question," all of which suggest that rhetoric deals with unethical or meaningless communication.

But rhetoric has a distinguished past, a useful present, and a promising future. Its roots stretch back 2500 years to the island of Sicily, where Corax of Syracuse developed methods to help local farmers plead their cases in court. By the fourth century BCE, Gorgias (c. 483–376 BCE) had become so renowned for instructing young Greek men in the ability to persuade audiences on any topic that Plato (c.429–347 BCE) criticized him for dazzling audiences with clever words rather than instructing them on ways to find the truth.

A common current definition of rhetoric is "the art of *effective* communication," with the word "effective" meaning successful. Communication that is effective succeeds in doing the job it was intended to do. An effective résumé, for instance, gets the writer an interview; an effective article gets published in its targeted magazine; an effective term paper, to many students, is one that receives a good grade.

But one of the earliest definitions of rhetoric comes from Aristotle, a Greek philosopher who lived from 384–322 BCE: "Rhetoric is the art of determining, in all situations, the best possible means of persuasion." Aristotle's definition points to other elements of rhetoric. By calling rhetoric an "art," Aristotle signifies that rhetoric is a learned skill, rather than an inherent talent. Aristotle also points out that rhetoric is situational; he recognizes that different situations require different rhetorical methods. The accomplished **rhetor** has learned how to tie his or her language to the persuasive needs of the situation.

Defining Rhetoric

Rhetor: a person who has developed skill at speaking or writing persuasively.

As part of this situational rhetoric, Aristotle focused on issues such as *style* and *delivery,* the ways in which words are presented in order to move a particular audience to action; today, as a student writer you are still—although you may not realize it—just as interested in finding ways to make your writing "flow" in an appealing way to classmates and teachers so that these audiences can understand the same drama, comedy, anger, or joy that you have experienced. At other times the elements of style and delivery can help to determine whether an audience will be moved to take your side on an issue, or to be more fully informed about a topic that you've covered. These desired responses are more possible when you carefully identify your audience and the *purpose* for your writing, and then choose an appropriate style and delivery—or what's called a *level of discourse*—for the message itself. In mathematical terms, the formula would look like this:

Audience + Purpose = Style/Delivery = Level of Discourse

For instance, it would be inappropriate to open a letter to the president of a college with the casual phrase, "Check this out." But it would just as strange to greet a friend on the street with an overly formal, "It is with great delight that I encounter you once more." This might seem like basic common sense, yet many times while making their ways through writing assignments writers slip into phrasing that doesn't fit the purpose. If the paper is for a history professor and about a key turning point in the Vietnam War, your purpose is to show what you know, and to prove that you know the material well. So if you were to use a too-casual style of commentary, away from a more appropriate style of reporting, and say "It's no wonder the American people started slamming the war after the government jerked them around," these words would suddenly stop fitting the message. A simple lapse into spoken language can make the subject matter appear as though it isn't being treated seriously.

Beyond matters of style and tone, in thinking about argument and persuasion it's also helpful to see how a successful argument isn't necessarily something to be *won,* but rather is something that opens the audience's mind to new ideas and, in turn, opens your mind as the arguer. In this way, argument is an ongoing process of **dialectic**, a method of deeply engaged critical reasoning defined through the centuries by such figures as Plato, Aristotle, Augustine, and Hegel. For early Greek philosophers, dialectic meant "to investigate through dialogue," to discover and learn through questioning. Later, dialectic became a synonym for argument itself.

Defining Rhetoric

Dialectic: a method of seeking the truth through the process of a dialogue in which the participants engage in critical reasoning.

Note how the word *dialectic* is very similar to the commonly used term *dialogue*— a conversation between two or more people—as opposed to *monologue,* a single person speaking. While the classic *lecture* (a monologue in which teachers dictate and students take notes) is an important part of college education, in many college classrooms today professors of any discipline are also skilled at using "Socratic questioning"—answering student questions with more questions—as a way to help students learn to find answers dialectically. Through dialectic, contemporary argument is a communal shaping and re-shaping of ideas held to be true and valuable. The process can be illustrated in this way:

Truth I: The initial point of view (opinion or **doxa**) of the messenger

Truth II: The counterviews of the audience that form as T1 is presented to it, and which the audience voices to the messenger

Truth III: An expanded and reshaped viewpoint, shared by both the messenger and the audience and made possible by the dialectical process that has taken place.

Defining Rhetoric

Doxa: in classical rhetoric, an audience's opinions/judgments of ideas generally held to be correct. (See an expanded definition in the "Thinking Critically" section at the end of this chapter.)

There's an old saying that truth is always in the middle between two stories—the common *facts* in A's version that match the same *facts* in B's version are true, while the remaining details in the two accounts are the sources of disagreement. But argument and the dialectical process are not always engaged in a search for *truth* so much as they seek to find a *common ground for agreement.* Finding that common ground comes through patience, skill, and relentless critical thinking—critical *interrogation,* as some teachers prefer to call it—about the issues being argued.

Why Rhetoric? Determining the Purposes of Persuasion

But why is rhetoric important to *you?* You may understand the power that an accomplished rhetor wields, but perhaps you don't see yourself in the role of a dictator or world figure. That doesn't matter; we all use rhetoric in many daily situations where it helps us succeed in attaining our goals. We're surrounded by rhetoric. Advertisers, politicians, friends and family, activists, teachers, religious leaders, and many others attempt to persuade all of us every day.

Advertising alone, for example, is a multibillion dollar industry in the United States. A company may spend millions of dollars and hire the most talented marketers available to design a campaign encouraging you to buy its newest cell phone; with a clear understanding of the methods of persuasion being used, you have an advantage in determining whether its product is, in fact, the best choice in meeting your needs. Rhetoric gives you the ability to recognize the claims others make and to evaluate them, thus empowering you to make up your own mind in any situation.

But while being fooled by others is regrettable, even Plato recognized that fooling ourselves is worse. We have all made decisions we later regretted. Furthermore, in an increasingly complex world, we have to make decisions on many levels: international, national, regional, professional, personal. The study of rhetoric, particularly in conjunction with its companion study of *dialectic,* helps us to understand complex issues better and evaluate evidence more carefully.

Finally, although it may be hard for you to believe right now, the study of rhetoric is *fun.* Any sport or leisure activity requires work: runners must build up their muscles and stamina to the point where they would consider taking on the challenge of a marathon; basketball players practice repetitive skills before they can successfully compete in a game; dancers use stretching and movement exercises to acquire the grace and poise they need.

Think of rhetoric as an intellectual exercise that will make you a better thinker and a more articulate speaker. Consider how it will broaden your worldview and give you the opportunity to understand others' opinions. Imagine the thrill you'll feel when the solution to a previously insurmountable problem suddenly materializes.

At that point, rhetoric becomes much more than a course you study in school; it becomes an essential element to living a fulfilling life.

Questions for Thinking and Writing

Why is rhetoric important to you? How do you use rhetoric in your daily life? What was one way you used it yesterday? How has someone tried to persuade you recently—and was the attempt effective?

The Communication Triangle: Analyzing the Elements of Communication

Aristotle recognized that three elements were needed in order for communication to occur: a communicator (either a speaker or writer), an audience, and a topic. He also recognized, as did most of the rhetoricians who preceded and followed him, that the key element in persuading an audience is awareness of that audience: their thoughts and feelings, the most effective methods of persuading them, and their current perceptions of the topic being discussed. Aristotle's most famous work, the *Rhetoric,* includes an extended discussion of the various types of audiences a speaker could encounter and the particular types of persuasion, or rhetorical methods, that would work most effectively with them.

The Communication Triangle is commonly used today to illustrate the interrelationships among the speaker or writer, the audience, and the topic, and the connections that need to be made to produce effective communication.

Aristotle's concept of persuasion recognized that audiences can be persuaded through the relationships among the three elements of the triangle: respect of the speaker or writer and belief in his credibility (**ethos**); appeals that are directed toward them and their perceived needs or desires (**pathos**); and the logic and knowledge demonstrated in the persuasive message itself (**logos**).

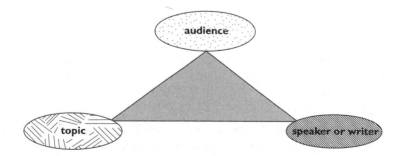

Figure 2.1   The Communication Triangle

Defining Rhetoric

Ethos, pathos, and **logos:** the three elements of The Communication Triangle. Ethos, or ethical appeal, refers to the writer's presentation of himself or herself as a person who deserves the reader's trust. Classical writers believed this trust was promoted by the writer's demonstration of good sense or wisdom, good moral character, and good will. Pathos refers to the writer's understanding of the audience and to adaptations the writer makes to accommodate the audience's beliefs and feelings. Logos, meaning "word" in Greek, refers to the actual arguments and examples the writer will use to make his or her case.

Positioning the Writer in the Communication Triangle

As a writer (the primary position you've been taking while reading this book), your position in the communication triangle requires that you consider the following:

- your understanding of the audience and the document you're producing for them, whether that audience is distinct individuals you actually know (a friendly letter to your mother; a note contesting a grade to your math teacher), a particular audience of which you may have some knowledge (an editorial concerning parking problems for your campus newspaper), or the so-called "general audience" (a letter supporting a bond issue for a daily newspaper).

- your understanding of the audience's take on the topic: what they already know about the topic, what they need to know about it, what their initial impression of the topic is, and whether they're likely to agree or disagree with what you have to say about it.

- your understanding of the best rhetorical methods to reach that audience. This includes everything from the specific points you'll argue to the precise vocabulary ("level of diction") you'll use.

- your understanding of the topic itself, which you've developed through experience, experiment, research, contemplation, logical analysis, discussion with others, writing, and other methods.

- your understanding of yourself in relation to the topic, taking into consideration any inclinations or biases you may have that influence your position. You'll also need to consider how to best present yourself to your audience so that they'll see you as knowledgeable and credible on this topic.

The three elements of the communication triangle intertwine to produce effective communication—communication that is successful in achieving the purpose for which it was intended. Successful rhetors pay close attention to these interrelationships in the writing they produce.

Examining the Ethos, Pathos, and Logos of an Essay

Following is an essay, "Rooms of Their Own," which first appeared in the *New York Times*. The author, Anna Quindlen, is a prolific writer who not only was a long-time columnist for the *Times* but has also written a number of very successful novels, among which are *One True Thing, Object Lessons,* and *Black and Blue*. Ms. Quindlen has most recently been an editorial writer for *Newsweek*.

As you read the essay, consider these questions, which will be discussed in depth afterward:

1. What is Quindlen's ethos, or ethical stance? Based on reading this one essay, what can you say about her background, current situation, and beliefs? How does she present herself in this essay to you, the audience?

2. What is the pathos, or pathetic (audience connection) stance, of this essay? What assumptions does Quindlen seem to be making about the backgrounds, current situations, and beliefs of the audience for her essay?

3. Does the logos of the essay, its actual message and the way it is presented, persuade you to accept Quindlen's ideas about the homeless and her solution to their problems as valid and acceptable?

Rooms of Their Own
Anna Quindlen — *New York Times*

When Ellen Baxter was working on a report about the homeless people of New York City, she went into shelters and subway stations and parks to talk to them about their lives. The problem was enormous but her conclusion was simple.

"It was so obvious to me that what they wanted was a place to live," she says. "They wanted a key and a room where they could lock the door."

That was 10 years ago, and in that time the number of homeless people has multiplied and the patience of the public has worn thin. It seems the homeless have always been with us, and it's begun to occur to us that lots of them are people we don't like very much.

Ten years ago some of the homeless were older people, disenfranchised by misfortune or fire or expensive building rehabilitations. Some were former mental patients sent to the streets by government policy that said large institutions were an affront to humanity but provided few small ones in their place. "Lady, could you spare a quarter," said the men, their faces vermilion from years of Thunderbird. If a wild woman zoomed by, shouting imprecations at President Kennedy and the Pope, you looked twice.

5   Today no one looks twice. The old homeless are still on the streets, but the holes in the societal safety net have spit out new companions. Young men roving the bus terminal, some of them just out of jail, and seemingly looking for a way back in. Young women pushing strollers in midtown at midnight, tired of the four walls of the welfare hotel and three kids under the age of 4. In one subway station a homeless man lies on the floor at the foot of the stairs and orders passers-by, "Put the money in the cup."

This has made people angry, and no wonder. Problem is, some of them get angry at the homeless. "Not in my neighborhood," we say about shelters, but it's already too late. If they're not in your neighborhood yet, sleeping in the doorways, looking through the dumpsters for dinner, they will be soon. To explain our antipathy we say that the problem is too big and intractable to solve.

While we've been saying that, people like Ellen Baxter have been quietly trying to solve it. In 1986, Baxter opened the Heights in a stolid gray apartment building with a panoramic view of the feed to the George Washington Bridge. The building is furnished with vanilla-and-gilt French provincial furniture, a donation from the Pierre Hotel.

There are 55 permanent tenants, veterans of such diverse venues as the 181st Street subway station, High Bridge Park and the Fort Washington Armory, where 800 beds may be lined up across the floor on any given night to welcome those who have no place to go. Visualizing it in the mind's eye makes it easy to understand why homeless people do not like shelters.

The people who live in The Heights, and the three other buildings Baxter now oversees, are people with problems. They are people, some of them, who have smoked crack and passed out drunk and spent time in psychiatric wards, and who may do so in the future.

10   But they once were homeless and now are living with leases, with keys, some with jobs, all with dignity. Their subsidized rent comes out of a welter of entitlement programs and, in some cases, their own wages. They still may not be people we like very much. That shouldn't matter, but it does. We like to like the people we help, to have a poster child. It is time to grow up about this. Public policy cannot be determined by our collective warm fuzzies.

We may have one of two motives in this matter, vastly different but leading us to the same place. We can demand that government finance more small permanent residences like The Heights because that is the right thing to do, because we have looked into the faces of homeless men and women and occasionally recognized ourselves. That probably requires more than most of us can find within ourselves at this point, after explaining to our children why the man is swearing at the fire hydrant, after having someone urinate in our doorway.

So there is another reason to demand that government support those groups that have found humane and permanent solutions. The Heights costs about $15 per person per day, including the cost of its staff of social workers and counselors. The armory, that vast expanse of temporary beds, costs at least twice that.

Look at it from a purely selfish point of view as well. You want the sidewalks and the parks to be clear again. You want to be left alone and not importuned for a dollar a dozen times a day. And up in Washington Heights, and in other quietly compassionate places all over New York, there are people who can help make that happen in a way that will not shame us as human beings.

Ethos   Looking first at the ethos of this article, Quindlen seems to be a person who knows, both through experience and research, about the homeless, and who has developed definite opinions about them, some of which may seem contradictory. While she states that the homeless "may not be people we like very much," she also says that helping them is "the right thing to do, because we have looked into the faces of homeless men and women and occasionally recognized ourselves." Her attitude toward the homeless may best be described as being ambivalent—she would like to help these people, even though she doesn't seem to be particularly sympathetic to the homeless as individuals.

But what else about Quindlen can we surmise from reading this one article? How old do you think she is? What is her educational level and economic standing? Does she live in an urban or rural area? You may have guessed that she's middle-aged, is well-educated and probably financially secure, and lives in an urban area: although she doesn't directly tell us any of these things, her writing carries clues about her background and situation.

She refers to President Kennedy and to "explaining to our children why the man is swearing at the fire hydrant," which would suggest that she's past young adulthood and is perhaps the mother of young children. Her sentence structure and vocabulary usage suggest higher education: She seems comfortable using words such as *disenfranchised, vermilion, antipathy, imprecations,* and *intractable* in her writing. She certainly isn't writing from the perspective of a person who is homeless herself, and her references to subways, apartment buildings, shelters, and bus terminals suggest that she spends a good part of her life in an urban environment.

Pathos   What about the pathos of her article, the assumptions Quindlen seems to be making about her audience? She seems to be speaking to people who share her ambivalence about the homeless, people who want to see an end that's both humane and practical to the problem of homelessness. Her audience is apparently both old enough and established enough to be able to help solve the problem, people who are able and willing to "demand that government support those groups that have found humane and permanent solutions." The message appears to be geared toward urban people such as herself, who have the same kinds of experiences with the homeless as she has, and to people who are similarly well-educated: She makes the assumption that her audience will be as familiar with words such as *antipathy* and *imprecations* as she is.

Do you see a pattern developing here?

We might believe that the author is simply writing for people who are much like herself, who share the same backgrounds and experiences. But for an accomplished writer like Anna Quindlen, awareness of audience encompasses more than that. Having an important message to present and realizing the need for persuasion, she focuses on particular aspects of herself and her background while writing this essay—those aspects that best connect with her audience and most effectively build *common ground* (a sharing of common interests and concerns, a feeling of identity with the author and her aims) with them.

Logos   Finally, let's look at the logos of the message, the knowledge expressed in the article and the way it is presented. Quindlen uses two kinds of *proofs* in her message: experiential and factual material. She keys in to her audience's knowledge of the homeless by focusing on some of her own experiences that may closely parallel their own: the man in the subway demanding money, the man swearing at the fire hydrant. But for her educated, knowledgeable audience she still needs specific references to people (Ellen Baxter), places (the George Washington Bridge, Fort Washington Armory), and numbers (55 permanent tenants, 800 beds) to give her essay the kind of credibility they expect.

One of Quindlen's most powerful rhetorical tools is her use of first- and second-person references to draw her audience into her topic. Some first-person references include "Not in **my** neighborhood"; "**we** say about shelters"; "**our** collective warm fuzzies"; "to explain **our** antipathy"; "in a way that will not shame **us** as human beings." Second-person references include "If they're not in **your** neighborhood yet . . . they will be soon"; "**You** want the sidewalks and the parks to be clear again." Using first- and second-person references is another way authors can develop common ground with the audience and lead them toward agreement with a position.

Using Rhetoric in Everyday Conversation

Audience analysis may seem more complicated than it actually is. We live in a complex society, one in which we encounter and need to interact with many people every day. Our communication patterns often change with the different relationships we have with these many people. For example, in the space of just an hour or two, you may present different facets of yourself and your personality to your roommate, your history teacher, your classmates, and the cashier at the college bookstore. We all continually change our communication patterns to fit the situations in which we find ourselves.

One way to illustrate the complex communication patterns among ethos, pathos, and logos is by examining the following samples of student writing. Students in a freshman composition course had the following assignment:

> Write two letters, one to your grandmother and one to your best friend, describing someone you met during your first weeks on campus whom you have begun to see regularly. You suspect that this relationship may turn into something serious. Your letters should include a physical description of the person as well as some information about the way you met him or her and the kinds of activities you have participated in since you met.

Amy's letters follow.

> Dear Grandma,
>   What is happening down in Florida? How is everyone doing? I am writing with the best news. I have met someone very special. I think that you would like him.
>   We met in class at school and he is very nice. He carried my bag to my car and even opened my door. He is such a polite young man. When you come up North I want you to meet him. I can't wait to see the look on your face—he is very cute.
>
> Love ya!
> Aim

> Yo Smokey—
>   What's up? I have met this guy who is so Hot! He has these lips that are sooo kissable and these arms that are so tight. Oh I just drool thinking about him.
>   The other night we went out and, girl, let me tell you, all eyes were on my man. I wasn't the only one checking him out, but I was the only one dancing with him. He can dance too—we were all over each other out on the floor. I can't wait until you come home. You can look, but no touching! I will send you a picture soon.

Notice how much these letters change when just one very important factor, the audience, changes? The basic content—the story of meeting the young man—is the same, but that's where the similarity ends. Details about his physical description and about the activities the couple has participated in change dramatically, and other changes are also evident.

The tone of the first letter is friendly but more formal ("What is happening down in Florida?") than the second ("What's up?"). Even the formatting of the letter changes. For example, the letter to Grandma uses standard letter formatting and punctuation in the address ("Dear Grandma,") and somewhat standard formatting in the closing ("Love ya! Aim"), while the second letter dispenses with standard formatting and punctuation in the address ("Yo Smokey—") and dispenses with language altogether in the closing.

What other differences do you notice? In constructing these letters, is Amy presenting herself dishonestly? Would she be embarrassed if the two letters were accidentally sent to the wrong recipients?

Rhetorically speaking, rather than being dishonest Amy is responding appropriately within the context of her relationships with her grandmother and her good friend, and tailoring her writing to effectively address and maintain those relationships. This is something most of us learned to do when young, and it's something most people do every day. So, in a manner of speaking, we're all rhetoricians every day of our lives.

Questions for Thinking and Writing

How many interactions with different people or groups of people have you had today? In what ways did you modify your communication patterns to adapt to these different audiences? How do your speech and writing change when you communicate with your parents? Your siblings? Your roommates? Your friends? Your teachers? Your teammates? Your co-workers?

Analyzing Essays for Ethos, Pathos, and Logos

The following essays, Stuart D. Bykofsky's "No Heart for the Homeless" and Steven VanderStaay's "Solutions Homeless People Seek," present perspectives on the homeless that differ significantly from Quindlen's. In order to focus your reading of these

TECHNIQUES FOR WRITERS 2-a

Audience Awareness

Choose one of the following options. Try to get actually into the situation and compose letters that would be very natural for you to write.

Option A
You've just completed your first week in college. Write two letters, one to your parents and one to your best friend, describing the major events of the past week.

Option B
You've discovered that attending college is far more expensive than you had anticipated, and that you're going to run short of cash very soon. Write two letters, one to your parents and one to the financial aid office of your school, requesting a loan.

essays, you may wish to refer to the **Critical Reading Questions** that follow Bykof-sky's and VanderStaay's essays before reading them: Bykofsky, pp. 39–40; Vander-Staay, pp. 45–46.

No Heart for the Homeless
Stuart D. Bykofsky

I am about to be heartless. There are people living on the streets of most American cities, turning sidewalks into dormitories. They are called the homeless, street people, vagrants, beggars, vent men, bag ladies, bums. Often they are called worse. They are America's living nightmare—tattered human bundles. They have got to go.

I don't know, exactly, when they got the *right* to live on the street. I don't know, exactly, when I *lost* the right to walk through town without being pestered by panhandlers. I do know I want them off my sidewalk. If you think I am heartless for saying that, can I send them to live on *your* sidewalk?

I am fed up with the trash they bring into my neighborhood. The pools of urine in apartment-house lobbies disgust me. I am fed up with picking my way down sidewalks blocked by plastic milk crates, stepping over human forms sprawled on steam gratings.

I also am fed up with newspaper columnists who periodically have a good cry in print over the plight of the street people—and the average citizen's callous reaction to them. I have yet to read that one of these columnists has taken a street person home for a bath and a meal. That happens only in movies like "Down and Out in Beverly Hills."

5   What are we, the heartless, supposed to do? In the Sermon on the Mount, Jesus urged his followers to "give to every one who begs from you." The horde of the homeless turns this plea into a joke. Walking to work this morning, I was approached eight times: "Mister, I'm hungry." "Can you help me out?" "You have any spare change?" "Got a quarter?" But what good would a quarter do? If I really mean to help, I should follow Jesus and give a dollar to everyone who asks. That would be $8 on my way to work—and $8 on the way home, because they are still there. That's $80 a week.

Early on, I felt pity for those in the streets, but their relentless begging has forced me to change *my* habits, my attitudes. Panhandlers have taught me to suspect anyone approaching me on the street. "Can I ask you something, sir?" a casually dressed man asks. Maybe he's a tourist needing directions.

Stuart D. Bykofsky, "No Heart for the Homeless," *Newsweek*, December 1, 1986. Reprinted by permission of the author.

Maybe he just wants to know the time. No. He wants access to my pockets. Tired of being hit like a money-access machine, I'm now deaf to people in the street. I'm not happy about that, but there it is.

I am amazed by their persistence. Since I walk the same route every day, I pass the same street people on the same gratings, or curled in the same makeshift, cardboard shelters. Every time I leave my apartment building, I mean *every time,* I am panhandled by begging sentinels more steadfast than Gurkhas. Every time, I ignore them. I wish I could make them disappear.

At 6 feet 3 and 185 pounds, I'm not frightened when one shuffles up to me, dull-eyed, asking alms. They do frighten my elderly neighbors. It is psychological assault. Why should they have to put up with it?

Don't tell me that's the price we pay for living in a democracy. Tell me why they are allowed to make the street their home—day and night, hot and cold—when I can't park a car at the curb for an hour without paying a meter. How is that possible? I find it ironical that my tax money keeps the street—their home—paved and clean. That makes me their landlord. I want to evict them.

Vagrancy Laws

10   No one has reliable statistics about their numbers across America, but authorities agree the homeless fall into three categories: (1) the economically distressed, who would work if they could find work; (2) the mentally ill, who can't work; (3) the alcoholic, the drug-addicted and others who won't work. Police once routinely arrested people sleeping in the streets, or the parks, or the railroad stations, as vagrants. Vagrancy laws were struck down because it shouldn't be a crime to be out of work. That seems right to me. No one should be arrested because he or she has no money. But by the same token, no one should be allowed to set up housekeeping on the sidewalk.

This is the nub of the problem. If I don't want them sleeping on the sidewalks, what is to be done?

People sleeping on the streets depress property values, decrease tourism, tarnish a city's reputation and inhibit customers from entering shops. In subtle ways, we already are paying the price for the homeless. I would rather pay higher taxes and get these people off the streets.

The unemployed are the easiest to help because they are able and willing to work. If they want a job, but society is unable to provide a job, then government should provide money for food and shelter to be delivered through welfare or a workfare program.

The mental patients, the "harmless schizophrenics," were turned loose when the courts decided no one should be locked up just because they were sick. Communities were to provide local facilities. Big surprise: they didn't. But some level of government must. The mentally incompetent who now have the "freedom" to die on cold streets must be steered to decent tax-supported homes or institutions that will care for them.

15   The drunk, the addicted and the just plain shiftless present an entirely different problem. They say they are on the streets because they have nowhere else to go. We must take that excuse away from them. New facilities do not have to be built. Every community has factories and warehouses that have been closed down. Nearly every community has abandoned houses. These can be converted at minimal cost into a shelter that provides light, heat and plumbing. Call them tax-supported flophouses, call them almshouses, I don't care.

People can't be *forced* to live there, of course. They have their rights. But so do we. Once we have made shelter available, we have the right to say this: the streets are not for sleeping anymore.

Critical Reading Questions

1. Quindlen uses first person in her article, but only in the plural: "We like to like the people *we* help." "That probably requires more than most of *us* can find within *ourselves* at this point." But Bykofsky uses a very emphatic singular first person from the outset: "*I* am about to be heartless." How does his use of first person make his *ethos* differ from Quindlen's? How does it affect the tone of his article?

2. Bykofsky gives us some very particular information about himself: "Walking to work this morning, I was approached eight times." "At 6 feet 3 and 185 pounds, I'm not frightened when one shuffles up to me." What else can you say about Bykofsky? Do you find any information in the article that would tell you about his education, his political leanings, his age?

3. Bykofsky tells us that he's "fed up with newspaper columnists who periodically have a good cry in print over the plight of the street people— and the average citizen's callous reaction to them." Might Anna Quindlen be one of the columnists to whom he refers? Can you imagine these two articles as a dialogue between the writers?

4. Bykofsky, like Quindlen, speaks directly to his readers, but the effect is very different. Are statements such as "If you think I am heartless for saying that, can I send them to live on *your* sidewalk?" or "Don't tell me that's the price we pay for living in a democracy" designed to establish Quindlen's type of common ground with readers? What kind of response is Bykofsky likely to get from his readers?

5. What examples does Bykofsky use to make his case against the homeless? Are they effective? What other kinds of proof does he use?

6. Bykofsky tells us that "authorities agree the homeless fall into three categories." Who might these "authorities" be? Are you more or less likely to accept his information as valid than you would be if he had given the names and titles of his authorities?

7. Bykofsky uses comparisons throughout his article. He tells us that panhandling homeless are "more steadfast than Gurkhas." What does he mean? He also discusses the rights of the homeless compared to his own loss of rights: "I don't know, exactly, when they got the right to live on the street. I don't know, exactly, when I lost the right to walk through town without being pestered . . . " and later, "Tell me why they are allowed to make the street their home—day and night, hot and cold—when I can't park a car at the curb for an hour without paying a meter." How accurate are these comparisons? How fair are they?

8. Bykofsky divides the homeless into three groups, and suggests a different solution in dealing with each group. Have any of his solutions been tried before? How likely are they to be successful?

Solutions Homeless People Seek

Steven VanderStaay

Homeless people seek solutions that account for their own experience. Persons homeless through loss of work see employment as their greatest need; others stress a safe and affordable home as the foundation upon which they can base other progress. Most recognize that effective drug and alcohol treatment must accompany job assistance and housing programs for people who need it.

Assumptions about such solutions vary widely among homeless people, depending—again—upon their experience. People recently homeless through accident or mishap tend to want "another chance," a little help in getting back on their feet. "I've always worked, always gotten by," one recently homeless man told me. "Now I just need that chance to show what kind of a worker I am."

Homeless people with little experience of middle-class success have less faith in the viability of hard work and perseverance to lift them out of destitution. As previous chapters have shown, many of these people remained poor while working hard and fell into homelessness despite their determination to do otherwise. They argue that the conditions of life, employment, and housing they face make middle-class notions of "boot-strap" success nearly impossible to achieve. Their feelings range from despair to anger, buttressing their view that only drastic measures can bring the changes they need to solve the problems they face. Disillusioned, they see homelessness as an urgent crisis of immense proportions few understand or care about. As a friend of mine puts it, "No one hears our cries."

These people cry for help beyond housing—for child care, medical attention, substance-abuse programs, and jobs. Surveys that cite high rates of personal problems among the homeless come as no surprise to homeless people themselves, many of whom freely admit personal difficulties that complicate their situations. "I need some help," "I'm still weak for it," "It was my fault I dropped out," are statements common to their stories. Those without debilitating problems see them in their family and friends, in the people who share their soup lines, and in the other homeless people they meet on the street.

5   But the idea that people should be punished for behavior they already suffer under makes no sense to homeless people. They view so-called austerity programs, designed to make emergency housing purposefully uncomfortable, as ludicrously cruel and counterproductive—measures akin to feeding starving children sour milk as punishment for missing breakfast. And that thousands of street addicts and alcoholics want rehabilitation they cannot get, strikes them as beyond comprehension.

Most homeless people I've interviewed also want to cut defense spending, the charitable assistance we send abroad, and tax breaks for the rich. They are nearly unanimous in wanting to substantially raise the minimum wage, increase support for dependent families, veterans, and the disabled, and in their desire for housing programs that integrate poor families into middle-class neighborhoods. Most see universal health care as an essential human right. They want schools that give a ghetto child a chance, streets that permit safe passage, a war on drugs that cares for the wounded, and job assistance programs that provide jobs, not assistance.

Most homeless people also mistrust the social service system. This is not to say they disagree with the idea of such services; rather, they fault the system for its failure to deliver them. They say that government and charitable funds earmarked for the poor and homeless rarely reach them, that caseworkers become adversaries, not advocates, and that job-training programs too often provide jobs for the trainers, not the trainees. It would be more effective, they argue, to receive assistance directly—either as employment, housing, or cash—rather than through service agencies where much of it is siphoned into salaries and operating expenses. Interestingly, it was a conservative administration—Nixon's—that actually proposed such a plan, the "Family Assistance Program." Of course, the plan met stiff opposition from Democrats and Republicans alike and was soundly defeated.

But one should resist the temptation to paint the suggestions raised by homeless people in the terms of party politics. Less concerned with affixing blame than finding solutions, most homeless people have little patience for the ideological battles that characterize public discussion of the crisis. As one man explained it to me, "Don't tell me I ain't got a job, I know that. And don't tell me why I ain't got one either. Tell me where I can get one."

Consequently, the solutions that homeless people suggest not only lack the political homogeneity common to those who speak for them, they point to new ways of thinking about the problem and the nation.

10   This is particularly evident in the frequent references homeless people make to communities. Whether speaking of family, neighbors, neighborhoods, or "the homeless," homeless people commonly speak of themselves in relation to a body of people who share their situation and who live where they do, and they frame their ideas in terms that are at once personal and community-based.

This sense of community is particularly evident in what may be the most salient characteristic of the solutions homeless people seek for themselves: the desire to help each other. I have heard versions of the following scenario, for example, from homeless men and women on both coasts, and in the North, South, and Midwest:

I think maybe if I could get some money I'd get a house and put some people up. Because, well, I can't say for you or for anybody else, but now that I've been homeless I'd see it as a waste of money to spend much on an apartment. You know, one of these bi-level apartments, six, seven hundred dollars a month. I'd rather get a place where I can put some people up, give 'em a place to stay where they can actually live—not permanent, but some place where a man or a woman can be long enough to get themselves together and get back on their feet. Where they can live. Have some rules, you know, but a place. Give 'em a door key and kind of work together.

Wishful thinking? Perhaps. But homeless assistance programs that succeed—even those that attract mainstream attention—speak to the viability of such ideas. "Study after study" has shown that "the homeless are different from other people," notes one essay on programs that work for homeless people: "They are profoundly alone." Accordingly, building support networks and community alliances is a key to their success.

It should be noted that this sense of alliances is much more than a vague wish for togetherness or cooperation: it is a strategic response to perilous conditions. Like survivors of a devastating earthquake or other natural disaster, homeless people have little choice but to take shelter together. Similarly, it is a mistake to assume these communities to be racially bound. Homeless people frequently say they have much more in common with other homeless people, regardless of race, than with any larger, housed community. And many of the communities homeless people form for themselves—whether a precarious "squat" in an abandoned building, or a cooperative household—are virtual models of integration.

The programs described in the testimonies that follow reaffirm these concerns. Whether the target population is homeless youth or homeless men, the programs that homeless people themselves advocate provide stability, opportunity, and the kind of community-building that fosters self-reliance and long-term structures of peer-support.

15   Community-based, long-term approaches of this nature are especially prevalent among shelters and programs established for women. One of many such organizations is the Elizabeth Stone House, which operates a residential mental health alternative, a battered women's program, and a transitional housing program in the Boston area. Stressing a "therapeutic community" and individual goal-setting to foster self-empowerment, the Elizabeth Stone House provides a broad range of programs and assistance options through which the women it serves work to meet their own needs. Furthermore, because the organization serves a broad population and sets no financial restrictions for admission to its programs, the communities and networks it fosters are themselves rich with opportunities for mutual assistance. Women combine households, make friends, and share support and encouragement across class and racial boundaries.

Elsewhere, informal communities of poor women have led cooperative, neighborhood campaigns to rescue buildings that threatened whole communities with homelessness. Many such efforts have generated new "community households" on the model of large, extended families. In them groups of precariously housed people combine resources, skills, and housing in small networks of mutual support.

Other communities combine peer support with opportunities for homeless people to work for their own betterment on a political level. Justice House, a radical Christian community of homeless people in Roanoke, Virginia, fosters rehabilitation and personal growth among its members, while encouraging lobbying, marches, and other direct action campaigns on behalf of homeless people. In this way organizations like Justice House build solidarity among homeless people while empowering their own participants through meaningful work and peer support.

But the communities to which homeless people refer are not merely those they have formed among themselves. While people with homes may not accept the homeless people in their streets as neighbors, the reverse is rarely true. Homeless people usually have a much more inclusive definition of community, which includes those with homes and those without.

This recognition is painful. It affirms the alienation and abandonment that homeless people feel. Similarly, reintegrating homeless people into other communities is no easy task. In many ways it is like welcoming veterans back from war: they return changed and scarred, sometimes disillusioned and bitter. Reintegration, moreover, means building housing instead of hotels, bringing jobs to poor communities, and accepting the poor as our neighbors. It means placing comparable schools in disparate neighborhoods, and considering new paradigms of cooperation, interdependence, and of the maintenance and distribution of resources.

20   Yet, while homelessness exposes the fragility of our lives and the vast inequalities of our society, it also points up the great resilience of people and their ability to create networks of support and connection under the most harrowing of circumstances. Solutions that work for homeless people draw strength and momentum from this resilience and ability.

Finally, allowing homeless people to work together for their own betterment is self-perpetuating. Solutions that build communities give meaning to people who suffer in isolation, creating contexts in which other difficulties can be overcome.

The testimonies that follow give witness to this. Each addresses a disability—drug addiction, unemployment, or destitution—and in each case rehabilitation occurs in the context of a community. This fact points up the initial absence of community in the inception of the problem, and the responsibility of the larger, societal "community" in the breakdown of its smaller, communal units.

Similarly, the testimonies often reframe the notion of a "solution." "Some people want to get back up into the mainstream where they can get that apartment, that washer and dryer, and keep them to themselves," explains Stewart Guernsey, a Boston-area lawyer who left Harvard's divinity school to form a cooperative household and advocacy center with a group of formerly homeless people. "But others have come to see that vision of independence as part of their problem."

This perspective generates what might be called New Movement solutions—cooperative, grass-root, self-help programs that place responsibility upon homeless people while entrusting them with the tools, services, and resources they need to better themselves. Although disparate, such programs share certain features: they tend to be formed through trial and error, to depend on peer support, to be long-term, to be "tight ships" with strict, consistent rules, to be small, and to employ few "experts"—though this is not universally true. Such programs have been shown to benefit both those who seek to (re)enter the mainstream and those who fit Mr. Guernsey's latter description and seek other alternatives.

25   The programs described in some of the testimonies that follow are not necessarily the best or most proven. But each is a program that speaks to the concerns of homeless people and one that homeless people eagerly speak for. There are not many such programs, though the "movement" is clearly growing. Those described here were chosen for the alternatives they suggest and the stories through which they are told.

However, it must be remembered that, with the proper context of support, homelessness need not have occurred for any of these people. To this end, efforts that strengthen family connections and community ties among people before they become homeless are implicitly advocated in each narrative. Homeless people, perhaps more fully than anyone else, recognize the value of a home and know that keeping one can mean the strength and support people need to maintain everything else.

Interestingly, there is evidence that the "new movement" of programs described here may become just such an effort. ACE, which began by organizing women in the so-called welfare hotels of New York City, has already changed its focus to the neighborhoods of Central Harlem, where many of the hotel residents come from. And Second Home, which initially sought to provide a refuge from the streets of Boston, has now begun a neighborhood boxing program as an alternative to the attractions of the local gangs who make those streets so violent.

It is said that some people are stronger where they've been broken. Perhaps, ultimately, this will be true of these immediate communities, and, by extension, of the larger communities of which they are a part.

Critical Reading Questions

1. Unlike Quindlen or Bykofsky, Steven VanderStaay limits his use of first person, for the most part, to references that establish the fact that his essay was produced through interviews with the homeless: "As a friend of *mine* puts it . . . ," "Most homeless people *I've* interviewed. . . . " He uses plural first person to establish common ground in only one sentence: "Yet, while homelessness exposes the fragility of *our* lives and the vast inequalities of *our* society. . . . " What is the effect of this switch toward the end of the article?

2. VanderStaay's limited use of first person makes his essay appear to be more objective than the previous two essays. Despite this, can you find any textual material that offers insights into his education, political leanings, etc.?

3. As its title suggests, "Solutions Homeless People Seek" focuses on self-images of the homeless and their situations. What aspects of the homeless, as seen from their own perspective, surprised you? How does this portrayal of the homeless situation differ from what you saw in Quindlen's and in Bykofsky's pieces?

4. Like Quindlen, VanderStaay uses the example of a successful shelter (Elizabeth Stone House) to illustrate an effective way to help the

homeless. How does Elizabeth Stone House differ from The Heights?

5. VanderStaay compares the cruelty of punishing people for being homeless as being "akin to feeding starving children sour milk as punishment for missing breakfast." How effective is this comparison?

6. Which of these three essays has given you the most information on the homeless? Have any of the essays changed your perceptions of the homeless? Which of the three seems to be the most effectively persuasive?

TECHNIQUES FOR WRITERS 2-b
Writing About the Homeless

The three essays presented in this chapter offer very different perspectives on the situation of America's homeless. They provide the research materials necessary for many possible student essays discussing varying aspects of homelessness and efforts being made by individuals to either understand or eradicate it. Here are three possible topics:

Essay A:

Compare and contrast the ethical and pathetic appeals presented in the three essays on the homeless. To what extent does each author use first person to establish common ground? What assumptions does each author seem to have about his or her audience? How effective is each author's use of first person in persuading you of the validity of his or her position about the homeless?

Essay B:

Themes of isolation, loss, community, deviance, and disorder (among many others) appear throughout the essays. Choose one theme that seems particularly important in understanding the situation of the homeless and trace references to that theme in two or three of the essays.

Essay C:

Each author offers some way or ways to deal with the situation of homelessness in America. Discuss the solutions presented in each essay, focusing on what you would find most or least effective in each.

Student Writing: Point/Counterpoint— Students Respond

Analyzing arguments is an important step in developing rhetorical skill. Analysis not only teaches you to discern both the what and the how of another's argument, it also points out ways that you can both develop and structure your own arguments. In this section, students respond to essays about education, and as you read these points and counterpoints, think of them as conversations—between writers and student writers— that get at the heart of what the best rhetoric really is: an open, honest dialogue on argumentative issues that leads to a deeper understanding of the complexity of those issues.

The first main essay, "Schools Cannot Raise America's Children," by Jamie Vollmer, lists responsibilities education has taken on over 100 years; two student responses to Vollmer's list follow. A young man who left college during his sophomore year writes the second main essay, "A Student's Farewell"; Sylvie Hang then responds to that essay. The third main piece is an e-mail message from an anonymous sender, and two student responses to that message point out flaws in the sender's argument. As you'll see, the student responses generated by these three key readings are strong in both logic and attitude, making them compelling readings in their own right.

Schools Cannot Raise America's Children
by Jamie Vollmer

America's public schools can be traced back to the year 1640. The Massachusetts Puritans who created these first schools assumed that families and churches bore the major responsibility for raising a child. The responsibility of the school was intended to be focused on:

1. Teaching basic reading, writing and arithmetic skills.
2. Cultivating values that serve a democratic society (some history and civics implied).

America's schools stayed focused for 260 years

At the beginning of this century, society began to assign additional responsibilities to the schools. Politicians, business leaders and policy makers began to see the schools as a logical site for the assimilation of newly arrived

Jamie Vollmer, "Schools Cannot Raise America's Children," *MEA Voice*, August 1998. Reprinted by permission of the author.

immigrants and the perfect place for the social engineering of the first generation of the "Industrial Age."

The practice of increasing the responsibilities of the nation's public
schools began then and has accelerated ever since.

From 1900 to 1920, we added:

- Nutrition.
- Immunization.
- Health

5   From 1920 to 1950, we added:

- Vocational education.
- The practical arts.
- Physical education.
- School lunch programs. (We take this for granted today. It was, how-
  ever, a significant step to shift to the schools the job of feeding Amer-
  ica's children, one-third of their daily meals.)

In the 1950s, we added:

- Safety education.
- Driver education.
- Stronger foreign language requirements.
- Sex education (topics escalate through the 1990s).

In the 1960s, we added:

- Consumer education.
- Peace education.
- Leisure education.
- Recreation education.

In the 1970s, the breakup of the American family accelerated and:

- Special education was mandated by the federal government.
- We added drug and alcohol abuse education.
- Parent education.
- Character education.
- School breakfast programs appeared. (Now, some schools are feeding
  America's children two-thirds of their daily meals. In some cases, these
  are the only decent meals the children receive.)

In the 1980s, the floodgates opened and we added:

- Keyboarding and computer education.

- Global education.
- Ethnic education.
- Multicultural/nonsexist education.
- English-as-a-second-language and bilingual education.
- Early childhood education.
- Full-day kindergarten.
- Preschool programs for children at risk.
- Child abuse monitoring became a legal requirement for all teachers.

10   And, finally, so far in the 1990s, we have added:

- HIV/AIDS education.
- Death education.
- Gang education in urban centers.
- Bus safety.
- Bicycle safety education.

And in most states, we have not added a single minute to the school year in decades.

Please note that as new responsibilities were added, few of the existing functions were removed; most of the added functions are highly valued by many Americans; and, arguably, all of these things may need to be taught.

As Americans we must decide the role of parents, schools and communities if we are to effectively prepare our children to succeed in the 21st century.

The bottom line: Schools cannot do it all. Schools cannot raise America's children.

The Hourglass Is Emptying

by Ben Minadeo

Of all the things in the world I'm afraid of, two things are at the top of my list: fruits and vegetables. Yeah, I realize that most people can handle those pretty well, and that there are plenty of other things to be afraid of and worry about. But you have no idea how much I despise fruits and vegetables. It's almost as if I was born to be a carnivore, to just rely completely on meat. Some people have told me that I've basically been on the Atkins Diet all my life, and this would explain why I'm so thin while my siblings, older and younger, are quite a bit heavier than I am. I guess I'm walking proof that the Atkins Diet really works.

Reprinted by permission of Ben Minadeo.

Avoiding fruits and vegetables for the past decade was my choice, and I'll probably have to pay for that later on in life. But if that's the case, then how many other kids who didn't eat right, like me, are going to have to pay for their choices, too? I'd say a few million, and in fact many are paying for it right now, given the huge increase of obesity in children.

For parents, it's difficult to get your kids to do anything you want them to; it's almost in their nature to resist. They kind of make you feel like Darth Vader when you push them to do something awful, like eat healthy food. So, because parents literally can't win these battles, schools are now required to teach health and nutrition classes, and for good reason. Too many parents just give up at a certain point on their kids, finding it easier to let them eat whatever they want to. In my case, at least meat offers lots of protein—but what if I preferred only potato chips and nachos? Health and nutrition classes, in my opinion, should definitely stay in the school system. They teach us what will happen to our bodies if we ignore all the nutritious stuff and go straight for the greasy, deep-fried stuff. I've taken the class three times at different schools, and it's had an effect. Last week I ate a salad with my burger, and I managed to keep it down.

In the article "Schools Cannot Raise America's Children," author Jamie Vollmer writes, "As Americans, we must decide the role of parents, schools and communities if we are to effectively prepare our children to succeed in the 21st century. The bottom line: Schools cannot do it all. Schools cannot raise America's children." I agree, schools *can't* raise children, not literally. However, they must play an important role in the process of preparing kids for life after high school. While it's true that parents do need to teach their children core knowledge and values, schools need to be a part in that teaching process. In contrast to what Vollmer claims, it's *parents* who "cannot do it all." We all know that there are too many kids out there who haven't been raised very well by their parents. What happens to them? Do they end up in jail at age 16? Schools can help reach these wayward souls and get them back on track when parents aren't there—or don't care.

And what about computer technology? The vast number of tech products that emerge each year is only increasing, meaning that the job market for video game designers, code programmers, hardware designers, and a dozen other fields is rapidly increasing too. Most parents don't have the money to buy expensive programs for drafting, or graphics-intensive equipment to design video games, let alone have the time or expertise to teach their kids how to use them. Schools have begun to offer classes that will give students valuable experience in a possible career field using technology, and these courses also let the students know if this is something they might want to do with the rest of their lives.

The point is that while it's true schools cannot raise our children alone, who else is going to teach kids the many things that parents can't? And if we were to get really logical, since kids are at school for a good chunk of the day, on most days of the year, why *shouldn't* schools use that time to teach the things the parents can't? The hourglass continues to drain each day, Mr. Vollmer. Do *you* want to teach your kids about all those things on your list?

* * *

Schools Must Raise America's Children
by Chris Arntson

At 14, I knew little of the evils of alcohol. One evening my father decided to enlighten me on the subject. "Don't drink, boy!" he exclaimed. "It doesn't taste good and it does nothing for you." Then he went to the refrigerator for another Miller High Life. After half a dozen more excursions into the kitchen, his personality began to change. His mood lightened, and his speech became more simplistic. He was happier and more loving, calm and relaxed; he became a better man in my eyes.

Many nights went exactly as this one had. After his first declaration against alcohol, my father showed me otherwise by his example. It wasn't until high school that I learned the truth about alcoholism: the impaired decisions, rotting livers, and mangled bodies of drunk-driving victims showed me that alcohol did not make my father a better man. It made him a hypocrite.

Reprinted by permission of Christian P. Arntson.

When is it no longer an option for parents to teach their children about important issues like alcoholism? My father taught me the wrong way, and I know I wasn't the only kid given the same false message. But school set me on the right path and provided me with a professional, stable atmosphere in which I could learn about the incredibly negative aspects of alcohol. There is a misconception in this country that issues like alcohol awareness should only be taught by parents, not burden the nation's public schools. But what happens to children when their parents can't— or won't—teach what they themselves have become victims of? A safety net has to be in place to catch those children and set them on a path to success. School caught me, and it will continue to catch the nation's children and set them on a path to success. School caught me, and it will continue to catch the nation's children when they need it.

In a historical overview entitled "Schools Cannot Raise America's Children" by Jamie Vollmer, the author lists the increasing responsibilities taken on by our country's public school system. As new responsibilities are added, few are removed, leading the author to conclude that "schools cannot do it all." While I agree that schools should not raise our children alone, I still need to point out that 21st century parents are much different from those in earlier times. Parents today work much more than those in the past, and gone are the days when one's income could support an entire family, leaving one parent at home. This situation leaves less time for family activities and less time for parents to teach their children. Vollmer argues that "as Americans we must decide the role of parents, schools and communities if we are to effectively prepare our children to succeed in the 21st century." But it looks to me like the decision has already been made: since both parents must work to stay afloat now, schools must pick up the slack.

What happens when parents do get enough precious time to educate their kids, but use it to teach the wrong ideas? For instance, I have a friend with racist parents, who make no effort to hide their idea that people of different races are of lesser value. Attitudes like this will undoubtedly influence the child, and my friend has confessed to me that he did begin to believe as his parents did—until he went to school. School showed him that all people, no matter what color, were equally capable in society. In the end, it was school that provided him the opportunity to learn about different cultures and ethnicities, not the wrongheaded myths that his parents taught.

Another aspect of Vollmer's overview is the fact that schools have had to add courses such as keyboarding and computer education to accommodate our technology-focused world. But this may be the only option because many families lack the finances to own a computer, and others can't teach their children much because the parents never used a computer themselves. In many cases, it's the children of a family who teach their parents how to use all of the technology in the house, so schools must be the place to support the community in ensuring that all children, both rich and poor, have the chance to learn on the tools of tomorrow.

Finally, let's take a look at the controversial subject of sex education in our schools. Many parents disagree with the idea of school being the source of such delicate information, but then again, many of those same parents don't want to explain sex to their kids either. So if children learn nothing from anyone, it will be all about having fun and feeling good and paying little attention to the risks and responsibilities that they don't know about. Schools create awareness and discuss everything from abstinence to what can happen as a result of having sex. A campaign of knowledge is much more valuable—and successful—than one of ignorance.

In today's hectic environment, parents have less and less time to teach their children about important social skills and topics. Our nation's school system has been called upon to teach our youth about the issues and challenges they will face in life, but some people like Jamie Vollmer have decided that this should not be the schools' responsibility. At the same time, America itself has decided that parents cannot possibly have the home lives they once did. Like it or not, school *has* to be that safety net to catch our children.

A Student's Farewell

by Chris

There are a few things I like about college, but a great many more that I don't. The positive aspects have kept me going through my first two years, but the negative ones have led me to decide that I won't be around for a third.

This university seems to be one big social club, and people are here to major in meet-your-future-spouse 101 or life-is-a-beer-swilling-frat-orgy 102. It's also very annoying to be surrounded by people whose sole interest in life is "making lots of money." Money controls everything here. Greek organizations and ROTC get more advertising than political debates, guest lecturers, literary gatherings, or even classes, for that matter. And why not? We've got to enforce those time-honored standards of racism, sexism, conformity, and general stupidity that have made going to college such a worthwhile endeavor for Americans in the past twelve years or so.

Don't let me give the impression that college is entirely pointless. The fact is, many of the faculty around here teach some pretty neat classes. And the key word there is *teach*—they don't just show up and lecture aimlessly; they try to share what they know. But that usually gets wasted on the ignorant slobs filling up the room, who could care less about learning anything. How many more minutes till class ends? Is this gonna be on the test? Why do you expect us to read the book? Can't you just cover the important parts? I skipped the last two weeks; can you tell me what we did?

If I was a teacher, I'd start screaming.

As a child, I built up a glorious vision for the concept of higher education. The very word, "college," conjured up images of lush campus courtyards filled with thousands of dedicated scholars willing to become, if not their country's leaders, then at least its benefactors. College was a place where young men and women went to gain *knowledge* as well as experience, in preparation for "real life." But now the academy is a place of ethical corruption and mental apathy. Due to the warped values that modern American society has instilled so thoroughly in our youth, the university has become just another industry, a big machine that accepts teenagers at one end and spits them out at the other as materialistic, selfish, and stupid adults. The intent of today's students is not the constant quest for knowledge and intellectual enlightenment, but material gain and social status. The old intellectual traditions are quickly dying out. Today's students see college only as a means to making money.

We're already living in a society that prefers to be apathetic and wants everything given to it with minimal effort. Reflecting this, students cheat on exams, have other people do their class work, and even plagiarize whole papers so they can get that all-important "A" and be done with it. Doesn't matter (or maybe they're too stupid to realize) that the "A" is completely pointless when it's obtained this way.

In the past, the academy was armed by learned professors who could spot these corrupt attitudes and turn them away. But too many people who call themselves "students," but are nothing more than crass consumers, have infiltrated the system completely and brought it down. A few *real* students remain, but no one is around to encourage them or praise their hard work. Apathy breeds apathy; the whole machine begins to feed on itself.

I commend this university for its fine job of churning out legions of unappreciative, unthinking robots, but I don't want to become one of them. So I'm leaving. I won't drop out, exactly; instead I'll travel around the country and try to find a *real* "academy of higher learning" where intellectual wealth is more important than materialism. Where students are scholars, who actually try to make a difference. Where people know the real meaning of "education."

I hope my search won't be wasted.

So long.

* * *

Farewell to You, Student

by Sylvie Hang

Imagine being stuck in a classroom full of slobs who could not care less about learning anything. Everyone's complaining and doodling in their notebooks and talking to the person in the next row, and no one is paying attention to the professor. That doesn't matter, because the professor just goes on lecturing for the rest of the semester anyway, and you're the only one listening to any of it.

This is how the author of "A Student's Farewell" portrays college life, but thank God the reality isn't like that at all. In real life, at the beginning of each new semester classes are packed to the max, but a couple of weeks later, those who choose not to be there have already dropped the class. The students still present are the ones who really want to listen and learn.

In his argument, Mr. Farewell claims that his university is just a big hangout club: you know, kind of like high school. He writes that "[t]his university seems to be one big social club. And people are here to major in meet-your-future-spouse 101 or life-is-a-beer-swilling-frat-orgy 102." Well, okay, that might be the case at some schools, but let's keep in mind that everyone needs to maintain a certain GPA in order to keep "hanging out" there. And who ever said that school had to be boring? If some people meet their spouses there, so what? If seniors drink a lot of beer (and don't drive of course), do we really care? The way I see it, as long as you can do what you need to do as a student, then go ahead and have some fun while you're at it.

Mr. Farewell claims that going to college will make a person "materialistic, selfish, and stupid. The intent of today's students is not the constant quest for knowledge and intellectual enlightenment, but material gain and social status." But I say he's wrong, and here's just one reason why: art majors. Some artists may be born with all the talent they need, but most have to learn techniques and design skills by attending classes with professional artists as their teachers. Even after graduation, art is *not* a profession where wealth and prestige are guaranteed. And art is one of the most unselfish of all professions because the product is shared with everyone. Yet no matter how difficult it can be for artists to make a living, they continue to do what they love, and they continue to learn along the way.

Additionally, Mr. Farewell writes that students are only in college to make money. Of course, some *are* in it for the money, but some are not. For example, we all know that teachers aren't paid nearly enough for the amount of work and dedication they put into their jobs, but there are many students majoring in education. Are those students going to college just for the salaries they'll make? No! They're trying to make a difference by teaching others the things that they themselves are learning. Once again, this sounds pretty unselfish, non-materialistic, and smart—contrary to what the author of "Farewell" claims.

Toward the end of his argument, that author also complains that "a few *real* students remain, but no one is around to encourage them or praise their hard work." Well, this is where teachers, parents, spouses, significant others, friends, and even children step into the picture. All of them have a role in encouraging students and giving them support in what they're doing. But the writer of "Farewell" is so blinded by his negative views that he forgets to give credit to all of these people who are so important.

He cleverly defines the "real" meaning of education as "intellectual wealth [being] more important than materialism," but isn't it funny that although he may know this, he doesn't do anything to encourage or create it? Instead, he *leaves* his school to go and look for a "real academy of higher learning." In his argument, the author seems to be describing himself without even knowing it. The whole message is about the negative aspects of college, but he himself is one of those students who don't want to be taught anything. He blames the school and the society for his own failure to contribute. Claiming to understand the real meaning of education and to be in search of others who understand it, too, he does not realize that many of his previous classmates were exactly what he's searching for. It's sad to say this, but maybe it was better for the writer to leave. He certainly showed a lot of apathy toward education.

* * *

Student E-mail

Dear Professor,

I have a few concerns regarding your English class that I feel I need to bring to your attention. I feel that you have very high expectations for our class and that you don't realize that we are a community college. I know you come from a university where the kids have mostly graduated with a 3.5 GPA and higher. They have a lot easier time understanding things and don't need as much attention paid to them. At our community college some of us only have GEDs and need a little more explanation. That is why we're not at a university. Community college is for students who need a little extra help with their work and don't have as easy of a time comprehending things. So please understand this and take it easier on us because we are not your high-standard university kids.

Sincerely,

Most of Your Class

* * *

Who's Better Than Whom?

by Shonté Terhune

When you think of a university student, do you think of a scholar? Do you think of someone who excelled in high school? Well, universities have a variety of students. There are some who were average and barely made it through high school, partied through their freshman year, never went to class, and eventually dropped out. Would you call them "quality students"?

When you think of a community college student, do you think of someone who couldn't succeed at the university level? In your mind, were they slackers in high school, troublemakers, baby mamas, and kids on probation? Some people do characterize students at two-year colleges in just these ways.

I attended a university for two years, and currently I attend a community college. And from my experience, students who attend universities are no different from community college students. If you don't have good study skills and good time management techniques, all of your merits in high school will mean nothing in either kind of higher learning setting. An average high school student can come to college and do better than an honor student.

Recently, I read an email that had been sent to a college English professor. The student claimed to have sent the message

Reprinted by permission of Shonté Terhune.

on behalf of the whole class but sent the email anonymously. The message made generalizations about community college students and their alleged standards, and it displayed a lack of confidence in what kind of people they are.

The writer refers to students with GEDs (General Equivalency Degrees) as if they need special attention. A GED is *equivalent* to a high school diploma, meaning that the person with a GED is no different from someone with a diploma. People with GEDs are admitted to universities and community colleges, and I wouldn't know how to recognize if a classmate had a GED unless she told me. Sure, there are some people who don't understand everything that is taught to them at every educational level—and that's why we're in school: to *learn* how to understand it. We have opportunities to ask questions, and help is provided through many offices on campus. Tutors can help with most subjects, and students with learning disabilities receive needed accommodations. I have gone to my own college's writing center to receive help with my writing process from tutors and teachers.

It's safe to assume that the person who wrote the email message thought very highly of university students and thought less of his or her self and peers. But as a former university student, I know that those students don't have "an easier time understanding things." Actually, they need just as much "attention" paid to them as community college students. But since they're at a university where there are often hundreds of students in a lecture hall instead of thirty in a small classroom, they receive *less* of the attention they need. It's hard to ask a question in a huge lecture hall and feel comfortable among those whose faces you barely recognize after the semester ends, and there's no way to interrupt a professor and ask for more explanation without feeling stupid. At a community college you can become much more familiar with your professors.

In life all of us as students must have confidence when trying to achieve our goals, and we can't believe that we're inferior to anyone. The person who wrote the anonymous email message had some obviously low self-esteem about learning capabilities. Why would we want our professor to "take it easy"

on our learning? How will we learn anything in depth? All
students, not just those at universities, should have high
standards. Apparently this writer wanted pity, thinking that
community college would be a way out of doing hard work. Anyone
who thinks they are less of a person because of where they attend
school, and then wants someone to pity them because they don't
want to put forth effort to benefit from their education, should
evaluate the reason for being in school. Advancing your education
means expanding your current knowledge and overcoming obstacles
in order to become successful.

* * *

The Community College Difference
by Amy Lamb

I'd like everyone reading this to take a moment and
visualize two things for me right now. First, picture a community
college student. When you have that image in your mind, imagine a
university student. I'd be willing to bet that there are some
definite differences in how you've perceived those two kids of
students. For example, you might have seen the community college
student as someone who didn't do well in high school, or maybe
didn't graduate at all. On the other hand, you may have seen the
university student as someone who excelled in high school
academics and sports and was just a good, well-rounded person
overall. The problem with those two views, however widespread
they may be, is that they aren't accurate.

Recently my class read an anonymous email message from a
student in an earlier semester who shared those stereotypical
views of college students. The anonymous writer claims that
"[university students] have a lot easier time understanding
things and don't need as much attention paid to them," and that
university students "have mostly graduated with a 3.5 [grade
point average] and higher," Of course, those statements go right
along with the ways that many people view students who go to
large universities. But those views are inaccurate and highly
stereotypical. In fact, I know quite a few students who blow the
stereotype right out of the water. In high school, my best friend

---

Reprinted by permission of Amy Lamb.

was always viewed as a kid who was really going places. She was really smart, involved with the National Honor Society and yearbook committee, and a varsity cheerleader among many other things. She graduated in the top 20 of our class of nearly 500, and she went to a state university. Is she fitting your picture of a typical university student? If so, hold on. Halfway through her first semester she had to seek tutoring to help her through her classes, and she ended the year with a GPA so low that she wouldn't even tell me what it was.

The next point made in the anonymous email message is a belittling of students who "only have GEDs and need a little more explanation." The writer goes on to say, "That is why we are not at a university." What really bothers me about these statements is how the writer uses the phrase "*only* have GEDs." There is nothing wrong or shameful about having a General Equivalency Degree, which many people are proud to have earned. And when I say *earned,* I mean just that. There is a lot of dedication and hard work that goes into attaining a GED, often more than goes into a regular high school diploma. And it's certainly not just students with GEDs who need extra explanation sometimes. I've got a high school diploma and I'm a fairly good student, and there are plenty of times when I need things explained to me more fully. And there's nothing wrong with that, either. We all need a little extra clarification sometimes.

The last point that the email writer makes is that "[c]ommunity college is for students who need a little extra help with their work and don't have as easy of a time comprehending things." This is another stereotypical statement about community colleges and their students. While it's true that two-year colleges may be home to a few students who aren't quite ready for the demands of university life, the vast majority of us are here for other reasons that have nothing to do with our intelligence levels or ability to do class work on our own. Personally, I chose a community college simply because it's more affordable than going off to a university where I would get the same education, and I'm closer to my home and family. I know other students who chose community college to get their General Education requirements finished with the benefit of smaller, more

personal classes before transferring to a four-year school for
their degrees. I even know students who have transferred *from* a
university *to* a community college! How's that for contradicting
the community college stereotype? Two-year schools aren't just
places for students who have difficulty with their classes;
you'll find that anywhere.

Thinking Critically

Doxa: In classical rhetoric, an audience's opinions/judgments generally held to be correct. Plato and Aristotle saw *doxa* as the opposite of true knowledge (*episteme*), leading to a division still taught by Western culture: Opinions vs. Facts. Today, we also include a third division: Beliefs. This three-part categorization breaks down as follows:

- *Facts:* hold no opinion by themselves, nor are they connected to beliefs; they exist as confirmed, observable information. For example, *water is two parts hydrogen and one part oxygen* is a fact, as is *the Mackinac Bridge connects the two Michigan peninsulas.*

- *Beliefs:* cannot be substantiated or corroborated by observation; they are derived from emotion-based faith in the issue. *More than a ten percent return on stock investments is a moral outrage when the elimination of workers' jobs creates the profit* is a belief—note how it values jobs over profits. *A new Methodist church will be good for the community, but a Buddhist temple will only attract strange "new age" people who will confuse our children* is also a belief based on more value-focused terms. (Can you spot them?)

- *Opinions:* can be supported by opinions ("expert testimony" from qualified sources) and by factual evidence arranged in a logical way. Typically that arrangement can be:
  - A syllogism (see an extended discussion of the syllogism in Chapter 8), in which two (or more) premises are stated, followed by a conclusion, for example:
    - *Major premise:* Ignoring the advice of a majority of scientific studies may lead to catastrophe.
    - *Minor premise:* The United States government is ignoring a majority of scientific studies confirming that global warming is taking place and that action must be taken immediately to slow it.
    - *Conclusion:* The U.S. government's lack of action may lead to catastrophe.
  - An enthymeme, a variation on the syllogism. For logicians an enthymeme is an argument in which the conclusion, a premise, or combination of conclusion and premise(s) are left unstated and the audience supplies the missing idea.

- *Premise I:* The United States government insists that global warming needs "further study" before any action is taken.
- *Conclusion:* By ignoring scientific evidence, the U.S. government is risking catastrophe.

In this case, the audience provides the statement. "A majority of scientific studies confirm that global warming is taking place and that action must be taken immediately to slow it." (Note that an enthymeme can't succeed if an audience is unaware of the information required to supply the missing piece.)

CHAPTER 3

Examining Argument Through Dialectic and Induction

Asking Different Kinds of Questions

In what fundamental way do these three questions differ?

1. What is the capital of California?
2. What is your favorite flavor of ice cream?
3. Should Affirmative Action be a factor in determining college admissions?

The first question here has one correct answer: Sacramento is the capital of California. To answer this question, all you need is knowledge—either knowledge you already possess, or knowledge that you could obtain through an encyclopedia, a map of California, or an Internet site. While a heated discussion could take place in a dorm room between Joe, who believes Sacramento is the capital, and Mike, who is certain that it's Los Angeles, the debate would be foolish because the correct answer is readily available. No matter how long Joe and Mike might discuss the question, the answer will not change even if Mike convinces Joe that Los Angeles is the capital.

The second question has many possible answers, because the answer depends entirely on personal preference. With this type of question, just as in the first type, argument would be senseless. Returning to our hypothetical roommates, let's imagine that Mike remarks that Rocky Road is his favorite ice cream. "Dude," Joe responds, "that's not true. Your favorite is Cherry Garcia. You ate almost a half a gallon of it yesterday." Again, there could be a drawn-out discussion over the issue, but what would be the point? Personal preferences are just that: personal. They vary with each individual.

The third question above, however, could be discussed at length by reasonable people who disagree over its answer. In fact, the question has been discussed at least since the 1970s, and it remains an argumentative topic in our country to this day. With all of the evidence for and against Affirmative Action that has been collected over time, forming a position on the third question requires not only knowledge, but also judgment. Because of this, the topic covered by the question is based on an **argumentative proposition.**

Defining Rhetoric

Argumentative proposition: a statement with which reasonable people can and do disagree.

Identifying Argumentative Propositions

Argumentative propositions are statements with which reasonable persons can agree or disagree. While individuals may believe that their positions on particular argumentative propositions are correct (wars have been fought over disagreements about argumentative propositions), they also recognize that valid arguments can be made *against* their positions on argumentative topics. Argumentative propositions are the only statements about which it is productive and worthwhile to argue.

Which of the following are argumentative propositions?

The chemical formula for water is H_2O.

All nine-year-olds should be permitted to drive automobiles.

My favorite poet is Maya Angelou.

Christianity is the one true faith.

The Chicago Cubs will win the next World Series.

Affirmative Action should be a factor in determining college admissions.

Taking these statements one at a time, let's see how you did with your answers.

The chemical formula for water is H_2O. (Agree/Disagree)

Like the previous example about the capital of California, people could argue this proposition, but not productively. The answer is readily available in any number of resources. This is not an argumentative proposition, but a *fact*.

All nine-year-olds should be permitted to drive automobiles. (Agree/Disagree)

No reasonable person could argue the validity of this statement. Many nine-year-olds cannot understand complex road signs, their feet most often can't reach the pedals of a car . . . the statement is patently absurd. Any reasonable person would consider this statement a *fallacy*.

My favorite poet is Maya Angelou. (Agree/Disagree)

We've already seen an example of this kind of statement. As in the example of the ice cream, this is a statement of *personal preference,* in this case based on an individual sense of *aesthetics.* It is *subjective,* and is therefore not open to *objective* discussion.

Even if the statement were phrased differently, as in *Maya Angelou is the best of the twentieth-century poets,* it still would not be open to objective argument because the term, "best," is equally tied to individual aesthetic preferences.

Christianity is the one true faith. (Agree/Disagree)

At first glance, this may appear to be an argumentative proposition. But religious arguments of this type do not fit into the category of argumentative propositions for two reasons.

First, many philosophers distinguish between systems of thinking based on *faith* and on *logic.* Often, accepting a particular religious doctrine requires belief in events and situations that appear to defy logic: belief in miracles or in prophecy would fall into this category. But the millions of people who embrace religion feel that the tenets of their faith transcend logical thinking. Many outstanding rhetoricians have also been devout followers of various faiths, and they have found no contradiction in dealing with religious matters on a faith basis and other matters on a logic basis.

The second problem in dealing with the "One true faith" statement as an argumentative proposition lies in supplying *evidence.* While a devout Christian could point to the *New Testament* to establish proof, a devout Jew would probably not accept the *New Testament* as a reliable source and point to the *Torah* as the qualified source of answers for religious matters. Without an established base of resources to supply evidence, statements based on religious doctrine can't work as argumentative propositions because they are grounded in faith and belief.

The Chicago Cubs will win the next World Series. (Agree/Disagree)

Sadly for Chicagoans, many baseball fans would consider this statement a fallacy. After all, the Cubs have not won the Series since 1908. While any team, any year, has the possibility of being a Series contender until the season's end proves otherwise, the above statement is only argumentative for as long as the Cubs' standing gives them any hope—which usually fades around the end of August. An argumentative proposition can have a shelf life: events or experimental findings can turn what was formerly a proposition into a fact or a fallacy.

Affirmative Action should be a factor in determining college admissions. (Agree/Disagree)

This is a classic argumentative proposition. While many people feel strongly, even passionately, in favor of or against the use of Affirmative Action in determining admission to colleges and universities, few would claim that there are no good arguments that contradict their position.

Because of the number and complexity of arguments surrounding Affirmative Action and its role in college admissions, a great deal of judgment is necessary in designing policies that address the issue both practically and ethically. It's unlikely

TECHNIQUES FOR WRITERS 3-a
Developing Argumentative Propositions

Write five statements that you believe are valid argumentative propositions. Compare your argumentative propositions with the propositions listed by a classmate. See if you can agree on the validity of all ten of your propositions.

If you're unsure of the validity of some of your propositions, discuss them with your professor and/or the class.

that one policy for dealing with Affirmative Action can be adopted that will satisfy all who have an opinion about it, but everyone connected to the issue must still make decisions thoughtfully and thoroughly.

Constructing Arguments: Using Pro/Con Grids to Support Positions

Once you're certain that your argumentative proposition is valid, you can start to determine the nature and number of arguments that either support or counter the statement you want to make. This is a good time to begin **brainstorming**, developing lists of possible arguments on either side. To help in organization, you may want to develop two separate lists, one for arguments in favor of your statement and one for arguments against it. At this point, don't worry about evaluating the arguments for their validity or importance; in brainstorming, you just want to list as many items as you can. Evaluation comes later.

Defining Rhetoric

Brainstorming: a technique for generating ideas, usually done in the early stages of writing. In brainstorming, the writer lists possible ideas without making any judgments about or changes in those ideas.

With your two lists, you'll be developing a **Pro/Con Grid.**

Defining Rhetoric

Pro/Con Grid: lists of arguments that support and oppose the statement in an argumentative proposition.

An initial pro/con grid on the Argumentative Proposition "Affirmative Action should be a factor in determining college admissions (Agree/Disagree)" might look something like this:

Pro

- promotes diversity on college campuses
- gives opportunities to people who might otherwise not have them
- helps to make up for past discrimination against groups
- gives colleges the right to determine qualifications for admission

Con

- can discriminate against some students through "reverse discrimination"
- could lower standards if less-qualified candidates gain admission
- often stigmatizes minorities—some people assume that all minorities are in college only because of Affirmative Action
- can increase resentment and backlash

You may feel at this point that you have enough arguments upon which to make a decision. Based at least on the balanced numbers in each list, you can argue either way: Affirmative Action should or should not be a factor in determining college admissions. But because initial brainstorming produces only information you already know (and often confirms what you already believe), you can't really be sure that you have assembled a complete list of possible arguments for and against Affirmative Action as a basis for college admissions. This would be a good time to discuss your list with another student whose pro/con grid on the same subject lists factors you haven't considered. In the discussion, your classmate might make the following comments:

- "Other groups, such as athletes, the children of alumni at particular colleges, or students with particular skills in things like theater or music, also get preference in college admissions. Would you want to see these preferences eliminated as well?"
- "Many studies have demonstrated that white students do much better on the kind of testing that is the basis of college admissions, like the SAT and ACT tests. Too much dependence on standardized testing discriminates against minorities."
- "Despite years of Affirmative Action, the playing field is not yet equal. Minorities still graduate from college less frequently and make less money in their careers than do whites."

- "Affirmative Action has led to the development of a new black middle class, which has been economically beneficial to the country as a whole."

- "As long as graduation requirements and professional certification stay rigorous, Affirmative Action won't lead to less-qualified people in various professions."

You might think that some of your classmate's points aren't valid; for example, you may believe that standardized testing is the best way to determine future college success. But remember that brainstorming isn't the place for evaluation, and you should include all possibly valid arguments on your lists. With this in mind, the following items go onto the "Pro" section of your grid:

- other groups (athletes, children of alumni, students with particular skills) also receive preferences

- standardized testing discriminates against minority populations

- the playing field is not yet equal—fewer minorities graduate from college, and they make less money than whites

- development of black middle class—good for country's economy

- AA will not lead to less-qualified people in professions

Discussing the topic with a classmate has helped because now you have more to work with. But in truth, you've only begun to delve into this issue.

Identifying the Themes of Argument: ③
Searching for Underlying Ideas

Philosophers going back at least as far as Aristotle recognized that arguments could be constructed based on a number of *themes,* or underlying ideas. Some of the previous arguments concerning Affirmative Action in college admissions are based on several contemporary themes for argument:

- *Social:* arguments about what most benefits society as a whole (i.e., promotes diversity on college campuses; will not lower standards)

- *Moral/ethical:* arguments that a society believes represent the right or correct way to behave (i.e., provides opportunities to people who might otherwise not have them; gives colleges the right to determine admission qualifications; helps to correct standardized testing discrimination against minorities; works toward leveling the playing field)

- *Legal:* arguments that conform to a society's laws (i.e., anti-discrimination of any kind)

- *Economic:* arguments about what promotes financial benefits (i.e., development of a black middle class)

- *Comparative:* arguments based on what other groups/societies have done to address the issue, and their successes or failures

- *Analogical:* arguments based on comparisons (i.e., other groups also receive preferences)

- *Historical:* arguments that address past practice or situations (i.e., helps to make up for past discrimination)

- *Psychological:* arguments about the way people think (i.e., stigmatizes minorities; can increase resentment, backlash)

Looking at your lists, you'll notice that they contain several *social* and *moral/ethical* arguments. Because the subject of Affirmative Action deals largely with the concept of fairness, this isn't surprising. But you might see other areas that your pro/con grid hasn't addressed yet. For example, you may wonder whether there are other legal arguments than the ones you've already listed, or how other groups or societies deal with Affirmative Action.

This would be a good time to do some initial research in the topic. While the following essays cannot provide all of the research necessary for a topic of this depth and breadth, they do present some of the most common arguments in favor of and against using Affirmative Action in determining college admissions.

Critical Reading Questions

As you read the essays, concentrate particularly on the following questions:

1. Which arguments, both supporting and opposing the use of Affirmative Action in determining college admissions, have already been discussed?

2. Which arguments, both supporting and opposing the use of Affirmative Action in determining college admissions, are new to this discussion?

A Defense of Affirmative Action
Thomas Nagel

The term *affirmative action* has changed in meaning since it was introduced. Originally it referred only to special efforts to ensure equal opportunity for members of groups that had been subject to discrimination. These efforts included public advertisement of positions to be filled, active

---

Thomas Nagel, "A Defense of Affirmative Action," *QQ: Report from the Center for Philosophy and Public Policy,* Vol. 1, No. 4, Fall 1981. Reprinted by permission of the author.

recruitment of qualified applicants from the formerly excluded groups, and special training programs to help them meet the standards for admission or appointment. There was also close attention to procedures of appointment, and sometimes to the results, with a view to detecting continued discrimination, conscious or unconscious.

More recently the term has come to refer also to some degree of definite preference for members of these groups in determining access to positions from which they were formerly excluded. Such preference might be allowed to influence decisions only between candidates who are otherwise equally qualified, but usually it involves the selection of women or minority members over other candidates who are better qualified for the position.

Let me call the first sort of policy "weak affirmative action" and the second "strong affirmative action." It is important to distinguish them, because the distinction is sometimes blurred in practice. It is strong affirmative action—the policy of preference—that arouses controversy. Most people would agree that weak or precautionary affirmative action is a good thing, and worth its cost in time and energy. But this does not imply that strong affirmative action is also justified.

I shall claim that in the present state of things it is justified, most clearly with respect to blacks. But I also believe that a defender of the practice must acknowledge that there are serious arguments against it, and that it is defensible only because the arguments for it have great weight. Moral opinion in this country is sharply divided over the issue because significant values are involved on both sides. My own view is that while strong affirmative action is intrinsically undesirable, it is a legitimate and perhaps indispensable method of pursuing a goal so important to the national welfare that it can be justified as a temporary, though not short-term, policy for both public and private institutions. In this respect it is like other policies that impose burdens on some for the public good.

Three Objections

5   I shall begin with the argument against. There are three objections to strong affirmative action: that it is inefficient; that it is unfair; and that it damages self-esteem.

The degree of inefficiency depends on how strong a role racial or sexual preference plays in the process of selection. Among candidates meeting the basic qualifications for a position, those better qualified will on the average perform better, whether they are doctors, policemen, teachers, or electricians. There may be some cases, as in preferential college admissions, where the immediate usefulness of making educational resources available to an individual is thought to be greater because of the use to which the education will be put or because of the internal effects on the institution itself. But by and large, policies of strong affirmative action must reckon

with the costs of some lowering in performance level: The stronger the preference, the larger the cost to be justified. Since both the costs and the value
of the results will vary from case to case, this suggests that no one policy of
affirmative action is likely to be correct in all cases, and that the cost of performance level should be taken into account in the design of a legitimate
policy.

The charge of unfairness arouses the deepest disagreements. To be
passed over because of membership in a group one was born into, where
this has nothing to do with one's individual qualifications for a position,
can arouse strong feelings of resentment. It is a departure from the ideal—
one of the values finally recognized in our society—that people should be
judged so far as possible on the basis of individual characteristics rather
than involuntary group membership.

This does not mean that strong affirmative action is morally repugnant
in the manner of racial or sexual discrimination. It is nothing like those
practices, for though like them it employs race and sex as criteria of selection, it does so for entirely different reasons. Racial and sexual discrimination are based on contempt or even loathing for the excluded group, a
feeling that certain contacts with them are degrading to members of the
dominant group, that they are fit only for subordinate positions or menial
work. Strong affirmative action involves none of this: It is simply a means
of increasing the social and economic strength of formerly victimized
groups, and does not stigmatize others.

There is an element of individual unfairness here, but it is more like the
unfairness of conscription in wartime, or of property condemnation under
the right of eminent domain. Those who benefit or lose out because of their
race or sex cannot be said to deserve their good or bad fortune.

10   It might be said on the other side that the beneficiaries of affirmative
action deserve it as compensation for past discrimination, and that compensation is rightly exacted from the group that has benefited from discrimination in the past. But this is a bad argument, because as the practice
usually works, no effort is made to give preference to those who have suffered most from discrimination, or to prefer them especially to those who
have benefited most from it, or been guilty of it. Only candidates who in
other qualifications fall on one or the other side of the margin of decision
will directly benefit or lose from the policy, and these are not necessarily, or
even probably, the ones who especially deserve it. Women or blacks who
don't have the qualifications even to be considered are likely to have been
handicapped more by the effects of discrimination than those who receive
preference. And the marginal white male candidate who is turned down can
evoke our sympathy if he asks, "Why me?" (A policy of explicitly compensatory preference, which took into account each individual's background of
poverty and discrimination, would escape some of these objections, and it

has its defenders, but it is not the policy I want to defend. Whatever its merits, it will not serve the same purpose as direct affirmative action.)

The third objection concerns self-esteem, and is particularly serious. While strong affirmative action is in effect, and generally known to be so, no one in an affirmative action category who gets a desirable job or is admitted to a selective university can be sure that he or she has not benefited from the policy. Even those who would have made it anyway fall under suspicion, from themselves and from others: It comes to be widely felt that success does not mean the same thing for women and minorities. This painful damage to esteem cannot be avoided. It should make any defender of strong affirmative action want the practice to end as soon as it has achieved its basic purpose.

Justifying Affirmative Action

I have examined these three objections and tried to assess their weight, in order to decide how strong a countervailing reason is needed to justify such a policy. In my view, taken together they imply that strong affirmative action involving significant preference should be undertaken only if it will substantially further a social goal of the first importance. While this condition is not met by all programs of affirmative action now in effect, it is met by those which address the most deep-seated, stubborn, and radically unhealthy divisions in the society, divisions whose removal is a condition of basic justice and social cohesion.

The situation of black people in our country is unique in this respect. For almost a century after the abolition of slavery we had a rigid racial caste system of the ugliest kind, and it only began to break up twenty-five years ago. In the South it was enforced by law, and in the North, in a somewhat less severe form, by social convention. Whites were thought to be defiled by social or residential proximity to blacks, intermarriage was taboo, blacks were denied the same level of public goods—education and legal protection—as whites, were restricted to the most menial occupations, and were barred from any positions of authority over whites. The visceral feelings of black inferiority and untouchability that this system expressed were deeply ingrained in the members of both races, and they continue, not surprisingly, to have their effect. Blacks still form, to a considerable extent, a hereditary social and economic community characterized by widespread poverty, unemployment, and social alienation.

When this society finally got around to moving against the caste system, it might have done no more than to enforce straight equality of opportunity, perhaps with the help of weak affirmative action, and then wait a few hundred years while things gradually got better. Fortunately it decided instead to accelerate the process by both public and private institutional action, because there was wide recognition of the intractable character of the problem posed by this insular minority and its place in the nation's history and collective consciousness. This has not been going on very long, but the results are already impressive, especially in speeding the advancement of blacks into the middle class. Affirmative action has not done much to improve the position of poor and unskilled blacks. That is the most serious part of the problem, and it requires a more direct economic attack. But increased access to higher education and upper-level jobs is an essential part of what must be achieved to break the structure of drastic separation that was left largely undisturbed by the legal abolition of the caste system.

15   Changes of this kind require a generation or two. My guess is that strong affirmative action for blacks will continue to be justified into the early decades of the next century, but that by then it will have accomplished what it can and will no longer be worth the costs. One point deserves special emphasis. The goal to be pursued is the reduction of a great social injustice, no proportional representation of the races in all institutions and professions. Proportional racial representation is of no value in itself. It is not a legitimate social goal, and it should certainly not be the aim of strong affirmative action, whose drawbacks make it worth adopting only against a serious and intractable social evil.

This implies that the justification for strong affirmative action is much weaker in the case of other racial and ethnic groups, and in the case of women. At least, the practice will be justified in a narrower range of circumstances and for a shorter span of time than it is for blacks. No other group has been treated quite like this, and no other group is in a comparable status. Hispanic-Americans occupy an intermediate position, but it seems to be frankly absurd to include persons of oriental descent as beneficiaries of affirmative action, strong or weak. They are not a severely deprived and excluded minority, and their eligibility serves only to swell the numbers that can be included on affirmative action reports. It also suggests that there is a drift in the policy toward adopting the goal of racial proportional representation for its own sake. This is a foolish mistake, and should be resisted. The only legitimate goal of the policy is to reduce egregious racial stratification.

With respect to women, I believe that except over the short term, and in professions or institutions from which their absence is particularly marked, strong affirmative action is not warranted and weak affirmative action is enough. This is based simply on the expectation that the social and economic situation of women will improve quite rapidly under conditions of full equality of opportunity. Recent progress provides some evidence for this. Women do not form a separate hereditary community, characteristically poor and uneducated, and their position is not likely to be self-perpetuating in the same way as that of an outcast race. The process requires less artificial acceleration, and any need for strong affirmative action for women can be expected to end sooner than it ends for blacks.

I said at the outset that there was a tendency to blur the distinction between weak and strong affirmative action. This occurs especially in the use of numerical quotas, a topic on which I want to comment briefly.

A quota may be a method of either weak or strong affirmative action, depending on the circumstances. It amounts to weak affirmative action— a safeguard against discrimination—if, and only if, there is independent evidence that average qualifications for the positions being filled are no lower in the group to which a minimum quota is being assigned than in the applicant group as a whole. This can be presumed true of unskilled jobs that most people can do, but it becomes less likely, and harder to establish, the greater the skill and education required for the position. At these levels, a quota proportional to population, or even to representation of the group in the applicant pool, is almost certain to amount to strong affirmative action. Moreover it is strong affirmative action of a particularly crude and indiscriminate kind, because it permits no variation in the degree of preference on the basis of costs in efficiency, depending on the qualification gap. For this reason I should defend quotas only where they serve the purpose of weak affirmative action. On the whole, strong affirmative action is better implemented by including group preference as one factor in appointment or admission decisions, and letting the results depend on its interaction with other factors.

20   I have tried to show that the arguments against strong affirmative action are clearly outweighed at present by the need for exceptional measures to remove the stubborn residues of racial caste. But advocates of the policy should acknowledge the reasons against it, which will ensure its termination when it is no longer necessary. Affirmative action is not an end in itself, but a means of dealing with a social situation that should be intolerable to us all.

Affirmative Action Must Go
Shelby Steele

There are many indications that affirmative action may soon provoke what it has never provoked before: a national debate on group preferences that will be so open and contentious that no important politician will be able to avoid a hard yea or nay position.

This has all been started by the threat of another of those California statewide initiatives in which some long-simmering public bitterness

Shelby Steele, "Affirmative Action Must Go," *The New York Times,* March 1, 1995, p. A19. Reprinted by permission of Carol Mann Agency.

explodes onto the ballot and is then argued out in the national village of talk radio. Next year, Californians are to vote on the appropriateness of preferential treatment by sex, race, and ethnic origin as a form of social redress. What an odd opportunity: to vote in secret on the idea that some citizens should be preferred over others in public employment, contracting, and higher education.

I wish my parents had had such a vote back in the 1950s, when I was languishing in a segregated elementary school created by white preferential treatment. My guess is that Californians will vote as my parents would surely have voted then: against preferences of any kind.

Significantly, most of the new interest in affirmative action seems to be political rather than social. The buzz is all about how the issue will wedge the Democrats into white male moderates on one flank and minorities and women on the other—an ugly resegregation of America's "civil rights" party that will make President Clinton even more vulnerable than he already is.

5   There is little talk about affirmative action as public policy. One reason, I think, is that affirmative action has always been what might be called iconographic public policy—policy that ostensibly exists to solve a social problem but actually functions as an icon for the self-image people hope to gain by supporting the policy. From the beginning, affirmative action could be cited as evidence of white social virtue and of emerging black power—the precise qualities that America's long history of racism had denied to each side.

Had America worked from the 1960s on to educate blacks to the same standards as whites, had it truly labored to eradicate discrimination, there would be more virtue and power on both sides of the racial divide today. The disingenuousness of affirmative action—born of the black struggle for freedom—can be seen in two remarkable facts: Middle-class white women have benefited from it far more than any other group, and 46 percent of all black children live in poverty.

The perniciousness of an iconographic social policy is that you cannot be against it without seeming to be against what it purports to represent. The white who argues against affirmative action looks like a racist and the black looks like an Uncle Tom. Iconographic policies perpetuate themselves by hiding behind what they represent. This is why, after twenty-five years, affirmative action is one of the least evaluated social policies in American history. The price for accepting its illusion of virtue and power is ignorance.

Not only do we blind ourselves to the workings of a social policy that becomes an icon, but in search of a flattering self-image we justify the policy by vague ideals like "diversity." And the emptiness of these ideals makes the policy unaccountable for any result it may have, so it remains an icon whether or not it accomplishes anything in the real world.

Diversity policies (today's euphemism for affirmative action) exist in virtually every important institution even though no one really knows what diversity means. Both proportionate and disproportionate representation reflect diversity; integration is one kind of diversity and segregation another. Here is an idealism that destroys accountability in social policy, and a language of willed ignorance in which the words mean only that the speaker has good intentions.

10   Still, as much as I loathe affirmative action—for the indignity and Faustian bargain it presents to minorities, for the hypocrisy and shameless self-congratulation it brings out in its white supporters—I must admit that it troubles me to see its demise so glibly urged from the political right. The Republican presidential aspirants are stumbling over one another to condemn it. While they are right to do so—and right is right even when it is nothing more than right—there is also the matter of moral authority. And this is something anyone who wants to dismantle affirmative action will have to earn.

I would ask those who oppose preferences to acknowledge and account for the reality of black alienation. As a black, I still fear discrimination, still have the feeling that it is waiting for me in public America. Discrimination does not justify preferential treatment, but I want to know that the person who stands with me against preferences understands the problem that inspired them.

To my mind there is only one way to moral authority for those of us who want affirmative action done away with: to ask that discrimination by race, gender, or ethnicity be a criminal offense, not just civil. If someone can go to jail for stealing my car stereo, he ought to do considerably more time for stifling my livelihood and well-being by discriminating against me.

If this means there will be many trials and lawsuits, so be it. When the pressure is put precisely on the evil you want to eradicate, then individuals and institutions will quickly learn not only what discrimination is but also what fairness is—and fairness is a concept so confused by decades of affirmative action that many now believe it can be reached only through discrimination.

Ending affirmative action must involve more than bringing down an icon. It must also involve an extension of democratic principles to what might be an extreme degree in a racially homogeneous society. But in a society like ours, discrimination is the greatest and most disruptive social evil. In a multiracial democracy of individuals, you have to make it a felony.

Affirmative Action and Campus Racism
Ernest van den Haag

Sufficient data are hard to come by, but it seems that racial incidents have increased recently, particularly in colleges. I should like to suggest two

Ernest van den Haag, "Affirmative Action and Campus Racism," *Academic Questions,* Summer 1989. Copyright © 1989 by Transaction Publishers. Reprinted by permission of the publisher.

propositions about cause and cure. The first is that racial incidents are unavoidable in multiracial societies, though such incidents can be minimized by education, or by criminal prosecution when violence is involved. The second is that racial incidents in our colleges are likely to increase as the effects of affirmative action practices are felt, as colleges pursue policies ostensibly meant to promote the perceived interests of racial minorities, and as minorities are given privileges withheld from others. This second proposition will be my focus here.

Affirmative action asks educational institutions to give preference in admissions, and employers to give preference in employment, to minorities. Blacks (and Hispanics) must be admitted, employed, and promoted even when, according to relevant tests used for all applicants, others are more qualified.

When segregation prevailed, few racial incidents occurred, since educational institutions were racially nearly homogeneous. But segregation placed blacks at a disadvantage; some of the best colleges would not admit them, despite merit, and they often had to content themselves with an inferior education.

After the Second World War segregation declined, while racial incidents increased only moderately. But Congress and the judiciary, always eager to "solve" problems which are about to disappear without their intervention, invented affirmative action as a means to compensate contemporary minorities for injustices done to minorities in the past. Unfortunately, the minority individuals who suffered unwarranted disadvantages in the past are not the ones to whom compensatory advantages are granted. The compensatory advantage goes to persons who resemble past victims of discrimination or oppression, in skin color or minority status, but are not themselves identified as victims of discrimination. On the other hand, the persons at whose expense the compensatory advantages are granted—i.e., whites, who, though no less meritorious, are not admitted or promoted so as to give preference to blacks—are not the ones who caused the past discrimination, nor can they be shown to have directly or indirectly profited from it.

5   Whatever the original intent behind affirmative action, in its final stage it has led educational institutions to admit a (disguised) quota of blacks who would not qualify by the criteria customarily applied to others.[1] Quotas are clearly inconsistent with the spirit of our educational institutions, which requires that there be no discrimination among members of actual or potential college populations, except on the basis of individual merit. This is what

---

[1]Administrative agencies and the judiciary had no difficulty overcoming the congressional prohibition of quotas that had helped the original civil rights legislation pass. Once the Civil Rights Act of 1964 was on the books they simply acted as though it instituted quotas. Later congressional action countenanced this "interpretation," although it is clearly contrary to the words of the law and to the original intent of Congress. [van den Haag's note.]

is meant by equality of opportunity or (originally) by nondiscrimination. The admission of blacks with lower qualifications than the whites they displace violates this spirit. It must unavoidably seem illegitimate to the majority.

To be sure, violations of equal opportunity have occurred in the past. But affirmative action institutionalizes a new discriminatory policy in the guise of compensating for a prior discriminatory policy. Whether favored blacks and Hispanics really benefit is dubious; it can be as harmful to be discriminated for as to be discriminated against. Many minority students feel uncomfortable in the majority environment, either because of background or insufficient qualifications. They tend to live together, apart from the rest of the college community. They take classes (e.g., black studies) that guarantee good grades without much effort. But, feeling uncomfortable, the black students tend to make demands for more black students, more black faculty, and a more black-oriented curriculum. Unwilling and unable to profit from the existing curriculum, they feel that courses of study should be adapted to minority demands. Often they are supported by guilt-ridden whites, particularly among the faculty. Indeed, it sometimes seems that demonstrations and occupations of college facilities by blacks constitute most of the campus "racial incidents" we are hearing about. Usually such demonstrations achieve concessions, however small the number of demonstrators, as well as impunity, however illegal the actions.

What is to be done? The admission of minority students less qualified than the majority students they replace cannot but increase friction within the student body. How could the preference extended to black students and faculty members not create bad blood and increase the number of racial incidents? The existence of numerous on-campus institutions to help minority students and dampen hostility to them will, if anything, increase the provocation. The minority is disliked not qua minority but qua preferred and privileged. The institutions that ostensibly exist to help minorities simply make the privileges more visible. The only way to diminish racial hostility, and thereby, the number of racial incidents in educational institutions, is to stop both discrimination against and preferment toward minorities, to treat all individuals equally regardless of race or sex, and to admit them solely on the basis of their individual merit.

Less formally, but quite as insistently, affirmative action is practiced by many universities in selecting and promoting black and Hispanic faculty members. The result is that black faculty members are often less qualified than white ones. Even well-qualified black degree holders suffer from the public perception that they got their degrees without meeting the same standards as whites. The perception, however unfair in some cases, does not help self-esteem, and those who are actually well qualified suffer. Among students, existing prejudices against blacks are confirmed when the students find that black faculty members are often less qualified than their white colleagues. Affirmative action has thus done as much injury to black scholars as to black students.

If colleges feel that blacks cannot meet ordinary admissions standards because they come from a deprived or disadvantaged environment—and surely this is true for some—the colleges can make suitable remedial efforts. They can tutor college-bound black high school students to help them meet admissions standards and to benefit from a college education, something only a few colleges now do. Tutoring efforts are economically unwise (returns are greater with the most rather than the least able) but politically wise: They may help produce proportional representation of blacks among the educated.

10   The greatest harm currently suffered by blacks is done by those who want to favor them. Indeed, a vested bureaucratic interest in affirmative action has grown up, and unfortunately many black political leaders benefit from this policy. Schools and corporations have hired affirmative action officers to establish and hide employment quotas, as well as to provide and hide other privileges for minorities. These employees cling to their roles and for the most part are unemployable in any other. Leaders benefit from the advantages of being "spokesmen" and from being able to mobilize the guilt feeling of whites profitably, while telling their supporters that they can pro-cure advantages without effort. In the long run blacks will have to pay for this demagogic leadership.

Since the foregoing remarks predictably will be called racist I should like to clarify the use of that term. I believe a person can properly be called a racist if he believes in the inferiority of one race to another, not in some activity or ability such as mathematics or baseball, but in a general sense; and further, if he believes that the "inferior" race should not be entitled to equal treatment, but subordinated to the "superior" one and discriminated against, i.e., deprived of advantages enjoyed by the superior race.

If this definition is accepted, I find nothing racist in my remarks or beliefs. On the contrary, I find affirmative action practices to be racist. Thus the racial incidents they inspire do not surprise me.

Racial Justice on the Cheap
Stephen L. Carter

I often feel that I should oppose all racial preferences in admission to college and professional school. But I don't. When the law school admission season rolls around during the winter, I find myself drawn to the folders of

Stephen L. Carter, "Racial Justice on the Cheap." From *Reflections of an Affirmative Action Baby* by Stephen L. Carter. Copyright © 1991 by Stephen L. Carter. Reprinted by permission of Basic Books, a member of Perseus Books, L.L.C.

applicants who are not white, as though to something rare and precious. Those folders I give an extra bit of scrutiny, looking, perhaps, for reasons to recommend a Yes. I am not trying to get the numbers right and I do not believe that the standards applied by colleges or professional schools are racist; rather, I find myself wanting others to have the same leg up that I had. The question is whether I can square this instinct with what I have said about the damage that preferences do. One of the principal mistaken emphases (or perhaps a public relations problem) of the modern diversity movement . . . is that it often seems in its rhetoric to press toward circumventing or eradicating standards, rather than training us and pushing us until we are able to meet them. There is an important distinction between this modern approach and the more traditional understanding of affirmative action as a program that would help a critical mass of us gain the necessary training to meet the standards of our chosen fields rather than seeking to get around them. Not the least of the difficulties is that the more time we spend arguing that various standards for achievement are culturally inappropriate, the more other people are likely to think we are afraid of trying to meet them.

My own view is that, given training, given a chance, we as a people need fear no standards. That is why I want to return the special admission programs to their more innocent roots, as tools for providing that training and that chance for students who might not otherwise have it. A college or university is not fulfilling its educational missions if it fails to take a hard look at the applicant pool to be sure that it is not missing highly motivated students—some of them people of color, some of them not—who might not be "sure things" but who show good evidence of being positioned to take advantage of what the school can offer. This means taking risks, but that is what higher educational institutions ought to be doing—not to fill a quota or to look good on paper or to keep student activists quiet, and certainly not to bring into the student body a group of students who will thereafter be called upon to represent the distinctive voices of oppressed people (imagine the brouhaha were a professor to take this idea seriously in calling on students in class discussion), but because the purveying of knowledge, the reason universities exist, is a serious enterprise, and one professors should undertake joyfully, even when it isn't easy and even when there is a risk of failure.

Of course, the students who are admitted because a school has decided to take a chance on them will not look as good on paper as those who are admitted because they are sure things; and the odds are that those with the better paper records will be the better performers, too, which is why grades and test scores are considered in the first place. The school, then, is admitting more than one group of students. Many students are admitted because of their paper qualifications, and these are the ones on which the school is likely to pin its highest hopes for academic attainment. The rest are admitted because they have benefited from one preference or another: legacy (as children of alumni are sometimes called), athlete, geography, even in some places music. And some receive a preference because of race.

All the beneficiaries of preferences, not just those who have earned a place through racial preferences, would have been excluded had only a paper record been used. But although every college has its stereotypes of the dumb jock and the stupid legacy, there is a qualitative difference between these characterizations and the conscious or unconscious racial nature of similar comments about the beneficiaries of racially conscious affirmative action. For just as a different standard for admission or hiring reinforces a double standard for the measurement of success, it also reinforces a double standard for the consequence of failure. When a person admitted because of membership in a special category does not succeed, that lack of success is often attributed to others in the same category. The stereotype of the dumb jock exists because of the widespread perception (a correct one) that athletes are frequently admitted on paper records for which other students would be rejected. When people of color are admitted in the same fashion, the damage is worse, because the double standard reinforces an already existing stereotype, and because the stereotype, like the program, sorts explicitly according to race. Consequently, if our success rate at elite colleges turns out to be lower than that of white students (as, thus far, it is), we can scarcely avoid having the fact noticed and, in our racially conscious society, remembered as well.

5   This risk is a predictable consequence of double standards and cannot be avoided. It can, however, be reduced. The best way to reduce the risk would be to eliminate racial preferences, and over time, as the competitive capacity of people of color continues to improve. A more immediate solution is for those students who are admitted as a consequence of affirmative action, while on the college campus and while in professional school and while pursuing their careers—in short, *for the rest of their professional lives*— to bend to their work with an energy that will leave competitors and detractors alike gasping in admiration. The way to turn this potential liability into a powerful asset is to make our cadre of professionals simply too good to ignore.

To accomplish this goal, the first thing that an opportunity-based affirmative action must do is to abandon the pretense that it will in any significant way compensate for present educational disadvantage. Programs of preferential admissions will not wipe away the lingering effects of struggling through the inner-city public schools about which the nation long ago ceased to care. To bring onto college campuses students whose academic abilities have been severely damaged by the conditions in which they have been forced to learn would be a recipe for failure. At best, affirmative action can take those students of color who have already shown the greatest potential and place them in environments where their minds will be tested and trained, the campuses of elite colleges and professional schools.

Besides, the evidence has long suggested, and recent studies have confirmed, that educational disadvantage is but one of a cluster of problems reducing the likelihood that students of color will attend or complete college. In the past decade, despite rising test scores, a higher rate of high school graduation, and affirmative action programs galore, college attendance by black students is down. In particular, the proportion of black youth aged eighteen to twenty-four who have been enrolled in college has plummeted. In 1976, 33.4 percent of that group were or had been enrolled in college, representing nearly half of black high school graduates; this compared very favorably with the 33.0 percent of white youth of the same age with enrollment experience, representing 40 percent of white high school graduates. Ten years later, although the high school graduation rate rose, the percentage of black youth with enrollment experience dropped to 28.6 percent, representing only 37.4 percent of high school graduates, while the equivalent percentages for white youth barely changed at all.

Debate over the causes of this decline continues, and some of the candidates—for example, the rising involvement with the drug culture, the large number of young black men caught up in the criminal justice system, and the appeal of competing career choices, such as the military—are beyond the control of educational institutions. (Besides, the drug culture and criminal justice arguments are plainly insufficient to explain why the rate of high school graduation would be *up* so sharply.) There is common agreement, however, that a principal difficulty is the high cost, especially at the nation's most exclusive universities, which makes alternative career choices more attractive. This is why preferential financial assistance (for all its obvious problems) might actually be a more logical and efficient solution than preferential admission. As this manuscript was being completed, a debate erupted over the decision (subsequently modified) by the United States Department of Education to deny federal funds to schools offering preferential financial aid packages on the basis of race.[1] This decision, defended on the ground that federal aid should be administered in a color-blind manner, created a dilemma for colleges interested in keeping both minority recruitment and academic standards at high levels. If one argues that affirmative action is impermissible, then schools are left with only the market mechanism—money—as a tool for enticing onto their campuses excellent students who are not white. A genuine believer in market solutions should allow participants in the market to bid for scarce resources—and by all accounts, first-rate students of color are such a resource. One

---

[1]The compromise resolution was that schools may not use federal funds for racially preferential scholarships but may fund such scholarships from other sources.

might want to argue that this bidding is not fair, but if colleges can rely on neither preferential admission nor bidding to attract students who are not white, they plainly can do no more than pay lip service to the ideal of "minority recruitment." . . .

With the proper goal in mind, then, a degree of racial consciousness *in college and perhaps professional school admission* can plausibly be justified—but just a degree, and just barely. The educational sphere is the place for action because the proper goal of all racial preferences is opportunity—a chance at advanced training for highly motivated people of color who, for whatever complex set of reasons, might not otherwise have it. So justified, the benefit of a racial preference carries with it the concomitant responsibility not to waste the opportunity affirmative action confers. What matters most is what happens *after* the preference.

10   I call this vision of professional achievement and racial preference the affirmative action pyramid, and it works much as the name implies: The role of preference narrows as one moves upward. And although I do not want to say arbitrarily *This is the spot,* what is clear is that as one climbs toward professional success, at some point the preferences must fall away entirely. Possibly a slight preference is justified in college admission, not as a matter of getting the numbers right, and certainly not as a matter of finding the right set of hitherto excluded points of view, but as a matter of giving lots of people from different backgrounds the chance—only the chance—to have an education at an elite college or university. But when that opportunity has been exercised, when the student has shown what he or she can do, the rationale for a preference at the next level is slimmer. So an even slighter affirmative action preference for professional school admission, while possibly justified on similar grounds, is less important, and a little bit harder to defend, than a program at the college level.

And when one's training is done, when the time comes for entry to the job market, I think it is quite clear that among professionals,[2] the case for preference evaporates. The candidate has by this time had six or seven or eight years of training at the highest level; it is a bit silly, as well as demeaning, to continue to insist that one's college and professional school performance is not a very accurate barometer of one's professional possibilities. The time has come, finally, to stand or fall on what one has actually achieved. And, of course, as one passes the point of initial entry and moves up the ladder of one's chosen field, all of the arguments run the other way; the time for preference has gone, and it is time instead to stand proudly on one's own record. The preferences cannot go on forever. Sooner or later, talent and preparation, rather than skin color, must tell.

---

[2]I make no claim here about the propriety of affirmative action in labor markets demanding less in the way of educational credentials.

In Defense of Joe Six-Pack
James Webb

Those who debate the impact of affirmative action and other social pro-grams are fond of making distinctions among white Americans along pro-fessional and geographic lines while avoiding the tinderbox of ethnic distinctions among whites. But differences among white ethnic groups are huge, fed by cultural tradition, the time and geography of migrations to the country, and—not insignificantly—the tendency of white Americans to dis-criminate against other whites in favor of their own class and culture.

In 1974, when affirmative action was in its infancy, the University of Chicago's National Opinion Research Center published a landmark study, dividing American whites into seventeen ethnic and religious backgrounds and scoring them by educational attainment and family income. Contrary to prevailing mythology, the vaunted White Anglo Saxon Protestants were even then not at the top.

A Greater Variation

The highest WASP group—the Episcopalians—ranked only sixth, behind American Jews, then Irish, Italian, German, and Polish Catholics. WASPs—principally the descendants of those who had settled the Midwest and the South—constituted the bottom eight groups, and ten of the bottom twelve. Educational attainment and income levels did not vary geographically, as for instance among white Baptists (who scored the lowest overall) living in Arkansas or California, a further indication that these differences are cul-turally rather than geographically based.

Family income among white cultures in the NORC study varied by almost $5,000 dollars, from the Jewish high of $13,340 to the Baptist low of $8,693. By comparison, in the 1970 census the variance in family income between whites taken as a whole and blacks was only $3,600. In addition, white Bap-tists averaged only 10.7 years of education, which was almost four years less than American Jews and at the same level of black Americans in 1970. This means that, even prior to the major affirmative action programs, there was a greater variation within "white America" than there was between "white America" and black America, and the whites at the bottom were in approx-imately the same situation as blacks.

5   These same less-advantaged white cultures by and large did the most to lay out the infrastructure of this country, quite often suffering educational and professional regression as they tamed the wilderness, built the towns, roads, and schools, and initiated a democratic way of life that later white

cultures were able to take advantage of without paying the price of pioneering. Today they have the least, socioeconomically, to show for these contributions. And if one would care to check a map, they are from the areas now evincing the greatest resistance to government practices.

It would be folly to assume that affirmative action has done anything but exacerbate these disparities. The increased stratification and economic polarization in American life since 1974 is well documented. In the technological age, with the shrinking of the industrial base, the decrease in quality of public education, and the tendency of those who "have" to protect their own and to utilize greater assets to prepare them for the future, the divergence in both expectation and reward among our citizens has grown rather than disappeared. The middle class has shrunk from 65 percent of the population in 1970 to less than 50 percent today. Its share of aggregate household income declined by 5 percent from 1968 to 1993, while the top 5 million households increased their incomes by up to 10 percent a year. A similar rift has occurred in the black culture, with dramatic declines at the bottom and significant gains among the top 5 percent.

Because America's current elites are somewhat heterogeneous and in part the product of an academically based meritocracy, they have increasingly deluded themselves regarding both the depth of this schism and the validity of their own advantages. The prevailing attitude has been to ridicule whites who have the audacity to complain about their reduced status, and to sneer at every aspect of the "redneck" way of life. In addition to rationalizing policies that hold the working-class male back from advancement in the name of an amorphous past wrong from which he himself did not benefit, the elites take great sport in debasing the man they love to call "Joe Six-Pack."

And what does "Joe Six-Pack" make of this?

He sees a president and a slew of other key luminaries who excused themselves from the dirty work of society when they were younger, feeling not remorse but "vindication" for having left him or perhaps his father to fight a war while they went on to graduate school and solidified careers.

10   He sees a governmental system that seems bent on belittling the basis of his existence, and has established a set of laws and regulations that often keep him from competing. His ever-more-isolated leaders have mandated an "equal opportunity" bureaucracy in the military, government, and even industry that closely resembles the Soviet "political cadre" structure, whose sole function is to report "political incorrectness" and to encourage the promotion of literally everyone but him and his kind.

He sees the meaning of words like "fairness" cynically inverted in the name of "diversity," while groups who claim to have been disadvantaged by old practices, and even those who have only just arrived in the country, are immediately moved ahead of him for no reason other than his race. In one of the bitterest ironies, he is required to pay tax dollars to finance special training for recent immigrants even as he himself is held back from fair competition and the "equal opportunity" bureaucracies keep him from receiving similar training, gaining employment, or securing a promotion.

He sees cultural rites buttressed by centuries of tradition—particularly the right to use firearms and pass that skill to future generations—attacked because many who make the laws do not understand the difference between his way of life and that of criminals who are blowing people away on the streets of urban America.

He watched the Democratic Party, once a champion of the worker-producer, abandon him in favor of special interests who define their advancement mostly through the extent of his own demise. To him "diversity" is a code word used to exclude him—but seldom better-situated whites—no matter the extent of his qualifications and no matter the obstacles he has had to overcome. The Republican Party, to which he swung in the last election, has embraced him on certain social issues, but has yet to support policies that would override the tendency of elites to simply protect their own rather than reverse the travails of affirmative action and the collapse of public education.

Out of the Casualty Radius

Finally, he sees the people who erected and continue to enforce such injustices blatantly wheedling and maneuvering themselves and their children out of the casualty radius of their own policies. A smaller percentage of whites in academia and the professions is acceptable, so long as their children make it. The public school system is self-destructing, but their children go to private schools and receive special preparatory classes to elevate college board scores. International peacekeeping is a lofty goal, so long as their children are not on the firing line. Continuous scrutiny is given to minority percentages in employment, but little or none is applied to how or why one white applicant was chosen over another.

15   Faced as he is with such barriers, it is difficult to fault him for deciding that those who make their living running the government or commenting on it are at minimum guilty of ignorance, arrogance, and self-interest. And it is not hyperbole to say that the prospect of a class war is genuine among the very people who traditionally have been the strongest supporters of the American system.

Racial Preferences? So What?

Stephen L. Carter

I

I got into law school because I am black.

As many black professionals think they must, I have long suppressed this truth, insisting instead that I got where I am the same way everybody else

Stephen L. Carter, "Racial Preferences? So What?" From *Reflections of an Affirmative Action Baby* by Stephen L. Carter. Copyright © 1991 by Stephen L. Carter. Reprinted by permission of Basic Books, a member of Perseus Books, L.L.C.

did. Today I am a professor at the Yale Law School. I like to think that I am a good one, but I am hardly the most objective judge. What I am fairly sure of, and can now say without trepidation, is that were my skin not the color that it is, I would not have had the chance to try.

For many, perhaps most, black professionals of my generation, the matter of who got where and how is left in a studied and, I think, purposeful ambiguity. Some of us, as they say, would have made it into an elite college or professional school anyway. (But, in my generation, many fewer than we like to pretend, even though one might question the much-publicized claim by Derek Bok, the president of Harvard University, that in the absence of preferences, only 1 percent of Harvard's entering class would be black.) Most of us, perhaps nearly all of us, have learned to bury the matter far back in our minds. We are who we are and where we are, we have records of accomplishment or failure, and there is no rational reason that anybody— employer, client, whoever—should care any longer whether racial preference played any role in our admission to a top professional school.

When people in positions to help or hurt our careers *do* seem to care, we tend to react with fury. Those of us who have graduated professional school over the past fifteen to twenty years, and are not white, travel career paths that are frequently bumpy with suspicions that we did not earn the right to be where we are. We bristle when others raise what might be called the qualification question—"Did you get into school or get hired because of a special program?"—and that prickly sensitivity is the best evidence, if any is needed, of one of the principal costs of racial preferences. Scratch a black professional with the qualification question, and you're likely to get a caustic response, such as this one from a senior executive at a major airline: "Some whites think I've made it because I'm black. Some blacks think I've made it only because I'm an Uncle Tom. The fact is, I've made it because I'm good."

5   Given the way that so many Americans seem to treat receipt of the benefits of affirmative action as a badge of shame, answers of this sort are both predictable and sensible. In the professional world, moreover, they are very often true: relatively few corporations are in a position to hand out charity. The peculiar aspect of the routine denial, however, is that so many of those who will bristle at the suggestion that they themselves have gained from racial preferences will try simultaneously to insist that racial preferences be preserved and to force the world to pretend that no one benefits from them. That awkward balancing of fact and fiction explains the frequent but generally groundless cry that it is racist to suggest that some individual's professional accomplishments would be fewer but for affirmative action; and therein hangs a tale.

For students at the leading law schools, autumn brings the recruiting season, the idyllic weeks when law firms from around the country compete to lavish upon them lunches and dinners and other attentions, all with the professed goal of obtaining the students' services—perhaps for the summer, perhaps for a longer term. The autumn of 1989 was different, however, because the nation's largest firm, Baker & McKenzie, was banned from interviewing students at the University of Chicago Law School, and on probation—that is, enjoined to be on its best behavior—at some others.

The immediate source of Baker & McKenzie's problems was a racially charged interview that a partner in the firm had conducted the previous fall with a black third-year student at the school. The interviewer evidently suggested that other lawyers might call her "nigger" or "black bitch" and wanted to know how she felt about that. Perhaps out of surprise that she played golf, he observed that "there aren't too many golf courses in the ghetto." He also suggested that the school was admitting "foreigners" and excluding "qualified" Americans.

The law school reacted swiftly, and the firm was banned from interviewing on campus. Other schools contemplated taking action against the firm, and some of them did. Because I am black myself, and teach in a law school, I suppose the easiest thing for me to have done would have been to clamor in solidarity for punishment. Yet I found myself strangely reluctant to applaud the school's action. Instead, I was disturbed rather than excited by this vision of law schools circling the wagons, as it were, to defend their beleaguered minority students against racially insensitive remarks. It is emphatically not my intention to defend the interviewer, most of whose reported questions and comments were inexplicable and inexcusable. I am troubled, however, by my suspicion that there would still have been outrage—not as much, but some—had the interviewer asked only what I called at the beginning of the chapter the qualification question.

I suspect this because in my own student days, something over a decade ago, an interviewer from a prominent law firm addressed this very question to a Yale student who was not white, and the student voices—including my own—howled in protest. "Racism!" we insisted. "Ban them!" But with the passing years, I have come to wonder whether our anger might have been misplaced.

10   To be sure, the Yale interviewer's question was boorish. And because the interviewer had a grade record and résumé right in front of him, it was probably irrelevant as well. (It is useful here to dispose of one common but rather silly anti-affirmative action bromide: the old question, "Do you really want to be treated by a doctor who got into medical school because of skin color?" The answer is, or ought to be, that the patient doesn't particularly care how the doctor got *into* school; what matters is how the doctor got *out*. The right question, the sensible question, is not "What medical school performance did your grades and test scores predict?" but "What was your medical school performance?") But irrelevance and boorishness cannot explain

our rage at the qualification question, because lots of interviewers ask questions that meet the tests of boorishness and irrelevance.

The controversy is not limited to outsiders who come onto campus to recruit. In the spring of 1991, for example, students at Georgetown Law School demanded punishment for a classmate who argued in the school newspaper that affirmative action is unfair because students of color are often admitted to law school on the basis of grades and test scores that would cause white applicants to be rejected. Several universities have considered proposals that would deem it "racial harassment" for a (white?) student to question the qualifications of nonwhite classmates. But we can't change either the truths or the myths about racial preferences by punishing those who speak them.

This clamor for protection from the qualification question is powerful evidence of the terrible psychological pressure that racial preferences often put on their beneficiaries. Indeed, it sometimes seems as though the programs are not supposed to have any beneficiaries—or, at least, that no one is permitted to suggest that they have any.

And that's ridiculous. If one supports racial preferences in professional school admissions, for example, one must be prepared to treat them like any other preference in admission and believe that they make a difference, that some students would not be admitted if the preferences did not exist. This is not a racist observation. It is not normative in any sense. It is simply a fact. A good deal of emotional underbrush might be cleared away were the fact simply conceded, and made the beginning, not the end, of any discussion of preferences. For once it is conceded that the programs have beneficiaries, it follows that some of us who are professionals and are not white must be among them. Supporters of preferences must stop pretending otherwise. Rather, some large segment of us must be willing to meet the qualification question head-on, to say, "Yes, I got into law school because of racial preferences. So what?"—and, having said it, must be ready with a list of what we have made of the opportunities the preferences provided.

Now, this is a costly concession, because it carries with it all the baggage of the bitter rhetorical battle over the relationship between preferences and merit. But bristling at the question suggests a deep-seated fear that the dichotomy might be real. Indeed, if admitting that racial preferences make a difference leaves a funny aftertaste in the mouths of proponents, they might be more comfortable fighting against preferences rather than for them.

15   So let us bring some honesty as well as rigor to the debate, and begin at the beginning. I have already made clear my starting point: I got into a top law school because I am black. Not only am I unashamed of this fact, but I can prove its truth.

As a senior at Stanford back in the mid-1970s, I applied to about half a dozen law schools. Yale, where I would ultimately enroll, came through fairly early with an acceptance. So did all but one of the others. The last school, Harvard, dawdled and dawdled. Finally, toward the end of the admission season, I received a letter of rejection. Then, within days, two different Harvard officials and a professor contacted me by telephone to apologize. They were quite frank in their explanation for the "error." I was told by one official that the school had initially rejected me because "we assumed from your record that you were white." (The words have always stuck in my mind, a tantalizing reminder of what is expected of me.) Suddenly coy, he went on to say that the school had obtained "additional information that should have been counted in your favor"—that is, Harvard had discovered the color of my skin. And if I had already made a deposit to confirm my decision to go elsewhere, well, that, I was told, would "not be allowed" to stand in my way should I enroll at Harvard.

Naturally, I was insulted by this miracle. Stephen Carter, the white male, was not good enough for the Harvard Law School; Stephen Carter, the black male, not only was good enough but rated agonized telephone calls urging him to attend. And Stephen Carter, color unknown, must have been white: How else could he have achieved what he did in college? Except that my college achievements were obviously not sufficiently spectacular to merit acceptance had I been white. In other words, my academic record was too good for a black Stanford University undergraduate, but not good enough for a white Harvard law student. Because I turned out to be black, however, Harvard was quite happy to scrape me from what it apparently considered somewhere nearer the bottom of the barrel.

My objective is not to single out Harvard for special criticism; on the contrary, although my ego insists otherwise, I make no claim that a white student with my academic record would have been admitted to any of the leading law schools. The insult I felt came from the pain of being reminded so forcefully that in the judgment of those with the power to dispose, I was good enough for a top law school only because I happened to be black.

Naturally, I should not have been insulted at all; that is what racial preferences are for—racial preference. But I was insulted and went off to Yale instead, even though I had then and have now absolutely no reason to imagine that Yale's judgment was based on different criteria than Harvard's. Hardly anyone granted admission at Yale is denied admission at Harvard, which admits a far larger class; but several hundreds of students who are admitted at Harvard are denied admission at Yale. Because Yale is far more selective, the chances are good that I was admitted at Yale for essentially the same reason I was admitted at Harvard—the color of my skin made up for what were evidently considered other deficiencies in my academic record. I may embrace this truth as a matter of simple justice or rail against it as one of life's great evils, but being a member of the affirmative action generation means that the one thing I cannot do is deny it. I will say it again: I got into law school because I am black. So what?

II

20   One answer to the "So what?" question is that someone more deserving than I—someone white—may have been turned away. I hardly know what to make of this argument, for I doubt that the mythical white student on the cusp, the one who almost made it to Yale but for my rude intervention, would have done better than I did in law school.* Nor am I some peculiar case: the Yale Law School of my youth trained any number of affirmative action babies who went on to fine academic performances and are now in the midst of stellar careers in the law.

Even in the abstract, what I call the "fairness story" has never struck me as one of the more convincing arguments against preferential policies. The costs of affirmative action differ from the costs of taxation only in degree, not in kind. People are routinely taxed for services they do not receive that are deemed by their government necessary to right social wrongs they did not commit. The taxpayer-financed "bailout" of the weak or collapsed savings-and-loan institutions is one example. Another is the provision of tax dollars for emergency disaster assistance after a hurricane devastates a coastal community. The people who bear the costs of these programs are not the people who caused the damage, but they still have to pay.

Like many, perhaps most, of America's domestic policies, affirmative action programs are essentially redistributive in nature. They transfer resources from their allocation in the market to other recipients, favored for social policy reasons. Much of the attack on affirmative action is fueled by the same instinct—the same American dream—that stands as a bulwark against any substantial redistribution of wealth. In America, most people like to think, it is possible for anyone to make it, and those who do not have been victims principally of their own sloth or lack of talent or perhaps plain bad luck—but not of anybody else's sinister plottings. Seymour Martin Lipset, among others, has argued plausibly that a stable democracy is possible only when an economically secure middle class exists to battle against radical economic reforms that the wealthier classes would otherwise resist by using means outside the system. In America, that middle class plainly

---

*It has always struck me as quite bizarre that so many otherwise thoughtful people on both sides of the affirmative action controversy seem to think so much turns on the question of how the beneficiaries perform. I would not dismiss the inquiry as irrelevant, but I am reluctant to say that it is the whole ball game. It may be the case, as many critics have argued, that the affirmative action beneficiary who fails at Harvard College might have performed quite well at a less competitive school and gone on to an excellent and productive career that will almost surely be lost because of the shattering experience of academic failure; but one must weigh this cost (and personal choice) against the tale of the student who would not have attended Harvard without affirmative action and who succeeds brilliantly there. It may be that those who do less well in school because of preferences outnumber those who do better, but such statistics are only the edge of the canvas, a tiny part of a much larger and more complex picture, and that is why I think the energy devoted to the qualification question is largely wasted.

exists, and racial preferences are among the radical reforms it is willing to resist.

Sometimes the fervent opposition of the great majority of white Americans to affirmative action is put down to racism, or at least racial resentment, and I do not want to argue that neither motivation is ever present. But affirmative action programs are different from other social transfers, and the way they differ is in the basis on which the favored and disfavored groups are identified. The basis is race, and sometimes sex—and that makes all the difference.

I say that race is different not because I favor the ideal of a color-blind society; indeed, for reasons I discuss [elsewhere], I fear that the rhetoric of color blindness conflates values that are best kept separate. Race is different for obvious historical reasons: the world in general, and this nation in particular, should know well the risks of encouraging powerful institutions to categorize by such immutable characteristics as race. Besides, even were race as a category less controversial, there is still the further fairness argument, that the sins for which the programs purportedly offer compensation are not sins of the current generation.

25   Many proponents of preferential policies, however, insist that the current generation of white males deserves to bear the costs of affirmative action. "White males," we are told, "have had exclusive access to certain information, education, experience, and contacts through which they have gained unfair advantage." In the words of a leading scholar, "[W]e have to say to whites, 'Listen, you have benefited in countless ways from racism, from its notions of beauty [and] its exclusion of minorities in jobs and schools.'" The argument has a second step, too: "For most of this country's history," wrote one commentator, "the nation's top universities practiced the most effective form of affirmative action ever; the quota was for 100 percent white males." The analogy is fair—indeed, it is so fair that it wins the endorsement of opponents as well as supporters of affirmative action—but what does it imply? For proponents of preferences, the answer is clear: if white males have been for centuries the beneficiaries of a vast and all-encompassing program of affirmative action, today's more limited programs can be defended as simply trying to undo the most pernicious effects of that one. That is how, in the contemporary rhetoric of affirmative action, white males turn out to deserve the disfavored treatment that the programs accord.*

But there is risk in this rhetoric. To make race the determining factor not simply of the favored group but of the disfavored one encourages an

---

*Even accepting this dubious rhetorical construct, it is easy to see that racial preferences call for sacrifices not from white males as a group but from the subgroups of white males most likely to be excluded by a preference benefitting someone else—that is, the most disadvantaged white males, those who, by hypothesis, have gained the least from racism.

analytical structure that seeks and assigns reasons in the present world for disfavoring one group. The simplest structure—and the one that has come, with mysterious force, to dominate the terms of intellectual and campus debate—is what Thomas Sowell has called "social irredentism," an insistence that all members of the disfavored dominant group bear the mantle of oppressor. Affirmative action, then, becomes almost a punishment for the sin of being born the wrong color and the wrong sex.

All of this carries a neat historical irony. The personalization of affirmative action, the specification of white males as the villains, has diluted the message of the black left of the 1960s and early 1970s, which often (but by no means always) joined forces with the white left to insist that the problems were systemic, not individual. In those halcyon days of campus radicalism, the race struggle was widely described as hand-in-glove with the class struggle. Racial justice was said to be impossible under capitalism, and the principal debate among radical students was over what form of socialism was best for black people—a separate society or an integrated one, central planning or local communities?

As for affirmative action, well, sophisticated nationalists understood that it was part of the problem. By funneling the best and brightest young black men and women into the white-dominated system of higher education, the critics argued, the programs would simply skim the cream from our community, co-opting into the (white) mainstream those who should have been our leaders. An attack on efforts to substitute enhanced educational opportunities for racial justice was a principal focus of Robert Allen's provocative 1969 book *Black Awakening in Capitalist America.* "The black student," Allen warned, "is crucial to corporate America's neocolonial plans." The best and brightest among black youth, he argued, instead of criticizing capitalism from the outside, would be trained to serve it from the inside. Nationalist reviewers agreed. For example, Anne Kelley wrote in *The Black Scholar* that "the emphasis on higher education for black students" was part of a "neocolonialist scheme" that was "designed to stabilize the masses."

But the language of protest is quite different now, and the success of affirmative action is one of the reasons; to paraphrase John le Carré, it is hard to criticize the system when it has brought you inside at its own expense. Affirmative action programs in education are designed to move people of color into productive roles in capitalist society, and the best sign that they are working is the way the argument has shifted. White males have replaced "the society" or "the system" or "the establishment" in the rhetoric of racial justice, perhaps because the rhetoric of justice is no longer under the control of genuine radicals. The modern proponents of preferences rarely plan to spend their lives in community organizing as they await the revolutionary moment, and there is no particular reason that they should. They are liberal reformers, not radical revolutionaries; with the collapse of communism as a force in the world, nobody seems to think any longer that the solution is to burn everything down and start over. On campuses nowadays, especially in the professional schools, the students of color seem about as likely as their white classmates to be capitalists to their very fingertips; they have no desire to kill the golden goose that the (white male) establishment has created. Or, to switch metaphors, today's affirmative action advocates want mainly to share in the pie, not to see it divided up in some scientific socialist redistribution.

III

30   Which helps explain, I think, why the "So what?" that I advocate is not easy to utter. Students of color are in the professional schools for the same reason white students are there: to get a good education and a good job. Because so many people seem to assume that the beneficiaries of affirmative action programs are necessarily bound for failure, or at least for inferiority, there is an understandable tendency for people of color to resist being thought of as beneficiaries. After all, who wants to be bound for failure? (Especially when so many beneficiaries of racial preferences really *don't* succeed as they would like.) Better not to think about it; better to make sure nobody else thinks about it either. Rather than saying, "So what?" better to say, "How dare you?"

I understand perfectly this temptation to try to make the world shut up, to pursue the fantasy that doubts that are not expressed do not exist. When I listen to the labored but heart-felt arguments on why potential employers (and, for that matter, other students) should not be permitted to question the admission qualifications of students of color, I am reminded uneasily of another incident from my own student days, a shining moment when we, too, thought that if we could only stifle debate on the question, we could make it go away.

The incident I have in mind occurred during the fall of 1978, my third year in law school, a few months after the Supreme Court's decision in *Regents of the University of California v. Bakke,* which placed what seemed to many of us unnecessarily severe restrictions on the operation of racially conscious admission programs. The air was thick with swirling critiques of racial preferences, most of them couched in the language of merit versus qualification. Everywhere we turned, someone seemed to be pointing at us and saying, "You don't belong here." We looked around and saw an academic world that seemed to be doing its best to get rid of us.

So we struck back. We called the critics racist. We tried to paint the question of our qualifications as a racist one. And one evening, when the Yale Political Union, a student organization, had scheduled a debate on the matter (the title, as I recall, was "The Future of Affirmative Action"), we demonstrated. All of us.

Our unanimity was astonishing. Then as now, the black students at the law school were divided, politically, socially, and in dozens of other ways. But on this issue, we were suddenly united. We picketed the Political Union meeting, roaring our slogan ("*We are not debatable! We are not debatable!*") in tones of righteous outrage. We made so much noise that at last they threw wide the doors and invited us in. In exchange for our promise to end the demonstration so that the debate could be conducted, we were offered, and we accepted, the chance to have one of our number address the assembly. That task, for some reason, fell to me.

35   I remember my rising excitement as I stood before the audience of immaculately attired undergraduates, many of them still in their teens. There was something sweet and naive and appealing about the Political Union members as they sat nervously but politely in their tidy rows, secure (or, perhaps, momentarily insecure) in their faith that a commitment to openness and debate would lead to moral truth. But I set my face against the smile that was twitching there, and tried to work up in its stead a glower sufficient to convey the image of the retributive fury of the radical black left. (Having missed those days in college, I thought perhaps to rekindle them briefly.) And while some of the kids seemed annoyed at the intrusion, others looked frightened, even intimidated, which I suppose was our goal. I spoke briefly, pointing out that it was easy for white people to call for color-blind admissions when they understood perfectly well that none of the costs would fall on them. I carefully avoided the word *racism,* but I let the implication hang in the air anyway, lest I be misunderstood.

And then we marched out again, triumphantly, clapping and chanting rhythmically as though in solemn reminder that should the Political Union folks get up to any more nonsense, we might return and drown them out again. (A few of the undergraduates and one of the speakers joined us in our clapping.) We were, for a shining moment, in our glory; the reporters were there, tapes rolling, cameras clicking; in our minds, we had turned back the calendar by a decade and the campuses were in flames (or at least awash with megaphones and boycotts and banners and an administration ready to compromise); the school would meet us with a promise of justice or we would tear it down!

Then all at once it was over. We dispersed, returning to our dormitory rooms and apartments, our law review and moot court activities, our long nights in the library to prepare for class and our freshly cleaned suits for job interviews, our political differences and our social cliques. We returned to the humdrum interests of law school life, and suddenly we were just like everybody else again. Absolutely nothing had changed. *Bakke* was still the law of the land. There was no magic, the campus was not in flames, and there had never been a shining moment. There was only the uneasy tension of our dual existence. The peculiar uncertainty provoked by affirmative action was still with us, and our outrage at being reminded of its reality was undiminished. And as for the eager young minds of the Political Union, I suppose they held their debate and I suppose somebody won.

IV

The demonstration at the Political Union seems very long ago now, not only in time but in place: Could that really have been Yale? Could that really have been *us*? (I look around at the chanting faces in my memory and pick out their subsequent histories: this one a partner in an elite law firm, that one an investment banker, this one a leading public interest lawyer, that one another partner, this one in the State Department, that one a professor at a leading law school, this one a prosecuting attorney, that one in the legal department of a Fortune 100 corporation, and so on.) We are not the people we were then, but the fact that the debate was held over our boisterous objections seems not to have diverted our careers. We are a successful generation of lawyers, walking advertisements, it might seem, for the bright side of affirmative action. Our doubts, seen from this end of the tunnel, seem vague and insubstantial.

At the time, however, the doubts, and the anger, were painfully real. I do not want to suggest that the doubts have persisted into our careers or those of other black professionals—I am as irritated as anybody else by the frequent suggestion that there lurks inside each black professional a confused and uncertain ego, desperately seeking reassurance—but it is certainly true that as long as racial preferences exist, the one thing that cannot be proved is which people of color in my generation would have achieved what they have in their absence.

40   At this point in the argument many of us are told, as though in reassurance, "Oh, don't worry, you're not here because of affirmative action—you're here on merit." But it is not easy to take this as quite the compliment it is presumably meant to be. In the first place, it continues the opposition of merit to preference that has brought about the pain and anger to begin with. More important, and perhaps more devastating, it places the judgment on how good we are just where we do not want it to be: in the minds and mouths of white colleagues, whose arrogant "assurances" serve as eloquent reminders of how fragile a trophy is our hard-won professional status.

Very well, perhaps we were wrong in our youthful enthusiasm to try to stifle debate, but that is not the point of the story. The point, rather, is that our outrage was misdirected. Even at the time of my glowering diatribe, I realized that not all of what I said was fair. Looking back, I have come to understand even better how much of my message—our message—was driven by our pain over Bakke and the nation's changing mood. "Don't you understand?" we were crying. "We have fought hard to get here, and we will not be pushed back!"

Our anguish was not less real for being misdirected. Whether one wants to blame racial preferences or white racism or the pressures of professional school or some combination of them all, our pain was too great for us to consider for an instant the possibility that victory in the battle to "get here" did not logically entail affirmative action. We were not prepared to discuss or even to imagine life without preferences, a world in which we would be challenged to meet and beat whatever standards for admission and advancement were placed before us. We wanted no discussion at all, only capitulation. All we saw was that the Supreme Court had given us the back of its hand in *Bakke* (we even wore little buttons: FIGHT RACISM, OVERTURN BAKKE) and the forces of reaction were closing in.

Now that I am a law professor, one of my more delicate tasks is convincing my students, whatever their color, to consider the possibility that perhaps the forces of reaction are *not* closing in. Perhaps what seems to them (and to many other people) a backlash against affirmative action is instead (or in addition) a signal that the programs, at least in their current expansive form, have run their course. Or perhaps, if the programs are to be preserved, they should move closer to their roots: the provision of opportunities for people of color who might not otherwise have the advanced training that will allow them to prove what they can do.

My students tend to disagree, sometimes vehemently. The bad guys are out there, they tell me, and they are winning. And one of the reasons they are winning, as I understand it, is that they get to set the rules. A couple of years ago, for example, a student complained to me that people of color are forced to disguise their true voices and write like white males in order to survive the writing competition for membership on the *Yale Law Journal.* One critic has argued that university faculties employ a "hierarchical majoritarian" standard for judging academic work—a standard that is not sensitive to the special perspective people of color can bring to scholarship. And all over the corporate world, I am led to believe, the standards of what counts as merit are designed, perhaps intentionally, to keep us out.

45   Nowadays, racial preferences are said to be our tool for forcing those bad guys—the white males who run the place, the purveyors, so I am told, of so much misery and the inheritors of so much unearned privilege—to acknowledge that theirs is only one way of looking at the world. Anyone who can't see the force of this argument is evidently a part of the problem. White people who ask whether the quest for diversity contemplates a lowering of standards of excellence are still charged with racism, just as in the old days. (The forces of reaction *are* closing in.) People of color who venture similar thoughts are labeled turncoats and worse, just as they always have been. (Don't they *know* that academic standards are a white male invention aimed at maintaining a eurocentric hegemony?) And through it all, the devotion to numbers that has long characterized the affirmative action debate continues.

Certainly the proportions of black people in the various professions are nothing to shout about. In my own field of law teaching, for example, a study prepared for the Society of American Law Teachers shows that only

3.7 percent of faculty members are black at law schools that are, as the report puts it in an unfortunate bit of jargon, "majority-run." In other professions, too, although the numbers have generally improved in recent years, the percentages of black folk remain small. On medical school faculties, for example, 1.9 percent of the professors are black. On university faculties generally, just 4 percent of the faculty members are black. For lawyers and judges, the figure is 2.3 percent. For physicians, 3.3 percent. Financial managers, 4.3 percent. (And, as long as we're at it, for authors, 0.4 percent, about 1 out of 250.)

But while we might agree on the desirability of raising these numbers, the question of strategy continues to divide us. To try to argue that purported racism in professional standards is not a plausible explanation for most of the data is to risk being dismissed for one's naïveté. And as to my oft-stated preference for returning to the roots of affirmative action: well, the roots, as it turns out, had the matter all wrong. My generation, with its obsessive concern with proving itself in the white man's world, pressed an argument that was beside the point. Had we but understood the ways in which our experiences differ from those of the dominant majority, it seems, we would have insisted on an affirmative action that rewrites the standards for excellence, rather than one that trains us to meet them.

Lies, Damn Lies, and Racial Statistics
Charles Krauthammer

Acceptance of Blacks, Latinos to UC Plunges
—Los Angeles Times, April 1

Admissions Plunge at U of California for Three Minorities
—New York Times, April 1

Black, Hispanic Admissions Plunge at Two Calif. Campuses
—Washington Post, April 1

The headlines were sensational, and the editorial writers were not far behind in drawing the politically correct conclusion: PROPOSITION 209 SHUTS THE DOOR (*New York Times*). In the relentless campaign against Proposition 209, which in 1996 abolished racial preferences in California, the "plunge" in minority students accepted for next fall at the University of

Charles Krauthammer, "Lies, Damn Lies, and Racial Statistics," *Time*, April 20, 1998, p. 32. © 1998 TIME Inc. Reprinted by permission.

California is political dynamite, alleged proof that the new color-blind admissions policy shuts the schoolhouse door in the face of minorities.

Of course, any plunge directly contradicts what proponents of affirmative action have been saying for 25 years: that under affirmative action there was no real academic discrepancy between minorities and whites admitted and that the students were all "qualified," with just marginal differences between them.

So fervently did affirmative-action proponents cling to these fictions that they went to great lengths to suppress the facts. In one famous case, in 1991, a Georgetown University law student who found and published the discrepancy between average white and black LSAT scores found himself reprimanded by the university for publishing the unmentionable.

Well, no matter. The facts are out. And affirmative-action proponents are eagerly waving them like a bloody shirt. At two elite University of California campuses, Berkeley and UCLA, black and Hispanic admissions are down significantly. On the basis of admissions, the number of black freshmen at Berkeley will decline 57% from 1997; the number of Hispanics, 40%. The drop at UCLA is 43% for blacks, 33% for Hispanics.

5   But the University of California has eight campuses, not two. How are blacks and Hispanics doing overall? University officials did not see fit to release the numbers until two days later, with the predictable result that the full story—the mitigating story—was buried. It turned out that at the University of California, the drop was far less dramatic: for blacks, not 57% but 17.6%; for Hispanics, not 40% but 6.9%.

Even these numbers do not tell the full story. This year there was a huge increase—to 6,846, or fully 15% of admissions—of those who did not identify themselves by race. (This is not surprising, given the fact that after Proposition 209 there was no advantage or disadvantage associated with race.) Not counting these students and looking just at those whose race we know for sure, black and Hispanic admissions at the UC system declined only slightly, from 17.7% to 17.2% of freshmen. (African Americans going from 3.7% to 3.3%; Hispanics remaining steady at about 14%.) This is shutting the schoolhouse door?

True, there was a significant drop in non-Asian minority admissions to the two most competitive UC schools. But there was a countervailing increase in such admissions at the less competitive schools. At UC–Riverside, for example, there was a 34% increase in black admissions and a 43% increase in Hispanic admissions.

What happened? Contrary to the avalanche of media stories, non-Asian minority students are not being shut out of the University of California. They are, instead and finally, being assigned to campuses that better fit their level of academic preparation.

Affirmative-action proponents decry as a national tragedy the fact that black admissions to Berkeley make up not 5.6% but 2.4% of the freshman class. But what happens after admission? Affirmative-action proponents don't tell you that the dropout rate for blacks at Berkeley is 42%, vs. 17% for whites.

10   Given the huge academic handicap burdening black students admitted under affirmative action—their average SAT scores were 288 points below the Berkeley average—this dropout rate is understandable. These students were arbitrarily thrown into an environment with students far more advanced academically. The result was predictable: failure. Even more tragic is the fact that these bright black students, as social theorist Thomas Sowell puts it, "were perfectly qualified to be successes somewhere else" but were instead "artificially turned into failures by being admitted to high-pressure campuses, where only students with exceptional academic backgrounds can survive."

But the welfare of these individual students is far less important to affirmative-action propagandists than puffing out their chests and boasting about admissions numbers. Consider: under affirmative action, nearly half the black freshmen at Berkeley don't make it. Under the new color-blind system, yes, the black freshman class is cut roughly in half (hence the headlines). What will happen to the less advanced half—those who didn't qualify academically and would probably have ended up among the 42% that drop out? They will likely end up at other UC campuses where they should do very well.

This is a national tragedy? On the contrary. This is showing respect for minority students, treating them as individuals, not statistics. This is caring about their future—academic success, graduation, career—not risking it by artificially assigning them to a school one notch too advanced just to satisfy the moral vanity of quota-driven bureaucrats and politicians.

TECHNIQUES FOR WRITERS 3-b
Pros and Cons

Read any three of the previous articles. Prepare a pro/con grid comprising only arguments that are new to this discussion: that is, include only arguments that haven't been presented earlier. If your reading has caused you to think of additional arguments, add those to your lists as well.

Expanding the Pro/Con Grid: Finding Support in Readings

Having read the previous articles, you probably realize that many more arguments exist on the controversial subject of Affirmative Action. After thinking about the issue, brainstorming/listing ideas, discussing it with a classmate, and reading more material on the topic, your pro/con grid might now look like this:

Pro

- promotes diversity on college campuses
  - **leads to more diversity in workplace and military applicants**
    - **important in global economy**
- gives opportunities to people who might otherwise not have them
- helps to make up for past discrimination against minorities
  - **social redress against "egregious racial stratification"**
    - **American caste system entrenched**
    - **would have taken hundreds of years to naturally correct the system**
- colleges have the right to determine admission qualifications
- *other groups (athletes, children of alumni, students with particular skills) also receive preferences*
- *standardized testing discriminates against minorities*
- *playing field is not yet equal—fewer minorities graduate from college; minorities make less money than whites*
  - **contemporary whites have benefited from past discrimination for centuries**
- *development of black middle class—good for country's economy*
- *will not lead to less-qualified people in professions*
  - **students admitted under AA guidelines still have to meet standard graduation requirements**
- 1978 *Bakke v. Regents of University of California* supported AA in college admissions
- **helps women as well**
- **"unfairness" exists in other legal decisions**
  - **military conscription**
  - **property condemnation**

Con

- discriminates against some students—reverse discrimination
  - **discriminates against people who were not responsible for past discrimination**
- Civil Rights Act mandates equality for all
  - **quotas against the law**
  - **AA considered racist by some**
- lowers standards if less qualified candidates gain admission
- stigmatizes minorities—all are assumed to be in college only because of AA
  - **minorities considered afraid of meeting standards**
- increases resentment, backlash
  - **increases number of racial incidents on campuses**
- leads to less-qualified professionals in fields like medicine and law
  - **today's society needs best and brightest in all areas**
- **discrimination was lessening on its own and would have disappeared even without AA**
- **admissions preferences should be based on class, not race**
- **AA only symbolic—icon of white hypocrisy and emerging black power**
- **no proof AA has truly accomplished anything**
- **problems should be addressed earlier**
  - **better elementary, high schools for minorities**

Now your pro/con grid has not only topics, but subtopics and sub-subtopics as well. It's beginning to reflect the complexity of the issue. But even though it has expanded and become much more complex, your grid still doesn't contain *every* possible argument ever made about Affirmative Action and college admissions. (In fact, you could work on the grid for a week and still not cover all the angles.)

At this point, you may feel that the topic has gotten away from you—that it's too confusing and complex to be handled by anything less than a 600-page book. It's time to focus.

Focusing the Issue: The Case Study

As we have stated earlier, the arguments surrounding Affirmative Action and its place in college admissions are both numerous and complex. Because of this, all of the individuals involved with the issue—government officials, college administrators, parents, students—require that the issue be addressed practically, ethically—and *fully.*

One way to begin to grasp an issue that is so complex is to focus more specifically on one aspect or situation involving that issue.

Here, you'll be introduced to the controversy surrounding the admissions policy of the University of Michigan in Ann Arbor, Michigan. U of M's admission policy included a 150-point system, of which 20 points could be awarded to applicants in underrepresented ethnic or racial groups. Administrators at U of M believed their system fell within the parameters of the 1978 ruling on *Bakke v. Regents of University of California,* in which Affirmative Action was ruled to be an acceptable factor in determining college admissions.

In 2003 the United States Supreme Court decided to review two cases concerning admissions to the U of M. One case specifically addressed the university's 150-point admissions system, while the other, *Grutter v. Bollinger,* was filed by Barbara Grutter, who was denied admission to the U of M law school despite having a grade point average and test scores higher than some minority applicants who were accepted. Lawyers, including two from the George W. Bush administration, filed a number of briefs pertaining to those cases.

As you read these materials, watch for places where you find the supporting evidence—either for or against Affirmative Action—particularly effective. Keep in mind that, although many writers have been involved in creating the pages you're reading, each of them was striving to create an argument that appealed to many kinds of readers on moral, ethical, and legal grounds.

Diversity Is Essential
Lee C. Bollinger

When I became president of the University of Michigan in 1997, affirmative action in higher education was under siege from the right. Buoyed by a successful lawsuit against the University of Texas Law School's admissions policy and by ballot initiatives such as California's Proposition 209, which outlawed race as a factor in college admissions, the opponents set their sights on affirmative-action programs at colleges across the country.

The rumor that Michigan would be the next target in this campaign turned out to be correct. I believed strongly that we had no choice but to mount the best legal defense ever for diversity in higher education and take special efforts to explain this complex issue, in simple and direct language, to the American public. There are many misperceptions about how race and ethnicity are considered in college admissions. Competitive colleges and universities are always looking for a mix of students with different experiences and backgrounds—academic, geographic, international, socioeconomic, athletic, public-service oriented, and, yes, racial and ethnic.

It is true that in sorting the initial rush of applications, large universities will give "points" for various factors in the selection process in order to ensure fairness as various officers review applicants. Opponents of Michigan's undergraduate system complain that an applicant is assigned more points for being black, Hispanic, or Native American than for having a perfect SAT score. This is true, but it trivializes the real issue: whether, in principle, race and ethnicity are appropriate considerations. The simple fact about the Michigan undergraduate policy is that it gives overwhelming weight to traditional academic factors—some 110 out of a total of 150 points. After that, there are some 40 points left for other factors, of which 20 can be allocated for race or socioeconomic status.

Race has been a defining element of the American experience. The historic *Brown v. Board of Education*[1] decision is almost 50 years old, yet metropolitan Detroit is more segregated now than it was in 1960. The majority of students who each year arrive on a campus like Michigan's graduated from virtually all-white or all-black high schools. The campus is their first experience living in an integrated environment.

5   This is vital. Diversity is not merely a desirable addition to a well-rounded education. It is as essential as the study of the Middle Ages, of international politics, and of Shakespeare. For our students to better understand the diverse country and world they inhabit, they must be immersed in a campus culture that allows them to study with, argue with, and become friends with students who may be different from them. It broadens the mind and the intellect—essential goals of education.

---

[1]In *Brown v. Board of Education* (1954) the U.S. Supreme Court unanimously decided that separating children in public schools on the basis of race was unconstitutional, violating the Fourteenth Amendment.

But Not at This Cost

Armstrong Williams

Back in 1977, when I was a senior in high school, I received scholarship offers to attend prestigious colleges. The schools wanted me in part because of my good academic record—but also because affirmative action mandates required them to encourage more black students to enroll. My father wouldn't let me take any of the enticements. His reasoning was straightforward: Scholarship money should go to the economically deprived. And since he could pay for my schooling, he would. In the end, I chose a historically black college—South Carolina State.

What I think my father meant, but was perhaps too stern to say, was that one should always rely on hard work and personal achievement to carry the

---

day—every day. Sadly, this rousing point seems lost on the admissions board at the University of Michigan, which wrongly and unapologetically discriminates on the basis of skin color. The university ranks applicants on a scale that awards points for SAT scores, high school grades, and race. For example, a perfect SAT score is worth 12 points. Being black gets you 20 points. Is there anyone who can look at those two numbers and think they are fair?

Supporters maintain that the quota system is essential to creating a diverse student body. And, indeed, there is some validity to this sort of thinking. A shared history of slavery and discrimination has ingrained racial hierarchies into our national identity, divisions that need to be erased. There is, however, a very real danger that we are merely reinforcing the idea that minorities are first and foremost victims. Because of this victim status, the logic goes, they are owed special treatment. But that isn't progress; it's inertia.

If the goal of affirmative action is to create a more equitable society, it should be need-based. Instead, affirmative action is defined by its tendency to reduce people to fixed categories: At many universities, it seems, admissions officers look less at who you are than what you are. As a result, affirmative-action programs rarely help the least among us. Instead, they often benefit the children of middle- and upper-class black Americans who have been conditioned to feel they are owed something.

5   This is alarming. We have finally, after far too long, reached a point where black Americans have pushed into the mainstream—and not just in entertainment and sports. From politics to corporate finance, blacks succeed. Yet many of us still feel entitled to special benefits—in school, in jobs, in government contracts.

It is time to stop. We must reach a point where we expect to rise or fall on our own merits. We just can't continue to base opportunities on race while the needs of the poor fall by the wayside. As a child growing up on a farm, I was taught that personal responsibility was the lever that moved the world. That is why it pains me to see my peers rest their heads upon the warm pillow of victim status.

Affirmative Action Backers Prepare Case
Patti Waldmeir

US business, labour, academic and military leaders have formed an unusual alliance to argue in favour of affirmative action before the US Supreme Court, which will soon hear its biggest racial preferences case in a generation.

Several top US corporations, including General Motors and Merck, will join other Fortune 500 companies in filing "friend of the court" briefs supporting the University of Michigan, which will defend its affirmative action programmes before the justices on April 1. Today is the deadline for filing such briefs, but the East Coast blizzard is expected to delay some filings until tomorrow.

The extraordinarily broad coalition supporting Michigan also includes the American Bar Association, the largest US lawyers' group; the AFL-CIO union federation; top US universities, law schools and education groups; former top-ranking military leaders; and politicians. But many conservative groups also plan to file briefs opposing Michigan's case. The US government has already filed its brief in opposition.

The court will hear two cases that involve the University of Michigan, and will be asked to decide whether public universities may consider race in admissions decisions without violating the constitution.

5   The court's previous 1978 ruling on the issue has been interpreted in contradictory ways by lower courts. That ruling allowed consideration of race in college admissions but banned racial quotas. Corporate supporters of Michigan's race-conscious admissions policies argue that without diverse student bodies at US universities, they cannot hire the diverse workforces needed to succeed in global business.

"Because our population is diverse, and because of the increasingly global reach of American business, the skills and training needed to succeed in business today demand exposure to widely diverse people, cultures, ideas and viewpoints," according to a brief to be filed by Fortune 500 companies. "Such a workforce is important to the firms' continued success in the global marketplace."

A spokesman for a group of former military chiefs said national security depended on being able to choose officers from a diverse student body: "It is an absolute imperative that we maintain a diverse officer corps to lead the most diverse fighting force on earth." The American Bar Association said that, without affirmative action, the legal profession could not achieve the required diversity.

Race Not Only "Bias" in College Admissions
Clarence Page

WASHINGTON – Stop the presses! I have run across what appears to be several classic examples of unfair preferential treatment in college admissions.

Clarence Page, "Race Not Only 'Bias' in College Admissions," *Chicago Tribune*, December 8, 2002, p. 11. Copyright, Tribune Media Services, Inc. All Rights Reserved. Reprinted with permission.

So shocking are they that I hesitate to report them for fear of widespread howling, heart palpitations and fainting spells.

But I feel it is my civic duty.

After all, some of these examples happened at the University of Michigan, whose race-conscious admissions policy the U.S. Supreme Court has decided to review.

5   That case, Grutter vs. Bollinger, is destined to be a big deal. It's the high court's first swing at race in college admissions since its famous 1978 Bakke vs. Regents of University of California opinion.

Then, Justice Lewis Powell's waffling decision tried to have it both ways. At best, it said that race can be a factor in college admissions as long as it was not the only factor. Twenty-five years later, lower courts—and the rest of America—disagree widely over how much of a "factor" is too much.

Now comes a new lead plaintiff, Barbara Grutter, who complains that she was turned down by the University of Michigan's law school in 1996 even though her 3.8 grade point average and high test scores were higher than most of the black students who were admitted.

She is joined by two white applicants, Jennifer Gratz and Patrick Hamacher, who were B students at Michigan high schools. They were turned down in the mid-1990s, while some black and Hispanic applicants with similar lesser academic records got in.

That much is not contested. If you think of college admissions as a reward for high grades and test scores and nothing else, pure and simple, it is easy to believe that Grutter and her fellow plaintiffs got shafted.

10   But there's another group of students whom the law school admitted even though they, too, had lower grades and test scores than Grutter. This second group happens to be white.

The same year that Grutter's application was rejected, 23 other white applicants were admitted to the law school, even though they had lower grade point averages and test scores than she did, according to the university's figures.

The two undergraduate plaintiffs in her case similarly were rejected while as many as 42 whites or Asians, which the university calls "non-underrepresented minorities," were admitted with both lower grades and lower test scores.

The same pattern of preferential treatment for some whites over others appeared in the 1998 case, Hopwood vs. University of Texas Law School. Cheryl Hopwood was one of four whites who felt the law school unfairly discriminated against them in favor of blacks and Hispanics. The U.S. 5th Circuit Court of Appeals agreed, declaring that race cannot be used as a factor.

The Supreme Court declined to review that case, even though more than 100 white students were admitted who had lower grade point averages or test scores than Hopwood did.

15   How does this happen? Because, as important as grades and test scores might be, they never have been the sole factors on which universities base their admissions.

The University of Michigan, for example, has 13 preference categories. They include geographic origins, talents, foreign origins, rural origins, family income and children of alumni over the age of 50. Race is one of those categories.

One friend, a Northwestern University professor, quips that he got into Princeton "under affirmative action for Greek kids from Albuquerque." Another friend, a Washington lawyer, says he got into Harvard under "affirmative action for Nebraskans."

My point is this: In comparison to the major boost that affirmative action has given to blacks and Latinos since the 1960s, it has not been a huge inconvenience to very many whites, including the plaintiffs in the Michigan case.

Michigan's undergraduate program, for example, received more than 25,000 applications this year for only 5,187 places. Even if affirmative action were eliminated, the odds for any particular white or Asian student would improve only marginally.

20   Yet it is a natural human tendency for everyone to suspect that they were the one who got shafted by racial quotas–and perceptions mean more than statistics in matters of politics and law.

Now 25 years after Bakke and almost 40 years after passage of the Civil Rights Act of 1964, it is time to reassess affirmative action. It is unfortunate that the reassessment is coming in the high court, which tends to wield a heavy hatchet, instead of legislatures, where it could be debated more thoroughly.

Sooner or later, I suspect that it will take the high court to force our politicians to come up with race-blind remedies we should have had all along for the social inequities every American of goodwill should want to end.

Affirmative Action Past Its Prime
Ruben Navarrette Jr.

DALLAS – The Supreme Court will soon have the chance to restrict the use of affirmative action in college and university admissions. It should. Not because, as some insist, admissions policies that give a boost to underrepresented minorities amount to "reverse discrimination" against whites. They do not. But because this civil rights relic often harms the very people it was intended to help.

First, let us separate fact from fiction. The fact is, reverse discrimination is fiction. Whites are not being systematically singled out and treated as second-class citizens because of some perceived inferiority. They aren't being denied educational opportunities on the basis of race or skin color. Nor are they able to point to institutions with a history of excluding people like them.

These are things that can be helpful in backing up a discrimination claim—not just in a court of law, but also in the court of public opinion. Individuals denied admission to a university have the right to feel aggrieved. Yet in order to merit some public remedy, their grievances have to pass the wince test.

The two cases headed for the high court—each challenging admissions policies at the University of Michigan—don't quite clear that hurdle. One cannot help but wince at the claim by the plaintiffs that their rights were somehow violated by a system of racial preferences that—at both the undergraduate level and the law school—has been known to produce instances where black and Hispanic applicants are accepted while whites with stronger academic credentials are rejected.

5   Under that system, undergraduate admissions at the University of Michigan are based on a "selection index" of up to 150 points. Most of those points are doled out on the basis of academics, but up to 20 points can be awarded for an additional factor such as the applicant being part of a underrepresented racial or ethnic group. The law school, meanwhile, considers not only grades and scores but also what it calls "soft variables" including an applicant's background and life experiences.

As the plaintiffs see it, the fact that they were white put them at a disadvantage and denied them equal protection of the law as provided by the Constitution.

That is a bold claim in light of the fact that—after all the talk of "selection indexes" and "soft variables"—just 8.4 percent of undergraduate students at the University of Michigan are black and 4.7 percent are Hispanic. At the law school, 6.7 percent of students are black and just 4.4 percent are Hispanic. Even allowing for the presence of Asian-American students, that still leaves a good chance that over half the students at both schools are white.

Not bad for a group "denied" equal protection.

Ah, memories. All this brings back images of a college admissions season almost 18 years ago when white high school classmates—whose grades and test scores were, incidentally, not as good as mine—marked my acceptance to Harvard by kindly informing me: "If you hadn't been Mexican, you wouldn't have gotten in."

10   Thinking back, I hang on the word Mexican? What happened to the popular lament: "Why can't we all just be Americans?"

The words of my friends stung at the time, but now, many years later, I don't worry about the stigma that some critics claim attaches itself to beneficiaries of affirmative action. After all, the first step to being happy and successful is not caring what anyone else thinks.

The real trouble with racial preferences goes much deeper. They subordinate the interests of the individual to that of the institution, making beneficiaries dependent on the kindness of strangers. They allow well-meaning college administrators to delude themselves into thinking that they can compensate for the educational failure of their counterparts at the K-12 level. Practiced with too much zeal, they lower standards by virtually assuring admission to the unqualified. Practiced with not enough, they enrich the few at the expense of the many by skimming the cream of the applicant pool while the vast majority of Hispanic and African-Americans students are stuck at the bottom.

All the while, they deflect attention away from the real issue by passing themselves off as a poor substitute for the educational reforms that might allow more black and Hispanic students to get into college on their own steam.

The minority advocacy groups who are so desperate to hold onto racial preferences have it backward. Instead of fighting to preserve these bureaucratic handouts, they should be fighting to free their constituencies from their grip.

Let's Reframe the Affirmative Action Debate on College Admissions

Dori J. Maynard

President George W. Bush's decision to wade into the legal wrangling over the University of Michigan's use of race in its admissions policy gives us a rare opportunity to take a fresh look at an issue that has needlessly polarized the nation for decades.

Bush, a third-generation Yale graduate, boasts at best an undistinguished academic record. He once bragged that his presidency was proof anyone with a "C" average could ascend to the highest office in the land. He was most likely admitted to college not on his academic performance, but on the basis of his family background.

He is not alone. According to media reports, Harvard accepts 40 percent of applicants who are the children of alumni. Even the most cursory look

Dori J. Maynard, "Let's Reframe the Affirmative Action Debate on College Admissions." Pacific News Service, February 7, 2003. Copyright © Pacific News Service. Reprinted by permission.

at the University of Michigan's selection guidelines makes clear that there are a number of factors that go into college admission—race being only one of them.

For example, children of alumni receive four points merely for their heritage. In-state students from underrepresented counties get 16 points. Applicants who are eligible for an athletic scholarship receive 20 points. The provost has the discretion to give a candidate 20 points. Socio-economically disadvantaged applicants of any race receive 20 points.

5   And yes, members of underrepresented racial and ethnic minorities receive 20 points.

However, according to the guidelines, the bulk of the decision is based on academics. In fact, only 27 percent of the maximum possible points an applicant can receive are based on non-academic criteria.

Scant attention has been paid by the media to other categories in the ranking system. The president has not criticized them. Instead, the focus has been solely on race.

As President Bush's own experience illustrates, this conversation should not be about race. Rather, it should be about an academic institution's right to decide the makeup of its student body. That it uses affirmative action in making that decision is a given. Look in the dictionary under affirmative, and you will find the word "positive." A racially diverse student body is just one factor that most schools view as positive.

It would certainly seem positive, for example, for a college or university to admit the children of alumni—particularly if those alumni have the resources to donate money to the school. In fact, University of Michigan guidelines state: "To recognize the continuing services and support provided to the University, points will be awarded for certain alumni relationships . . . "

10   It also seems positive for a college or university to admit an athlete who could improve the team and raise the school's profile. Again, the guidelines state: "In anticipation of their contributions to the University and in recognition of the tradition and national prominence of Michigan intercollegiate athletics, applicants being officially recruited and considered for athletic scholarships should have 20 points added to their score."

It is clear that the white plaintiffs in the University of Michigan case were not necessarily rejected in favor of a student of color.

This should not come as a surprise to applicants. The University of Michigan has stood by its desire to have a diverse student population in all senses of the word.

"It is our sincere belief that this mixture contributes to the education of our students, as well as fulfills the University's mission to prepare society's future citizens and leaders," the guidelines state.

Now that President Bush has joined the debate, it can only be hoped that he will bring the insight of his experience to the conversation. Then, as we look at college admission policies, we can weigh all the benefits of a diverse campus, including those of class, gender and geography.

15   For years, people of color have been told to stop playing the race card. Maybe it is time we all stopped playing the race card, and realize that there are a variety of factors that can lead to college admission.

As a nation, we must continue to have a dialogue on race. But we should not allow a university's right to decide the makeup of its student body to be a proxy for that discussion. Nor should a college's admissions plan be sacrificed in our struggle to reconcile the past, make sense of the present and move on to the future.

What I Think: College Admissions and Affirmative Action

Melisa Gao

With the college admissions process becoming increasingly competitive, the slightest edge can make the difference between a thin envelope and a thick one. I felt the pressure last year when I was applying, and I did wonder if my ethnic background ever played a role in decisions. Being of Chinese descent, I am part of the "over-represented minority" that, along with Caucasians, is allegedly hurt by affirmative action. Though I did not apply to the University of Michigan, where being African-American would have earned me an extra 20 points out of 150, the colleges reviewing my application undoubtedly gave preference to students of certain backgrounds—and thus I was indirectly placed at some disadvantage.

But the truth is, I benefited from affirmative action. And so does every single college applicant today.

Rejection is hard to swallow, and it's tempting to point fingers. It's easy to say, "I didn't get in because these people took my spot. It's even easier to say, "I would have gotten in if I were [insert underrepresented minority of your choice]." And there may be some truth to that. Affirmative action is an imperfect system—but hey, the college admissions process itself is imperfect, as is any attempt to determine the relative merit of a pool of candidates using ambiguous criteria. The specific problem people have with affirmative action is that it allows a systematic preference for something that does not represent "merit"—that is to say, race. In an ideal world, admissions would not take race into account, but the process today is far from color-blind. Surely, then, affirmative action helps people at the expense of others. On the contrary: I contend that every student benefits. At college I live next door to an African-American, across the hall from someone who's half-Chinese and around the corner from an Indian boy. Two doors down, a girl who is half-Japanese rooms with a Nigerian. Downstairs there's a boy from Ecuador and someone from South Korea. And when together, those racial differences don't matter. We're just a bunch of college freshmen, hanging out and learning from each other's vastly different experiences.

Diversity is something that every college aims for and touts to prospective students. But I've found it's not overrated in the least. Interacting with and learning from people of different backgrounds—geographic, economic, or racial—is perhaps the most valuable experience one can have, because that's what life is all about. It's not something a professor can teach; it's not something one can learn from a textbook or presentation. Colleges do all their students a favor by trying to achieve diversity, and if the only way is through the flawed process of affirmative action, then I hope the government will not take that away from us.

High Noon for "Diversity"
George F. Will

The late Justice William Brennan reportedly said that the most important word in the Supreme Court is not "justice" or "equality" or "law" but "five." Soon the Supreme Court, and perhaps Justice Sandra Day O'Connor as the decisive fifth vote, will decide whether racial preferences will be part of American higher education forever, or whether America will continue its long, meandering march to a colorblind society.

The result may turn on how she construes fidelity to her departed friend Justice Lewis Powell. He did more than anyone else to make the word "diversity" ubiquitous.

The court will be ruling on the constitutionality of the racial preferences used at the University of Michigan and its law school. Undergraduate applicants get 20 points added to their scores (150 is the maximum; a perfect 1600 SAT result earns just 12 points) if they are African–Americans, Hispanics or Native Americans. The university says preferences granted to these races are not racial preferences but diversity preferences.

It cites as justification Powell's opinion in the 1978 *Bakke* decision. He said that although racial quotas are unconstitutional, race can be a "plus factor" in admissions decisions, and not merely, or primarily—or even at all—as a remedial measure. Preferences, meaning the radical idea of group as opposed to individual rights, could be used to promote "diversity" for its putative educational value.

George F. Will, "High Noon for 'Diversity'," *Newsweek*, May 26, 2003, p. 76. Reprinted by permission of the author.

5   The pedagogic justification of diversity based on race is, to say no more, murky. But the murkiness makes it immortal. Racial preferences *as a remedy for past discrimination* must eventually be considered things of the past. But the value of diversity can be invoked a century from now. Indeed, many people favor the "diversity" rationale for racial preferences precisely because it need never go out of style.

John C. Jeffries Jr. in his fine biography of Powell describes this exchange during the justices' deliberations about *Bakke:*

"[John Paul] Stevens said that preferences might be acceptable as a temporary measure but not as a permanent solution. Powell agreed. The problem was one of transition to a color-blind society. Perhaps, Stevens added, blacks would not need these special programs much longer, but at this point [Thurgood] Marshall broke in to say that it would be another hundred years. This remark left Powell speechless."

What would Powell make of the many permutations of the "diversity" rationale for racial preferences in the almost quarter of a century since then? As John D. Skrentny, a professor of sociology at the University of California, San Diego, noted in the winter 2002 issue of The Public Interest quarterly:

"Powell chose to embrace the 'diversity' rationale for affirmative action precisely because it avoided the question of which groups had suffered sufficient discrimination to warrant preferential treatment—any underrepresented group could add to the diversity of a student body . . . Powell suggested that a constitutional 'diversity' preference might, in some circumstances, offer preference to an Italian American."

10   Or to those who today are even more severely penalized than whites by racial preferences like Michigan's—Asian-Americans. But as Powell wrote in his *Bakke* opinion:

"There is no principled basis for deciding which groups would merit 'heightened judicial solicitude' and which would not. Courts would be asked to evaluate the extent of the prejudice and consequent harm suffered by various minority groups. Those whose societal injury is thought to exceed some arbitrary level of tolerability then would be entitled to preferential classifications at the expense of other groups."

So "diversity" severed preferences from remediation. And 11 years later Powell was confronted with evidence of how a regime of racial preferences can spin toward absurdity. In 1989, two years after he retired from the court, in a case from Richmond, Va., his home, the court struck down that city's program of racial set-asides in awarding contracts. The court—O'Connor wrote the opinion—held that the program had no rational basis for including, for example, Eskimos as a group deserving recompense for past discrimination. There were no Eskimos in Richmond.

Jeffries writes about the "special friendship" between Powell, the courtly Virginia Democrat, and O'Connor, the Arizona Republican cowgirl who called him "sweet, kind, courteous and thoughtful." Jeffries says the two "often talked and visited, both about personal matters and about the Court." In her graceful eulogy at Powell's funeral in 1998, O'Connor spoke of the delight of dancing with him, and recalled that he said his tombstone would read "HERE LIES THE FIRST SUPREME COURT JUSTICE TO DANCE WITH ANOTHER JUSTICE."

Perhaps O'Connor, who so often is the decisive vote on this closely divided court, will get the nation off the path of open-ended and eternal racial preferences. Her friend inadvertently put the nation on that path when, generously but improvidently, he helped affirmative action spread beyond the narrow *and temporary* function of remediation for past discrimination.

Affirmative Action: The Court Muddies the Waters
Robert J. Bresler

In its 2002–03 term, the Supreme Court opened the door to more contention and confusion over the issues of affirmative action and gay rights. In three landmark decisions, the Court assured the country that our tiresome culture wars will continue, with even greater intensity. As discussed in my last column, the case of Lawrence v. Texas, overturning that state's homosexual sodomy law, has opened up the possibility of judicial authorization of gay marriage. This issue promises to stay around for a long while.

At the same time, the Court declined to put the question of racial preferences to rest in college admissions practices. The Court previously had established a very high standard for any racial preference initiative. Such programs would have to serve a compelling state interest and must be narrowly tailored to meet that compelling interest. To the surprise of many, the Court did not take its lead from the Fifth Circuit Court of Appeals decision (Hopwood v. Texas) and declare that racial diversity was not a compelling justification for racial preferences.

Instead, two University of Michigan affirmative action cases (Grutter v. Bollinger and Gratz v. Bollinger) have further muddied the waters by assuring an endless parade of affirmative action lawsuits. On June 23, the Supreme Court upheld the affirmative action policy of the University of Michigan Law School (Grutter) and overturned the affirmation policy of the undergraduate college (Gratz). Justice Sandra Day O'Connor cast the

Robert J. Bresler, "Affirmative Action: The Court Muddies the Waters." Reprinted from *USA Today Magazine,* November 2003. Copyrighted by the Society for the Advancement of Education, Inc.

swing vote in both cases. In Gratz, the Court dismissed a blatant racial preference scheme that gave a number of points to all applicants in certain racial categories—in violation of the equal protection clause of the Fourteenth Amendment. Yet, this obvious quota system was only struck down by a five-to-four vote.

In Grutter, the outcome was quite different and more disturbing. O'Connor, writing for another five-to-four majority, endorsed the idea that student body diversity was a compelling state interest justifying the use of race in university admissions and ignored the lower court opinion in Hopwood. The Court majority bought the diversity rationale in the face of extensive research that such a policy does not promote tolerance or understanding for the views of others. Students frequently separate themselves by race, and minority students often exhibit a militancy they never embraced in their more integrated high schools.

5   While championing racial diversity, higher education has produced greater ideological and political uniformity than experienced even in the so-called "McCarthy Era" of the 1950s. Conservative Republicans are a rare breed on most university faculties. Intellectual diversity, essential to a fine education, is perfunctorily saluted and ignored.

O'Connor and the liberal majority in Grutter accepted the diversity rationale as compelling and found the Michigan Law School's racial preference program to be narrowly tailored to fit that need. The Law School, unlike the undergraduate college, did not rely on a fixed numerical formula to benefit minority applicants. Instead, it used the vague concept of a "critical mass" of minority students that allegedly would prevent such individuals from feeling isolated and would challenge all students to reexamine stereotypes. O'Connor noted that "the Law School engages in a highly individualized, holistic review of each applicant's file, giving serious consideration to all the ways an applicant might contribute to a diverse educational environment." She found the Law School policy acceptable since it focused on "academic ability coupled with a flexible assessment of applicant's talents, experiences, and potential to contribute to the learning of those around them and did not define diversity solely in terms of racial and ethnic status."

In his Grutter dissent, Chief Justice William Rehnquist was baffled by the critical mass concept. He pointed out that an adequate critical mass for African-American students was between 91 and 108 and for Native Americans it was between 13 and 19. The Law School, Rehnquist noted, gave no explanation for such disparities and had no explanation as to why admission standards for Hispanics were higher than for African-Americans.

Grutter certainly will require more work for university admissions officers who will have to meet all its standards. Universities and colleges will have to demonstrate that they have provided "a highly individualized, holistic review of each applicant's file." Competitive colleges and universities receive tens of thousands of applications each year. How can admissions possibly provide such a review without yielding to the temptation of merely a superficial compliance with Grutter? This problem, plus the formless nature of what constitutes a "critical mass," will open the door to endless litigation from disappointed applicants. Consequently, the Court has guaranteed that the diversity battle over affirmative action will rage unabated. Lower courts certainly will give Grutter different interpretations, and schools will be at a loss to know what admission policies are legal. This is good news for lawyers and more work for the courts.

The controversy will intensify in the political arena. While many politicians try to avoid taking a clear stand on the issue, the opponents of racial preferences will not let Grutter be the final word, even if that word had been clearer. Emboldened by polls that show the overwhelming number of both white and black people to be opposed to such preferences, they will take the battle to the states. Already, voters in California and Washington state have passed initiatives banning racial preferences and the Florida legislature did the same. Ward Connerly, the architect of Proposition 209, the California initiative, is planning to put a similar one on the ballot in Michigan in 2004.

10   While much time and energy is expended in this fight, minority education suffers. Affirmative action allows liberal administrators to feel good, but does little for minority students. Accepting students who are not competitive with their peers does them no favor. When racial preferences were eliminated, the graduation rate for minorities in the University of California system increased. Students were accepted onto campuses where they had a better chance to excel. If the Supreme Court cannot see these issues clearly, perhaps the voters will.

Validation of the University of Michigan's Affirmative Action Program by the U.S. Supreme Court

Mac A. Stewart

On June 23, the Supreme Court announced its anxiously awaited decision in two lawsuits challenging admissions policies at the University of Michigan. National reactions were immediate and mixed. U of M President May Sue Coleman called the decisions "a tremendous victory for the Uni-

Mac A. Stewart, "Validation of the University of Michigan's Affirmative Action Program by the U.S. Supreme Court," *The Negro Educational Review*, Vol. 54, No. 3/4 (July 2003), p. 59. Reprinted by permission of the author.

versity of Michigan, for all of higher education, and for hundreds of groups and individual who supported us". Ward Connerly, founder and chairman of the American Civil Rights Institute, in an article entitled "Murder at the Supreme Court", concluded:

> The Grutter and Gratz decisions, taken together, represent a sad and tragic chapter in American history. June 23, 2003 was the day that the concept of academic meritocracy and the principle of equal treatment were murdered by a majority of the Supreme Court so that the goal of 'diversity' might live. Adding insult to injury is the fact that the head of the death squad was a woman appointed by a president who believed in the principles of personal freedom, merit, and equal treatment as much as, if not more than, any president in our nation's history. What a shame!

Connerly was, of course, referring to Justice Sandra Day O'Connor, and the virulence of his rhetoric, characterizing the Court's decision as "murder" by a "death squad," can easily provoke opponents to waste their energy in responding in kind. In the long run, it will be much more productive, I believe, to listen closely to what the Supreme Court has determined and move forward from these decisions in ways consistent with the law as now understood and in ways that will benefit universities and their diverse constituencies. What will such a positive course of action require?

First, colleges and universities need to review their current admission policies to insure that they follow not only the letter but the spirit of the law. The fundamental basis for the Court's reaffirmation of Bakke is that diversity, including but not limited to, racial and ethnic diversity, can be considered in forwarding the goal of free and vigorous discussion. Institutions need to revise current policies to be more inclusive.

5   Second, institutions should be prepared to evaluate individuals as individuals. We have long understood that education affects the whole person and that the changes effected by education are qualitative as well as quantitative. That is, a well educated person is not merely someone who knows more than he or she did before. Such a person has greater understanding and can make better judgements about the world than before. Yet too often our admissions decisions have been based on predominantly quantitative measures, such as test scores and high school rank. Too often we have measured the quality of an institution by the quantifiable criteria used in such national rankings as those in *Newsweek* and *U.S. News & World Report*. Such measures have an important role, but we need to develop and acknowledge other qualitative ways to decide among individual applicants.

Third, we need to be ready to pay for these changes. They will require more labor-intensive judgements and the investment of more human time. These can be costly, especially at large universities like my own. I agree with President Coleman that the Court's decision was a tremendous victory. I congratulate the University of Michigan for staying the course and all its supporters for their important contributions. Now let us move forward to carry out the law.

'Diversity' . . . D'oh!

John J. Miller

The Supreme Court delivered a huge blow to equal opportunity on June 23, but the two cases involving "diversity" at the University of Michigan may have been lost well before then. That's because the Center for Individual Rights, the Washington, D.C.-based law firm handling the litigation, made a tactical decision early on not to challenge Michigan's claim that racial and ethnic diversity improves the quality of higher education. "We didn't have the resources to turn it into an issue," says Curt Levey of CIR. "Besides, people out there have a sense that diversity is valuable, and we didn't want to get into a debate over that. We wanted to focus on the legal principles."

As it turned out, legal principle had little to do with what the Supreme Court decided. As Justice Sandra Day O'Connor wrote in her majority opinion, "The Law School's educational judgment that such diversity is essential to its educational mission is one to which we defer." CIR deferred as well. In 2000, as CIR and Michigan were wrangling in federal district court, CIR's lead trial attorney, Kirk Kolbo, allowed that "racial diversity . . . is something that's valuable, maybe even important."

It is impossible to know whether this concession affected the outcome of the case; second-guessing is easy. What's more, responsibility for an outrageous decision must lie squarely with the five justices who rendered it, and in particular O'Connor. Another culprit is the Bush administration, which submitted a feeble amicus brief and greeted the eventual decisions with troubling approval. "I applaud the Supreme Court for recognizing the value of diversity on our nation's campuses," said President Bush. "Today's decisions seek a careful balance between the goal of campus diversity and the fundamental principle of equal treatment under the law." The Michigan rulings may "seek" such a thing, but they do not achieve it. They don't even come close. They represent a near-total win for the supporters of racial preferences.

"Failing to take on the diversity argument was a big mistake," says Ward Connerly of the American Civil Rights Institute. It's a blunder conservatives can no longer afford to make. For more than a decade, conservatives have waged a slow but successful legal offensive against preferences in contracting and voting; the Supreme Court's acceptance of "diversity" as a rationale for state-sponsored racial discrimination puts these gains in jeopardy. The Left now will try to expand the "diversity" argument beyond the confines

John J. Miller, "'Diversity'... D'oh," *National Review,* Vol. 55, No. 14 (July 28, 2003), pp. 17–18. © 2003 by National Review, Inc., 215 Lexington Avenue, New York, NY 10016. Reprinted by permission.

of higher education. Pretty soon, it will be offered as a rationale for set-aside contracts, racial gerrymandering, and the composition of magnet schools in K-12 systems. Can "diversity" for gays be far behind? Conservatives who thought they were on the verge of a game-winning touchdown with the Michigan cases now find that they've thrown an interception—and the other team is sprinting down the field.

5   The Center for Individual Rights is a first-rate public-interest law firm; it was the key force behind the 1996 Hopwood decision, which restricted the use of racial preferences at the University of Texas and which, until June, was the most important federal court decision on preferences in education since Bakke in 1978. So the Michigan plaintiffs were in good hands when they hooked up with CIR and filed their lawsuits six years ago. The Hopwood case was won on pure law, with no mention of the social-science gobbledygook underpinning Michigan's key claim that diversity is essential to intellectual growth. But Michigan's innovation was a neces- sary one if racial preferences were to survive far into the 21st century: With bigotry an ever-decreasing feature of American life, the old justifi- cations for preferences were losing their punch. They needed a new rea- son for being, and they got it from Patricia Gurin, a Michigan psychology professor who produced a flurry of research on the supposed benefits of diversity in Ann Arbor.

Gurin's conclusions have been picked apart in exhaustive critiques by the Center for Equal Opportunity (CEO) and the National Association of Scholars and contradicted in separate research by political scientists Stan- ley Rothman, Seymour Martin Lipset, and Neil Nevitte. Yet Michigan's entire case rested on her claims. Still, CIR believed Gurin's work was irrel- evant. "Whether diversity is a compelling state interest is a legal question, not an empirical one," says CIR's Levey. Questions of principle shouldn't play second fiddle to the soft claims of social science, after all.

And so CIR made a very sound constitutional argument against the use of racial preferences in higher education, ignoring what social science might have to say on the matter. "If people followed the normal rules of logic, CIR should have won going away," says one conservative involved in the cases. "But judges aren't normal people and they don't always follow logic."

"I say this more in sadness than in anger, but CIR made a tactical error," says Peter Wood of Boston University. "They should have con- fronted the diversity argument." This would not have been difficult. Fol- lowing the oral arguments in April, it was reported in the press that a University of Michigan survey of its own students showed "diversity" hav- ing a negative impact on campus. Naturally, this piece of information did not find its way into Michigan's court presentations. It was briefly assumed by some that the university had suppressed the survey results—

until administrators said they had provided the report to CIR years earlier. "We had the material in our files," says Levey. "We overlooked it."

When the Michigan decisions were handed down, CIR claimed a partial victory because the Court struck down the university's system of undergraduate admissions. "Overall, I think this is a big step forward," said CIR president Terence Pell in a video clip shown on the PBS NewsHour. "I think what we are seeing today is the beginning of the end of race preferences." CIR is virtually alone in this view, because in upholding Michigan's law-school admissions, five justices enshrined diversity in the Constitution. "We were wiped out," says Michael Greve, who headed CIR until 2000 and conceived the original lawsuits. "Anything else is spin."

10   Not everyone on the right is as glum as Greve. The rulings were a major disappointment, but many conservative lawyers believe they leave the door open for more worthwhile litigation. "If the Left were in our position, it would not give up," says Roger Clegg of CEO. "It would act like one of those whack-a-mole games you see at Chuck E. Cheese: You hit it in one place, but it pops up in another. That's what we should do." If the makeup of the Court changes in the next few years, perhaps the justices would even reverse themselves. They've done it before, and they're more likely to do so when a ruling is fresh and controversial than after it's perceived as old and settled. O'Connor suggested that preferences should be gone for good in 25 years, but waiting that long may be exactly the wrong approach. Another quarter-century might entrench them even further. At the very least, the Michigan rulings provide conservatives with a solid reason for opposing White House counsel Alberto Gonzales as a nominee to the Supreme Court: He had much to do with the weakness of the administration's brief, and the positive air of its response to the rulings.

Conservatives may be able to limit the damage from the Michigan cases if they have a hand in determining how the rulings will be enforced. One reason the law school's admission system passed muster with O'Connor is that it engaged in a "highly individualized, holistic review" of all applicants. This will be difficult to duplicate for undergraduates, however, because the volume of applications is many times larger. Michigan is already assuring everybody that this is what it will do, but that doesn't mean it will succeed. "Just because they glance over an application doesn't mean they've given it serious attention," says one Bush-administration official. "And that's what the Court is now requiring."

Finally, there are political solutions. These haven't worked well for conservatives in the past, but it's important to note that the Supreme Court didn't say universities must use preferences to achieve diverse student bodies; it merely said they may use them. The last real attempt in Congress to rein in preferences came eight years ago, when presidential candidate Bob Dole offered a bill to restrict them. It fared about as well as

Dole's 1996 campaign; since then, many Republicans have tried to make peace with preferences, in the belief that fighting against them riles up their opposition more than it pleases their own troops.

One political approach has worked, however. In 1996, California voters passed a sweeping ban on racial preferences in their state. Two years later, voters in Washington followed suit. Ward Connerly led both ballot initiatives. Just a few days after the Michigan rulings were announced, Connerly was clearing his schedule and making travel plans—for Ann Arbor. The fight against race preferences will go on.

TECHNIQUES FOR WRITERS 3-c

Analyzing an Argument

Choose one of the articles from the previous selection and analyze it, based on the material in this chapter and class discussion. The analysis will include brief sections of summary as you discuss some of the author's major points, but it isn't a response paper in which you have to debate those points. Hold off on your opinion; what counts here is your ability to demonstrate what you know about the elements of argument and how they've been applied in the article.

In your analysis, focus on such matters as the following:

- What is the *argumentative proposition* that is the basis of the article?
  - What are the major points the author makes to support his/her position?
  - Does the author mention any points made by the opposition against his/her position? If so, what are they? How does the author argue against them?
  - What evidence based on logic does the author make?
  - What evidence based on emotion does the author make?
  - How does the author presents herself or himself in this essay (*ethical stance*)?
  - What assumptions does the author seem to be making about the audience (*pathetic stance*)?
  - Is the argument *effective?* Why or why not?

Student Writing: Argument Analysis

Following are two student papers analyzing Stephen Carter's "Racial Justice on the Cheap."

Analysis of "Racial Justice on the Cheap"

Mary Best

The argumentative proposition for this article is that affirmative action gives minorities and students with other preferences the chance to further their educations. Stephen Carter argues that colleges and universities should take risks in admitting students that might not be "sure things" but show good evidence of taking advantage of what the college or university can offer.

The author also states arguments from the opposing side. He states that "students admitted because a school decided to take a chance on them will not look as good on paper as those who are admitted because they are sure things." Carter also states that the "odds are those with better paper records will be better performers." He argues against this by stating that "the best way to reduce the risk would be to eliminate racial preferences."

Evidence based on logic includes his comment that "studies have shown that educational disadvantage is one of a cluster of problems reducing the likelihood that students of color will attend or complete college." The author states some statistics concerning the percentage of black youth from the ages of eighteen to twenty-four that have enrolled in college. Other evidence of logic is Carter's statement that "in 1976, 33.4 percent of that group [were or had] been enrolled in college, this representing nearly half of the black high school graduates." This is compared to "33.0 percent of the white youth . . . representing 40 percent of white high school graduates." Ten years later, black enrollment was only 28.6 percent.

The author uses evidence based on emotion in the very beginning of the article when he says that he is "drawn to the folders of applicants who are not white." He also plays on emotions when he talks about the different stereotypes that are used in colleges and universities. Evidence of this is "dumb jocks and stupid legacy." The author's solution offers evidence

---

Reprinted by permission of Mary Best.

based on emotions. He states that "students who are admitted as a consequence of affirmative action, while on college campus and while in professional school and while pursuing their careers," basically, "for the rest of their professional lives . . . bend to their work with an energy that will leave competitors and detractors alike gasping in admiration."

Carter feels that he should oppose all racial preferences, but he doesn't. He states "the proper goal of all racial preferences is opportunity." He feels it's a chance at advanced training minorities, for whatever set of reasons, might not otherwise have. The author states that "a college or university is not fulfilling its educational missions if it fails to take a hard look at the applicant pool to be sure that it is not missing highly motivated students, some of them people of color," some of them not people of color.

The author seems to assume that the audience is somewhat educated in general on this topic. He uses statistics to show the audience that college attendance by black students is down. The article could also be confusing to people who aren't well educated because of some of its wording.

I believe that the article is effective. Carter uses evidence to support his position and the opposing position. This allows audience members who might not have a position to choose one, while not making those who have a position feel like they have to be on the same side as the author.

* * *

Analysis of "Racial Justice on the Cheap"
Curtis Dale

The argumentative proposition for "Racial Justice on the Cheap" is that racial preference in admission to college and professional schools is good, but after school, as one climbs toward professional success, at some point the preference must fall away entirely. The author's major points are that he doesn't believe the standards applied by colleges are racist; he wants others to have the same hand up that he had. Carter believes that the admissions programs should be tools for providing training

---

Reprinted by permission of Curtis Dale.

and a chance for students who otherwise might not have them. After college, the time has come, finally, to stand or fall on what one has actually achieved. Among professionals, the case for preference evaporates.

Carter also states points opposing this view. He states that the odds are that those students with better records will be better performers. Athletes are frequently admitted on paper records for which other students would be rejected. He also says that if the success rates for minority students at elite colleges turn out to be lower that those of white students, that fact will be noticed, and in our racially-conscious society, remembered as well.

Carter uses logic to persuade his audience by saying that despite rising test scores, a higher rate of high school graduations, and affirmative action programs, college attendance by black students is down from 1976 to 1986. The common reason given for this is the high cost of attending a college or university. Carter uses emotion to persuade his audience by saying that minorities need fear no standards. A college or university is not fulfilling its educational mission if it fails to take a hard look at the applicant pool to be sure that it is not missing highly motivated students who might otherwise not get the chance to better themselves and their educations.

Carter urges high schools and colleges to properly train and push students to meet and exceed the standards. He believes it is a positive thing for our society to give lots of people from different backgrounds the chance to excel in college so that society as a whole will eventually improve.

The author presents himself as a black man who benefited from racial preferences in college admissions. He knows that without the current system, he might not have been able to get the education he did to reach his full potential. Carter assumes that his readers are intelligent and well-educated, and are not completely in favor of preferences.

I feel the argument was very effective. He states his own viewpoint as well as many opposing viewpoints. I thought his essay was a little hard to follow, but after reading it a few times, I found it extremely effective. It changed my mind on the topic, and probably that of many others as well.

Writing a Dialogue: Creating Support Through Dialectic

Having worked through all of the steps in planning an argument on Affirmative Action, you can see the number and variety of arguments that support and oppose argumentative propositions. This is the nature of argumentative propositions, especially those based on issues that have been debated over many years or decades. And some issues, like the citizen's duty to the state or the effectiveness of the death penalty, have been argued for centuries. The complexity of such issues causes them to continue as argumentative propositions over time and distance.

One way you can clarify the issues comprising any argumentative proposition is to write your own dialogue. Think of your dialogue as an extended prewriting exercise that can help you to generate more ideas for your expanded argument.

Dialectic: Using Dialogue to Examine an Issue

From its earliest times, one criticism of rhetoric has been that, in its search for persuasive arguments, it has not truly looked at the value of those arguments. An even earlier philosophical concept, *dialectic* (defined in Chapter 2), attempted to evaluate arguments according to their value, rather than their persuasive ability.

Plato, the student of Socrates and the teacher of Aristotle, was more concerned with determining the basic "truth" or "goodness" of the issues being argued in his time. Plato disdained rhetoric and saw it as pandering to the masses. He believed that every issue did have one "ideal" answer, and that the best way to arrive at that ideal answer was through thoughtful dialogue, which he described as "leisurely discussion . . . stargazing, if you will, about the nature of things" (*Phaedrus*).

Plato's extensive writings consist of dialogues (commonly called *dialectics*) between Socrates and his students, the young men of Athens who followed Socrates and hoped to acquire wisdom through association with "the wisest man in Athens."

Socrates taught not by lecture, but through questioning. In this way, he hoped to elicit the truth of any issue from and through his students. While many readers of the dialectics have accused Socrates of manipulating followers into adopting his own ideas, careful reading suggests that Socrates really did believe what he maintained: through dialectic, both speakers gain new insights and become more knowledgeable. In many of the works of Plato we see Socrates discovering the "truth" through dialectic, right along with his students.

The following excerpt from Plato's dialectic *Crito* examines the thoughts of Socrates as he awaits execution. After Socrates taught his students to question, they began questioning many things—including the political and religious leadership of their time. In response, the Athenian government accused Socrates of corrupting the youth of Athens and sentenced him to death. Because the execution had been delayed, one of Socrates' old friends, Crito, visited him in prison, offering to help him escape. Socrates' response, which may surprise you, examines his view of the responsibility the individual owes to his country.

As you read *Crito,* look for Socrates' and Crito's arguments, but also at the format of the dialectic itself.

Crito

Plato
Translated by Benjamin Jowett

Persons of the Dialogue
> SOCRATES
> CRITO

Scene

The Prison of Socrates.

SOCRATES   Why have you come at this hour, Crito? it must be quite early.
CRITO   Yes, certainly.
Soc.   What is the exact time?
CR.   The dawn is breaking.
5   Soc.   I wonder the keeper of the prison would let you in.
CR.   He knows me because I often come, Socrates; moreover. I have done him a kindness.
Soc.   And are you only just come?
CR.   No, I came some time ago.
Soc.   Then why did you sit and say nothing, instead of awakening me at once?
10   CR.   Why, indeed, Socrates, I myself would rather not have all this sleeplessness and sorrow. But I have been wondering at your peaceful slumbers, and that was the reason why I did not awaken you, because I wanted you to be out of pain. I have always thought you happy in the calmness of your temperament; but never did I see the like of the easy, cheerful way in which you bear this calamity.
Soc.   Why, Crito, when a man has reached my age he ought not to be repining at the prospect of death.
CR.   And yet other old men find themselves in similar misfortunes, and age does not prevent them from repining.
Soc.   That may be. But you have not told me why you come at this early hour.
CR.   I come to bring you a message which is sad and painful; not, as I believe, to yourself but to all of us who are your friends, and saddest of all to me.

From *Crito,* from *Dialogues of Plato,* translated by Benjamin Jowett. New York: D. Appleton and Company, 1898.

15 Soc.   What! I suppose that the ship has come from Delos, on the arrival of which I am to die?

Cr.   No, the ship has not actually arrived, but she will probably be here to-day, as persons who have come from Sunium tell me that they have left her there; and therefore to-morrow, Socrates, will be the last day of your life.

Soc.   Very well, Crito; if such is the will of God, I am willing; but my belief is that there will be a delay of a day.

Cr.   Why do you say this?

Soc.   I will tell you. I am to die on the day after the arrival of the ship?

20 Cr.   Yes; that is what the authorities say.

Soc.   But I do not think that the ship will be here until to-morrow; this I gather from a vision which I had last night, or rather only just now, when you fortunately allowed me to sleep.

Cr.   And what was the nature of the vision?

Soc.   There came to me the likeness of a woman, fair and comely, clothed in white raiment, who called to me and said: O Socrates— "The third day hence, to Phthia shalt thou go."

Cr.   What a singular dream, Socrates!

25 Soc.   There can be no doubt about the meaning Crito, I think.

Cr.   Yes: the meaning is only too clear. But, O! my beloved Socrates, let me entreat you once more to take my advice and escape. For if you die I shall not only lose a friend who can never be replaced, but there is another evil: people who do not know you and me will believe that I might have saved you if I had been willing to give money, but that I did not care. Now, can there be a worse disgrace than this— that I should be thought to value money more than the life of a friend? For the many will not be persuaded that I wanted you to escape, and that you refused.

Soc.   But why, my dear Crito, should we care about the opinion of the many? Good men, and they are the only persons who are worth considering, will think of these things truly as they happened.

Cr.   But do you see. Socrates, that the opinion of the many must be regarded, as is evident in your own case, because they can do the very greatest evil to anyone who has lost their good opinion?

Soc.   I only wish, Crito, that they could; for then they could also do the greatest good, and that would be well. But the truth is, that they can do neither good nor evil: they cannot make a man wise or make him foolish; and whatever they do is the result of chance.

30 Cr.   Well, I will not dispute about that; but please to tell me, Socrates, whether you are not acting out of regard to me and your other friends: are you not afraid that if you escape hence we may get into trouble with the informers for having stolen you away, and lose either the whole or a great part of our property; or that even a worse evil may happen to us? Now, if this is your fear, be at ease; for in order to save you, we ought surely to run this or even a greater risk; be persuaded, then, and do as I say.

Soc.   Yes, Crito, that is one fear which you mention, but by no means the
only one.

Cr.   Fear not. There are persons who at no great cost are willing to
save you and bring you out of prison; and as for the informers, you
may observe that they are far from being exorbitant in their
demands; a little money will satisfy them. My means, which, as I am
sure, are ample, are at your service, and if you have a scruple about
spending all mine, here are strangers who will give you the use of
theirs; and one of them, Simmias the Theban, has brought a sum of
money for this very purpose; and Cebes and many others are willing
to spend their money too. I say, therefore, do not on that account
hesitate about making your escape, and do not say, as you did in the
court, that you will have a difficulty in knowing what to do with
yourself if you escape. For men will love you in other places to which
you may go, and not in Athens only; there are friends of mine in
Thessaly, if you like to go to them, who will value and protect you,
and no Thessalian will give you any trouble. Nor can I think that you
are justified, Socrates, in betraying your own life when you might be
saved; this is playing into the hands of your enemies and destroyers;
and moreover I should say that you were betraying your children; for
you might bring them up and educate them; instead of which you go
away and leave them, and they will have to take thei r chance; and if
they do not meet with the usual fate of orphans, there will be small
thanks to you. No man should bring children into the world who is
unwilling to persevere to the end in their nurture and education.
But you are choosing the easier part, as I think, not the better and
manlier, which would rather have become one who professes virtue
in all his actions, like yourself. And, indeed, I am ashamed not only
of you, but of us who are your friends, when I reflect that this entire
business of yours will be attributed to our want of courage. The trial
need never have come on, or might have been brought to another
issue; and the end of all, which is the crowning absurdity, will seem
to have been permitted by us, through cowardice and baseness, who
might have saved you, as you might have saved yourself, if we had
been good for anything (for there was no difficulty in escaping);
and we did not see how disgraceful, Socrates, and also miserable all
this will be to us as well as to you. Make your mind up then, or
rather have your mind already made up, for the time of deliberation
is over, and there is only one thing to be done, which must be done,
if at all, this very night, and which any delay will render all but
impossible; I beseech you therefore, Socrates, to be persuaded by
me, and to do as I say.

Soc.   Dear Crito, your zeal is invaluable, if a right one; but if wrong,
the greater the zeal the greater the evil; and therefore we ought to
consider whether these things shall be done or not. For I am and
always have been one of those natures who must be guided by

reason, whatever the reason may be which upon reflection appears to me to be the best; and now that this fortune has come upon me, I cannot put away the reasons which I have before given: the principles which I have hitherto honored and revered I still honor, and unless we can find other and better principles on the instant, I am certain not to agree with you; no, not even if the power of the multitude could inflict many more imprisonments, confiscations, deaths, frightening us like children with hobgoblin terrors. But what will be the fairest way of considering the question? Shall I return to your old argument about the opinions of men, some of which are to be regarded, and others, as we were saying, are not to be regarded? Now were we right in maintaining this before I was condemned? And has the argument which was once good now proved to be talk for the sake of talking; in fact an amusement only, and altogether vanity? That is what I want to consider with your help, Crito: whether, under my present circumstances, the argument appears to be in any way different or not; and is to be allowed by me or disallowed. That argument, which, as I believe, is maintained by many who assume to be authorities, was to the effect, as I was saying, that the opinions of some men are to be regarded, and of other men not to be regarded. Now you, Crito, are a disinterested person who are not going to die to-morrow— at least, there is no human probability of this, and you are therefore not liable to be deceived by the circumstances in which you are placed. Tell me, then, whether I am right in saying that some opinions, and the opinions of some men only, are to be valued, and other opinions, and the opinions of other men, are not to be valued. I ask you whether I was right in maintaining this?

CR.   Certainly.

35   SOC.   The good are to be regarded, and not the bad?

CR.   Yes.

SOC.   And the opinions of the wise are good, and the opinions of the unwise are evil?

CR.   Certainly.

SOC.   And what was said about another matter? Was the disciple in gymnastics supposed to attend to the praise and blame and opinion of every man, or of one man only— his physician or trainer, whoever that was?

40   CR.   Of one man only.

SOC.   And he ought to fear the censure and welcome the praise of that one only, and not of the many?

CR.   That is clear.

SOC.   And he ought to live and train, and eat and drink in the way which seems good to his single master who has understanding, rather than according to the opinion of all other men put together?

CR.   True.

45 SOC.   And if he disobeys and disregards the opinion and approval of the
one, and regards the opinion of the many who have no understanding,
will he not suffer evil?

CR.   Certainly he will.

SOC.   And what will the evil be, whither tending and what affecting, in
the disobedient person?

CR.   Clearly, affecting the body; that is what is destroyed by the evil.

SOC.   Very good; and is not this true, Crito, of other things which we
need not separately enumerate? In the matter of just and unjust, fair
and foul, good and evil, which are the subjects of our present
consultation, ought we to follow the opinion of the many and to fear
them; or the opinion of the one man who has understanding, and
whom we ought to fear and reverence more than all the rest of the
world: and whom deserting we shall destroy and injure that principle
in us which may be assumed to be improved by justice and
deteriorated by injustice; is there not such a principle?

50 CR.   Certainly there is, Socrates.

SOC.   Take a parallel instance; if, acting under the advice of men who
have no understanding, we destroy that which is improvable by health
and deteriorated by disease— when that has been destroyed, I say,
would life be worth having? And that is— the body?

CR.   Yes.

SOC.   Could we live, having an evil and corrupted body?

CR.   Certainly not.

55 SOC.   And will life be worth having, if that higher part of man be
depraved, which is improved by justice and deteriorated by injustice?
Do we suppose that principle, whatever it may be in man, which has to
do with justice and injustice, to be inferior to the body?

CR.   Certainly not.

SOC.   More honored, then?

CR.   Far more honored.

SOC.   Then, my friend, we must not regard what the many say of us: but
what he, the one man who has understanding of just and unjust, will
say, and what the truth will say. And therefore you begin in error when
you suggest that we should regard the opinion of the many about just
and unjust, good and evil, honorable and dishonorable. Well, someone
will say, "But the many can kill us."

60 CR.   Yes, Socrates; that will clearly be the answer.

SOC.   That is true; but still I find with surprise that the old argument is,
as I conceive, unshaken as ever. And I should like to know Whether I
may say the same of another proposition— that not life, but a good
life, is to be chiefly valued?

CR.   Yes, that also remains.

SOC.   And a good life is equivalent to a just and honorable one— that
holds also?

CR.   Yes, that holds.

65 SOC.   From these premises I proceed to argue the question whether I
ought or ought not to try to escape without the consent of the
Athenians: and if I am clearly right in escaping, then I will make the
attempt; but if not, I will abstain. The other considerations which you
mention, of money and loss of character, and the duty of educating
children, are, I fear, only the doctrines of the multitude, who would be
as ready to call people to life, if they were able, as they are to put them
to death— and with as little reason. But now, since the argument has
thus far prevailed, the only question which remains to be considered
is, whether we shall do rightly either in escaping or in suffering others
to aid in our escape and paying them in money and thanks, or whether
we shall not do rightly; and if the latter, then death or any other
calamity which may ensue on my remaining here must not be allowed
to enter into the calculation.

CR.   I think that you are right, Socrates; how then shall we proceed?

SOC.   Let us consider the matter together, and do you either refute me if
you can, and I will be convinced; or else cease, my dear friend, from
repeating to me that I ought to escape against the wishes of the
Athenians: for I am extremely desirous to be persuaded by you, but
not against my own better judgment. And now please to consider my
first position, and do your best to answer me.

CR.   I will do my best.

SOC.   Are we to say that we are never intentionally to do wrong, or that
in one way we ought and in another way we ought not to do wrong, or
is doing wrong always evil and dishonorable, as I was just now saying,
and as has been already acknowledged by us? Are all our former
admissions which were made within a few days to be thrown away?
And have we, at our age, been earnestly discoursing with one another
all our life long only to discover that we are no better than children?
Or are we to rest assured, in spite of the opinion of the many, and in
spite of consequences whether better or worse, of the truth of what
was then said, that injustice is always an evil and dishonor to him who
acts unjustly? Shall we affirm that?

70 CR.   Yes.

SOC.   Then we must do no wrong?

CR.   Certainly not.

SOC.   Nor when injured injure in return, as the many imagine; for we
must injure no one at all?

CR.   Clearly not.

75 SOC.   Again, Crito, may we do evil?

CR.   Surely not, Socrates.

SOC.   And what of doing evil in return for evil, which is the morality of
the many—is that just or not?

CR.   Not just.

SOC.   For doing evil to another is the same as injuring him?

80 CR.   Very true.

SOC. Then we ought not to retaliate or render evil for evil to anyone, whatever evil we may have suffered from him. But I would have you consider, Crito, whether you really mean what you are saying. For this opinion has never been held, and never will be held, by any considerable number of persons; and those who are agreed and those who are not agreed upon this point have no common ground, and can only despise one another, when they see how widely they differ. Tell me, then, whether you agree with and assent to my first principle, that neither injury nor retaliation nor warding off evil by evil is ever right. And shall that be the premise of our agreement? Or do you decline and dissent from this? For this has been of old and is still my opinion; but, if you are of another opinion, let me hear what you have to say. If, however, you remain of the same mind as formerly, I will proceed to the next step.

CR. You may proceed, for I have not changed my mind.

SOC. Then I will proceed to the next step, which may be put in the form of a question: Ought a man to do what he admits to be right, or ought he to betray the right?

CR. He ought to do what he thinks right.

85 SOC. But if this is true, what is the application? In leaving the prison against the will of the Athenians, do I wrong any? or rather do I not wrong those whom I ought least to wrong? Do I not desert the principles which were acknowledged by us to be just? What do you say?

CR. I cannot tell, Socrates, for I do not know.

SOC. Then consider the matter in this way: Imagine that I am about to play truant (you may call the proceeding by any name which you like), and the laws and the government come and interrogate me: "Tell us, Socrates," they say; "what are you about? are you going by an act of yours to overturn us— the laws and the whole State, as far as in you lies? Do you imagine that a State can subsist and not be overthrown, in which the decisions of law have no power, but are set aside and overthrown by individuals?" What will be our answer, Crito, to these and the like words? Anyone, and especially a clever rhetorician, will have a good deal to urge about the evil of setting aside the law which requires a sentence to be carried out; and we might reply, "Yes; but the State has injured us and given an unjust sentence." Suppose I say that?

CR. Very good, Socrates.

SOC. "And was that our agreement with you?" the law would say, "or were you to abide by the sentence of the State?" And if I were to express astonishment at their saying this, the law would probably add: "Answer, Socrates, instead of opening your eyes: you are in the habit of asking and answering questions. Tell us what complaint you have to make against us which justifies you in attempting to destroy us and the State? In the first place did we not bring you into existence? Your father married your mother by our aid and begat you. Say whether you have any objection to urge against those of us who regulate marriage?" None, I should reply. "Or against those of us who regulate the system of nurture and education of children in which you were trained? Were not the laws, who have the charge of this, right in commanding your father to train you in music and gymnastic?" Right, I should reply. "Well, then, since you were brought into the world and nurtured and educated by us, can you deny in the first place that you are our child and slave, as your fathers were before you? And if this is true you are not on equal terms with us; nor can you think that you have a right to do to us what we are doing to you. Would you have any right to strike or revile or do any other evil to a father or to your master, if you had one, when you have been struck or reviled by him, or received some other evil at his hands?— you would not say this? And because we think right to destroy you, do you think that you have any right to destroy us in return, and your country as far as in you lies? And will you, O professor of true virtue, say that you are justified in this? Has a philosopher like you failed to discover that our country is more to be valued and higher and holier far than mother or father or any ancestor, and more to be regarded in the eyes of the gods and of men of understanding? also to be soothed, and gently and reverently entreated when angry, even more than a father, and if not persuaded, obeyed? And when we are punished by her, whether with imprisonment or stripes, the punishment is to be endured in silence; and if she leads us to wounds or death in battle, thither we follow as is right; neither may anyone yield or retreat or leave his rank, but whether in battle or in a court of law, or in any other place, he must do what his city and his country order him; or he must change their view of what is just: and if he may do no violence to his father or mother, much less may he do violence to his country." What answer shall we make to this, Crito? Do the laws speak truly, or do they not?

90   Cr.   I think that they do.

Soc.   Then the laws will say: "Consider, Socrates, if this is true, that in your present attempt you are going to do us wrong. For, after having brought you into the world, and nurtured and educated you, and given you and every other citizen a share in every good that we had to give, we further proclaim and give the right to every Athenian, that if he does not like us when he has come of age and has seen the ways of the city, and made our acquaintance, he may go where he pleases and take his goods with him; and none of us laws will forbid him or interfere with him. Any of you who does not like us and the city, and who wants to go to a colony or to any other city, may go where he likes, and take his goods with him. But he who has experience of the manner in which we order justice and administer the State, and still remains, has entered into an implied contract that he will do as we command him. And he who disobeys us is, as we maintain, thrice wrong: first, because in disobeying us he is disobeying his parents; secondly, because we are the authors of his education; thirdly, because he has made an agreement with us that he will duly obey our commands; and he neither obeys them nor convinces us that our commands are wrong; and we do not rudely impose them, but give him the alternative of obeying or convincing us; that is what we offer and he does neither. These are the sort of accusations to which, as we were saying, you, Socrates, will be exposed if you accomplish your intentions; you, above all other Athenians." Suppose I ask, why is this? they will justly retort upon me that I above all other men have acknowledged the agreement. "There is clear proof," they will say, "Socrates, that we and the city were not displeasing to you. Of all Athenians you have been the most constant resident in the city, which, as you never leave, you may be supposed to love. For you never went out of the city either to see the games, except once when you went to the Isthmus, or to any other place unless when you were on military service; nor did you travel as other men do. Nor had you any curiosity to know other States or their laws: your affections did not go beyond us and our State; we were your especial favorites, and you acquiesced in our government of you; and this is the State in which you begat your children, which is a proof of your satisfaction. Moreover, you might, if you had liked, have fixed the penalty at banishment in the course of the trial— the State which refuses to let you go now would have let you go then. But you pretended that you preferred death to exile, and that you were not grieved at death. And now you have forgotten these fine sentiments, and pay no respect to us, the laws, of whom you are the destroyer; and are doing what only a miserable slave would do, running away and turning your back upon the compacts and agreements which you made as a citizen. And first of all answer this very question: Are we right in saying that you agreed to be governed according to us in deed, and not in word only? Is that true or not?" How shall we answer that, Crito? Must we not agree?

CR.   There is no help, Socrates.

SOC.   Then will they not say: "You, Socrates, are breaking the covenants and agreements which you made with us at your leisure, not in any haste or under any compulsion or deception, but having had seventy years to think of them, during which time you were at liberty to leave the city, if we were not to your mind, or if our covenants appeared to you to be unfair. You had your choice, and might have gone either to Lacedaemon or Crete, which you often praise for their good government, or to some other Hellenic or foreign State. Whereas you, above all other Athenians, seemed to be so fond of the State, or, in other words, of us her laws (for who would like a State that has no laws?), that you never stirred out of her: the halt, the blind, the maimed, were not more stationary in her than you were. And now you run away and forsake your agreements. Not so, Socrates, if you will take our advice; do not make yourself ridiculous by escaping out of the city.

"For just consider, if you transgress and err in this sort of way, what good will you do, either to yourself or to your friends? That your friends will be driven into exile and deprived of citizenship, or will lose their property, is tolerably certain; and you yourself, if you fly to one of the neighboring cities, as, for example, Thebes or Megara, both of which are well-governed cities, will come to them as an enemy, Socrates, and their government will be against you, and all patriotic citizens will cast an evil eye upon you as a subverter of the laws, and you will confirm in the minds of the judges the justice of their own condemnation of you. For he who is a corrupter of the laws is more than likely to be corrupter of the young and foolish portion of mankind. Will you then flee from well-ordered cities and virtuous men? and is existence worth having on these terms? Or will you go to them without shame, and talk to them, Socrates? And what will you say to them? What you say here about virtue and justice and institutions and laws being the best things among men? Would that be decent of you? Surely not. But if you go away from well-governed States to Crito's friends in Thessaly, where there is great disorder and license, they will be charmed to have the tale of your escape from prison, set off with ludicrous particulars of the manner in which you were wrapped in a goatskin or some other disguise, and metamorphosed as the fashion of runaways is— that is very likely; but will there be no one to remind you that in your old age you violated the most sacred laws from a miserable desire of a little more life? Perhaps not, if you keep them in a good temper; but if they are out of temper you will hear many degrading things; you will live, but how?— as the flatterer of all men, and the servant of all men; and doing what?— eating and drinking in Thessaly, having gone abroad in order that you may get a dinner. And where will be your fine sentiments about justice and virtue then? Say that you wish to live for the sake of your children, that you may bring them up and educate them— will you take them into Thessaly and deprive them of Athenian citizenship? Is that the benefit which you would confer upon them? Or are you under the impression that they will be better cared for and educated here if you are still alive, although absent from them; for that your friends will take care of them? Do you fancy that if you are an inhabitant of Thessaly they will take care of them, and if you are an inhabitant of the other world they will not take care of them? Nay; but if they who call themselves friends are truly friends, they surely will.

95   "Listen, then, Socrates, to us who have brought you up. Think not of life and children first, and of justice afterwards, but of justice first, that you may be justified before the princes of the world below. For neither will you nor any that belong to you be happier or holier or juster in this life, or happier in another, if you do as Crito bids. Now you depart in innocence, a sufferer and not a doer of evil; a victim, not of the laws, but of men. But if you go forth, returning evil for evil, and injury for injury, breaking the covenants and agreements which you have made with us, and wronging those whom you ought

least to wrong, that is to say, yourself, your friends, your country, and us, we shall be angry with you while you live, and our brethren, the laws in the world below, will receive you as an enemy; for they will know that you have done your best to destroy us. Listen, then, to us and not to Crito."

This is the voice which I seem to hear murmuring in my ears, like the sound of the flute in the ears of the mystic; that voice, I say, is humming in my ears, and prevents me from hearing any other. And I know that anything more which you will say will be in vain. Yet speak, if you have anything to say.

CR.   I have nothing to say, Socrates.

SOC.   Then let me follow the intimations of the will of God.

Critical Reading Questions

1. What reasons does Crito give to urge Socrates to escape?

2. Although most of Plato's dialectics begin with some introductory material that gives us background information about the situation and characters, *Crito* contains more introductory material than is customary. At what point does Socrates' dialectic (his actual questioning of Crito) begin?

3. What analogy (comparison) does Socrates use early in his dialectic? Is it effective in illustrating his point?

4. To what degree does Socrates value popular opinion? Expert knowledge?

5. Socrates makes this often-quoted statement to Crito: "[T]he really important thing is not to live, but to live well." What, specifically, does Socrates mean by living well?

6. Many people today have adopted "situational ethics," the idea that in judging someone's actions, one should consider the situation in which those actions occur. How would Socrates respond to the idea of situational ethics?

7. What are Socrates' major arguments in defending his position to stay in Athens and submit to execution?

8. How would you characterize Socrates' questioning method?

The next selection is a dialogue between Ernest van den Haag, a philosophy teacher, and Gay Talese, an author who has written often about American sexual attitudes. The topic of the selection, pornography, is as controversial today as it was when van den Haag and Talese discussed it.

What Is a Civil Libertarian to Do When Pornography Becomes So Bold?

Moderated by Walter Goodman

As pornography has proliferated across the land, from centers of sexual technology such as New York and Los Angeles to less advanced communities, a suspicion that something may be awry has begun to nag at even that enlightened vanguard which once strove to save Lady Chatterley from the philistines. Having opened the door to sex for art's sake, they have found that it is no longer possible to close it against sex for profit's sake.

Where does duty lie today for the dutiful civil libertarian confronted by efforts around the country to prosecute the purveyors of porn? One may wish that Al Goldstein, an avant-garde publisher of the stuff, would go away, but no civil libertarian can cheer the efforts by lawmen in Wichita, Kansas, to have him put away. One might doubt that Harry Reems, who has filled many X-rated screens, is contributing much to the art of the cinema, yet no civil libertarian wants the assistant U.S. Attorney in Memphis, Tennessee, to clap him in irons. What to do?

To grapple with this matter, I brought together two figures known to have provocative—and sharply conflicting—views on the subject: author Gay Talese, whose ongoing research for a book about sex in America includes the management of two New York City massage parlors, and psychoanalyst Ernest van den Haag, adjunct professor of social philosophy at New York University and a favorite "expert witness" of pornography prosecutors everywhere.

Our conversation began with an effort by Professor van den Haag to identify the animal which he believes ought to be locked up:

5 VAN DEN HAAG   I would call pornographic whatever is blatantly offensive to the standards of the community.

TALESE   But does the public have the right to ban *Ulysses* because some people find it offensive?

VAN DEN HAAG   I think anyone who reads *Ulysses* for the sake of pornographic interests ought to get a medal! The characteristic focus of pornography is precisely that it leaves out all human context and reduces the action to interaction between organs and orifices—and that I find obscene, degrading to sex and dehumanizing to its audiences.

TALESE   So if you have a picture of a girl, including the genitals, then that is pornographic.

VAN DEN HAAG   Not necessarily.

10   TALESE   But if she's making love it would be?

VAN DEN HAAG   I'm not even opposed to that altogether. But, if the lovemaking picture focuses on the operation of the genitals . . .

TALESE   You mean if it shows the genitals while the love-making is going on?

VAN DEN HAAG   If the genitals are shown incidentally, that does not greatly disturb me. But if it is clearly focused on the operation of the genitals and the persons are only shown incidentally, then I think the stuff is pornographic.

TALESE   There's no agreement on a definition at all, even by the people who want to ban it. Obscenity is the one crime that cannot be defined. Unlike murder, burglary, forgery, the word means different things to different people—to judges, to newspaper editors, to pornographic film-makers.

15   VAN DEN HAAG   That's why we have courts of law and lawyers.

TALESE   And it means different things to different lawyers—it's the most imprecise of crimes.

VAN DEN HAAG   Gay, if you were to see a man walking down the street, fully clothed except that his genitals were exposed, would you regard that as obscene?

TALESE   On the issue of whether the cop on the beat has the right to stop public behavior that is unseemly and offensive we have no quarrel. But no policeman ought to have the right to stop two homosexuals in a Holiday Inn in Teaneck, New Jersey, from doing whatever they want together. They have that right, and I have the right to see a film or a play even if it is considered offensive by Sidney Baumgarten of the Mayor's Midtown Enforcement Project. I don't want policemen to tell me what is moral or immoral in my private life. I think we have too much government and where sex is concerned, I want next to no government.

VAN DEN HAAG   I certainly agree, Gay, that you or I should be allowed to indulge in sexual acts in our homes. That's our business. I am not in the least disturbed about that. But when anyone can see the spectacle we are no longer dealing with a private matter, but with a public matter.

20   TALESE   If I want to pay five dollars to go into a theater to go see "Deep Throat," that's a private matter.

VAN DEN HAAG   Then you regard a public spectacle as a private act.

TALESE   How about buying a book?

VAN DEN HAAG   If it is publicly available to anyone who pays the price, it's a public matter.

TALESE   So, according to you, I have the right to read *Ulysses* or *The Story of O* or *The Sex Life of a Cop* in my home—only I shouldn't be allowed to get it into my home in the first place.

25   VAN DEN HAAG   The police should not come into your home and check what you're reading—but the police can accuse a seller of selling something pornographic. The matter can then be brought up before a jury and if the jury feels that what the seller sold publicly is pornography, then the seller can be convicted.

TALESE   So you'd ban such magazines as *Playboy* or *Oui* or *Screw*?

VAN DEN HAAG   I have testified against *Screw* and I am in favor of banning it. As for *Playboy* and so on, I would leave those to juries, in particular communities. If I'm invited as an expert to testify about the effects they will have on a particular community, I will testify that these effects are deleterious, but it is not for me to decide whether they should be prohibited or not.

GOODMAN   Ernest, why should it be any more the business of a jury what Gay likes to read or watch than it is what he likes to do in bed?

VAN DEN HAAG   Gay's view—one that is widespread—is that society consists of individuals, each independent of each other, and that the task of the government is merely to protect one individual from interference by others. That is not my view. My view is that no society can survive unless there are bonds among its members, unless its members identify with each other, recognize each other as humans and do not think of each other simply as sources of pleasure or unpleasure. For once they do, then they may come to think of people as kinds of insects. If one disturbs you, you kill it. Once you no longer recognize that a person is fully human, like yourself, you can do what the Germans did to the Jews—use the gold in their teeth. Human solidarity is based on our ability to think of each other not purely as means, but as ends in ourselves. Now the point of all pornography, in my opinion, is that it invites us to regard the other person purely as a subject of exploitation for sexual pleasure.

GOODMAN   Gay, am I right in assuming that you don't agree that pornography has such dire consequences?

30   TALESE   Government interference in these areas is usually justified on the grounds that obscenity is harmful to the morals of society, harmful to family life, harmful to juveniles. But in fact there is no proof that exposure to pornography leads to anti-social behavior. There is no proof that watching a pornographic movie leads anybody to go out and commit rape.

VAN DEN HAAG   You're not getting my point. I do not maintain that reading pornography leads to an increase in crime. It may, but I don't think there's conclusive evidence either way. I feel that the main damage pornography does is not to the individual but to the social climate.

TALESE   Tell me how.

VAN DEN HAAG   You and I both write books, and our books are somehow meant to influence what people feel and think. Sexual mores, you certainly will agree, have changed over the past century. Why have they changed? Basically because of the ideas of people who write books, make movies, produce things. The biology of sex hasn't changed. What has changed is our perception of it and our reaction to it. So I don't think it can be denied that books do have an influence. If that is so, we come to the question of whether the government has the right or duty to limit it. Here my point is a very simple one. Every community has a right to protect what it regards as its important shared values. In India, I would vote for the prohibition against the raising of pigs for slaughter. In the United States, where a certain amount of sexual reticence has been a central value of traditional culture, I would vote for the rights of communities to protect their sexual reticence.

TALESE   And I'm saying that the government should not have the right to deal with this "crime" that it cannot define. The Supreme Court has never been able to define what is obscene to the satisfaction of most Americans. If you are going to give government the power to tell us what is obscene and to restrict our freedom to read books, see films or look at pictures, if you give government that kind of power over the individual, you are not going to maintain a democracy.

35 VAN DEN HAAG   I am for freedom, too, but you ignore the fact that freedom can be used for good or bad. For instance, if the Weimar Republic had banned its political pornographers such as Hitler, then perhaps six million Jews would not have been killed. The dogmatic insistence on freedom as the only value to be protected by the government disregards such things as survival and community traditions which are essential to survival.

TALESE   But you seem to forget that Hitler himself opposed pornography. Almost the first thing he did on taking power was to ban *Ideal Marriage*, a classic work on sex and marriage.

GOODMAN   Would you put any limits at all on individual liberties in this area, Gay?

TALESE   I believe there should be censorship—in the home. I have two daughters, and in my home I do exercise censorship. I subscribe to magazines and newspapers that I do not leave on the coffee table. But I do not want government to tell me what I can have in my house or what I can have my daughters read.

VAN DEN HAAG   I congratulate you on having this family that you describe. Let me point out that many American families are not so structured. Not all parents are able to exercise such parental discipline.

40 GOODMAN   But isn't Gay's response to government intrusions into family life in accord with your own principles as a conservative?

VAN DEN HAAG   In an ideal society, things that we now regulate by law, would be regulated by custom and by the authority of parents. We don't live in this ideal society. The authority of parents has been undermined by all kinds of things, starting with progressive education. If we could strengthen the hand of parents and integrate families more, that would be much better. I have found no way of doing so for the time being.

TALESE   So you're willing to give this power to a policeman.

VAN DEN HAAG   I am not proposing that we trust the government with the power of censorship. I'm opposed to censorship, opposed to prior restraint which is unconstitutional. I am in favor of traditional American legislation. Whereby each state, and more recently each community, may determine for itself what it wishes and what it does not wish to be publicly sold. In each case, Ralph Ginzburg or Al Goldstein or you or anyone can publish whatever he wishes. Until the bounds have been exceeded . . .

TALESE   What bounds! It's all so hypocritical. One night these people have been at an American Legion smoker enjoying hard-core porn and the next day they are deciding to put a pornographer in jail. What a member of the jury is likely to say in public has nothing to do with the way he behaves in private. That seems to me socially unhealthy. Many of the people who would go on record to have Times Square closed down because it has too many massage parlors patronize the places. We're dealing here with something very private—sexual desires. Very private.

45 GOODMAN   But is the expression of these desires around an area such as Times Square really all that private? It seems pretty public to me.

TALESE   Sure, Times Square has always been a center of public entertainment. What some people can't stand is that it is today a center of entertainment for the working class instead of for the elite. There are two kinds of pornography. You have the pornography for the working man, like the 42nd Street peep shows, and you have the "legitimate theater," where the elite can see "Let My People Come," "Oh, Calcutta!" or the works of Edward Albee or Arthur Miller or Tennessee Williams. The government does not as readily interfere with the pornography of the elite as it does with the pornography of the man who buys his magazine at the corner newsstand, which is the museum of the man in the street, or the man who pays 25 cents to see copulating couples in a coin-operated machine. Pornography is primarily denied to the blue collar classes. That has always been the case. Strong government tries always to control the masses—just as much in China and Cuba as in Times Square. The people who get their pleasure from going to an art gallery to look at Goya's "The Naked Maja" aren't bothered by government.

GOODMAN   Ernest, under your definition of pornography, is there any difference between a picture of a copulating couple on a museum wall and in the centerfold of a girly magazine?

VAN DEN HAAG   Yes, effect and intent are different, and I think the courts are correct in taking the context into consideration. That is, if Hugh Hefner had put "The Naked Maja" in *Playboy* a few years ago, it might have become pornographic in that context though Goya had not intended it that way.

TALESE   So pornography is all right for the elite, but not for the working man.

50   VAN DEN HAAG   It may appear that way, but the reason, as you yourself
        pointed out, is that the working man gets his pornography in a more
        public way. A theater at which you've made a reservation and paid $10
        is much less public than the 25-cent arcade; therefore, there is more
        justification, if you are against pornography, to intervene against one
        than against the other.
     GOODMAN   You don't deny, Gay, that Times Square has in fact become a
        place of public pornography.
     TALESE   Yes, our sensibilities are assaulted. I wish the 42nd Street
        pornographer would be more subtle. But people have as much right to
        put a quarter in a machine as to pay $5 for "Deep Throat" or $10 for
        "Let My People Come." I do not want to give to law enforcement
        officials the right to clean up Times Square, to deny pornography to
        those who want it. If crimes are being committed, people being
        mugged, that should be prevented. But nobody is forced to go into a
        peep show or a massage parlor or to pay for sex with a prostitute.
     GOODMAN   I take it you're opposed to laws against prostitution.
     TALESE   I would really like to see prostitution legalized, but I know that
        would be the worst thing for prostitution, because it would mean that
        women would have to be fingerprinted.
55   VAN DEN HAAG   You would simply decriminalize it.
     TALESE   I would like to see that happen.
     GOODMAN   And you, Ernest?
     VAN DEN HAAG   For call girls yes; for street prostitution no.
     GOODMAN   Isn't that a trifle elitist, as Gay terms it?
60   VAN DEN HAAG   No. A call girl is an entirely private proposition. You call
        her. In the case of the street prostitute, the initiative must come from
        the soliciting girl, and that makes a difference.
     TALESE   Have you ever been assaulted by a prostitute on the street? All the
        girls do is ask a question.
     VAN DEN HAAG   There's more to it than that. In the United States, for
        some reason, prostitution has always been connected with crime. The
        sort of thing that exists around Times Square attracts not only
        prostitutes and their customers, but people who prey on prostitutes
        and customers and make the whole area unsafe. I believe that crime
        must not only be prosecuted; it must also be prevented.
     TALESE   What offends the white New Yorker, the customer on his way to
        the bus terminal, about Times Square is that he walks through the
        neighborhood and sees the great number of blacks there—the black
        prostitutes and black pimps. That's what makes people fearful. There
        is more crime all over the country today, but it has nothing to do with
        prostitutes working Eighth Avenue. You see, I don't think it's a crime
        to have sex with a person. The prostitutes are there, on the street in
        great numbers, because men—not the children Ernest is legitimately
        concerned about but middle class married white men—want them.
        For some reason, they find prostitutes necessary. That's their private
        affair. I don't want to have Times Square become acceptable to Franco
        Spain. I don't want government to clean it up.

VAN DEN HAAG   You're saying that people should be allowed to have what they want. But should people be forced to have what they don't want! Suppose that a town in Ohio votes that it doesn't want prostitutes on its streets or pornographic movies? You are in favor of pornography in principle, regardless of what the majority wants.

65   TALESE   I am in favor of freedom of expression.

VAN DEN HAAG   The men who wrote Article 1 of the Bill of Rights intended to make sure that the government would not suppress opposition. They did not intend to include such things as pornography.

TALESE   They wrote that Congress shall make no law abridging freedom of speech or the press; they didn't add, "except when it comes to sexual expression."

GOODMAN   Gentlemen, I am not sure how much light we have shed on pornography but your respective positions are clear as day. And I thank you.

TECHNIQUES FOR WRITERS 3-d
Writing a Dialogue

Write an argumentative proposition on a topic that engages your interest. Selecting the topic is important. You need something definitely argumentative, with enough depth to give you plenty of supporting arguments with which to work.

Develop a pro/con grid that adequately presents all of the arguments you can think of on both sides of the issue, considering social, moral/ethical, legal, economic, comparative, historical, and psychological arguments.

Establish the personalities of the two characters you will create for your dialogue—their names, ages, motivations, backgrounds. You might not actually use this information in your essay itself, but doing this will help you to form language for these characters that rings true. Create characters who would be likely to discuss the topic you have chosen.

Establish the setting (characters, time, place) in a short paragraph; then switch to script format. One of your characters should introduce the topic quite early in your paper, and if you have spent enough time developing your pro/con grid, your paper will really take off from this point. Don't make the dialogue one-sided; not all of the good arguments should represent one side of the issue. The character who represents your viewpoint shouldn't be engaged in a battle of wits with an unarmed opponent.

Remember, a good dialogue carefully examines both sides of an argumentative proposition—don't be surprised if your own beliefs are called into question as you write it. If this happens, then you're beginning to truly understand the complex nature of argument.

© United Feature Syndicate, Inc.

Peer Revision: Refining and Developing a Draft

Revision: To many students, this word sounds like punishment for not having written well the first time. But to professional writers, revision is a natural and welcome part of the writing process, along with invention and drafting. For many writers, the revision process can take more time and energy than the original drafting process itself.

Consider these examples. Russian writer Leo Tolstoy is said to have revised *War and Peace,* a novel of more than 1,500 pages, five times. Ernest Hemingway, known for the "simplicity" and "natural style" of his prose, revised the last page of his novel, *A Farewell to Arms,* 39 times. (It's said that Hemingway would sometimes type a single line, read it, and then tear up the whole page.) Perhaps what makes a writer great is not a "gift" or a natural ability at writing, but a willingness to revise.

Writers in the workplace commonly ask colleagues to critique major writing projects such as proposals, important correspondence, and final reports. Many professional writers participate in writers' groups, where they read and critique each other's drafts. And you may have already found that your writing can be improved with the help of classmates during feedback sessions. Engaging in peer revision with a classmate is a good way to find areas in your paper that need revision.

Occasionally, students will object to peer revision because they feel that editing student writing is the job of the teacher, who, after all, brings much more training and experience to the task. But these students haven't considered their role as an audience. Anyone can be an editing audience for a given text, pointing out where writing becomes unclear, where an idea needs more expansion, where a point bogs down. The task of peer editors isn't to judge a draft and possibly hurt the writer's feelings, but to offer suggestions that the writer may or may not follow.

To assist you in the job of peer editing, this book includes peer revision sheets to cover the particular specifications for each of the major writing assignments. The revision sheet for the dialogue assignment follows.

Peer Revision Questions—Dialogue

1. Does the format of the dialogue fit the assignment (introductory paragraph explaining time, place, characters, and situation; two characters; script format)?
2. Are the situation and characters plausible for the topic?
3. Do both characters have complete, valid arguments?
4. What argumentative proposition is the dialectic based on?
5. Has the author covered all possible arguments for his/her topic? Consider the following types of argument:

social	moral/ethical	legal
economic	comparative	historical
psychological	others?	

6. What other arguments should the author incorporate into her/his dialogue?
7. Is the dialogue understandable and easy to follow?
8. Do any editing errors need to be changed? What are they?
9. What other suggestions do you have for improving this draft?

Student Writing: Dialogue

Following are two student samples of dialogues: Sandy Smaltz's paper on Affirmative Action and college admissions and Justin Bauer's dialogue on gambling. As you read the essays, determine whether they do a good job of fairly presenting the major arguments on both sides of their topics. Can you think of any major arguments missing from either of the dialogues?

```
            Affirmative Action: What's Your Point?
                      Sandra Smaltz
      (Scene: Two friends having lunch at a local restaurant. Adam
and India are seated at a corner table for two during the late
```

Reprinted by permission of Sandra Smaltz.

afternoon hours, just before business picks up for the evening. Spring Break is approaching and midterms are just about finished. Adam is 23 and a college senior; India is 21 and a sophomore. They have finished their meal and are lingering over coffee as the conversation begins.)

Adam: I can't wait for Spring Break! My brain is fried with all the cramming for exams. What are your plans this year?

India: I hear you . . . this is the first time I've left campus in a week! I'm heading home for break, just to kind of catch up with my friends and family. What about you?

Adam: I'll be heading out but I'm going to be visiting a couple of schools that I've applied to for graduate school.

India: Speaking of that, what do you think CJ's chances are of getting into law school?

Adam: Are you kidding me? With his academic record and the fact that he's black, he's practically guaranteed a slot.

India: I agree with you that he's got great grades, but what does his being black have to do with anything?

Adam: India, haven't you heard about affirmative action? I mean, come on, the guy's going to get into whichever law school he wants just because he's black. Let's face it, colleges have to have a certain number of minority students and not that many minorities apply to go to law school or other graduate level programs.

India: I admit that sounds unfair, but the fact that he's black isn't the only factor considered when one applies to graduate schools. You have to admit that there has long been a bias against blacks and that affirmative action is one way to address the problem.

Adam: I agree with that but at what point does affirmative action actually become reverse discrimination? Where is the line drawn? I can't imagine how it must feel to know that you are admitted to a program or hired for a job based solely on the color of your skin. What about those people who are turned away because they aren't a minority? How is this fair to them?

India: In theory, it doesn't sound like it is. However, the people who have benefited most from affirmative action policies

are white women and middle-class blacks. The people who need
affirmative action the most are not the ones benefiting from it.

Adam: Be that as it may, why shouldn't we all be judged on
our own individual merit rather than some outward symbol of our
race? If CJ is successful in getting into law school, how does
he know that he was the best candidate for the position he
received? Was there someone more qualified for the position who
was white?

India: What if there was? Let's be real, blacks don't have
that many educational opportunities to begin with and what's
wrong with helping them along so they can help others?
Affirmative action was designed to ensure that blacks had
access to the equal opportunities that had long been denied
them. It's just making sure that they have a fair shot at
success.

Adam: Again, we're getting back to what's fair. The
definition of "fair" depends on who you're talking to and not on
any one specific meaning. Is the only way that we can have
"fairness" for blacks is to discriminate against whites?

India: On one hand, you could be right; on the other hand,
blacks have faced overt discrimination for so long, maybe it's
time to fix the system and do away with it. Those policies were
never intended to discriminate against whites, but some will
undoubtedly pay that price. Face it, Adam, with minorities
increasing in numbers here in the U.S., affirmative action
policies are here to stay, at least for the time being.

Adam: That may be the case, but if those minorities who are
admitted via affirmative action policies are products of a lesser
quality educational background, does that mean we have to lower
our standards so that "fairness" can be achieved? What does that
do to the quality of the classes we take and how our professors
teach? If the bar is lowered, doesn't the quality of the
education also decline?

India: Affirmative action doesn't lower the bar, it simply
adds another rung to a ladder. Everyone gets preference for some
reason or another, whether your parents were alumni of a school,
or your grades were outstanding, or you got an athletic

scholarship. All of those could be perceived as preferential treatment.

Adam: That's different. Those people were outstanding in some area; just being black doesn't make you different.

India: I don't agree. Being black can mean a lot of things like a lack of educational advantages, for instance. Ever since the Jim Crow laws, educational opportunities for blacks have not been the same as those for whites, even though that disparity is not supposed to exist. If true equality existed for all people, affirmative action would not be a necessary policy.

Adam: If that's the case, why are we focusing on affirmative action at the college level? Why aren't we doing something to fix the schools that aren't providing the best education in the first place? Why try to remedy the situation later on with a policy that has such negative effects in spite of its good intentions?

India: That's a good idea, but it will take a long time to actually see the results of the needed changes. In the meantime, affirmative action policies still need to be in place. Those who benefit from affirmative action are just asking for an opportunity. They are willing to do the work once they get their foot in the door, but getting it there in the first place is more difficult without additional resources.

Adam: I can see your point. While I agree there is a disparity in equal education, I just don't think that affirmative action programs are the way to fix it. They have passed their prime for effectiveness.

India: You may be right, but until something better comes along, it will have to do. I just hope that CJ gets into the school of his choice and they really look at him as a whole person, not just one who is black.

Adam: I hear you . . . hey, let's get going and head back. I want to see CJ before he leaves and wish him luck.

India: Good idea, it may also keep you in his good graces for the next time you need a good lawyer!

* * *

Wanna Bet?

Justin Bauer

(Scene: A room in an apartment. The time is around 8:30 p.m. The room is dark except for two table lamps at the end of the couch. Jack Black, the owner of the apartment, and his friend Alicia Nebber walk into the room and sit on the couch. Jack, who is nineteen years old, is a college sophomore, and Alicia is twenty years old and a junior. Jack turns to Alicia and begins a conversation.)

Jack: So, Alicia, what do you want to watch on television?

Alicia: I'm not really sure. We could put in a movie and watch it. Maybe *Cruel Intentions* or *Face-off*?

Jack: Nah . . . I'm not really in the mood for a movie. How about we just turn the tube on and flip through the channels?

Alicia: I guess. How come it always has to be your way, Jack? (laughs) I'm just kidding. (Jack turns on the television.)

Jack: Let's see what we got here. Drew Carey is on. No, I don't feel like watching that. Do you want to watch *Seinfeld*?

Alicia: No, I don't feel like watching that. Keep flipping.

Jack: Let's see what's on ESPN. (Flips to ESPN.) Hey! Cool! It's the *World Series of Poker*! I love watching this. It's amazing to see so much money change hands in a matter of a few minutes.

Alicia: How can you enjoy watching this? It's so repetitive and boring. They make a bet, then get a new card and bet again. Aside from being boring, it's not worth playing. It's way too easy to lose all your money.

Jack: It may be boring to watch it on TV, but it's a lot of fun when you actually play it. Have you ever played poker?

Alicia: Yes, I've played it, and I don't find it any more exciting that way. Frankly, I don't find gambling of any kind worth the time of day.

Reprinted by permission of Justin Bauer.

Jack: I'll bet you ten bucks that the only time you played poker you lost a bunch of money. That seems like the only logical reason for you to think the way you do.

Alicia: Like I said, I don't like to gamble. But if I did, you would be out ten bucks. The last and only time I played I came out even. I'm glad gambling is illegal in most places. In my opinion, it should be illegal everywhere.

Jack: How can you say that? Many people have prospered from gambling. There are actually many people who make their livings playing poker. For example, these guys here on TV have probably made hundreds of thousands, if not millions, of dollars just by playing poker.

Alicia: But there are far many more people who have lost all their money to casinos. Telling them that they could win millions won't do them any good.

Jack: But that's their own fault. If they bring everything they have to the casino and lose it all, they're the stupid ones. You should only put down on the table what you can afford to lose.

Alicia: But what about the people who are gambling addicts? It's just like being an alcoholic. They can't stop themselves from gambling. They just keep thinking, "One more game and I'll win and be right back in the game. Just let me go get some more money first." They have a problem, and all the casinos do is put more wood on the fire for them. Most of the time it is the people who are already poor and hoping to strike it rich who end up losing even more. Their gambling problem wouldn't just affect them either. What if they had a family? They could bring the whole family into trouble. If casinos were outlawed all together, there would be a lot less people who lose everything.

Jack: I don't disagree that there are people out there with gambling problems, but help is available to them. There are lots of clubs and organizations that they can join to help them get over their addiction. Like I said before, it's their own fault and it's up to them to get it fixed. If a person is already poor, then they shouldn't be there in the first place. I agree you're right about their family—it could hurt them as well. But the family should also be there to help the addict.

Alicia: But there are many people who don't have the strength to go to meetings and admit it, so it's hard for them to piece their life back together.

Jack: So you think we should just shut down the casinos altogether?

Alicia: Yes, I do. It would save a lot of people from losing all their money and living on the streets.

Jack: Well, that seems very unethical. Do you agree that there are many people who go to the casino and win money?

Alicia: Well, yeah, I guess.

Jack: Well, why should those people be prevented from winning because there are others that are losing? Why should everyone be punished for the problems of a few? Think of it this way. In the many years since airplanes began flying, there have been a number of accidents where hundreds of people have died. According to your logic, the airplane business should be shut down as well, right?

Alicia: I guess when you put it that way, I see your point. But you have to admit that a casino can be detrimental to the community in which it is located.

Jack: How do you figure that?

Alicia: Casinos bring with them all kinds of problems. With all that money floating around, casinos are bound to attract crooks. Not only can people go in and cheat at the games and steal money from the casino itself, they can also steal money from other people. If there are people in this world who will kill you for your sneakers, there are definitely people who will kill you for all the money you just won from a casino. All a person would have to do is watch someone in the casino win all their money, and then follow them home when they leave. Anyone who wins a lot of money in a casino is bound to attract a lot of attention.

Jack: I'll agree with you on that point, but that can also happen to someone coming out of a bank. It's not a problem just associated with casinos. While we're talking about the effects of a casino on the public, let's look at the good side. A casino is a place of business, and what do all businesses need? Workers! Casinos need a massive workforce to keep them running properly. Even small casinos can have sixty or more people working in them at any given time. With most casinos being open twenty-four hours a day, this would provide a lot of jobs. And we both know that there are a lot of unemployed people out there. If gambling was legalized in all fifty states and there were more casinos, imagine how many jobs it would create.

Alicia: I suppose you're right; it would create a lot of jobs. But that doesn't mean that the people who are unemployed will try to get the jobs. They might just try and win so they don't have to work. Then they might end up losing everything.

Jack: Again, why should everyone be punished for the mistakes of a few? And another thing, casinos would bring a lot of money into the community. The closest casino is about an hour away from here, which means I have to drive there. That gives money to the gas stations around here and helps them out. When I'm down there, I usually like to eat something, which will help out their restaurants. The tourism in a city would be greatly increased by having a casino there. While we're on the topic of making money, what about if they made government-owned casinos? Then all the profits would be used to help the government. That could help a lot to reduce our taxes and get rid of the national debt. If people are going to go to a casino anyway, why don't they go to one that will help them even if they lose?

Alicia: I guess I can't really argue with that, and a government-owned casino actually sounds like a good idea. Maybe you're right. Legalizing gambling might be a good idea, but it's still not for me. We've spent enough time arguing about this . . . what else is on TV?

Jack: Thank you. I knew you would see it my way. But I still think that deep down inside you're a hardcore gambler. I'll bet you dinner and a movie that I can get you gambling within the next hour.

      Alicia: You're on! . . . Wait a minute . . . You tricked me!

CHAPTER 4

Writing Inductive Essays and Mediated Arguments

Generating Ideas Through Stasis Theory

Generating ideas is crucial to developing effective arguments. In Chapter 3 you were introduced to invention, or idea generation, through brainstorming and pro/con lists. But these aren't the only effective invention techniques available to you as a writer. Preparing a well-developed argument requires using multiple invention techniques, because the generation of solid ideas is basic to good rhetoric.

Cicero's Method for Analysis/Prewriting

In the first century BCE, the Roman rhetorician Cicero devised four levels, which he called *stases,* of argument formation. More than two thousand years later his method still works well as a way to think about, plan, and construct an argument and analysis. In considering the topic you've chosen for your argument, try to respond to each of the following questions.

- Conjecture
  - What is the issue you're addressing?
  - Where and how does it exist?
  - Where did it come from?
  - How did it begin?
  - What is its main cause?
  - How can it be changed?
- Definition
  - What kind of issue is it—economic, social, political, moral, other? Explain.
  - To what larger class of similar issues does it belong?

TECHNIQUES FOR WRITERS 4-a
Applying Stasis Theory to an Argument

Write responses to Cicero's stasis theory questions (listed here) for the topic about which you will be writing. Your responses should be as long and thoroughly-developed as you can possibly make them.

- What are its individual parts?
- How are those parts related?

- Quality (*each question followed by the question "Why?"*)
  - Is this a good or bad thing?
  - Should it be encouraged or discouraged?
  - Is it right or wrong?
  - Is it honorable or dishonorable?
  - What is it better than?
  - What is it worse than?
  - Is it more desirable than an alternative?

- Procedure
  - If a change were to come about in connection to this issue, how would that change take place?
  - Who would be affected? How?
  - What would be the result(s) of that change?
  - Who would benefit most?
  - In what way(s) would they benefit?

Freewriting

In freewriting, an idea generation technique developed by Peter Elbow (in *Writing Without Teachers*), you write about your topic for a specified period of time (usually five or ten minutes) without stopping. Freewriting is free in that you do not worry about organization, grammar, or mechanics while writing; your purpose is to simply get down as much as you know about a particular topic in the time specified.

If you run out of things to say, still continue writing, even if you find yourself writing such things as, "I don't know what to say," "I don't know what to say," "This is stupid," or "Why is my teacher asking me to do this?" Read your freewrite only after the allotted time has passed.

A major reason for freewriting is to generate ideas. But beyond that, it can help you to select a topic: if your freewrite contains many comments like "I don't know what to write," you may wish to select another topic.

The following five-minute freewrite was written by Susan on the topic of gay marriage. Matt's five-minute freewrite on hunting follows:

```
                    Susan's Freewrite
     Should gay marriages be allowed? Who should be the judge of
that? My brother-in-law is one person that I know would disagree
with gay marriages. He believes it is wrong and that a sin would
be committed. God did not intend for a woman and woman to become
a couple nor a man and a man. I see his points, but I believe
that if two people love each other unconditionally, no matter if
they're the same sex, that they should be allowed to enter into a
marriage. But then comes the issues with children. How kids look
for the mother/father figure in a family. Well, if there is not a
man or a woman in the household but instead a man/man and
woman/woman, then I believe there might be an issue.
```

```
                    Matt's Freewrite
     People are always dogging hunting, claiming it's inhumane
and cruelty to animals. Would you like it if I shot you in your
own home? In truth, hunting benefits all of us. There is hunting
for a reason. The early settlers hunted for food and survival.
Today we don't quite need to hunt for survival, but it certainly
helps us. No more buying $20 steaks—just turn on the grill and
flame up a nice piece of venison steak. Not only does hunting cut
costs of food, but it helps maintain populations. Looking at just
one species, the whitetail deer population is affected
dramatically when it comes to hunting. Without hunting
overpopulation would set in in no time.
```

Mapping

Mapping (sometimes called clustering) is a form of organized brainstorming. In mapping, you generate ideas on your topic, placing them in a diagram beginning with your major subtopics and working down from there.

Matt developed his ideas about hunting when he produced the following mapped diagram:

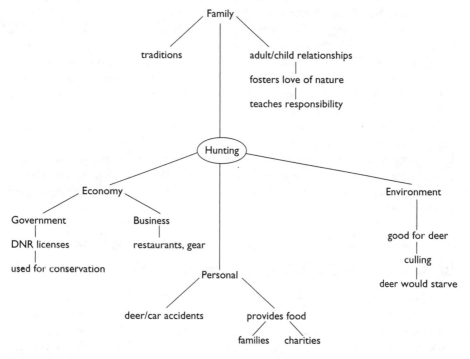

Matt's Map

A Writing Note About Invention

While early rhetoricians may have seen invention as the first stage of developing an argument, contemporary composition theorists believe that idea generation can occur at any stage of writing: before anything is actually written, during the drafting process, or even while the paper is being revised or edited. For example, you may decide while working on the final draft of a research paper that one of your arguments isn't supported sufficiently. To do a good job, you might need to find another source or two to back up the argument you are making, thus taking you back to the idea generating part of the process.

Some students resist suggestions to generate more ideas once they've begun writing their essays. These students may prefer processes that develop in linear patterns. But writing is often very messy—it involves repeating and re-repeating steps in what composition theorists call a *recursive* process. Your willingness to re-see and rework something that you may consider already completed is central to becoming a good writer.

Generating Ideas Through the Canons of Rhetoric

Invention was the first of five central tasks, called the Canons of Rhetoric, that Aristotle considered crucial to developing effective arguments. Two of Aristotle's Canons, *Memoria* (Memory—techniques for committing a speech to memory) and *Pronuntiatio* (Delivery—techniques for using one's voice and body effectively while speaking), were directly related to the presentation of oral arguments and are discussed in Chapter 10 on oral argument. Aristotle's second and third Canons, however, are relevant in developing both written and oral arguments.

- *Dispositio*—Arrangement. Arrangement consists of determining the most effective sequencing of the elements of an argument. A detailed description of Aristotle's and Cicero's principles of arrangement follows.

- *Elocutio*—Style. Style is concerned with determining the words, phrases, and ornamental flourishes that would best present the argument to its intended audience. Some elements of contemporary style are covered in Appendix 2.

Arrangement

Aristotle recognized that the arrangement of the various parts of an argument, its strategic plan, was crucial in leading an audience to accept the statements being made. His five-part arrangement strategy, which was designed to ease an audience into gradual adoption of the speaker's position, is considered effective in written arguments as well.

The *introduction,* or *exordium,* has two goals: to introduce your topic and to begin developing goodwill between you and your readers. You may have noticed that many speeches begin with a joke or an amusing anecdote. It's equally important with an audience of readers to develop a good relationship; thus, the introduction to a written argument must take into account reader involvement.

In the *statement of facts or circumstances,* or *narratio,* you give a detailed description of the issue or the situation you wish to address. This is followed by the *confirmatio,* or *statement of proof,* in which you lay out all the evidence at your disposal, which can include anything from scientific experiments to testimony from experts to logical conclusions.

Inexperienced writers often believe this is enough to convince readers. But any audience is likely to include members who are skeptical of or even opposed to the position being argued; after all, what is the point of presenting arguments to people who already agree with your position? For this reason, Aristotle recognized that *refutatio,* or the *discrediting of opposing views,* was as essential as presenting a good case. To excel at refutation, you must be clearly aware of all the arguments that oppose your position.

Finally, an argument must contain a *conclusion,* or *peroratio.* Often the conclusion contains a summary of the major points that were presented. But it's also a good place to confirm the goodwill already established with the audience, through appeals to the audience's emotions and further establishing of your good character (ethos). Conclusions often also include suggestions about the course of action that should be followed by the audience.

Cicero expanded Aristotle's arrangement model by adding *partitio,* or *division* of the issue into its discrete parts. In *partitio,* the writer takes time to emphasize key aspects of the problem being addressed by the argument, thus giving readers a clearer understanding of the problem itself and helping to persuade them even more convincingly. In contemporary terms, Cicero's pattern of arrangement can be outlined this way:

Exordium (Introduction)
Giving readers an overview of the situation. What has prompted the writer to write this argument?

Narratio
Telling readers the story or stories connected to the situation, and providing them with the important who, what, when, where, why, and how aspects of those stories.

Partitio
Breaking the problem down into separate, distinct parts or aspects. This can help readers to see, for example, how a complex situation is a result of several causes, or to understand how the problem has grown over time, or to recognize how seemingly logical arguments collapse upon closer inspection.

Confirmatio
Stating the specific argument and providing details to support it. Often, this part of the argument is a call to action or a plea for changed attitudes, although it can also be a defense of one's intentions or motives (as the following example by Martin Luther King, Jr., will show).

Refutatio   Identifying the anticipated counterarguments that will arise in response to the points made in the *confirmatio,* and refuting those points systematically through the use of rational and/or emotional appeals.

Peroratio (**Conclusion**)   Signaling to readers that the argument is coming to a close, and making final appeals that also help to reinforce the writer's position character (ethos).

The following argument, presented as a letter, illustrates the way in which the Canon of arrangement developed by Aristotle and Cicero can produce a powerfully convincing argument. In 1963, Dr. Martin Luther King was arrested for leading a civil rights demonstration in Birmingham, Alabama. Eight prominent clergymen had written to King asking him to end the demonstrations. His "Letter from Birmingham Jail," a response to their request, clearly illustrates the way in which formal arrangement can enhance an argument's rhetorical power.

Examining Cicero's Model of Argument Arrangement

Martin Luther King Jr., Letter from Birmingham Jail

1. *Exordium*, **or introduction.**
April 16, 1963
Birmingham, Ala.

MY DEAR FELLOW CLERGYMEN:
    While confined here in the Birmingham City Jail, I came across your recent statement calling our present activities "unwise and untimely." Seldom, if ever, have I sought to answer all the criticisms that cross my desk, my secretaries would be engaged in little else in the course of the day, and I would have no time for constructive work. But since I feel that you are men of genuine goodwill and your criticisms are sincerely set forth, I would like to answer your statement in what I hope will be patient and reasonable terms.
2. *Narratio*, **or detailed description of the issue.**
    I think I should give the reason for my being in Birmingham, since you have been influenced by the argument of "outsiders coming in." I have the honor of serving as president of the Southern Christian Leadership Conference, an organization operating in every Southern state, with headquarters in Atlanta, Georgia. We have some eighty-five affiliate organizations

---

Martin Luther King Jr., "Letter from Birmingham Jail." Reprinted by arrangement with the Estate of Martin Luther King Jr., c/o Writers House as agent for the proprietor New York, NY. Copyright 1963 Martin Luther King Jr., copyright renewed 1991 Coretta Scott King.

all across the South—one being the Alabama Christian Movement for Human Rights. Whenever necessary and possible we share staff, educational and financial resources with our affiliates. Several months ago our local affiliate here in Birmingham invited us to be on call to engage in a nonviolent direct action program if such were deemed necessary. We readily consented and when the hour came we lived up to our promises. So I am here, along with several members of my staff, because I have basic organizational ties here.

Beyond this, I am in Birmingham because injustice is here. Just as the eighth century prophets left their little villages and carried their "thus saith the Lord" far beyond the boundaries of their home towns; and just as the Apostle Paul left his little village of Tarsus and carried the gospel of Jesus Christ to practically every hamlet and city of the Graeco-Roman world, I too am compelled to carry the gospel of freedom beyond my particular home town. Like Paul, I must constantly respond to the Macedonian call for aid.

3. *Partitio*, or division of the issue into its discrete parts.

Moreover, I am cognizant of the interrelatedness of all communities and states. I cannot sit idly by in Atlanta and not be concerned about what happens in Birmingham. Injustice anywhere is a threat to justice everywhere. We are caught in an inescapable network of mutuality, tied in a single garment of destiny. Whatever affects one directly affects all indirectly. Never again can we afford to live with the narrow, provincial "outside agitator" idea. Anyone who lives inside the United States can never be considered an outsider anywhere in this country.

5   You deplore the demonstrations that are presently taking place in Birmingham. But I am sorry that your statement did not express a similar concern for the conditions that brought the demonstrations into being. I am sure that each of you would want to go beyond the superficial social analyst who looks merely at effects, and does not grapple with underlying causes. I would not hesitate to say that it is unfortunate that so-called demonstrations are taking place in Birmingham at this time, but I would say in more emphatic terms that it is even more unfortunate that the white power structure of this city left the Negro community with no other alternative.

In any nonviolent campaign there are four basic steps: 1) Collection of the facts to determine whether injustices are alive. 2) Negotiation. 3) Self-purification and 4) Direct action. We have gone through all of these steps in Birmingham. There can be no gainsaying of the fact that racial injustice engulfs this community.

4. *Confirmatio*, or statement of the author's specific argument. (Here, notice how, as part of a defense of the motives behind the Birmingham protests, Dr. King also employs *narration*. Components of Cicero's arrangement pattern will often overlap in this way.)

Birmingham is probably the most thoroughly segregated city in the United States. Its ugly record of police brutality is known in every section of this country. Its unjust treatment of Negroes in the courts is a notorious reality. There have been more unsolved bombings of Negro homes and churches in Birmingham than any city in this nation. These are the hard, brutal and unbelievable facts. On the basis of these conditions, Negro leaders sought to negotiate with the city fathers. But the political leaders consistently refused to engage in good faith negotiation.

Then came the opportunity last September to talk with some of the leaders of the economic community. In these negotiating sessions certain promises were made by the merchants—such as the promise to remove the humiliating racial signs from the stores. On the basis of these promises Rev. Shuttlesworth and the leaders of the Alabama Christian Movement for Human Rights agreed to call a moratorium on any type of demonstrations. As the weeks and months unfolded we realized that we were the victims of a broken promise. The signs remained. Like so many experiences of the past we were confronted with blasted hopes, and the dark shadow of a deep disappointment settled upon us. So we had no alternative except that of preparing for direct action, whereby we would present our very bodies as a means of laying our case before the conscience of the local and national community. We were not unmindful of the difficulties involved. So we decided to go through a process of self-purification. We started having workshops on nonviolence and repeatedly asked ourselves the questions: "Are you able to accept blows without retaliating?" "Are you able to endure the ordeals of jail?" We decided to set our direct-action program around the Easter season, realizing that with the exception of Christmas, this was the largest shopping period of the year. Knowing that a strong economic withdrawal program would be the by-product of direct action, we felt that this was the best time to bring pressure on the merchants for the needed changes. Then it occurred to us that the March election was ahead and so we speedily decided to postpone action until after election day. When we discovered that Mr. Connor was in the run-off, we decided again to postpone action so that the demonstrations could not be used to cloud the issues. At this time we agreed to begin our nonviolent witness the day after the run-off.

This reveals that we did not move irresponsibly into direct action. We too wanted to see Mr. Connor defeated; so we went through postponement after postponement to aid in this community need. After this we felt that direct action could be delayed no longer.

5. *Refutatio*, or naming and refuting counterarguments. (Here, once again, notice how components of Cicero's arrangement pattern can overlap. This time, it's *partitio*—breaking the argument down into distinct aspects—that comes into play as part of the refutation strategy.)

10   **You may well ask: "Why direct action? Why sit-ins, marches, etc.? Isn't negotiation a better path?"** You are exactly right in your call for negotiation.

Indeed, this is the purpose of direct action. Nonviolent direct action seeks to create such a crisis and establish such creative tension that a community that has constantly refused to negotiate is forced to confront the issue. It seeks so to dramatize the issue that it can no longer be ignored. I just referred to the creation of tension as a part of the work of the nonviolent resister. This may sound rather shocking. But I must confess that I am not afraid of the word tension. I have earnestly worked and preached against violent tension, but there is a type of constructive nonviolent tension that is necessary for growth. Just as Socrates felt that it was necessary to create a tension in the mind so that individuals could rise from the bondage of myths and half-truths to the unfettered realm of creative analysis and objective appraisal, we must see the need of having nonviolent gadflies to create the kind of tension in society that will help men to rise from the dark depths of prejudice and racism to the majestic heights of understanding and brotherhood. So the purpose of the direct action is to create a situation so crisis-packed that it will inevitably open the door to negotiation. We, therefore, concur with you in your call for negotiation. Too long has our beloved Southland been bogged down in the tragic attempt to live in monologue rather than dialogue.

One of the basic points in your statement is that our acts are untimely. Some have asked, "Why didn't you give the new administration time to act?" The only answer that I can give to this inquiry is that the new Birmingham administration must be prodded about as much as the outgoing one before it acts. We will be sadly mistaken if we feel that the election of Mr. Boutwell will bring the millennium to Birmingham. While Mr. Boutwell is much more articulate and gentle than Mr. Connor, they are both segregationists, dedicated to the task of maintaining the status quo. The hope I see in Mr. Boutwell is that he will be reasonable enough to see the futility of massive resistance to desegregation. But he will not see this without pressure from the devotees of civil rights. My friends, I must say to you that we have not made a single gain in civil rights without determined legal and nonviolent pressure. History is the long and tragic story of the fact that privileged groups seldom give up their privileges voluntarily. Individuals may see the moral light and voluntarily give up their unjust posture; but as Reinhold Niebuhr has reminded us, groups are more immoral than individuals.

We know through painful experience that freedom is never voluntarily given by the oppressor; it must be demanded by the oppressed. Frankly, I have never yet engaged in a direct action movement that was "well timed," according to the timetable of those who have not suffered unduly from the disease of segregation. For years now I have heard the word, "Wait!" It rings in the ear of every Negro with a piercing familiarity. This "Wait" has almost always meant "Never." We must come to see with the distinguished jurist of yesterday that "justice too long delayed is justice denied."

We have waited for more than three hundred and forty years for our constitutional and God-given rights. The nations of Asia and Africa are moving with jet-like speed toward the goal of political independence, and we still creep at horse and buggy pace toward the gaining of a cup of coffee at a lunch counter. I guess it is easy for those who have never felt the stinging darts of segregation to say, "Wait." But when you have seen vicious mobs lynch your mothers and fathers at will and drown your sisters and brothers at whim; when you have seen hate filled policemen curse, kick, brutalize and even kill your black brothers and sisters with impunity; when you see the vast majority of your twenty million Negro brothers smothering in an airtight cage of poverty in the midst of an affluent society; when you suddenly find your tongue twisted and your speech stammering as you seek to explain to your six-year-old daughter why she can't go to the public amusement park that has just been advertised on television, and see tears welling up in her eyes when she is told that Funtown is closed to colored children, and see the depressing clouds of inferiority begin to form in her little mental sky, and see her begin to distort her little personality by unconsciously developing a bitterness toward white people; when you have to concoct an answer for a five-year-old son asking in agonizing pathos: "Daddy, why do white people treat colored people so mean?"; when you take a cross-country drive and find it necessary to sleep night after night in the uncomfortable corners of your automobile because no motel will accept you; when you are humiliated day in and day out by nagging signs reading "white" and "colored"; when your first name becomes "nigger," your middle name becomes "boy" (however old you are) and your last name becomes "John," and your wife and mother are never given the respected title "Mrs."; when you are harried by day and haunted by night by the fact that you are a Negro, living constantly at tip-toe stance never quite knowing what to expect next, and plagued with inner fears and outer resentments; when you are forever fighting a degenerating sense of "nobodiness"; then you will understand why we find it difficult to wait. There comes a time when the cup of endurance runs over, and men are no longer willing to be plunged into an abyss of despair. I hope, sirs, you can understand our legitimate and unavoidable impatience.

You express a great deal of anxiety over our willingness to break laws. This is certainly a legitimate concern. Since we so diligently urge people to obey the Supreme Court's decision of 1954 outlawing segregation in the public schools, it is rather strange and paradoxical to find us consciously breaking laws. One may well ask: "How can you advocate breaking some laws and obeying others?" The answer is found in the fact that there are two types of laws: There are just and there are unjust laws. I would agree with Saint Augustine that "An unjust law is no law at all."

15   Now, what is the difference between the two? How does one determine when a law is just or unjust? A just law is a man-made code that squares with

the moral law or the law of God. An unjust law is a code that is out of harmony with the moral law. . . .

An unjust law is a code that a majority inflicts on a minority that is not binding on itself. This is difference made legal. On the other hand a just law is a code that a majority compels a minority to follow that it is willing to follow itself. This is sameness made legal.

Let me give another explanation. An unjust law is a code inflicted upon a minority which that minority had no part in enacting or creating because they did not have the unhampered right to vote. Who can say that the legislature of Alabama which set up the segregation laws was democratically elected? Throughout the state of Alabama all types of conniving methods are used to prevent Negroes from becoming registered voters. . . .

These are just a few examples of unjust and just laws. There are some instances when a law is just on its face and unjust in its application. For instance, I was arrested Friday on a charge of parading without a permit. Now there is nothing wrong with an ordinance which requires a permit for a parade, but when the ordinance is used to preserve segregation and to deny citizens the First-Amendment privilege of peaceful assembly and peaceful protest, then it becomes unjust. . . .

We can never forget that everything Hitler did in Germany was "legal" and everything the Hungarian freedom fighters did in Hungary was "illegal". . . .

20   **In your statement you asserted that our actions, even though peaceful, must be condemned because they precipitate violence.** But can this assertion be logically made? Isn't this like condemning the robbed man because his possession of money precipitated the evil act of robbery? Isn't this like condemning Socrates because his unswerving commitment to truth and his philosophical delvings precipitated the misguided popular mind to make him drink the hemlock?...

6. *Peroratio*, or conclusion.

— *summary*

I hope the church as a whole will meet the challenge of this decisive hour. But even if the church does not come to the aid of justice, I have no despair about the future. I have no fear about the outcome of our struggle in Birmingham, even if our motives are presently misunderstood. We will reach the goal of freedom in Birmingham and all over the nation, because the goal of America is freedom. Abused and scorned though we may be, our destiny is tied up with the destiny of America. Before the pilgrims landed at Plymouth we were here. Before the pen of Jefferson etched across the pages of history the majestic words of the Declaration of Independence, we were here. . . .

— *emotional appeals*

I must close now. But before closing I am impelled to mention one other point in your statement that troubled me profoundly. You warmly commended the Birmingham police force for keeping "order" and "preventing violence." I don't believe you would have so warmly commended the police force if you had seen its angry violent dogs literally biting six unarmed, nonviolent Negroes. I don't believe you would so quickly commend the policemen if you would observe their ugly and inhuman treatment of Negroes here in the city jail; if you would watch them push and curse old Negro women and young Negro girls; if you would see them slap and kick old Negro men and young boys; if you will observe them, as they did on two occasions, refuse to give us food because we wanted to sing our grace together. I'm sorry that I can't join you in your praise for the police department. . . .

I wish you had commended the Negro sit-inners and demonstrators of Birmingham for their sublime courage, their willingness to suffer and their amazing discipline in the midst of the most inhuman provocation. One day the South will recognize its real heroes. They will be the James Merediths, courageously and with a majestic sense of purpose, facing jeering and hostile mobs and with the agonizing loneliness that characterizes the life of the pioneer. They will be old oppressed, battered Negro women, symbolized in a seventy-two year old woman of Montgomery, Alabama, who rose up with a sense of dignity and with her people decided not to ride the segregated buses, and responded to one who inquired about her tiredness with ungrammatical profundity; "my feet is tired, but my soul is rested". . . .

— *establishing character*

Never before have I written a letter this long, (or should I say a book?). I'm afraid it is much too long to take your precious time. I can assure you that it would have been much shorter if I had been writing from a comfortable desk, but what else is there to do when you are alone for days in the dull monotony of a narrow jail cell other than write long letters, think strange thoughts, and pray long prayers?

25   If I have said anything in this letter that is an overstatement of the truth and is indicative of an unreasonable impatience, I beg you to forgive me. If I have said anything in this letter that is an understatement of the truth and is indicative of my having a patience that makes me patient with anything less than brotherhood, I beg God to forgive me.

I hope this letter finds you strong in the faith. I also hope that circumstances will soon make it possible for me to meet each of you, not as an integrationist or a civil rights leader, but as a fellow clergyman and a Christian brother. Let us all hope that the dark clouds of racial prejudice will soon pass away and the deep fog of misunderstanding will be lifted from our fear-drenched communities and in some not too distant tomorrow the radiant stars of love and brotherhood will shine over our great nation with all their scintillating beauty.

Yours for the cause of Peace and Brotherhood, Martin Luther King, Jr.

Writing the Inductive Essay

In an inductive essay, you take a position either supporting or opposing an argumentative proposition. The purpose of the inductive essay is to persuade your reader. Although your actual audience for this essay will be your teacher and perhaps some of your classmates, as you write, imagine a more general audience: a group of educated, reasonable people who may not agree with you but are open to persuasion on your position.

Inductive arguments are based primarily on *logical appeals:* that is, evidence such as facts, statistics, testimony from experts, comparisons to other situations, and examples. In a formal research paper, you would need to cite carefully any material you had taken from outside sources. For this paper, however, you will need to use only the ideas and arguments you have already developed (i.e., in your pro/con grid, dialogue, stasis theory exercise, and/or freewriting/mapping exercises) without depending on specific information from outside sources. That will come later.

Most inductive arguments also depend on *emotional appeals* to some extent. Emotional appeals include your presentation of yourself as a reliable, reasonable person (ethos) as well as your use of language, particularly in your introduction and conclusion, that is intended to provoke an emotional response that will move your audience toward your position (more on language in Appendix 2). Another example of an emotional appeal would be a short narrative that illustrates the point you wish to make.

In planning your essay, follow the seven-step Ciceronian arrangement method, paying particular attention to the requirements of each step. In presenting the arguments that will appear in your statement of proof, ask yourself whether they can be arranged in some logical sequence. One common arrangement for arguments follows their relative importance: the strongest arguments are reserved for the beginning and the end of the essay.

TECHNIQUES FOR WRITERS 4-c

The Inductive Essay

Write a three–to–five page essay in which you support an argument. Use the material from your invention techniques and/or dialogue as prewriting for your inductive essay.

Carefully select three to five of your major arguments, making sure to select points that you can support with fully developed paragraphs, and use those in your inductive essay.

(continued on next page)

The Inductive Essay *(continued)*

Arrange your essay following Cicero's model. Be sure it includes the following:

- introduction
- detailed description of the issue
- division of the issue into its discrete parts (if applicable)
- statement of the author's specific arguments
- naming and refuting of counter-arguments
- conclusion

In your detailed description of the issue, you need to define any key terms included in your argumentative proposition. For example, if you're writing in favor of gun control, you need to define what, precisely, you mean by gun control: owner registration, limitations on types of weapons allowed, prohibition of handguns? All can be considered "gun control." What, specifically, are you advocating in your essay?

Remember your refutation. An inductive essay without refutation is incomplete.

Keep in mind that the purpose of an inductive essay is to persuade. You'll be more likely to sway your audience if you present yourself as a reasonable person who is very knowledgeable on your topic.

Peer Revision Questions—Inductive Essay

Title of Paper:

1. Does the introduction both interest the reader and give some idea of the direction the author will take in the paper?
2. Does the author describe the issue sufficiently? If necessary, has the author divided the issue into discrete parts?
3. What are the author's major arguments?
4. Comment on the author's arrangement. Do any of the elements of arrangement need expansion in this essay?
5. What counterarguments does the author refute? Is the refutation effective?
6. Is anything unclear in the paper? What, if anything, needs to be clarified?
7. What grammatical/mechanical errors does the author need to clear up?

Student Writing: Inductive Essay

Following are two student inductive essays: Sandra Smaltz's on affirmative action and T. J. Kinkle's on uniforms in public schools. As you read them, look for both supporting arguments and refutation of opposing arguments.

Affirmative Action: The Great Leveler in College Admissions
Sandra Smaltz

Picture this: a law school is looking at two applications. One is from a white male with an outstanding academic record; the other is from a black male who also has an outstanding academic record. Which student will get into law school? On the surface, one would say both students are deserving; however, in this case, the black student, by virtue of being black, is the one admitted. Is this unfair or fairness too long denied? This question is central to the debate over affirmative action policies in education, particularly in higher education settings.

Discrimination started with the practice of enslaving blacks and forcibly bringing them to the United States. Black men, women, and children were regarded as property, not human beings. Their very right to exist was held in the hands of their masters who could dispose of them with impunity. When slavery ended blacks, while technically free, could not escape the bounds of discriminatory practices so deeply rooted in the white psyche. Jim Crow laws were passed, which maintained white superiority while subjugating the black minority. The Civil Rights Movement was a direct challenge by blacks to those laws and an attempt to obtain the rights that had been legally theirs for many years. Although these laws have since been constitutionally challenged and repealed, the concept of true racial equality still eluded the American public. Over the years, some attempts have been made to atone for and remedy the many injustices perpetrated upon the black race. One of the many policies to develop out of an attempt to rectify this situation is affirmative action.

Affirmative action is a policy with many definitions and nuances of meaning and practice. In a higher educational setting, affirmative action commonly refers to the practice of weighted admissions for black students. But knowing what affirmative action is and how it works are two different things. The American public tends to question: What are the preferences afforded to black students? What are the reasons for such a practice; why is it necessary? And, is affirmative action policy effective in its intent?

Reprinted by permission of Sandra Smaltz.

Affirmative action, as practiced in college and university admissions, takes the form of preferential admissions. Preference is given to minorities as one of the factors weighed when applications are evaluated. The preference can take the form of extra points, additional merit, or other such preferential considerations. By law, schools cannot have formal admission quotas for minorities. Many schools, however, are trying to increase the diverse nature of their student bodies in order to facilitate a richer learning experience for all students, regardless of race. Black students are not the only recipients of preferences in higher education. Preferences are also given to children of alumni, outstanding athletes, and others; being black simply adds another preference to the long list already in place.

The reasoning for black preferences is apparent when one examines the disparity in educational quality afforded black students versus white students. Although the idea of "separate but equal" has long gone by the wayside, schools are seeing a resurgence in segregation simply because of exurban development. White families are moving out of the city towards the suburbs and beyond (exurbia). The schools set up in these outlying areas are predominantly white, leaving the inner city schools to become predominantly black. Black families, usually of a lower socioeconomic status, tend to not have the means to make the same move and are thus subject to their circumstances. What is the difference in educational opportunities? Schools in the inner city often have a harder time attracting quality educators; many teachers simply do not want to assume the additional personal risk associated with working in an inner city environment.

Oftentimes, the school has to settle for who it can get as opposed to who is best for the job. Another factor that comes into play is economics. With exurban development, the tax base for desperately needed funds is gradually eroding, leaving schools with less funding to adequately confront the educational needs of inner city students. With many black students facing such an educational deficit, the need for affirmative action policies becomes clear. Black students often have the same drive to be successful as white students; what they need is a leg up in the educational system to get them into college to prove it.

Whether or not the current system is effective is another aspect of the affirmative action debate. While it is true that the majority of people helped by affirmative action policies are white women and middle-class blacks, the system affords some measure of benefit for those of a lower socioeconomic standing. The number of black students attending college has increased dramatically since affirmative action policies were put into effect. This increase is reflective of the success of such policies as well as the necessity for their continuation.

Opponents of affirmative action do not agree with the idea of weighted admission policies, or any other affirmative action measure. They maintain that affirmative action policies create an environment likely to foster reverse discrimination. Although the policies were never intended to discriminate against whites, some will undoubtedly pay that price. Conversely, the policy's effectiveness in raising the number of black students far outweighs the perception of discrimination by whites. Additionally, white students tend to apply to far more colleges and universities than do black students and are, therefore, more likely to be accepted by more than one school.

Another argument offered by opponents of affirmative action is the question of the validity of personal merit. Opponents would prefer that each student, regardless of race, be evaluated on the basis of individual merit. This situation mirrors the one presented at the beginning of this essay. Which student would you choose to admit if there were only one slot available and each candidate is identical in every way, except race? This dilemma is one that affirmative action seeks to address. To a great degree, students, whether black or white, are evaluated on merit. Preferences come into play when other factors have already been considered. Affirmative action does not mean that a college or university is mandated to accept a failing student just because he or she is black.

With the minority population in the U.S. continually on the rise, affirmative action policies are here to stay, at least for the time being. The policies' effectiveness, demonstrated in the creation of a diverse learning community at the post-secondary educational level, stands as testimony to their necessity and success. Proponents and opponents alike would like the necessity for affirmative action policies to evaporate, albeit for different reasons. However, until such time as we have achieved the true equality called for in the Constitution, affirmative action policies are necessary to ensure some measure of equal opportunity exists for black students.

* * *

The Great Debate Over School Uniforms
T. J. Kinkle

School uniforms are not an uncommon sight around the world. Many countries like China, Japan, the United Kingdom and many more require students to wear uniforms. Even in the United States private schools require their students to wear uniforms. But does that mean that public school students should also be required to wear them? This has been a debatable topic among parents, school staff, and boards of education across the nation for years. Should the students' rights be overlooked by forcing them to dress alike? I for one do not think that uniforms will solve the problems school administrators are looking to solve.

Some people believe that school uniforms will decrease the expenses for parents but in fact it is the opposite. This clearly is not a practical argument to support school uniforms. It is no longer like the 1940s when students had their nice school clothes, then changed into their normal clothes. Most students wear the same clothes in and out of school. So if a student is required to wear a uniform to school parents have to spend twice the amount of money. This is not a perfect world; there are less fortunate people who have little money. If these people can barely feed and clothe their kids how are they to be expected to provide even more clothes? One might say that the government could provide a program in which taxes could help pay for school clothes. But because the U.S. has such a huge deficit and taxes are already disliked, that idea would

Reprinted by permission of Travis Kinkle.

never pass. Simply said school uniforms are not financially efficient and can cause some serious problems.

Another argument against school uniforms is that students might rebel. People say that school uniforms would help decrease disciplinary actions. I know that the kids in my high school would not stand for such a thing and would rebel. Many different "groups" of students absolutely hate the types of clothes that the uniforms consist of. I for one was one of these kids. Khakis and polo shirts were not a big part of the so-called Goth wardrobe. These students would rebel along with other groups of students. In reality it would only cause more of a disruption and a higher rate of disciplinary actions.

One of the strongest arguments and one of the most debated is whether or not it infringes on the students' rights. The First Amendment guarantees the protection of the freedom of speech, press, and protest. Dress codes go against freedom of speech because clothing is how most kids speak their minds. In *Tinker v. Des Moines Independent Community School District* in 1969, the Supreme Court ruled that the school could not ban black arm bands. Why should it stop at arm bands? What is the difference between black armbands that protested Vietnam and normal person's clothes that can symbolize many important things? If the government tried to place a uniform standard on the country itself no one would stand for that. There is no difference in that and making students wear school uniforms.

There are many other arguments on both sides that have valid points and some that are not valid. But when it comes down to it, what do the students want? This is the time when they have no worries, the time that they will look back on for the rest of their lives. Let them express themselves and let them learn from life. Let them enjoy being free while they can. Students for decades have been told that this is a free country. Well then make it a free country and let them wear the clothes that help them express themselves and help promote creativity. They only get one childhood and one trip through being a teenager. Let them enjoy it as much as they can while they can.

Mediating an Argument: Finding Resolution

The next three passages illustrate students' developing understanding of argument through the first half of a semester:

■ In the beginning of the semester, I thought that an argument was just a disagreement between two people and that was it. While it can be that, there's much more to an argument. My definition of argument has changed greatly through the semester, and now I have a new and improved one. Ready?

An argument is a difference in opinion between two or more people or groups.

To argue effectively, neither side will flat-out tell the others that they're wrong, or make them feel inferior. Instead, you try to support your opinions and viewpoints with a positive and appealing ethos, a powerful and confident voice, compelling facts, reasoned counterarguments, and plenty of appeals to common ground and anticipation of objections. You will acknowledge when you agree with the opposition, but persuade them to see that your points are better. In the end, depending on how effectively you have argued and proven your case, you may get the other person to say, "Wow, I never thought about that."

And guess what? You just won your argument.

■ Argument is a difference of opinion, belief, or emotions between people or groups where Side A of the argument tries to persuade Side B to feel or believe the same way A does. They do this not by berating or belittling or accusing the other side of being wrong, but by a very organized and deliberate kind of persuasion where you set out ideas or appeals that really affect the other side and allow them to feel that they are forming their own opinions on the subject. Throughout this process, the other side doesn't realize that they are changing their minds until the end and then it's like *hey, this person really does know what they are talking about so I think I should really reconsider my stand on the issue.* When arguing, you need to make your audience feel like they still hold the power, and that they are forming the opinions and making the decisions of their own free will.

(This student's definition of argument at the beginning of the semester: "An argument is just a difference of opinion where you take one side and explain it.")

■ Argument is a stance or position that one holds, based on facts and strong opinions that appeal to readers and listeners because of the strength of the claims being made and supported. You can argue opinions more logically than you can argue beliefs, but all arguments need to be well organized by planning and constructing them carefully. Development of the argument is crucial, and looking at what rhetoricians like Cicero offered for doing this will help you to think about the issue and break it down into specific areas before presenting your stance to an audience. Using examples, details, explanations, and "showing rather than telling" will help the argument to be much more effective than just saying, "look, this is what I think." You also need to judge your audience and decide what kinds of emotional and rational appeals are going to reach them. When you know your audience, you can anticipate their objections and establish common ground with them to show that you understand their position, too—and if all of your claims are supported logically and convincingly, then what else is there for them to counterargue? If all else fails, then at least they have thought about the issue in a new light and a different perspective, even though you may not have convinced them to change their minds or to take the action you've suggested.

The students who wrote these definitions display a great deal of development in their understanding of the complexity and difficulty involved in writing effective arguments. They recognize the importance of such argumentative elements as understanding audience, providing sufficient support, and offering refutation. They understand that an audience is persuaded both by logic and emotion. And they realize that an effective argument doesn't belittle or insult an audience.

But what if we could take argument one step further? We've already discussed the differences in Plato's and Aristotle's views on the purpose of argument; Aristotle wished to persuade, while Plato's dialogues were presented as a search for the truth. Is it possible to envision an argumentative system that incorporates both of those goals?

The argument patterns we've already studied depend on concepts that were developed more than 2500 years ago. But society has developed in many ways since then. Technological advances have brought to the forefront arguments that never could have existed before (i.e., cloning, environmental issues). Various forms of government have been developed, and sometimes abandoned. Our society is much more diverse than the society of ancient Greece, and we've learned over time to recognize, tolerate, and finally celebrate the many ways in which people differ.

Recognizing these major changes in contemporary life, philosopher Kenneth Burke (1897–1993) proposed a "New Rhetoric," one based on cooperation rather than persuasion. In Burke's rhetoric, cooperation is achieved through **identification** with those holding opposing views: ideally, mutual understanding comes about when both parties understand and relate to the opposing position.

Defining Rhetoric

Identification: rhetorical process in which the audience is persuaded so completely that its ideas exist as one with the writer's.

Psychologist Carl Rogers recognized this in his work on interpersonal relationships. He urged his patients to develop nonthreatening forms of argument by attempting to understand opposing points of view and by searching for common ground to resolve conflicts.

You've already encountered the concept of common ground in Aristotle (in Chapter 3), who recognized the necessity of finding areas of agreement in order to develop effective arguments. But the "New Rhetoric" views common ground as much more than that: it's the starting point for developing a resolution that truly takes into account the values and concerns of both sides. It's the basis for finding ways to negotiate and compromise, to come to some kind of mediated agreement, instead of to win arguments.

No one likes to lose, and often solutions that don't take into account the values and feelings of all parties involved lead to misunderstanding and conflict. The "New Rhetoric" suggests a different perspective in dealing with argumentative propositions—one that encompasses both Aristotle's desire for persuasion and Plato's search for truth. If an argumentative proposition is defined as "a statement with which reasonable people can and do disagree," then there must be good, valid arguments on both sides of the proposition. A truly effective **mediated argument** promotes new understanding of argumentative topics not only for the audience, but for *the writer* as well.

Defining Rhetoric

Mediated argument: an argument that not only presents both sides of an issue, but that also establishes common ground between the opposing sides and offers a resolution that considers the goals and values of both positions.

Analyzing a Mediated Argument

A mediated argument includes the following elements:

- an introductory section that explains and defines the issue being discussed

- complete and impartial analysis of the major arguments comprising *both positions* on the issue

- a statement that establishes the values and interests both sides share—their common ground. In finding common ground, it's necessary to assess goals and values from a perspective broader than the argumentative issue itself. For example, both those who support and those who oppose Affirmative Action value higher education and equal opportunity, although they disagree on how to achieve these goals, and both hope that the benefits of a college-educated populace will lead to prosperity and to a better quality of life. A mediated argument builds on such areas of agreement.

■ a proposal that recognizes the interests of both parties. Devising and presenting such a proposal is central to the mediated argument. While the proposal may not (and probably will not) completely satisfy those who hold opposing positions on the issue, it's important that both sides feel that their values and interests have been recognized and accommodated.

Roger Rosenblatt's article titled "How to End the Abortion War" is an argument that presents a mediated position on one of the most vehemently contested topics of our time—abortion. An analysis of Rosenblatt's article as a mediated argument follows.

How to End the Abortion War
Roger Rosenblatt

The veins in his forehead bulged so prominently they might have been blue worms that had worked their way under the surface of his skin. His eyes bulged, too, capillaries zigzagging from the pupils in all directions. His face was pulled tight about the jaw, which thrust forward like a snowplow attachment on the grille of a truck. From the flattened O of his mouth, the word "murderer" erupted in a regular rhythm, the repetition of the r's giving the word the sound of an outboard motor that failed to catch.

She, for her part, paced up and down directly in front of him, saying nothing. Instead, she held high a large cardboard sign on a stick, showing the cartoonish drawing of a bloody coat hanger over the caption, "Never again." Like his, her face was taut with fury, her lips pressed together so tightly they folded under and vanished. Whenever she drew close to him, she would deliberately lower the sign and turn it toward him, so that he would be yelling his "murderer" at the picture of the coat hanger.

For nearly twenty years these two have been at each other with all the hatred they can unearth. Sometimes the man is a woman, sometimes the woman a man. They are black, white, Hispanic, Asian; they make their homes in Missouri or New Jersey; they are teenagers and pharmacists and college professors; Catholic, Baptist, Jew. They have exploded at each other on the steps of the Capitol in Washington, in front of abortion clinics, hospitals, and politicians' homes, on village greens and the avenues of cities. Their rage is tireless; at every decision of the United States Supreme Court or of the President or of the state legislatures, it rises like a missile seeking only the heat of its counterpart.

This is where America is these days on the matter of abortion, or where it seems to be. In fact, it is very hard to tell how the country really feels about abortion, because those feelings are almost always displayed in political arenas. Most ordinary people do not speak of abortion. Friends who gladly debate other volatile issues—political philosophy, war, race—shy away from the subject. It is too private, too personal, too bound up with one's faith or spiritual identity. Give abortion five seconds of thought, and it quickly spirals down in the mind to the most basic questions about human life, to the mysteries of birth and our relationship with our souls.

5   We simply will not talk about it. We will march in demonstrations, shout and carry placards, but we will not talk about it. In the Presidential election of 1992, we will cast votes for a national leader based in part on his or her position on abortion. Still, we will not talk about it.

The oddity in this unnatural silence is that most of us actually know what we feel about abortion. But because those feelings are mixed and complicated, we have decided that they are intractable. I believe the opposite is true: that we are more prepared than we realize to reach a common, reasonable understanding on this subject, and if we were to vent our mixed feelings and begin to make use of them, a resolution would be at hand.

Seventy-three percent of Americans polled in 1990 were in favor of abortion rights. Seventy-seven percent polled also regard abortion as a kind of killing. (Forty-nine percent see abortion as outright murder, 28 percent solely as the taking of human life.) These figures represent the findings of the Harris and Gallup polls, respectively, and contain certain nuances of opinion within both attitudes. But the general conclusions are widely considered valid. In other words, most Americans are both for the choice of abortion as a principle and against abortion for themselves. One has to know nothing else to realize how conflicted a problem we have before and within us.

The fact that abortion entails conflict, however, does not mean that the country is bound to be locked in combat forever. In other contexts, living with conflict is not only normal to America, it is often the only way to function honestly. We are for both Federal assistance and states' autonomy; we are for both the First Amendment and normal standards of propriety; we are for both the rights of privacy and the needs of public health. Our most productive thinking usually contains an inner confession of mixed feelings. Our least productive thinking, a nebulous irritation resulting from a refusal to come to terms with disturbing and patently irreconcilable ideas.

Yet acknowledging and living with ambivalence is, in a way, what America was invented to do. To create a society in which abortion is permitted and its gravity appreciated is to create but another of the many useful frictions of a democratic society. Such a society does not devalue life by allowing abortion; it takes life with utmost seriousness and is, by the depth of its conflicts and by the richness of its difficulties, a reflection of life itself.

10   Why, then, are we stuck in political warfare on this issue? Why can we not make use of our ambivalence and move on?

The answer has to do with America's peculiar place in the history of abortion, and also with the country's special defining characteristics, both ancient and modern, with which abortion has collided. In the 4,000-year-old history extending from the Greeks and Romans through the Middle Ages and into the present, every civilization has taken abortion with utmost seriousness. Yet ours seems to be the only civilization to have engaged in an emotional and intellectual civil war over the issue.

There are several reasons for this. The more obvious include the general lack of consensus in the country since the mid-60's, which has promoted bitter divisions over many social issues—race, crime, war, and abortion, too. The sexual revolution of the 60's resulted in the heightened activity of people who declared themselves "pro-choice" *and* "pro-life"—misleading terms used here principally for convenience. The pro-life movement began in 1967, six years before *Roe v. Wade*. The women's movement, also revitalized during the 60's, gave an impetus for self-assertion to women on both sides of the abortion issue.

But there are less obvious reasons, central to America's special character, which have helped to make abortion an explosive issue in this country.

Religiosity. America is, and always has been, a religious country, even though it spreads its religiosity among many different religions. Perry Miller, the great historian of American religious thought, established that the New England colonists arrived with a ready-made religious mission, which they cultivated and sustained through all its manifestations, from charity to intolerance. The Virginia settlement, too, was energized by God's glory. Nothing changed in this attitude by the time the nation was invented. If anything, the creation of the United States of America made the desire to receive redemption in the New World more intense.

15   Yet individuals sought something in American religion that was different, more emotional than the religion practiced in England. One member of an early congregation explained that the reason he made the long journey to America was "I thought I should find feelings." This personalized sense of religion, which has endured to the present, has an odd but telling relationship with the national attitude toward religion. Officially, America is an a-religious country; the separation of church and state is so rooted in the democracy it has become a cliché. Yet that same separation has created and intensified a hidden national feeling about faith and God, a sort of secret, undercurrent religion, which, perhaps because of its subterranean nature, is often more deeply felt and volatile than that of countries with official or state religions. . . .

Individualism. Two basic and antithetical views of individualism have grown up with the country. Emerson, the evangelist of self-reliance and nonconformity, had a quasi-mystical sense of the value of the individual self. He described man as a self-sufficient microcosm: "The lightning which explodes and fashions planets, maker of planets and suns, is in him." Tocqueville had a more prosaic and practical view. He worried about the tendency of Americans to withdraw into themselves at the expense of the public good, confusing self-assertion with self-absorption.

Abortion hits both of these views of the individual head on, of course; but both views are open to antipodal interpretations. The Emersonian celebration of the individual may be shared by the pro-choice advocate who sees in individualism one's right to privacy. It may be seen equally by a pro-life advocate as a justification for taking an individual stance—an antiliberal stance to boot—on a matter of conscience. . . .

To those who believe in abortion rights, the "public good" consists of a society in which people, collectively, have the right to privacy and individual choice. Their vision of an unselfish, unself-centered America is one in which the collective sustains its strength by encouraging the independence of those who comprise it. Logically, both camps rail against the individual imposing his or her individual views on society at large, each feeling the same, if opposite, passion about both what society and the individual ought to be. Passion on this subject has led to rage.

Optimism. The American characteristic of optimism, like that of individualism, is affected by abortion in contradictory ways. People favoring the pro-life position see optimism exactly as they read individual rights: Every American, born or unborn, is entitled to look forward to a state of infinite hope and progress. The process of birth is itself an optimistic activity.

20   Taking the opposite view, those favoring abortion rights interpret the ideas of hope and progress as a consequence of one's entitlement to free choice in all things, abortion definitely included. If the individual woman wishes to pursue her manifest destiny unencumbered by children she does not want, that is not only her business but her glory. The issue is national as well as personal. The pro-choice reasoning goes: The country may only reach its ideal goals if women, along with men, are allowed to achieve their highest potential as citizens, unburdened by limitations that are not of their own choosing.

Even the element of American "can-do" ingenuity applies. The invention of abortion, like other instruments of American optimism, supports both the pro-life and pro-choice stands. Hail the procedure for allowing women to realize full control over their invented selves. Or damn the procedure for destroying forever the possibility of a new life inventing itself. As with all else pertaining to this issue, one's moral position depends on the direction in which one is looking. Yet both directions are heaving with optimism, and both see life in America as the best of choices.

Sexuality. The connection of abortion with American attitudes toward sexuality is both economic and social. The American way with sex is directly related to the country's original desire to become a society of the middle class, and thus to cast off the extremes of luxury and poverty that characterized Europe and the Old World. The structure of English society, in particular, was something the new nation sought to avoid. Not for Puritan America was the rigid English class system, which not only fixed people into economically immobile slots but allowed and encouraged free-wheeling sexual behavior at both the highest and lowest strata.

At the top of the English classes was a self-indulgent minority rich enough to ignore middle-class moral codes and idle enough to spend their time seducing servants. At the opposite end of the system, the poor also felt free to do whatever they wished with their bodies, since the world offered them so little. The masses of urban poor, created by the Industrial Revolution, had little or no hope of bettering their lot. Many of them wallowed in a kind of sexual Pandemonium, producing babies wantonly and routinely engaging in rape and incest. Between the two class extremes stood the staunch English middle class, with its hands on its hips, outraged at the behavior both above and below them, but powerless to insist on, much less enforce, bourgeois values.

This was not to be the case in America, where bourgeois values were to become the standards and the moral engine of the country. Puritanism, a mere aberrant religion to the English, who were able to get rid of it in 1660 after a brief eighteen years, was the force that dominated American social life for a century and a half. Since there has been a natural progression from Puritanism to Victorianism and from Victorianism to modern forms of fundamentalism in terms of social values, it may be said that the Puritans have really never loosened their headlock on American thinking. The Puritans offered a perfect context for America's desire to create a ruling middle class, which was to be known equally for infinite mobility (geographic, social, economic) and the severest forms of repression.

25   Abortion fits into such thinking more by what the issue implies than by what it is. In the 1800's and the early 1900's, Americans were able to live with abortion, even during periods of intense national prudery, as long as the practice was considered the exception that proved the rule. The rule was that abortion was legally and morally discouraged. Indeed, most every modern civilization has adopted that attitude, which, put simply, is an attitude of looking the other way in a difficult human situation, which often cannot and should not be avoided. For all its adamant middle-classedness, it was not uncomfortable for Americans to look the other way, either—at least until recently.

When abortion was no longer allowed to be a private, albeit dangerous, business, however, especially during the sexual revolution of the 60's, America's basic middle-classedness asserted itself loudly. Who was having all these abortions? The upper classes, who were behaving irresponsibly, and the lower orders, who had nothing to lose. Abortion, in other words, was a sign of careless sexuality and was thus an offense to the bourgeois dream.

The complaint was, and is, that abortion contradicts middle-class values, which dictate the rules of sexual conduct. Abortion, it is assumed, is the practice of the socially irresponsible, those who defy the solid norms that keep America intact. When *Roe v. Wade* was ruled upon, it sent the harshest message to the American middle class, including those who did not oppose abortion themselves but did oppose the disruption of conformity and stability. If they—certainly the middle-class majority—did not object to *Roe v. Wade* specifically, they did very much object to the atmosphere of lawlessness or unruliness that they felt the law encouraged. Thus the outcry; thus the warfare. . . .

If we could find the way to retrieve this kind of conflicted thinking, and find a way to apply it to the country's needs, we might be on our way toward a common understanding on abortion, and perhaps toward a common good. Abortion requires us to think one way and another way simultaneously. Americans these days could make very good use of this bifurcated way of thinking.

This brings me back to the concern I voiced at the beginning: Americans are not speaking their true minds about abortion because their minds are in conflict. Yet living with conflict is normal in America, and our reluctance to do so openly in this matter, while understandable in an atmosphere of easy polarities, may help create a false image of our country in which we do not recognize ourselves. An America that declares abortion legal and says nothing more about it would be just as distorted as one that prohibited the practice. The ideal situation, in my view, would consist of a combination of laws, attitudes, and actions that would go toward satisfying both the rights of citizens and the doubts held by most of them. . . .

30   What most Americans want to do with abortion is to permit but discourage it. Even those with the most pronounced political stands on the subject reveal this duality in the things they say; while making strong defenses of their positions, they nonetheless, if given time to work out their thoughts, allow for opposing views. I discovered this in a great many interviews over the past three years.

Pro-choice advocates are often surprised to hear themselves speak of the immorality of taking a life. Pro-life people are surprised to hear themselves defend individual rights, especially women's rights. And both sides might be surprised to learn how similar are their visions of a society that makes abortion less necessary through sex education, help for unwanted babies, programs to shore up disintegrating families and moral values, and other forms of constructive community action. Such visions may appear Panglossian, but they have been realized before, and the effort is itself salutary. . . .

Already 73 percent of America finds abortion acceptable. Even more may find it so if they can tolerate living in a country in which they may exercise the individual right not to have an abortion themselves or to argue against others having one, yet still go along with the majority who want the practice continued. The key element for all is to create social conditions in which abortion will be increasingly unnecessary. It is right that we have the choice, but it would be better if we did not have to make it.

Were this balance of thought and attitude to be expressed publicly, it might serve some of the country's wider purposes as well, especially these days when there is so much anguish over how we have lost our national identity and character. The character we lost, it seems to me, was one that exalted the individual for what the individual did for the community. It honored and embodied both privacy and selflessness. A balanced attitude on abortion would also do both. It would make a splendid irony if this most painful and troublesome issue could be converted into a building block for a renewed national pride based on good will. . . .

Taking a stand against abortion while allowing for its existence can turn out to be a progressive philosophy. It both speaks for moral seriousness and moves in the direction of ameliorating conditions of ignorance, poverty, the social self-destruction of fragmented families, and the loss of spiritual values in general. What started as a debate as to when life begins might lead to making life better.

35   The effort to reduce the necessity of abortion, then, is to choose life as wholeheartedly as it is to be "pro-life." By such an effort, one is choosing life for millions who do not want to be, who do not deserve to be, forever hobbled by an accident, a mistake or by miseducation. By such an effort, one is also choosing a different sort of life for the country as a whole—a more sympathetic life in which we acknowledge, privileged and unprivileged alike, that we have the same doubts and mysteries and hopes for one another.

Earlier, I noted America's obsessive moral character, our tendency to treat every question that comes before us as a test of our national soul. The permit-but-discourage formula on abortion offers the chance to test our national soul by appealing to its basic egalitarian impulse. Were we once again to work actively toward creating a country where everyone had the same health care, the same sex education, the same opportunity for economic survival, the same sense of personal dignity and worth, we would see both fewer abortions and a more respectable America.

Examining "How to End the Abortion War" as a Mediated Argument

In "How to End the Abortion War," Rosenblatt has chosen a topic that seems to offer no opportunity for mediated resolution. The images Rosenblatt uses to begin his article—of pro-life and pro-choice supporters waged in a virtual war—illustrate the polarity with which many Americans view abortion.

Yet Rosenblatt is able to discern common ground between these two opposing positions, beginning with this statement: "both camps rail against the individual imposing his or her individual views on society at large, each feeling the same, if opposite, passion about both what society and the individual ought to be." Viewing abortion as a classic argument between the rights of the individual and those of society gives Rosenblatt a platform for pointing out other points with which both sides agree.

One of those points is optimism, which he sees as a defining American characteristic. He argues that both supporters and opponents of abortion "are heaving with optimism, and both see life in America as the best of choices." This idea leads, according to Rosenblatt, to Americans' belief in continual "hope and progress."

Rosenblatt also finds common ground by arguing that the majority of Americans support abortion rights while discouraging its practice. He foreshadows his coming resolution when he proposes the following:

> If we could find the way to retrieve this kind of conflicted thinking, and find a way to apply it to the country's needs, we might be on our way toward a common understanding on abortion, and perhaps toward a common good. Abortion requires us to think one way and another way simultaneously. Americans these days could make very good use of this bifurcated way of thinking.

Rosenblatt's proposal is that we, as a society, permit but discourage abortion. While he doesn't lay out any specific plan for accomplishing this goal, he does point to directions necessary for beginning the process. In another section of the essay, he says:

> I think it is time for Congress to make a law like *Roe v. Wade* that fully protects abortion rights, but legislates the kind of community help, like sex education, that would diminish the practice.

Will such a solution completely satisfy the man shouting "murderer" or the woman carrying the cardboard sign who Rosenblatt presents at the beginning of his article? Probably not. But Rosenblatt's proposal accomplishes what a mediated argument sets out to do: it presents a mediated solution that takes into consideration the values and interests of both parties in a dispute.

Writing the Mediated Argument

The mediated argument is rhetorical in that its purpose is to persuade, but it's also dialectic in that it attempts to present both sides of an issue equally. In developing a well-researched and structured argument, you may find your own position on a topic changing: this isn't a negative outcome. Learning the goals and values that underlie

TECHNIQUES FOR WRITERS 4-d
The Mediated Argument

Write a five to eight page mediated argument, using the material from your invention techniques and/or dialogue/inductive essay(s) as your prewriting. Your argument will need to include the following:

- an introduction that explains and defines the issue being discussed
- a complete and impartial analysis of the major arguments comprising *both positions* on the issue
- a statement that establishes the values and interests both sides share—their common ground
- a proposal or solution that recognizes the interests of both parties.

Be sure that *both positions* on the subject are equally represented in your paper: while it's often difficult to effectively present a position which you do not hold, a mediated argument requires fair representation.

Think about your common ground in broad terms: do both sides desire fairness, security, opportunity? And remember, your proposal must recognize both sides' interests. An otherwise well-written mediated argument can be destroyed by a one-sided solution.

Keep in mind the elements of argument you have studied so far. Think of your audience as readers who are concerned about your topic, are open to new ideas, and would like to see some resolution; adjust your style to meet their needs.

an opposing position leads to deeper understanding of the complex issues we face today.

Peer Revision Questions—Mediated Argument

1. Comment on the effectiveness of the introduction.
2. Has the author presented sufficient argument/evidence for both sides of his/her topic? Can you suggest other arguments/evidence that should be added?
3. What common ground has the author offered?
4. What is the author's resolution of the argument? Is the resolution effective in taking into account both sides of the argument?
5. What grammatical/mechanical errors need correcting?
6. Any other comments?

Student Writing: Mediated Argument

Following is Sandra Smaltz's mediated argument on affirmative action.

Affirmative Action, or Not
by Sandra Smaltz

When applying to a school of higher education, students have a
reasonable expectation of acceptance. This acceptance is based on
the assumption that the basic entry requirements have been met; or,
is it? Colleges and universities nationwide cite affirmative action
policies as a means of diversifying their campuses. Affirmative
action, as practiced in college and university admissions, takes
the form of preferential admissions. Preference is given to
minority students as one of the factors weighed when applications
are evaluated. The preference can take the form of extra points,
additional merit, or other such preferential considerations. By
law, schools cannot have formal admission quotas for minorities
unless past practices of discrimination warrant intervention by a
court. The basic arguments surrounding the debate over affirmative
action are equality versus justice, expectation versus merit,
preferences versus reverse discrimination, and unequal education
versus effectiveness.

For proponents of affirmative action, the most powerful
reasoning cited for maintaining affirmative action programs is
equality and the ability of everyone, regardless of race, to have
an opportunity to obtain the American Dream. Discrimination
started with the practice of enslaving blacks forcibly brought to
the United States for that very purpose. Black men, women, and
children were regarded as property, not human beings. Their very
right to exist was held in the hands of their owners who could
dispose of them without impunity. Even with the ending of
slavery, blacks could not escape the bounds of discriminatory
practices so deeply rooted in the white psyche. Jim Crow laws
were passed; these later were challenged during the Civil Rights
Movement of the 1960s. Due in large part to the Civil Rights
Movement, legal inequalities (or *du jour* discrimination) have

been addressed. However, inequalities in social and economic arenas (de facto discrimination) still exist. One of the many policies to develop out of an attempt to rectify this situation is affirmative action. Proponents of affirmative action seek to better society as a whole by supporting policies that give those individuals who formerly suffered discrimination the chance to achieve their educational goals.

Opponents disagree, citing slavery as the mistake of past generations, making it no longer a valid excuse for special treatment. With the exception of court orders in which intent to discriminate is proven, opponents feel there is no need for voluntary affirmative action programs such as admissions preferences. Opponents would prefer that individuals be evaluated for admission based on merit alone, not race. However, this argument seems somewhat disingenuous when one looks at the preferences given for athletic ability, legacy admissions, and talents in the arts. Being black would simply add another preference to the long list already in place.

With preferences in place, what expectations do blacks have of affirmative action policies? First and foremost, they do not expect handouts or "freebies." The vast majority of black students want the same thing as all other students, the chance to try. What they are seeking is what President Kennedy intended in his 1961 executive order, the ability to apply and then be judged on merit. The intent of the executive order was to encourage blacks and other minorities to apply to colleges that they might not have otherwise, citing racial concerns. Blacks expect the same degree of fairness that whites take for granted in the application process. If this fairness is not normally present, then affirmative action policies level the playing field for all players, including blacks. To a great degree students, whether black or white, are evaluated on merit. Preferences come into play when other factors have already been considered. Affirmative action does not mean that a college or university is mandated to accept a failing student just because he or she is black.

Opponents maintain that affirmative action policies go against the American ideal of fairness and open market competition. They feel that individuals should be judged on merit alone; race should not be a factor in admission policies for any reason. While this line of reasoning would work well in an ideal world where all were treated fairly all of the time, it brings to question how other students perceive a successful minority applicant upon admission. Opponents of affirmative action often view minority students with a degree of suspicion, as if their admission was somehow tainted and they truly have no business being there. If the intent of President Kennedy's executive order was simply to encourage fairness and increase minority applications to colleges and universities, why have affirmative action policies gone so much further? Litigation has brought affirmative action to where it is now. Regardless of the standards for admission set by a college or university, opponents maintain that threats of litigation have forced artificial criteria for admissions not previously considered necessary.

Proponents maintain that admission preferences are necessary to ensure the diversity of a college or university's student body. In general, more whites than blacks apply to college in the first place. In preferential admission policies for blacks, being black is only one of the factors weighed when applications are evaluated. The Supreme Court has ruled that formal admission quotas cannot be established; however, targeting specific minorities and individuals for admission is permissible.

Those seeking to end affirmative action would lament the idea of whether or not the preferences were "fair." Due in part to litigation and aggressive affirmative action policies, they argue that the idea of what is "fair" has now become subjective and discriminatory, causing reverse discrimination. They perceive minorities as using their minority status as an advantage, to be placed above personal qualifications. Although the policies were never intended to discriminate against whites, some will undoubtedly pay that price.

The reasoning behind affirmative action policies in college and university admissions is apparent when one examines the disparity in educational quality afforded black students versus that of white students. Although the idea of "separate but equal" has long gone by the wayside, schools are seeing a resurgence in segregation simply because of exurban development. White families are moving out of the city towards the suburbs and beyond (exurbia). The schools set up in these outlying areas are predominantly white, leaving the inner city schools to become predominantly black (de facto segregation). Black families, usually of a lower socioeconomic status, tend to not have the means to make the same move and are thus subject to their circumstances. What is the difference in educational opportunities? Schools in the inner city often have a harder time attracting quality educators; many teachers simply do not want to assume the additional personal risk associated with working in an inner-city environment.

Oftentimes, the school has to settle for who it can get as opposed to who is best for the job. Another factor that comes into play is economics. With exurban development, the tax base for desperately needed funds is gradually eroding, leaving schools with less funding to adequately confront the educational needs of inner city students. With many black students facing such an educational deficit, the need for affirmative action policies becomes clear. Minority students who have experienced educational deficits often have the same drive to be successful as white students; what they need is a leg up in the educational system to get them into college to prove it. With academic support services as a temporary measure to get them started, they can and do achieve success in college.

While educational disparities do exist, opponents note, the effectiveness of affirmative action policies is another aspect of the affirmative action debate. Regardless of intent, the majority of those helped by affirmative action policies are middle-class blacks and white women, while the majority of those needing the help are much poorer. While the number of blacks entering colleges and universities has increased, their graduation rates are still far lower than those of whites. The other argument put forth by institutions of higher learning is that affirmative action is necessary to ensure a diverse student body on campus. While this seems a worthy goal, the reality is that students tend to associate with their own kind; in essence, black students hang out with other blacks students, white students tend to hang out with other white students, and so on. Where is the benefit of having a diverse student body in the face of de facto segregation? If the intent was to ensure a variety of viewpoints would be discussed in classes, what about the fact that many students speak up and tell the professor what he or she wants to hear, not necessarily what they truly think? Where is the diversity in this equation?

Regardless of all of the arguments for or against affirmative action, both sides agree on some basic tenets. First, proponents and opponents alike would like the necessity for affirmative action policies to evaporate. The question is how to go about creating an environment where the need for affirmative action no longer exists. Second, when one segment of the society is bettered, the society as a whole also benefits. An educational system that works is paramount to societal change. Changing the environment, in this case, the educational disparities, changes attitudes. The more successful that students are early on, the more they will be educationally competitive when it comes time to enter a college or university. Third, both sides want to be treated fairly. The question is what is "fairness" and how does one determine its distribution. In the ideal world, everyone would have the same chance to achieve the American dream, regardless of race. This dream can be one of home ownership, job opportunities, or educational goals.

The answer to all three requires both public input and spending money on the country's educational system. Public investment in programs such as Head Start, literacy initiatives, job training, parenting classes, and student loans will assist students in gaining that competitive edge. Second, urban planners are working hard to entice middle-class individuals and families back into the inner city. Entire areas are being refurbished and rebuilt, increasing the tax base and the diversity of the population. The hope is that this resurgence in city dwelling will also increase the diversity and quality of inner-city schools.

With the minority population in the U.S. continually on the rise, affirmative action policies are here to stay, at least for the time being. With the educational disparities inherent in the public school system across the country, those policies are still necessary. Each of us would like to see ourselves as fair and equitably judged. However, until such time as we have achieved the true equality called for in the Constitution, affirmative action policies are necessary to ensure some measure of equal opportunity exists for black students.

Section 2

Enriching and Expanding Arguments

CHAPTER 5

Developing Arguments Through Rhetorical Strategies

PANIC! This is a common student response to a paper assignment that begins with the words, "Write an 8–10 (or 10–12; or 12–15)-page paper . . . " Many college writers, even those who are quite comfortable with their writing ability, freeze at the thought of writing a paper whose length exceeds a few pages.

For other writers, the panic doesn't hit until the paper is in its "final revision" stage, and the draft for a ten-page paper comes to only seven or eight pages of typed text. You know what happens next: margins expand by a quarter- or half-inch on each side, fonts bump up by a half size, the leading between lines increases. And often, a bunch of filler phrases get injected into sentences—e.g., "due to the fact that" replaces "because"; "it came to their attention" replaces "they discovered." Usually, the result is a brief comment from the teacher when the paper comes back: "Wordy," "Unfocused," or even "Less language, more substance."

Chapters 3 and 4 provided you with detailed instructions on how to develop a pro/con grid listing the most important points that support or oppose your argument. But while a well-developed pro/con grid provides a good start on the "what" of an argument, it doesn't give all the help you need on the "how" of that argument—the steps needed to produce an argument that is more than just a listing of statements which either support or oppose a topic.

Aristotle's *Topoi*: Identifying Classical Argument Strategies

In the *Rhetoric*, Aristotle provided a list of strategies—the ***topoi***—for developing arguments beyond the "list" stage. *Topos* means "place" in

Greek, and the *topoi* are places or areas of thought from which you can develop arguments. Aristotle's *topoi* provide you with fresh approaches to a topic, which can help you to develop your argument by providing an analytical structure for the information on your pro/con grid.

Defining Rhetoric

Topoi (plural form of *topos,* meaning "place" in Greek): argument strategies that can be used to develop essays.

Aristotle discussed twenty-eight *topoi* in the *Rhetoric,* many of which will be discussed here. (In this chapter, you'll find strategies related to definitions, relationships, comparisons, and feasibility, while Chapter 7 deals with strategies that directly relate to research.) You would never include all of these argument strategies in any one argument, but they provide a good checklist of ways to organize your information into a structured essay.

Definitions

Many disagreements hinge on the failure to define terms. For example, imagine two people arguing at length about gun control—one strongly favoring and one strongly opposing the topic. Several minutes into the argument, the following interchange occurs:

Pro: I honestly don't see why you would oppose registration of firearms and a short waiting period before being able to purchase a handgun.

Con: I don't oppose that.

Pro: I thought you were against gun control.

Con: I am—I'm against depriving law-abiding citizens of their right to own guns.

Pro: That's not what I meant by gun control. I meant registration and a waiting period.

Con: Why didn't you say so?

Because a term as complex as "gun control" can have many possible definitions, a definition of the term should appear very early, preferably in the introduction, in any argument on this topic.

This is equally true concerning a topic as complex as the use of Affirmative Action for determining college admissions. Affirmative Action policies have included such practices as establishing a percentage of minority students that will be admitted, adding a specified number of points for minority admissions, or automatically admitting a certain percentage of students from each high school in the state.

Without a clear definition of Affirmative Action, any argument concerning its place in determining college admissions would be very weak.

Category and Distinguishing Characteristics   One way to define a topic is by telling what it is (its *category*) and listing the elements that make it different from other members of its category (its *distinguishing characteristics*). For example, you might define a hammer this way:

> A hammer is a hand tool. It consists of a head commonly made of metal and a handle commonly made of wood or heavy fiberglass. It's used for striking.

The first sentence of the definition places hammers into the category of hand tools, along with other items such as wrenches, saws, and pliers. The second and third sentences list characteristics that distinguish hammers from other hand tools: the composition of their components and their usage.

Another example of this type of definition follows:

> A guitar is a musical instrument with a large sound box and (usually six) strings. It can be played by strumming or plucking.

Into what category does this definition place guitars? What distinguishing characteristics differentiate guitars from other musical instruments?

Of course, most definitions common in argumentative writing are more complex than these. Thomas Nagel, in "A Defense of Affirmative Action" (see p. 70), uses both category and distinguishing characteristics in the definition that appears early in his article:

> The term *affirmative action* has changed in meaning since it was first introduced. Originally it referred to only special efforts to ensure equal opportunity for members of groups that had been subject to discrimination. These efforts included public advertisement of positions to be filled, active recruitment of qualified applicants from the formerly excluded groups, and special training programs to help them meet the standards for admission or appointment. There was also close attention to procedures of appointment, and sometimes to the results, with a view to detecting continued discrimination, conscious or unconscious.
>
> More recently the term has come to refer also to some degree of definite preference for members of these groups in determining access to positions from which they were formerly excluded. Such preference might be allowed to influence decision only between candidates who are otherwise equally qualified, but usually it involves the selection of women or minority members over other candidates who are better qualified for the position.
>
> Let me call the first sort of policy "weak affirmative action" and the second "strong affirmative action." It is important to distinguish between them, because the distinction is sometimes blurred in practice. It is strong affirmative action—the policy of preference—that arouses controversy. Most people would agree that weak or precautionary affirmative action is a good thing, and worth its cost in time and energy. But this does not imply that strong affirmative action is also justified.

Nagel presents two definitions of Affirmative Action, an earlier one and a more recent one, before extending the definition further by separating the definitions and renaming each. He *stipulates* that, for the purposes of his discussion in this article, he will define the earlier Affirmative Action policy as "'strong affirmative action'" and the later policy as "'weak affirmative action.'" When you present your own definition of a word or term or specify which already-existing definition you are using, you create a *stipulative definition.*

TECHNIQUES FOR WRITERS 5-a
Writing Definitions

Write a one-sentence definition for each of the following words or terms, using the following pattern: *A(n)* _____ *is a(n)* _____ *that* _____. (Ex.: *A computer is a machine that processes large amounts of coded data.*)

tsunami	catalytic converter	DVD player
college degree	wrench	patriot
geek	success	tuba

Relationships

Arguments based on relationships look at the connections or presumed connections between two events, situations, or qualities. Being able to discern relationships is central to acquiring knowledge.

Similarity and Difference
Comparing similarities and differences is an analytic method that develops very early in the minds of children. A very young child

TECHNIQUES FOR WRITERS 5-b
More Definitions

Write one-sentence definitions for five words used regularly in your major field of study, the career field you plan to enter, or a sport, hobby, or interest you pursue.

might learn the word "doggie" in reference to the family's beagle. Then, on encountering a neighbor's cat for the first time, the child, seeing the similarity between the two animals, might call the cat "doggie." Once the parents explain, probably in words something like, "No, this is a *kitty.* See how different her fur is? Listen to how she purrs," the child learns that despite the similarities between a cat and a dog, there are enough differences to distinguish them as separate animals. (What would the likely outcome be when the child encounters another neighbor's ferret?)

Because looking for similarities and differences is a natural cognitive function, particularly when encountering something new, you can use these elements of comparison to help readers see an argument in a new light. For example, if you argue that Affirmative Action is the same as other preferences commonly used in college admissions, such as athletic scholarships, legacies (preference for the children of alumni), or grants for students with particular skills, such as music or theater, you're using similarity. Another argument of similarity would be to compare the "unfairness" of Affirmative Action to the "unfairness" of other legal decisions such as military conscription (the draft), arguing that if military conscription, while unfair to individuals, has been accepted because it promotes the good of society, then the same can be said for Affirmative Action.

On the other hand, you can also make a good argument by focusing on the ways in which two things differ. For example, you might contrast Affirmative Action policies on a particular campus with quotas, which are clearly against the law. In this case, you would argue that awarding points to minority applicants (a common Affirmative Action policy) differs significantly from assigning a certain percentage of positions to minority students. By explaining the difference, you would counter/refute the argument that Affirmative Action establishes quotas.

Degree   The relationship of degree focuses on *more* or *less* rather than on similarity or difference. An understanding of degree develops quite early in childhood as well; children learn the meanings of such terms as "taller" or "shorter" while very young. In argument, degree is often used in determinations of "better" (more to the good) or "worse" (less to the good). The argument that Affirmative Action provides an atmosphere that familiarizes students with diversity, thus benefiting society, is an example of argument of degree, since its basis is that a society that embraces diversity is better than a society that does not.

Another argument based on degree would be that the University of Michigan admissions policy, which added 20 points to the applications of minority students, provided too great a preference for minorities. This argument might then conclude that *less* preference would be acceptable.

You have probably seen arguments of degree frequently in advertising. Companies whose products are leading sellers often trumpet that fact, implying that if more people use Brand A than Brand B, Brand A must be superior. If you argued that

Affirmative Action must be a good policy because so many universities and colleges use it, you would be using argument of degree.

Cause and Effect
Mark Twain once said that if a cat jumps on a hot stove, it will never jump on a hot stove again—but it will never jump on a cold stove, either. This statement shows both the power and the danger of the cause-and-effect argument.

A cause-and-effect argument makes the case that doing one thing will cause another thing to happen. The concept of cause and effect, like the concepts of similarity and difference or more and less, develops very early in childhood. Even babies can learn, remarkably quickly, what specific cries or behaviors will elicit the reactions they wish from their parents.

But cause and effect often leads to misunderstanding, particularly in regards to stereotyping. The child who reaches out to pet a dog and is bitten may fear all dogs for a very long time after the event. Often not even the parents' careful explanations about the warning signals dogs give or about the trustworthiness of particular dogs are enough to overcome the child's fear that the previous action (petting a dog) will lead to the same unwanted effect (getting bitten).

To use cause and effect in developing an argument, you need to prove that the cause actually produced the effect. Because one event precedes another does not mean that the first event caused the second—*post hoc, ergo propter hoc* fallacies are based solely on chronology, on the fact that one event preceded another, with no actual proof of cause (see pp. 214–215). For example, the statement, "Of course it's raining—I just washed my car" implies that washing the car led to the arrival of the rain, a logical impossibility.

LOOKING CRITICALLY: THE *POST HOC* FALLACY Consider this argument and, with a classmate or group, see how many reasons you can find for the argument not holding up:

1. This company never had a woman CEO in its 120 years of existence.
2. Two years ago, the company hired a woman as the new CEO.
3. The company's stock value has dropped to its lowest level in history.
4. Clearly, women CEOs can't run companies like this one.

It will help your analysis if you make the company a specific kind: a manufacturer, a retailer, a publisher, or anything else. Then factor in the variables that are unique to this kind of firm.

The argument that diversity on college campuses promotes the development of a black middle class by providing more diversity in the workplace is a cause-and-effect argument in favor of Affirmative Action; the argument that Affirmative Action leads to fewer career opportunities for white students and to the emergence of less-qualified people in various professions is a cause-and-effect argument against it.

If/Then Arguments   A complete definition of the *syllogism* appears in Chapter 8, on deductive arguments. The if/then argument is a form of syllogistic thinking that states *if* something is true, *then* something else must be true. For example, *if* you know that all professors at your school's main campus have doctorates, *then* you know that your math professor must have a doctorate, as illustrated in the following syllogism:

Major Premise:	All professors at this campus have doctorates.
minor premise:	My math professor teaches at this campus.
Conclusion:	My math professor has a doctorate.

Similarly, *if* you know that all Snickers candy bars are "packed with peanuts," *then* you know that the Snickers bar you just picked up at the local convenience store will contain plenty of peanuts.

An argument in favor of Affirmative Action based on the if/then argument might be that *if* colleges and universities have the right to determine the qualifications necessary for admission, *then* they have the right to include Affirmative Action as one of those qualifications.

If/then arguments can also be used with opposites, based on the thinking that if something is good, then its opposite must be bad; for example, *if* health is good, *then* illness must be bad, or *if* wealth is good, *then* poverty must be bad. Of course, in making an argument based on opposites, both the writer and the reader must agree on the benefits and liabilities of the two qualities being compared, as well as on how the particular situation fits those qualities.

You could use this type of if/then argument to either support or oppose Affirmative Action, based on the statement, "*If* equal opportunity is good, *then* unequal opportunity is bad." Affirmative Action could be portrayed as supporting inequality by being unfair to white students, or as supporting equality by helping to lessen inequality between white and minority students. Another example of an if/then argument that supports Affirmative Action would be the following:

> Affirmative Action in determining college admissions is often seen as being unfair to white applicants. If American society were an equal playing field, this would be true. But this is not the case. A smaller percentage of minorities graduate from college than whites, and minorities, on average, make less money than whites. Because of the inequities in our social system, Affirmative Action in determining college admissions is still necessary.

Feasibility

Often, the argument is made that, although a certain policy or action might be beneficial, it's just not feasible or possible. For example, an individual opposing a tax increase that would pay for a new high school might argue that although the benefits of a new school are obvious, taxpayers simply can't afford to pay higher taxes while the local economy is in a slump. On a much larger scale, you could argue that equality for all is an ideal that unfortunately can never be realized: no society has been able to attain absolute equality for all its citizens.

One way to argue feasibility is by showing that a challenge more difficult than the one currently proposed has already been accomplished: if it's possible to accomplish a more difficult challenge, a less difficult one can surely be accomplished as well. This type of argument is commonly seen in such expressions as "If we can send a man into space, we can . . . " Any appropriate challenge can complete the statement (i.e., " . . . invent automobiles more favorable to the environment" or " . . . end poverty in our cities").

In the eighteenth and nineteenth centuries, one argument against the abolition of slavery was that blacks would never be able to succeed in white culture: their experiences as slaves would make them unable to compete economically. A supporter of Affirmative Action could use feasibility in arguing that since blacks have, over time, been able to approach economic equity with whites, establishing Affirmative Action policies in college admissions would make it possible for them to take the final, more possible step of achieving complete equity.

Example   Another argument based on feasibility is the example; after all, if something has happened once, it's possible for it to happen again. Aristotle focused on legal precedents (as are cited in courtrooms) as examples, while other rhetoricians have used hypothetical situations (i.e., New Testament parables). But one of the most commonly used strategies is the personal example; in addition to providing feasibility to an argument, a personal example can contribute to making an argument compelling in other important ways.

We've all heard personal examples throughout our lives, from stories our parents told us about their experiences as children (perhaps hoping that we would learn from their mistakes) to interviews of accident survivors on news programs. Although the telling of one person's story is certainly not representative of all experience, when you present a personal example you put a "face" on an argument, appealing to its *pathetic*, or emotional, component.

A personal example can comprise an entire argument. (Chapter 9 contains some exceptionally effective arguments composed almost entirely of personal examples: i.e., Langston Hughes' "Salvation" and Ron Kovic's *On Patrol*.) But short examples of as little as two or three sentences can also be used to develop arguments within essays. Stephen L. Carter, in his article supporting Affirmative Action, "Racial Preferences? So What?" (p. 87), uses personal example several times to illustrate his point, beginning in his introduction with an example from his own life:

> I got into law school because I am black.
>
> As many black professionals think they must, I have long suppressed this truth, insisting instead that I got where I am the same way everybody else did. Today I am a professor at the Yale Law School. I like to think that I am a good one, but I am hardly the most objective judge. What I am fairly sure of, and can now say without trepidation, is that were my skin not the color that it is, I would not have had the chance to try.

Later in the essay, Carter uses an example of a woman interviewing for a prospective internship with a large law firm:

> The immediate source of Baker & McKenzie's problems was a racially charged interview that a partner in the firm had conducted the previous fall with a black third-year student at the school. The interviewer evidently suggested that other lawyers might call her "nigger" or "black bitch" and wanted to know how she felt about that. Perhaps out of surprise that she played golf, he observed that "there aren't too many golf courses in the ghetto." He also suggested that the school was admitting "foreigners" and excluding "qualified" Americans.

Carter includes an extended narrative about his college graduation as a personal example toward the end of his essay:

> The incident I have in mind occurred during the fall of 1978, my third year in law school, a few months after the Supreme Court's decision in *Regents of the University of California v. Bakke,* which placed what seemed to many of us unnecessarily severe restrictions on the operation of racially conscious admission programs. The air was thick with swirling critiques of racial preferences, most of the couched in the language of merit versus qualification. Everywhere we turned, someone seemed to be pointing at us and saying, "You don't belong here." We looked around and saw an academic world that seemed to be doing its best to get rid of us.
>
> So we struck back. We called the critics racist. We tried to paint the question of our qualifications as a racist one. And one evening, when the Yale Political Union, a student organization, had scheduled a debate on the matter (the title, as I recall, was "The Future of Affirmative Action"), we demonstrated. All of us.
>
> Our unanimity was astonishing. Then as now, the black students at law school were divided, politically, socially, and in dozens of other ways. But on this issue, we were suddenly united. We picketed the Political Union meeting, roaring our slogan (*"We are not debatable! We are not debatable!"*) in tones of righteous outrage. We made so much noise that at last they threw wide the doors and invited us in. In exchange for our promise to end the demonstration so that the debate could be conducted, we were offered, and we accepted, the chance to have one of our number address the assembly. That task, for some reason, fell to me.
>
> I remember my rising excitement as I stood before the audience of immaculately attired undergraduates, many of them still in their teens. There was something sweet and naïve and appealing about the Political Union members as they sat nervously but politely in their tidy rows, secure (or, perhaps, momentarily insecure) in their faith that a commitment to openness and debate would lead to moral truth. But I set my face against the smile that was twitching there, and tried to work up in its stead a glower sufficient to convey the image of the retributive fury of the radical black left. (Having missed those days in college, I thought perhaps to rekindle them briefly.) And while some of the kids seemed annoyed at the intrusion, others looked frightened, even intimidated, which I suppose was our goal. I spoke briefly, pointing out that it was easy for white people to call for color-blind admissions when they understood perfectly well that none of the costs would fall on them. I carefully avoided the word *racism,* but I let the implication hang in the air anyway, lest I be misunderstood.

And then we marched out again, triumphantly, clapping and chanting rhythmically as though in solemn reminder that should the Political Union folks get up to
any more nonsense, we might return and drown them out again. (A few of the undergraduates and one of the speakers joined us in our clapping.) We were, for a shining
moment, in our glory; the reporters were there, tapes rolling, cameras clicking; in our
minds, we had turned back the calendar by a decade and the campuses were in flames
(or at least awash with megaphones and boycotts and banners and an administration
ready to compromise); the school would meet us with a promise of justice or we
would tear it down!

Then all at once it was over. We dispersed, returning to our dormitory rooms and
apartments, our law review and moot court activities, our long nights in the library to prepare for class and our freshly cleaned suits for job interviews, our political differences and
our social cliques. We returned to the humdrum interests of law school life, and suddenly
we were just like everybody else again. Absolutely nothing had changed. *Bakke* was still the
law of the land. There was no magic, the campus was not in flames, and there had never
been a shining moment. There was only the uneasy tension of our dual existence. The peculiar uncertainty provoked by affirmative action was still with us, and our outrage at being
reminded of its reality was undiminished. And as for the eager young minds of the Political Union, I suppose they held their debate and I suppose somebody won.

Carter's use of examples—from his own and another's experiences—illustrates
the points he's making about Affirmative Action in a way that straightforward argumentative prose cannot. While a good example doesn't actually *prove* anything (even
many random examples that point to the same conclusion aren't actually proof), presenting a compelling example is often the best way to help someone see a situation
from your perspective.

Finding Argument Strategies

You've probably encountered the strategies described here many times already in your
reading and in discussions with others, without actually recognizing them as a class.
In "Farewell to Fitness," Mike Royko uses a number of the argument strategies discussed in this chapter to illustrate the point he wishes to make about Americans' quest
for physical fitness.

Farewell to Fitness

Mike Royko

At least once a week, the office jock will stop me in the hall,
bounce on the balls of his feet, plant his hands on his hips,
flex his pectoral muscles and say: "How about it? I'll reserve a

Personal
Example

racquetball court. You can start working off some of that. . . ." And he'll jab a finger deep into my midsection.

Personal Example

It's been going on for months, but I've always had an excuse: "Next week, I've got a cold." "Next week, my back is sore." "Next week, I've got a pulled hamstring." "Next week, after the holidays."

But this is it. No more excuses. I made one New Year's resolution, which is that I will tell him the truth. And the truth is that I don't want to play racquetball or handball or tennis, or jog, or pump Nautilus machines, or do push-ups or sit-ups or isometrics, or ride a stationary bicycle, or pull on a rowing machine, or hit a softball, or run up a flight of steps, or engage in any other form of exercise more strenuous than rolling out of bed.

This may be unpatriotic, and it is surely out of step with our muscle-flexing times, but I am renouncing the physical-fitness craze.

5   Oh, I was part of it. Maybe not as fanatically as some. But about 15 years ago, when I was 32, someone talked me into taking up handball, the most punishing court game there is.

From then on it was four or five times a week—up at 6 a.m., on the handball court at 7, run, grunt, sweat, pant until 8:30, then in the office at 9. And I'd go around bouncing on the balls of my feet, flexing my pectoral muscles, poking friends in their soft guts, saying: "How about working some of that off? I'll reserve a court," and being obnoxious.

Personal Example

This went on for years. And for what? I'll tell you what it led to: I stopped eating pork shanks, that's what. It was inevitable. When you join the physical-fitness craze, you have to stop eating wonderful things like pork shanks because they are full of cholesterol. And you have to give up eggs benedict, smoked liverwurst, Italian sausage, butter-pecan ice cream, Polish sausage, goose-liver paté, Sara Lee cheesecake, Twinkies, potato chips, salami-and-Swiss-cheese sandwiches, double cheeseburgers with fries, Christian Brothers brandy with a Beck's chaser, and everything else that tastes good.

Cause and Effect

Similarity and Difference

Instead, I ate broiled skinless chicken, broiled whitefish, grapefruit, steamed broccoli, steamed spinach, unbuttered toast, yogurt, eggplant, an apple for dessert and Perrier water to wash it down. Blahhhhh!

You do this for years, and what is your reward for panting and sweating around a handball-racquetball court, and eating yogurt and the skinned flesh of a dead chicken?

If/Then

10   —You can take your pulse and find that it is slow. So what? Am I a clock?

—You buy pants with a narrower waistline. Big deal. The pants don't cost less than the ones with a big waistline.

—You get to admire yourself in the bathroom mirror for about 10 seconds a day after taking a shower. It takes five seconds to look at your flat stomach from the front, and five more seconds to look at your flat stomach from the side. If you're a real creep of a narcissist, you can add another 10 seconds for looking at your small behind with a mirror. | If/Then

That's it.

Wait, I forgot something. You will live longer. I know that because my doctor told me so every time I took a physical. My fitness-conscious doctor was very slender—especially the last time I saw him, which was at his wake. | Cause and Effect

15   But I still believe him. Running around a handball court or jogging five miles a day, eating yogurt and guzzling Perrier will make you live longer.

So you live longer. Have you been in a typical nursing home lately? Have you walked around the low-rent neighborhoods where the geezers try to survive on Social Security? | If/Then

If you think living longer is rough now, wait until the 1990s, when today's Me Generation potheads and coke sniffers begin taking care of the elderly (today's middle-aged joggers). It'll be: "Just take this little happy pill, gramps, and you'll wake up in heaven."

It's not worth giving up pork shanks and Sara Lee cheesecake.

Nor is it the way to age gracefully. Look around at all those middle-aged jogging chicken-eaters. Half of them tape hairpieces to their heads. That's what comes from having a flat stomach. You start thinking that you should also have hair. And after that comes a facelift. And that leads to jumping around a disco floor, pinching an airline stewardess and other bizarre behavior. | If/Then

20   I prefer to age gracefully, the way men did when I was a boy. The only time a man over 40 ran was when the cops caught him burglarizing a warehouse. The idea of exercise was to walk to and from the corner tavern, mostly to. A well-rounded health-food diet included pork shanks, dumplings, Jim Beam and a beer chaser. | Similarity and Difference

Anyone who was skinny was suspected of having TB or an ulcer. A fine figure of a man was one who could look down and not see his knees, his feet or anything else in that vicinity. What do you have to look for, anyway? You ought to know if anything is missing.

A few years ago I was in Bavaria, and I went to a German beer hall. It was a beautiful sight. Everybody was popping sausages and pork shanks and draining quart-sized steins of thick beer. Every so often they'd thump their magnificent bellies and smile happily at the booming sound that they made.

Compare that to the finish line of a marathon, with all those emaciated runners sprawled on the grass, tongues hanging out, wheezing, moaning, writhing, throwing up.

If that is the way to happiness and a long life, pass me the cheesecake.

25   May you get a hernia, Arnold Schwarzenegger. And here's to you, Orson Welles.

(marginal notes)
Personal Example

Similarity and Difference

TECHNIQUES FOR WRITERS 5-c
Topoi at Work

Roger Rosenblatt uses many argument strategies in his mediated argument "Ending the Abortion War" (pp. 179–185). Identify the strategies he is using in the following passages:

a. "She, for her part, paced up and down directly in front of him, saying nothing. Instead, she held high a large cardboard sign on a stick, showing the cartoonish drawing of a bloody coat hanger over the caption, 'Never again.' Like his, her face was taut with fury, her lips pressed together so tightly they folded under and vanished."

b. "In the 4,000-year-old history extending from the Greeks and Romans through the Middle Ages and into the present, every civilization has taken abortion with utmost seriousness. Yet ours seems to be the only civilization to have engaged in an emotional and intellectual civil war over the issue."

c. "Officially, America is an a-religious country; the separation of church and state is so rooted in the democracy it has become a cliché. Yet that same separation has created and intensified a hidden national feeling about faith and God, a sort of secret, undercurrent religion, which, perhaps because of its subterranean nature, is often more deeply felt and volatile than that of countries with official or state religions."

TECHNIQUES FOR WRITERS 5-d

Finding the *Topoi*

Choose an article from Section 4: "Rhetoric Today: Contemporary Issues," and determine which argument strategies the author used to develop his or her argument. In a short essay (500–750 words), discuss the author's use of strategies, focusing particularly on whether or not the strategies used clarified the argument and made it more persuasive.

TECHNIQUES FOR WRITERS 5-e

Using the *Topoi*

Using the topic you're currently writing about or one you've written about before, select three argument strategies already presented in this chapter (similarity/difference; degree; cause and effect; if/then; feasibility; example) that could reasonably be used to develop that argument. Write three extended paragraphs for that topic, using a different strategy in each paragraph.

Assumptions: Identifying the Ideas that Underlie Arguments

Assumptions can be defined as statements made without any evidence provided, but that are presumed to be true. Assumptions can further be understood as ideas and beliefs that lie beneath the surface of the argument. Assumptions are subtle persuaders—you might not recognize them in the arguments you hear, or even in the arguments you make.

Defining Rhetoric

Assumption: a statement in an argument that is accepted as truth, without any proof or evidence having been given.

*guess what
might be*

Assumptions are called *explicit* when they're actually stated, and *tacit* or *implicit* when they're only implied. A good example of explicit assumption can be found in the Declaration of Independence (see Chapter 8):

> We hold these truths to be self-evident, that all men are created equal, that they are endowed by their Creator with certain unalienable Rights, that among these are Life, Liberty and the pursuit of Happiness . . .

While Jefferson referred to self-evident truths, he was really listing assumptions, beliefs that he chose to present as truths. Many in Jefferson's time didn't believe that all were created equal; certainly King George of England held himself above his subjects. And with the institution of slavery firmly entrenched in many of the colonies (Jefferson himself held slaves), liberty for all was not seen as an unalienable right. Calling these assumptions self-evident truths was a good introduction to the radical and revolutionary ideas Jefferson would be presenting in his declaration.

But many assumptions are only implied. How many assumptions can you find in the following sentence?

> The Department of Children and Family Services needs to be much more effective in removing children from homes where they are being abused and neglected and placing them in foster care.

To accept the validity of the sentence, you need to accept as true a number of assumptions that are implied, but not proved or validated, within the sentence. The most obvious one may be that the Department of Children and Family Services is *not* being effective in its job of removing children from homes where they're being abused and neglected, and that they're capable of becoming *more effective* in doing so. But other assumptions are inherent in what may seem to be a straightforward statement.

The sentence assumes that at least some children are currently living in homes where they are being abused or neglected. It also implies that the terms "abuse" and "neglect" can be defined in ways that are accepted as standard, and that the Department of Children and Family Services is able to clearly identify and determine what constitutes abuse and neglect of children. But many different cultures, religions, and individual families would argue that what one person sees as abuse is in fact discipline, or what another sees as neglect is actually acceptable behavior within the bounds of good parenting.

Other assumptions inherent in the statement include the following:

- the Department of Children and Family Services has the right and duty to intervene when it believes that children are not being properly cared for.
- children should be removed from homes in which it is believed that they are not being properly cared for.

- foster homes are a better environment for children who have been abused or neglected in their own homes.
- good foster homes are available for all the children who need them.

All four of these assumptions have been challenged in court cases brought by individuals and groups who believe that family beliefs and values should take precedence over government regulations when the issue at stake is individual family autonomy. What at first may seem to be a clear, straightforward statement is, in fact, made up of many assumptions that may not be held by all, or even a majority, of those reading the sentence.

Assumptions Underlying the Abortion Controversy

One of the most hotly contested issues of our time is abortion, with those who favor a woman's right to abortion calling themselves "pro-choice" and those who oppose all or most abortions calling themselves "pro-life." These terms call up assumptions that are very misleading in themselves. Those who favor abortion would never see themselves as the enemies of life, and those who oppose abortion don't see themselves as opposed to women making choices.

But different assumptions about life and its beginnings lie at the base of the serious differences between the pro-life and pro-choice movements. To most of those who would call themselves pro-life, human life—with all the rights and protections that come with being human—begins at the moment when egg and sperm connect. Aborting a fetus even one day after conception is equal to murder to many dedicated pro-lifers, and it's as serious a crime as killing a child who's already several years old. In contrast, most whose position on abortion is pro-choice argue that human life doesn't actually exist until the fetus is capable of living on its own. Until then, the pro-choice side argues, pregnant women have the right to choose to terminate the pregnancy. (As medical advancements make life possible for babies born more and more prematurely, adjustments will likely have to be made to this argument.)

The pro-life movement will never be persuaded by arguments about the rights of women: they see the fetus as a child and argue that the right of a child to life takes precedence over the right of a woman to decide whether or not to become a mother. Similarly, pro-choice adherents feel that banning abortion places a hardship on women who are forced to become mothers before they are emotionally or financially able to take on such a burden. Because they don't see the unviable fetus as a child, this hardship is seen as unfair and discriminatory.

Tacit assumptions can be used to cloud the issues in an argument. As a careful reader, you need to be aware of the rhetorical impact of tacit assumptions, and look for these assumptions in the arguments you read. As a careful writer, you should use assumptions judiciously and consciously, always being aware of whether what you're writing is factual or assumed.

TECHNIQUES FOR WRITERS 5-f

Finding Assumptions

Find any assumptions that underlie the following statements:

a. Because Saddam Hussein had the capability and intent to produce weapons of mass destruction, removing him from power in Iraq was necessary for the security of the United States.

b. Prosecuting those who download music from the internet will lead to less illegal sharing of music.

c. People who neglect or abuse animals should be prosecuted to the same extent as those who neglect or abuse children.

d. Reinstituting prayer in school will help curtail the discipline problems plaguing our schools.

e. Standardized testing in elementary and high schools is an effective way to promote student learning.

Logical Fallacy: Learning How *Not* to Argue

Catherine Zeta-Jones sells cell phone contracts, although she has no particular expertise in telecommunications. Howie Long has been a long-term spokesperson for Radio Shack, despite having no academic credentials or other expertise in the field of electronics. Both are successful not because of any specialized knowledge of the products they represent, but because they're attractive, well-known celebrities.

In political campaigns, advertising often focuses more on candidates' personal lives than on their voting records. Negative ads regularly quote candidates out of context or offer intentionally misleading interpretations of their backgrounds or positions. This leaves voters with slanted views of candidates, making it difficult for them to assess the relative merits of those running for office.

Our discussion of argument so far has focused on *how* to reason well; the logical fallacies, on the other hand, give us some guidelines for how *not* to reason. While **logical fallacy,** or false reasoning, is commonly seen in written (opinion pages in newspapers), spoken (political speeches), and visual (advertising copy) arguments, its effectiveness is diluted when directed toward a person (like your writing instructor) who has studied and understands logical fallacy. Although logical fallacy is commonly used to divert attention from the real, substantial points of an argument, using fallacies is unfair and can detract from the real merits of your work. Once a discerning reader discovers fallacy, he or she is likely to dismiss or distrust the remainder of your argument.

Defining Rhetoric

Logical fallacy: flawed reasoning based on such mistakes as oversimplification or unfair comparison.

Though rhetoricians don't agree on the number of fallacies, and it's probably not important that you remember them by name, the following list is provided to make you aware of the kinds of arguments that are considered fallacious.

1. *Hasty generalization* is a general term for a pattern of careless thinking that masquerades as thoughtful reasoning. In hasty generalization, assumptions are based on insufficient evidence or on evidence that isn't really representative of the majority of cases. Stereotypes are examples of hasty generalization.
   - Example: We'd better watch that man wearing the turban. He could be a terrorist.
   - Example: Football linemen are athletic but not intelligent.

   Hasty generalization can result when one member of a set is judged by the general characteristics of the set, or when a set is judged by one of its members.
   - Example: I read in *Newsweek* that doctors' average salaries are pretty high. My neighbor, Dr. Smith, must be really rich.
   - Example: Dr. Smith is one of the wealthiest men in town, so Dr. Mandrel must be wealthy too.

   The *either/or* fallacy is a type of hasty generalization in which the number of choices a reader has on a given argument is oversimplified.
   - Example: If you don't support our party's policies, you are a traitor.
   - Example: America: Love It or Leave It.

   The second example illustrates what's commonly called "Bumper Sticker Logic," in which an extremely complicated issue (the responsibilities of a patriotic citizen) is minimized to a statement small enough to fit on a bumper sticker. In all forms of hasty generalization, complex issues are treated in an oversimplified manner that does not recognize the complexity that causes them to be argumentative.

2. *Post hoc ergo propter hoc* (in Latin, "after this, therefore because of this") fallacies are commonly seen in cause and effect arguments. As you saw earlier with the female CEO example, in a post hoc fallacy, an effect is attributed to a cause solely because one event precedes the other.
   - Example: I told you the seers were right. Didn't the volcano stop erupting last week after we tossed in those virgins?
   - Example: I didn't study for my chemistry test last week and still did well. No sense studying for next week's test.

3. *Non sequitur,* which translates as "It does not follow" in Latin, occurs when no logical relationship exists between two or more ideas that are represented as being related.

   ■ Example: Although it has been demonstrated that inner city clinics need better facilities, I will not support appropriations for improving their facilities as long as doctors charge such exorbitant fees.

   Although both parts of the above statement relate to medical costs, doctors' fees are not used to improve clinic facilities. The argument does not follow.

4. An *argument to the person* (also called *argument ad hominem*), avoids an issue by focusing on irrelevant positive or negative references to an individual supporting or opposing a particular position.

   ■ Example: Madonna is way too old to wear those jeans. I'm not buying anything from a company that's so clueless about basic fashion sense.

   ■ Example: How can we trust Senator Merriweather's work on economics when we know he's been cheating on his wife for years?

   ■ Example: How can this person be the Commander in Chief of our armed forces? He experimented with marijuana in college and avoided military service.

5. In *argument to the people* (also called *argument ad populum*), a writer or speaker arouses emotion in an audience by an appealing to their biases, whether those biases are for or against the topic.

   ■ Example: Although Medicare is an important program for the elderly and the infirm, increasing Medicare eligibility is nothing more than a liberal plan to promote big government.

   ■ Example: Curtailing freedom of speech may be necessary to maintain our national security.

   In these examples, emotion-laden buzzwords ("liberal," "security") are used to evoke a response in readers.

6. *Begging the question* occurs when the persuader assumes the validity of an unproven premise: that is, when an assumption is taken as a fact. It can be signaled by introductory statements like "Everybody knows . . . " or "History tells us . . . "

   ■ Example: Because the death penalty deters murderers, it should be the mandatory sentence for all convicted killers.

   Unless it's been proven that the death penalty does in fact deter murderers (which is a highly contested argument in itself), the example *begs the question.*

7. An *appeal to ignorance* is based on the assumption that something is true if it hasn't been proven false.

   ■ Example: UFOs must be alien spacecraft, because scientists have not proven that they aren't.

   Sometimes it's difficult to see where valid use of the *topoi* ends and fallacies begin. For example, at what point does presenting yourself or another person as straw man —

a reliable supporter of an issue become argument to the person? At what point does the use of a relevant case study become a hasty generalization? How much proof is necessary to distinguish a valid cause-and-effect relationship from a post hoc fallacy?

The only way to judge the validity of an argument is to look at the whole argument: does the writer produce compelling evidence or rely solely on developing ethos? Does the writer use only generalization, or back up the argument with specific evidence? Does the writer support claims of cause with logical explanation? Valid arguments will stand on their own merits, without resorting to trickery or diversion, while weak ones will divert reader attention by resorting to fallacies—intentionally or not.

TECHNIQUES FOR WRITERS 5-g
Identifying and Understanding Fallacies

Write five sentences that you believe to be fallacious, using several of the logical fallacies described above. Switch papers with a classmate: see if he or she can identify the fallacy illustrated in each of your sentences.

Introductions: Creating Audience Interest

How would you evaluate the following paragraph as the introduction to an argument?

> In today's complex world, Affirmative Action is a very controversial issue. Many argue strongly in favor of Affirmative Action, citing study results and other evidence to support their position, while many others are equally opposed to Affirmative Action and support their beliefs with similarly extensive evidence. This paper looks at the arguments for and against Affirmative Action with the goal of reaching some understanding of the complexities of this very controversial issue.

Is the paragraph direct and to the point? Without a doubt. Does it state the topic and give some idea of the arrangement of the paper that is to follow? Definitely. But now the big question: Would you really *want* to read the paper?

While the paragraph does follow two of the goals of an introduction—to identify (literally, *introduce*) the topic and give some idea of the content and arrangement of the paper that will follow—it doesn't reach the crucial goal of interesting readers enough to encourage them to continue reading. In the real world of writing, an audience won't continue reading something that doesn't generate interest (unless, of course, they're required to read it).

The above introduction fails because it's generic and formulaic. If you substitute the words "Affirmative Action" with "animal rights," "gun control," "cloning," or any other argumentative topic, the paragraph becomes equally meaningful—and equally generic. The introduction might *address* the topic, but it doesn't *introduce* readers to the paper's purpose, scope, and depth. In fact, because the "intro" is so shallow, most readers will rightfully guess that the paper that follows is shallow, too.

There are, however, many ways you can avoid writing generic introductions. The following student examples illustrate just a few.

> As church bells rang joyfully, the young couple, holding hands, stepped out of the chapel into a beautiful, sunny day. They raised their hands to their eyes, partly to block the sun's strong rays, partly to fend off the handfuls of rice being flung their way by their cheering friends. Dashing toward a white limousine bedecked with paper carnations and a sign saying "Just Married," they smiled and waved before making their escape. It was a beautiful sight, but should this day be happening for Judy and Jennifer? Should the law permit this gay couple to marry?

This introduction illustrates a common, and often effective, way to begin an argumentative paper—with a *narrative* that leads the reader into the topic. But, in addition, the last two sentences offer a twist that makes readers realize that the subject of the paper won't be what they expected. This introduction states the topic and gives some idea of the direction the paper will take without being generic.

Another way to begin a paper with a narrative is by portraying a hypothetical outcome to a current problem:

> Early on the morning of October 15, 2072, Susie Simmons dragged herself out of bed and sleepily headed downstairs for breakfast. She quickly ingested the energy bar her mother handed her while going over notes for the test on the history of the space colony on Mars that she would be taking first period. Mrs. Simmons reminded Susie that she had only two minutes before the airbus would arrive at their door—she needed to spend that time getting into her solar protection suit and oxygen mask. Susie groaned. She hated her solar protection suit—not only was it last year's model, but she thought it made her look fat.

The next introduction uses questions to interest a reader in the topic:

> Do you like to spend a warm summer afternoon in the shade? Are you fond of birds and squirrels? Do you love the smell of pine needles? Does the sight of a 200-year-old oak fill you with wonder? Most of all, do you like to breathe? If you answered "yes" to any of the above questions, you will be horribly alarmed by the forestry guidelines recently proposed by the current administration.

Beginning a paper with a set of startling statistics can also be effective.

> Five million deaths, 400,000 of them in the United States. Reduction in lifespans aver-
> aging 15%. Fifty billion dollars in U.S. health care expenses and 47 billion in lost earn-
> ings and productivity. More than 168,000 fires in the U.S. alone. Smokers complain
> that $5.00 a pack is too expensive for cigarettes. But the real expense of cigarettes far
> exceeds their price.

Many successful writers have begun essays and articles with relevant and powerful quotes from other sources:

> "Human beings and the natural world are on a collision course. Human activities inflict
> harsh and often irreversible damage on the environment and on critical resources. If not
> checked, many of our current practices . . . may so alter the living world that it will be
> unable to sustain life in the manner that we know. Fundamental changes are urgent if
> we are to avoid the collision our present course will bring about (Union of Concerned
> Scientists)." Predictably dire warnings from the Sierra Club or Greenpeace? If only that
> were true. This warning is the introduction to a paper signed by 1700 scientists, many
> of whom were Nobel laureates.

These examples comprise only a few of the creative ways to introduce argumentative essays: your options are limited only by your own creativity. One further
note about writing your introduction: there is no law stating that an introduction
must be written *first*. Many of our students have found to their distress that the introductions they labored over early in their writing process became irrelevant after the
paper itself was completed. We encourage you to discover the advantages of waiting
until a work has been fully developed, sometimes even completely written, before
tackling the job of writing your introduction.

TECHNIQUES FOR WRITERS 5-h
Focusing on Introductions

Read the introductions of several of the selections from Section 4, paying
particular attention to the introductory techniques the authors used. Write
one-paragraph critiques on the effectiveness of the introductory techniques
used for three of those selections.

TECHNIQUES FOR WRITERS 5-i
Writing Introductions

For the draft of the paper you're currently writing or for a revision of a paper you wrote earlier, compose three 1-paragraph introductions. Use three of the introductory techniques discussed above, or write your introductions using other techniques that you would consider particularly effective.

CHAPTER 6

Reading Rhetorically: Case Studies on Popular Music

Analyzing the "Sellout" Argument in Popular Music

How can I convince her (Faker!) that I'm invented, too?
I am smitten; I'm the real thing (I'm the real thing)
We all invent ourselves, and—uh—you know me.

—R.E.M., "Crush with Eyeliner"

I don't know why people pay such tribute to Madonna. She had a lot of great disco records, and certainly sustained that for a long time. . . . She just wanted to be up there, and it worked. But it was never rock 'n' roll.

—Chrissie Hynde of the Pretenders

[We called our band] the Originals, but there was another group, up in the east end, called the Originals, so we had to change our name to the *New* Originals. Then they changed *their* name to the Regulars, and we thought, "Well, we could go back to the Originals—but what's the point?

—Dialog in the rock documentary parody, This Is Spinal Tap

These three epigraphs reflect an idea that has been around as long as popular music has existed. Michael Stipe of R.E.M., with his "Crush" lyrics, indicates his awareness that rock musicians should have an authentic self, but he interrupts his own claim of authenticity by reminding himself that he's a "faker" before going on with a counter-argument that he's "the real thing." After that, he seems to become confused by the two clashing ideas. Chrissie Hynde, on the other hand, uses a rhetorical pattern of past-tense verb forms to construct Madonna as someone no longer relevant because she "was never rock 'n' roll." And finally, the parodic "metal band" Spinal Tap pokes fun at the whole notion of originality itself in popular music.

Clearly, there's more going on in popular music than just lyrics and chords, and this chapter will provide you with several case studies aimed at helping you to think and write about some of the debates taking place about the music. Longtime music critic Dave Marsh has written that contemporary music fans "feel empowered by the very rhetoric of the music to make judgments—sometimes punitive judgments—about their heroes. Furthermore, they not only expect to be entertained but expect to have certain 'needs' met in the process." What all of this provides for you, as a student of rhetoric and composition, is a chance to explore the role of ethos (defined and discussed in Chapter 2), an ancient concept, in a contemporary setting.

When looking carefully at the constructions of an "authentic" or "real" ethos in musical performers, you engage in a technique called a *close reading* or **rhetorical analysis.** This kind of thorough and systematic examination of the issue helps others to follow your exact line of argument and to see your supporting evidence in enhanced detail. Of course, this doesn't guarantee that the audience will necessarily accept your analysis unchallenged, but as you read earlier in the introduction to this book, being faced with a vigorous challenge can be one of the main benefits of the dialectical process for a writer.

Defining Rhetoric

Rhetorical Analysis: a thorough and systematic examination of all positions of an issue.

Each of the case studies in this chapter provides you with a situation to consider through close reading and rhetorical analysis. As you take in the information, reflect on the positions you begin to form (you may want to write a brief journal entry to record your impressions). What issues of authenticity or "realness" are contained in each scenario? Are those issues important? How do they apply to situations outside music?

Case #1: Osbourne, Seger, and "Corruption"

Critic Larry Grossberg has explained that the rhetoric of popular music "easily and often slides into a narrative war between authentic youth cultures and corrupting commercial interests." This "war" is a complex one. For instance, Ozzy Osbourne, an influential pioneer of heavy metal and founder of the annual Ozzfest concert series, is still a relevant figure in contemporary music culture, so when his song "Crazy Train" first blasted from TV sets to help sell the Mitsubishi Montero, his fans made a complex adjustment in their rhetoric so that Ozzy *the man* wasn't blamed for the commercial use of Ozzy *the music.* "Mitsubishi corrupted Ozzy's music by using it to sell cars" was the preferred explanation over "Ozzy corrupted his music by selling it to Mitsubishi." (As a writer, you already understand how the order of ideas in a sentence has a huge impact on how the sentence creates meaning.)

Yet when consumers heard musician Bob Seger on TV, too, singing that Chevy trucks were "Like a Rock," more than one journalist asked Seger how he could allow this to happen when so many other artists had protested the increasing corporate "misuse" of rock music. Seger explained that he genuinely *liked* Chevy trucks, and that many of his fans drove Chevy trucks, so they would understand. But unlike the protecting shield that formed around Ozzy Osbourne, the rhetoric by fans and music journalists presented here made no adjustments for Bob Seger. In their view Seger had sold out to General Motors, and worse, he helped to pave the way for even more corporate "corruptions" of rock.

Case #1 Question for Thinking and Writing

Why did Ozzy Osbourne get rhetorical protection that Bob Seger didn't?

Case #2: Warner/Manson

According to Brian Warner, better known by his stage name, Marilyn Manson, "I never identified with [Kiss and Alice Cooper] . . . because both of those bands were always very specific that their show was an act. I wanted to meet what was on stage. I didn't want to meet some old guy who plays golf." Asked to speculate about any possible contradictions in these words, Warner has explained that he is different from them in that he "can't wake up and not be Marilyn Manson. It's not like I turn off Marilyn Manson and I'm an everyday guy who goes and has another job and doesn't think about any of this stuff. Marilyn Manson is the most real thing that can come from me."

Warner/Manson won't admit any possibility of his "real" identity being just an act, equal to the same theatrics of Kiss and Cooper that alienated him in his youth. Behind his gothic mask of death-pale makeup and black lipstick, with a clouded contact lens covering one iris, Warner's "Marilyn Manson" persona feels free to assert his "realness." In one early song, Manson addressed his individuality with these lyrics:

> You want to look like me, you want to act like me
> You've got no sense of your own identity . . .
> Imitation's not a flattery, you're a pitiful thief.

Yet some music fans have pointed out similarities between the names *Marilyn Manson* and *Alice Cooper,* and others see a connection between Warner/Manson and musician David Bowie with his own stage persona, Ziggy Stardust, in the 1970s. Bowie, describing his adolescence, speaks of being "painfully shy, withdrawn. I didn't really have the nerve to sing my songs on stage, and nobody else was doing them. I decided to do them in disguise." Picking up on this admission, a film about the glam-rock era, *Velvet Goldmine,* presented its Bowie-esque character "Brian Slade" (Jonathan Rhys Meyers) announcing that "[r]ock and roll is a prostitute. It should be tarted up, performed. The music is the mask." Given all of this, some fans wonder why Brian Warner continues to defend the "genuine" status of his Marilyn Manson stage persona.

Case #2 Questions for Thinking and Writing

On what grounds can Brian Warner defend the argument that Marilyn Manson is his real self? Why do you suppose he thinks it's important to take this position?

Case #3: "The Milli Vanilli Affair"

In the 1980s, two handsome young men named Rob Pilatus and Fabrice Morvan made up a group called Milli Vanilli that put out a few songs like "Blame It On the Rain" and "Girl You Know It's True." Each song was a catchy track highlighting appealing tenors, and the promotional MTV videos revealed the singers' fine Afro-European looks, long braids, and smooth dance moves. Milli Vanilli sold millions of albums because of those songs and videos, and Rob and Fab (as the group's fans knew them) became huge celebrities.

But all of this ended when a record producer, Frank Farian, went public with information that Rob and Fab had never sung a note of those top-selling tracks. It was all just a lip-sync performance—moving to tape, even in their live "concerts." Even those long braids were only hair extensions. Milli Vanilli, in truth, was a studio concept, an invented image. The real singers weren't as attractive as Rob and Fab, so those two young men had been hired as faces for the vocals. Farian publicized this information because, as he saw it, Rob and Fab had taken their "own" stardom much too far, becoming not merely a part of the lie, but all of it, showing disrespect for their benefactor back in the studio. They even demanded a chance to *actually sing* on "their" next album.

When the truth came out, Rob Pilatus and Fabrice Morvan were derided and mocked around the world. In the United States, Arsenio Hall made Rob and Fab the focus of his most cutting jokes on his late-night talk show, and after the National Academy of Recording Arts and Sciences made them return the Grammy Award they'd received for Best New Artist, the humiliation was complete. Rob and Fab went into seclusion, and in 1998, Rob Pilatus committed suicide in a hotel room in Germany.

But nearly 20 years before the sordid "Milli Vanilli Affair" as at least one music historian has called it, a man named Malcolm McLaren, who owned a small clothing shop in England, decided to start a punk band called the Sex Pistols. McLaren would not be a musician or songwriter; he would serve only as the band's creator. The Sex Pistols were nowhere near as commercially successful as Milli Vanilli, yet its lead singer, "Johnny Rotten" (whose real name was John Lydon), would become a punk legend who eventually found himself connected—through a Neil Young lyric—to 1990s punk/grunge suicide Kurt Cobain.

Like Lydon, the band's bass player, "Sid Vicious" (whose real name was John Ritchie), would become a legend in a different way after he murdered his girlfriend and then overdosed on heroin three months later while awaiting trial. Today the Sex Pistols are famous as authentic founders of punk music, even though they, like Milli Vanilli, recorded and toured for little more than a year, and even though, as critic Greil Marcus has written: "Punk began as fake culture, a product of McLaren's fashion sense, his dreams of glory, his hunch that the marketing of sadomasochistic fantasies might lead the way to the next big thing." Or, as one of our students recently put it, "The Sex Pistols were just an early 'boy band,' like N' Sync or the Backstreet Boys."

To most popular music fans around the world, Milli Vanilli clearly was a fraud, a fake, a manufactured facade that quickly crumbled. Milli Vanilli was obviously a sham, a joke, an embarrassment. But the Sex Pistols' founder, Malcolm McLaren, was a pure genius, taking four raw kids off the street, putting instruments and a microphone into their hands and telling them to make some noise with no smooth edges, no melodies, and limited commercial appeal. Although they had been carefully put together by McLaren, the Sex Pistols were never perceived by fans as invented; instead, the perception was that each of its members invented him*self,* especially Lydon and Ritchie—"Rotten" and "Vicious." Like Milli Vanilli, the Sex Pistols couldn't sing or play—but that was supposed to be the whole point.

Case #3 Questions for Thinking and Writing

What charges can be made against Milli Vanilli that could not also be made against the Sex Pistols? Can the depiction of the Sex Pistols as "an early boy band" be defended logically? What specific aspects of the case study here do you find to be most important in evaluating the status of each of the two music groups? (You may want to do some internet research to become more familiar with each group.)

TECHNIQUES FOR WRITERS 6-a

Rhetoric Online: Rap Lyrics in School

For years, television and radio talk shows have addressed the cultural and social influences of rap music and hip-hop culture. With a growing number of educators beginning to incorporate rap lyrics into literature and writing courses as well as other disciplines (e.g., psychology and sociology), the music has been portrayed as especially controversial. For this case study, go online and use a service such as Google.com to search for the following strings. The first entry will locate a transcript of an especially lively TV debate:

- O'Reilly Jeffrey Duncan-Andrade
- *rap lyrics classroom*
- rap literature college controversy
- *hip-hop higher education*

Once you find the music being discussed or debated, make notes or underline passages where you see authors, commentators, or guests showing concern over the validity of rap as a real instructional device.

Questions for Thinking and Writing

Based on specific evidence you gathered during your research for "Techniques for Writers" exercise 6-a (p. 224), what is the overall consensus on the use of rap in school classrooms? What rhetorical strategies have your sources employed in forming their depiction of rap? Is that depiction solely negative, or would you label it as fair and accurate? On what grounds would you yourself defend or condemn the use of rap in the classroom if you were to publish your own opinions online?

Case #4: Extended Case Study: Metallica—The Ultimate Sellout?

There's very few outside factors involved. It's not your typical "Give the people what they want" or "Yeah, we're here to play rock and roll for you and party all day," or any of that. This is *our* [music], and we wanna do what's right for us, what we feel good about. If you like it, you're invited along. If you don't, well, there's the door.

—Lars Ulrich of Metallica

And my ties are severed clean; the less I have, the more I gain
Off the beaten path I reign: rover, wanderer, nomad, vagabond—call me what
    you will.

—Metallica, "Wherever I May Roam"

By all accounts, the formation of the heavy metal band Metallica is credited to drummer Lars Ulrich, a Danish junior-ranked tennis player and rabid fan of what was called, in the late 1970s and early '80s, the "New Wave of British Heavy Metal." Abandoning his tennis racquet for a drum set after his parents' move to Los Angeles and the States, Ulrich taught himself drumbeats by following along with recordings, then advertised his desire to join with other musicians in performing cover versions of the songs he loved.

James Hetfield, a fellow teenaged admirer of the New-Wave genre who had picked up the guitar after many years of despised piano lessons, responded to Ulrich's ad; the first realization the two fledgling musicians had, after jamming together, was that Hetfield couldn't sing and Ulrich's drumming skills were even worse.

Untrained and raw but having chosen the name *Metallica* for themselves, Ulrich and Hetfield recruited two other teens to cut a demo song for a compilation album to be released by a local independent record label. The music followed a tempo faster and louder than anything previously recorded by an American metal band. The record was a local success, and the group—praised by area fans and critics alike for this new form of "thrash" metal—found steady work.

Having developed a following by playing faster and louder than its rivals, Metallica traveled to Denmark to record its second album, *Ride the Lightning*. The title of this work, prison slang for execution by electric chair, reflected a new political content to the band's songs because the proceeds from its sales bought the band members their first television set, which provided CNN as a supplier for news-based themes. Metallica also went "experimental" on the new album, slowing its tempo and introducing acoustic guitar to the lead-in for its anti-suicide song, "Fade to Black." Many of the group's fans, sensing an impending crossover to mainstream metal, voiced collective displeasure.

For Metallica's next two albums the group allowed shortened "radio edit" versions of two of its songs to be released as singles, and then abandoned a pledge never to make MTV videos as promotional tools. In 1988 the band commissioned a video for its song "One," which was then nominated for a Grammy Award; although it didn't win in its category, the band performed live for the tuxedo-and-ballgown set at the ceremony.

Metallica entered the 1990s with a lucrative recording contract, high-powered management representation, two video collections in the stores, royalties pouring in from clothing and memorabilia sales, and a touring entourage of 18 trucks and 60 full-time employees who followed the musicians to the best hotels as they traveled the U.S. and Europe. After losing at the 1989 Grammys, the band won two awards before recording a sixth album, *Metallica*, that contained short, formulaic songs perfect for radio play. Five of the songs were accompanied by MTV videos and one was a tender love ballad.

The album's producer, Bob Rock, was best known for making slick, radio-friendly music with no rough edges, and *Metallica* (otherwise known as "the black album") arrived in stores at the number-one spot on the *Billboard* sales charts. Its 1993 follow-up, *Binge and Purge,* was a combination music/videotape/book package with a retail price of $90. Two British biographers wrote that the band "had clearly been transformed into the kind of highly-polished corporate money machine they once existed to rebel against. They were just another fat turkey on the production line, bearing no resemblance to their former selves."

> Living on your knees: Conformity / Or dying on your feet for honesty. . .
> Following our instinct: Not a trend / Go against the grain until the end.
>
> —*Metallica, "Damage Inc."*

Metallica's 1996 album, *Load,* alienated millions more of the band's fans. The band's barbed-hook logo had been replaced by a softer, rounded set of capital letters—but this was not the only thing that was visually shocking. Every member of the group had cut off his long hair, and guitarist Kirk Hammett's appearance was the most severely altered. In contrast to the short college-athlete haircuts of his three bandmates, Hammett had trimmed his waist-length curls to a tight Afro style while also piercing his lower lip with a silver spike, having his stomach and left side tattooed, and hiding his eyes behind gobs of black mascara.

Internet discussion forums immediately burned with howls of confusion and alarm from the band's core fans. But more was to follow. The group's final release of the twentieth century, *S&M,* was a live recording with the San Francisco Symphony, an event that caused many *orchestra* patrons to howl in protest. And as the twenty first century began, a surreal picture played out as Lars Ulrich, the band's outspoken drummer and founder, testified before Congress after filing suit against the internet music-file sharing site Napster for distributing copies of the band's contribution to the *Mission Impossible 2* soundtrack.

TECHNIQUES FOR WRITERS 6-b

Rhetoric Online: The Look of a Logo

Go online and use the "Images" link on a service like Google.com to enter the search terms "Metallica logo" and locate a photo of the band's original barbed-hook logo and another of its softer, gentler replacement. Looking at the new logo through the eyes of a longtime fan of the band, what crucial aspects of the band's image, or the image of its music, were lost by the change? Is this purely an aesthetic argument, or can you back it up with similar examples from art, architecture, and/or design?

Metallica played a big role in generating a court-ordered Napster shutdown in July 2000, and in a *Rolling Stone* interview conducted that same month Ulrich raised key questions and issues about capitalism and private property. (Notice how Ulrich's questions follow the *stasis* methodology prescribed by Cicero—see Chapter 4.)

> What's the issue about? It's about choice, everything this country stands for. I should have the choice to decide what happens to my music. . . . When I bought my Suburban a few months ago, and it was $51,000 and I thought that was expensive, does that give me the right to just steal it? If I have a right to free music through my computer, well, what about the guy who doesn't have a computer? Should we remove the cash registers from Tower Records? How's this gonna work?

As the drama unfolded, discussion boards filled with messages from fans who wanted to voice their opinions: "Metallica: Masters of Money" read one of the more creative subject headers, playing on the band's early album titled *Master of Puppets*. Another simply read "Another Bunch of Old-Fart Sellouts!" The latter fan quickly qualified her choice of words by categorizing *herself* as an "old fart" too (at age 27!), then offered a lengthy comparison between Metallica and the Rolling Stones, a band she saw as having once been "genuinely about the music, but now they're all about money."

Case #4 Questions for Thinking and Writing

Often, accusing a musical act of "selling out" to corporate interests is an easy argument to make, while looking objectively at the realities of music as a *job*, rather than an *art*, is more difficult. On what grounds could you make an argument in defense of Metallica's growth and accomplishments as professional musicians? What are a musician's chances for a successful career if s/he insists on remaining "untainted" by the music industry? Why do music fans insist on "realness" from the musicians they admire? In hip-hop, where being "the realest" is a boast made by many rappers to attract fans and sell music, is this a separate set of values from the ones held by fans of rock? What distinctions exist between a chart-topping "real" rapper and a chart-topping "sellout" act in rock?

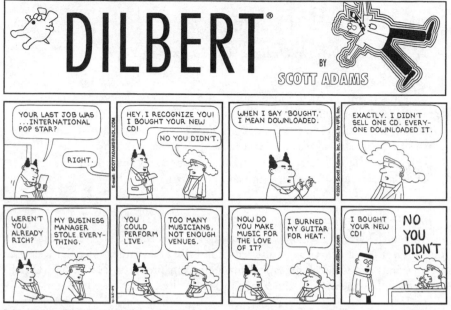

© Scott Adams/Dist. by United Feature Syndicate, Inc.

Questions for Thinking and Writing: Analyzing Issues of Ethos

Looking at any or all of the musical acts described in this chapter so far, how does the ancient rhetorical issue of ethos apply to modern-day performers? Which of these acts do you see as more genuine than others? Do you see any as completely fraudulent or "fake"? While reading so far, were you reminded of other musicians not described in this chapter? How do they compare or contrast with the ones you've read about here?

Analyzing Arguments on Music Downloading

Since January 1999 and the advent of a little computer program called Napster, the controversy over peer-to-peer file swapping—especially music files—has grown from a murmur to a roar. Issues of morality and integrity, ethics and legality, copyright and technology have swarmed around the music industry's cries of foul play as the Internet has continued to grow and even more programs like Napster have come along to replace the original. Free, unregulated services such as Kazaa (PC) and Poisoned (Mac) have provided unlimited file downloading for users willing to take a chance on being sued by the Recording Industry Association of America, while a number of pay services such as the Apple iTunes Store have sold millions of single songs and whole albums to those who agree, with Lars Ulrich, that musicians should be paid for their labors.

What follows now is an assortment of arguments and overviews of the downloading controversy. Using all of the techniques and strategies you have learned so far, follow these arguments closely in order to form your own opinion and support it with logical, specific evidence.

Metallica, how could you?
Brian Lew

"We'll never stop, we'll never quit/'Cause *you're* Metallica!"

That's the war cry of fan camaraderie Metallica's James Hetfield conjures up when the band performs their anthem "Whiplash." In 18 years Metallica has risen from an obscure underground band to one of rock's most perennially successful groups.

Today, "indie" doesn't mean much of anything; back then, it did. In the early 1980s, before Metallica even recorded their debut album, the band had established a worldwide following via an underground tape-trading network. In modern parlance, we would call it illegal and unrestricted copying and distribution of their songs; the announcement of Metallica's lawsuit against Napster and various colleges on the grounds of copyright infringement by users of Napster's software struck me as stunningly ironic in light of the band's history.

Come with me back to the Stone Age times of the early '80s, a time when VCRs were the size of small cars and we learned about computers in movies like "War Games" and "Tron." There was a thriving heavy-metal underground at this time. Mainstream metal was dominated by hair bands like Mötley Crüe, Bon Jovi and Poison. As with other underground scenes, this underground was born out of hatred for the mainstream of the day. The unwashed image of Motorhead was the aesthetic of this scene, not the spandex and hairspray of Mötley Crüe.

5   A big part of this scene was tape trading. Tape traders networked via the pen-pals section in English hard-rock magazines like *Kerrang!* and the now-defunct *Sounds*. There were few independent record labels at that time catering to the metal crowd; we traded demos and live tapes by dozens of bands who didn't have a record out. The metal underground was just as legitimate as any punk scene, especially in the San Francisco Bay Area. Some of the bands eventually had limited success; a few are still stumbling along (shout-outs go to Anthrax, Megadeth and Slayer), but most of these bands never put out more than an album or a single, and the majority are

Brian Lew, "Metallica, how could you?" This article first appeared in Salon.com, at http://www.salon.com. An online version remains in the Salon archives. Reprinted with permission.

now long forgotten (special shout-outs go to Jaguar, Blitzkrieg, Control and Anvil Chorus).

Back in the Stone Age, tape trades took weeks to complete as letters and packages were sent and received. Communication at that time was done by means of a now-ancient art that required the participant to be familiar with the technology of envelopes and postage. Bands would get famous without even having played a show or releasing a record, but simply on the strength of their tape getting distributed to tape traders around the world.

In 1982, an upstart band called Metallica provided a few tape-trading friends with a demo tape of seven songs, called "No Life 'Til Leather." Dubbed and re-dubbed and re-re-dubbed, the tape made its way from California to Chicago, to New York, to England, to Holland, to Germany. Within months, the band had fans worldwide—without the benefit of a publicist, an A&R person or a marketing budget. It's anybody's guess how many people were actually involved in this tape-trading network, but a good number of these charter Metallica fans were budding rock journalists who wrote for the various underground metal zines and magazines of the time (added shout-outs go to *Metal Mania, Whiplash, Aardschok* and *Metal Forces*); their enthusiasm for this unknown California band was very soon transmitted to thousands of their readers.

The rest, as they say, is history. *Kill 'Em All* was a sensation; *Master of Puppets* ended up in the Top 40 album chart; a few years later, *Metallica* would sell 12 million copies.

Despite its huge success, Metallica has tended to respect its roots. The band members realized the valuable role concert bootlegs played in building their loyal and enduring fan base. As recently as 1996, the band allowed fans to tape concerts from special taping sections. . . . In a 1997 *Musician* cover story on the commercial bootleg industry, band co-manager Peter Mensch said that by allowing fans to tape their shows, Metallica effectively killed the demand for commercial bootlegs; fans were allowed access for free to what they would otherwise buy.

10   Of course, concert bootlegs are different from pirated versions of songs lifted directly from officially released albums and singles. Pirated versions of officially released material cut directly into money, and it's not called the "music business" for nothing.

Fast forward to April 13, 2000, and the announcement that Metallica and their representatives had filed a lawsuit against the software company Napster and the University of Southern California, Yale and Indiana University.

Napster is a program that lets people swap music files (relatively) quickly and easily. The company says, in effect, that its software helps new bands distribute their music and that it's not the company's fault that users are abusing the technology to distribute copyrighted songs. Metallica argued that the program stole their intellectual property. They also contended that the universities were a partner in this because college students using the schools' networks seemed to be the biggest users of Napster's software....

Personally, I'm torn. The Internet allows such rapid dissemination of information that it potentially can be an incredible way to distribute music. When I think back about how it used to take weeks to receive a cassette of new songs by a band through the mail, it's astounding that the same task now takes only minutes or even seconds.

On the other hand, since I happen to work as the copyright and licensing person for a major book publisher, I completely understand Metallica's position. The songs *do* belong to them. They worked hard to create them and registered them for copyright protection.

15   But Napster isn't doing the actual pirating of the songs; it's the users who are the culprits. Can the company and universities really be held accountable? Should Xerox machines be held accountable for the magazine articles and book chapters illegally copied on them? Should Kinko's? I don't know.

In the end, success is a double-edged sword. Twenty years ago, we swapped music. Today, the same thing is referred to with words like "commodity" and "goods"—both part of the wording in Metallica's press release concerning the lawsuit. After 50 million-plus albums, the band's music *is* a commodity now.

The tape-trading days of the early '80s were very innocent. It was all for the love of the commodity—er, music. To their credit, Metallica are one of the few to claw their way out of that metal underground scene; it's also to their credit that they're still going strong. Still, the fact that they're attempting to crush something that would allow a young upstart band the same kind of underground exposure once afforded them is ironic.

Beyond the legal issues, I think the Internet has also taken some of the mystery and excitement out of discovering new music. Yes, it's definitely making it more convenient, but with convenience can come apathy. There's something compelling about taking the time and making the effort to dub a cassette. (Adjust those levels! Do you want Dolby with that?) You put it into an envelope, throw it into the nearest mailbox and have it delivered to a far-off destination. Once there, another music lover opens the package, pops it into a tape deck and the magic of sharing happens. Yes, the Internet is about sharing information, but downloading a file onto your hard drive and opening the file in Real Audio just isn't as exciting to me.

Press eject and give me the tape.

TECHNIQUES FOR WRITERS 6-c
Rhetoric Online: A Drummer's Lament

Lars Ulrich, the drummer for Metallica, joined the conversation about music downloading by publishing an essay titled "It's Our Property" in the June 5, 2000, issue of *Newsweek*. Using your college library's online database search, or a Web-search resource such as Google, locate a copy of Ulrich's essay and print it for inclusion as a possible source for an argument on the topic of music downloading. The library search can simply include "Ulrich" as the author last name and "Property" as a title keyword, while the string

> lars ulrich "it's our property"

will locate any full-text versions of the essay that may be reproduced free on the Web. You may also want to search for "ulrich napster" or "metallica napster" to locate a wealth of published material covering this musician's legal campaign to shut down the original (free) version of Napster.com in the late 1990s.

The Artists: It's the Music, Stupid
Lorraine Ali

The music industry can sue every middle-schooler from Poughkeepsie to Palo Alto, but record labels will not cure their woes if they continue to churn out cut-rate albums at top-rate prices. For the past five years, they've been pedaling anti-art: boy bands, Britney and "The Thong Song." Judging by sales numbers, kids finally figured that a lot of artists were only as good as their Svengalis, or that an entire album by 98 Degrees was really just a single with filler.

"Who expects a 12-year-old girl to buy a $20 record with her baby-sitting money for one good song?" says singer-songwriter Michelle Branch, 20, whose 2001 single "Everywhere" [was] one of the top swaps. As a teen, she lifted some of her favorite singles off the Internet. "Why not download the one song you like?"

Few top-grossing musicians want to criticize file sharing since Lars Ulrich of Metallica was verbally attacked by fans and peers for condemning piracy at a Senate hearing in 2000. In fact, many labels didn't want their artists speaking to *Newsweek* for this story. It's likely that rappers Eminem and 50 Cent now agree with Ulrich because, as top sellers, they stand to lose millions. But opinions differ radically depending on an artist's success. Punk upstarts like the Ataris—who have nothing to lose—have embraced file swapping. The spiky-haired outfit used Napster and MP3.com to promote its first three independent albums and build up a fan base before signing with Columbia. . . . When its cover of Don Henley's "Boys of Summer" became a hot download, the band's members couldn't have been happier. "If our single is downloaded, then maybe they'll buy the whole album," says Ataris singer Kris Roe. "And if they download the whole record, then maybe they'll come see us play. We just want to be heard."

For midrange artists who feel loyal to their fans *and* their major labels, file sharing can be a fence-sitter. Ideologically, they still relate to the "get stuff free" ethos of fans and once relied on swappers to promote their music. But now they stand to lose a chunk of their income. S-Curve Records' Fountains of Wayne worry about high-volume swaps of their single "Stacy's Mom." "We want new fans," says Fountain's Adam Schlesinger. "But we don't want to stop playing music because the business falls apart around us."

5   Ironically, file sharing may play a large part in artists' salvation. It's an alternative to stale radio playlists, levels the field for lesser-known acts and makes kids excited about discovering "new" artists—no hype or slick packaging required. "There's no other place where you have that option," says Branch. "You find it on your own, and it becomes your own."

Students Shall Not Download. Yeah, Sure.
Kate Zernike

STATE COLLEGE, Pa., Sept. 17 — In the rough and tumble of the student union here at Pennsylvania State University, the moral code is purely pragmatic.

Thou shalt not smoke — it will kill you.

Thou shalt not lift a term paper off the Internet — it will get you kicked out.

Thou shalt not use a fake ID — it will get you arrested.

5   And when it comes to downloading music or movies off the Internet, students here compare it with under-age drinking: illegal, but not immoral. Like alcohol and parties, the Internet is easily accessible. Why not download, or drink, when "everyone" does it?

This set of commandments has helped make people between the ages of 18 and 29, and college students in particular, the biggest downloaders of Internet music.

"It's not something you feel guilty about doing," said Dan Langlitz, 20, a junior here. "You don't get the feeling it's illegal because it's so easy." He held an MP3 player in his hand. "They sell these things, the sites are there. Why is it illegal?"

Students say they have had the Internet for as long as they can remember, and have grown up thinking of it as theirs for the taking. The array of services available to them on campus has only encouraged that sense.

Penn State recently made the student center, known as the Hub, entirely wireless, so students do not even have to dial up to get on the Internet. In comfortable armchairs, they sit clicking on Google searches, their ears attached to iPods, cellphones a hand away. A swipe of a student ID gets them three free newspapers. They do not need cash — only a swipe card, the cost included in their student fees — to buy anything from a caramel caffè latte to tamale pie at an abundance of fast food counters. There is a bank branch and a travel agency, and a daily activities board lists a Nascar simulator as well as rumba lessons.

10   Many courses put all materials — textbook excerpts, articles, syllabuses — online. Residence halls offer fast broadband access — which studies say makes people more likely to download. "It kind of spoils us, in a sense, because you get used to it," said Jill Wilson, 20, a sophomore.

The ease of going online has shaped not only attitudes about downloading, but cheating as well, blurring the lines between right and wrong so much that many colleges now require orientation courses that give students specific examples of what plagiarism looks like. Students generally know not to buy a paper off the Internet, but many think it is O.K. to pull a paragraph or two, as long as they change a few words.

"Before, when you had to go into the library and at least type it in to your paper, you were pretty conscious about what you were doing," said Janis Jacobs, vice-provost for undergraduate education here. "That means we do have to educate students about what is O.K. It's the same whether you're talking about plagiarizing a phrase from a book or article or downloading music — it all seems free to them."

Last year and again last week, the university sent out an e-mail message reminding students that downloading copyrighted music was illegal, and pleading with them to "resist the urge" to download. It also warned students that it had begun monitoring how much information students are downloading, and that they could lose their Internet access if their weekly use exceeded a limit administrators described as equivalent to tens of thousands of e-mail messages sent.

This year, all students had to take an online tutorial before receiving access to their e-mail accounts, acknowledging that they had read and agreed to university policy prohibiting the downloading of copyrighted material. At the same time, realizing the difficulties of stopping downloading, Penn State's president, Graham B. Spanier, is hoping to try out a program this spring where the university would pay for the rights to music, and then allow students to download at will.

15   To students, the crackdown seemed like a sudden reversal.

"Up until recently, we were not told it was wrong," said Kristin Ebert, 19. "We think if it's available, you can use it. It's another resource."

When representatives from the technology services department told students about the bandwidth monitoring, Ms. Ebert said, they outlined the reasonable limits in terms of movies downloaded. "They weren't encouraging it, but they used it as a frame of reference," she said. "They were aware, but they weren't doing anything to correct it." Penn State has taken a harder line than most other campuses. But whether here or at other campuses, students do not seem to be grasping the moral message.

According to a study by the Pew Internet and American Life Project last spring, 56 percent of college students download music, compared with about 25 percent of nonstudents, and those students are more likely than downloaders in general — 80 percent to 67 percent — to say they do not care that the music is copyrighted when they download it. (The study came before recent lawsuits by the recording industry against 261 people it says have shared copyrighted music over the Internet. But researchers defend the report's relevancy, saying it came after the industry had shut down Napster and begun a widespread advertising campaign against downloading.)

Similarly, studies by the Center for Academic Integrity show a decline in traditional peering-over-someone's-shoulder cheating, but a steady rise in Internet plagiarism from 1999 to 2003. Here, the warnings against plagiarism seem to have sunk in better than those about downloading. But even some of the lessons about plagiarism came as a surprise to students who had freely used the Internet in high school.

20   "When I came in, I didn't expect any of this to be plagiarism," said Maria Sansone, 22, a senior. "The idea you had to cite what you took off the Internet was new. I think a lot of people don't know where to draw the line."

Elizabeth Kiss, director of the Kenan Institute for Ethics at Duke University, said she suspected that older generations were not more ethical, just less techno-savvy. "I don't think we've done a very good job of making the argument that it's different if it's copyrighted," Ms. Kiss said. "If students haven't grown up with that being a conversation, they're not thinking about it."

Ann Morrissey, 19, confessed that she had not even listened to all the songs she had downloaded. "I have 400 songs, I listen to 20," she said. "I don't know why," she added, then laughed self consciously, and answered herself, "You can, and it's cool to have them." She, like others, does not see the harm done, and remains suspicious of the recording industry. "How are you going to make downloading illegal when you can still smoke legally and give yourself lung cancer?" Ms. Morrissey asked. "There are a lot worse issues you could focus on."

The university has sent warnings about exceeding bandwidth to a couple of hundred students. But on a campus with 42,000 students, punishment seems remote to many. "No one close to home has gotten in trouble," said Andrew Ricken, a junior.

A common analogy — downloading music is like stealing a CD — does not sway students. Many argue that they are spending more money on music. "I never went out and bought CD's; now I go to concerts, because I know what kind of music people play," said Kristen Lipski, 20. "If you can get your music out to a big group of people to listen to, they'll go to your CD, go to your concert, spend money on posters. It's really expensive, especially for college students, to buy the whole CD."

25   Mr. Langlitz was on his way to a concert downtown by Taking Back Sunday, a band he said he would never have heard without downloading. "A lot of the bands I know about aren't that well-known," he said. "Before I saw their CD's, I had them in my computer."

These are the same arguments adults make. But while adults who remember the days of LP's seem willing to pay 99 cents a song, students see any transition from free as a denial of basic right. "A dollar a song is just not worth it," said Edwin Shaw, a 20-year-old junior walking across campus with his MP3 player and trying to confirm which night the Red Hot Chili Peppers were playing on campus.

At best, the new warnings seemed to have some students negotiating new rules. At a table with friends, John Dixon was debating whether he would be caught if he traded songs only with his roommates on their local area network, off campus. Just to be safe, he is sticking mostly to downloading music from CD's. He is not sharing his files — not because he sees it as illegal, but because he hears that the record industry is going mainly after sharers, not downloaders. "The risk is higher," Mr. Dixon said.

Ms. Wilson, too, is not sharing, though she has continued downloading. "That doesn't make it right," she said. "But it's not that big a deal, right?"

TECHNIQUES FOR WRITERS 6-d

In Depth

Using the following two quotes and the three epigraphs that appear at the beginning of the chapter as your context, consider the earlier case of Brian Warner/Marilyn Manson. By referring to the five context quotes, explain how Warner/Manson is an "authentic" or "genuine" performer, or construct an argument to show that he is a fraud.

> The point was to be non-competitive, to say, 'I don't have to prove anything. This is me. I walked in here, off the street, and this is it. I'm not an actor. I'm in a rock band. I'm not going to compromise myself to look or be something to make you accept me.
>
> —*Chrissie Hynde of The Pretenders*

> We're not like Kiss. We break real guitars, not the fake stuff.
>
> —*Rick Nielsen of Cheap Trick*

TECHNIQUES FOR WRITERS 6-e

 Rhetoric Online: **Music Downloading—The Real Deal?**

Conduct online research and find more valid arguments, like those in one of the "Extended Readings" sections of this chapter, regarding the ethics of free music downloading— some in support of the practice, others against. These arguments should contain evidence of the rhetorical elements of ethos, pathos, and logos that were discussed in Chapter 1. In what ways do free music downloads work against the idea of a musician's authenticity as the creator of his or her songs? In what ways do copyright laws support the idea of authenticity?

TECHNIQUES FOR WRITERS 6-f

Sellout, or Fraud?

Write a two-page paper about two musicians: one whom you find to be a "sellout" and a fraud, another whom you admire for being "real." What are your criteria for making each of these judgments? (If your instructor will be reading this, remember to provide enough background so that s/he will have a clear introduction to these performers.)

TECHNIQUES FOR WRITERS 6-g
Rockin' Rush

Read the following article, "Rockin' Rush: Radio Pirate," and notice how the author turns the discussion of Rush Limbaugh's use of rock music into an argument against rock music itself. With this article as a model, craft a similar argument about the alleged "misuses" of any genre of popular music. As an alternative, write a brief argument that tries to prove a disconnect between a conservative Republican radio program and rock music. Can you defend this argument?

Rockin' Rush: Radio Pirate
David Corn and Sam Munger

Every weekday millions of Americans awaiting a fix of right-wing raving switch on their radios and hear the distinctive, funky bass riff from new-wave rocker Chrissie Hynde's song "My City Was Gone." Then the 1984 Pretenders tune fades, and the conservative tirades of Rush Limbaugh begin. As Limbaugh's three-hour gabfest continues, he routinely pumps up the show with snippets of music from past and present rock artists: Pearl Jam, Stone Temple Pilots, Jimi Hendrix, Blur, Depeche Mode, Bob Marley, Garbage. His aim, presumably, is to inject hipness into his conservatism. That he gets away with it so readily is proof of how depoliticized rock music has become. A Christian Coalition—loving, family-values advocate playing T. Rex's licentious "Bang a Gong (Get It On)"? No problem. ("One of my favorites," said Limbaugh, a former deejay.) And neither does it seem to be a problem that Limbaugh, that fierce champion of property rights, has apparently expropriated Hynde's music as his theme song in violation of copyright law. He's a radio pirate.

Recently, Limbaugh discussed on air how he came to hijack Hynde's lament over the mallification of America ("My pretty countryside/had been paved down the middle/by a government that had no pride"). Recalling the days when he was first firing up his show, Limbaugh noted that he tried

David Corn and Sam Munger, "Rockin' Rush: Radio Pirate." Reprinted with permission from the August 25, 1997 issue of *The Nation*. For subscription information, call 1-800-333-8536. Portions of each week's *Nation* magazine can be accessed at http://www.thenation.com.

a number of rock songs for his theme music. A few callers griped that a "conservative guy" should not be identified with a rock-and-roll sound. To "tweak" these fans, Limbaugh searched for "the hardest-pounding bass line" he could find and selected "My City Was Gone." Was he aware he had picked the work of an animal rights activist and an ideological opponent? He sure was. He relished that: "It was icing on the cake that it was [written by] an environmentalist, animal-rights wacko—and an anti-conservative song. . . . It is anti-development, anti-capitalist. . . . Here I am going to take a liberal song and make fun of [liberals] at the same time."

But Limbaugh never licensed his show's use of the song, according to Hynde and her manager, Gail Colson. Asked about Limbaugh's conscription of "My City Was Gone," several music licensing experts maintained that if a radio show adopts a recorded song as its theme, it must receive permission from the music publisher and the record label. (Labels often require approval by the artist, and Hynde, in addition, retains publishing rights to her songs.) As Kohn on Music Licensing, a prominent industry text, notes, "The making of recordings of introductory musical themes…as part of syndicated radio shows . . . [requires] permission from the copyright owners." Besides a license, Limbaugh would need permission to alter the song—which he has done by editing it to a seventy-five-second-long instrumental excerpt. Assuming these experts are correct, Limbaugh has stolen the intellectual property of another.

Years ago, when Limbaugh was coming into phenom status, Hynde received letters from fans who were flabbergasted to discover her art associated with the right's number-one mouth. At airports, people approached her and complained. Hynde, who has lived in England since 1973, was unfamiliar with the Limbaugh show. "From what I understood," she says, "I wouldn't be endorsing his show. I went to Kent State and we burned down the R.O.T.C. building." She asked Colson to investigate. Colson says she checked and was told Hynde could do nothing to nix this use of her song. Colson seems to have received bad advice. And until this summer, neither she nor Hynde realized that the Limbaugh show was playing an edited version of the track. "If he's redoing the song, he must license it," Colson remarks. "And there is no way we have ever cleared a license or even been asked for one." (Hynde, as the publisher and writer, does receive performance royalties through ASCAP for the airplay on Limbaugh's show.) Limbaugh did not respond to inquiries regarding "My City Was Gone."

5   "I'm sure if I heard this show," Hynde notes, "it would piss me off and I would say, get my song off right away. . . . He's obviously very clever. If he just played the Carpenters, it wouldn't cause any controversy. So now he plays rock and he's bold and a rebel. I probably should have done more when people were rushing at me in the airports. But since I had not heard the show I said, 'Oh fuck it.' That's a lazy attitude, I know. I only wanted to

be a rock singer, but I am associated with speaking my mind." Now Colson, in response to this article, has asked Hynde's label and publishing rep to research the matter. "It would be wonderful if we could get him," she says.

Few of the other musicians whose songs have been less formally recruited into Limbaugh's conservative cavalcade feel compelled to complain. The Nation surveyed twenty such artists and asked what they thought of their discs being played by Limbaugh. Most had nothing to say. The publicist for the Wallflowers (which is led by Jakob Dylan, son of Bob) replied, "I talked to the band's management, and we've decided to pass." A spokesman for Garbage said the band members "have no comment either way and don't wish to say anything. They think of themselves as apolitical and they just don't want to be in those kinds of stories." Eric Clapton, the Dave Matthews Band (fronted by a marijuana aficionado), Peter Gabriel (a human rights activist), Stone Temple Pilots, Seal, Pearl Jam (abortion-rights proponents), Reel Big Fish and the Rolling Stones declined comment. So did Bob Seger. (When Rush played a nugget of Seger's "The Fire Inside," he dedicated that day's program "to all the longhaired, maggot-infested, dope-smoking FM types.") A spokesman for Bush and Depeche Mode replied, "Both groups have the same things to say: We don't share the politics, but music's for everybody." And June Pointer of the Pointer Sisters politely responded, "Naturally when anybody likes our music, we're flattered. I believe in God's world there's room for all of us." Her manager added, "Read between the lines."

Last year, one musician nearly went after Limbaugh. When Joan Osborne was told Limbaugh had played her song "Right Hand Man," she was upset and considered issuing a public statement. Danny Goldberg, the president of her label, Mercury provided Fairness & Accuracy in Reporting with a small grant to search past Limbaugh broadcasts. FAIR found that Limbaugh had indeed played the tune, but only once. Osborne decided not to howl about this one-time offense.

Is Limbaugh a hypocrite for spicing up his program with drug anthems like "Purple Haze"? Probably. But rock music as a genre has become so content-neutral that the obvious contradictions between Limbaugh-ism and the values expressed in the music he airs do not rate high on today's outrage-o-meter. After all, for years rock has been selling soda, banking services and overpriced sneakers manufactured by underpaid workers abroad. Why not right-wing rants? "Rock music was once political and countercultural," Hynde says. "Now music is music. The whole of popular culture has gone more mainstream. And even conservatives want to be hip." Limbaugh shows how easy that is. While Hynde may have the power to make him pay for swiping one song—hers—there's not much to inhibit Limbaugh's rampant exploitation of rock music. Rush can rock—and that's less a comment on him than on the neutered culture of rock.

TECHNIQUES FOR WRITERS 6-h

Rhetoric Online: **The Professor and the Walkman**

The late professor Allan Bloom had a surprise best-seller with his book, *The Closing of the American Mind.* One aspect of this book was Bloom's strong opinion against college students, their music, and the Sony Walkmen that were popular at the time. Go online and use a service such as Google.com to enter these search strings:

- *allan bloom music*
- bloom "they find they are deaf"

Several Web sites may have a full-text copy of the author's essay titled simply, "Music," while others will offer analysis, critique, and commentary on the professor's views. After perusing a dozen or so of the better-quality online resources of information, can you identify Bloom's main argument? If so, do you find that you agree, or disagree, with his opinion? In what ways do you think the author's views were influenced by the rapidly increasing use of portable music listening technology? What would Bloom say about the Apple iPod if he were still alive today?

CHAPTER 7

Thinking Critically About Research

Believe nothing, no matter where you read it, or who said it, no matter if I have said it, unless it agrees with your own reason and your own common sense.

—Buddha (568–488 BCE)

Many research projects direct writers to "incorporate" source materials with their own opinions. The word "incorporating" has more than one meaning, but we'd like to call your attention to just one definition: "to combine or blend into a unified whole; unite" (*The American Heritage Dictionary*). This definition states the essence of what incorporating research into writing should involve: blending and uniting *your* ideas and knowledge with the research you've found into a unified, whole essay.

Too often students begin research writing with the research itself. Once they've been assigned or have chosen a topic, they head out to the library or to the Internet to gather materials. Too often the papers they produce are merely the ideas and knowledge of others cobbled together into eight, ten, or twenty-five pages devoid of the voice of the student who wrote them. At their best, these kinds of papers are merely words assembled together to achieve an acceptable grade. At their worst, these papers are plagiarized versions of others' work.

But this does not need to be the case. Research writing can be enlightening, empowering, and even exciting when it reflects the perspective of the writer. But to produce such a paper, first you need to determine the *purpose* of your assignment.

Defining the Purposes of Research Writing

Research papers are written for various purposes. The following list includes many of the most commonly assigned types of research paper:

- Exposition
  - Presents information on a particular topic—often assigned to assess students' knowledge and understanding
- Argument
  - Presents a position on a topic, usually following either the inductive or mediated patterns discussed in Chapters 3, 4, and 5
- Analysis
  - Cause and effect
    - Suggests the likely cause of a particular event or phenomenon or hypothesizes the outcome of a particular course of action
  - Comparison and/or Contrast
    - Assesses the relative benefits and disadvantages of two or more similar items or procedures, generally leading to a recommendation
- Feasibility
  - Assesses the likelihood of success for a particular plan of action
- Proposal
  - Assesses possible solutions to a problem and offers a recommendation

Developing a Research Plan

Whatever the purpose of the paper you are writing, you should invest some time in generating ideas before beginning your search for appropriate research. If your paper is an argument, consider developing a pro/con grid (see Chapter 3) that lists arguments supporting and opposing your topic. Your argument may follow the inductive or the mediated pattern, but either way your pro/con grid should include a number of arguments that represent both positions.

For arguments and all other types of research papers, it is wise to freewrite and map your topic (Chapter 4) as part of your idea generation process.

Research Questions

If well done, your freewrite and map diagram should begin to suggest some of the questions you will need to answer in order to produce a well-researched paper on your topic. In examining the freewriting and mapping he had done on the topic of hunting (Chapter 4), Matt realized that his initial research should probably begin with materials that would give answers to the following:

1. Number of hunters in the United States.
2. Numbers of deer in the United States, over past 200 years. Are numbers increasing or decreasing?
3. Annual income for resorts, restaurants, sporting goods stores, etc., brought in by hunters.

4. Annual attendance at hunters' safety classes.

5. Number of deer/car accidents in the United States per year. Number of injuries, fatalities, from those accidents. Annual expense for auto repairs caused by deer/car accidents.

6. Number of deer that die annually in accidents or of starvation.

Libraries and the Internet can seem daunting at times, with limitless amounts of information available on practically any topic. Taking the time to develop a research plan *before* you access the library or Internet will give you an advantage in efficiently finding information that meets your needs.

TECHNIQUES FOR WRITERS 7-a
Developing a Research Plan

Use freewriting, mapping, and research questions to develop a research plan for the specific topic about which you will be writing:

1. For five minutes, write freely about your topic. Don't worry about grammar or punctuation. If you run out of things to say, write "I don't know what to say" or something similar. Don't read your freewrite until the five minutes are up.

2. Mark any possible subtopics you have generated during your freewrite. Use these and any other subtopics you can think of as initial points to construct a map diagram on your topic.

3. After examining your map diagram, produce a list of five to ten of the initial questions you'll need to answer when you begin to research your topic.

If you haven't yet made a decision about a topic from a number of possibilities, doing these activities with two or three of your most likely topics can help you decide which topic would be the most feasible and interesting to pursue.

Comparing the Qualities of Varieties of Sources

One way to classify the various sources available to you is to consider a source *primary research* if it is information you have produced or analyzed yourself and *secondary research* if it is information that has been summarized, paraphrased, or quoted from a printed or otherwise already prepared source. Using this classification system, material gathered from the following sources would be considered primary research:

- interviews (personal, telephone, e-mail)
- personal and e-mail letters of inquiry
- researcher-conducted surveys and questionnaires

    Material gathered from the following sources is considered secondary research:

- books
- magazines and newspapers
- journals
- Internet and information services (i.e., FirstSearch, ERIC) articles
- professional literature (i.e., brochures, manuals)
- films, music, television, and radio programs

    Whether the source is primary or secondary, research gains its validity when it is based on one of the categories of research-based *topoi* discussed below.

Research-based *Topoi:* Strategies for Validating Sources

In Chapter 5, we discussed a number of Aristotle's *topoi,* strategies used to develop and support an argument. But Aristotle recognized that, in order to construct a convincing argument, communicators must incorporate material and ideas from outside their own set of ideas or thought processes. The following *topoi* are strategies that can help you to determine the validity of your research.

Authority

The American Heritage Dictionary defines "authority" as "an accepted source of expert information." Authority can involve primary (interview, survey) or secondary (Internet, journal article, book) research. An authority is an individual whose knowledge and ability are recognized by colleagues or peers, whether in skateboarding, orchid cultivation, cardiology, or any other subject. Sometimes authorities are called upon to testify in such formal argumentative venues as courtrooms and legislative assemblies. That's why, in talking about research, teachers often refer to "expert testimony" as a means of support for the main topic or argument.

    But authorities can, and do, disagree. Every field has areas of dispute, with authorities promoting the various positions in any controversy. In incorporating research from authorities into your writing, it's important to establish their credentials and to determine whether they are representative of their field. To establish credentials, look for such information as earned degrees, employment backgrounds, publication records, and membership in recognized organizations. Then compare your potential source's work with that of other authorities in the field. If you find major discrepancies in a source, reconsider using it in your research.

Laws

Legal opinions have appeared everywhere from biblical injunctions (the Old Testament contains books listing nothing but the laws of the day) to constitutional language, to local statutes, to written contracts. In Chapter 3 on Affirmative Action and college admissions, for example, we can follow a trail of laws and court decisions ranging from the Civil Rights Act of 1964 to *Grutter v. Bollinger* (the 2003 Supreme Court ruling concerning the University of Michigan's admissions policy) and beyond.

But it's important to realize that an argument does not end once someone creates a law concerning that argument. Laws can become outdated or contradictory, and all laws are subject to discussion and continual change—or removal from the legal code. Even the justices of the Supreme Court have occasionally reversed decisions made by earlier Supreme Courts. Using laws as part of your support for an argument can be very persuasive, but this doesn't mean your argument is airtight and safe from challenge and refutation. Martin Luther King's famous "Letter from Birmingham Jail" (see Chapter 4), for instance, contains a lengthy argument in defense of breaking laws when those laws are unjust.

Facts and Statistics

It may appear that facts and statistics rely entirely on logic, but this isn't the case. Facts and statistics need to be analyzed and interpreted before you include them in your argument, because sometimes the analysis will show how bias and manipulation of the information can occur.

For example, if the National Plywood Association presented statistics based on a survey of its members and stated that, based on those statistics, most Americans favor cutting down forests, the statistics would be misleading, because NPA members are not a representative sample of Americans in general. The same would be true if People for the Ethical Treatment of Animals, using a sampling of PETA members, declared that most Americans oppose using animals for research. The logical fallacy here, sometimes called a *hasty generalization,* comes from the sample size being both too small and too biased toward one outcome.

Another reason to be careful with facts and statistics is that readers can often misunderstand the difference between numbers and on percentages. The following article from the educational journal *Phi Delta Kappan* discusses ways in which readers can be misled through statistics.

Tips for Readers of Research: Numbers Versus Percentages

Gerald W. Bracey

Some things are important enough to be repeated, in part because they keep cropping up again and again. Herewith a repeat: be aware of whether you are dealing with percentages or numbers. The two often present different pictures of a condition or a trend. Anyone who visited the U.S. Department of Education's website (www.ed.gov) in November 2002 would have seen a graph (reproduced below) comparing spending increases in three federal departments.

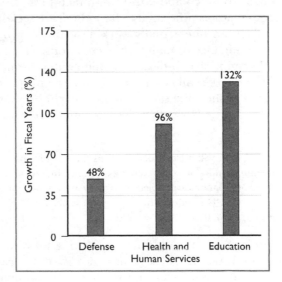

The immediate visual impression the chart gives is that President Clinton's second term and the first half of President Bush's first term have favored education over everything else. But these are percentages. The numbers present a different picture.

President's Proposed Budget Fiscal Year 2003

Health & Human Services	$459 billion
Defense	$368 billion
Education	$48 billion

From Gerald W. Bracey, "Tips for Readers of Research: Numbers Versus Percentages," *Phi Delta Kappan,* January 2003, pp. 410–411. Reprinted by permission of Phi Delta Kappa International.

Doubling the budget for the Department of Education to $96 billion would be the equivalent of only a little more than a 10% increase in the budget for the Department of Health and Human Services or a 13% increase in the budget for the Department of Defense. In the chart, the "Historic Increases" are expressed in percentages, which are a measure of *rate* of increase. The budget, though, is in terms of *numbers*—how many dollars are involved.

Jobs, Jobs, Jobs: Numbers Versus Percentages Again

One place where numbers and percentages have been repeatedly confused—sometimes for political and ideological purposes—is in the arena of jobs. We hear that today's students will be "knowledge workers." We hear that the "fastest-growing" jobs are all high-tech, high-skill areas.

5   We don't hear so much about the "high-tech jobs" anymore—except when we hear that people who used to have them are seeking employment elsewhere. In fact, no one actually working with job growth ever made claims for the dominance of high-tech occupations. The most recent projections for jobs continue to indicate that high-skill jobs and jobs requiring at least a college degree will continue to grow as a proportion of all jobs, but will continue to show the same slow growth they have shown over the last few decades. In the November 2001 *Monthly Labor Review*, economist Daniel Hecker wrote:

> Most new jobs, however, will arise in occupations that require only work-related training (on-the-job training or work-related experience in a related occupation), even though these occupations are projected to grow more slowly on average [than in previous projections]. This reflects the fact that these occupations accounted for about 7 out of 10 jobs in 2000.

Hecker's projections for the 10 fastest-growing jobs from 2000 to 2010 are displayed in Table 1. These numbers reveal several things. First, although the dot-com bubble has "burst," high-tech occupations still dominate the projections for rapid growth. Second, most, but not all, of these jobs pay pretty well; the majority are in the top quartile of pay for all jobs. Third, the nation is aging; hence, the rapidly growing need for personal and home-care aides and medical assistants, who earn only low wages.

Hecker's projections for the 10 occupations that will offer the largest numbers of jobs are displayed in Table 2, and they look quite different. Truck and tractor-trailer drivers are 11th, followed by elementary school teachers.

These numbers are revealing as well. They show that retail sales, the occupation that accounts for the largest number of jobs in 2000, will also account for the largest number of jobs in 2010. Moreover, retail sales account for more jobs in 2000 than the top 10 fastest-growing jobs combined and will come close to doing so in 2010 as well. Retail sales will add more jobs than any of the fastest-growing categories, but, because it is starting from such a large base, its percentage growth is small, just 12%.

10   These numbers also show that eight of the top 10 occupations with lots of jobs don't pay well: they place in the third or fourth quartile of pay for all jobs. . . .

TABLE 1 Ten Fastest-Growing Jobs, 2000–2010, in Thousands

Occupation	2000	2010	Percent Change	Quartile Rank For Earnings
Computer software engineers, applications	380	760	100	1
Computer support specialists	506	996	97	2
Computer software engineers, systems	317	601	90	1
Network computer systems administrators	229	416	82	1
Network and communications systems analysts	119	21	77	1
Desktop publishers	38	63	67	2
Database administrators	106	176	66	1
Personal and home-care aides	414	672	62	4
Computer systems analysis	431	689	60	1
Medical assistants	329	516	57	3
Totals	2,869	5,100		

TABLE 2 Ten Occupations Offering Most Jobs, 2000–2010, in Thousands

Occupation	2000	2010	Percent Change	Quartile Rank For Earnings
Retail sales	4,109	4,619	12	4
Cashiers	3,325	3,799	14	4
Office clerks (general)	2,705	3,135	16	3
General and operations managers	2,398	2,761	15	1
Janitors and cleaners (excluding maids and housekeepers)	2,348	2,665	13	4
Food preparation (including fast food)	2,206	2,879	30	4
Registered nurses	2,194	2,755	26	1
Laborers and material movers	2,084	2,373	14	3
Waiters and waitresses	1,983	2,347	18	4
Customer service reps	1,946	2,577	32	3
Totals	25,298	29,910		

In fact, given the high proportion of people attending college and completing college, we can say for certain that some college graduates will have to take jobs for which they need no college. Such a conclusion is reinforced by looking at the data displayed in Table 3.

TABLE 3 Most Significant Source of Education or Training, in Thousands

	Employment		Percentage	
Most Significant Source	*2000*	*2010*	*2000*	*2010*
First professional degree*	2,034	2,404	1.4	1.4
Doctoral degree	1,492	1,845	1.0	1.1
Master's degree	1,426	1,845	1.0	1.0
Bachelor's or higher (plus work experience)	7,319	8,741	5.0	5.2
Bachelor's degree	17,801	21,807	12.2	13.0
Associate's degree	5,083	6,710	3.5	4.0
Postsecondary vocational award	6,678	7,891	4.6	4.7
Work experience in related occupation	10,456	11,559	7.2	6.9
Long-term on-the-job training**	12,435	13,373	8.5	8.0
Moderate-term on-the-job training	27,671	30,794	19.0	18.4
Short-term on-the-job training	53,198	60,871	36.5	36.3

*A first professional degree, such as a law degree, is any professional degree requiring three or more years of continuous study.

**In the Bureau of Labor Statistics system, long-term training is more than one year, moderate-term training is one month to one year, and short-term training is one week to one month.

Short-term on-the-job training dominates the list in both 2000 and 2010. Indeed, the second-largest category consists of jobs that require "moderate-term on-the-job training." Currently, almost 21% of jobs require at least a bachelor's degree, and 8% require an associate's degree or some vocational certificate. But fully 71% qualify people through on-the-job training. The proportion of jobs requiring academic degrees is projected to grow slightly over the decade, while the proportion that require on-the-job training will decline slightly. But the projections hardly show a revolutionary shift in job requirements. . . .

Following General Research Guidelines

■ Go for a quantity of information. If your assignment requires eight sources, find sixteen. It's much better to discard less useful sources than to try to force weak research to work for you.

- Be sure that your research includes several kinds of sources. Sixteen journal articles or 16 Web sites comprise equally weak research: neither gives insight into the full range of information available on any topic.

- Assess the quality of your research. Is it current? In today's fast-paced flow of information, a source even five years old can be outdated. However, you can certainly use sources that are even decades old as examples of their time, as historical information, or as points of contrast to the current day. Can you determine whether the author or authors are experts in the field? Is any of the information inconsistent or illogical? Does it agree with other research you have found? Are claims too good to be true? The magnitude of easily accessible information available on the Internet presents its own challenges in finding good research, because it may take a considerable amount of detective work to determine the reliability of the information you find.

- Be sure you understand what your sources are saying. Journal articles, for example, are written for experts in their fields, and while an article from *JAMA* (*Journal of the American Medical Association*) may look impressive on a Works Cited page, its effect will be greatly diminished if your incorporation of material from that source shows little actual comprehension of the information.

- Carefully document your source, both within the paper and on your Works Cited page, using the documentation format specified by your teacher. Documentation is not a place to display creativity. Good documentation requires attention to detail and careful modeling of examples. This textbook provides a basic listing of MLA and APA formats for commonly used sources, but your teacher may also direct you to a handbook or online guide for a more comprehensive list.

Following Guidelines for Electronic Research

Often, when students are assigned a research project, they immediately turn to the Internet. While the Internet is an almost inconceivably vast and quick source of information, often dozens of sites must be sorted through before any truly useful information can be found and many Web sites are too commercial, personal, or biased to use for serious research. An extreme example of this appears at the Web site martinlutherking.org, which at first glance may appear to be a high school-level resource for information about the Civil Rights leader—but on closer examination (following the links at the bottom of the home page) is maintained by a white supremacist organization called Stormfront.

Dubious sources are not a problem, however, with electronic databases such as Wilson Select, FirstSearch, or General Reference Center Gold. These databases access only selected sources, filtering out much of the inappropriate or unusable information you would find in sites accessed through Internet search engines such as Google or Yahoo.

Research Basics: Electronic Databases

1. Go to your school's home page on the Web.

2. Follow links to the Library page.

3. Click on links provided to online resources (typically, catalogs of books and periodicals).

4. If necessary, log in with your library card number or student ID. Typically, this step will only be required if you're accessing your school's library from an off-campus location.

5. If you're looking for books, the search screen that will open should be fairly self-explanatory. If you're searching for periodicals and articles, then you'll typically see a list of the databases that your school's library subscribes to. Each database will offer a slightly different service; for example, OCLC FirstSearch provides *full-text* articles, while other databases, such as General Reference Center Gold, often provide only partial information, such as abstracts and summaries.

6. After selecting a main database, you may be presented with a pop-up menu containing even more choices. If so, make your selection from that menu.

7. Enter your search terms. Typically, a database will offer you several search fields to narrow your topic. For example, if you are researching the contested national election of 2000, you can enter "Election 2000" in the first box, "Supreme Court" in the second, and "Bush and Gore" in the third. The resulting "hits" (search results) will be ones that contain only those three key items.

8. Click "Search." Your returns will show up in a list, with a total number of results typically listed at the top or bottom of the page.

9. Scan through the list of results. When you see an article that looks promising, click on one of the viewing options offered to you. Many databases allow you to "View article in HTML" or "View article as PDF file." HTML (hypertext markup language) is basic Web format, which opens much faster; PDF is an Adobe Acrobat Portable Document Format, which tends to open more slowly, but will often show the document exactly as it appeared, including illustrations, ads, and original pagination.

10. From here, many school libraries have their systems set up so that you can e-mail articles to yourself, rank and select some articles while eliminating others, or print an article after you've scanned it thoroughly for content. (Many schools allow you to print only a limited number of pages, after which you'll be charged a small fee for each extra page.) *Be sure to get the basic citation information from the document*—author, title, publication name, date, page range. You'll need these for your Works Cited or References page. (Many students who forget this step have to go back and retrace their steps later in order to get the information.)

See the following figures for examples of what you may see onscreen during your electronic search process:

Election 2000 Revisited.
Author: Franck, Matthew J. **Source:** Presidential Studies Quarterly v. 33 no1 (Mar. 2003) p. 238-42 **Libraries Worldwide:** 819
, ⬛ View Full Text in PDF format (WilsonSelectPlus) ⬛ View Full Text in HTML format (WilsonSelectPlus)

Supreme Democracy: Bush v. Gore Redux.
Author: Guinier, Lani. **Source:** Loyola University Chicago Law Journal v. 34 no1 (Fall 2002) p. 23-76 **Libraries Worldwide:** 277
, ⬛ View Full Text in PDF format (WilsonSelectPlus) ⬛ View Full Text in HTML format (WilsonSelectPlus)

Bush V. Gore and the French Revolution: A Tentative List of Some Early Lessons.
Author: Levinson, Sanford. **Source:** Law and Contemporary Problems v. 65 no3 (Summer 2002) p. 7-39
Libraries Worldwide: 1181 ⬛ MOTT COMMUN COL LIBR , ⬛ View Full Text in PDF format (WilsonSelectPlus)
⬛ View Full Text in HTML format (WilsonSelectPlus)

Figure 7.1 Sample result from *article* search terms entered into Wilson Select Plus. Reprinted by permission of OCLC. FirstSearch is a registered trademark of OCLC Online Computer Library Center, Inc.

It is, of course, possible that both high courts were wrong: the Florida Supreme Court in rewriting its state's election laws, invading the province of executive discretion, torturing its state constitution to find grounds for its impulses, and abusing its equitable power to fashion remedies, and the U.S. Supreme Court in intervening at all in an election conducted under state laws authoritatively interpreted by a state's highest court and discovering a wholly new species of constitutional violation to justify its intervention (the unequal treatment of similar ballots under the eyes of different examiners during a statewide recount). Yet those who would largely ignore the subject of the state court's behavior, to focus on that of the national court, owe readers two things.

Figure 7.2 Sample quote from the first source shown in Figure 7.1.

> AUTHOR: Matthew J. Franck
>   TITLE: Election 2000 Revisited
> SOURCE: Presidential Studies Quarterly 33 no1 238-42 Mr 2003

Figure 7.3 Vital information to record for this source.

> ⊚ http://newfirstsearch.oclc.org/WebZ/FTFETCH?sessionid=sp07

Figure 7.4 The URL (Web address) to include with the information in Figure 7.3. Note: End the URL after the "org," because the rest is internal Library information.

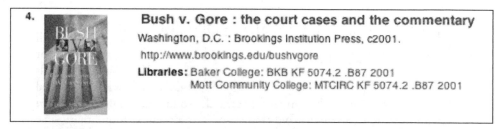

4. **Bush v. Gore : the court cases and the commentary**
Washington, D.C. : Brookings Institution Press, c2001.
http://www.brookings.edu/bushvgore
Libraries: Baker College: BKB KF 5074.2 .B87 2001
       Mott Community College: MTCIRC KF 5074.2 .B87 2001

Figure 7.5 First sample result listing from "Library Catalog/FALCON *book* search. Note: Look after the word "Libraries" to see if the book is owned by your school's library. Screenshot Copyright 2004, Dynix Corporation. Reprinted by permission. Cover of *Bush v. Gore* reprinted by permission of The Brookings Institution Press.

Bush v. Gore : the court cases and the commentary /

Washington, D.C. : Brookings Institution Press, c2001.

Subjects	• Bush, George W. (George Walker), 1946- -- Trials, litigation, etc.
	• Gore, Albert, 1948- -- Trials, litigation, etc.
	• Contested elections -- United States.
	• Contested elections -- Florida.
	• Presidents -- United States -- Election -- 2000.
Web Location	http://www.brookings.edu/bushvgore
Description:	xiv, 344 p. ; 23 cm.
Summary:	"In the first half of this volume gathers what we and the editors at the Brookings Institution Press believe to be the most important legal documents in the Bush-Gore confrontation...The book begins with the early advisory rulings on the recounts by Florida state officials. It moves on to the intermediate court rulings and ends with the critical decisions in early December by the Florida Supreme Court and the United States Supreme Court. We have included the dissents in all the major cases...The second half of the book consists of contemporary commentaries on the controversy. These include columns, mazagine articles, editorials and also a few news stories that shed important light on the issues at stake" – p.2.
ISBN:	0815701071 (alk. paper)
Notes:	Includes index.
Additional Authors:	Dionne, E. J.
	Kristol, William.
Additional Title:	Bush versus Gore
	Bush vs. Gore

(Add to my list)   (Request Item)

Copy/Holding information

Location	Call No.	Status
MCC - Flint	KF 5074.2 .B87 2001	Checked In

(All Locations)

Figure 7.6 Detailed information after clicking on book title shown in the Figure 7.5. Note: Look at the bottom of the details to find the book's call number (shelf location) and to see whether it's currently checked in and available to you. Screenshot Copyright 2004, Dynix Corporation. Reprinted by permission. Cover of *Bush v. Gore* and excerpt from page 2 reprinted by permission of The Brookings Institution Press.

Evaluating Web Sites for Validity, Reliability, and Credibility: An Example

The Internet is an inexhaustible source of information, but because of the wide range of materials found on the Web, using it for research requires additional knowledge to ascertain the validity, reliability, and credibility of information found there. The following information will help you to become a better Internet researcher.

Your general subject: Quality of American cars, 1960–Present

Your thesis: By returning to the features that appealed to buyers in past decades, American car companies can rebuild the market share they lost during the era of "generic box" vehicle styling.

Your first case study as support: Ford Mustang.

1. **Scan the domain name for preliminary information.** After searching for the specific term, "Ford Mustang," scan through the domain names in the URLs that appear as search returns. The domain name will often reveal a great deal of information. For example:

   www.fordvehicles.com/cars/mustang

   www.fordheritage.com/mustang

   www.powertoysforpowerboys.net/mustang

   www.aol.com/users/~jimsmith/mustangsrule

   The first domain name belongs to Ford Motor Company, and is the section of its main Web site dedicated to information about a specific vehicle, the Mustang. The second domain name is less clear, and will need investigation—clicking on it takes you to another section of Ford Motor Company's Web site, this one dedicated to the Mustang's history through all of the car's various body styles and engine sizes. The third domain name pretty clearly indicates that it is *not* owned by Ford: it ends in ".net" rather than ".com," and its name alone reveals a specific way of looking at the car as a *power toy* for "power boys" rather than a vehicle. Finally, the fourth domain name belongs to AOL, a mass Internet provider to millions of users—including someone named Jim Smith, whose personal opinion is that "Mustangs rule." (The latter two Web sites here are hypothetical examples.)

   Domain names end in suffixes such as *.com* (commercial/for-profit), *.org* (nonprofit), *.net* (Internet or network), *.edu* (education), *.gov* (government), and country specifications such as *.uk* (United Kingdom/England), *.jp* (Japan), and *.de* (Deutschland/Germany). But suffixes alone can't reveal whether a Web site is valid, reliable, and credible. Many colleges and universities give their students personal Web space with ".edu" domains, and students can post any materials they like—including highly dubious research findings—on that Web space. Nonprofit ".org" domains are essentially for sale to anyone who pays for them, so a Web site called martinlutherking.org, for example, can be (and is) an anti-Civil Rights propaganda tool owned by a white supremacy group. Thus, you need to investigate further than the domain-name scan.

2. **Scan the home page, then read the "About Us" link.** Unless its ownership is very obvious, a professionally assembled Web site will always include a link at the bottom of the home (main) page that takes users to a page of background information about the site's owners. Most often this link is titled "About Us," but variations can include "Who We Are," "More About [Company or Site Name]," "Our History," and the like. No matter what it's called, you want to click on this link after scanning the home page and determining that the site might be a useful resource for your research project. In our Mustang example, the site at fordvehicles.com is obviously owned by Ford Motor Company, but even so, the bottom of the Mustang's home page reveals "© 2005 Ford Motor Company"—and clicking on the copyright phrase takes viewers to the Ford home page. The second site at fordheritage.com is less clear in its ownership, and because the blue oval Ford logo can be pasted onto anyone's Web site, scrolling down to the bottom of the page once again reveals "© 2003 Ford Motor Company." As before, clicking on those words takes viewers directly to the Ford home page.

The third site, powertoysforpowerboys, looks professional enough, but pretty quickly clues start to add up about its reliability. Clicking on the "General Info" link at the side of the page (rather than at the bottom) does nothing—the link is broken. Scanning through the main page's text reveals a lot of first-person references: "my passion," "I enjoy," "contact me," and others. But most seriously, a number of blatant misspellings and grammar problems ("i have always luvd the mustangs style") reveal that the site is *not* professional and should not be used as a source of information. Finally, the fourth site at AOL, put together by Jim Smith, isn't completely unreadable in its combination of orange text on a yellow background, and it does have a "More about me" link at the bottom of the page. But clicking on it reveals only that he is married, enjoys NASCAR and drag races, and also builds outdoor furniture—which can be viewed at another page on his site. Jim's main page about Mustangs does contain links to reviews of the car (all positive) and to many photographs of Mustangs through the years, but as these photographs have been taken from Ford Motor Company's Web site anyway, you're much better off going there and leaving Jim to his furniture.

3. **Use Google to determine who else finds the site valid, reliable, and credible.** The Google search engine (http://www.google.com) is a powerful resource in determining the overall value of Web sites as research materials, not only in its ability to find the sites themselves, but also by offering tools for cross-referencing the results. Once you've found a Web site that, based on the first two evaluation criteria here, seems sound, copy its URL (Web address) and then paste that URL into the Google search field. Google will then offer you four choices, as shown here:

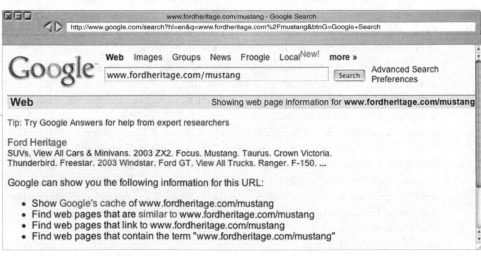

Google is a trademark of Google Inc.

Clicking on the first choice, "Google's cache," will show the site itself. (Useful for times when a server has crashed or been taken offline, and you want to see how the Web site appeared while it was up.) Clicking on the second choice can be quite rewarding, as it often leads you to other sites that can provide you with even more of the kinds of information you're seeking. In this case, for example, Google's "similar to" tool leads to a Ford-owned site specializing in the Mustang's *design*—exactly your focus. (See the third return in the picture below.)

Google is a trademark of Google Inc.

Clicking the "link to" tool can be valuable in determining what kinds of organizations and individuals provide links to the site you're investigating. In our Mustang example, it's not surprising to find that the "link to" search reveals a list of about 20 car enthusiasts and historians, but in the case of a deceptive Web site such as martinlutherking.org, mentioned earlier, using the "link to" tool reveals hundreds of hate sites and a number of school and city library pages cautioning users to evaluate Web sources carefully. Finally, clicking the "contain the term" tool can, like the "similar to" tool, reveal other potentially useful sources of information for your project, as the listing will contain many organizations with interests and expertise equivalent to the site you're investigating.

4. **For absolute confirmation, use "whois" to determine ownership, then run a Google search on the owner listed.** Occasionally, even a careful application of the first three evaluation criteria here won't be enough for you to be able to confirm, with absolute certainty, that a site's owners are valid and reliable. In our Mustang example, there's no need to dig deeper because the car's manufacturer is well known, all links have confirmed that Ford is the parent sponsor for the Mustang section of Ford's Web site, and nothing has happened in our searching

to make us question (a) what kind of company Ford is or (b) whether it's truly the site's owner.

But sometimes things aren't quite as clear. For example, a student researching the general subject "child abuse" will likely receive search returns from the domain child.com, and clicking on the "About Us" link at that site's home page reveals that the site is an online component of *Child* magazine. Searching for *Child* magazine, in turn, returns the domain childmagazine.com—and clicking on that link takes you right back to the Web site at child.com. The articles and information at the site seem excellent as potential sources for your argument, but the issue remains: who owns this site? Can the owners be confirmed as valid, reliable, and credible? Because the investigation so far has just taken you in a circle, you need to become familiar with another tool, known as a "whois" search. By using the search function at any free whois Web site—some recent examples include easywhois.com and betterwhois.com—you can do an ownership and registration search for any domain. Simply type the name of the domain (e.g., *child.com*) in the search box.

5. **Determine the site's main focus and potential bias.** Essentially, Web sites exist for one of two main reasons: to *inform* or *persuade* viewers who visit them. And either of those tasks can be done in an *objective* or *subjective* fashion—in other words, with or without *bias,* or preference. Our friend Jim Smith at AOL, for example, reveals his bias from the start with the domain name mustangsrule. Ford Motor Company, on the other hand, can't reasonably be expected to present an unbiased history of the car's design and performance. Certainly not everyone found each of the Mustang's various body styles appealing or even desirable, but you won't learn this from its manufacturer's Web site. Does this mean that, after all of the reliability testing you've done, you have to throw away the source? No, but it does mean that you should acknowledge the bias when you use the source as support for your argument. By acknowledging what you see, you build

TECHNIQUES FOR WRITERS 7-b

Rhetoric Online: Ownership and Reliability

Use a service such as Google.com to locate a free whois search site and determine the ownership of the child.com Web site. Then run a separate search, again on a service such as Google, for the company name listed by your whois results as the Registrant or Owner.

Based on what you find, would you say that information found on the child.com site is solid and reliable? Why or why not?

a positive ethos, which helps to make your argument even stronger. Failing to acknowledge bias—or pretending it isn't there—creates a negative ethos and in turn makes the argument weaker.

In general, follow this rule: *Don't just collect Web sources—research them.* An argument supported by *research* should reflect what the word entails: investigation, questioning, searching. If a Web site provides a link to an article, are you sure that the *whole* article is there? If all of the articles listed as links are positive, are you seeing the full picture of the issue? If the links span a long period of time with a gaping hole in the middle, do you really think that nothing was written about the issue during those years? If a court case is summarized and presents only the plaintiff's account of events, is it really feasible that no one recorded what the defendant said? These are only a few examples of the kinds of *critical questioning* that you need to bring to the research process, especially when evaluating potential bias from Web sources.

6. **Know the difference between an "article from a Web site" and an article in an online publication.** Anyone can copy, paste, and edit text on a computer. In fact, due to page space considerations, we've found it necessary to delete some of the extraneous information in the photos of Web pages in this chapter. We haven't changed the accuracy of the core information, nor have we edited any of the text that does appear in the photos, and when you visit the sites yourself, you'll see what's been deleted. In other words, we have nothing to hide, and no reservations in telling you about the selective editing that's been necessary. But this isn't always the case when the people who construct Web sites provide articles, essays, and other source materials to viewers in an effort to inform or persuade them. Our friend Jim Smith at AOL can do a number of things in an effort to persuade us that "Mustangs rule" and always have. He can:

- Attribute a review written by a friend or neighbor—or himself—to a respected automotive publication.
- Reproduce a review that weighed both positive and negative aspects of a model year, but delete all of the negative references—or change them to positives.
- Reproduce only articles from fan magazines, which themselves don't print negative reviews or comments about the car.
- Paraphrase reviews inaccurately.
- Provide links to the original articles for verification, but alter the URLs so that clicking on them produces a "404: Not Found" message.
- Fail to provide links to the original articles, or fail to attribute the articles to any specific authors or publications.

For all of these reasons, you should forget about Jim Smith, and in general avoid the "articles from Web sites" approach to research.

Instead, use *online publications*—Internet versions of publications that also appear in print. For example, www.nytimes.com is the online version of the *New*

York Times, known as "the newspaper of record" or "the nation's newspaper," while www.autonews.com is the Web's home to *Automotive News,* an industry publication, and www.caranddriver.com is *Car and Driver* magazine's online twin. By insisting on these kinds of sources instead of generic "articles from Web sites," you're assured that you'll be looking at those articles in exactly the form in which they originally appeared. (Note that some online publications charge a fee for archived materials—in which case you should first ask your school's reference librarian if the publication is available in the library's collection.)

TECHNIQUES FOR WRITERS 7-c

Rhetoric Online: **Real Research Evaluation Worksheet**

Your general subject: ————————————————————————————
Your thesis: ————————————————————————————————
Your specific Web search: ——————————————————————————

In two to three detailed and well-developed pages, please provide answers to the following questions. (Be sure to refer to the preceding section of this chapter for specific terminology and techniques, as your goal is to demonstrate your understanding of the information there.)

1. After scanning the domain names for preliminary information, what were three of your main observations?

2. After scanning the home page and following the "About Us" link, what did you learn about two of the potential sources?

3. After using Google to determine who else finds one of your potential sources to be valid, reliable, and credible, what were the overall results of your investigation?

4. What were the results of your "whois" search to determine ownership on one of the sources, if ownership was not obvious? (If it was, explain why/how.)

5. How would you describe the main focus of two of your potential sources? Do either of them reveal any bias that suggests you should avoid using the source?

6. How have you determined whether three of your potential sources are merely "articles from Web sites" or articles from online publications?

7. In general, how satisfied are you that your investigation of the potential sources you've described has found them to be valid, reliable, and credible?

Incorporating Summary, Paraphrase, and Direct Quotation

After gathering your research, you incorporate it into your essay through *summary, paraphrase,* and *direct quotation.* You may also be required to include tables, graphs, charts and other visuals. All research needs to be carefully cited using **parenthetical citation format,** which places relevant citation information within parentheses in the essay. (See full directions following.) A complete citation of each source must also appear on your Works Cited list at the end of the paper.

Defining Rhetoric

Parenthetical citation format: a method of documentation in which relevant citation information (i.e., author's last name, page number) is placed within parentheses immediately after the cited material.

The following information is based on MLA (Modern Language Association) documentation format, but your teacher may require that you use the APA documentation format that appears later in this chapter—or perhaps a different system such as *The Chicago Manual of Style.*

Summary and Paraphrase

A summary is a condensed version of an author's work, while a paraphrase is a retelling of the original. With both summaries and paraphrase, you set aside the original work so that you're not copying it, then write your understanding of the information *in your own words.* Because a research-supported paper should consist mainly of *your* ideas and *your* writing voice, both summary and paraphrase are important tools for avoiding a paper that's bogged down by endless quotes, although you still need to include parenthetical source citations when using them.

What, exactly, is meant by *in your own words?* Misunderstanding this short phrase can have serious consequences for students when summaries and paraphrases that resemble the original work too closely are labeled by teachers as plagiarism. **Plagiarism** is the intentional or unintentional incorporating of an author's work in a way that makes it look like your own writing and your own ideas. But disagreements can sometimes arise over how much of the original author's vocabulary or sentence structure constitutes plagiarism.

Defining Rhetoric

Plagiarism: as defined by the Council of Writing Program Administrators, "plagiarism occurs when a writer deliberately uses someone else's language, ideas, or other original (not common knowledge) material without acknowledging its source . . . or submitting someone else's text as one's own or attempting to blur the line between one's own ideas or words and those borrowed from another source." (Source: *Council Statement on Plagiarism.*) While the WPA guidelines make distinctions between "intentional" and "accidental" plagiarism, many instructors do not—so it's important to read your course syllabus and understand the plagiarism policy set forth by your particular instructor and learning institution.

Summarizing Without Plagiarizing

Constructing summaries and paraphrases while looking at the original is pretty much an invitation to disaster. A summary or paraphrase written in this way might not be an exact duplicate of the original, but it usually stands out from the rest of the essay as a reflection of the original author's writing style, not the student's writing style. Looking at some examples will help you to see the difference between plagiarized and non-plagiarized summaries and paraphrases.

The following excerpt is from Stephen L. Carter's "Racial Justice on the Cheap" (p. 87):

> With the proper goal in mind, then, a degree of racial consciousness *in college and perhaps professional school admission* can plausibly be justified—but just a degree, and just barely. The educational sphere is the place for action because the proper goal of all racial preferences is opportunity—a chance at advanced training for highly motivated people of color who, for whatever complex set of reasons, might not otherwise have it. So justified, the benefit of a racial preference carries with it the concomitant responsibility not to waste the opportunity affirmative action confers. What matter most is what happens *after* the preference.
>
> I call this vision of professional achievement and racial preference the affirmative action pyramid, and it works much as the name implies: The role of preference narrows as one moves upward. And although I do not want to say arbitrarily *This is the spot,* what is clear is that as one climbs toward professional success, at some point the preferences must fall away entirely. Possibly a slight preference is justified in college admission, not as a matter of getting the numbers right, and certainly not as a matter of finding the right set of hitherto excluded points of view, but as a matter of giving lots of people from different backgrounds the chance—only the chance—to have an education at an elite college or university. But when that opportunity has been exercised, when the student has shown what he or she can do, the rationale for a preference at the next level is

slimmer. So an even slighter affirmative action preference for professional school admission, while possibly justified on similar grounds, is less important, and a little bit harder to defend, than a program at the college level.

And when one's training is done, when the time comes for entry to the job market, I think it is quite clear that among professionals, the case for preference evaporates. The candidate has by this time had six or seven or eight years of training at the highest level; it is a bit silly, as well as demeaning, to continue to insist that one's college and professional school performance is not a very accurate barometer of one's professional possibilities. The time has come, finally, to stand or fall on what one has actually achieved. . . .

To summarize or paraphrase this excerpt of Carter's article, you would rewrite it in your own words, including his major ideas and attributing the summary or paraphrase using appropriate documentation. Simply reproducing the excerpt or any part of it, intentionally avoiding quotation marks or any documentation for the source, would constitute plagiarism. But the following paraphrase of the first paragraph of Carter's article would also be considered plagiarized:

> According to Stephen L. Carter, if we have the correct goal in mind, a certain amount of racial consciousness in college admission and maybe in professional school admission could be accepted, but just barely. Because the correct goal of racial preferences is opportunity, the educational sphere is the best place for action because it gives highly motivated minorities who would not have the opportunity a chance to receive advanced training. But benefiting from racial preference brings with it the responsibility not to waste the opportunity given by affirmative action. What is important is what happens later in life (87).

Many students might argue that the paragraph is not plagiarized. After all, it isn't written in Carter's exact words, and it is attributed to him by both name and page number. *But inserting synonyms and restructuring phrases and clauses is not enough to make a summary or paraphrase valid.* Although the above paraphrase differs markedly from the original, it still relies too closely on Carter's style to be considered acceptable.

A Workable Method

To ensure that your summaries and paraphrases are not plagiarized, you must distance yourself physically from the source material. You can't plagiarize something you don't see, and writing summaries and paraphrases without having the original before your eyes motivates you to reread the original until you truly understand the points the author is making. And as we mentioned earlier, a thorough understanding of your material is a feature of good research writing.

Try this technique with the Carter paragraph we've been examining. Read the paragraph once, twice, or as many times as needed to make sure you clearly understand the author's point. Then, after closing the book or placing it in your backpack, write your paraphrase.

An acceptable paraphrase might look like this:

Stephen L. Carter believes that racial preferences are justified only when they serve one goal: providing opportunity to those who would not otherwise have it. For that reason, he believes that affirmative action is somewhat justified in determining college admission and even less justified in professional school admission. He also states that those who receive the benefits of affirmative action have the responsibility of putting that opportunity to work after they have graduated (87).

If your paraphrases, like the one above, accurately convey an author's main ideas without using his or her vocabulary and sentence structure—then you're on the way to worry-free research writing.

TECHNIQUES FOR WRITERS 7-d
Summary and Paraphrase

Carefully read the following excerpt from George Orwell's "Politics and the English Language," taking notes on his major ideas. (Don't forget to enclose within quotation marks any phrases or sentences taken directly from the text.) While Orwell's essay discussed political language as it was used in the 1940s, it's still frequently referenced as an indictment of contemporary political language.

> In our time, political speech and writing are largely the defence of the indefensible. Things like the continuance of British rule in India, the Russian purges and deportations, the dropping of the atom bombs on Japan, can indeed be defended, but only by arguments which are too brutal for most people to face, and which do not square with the professed aims of political parties. Thus political language has to consist largely of euphemism, question-begging and sheer cloudy vagueness. Defenceless villages are bombarded from the air, the inhabitants driven out into the countryside, the cattle machine-gunned, the huts set on fire with incendiary bullets: this is called *pacification*. Millions of peasants are robbed of their farms and sent trudging along the roads with no more than they can carry: this is called *transfer of population or rectification of frontiers*. People are imprisoned for years without trial, or shot in the back of the neck or sent to die of scurvy in Arctic lumber camps: this is called *elimination of unreliable elements*. Such phraseology is needed if one wants to name things without calling up mental pictures of them.

Using only your notes, write a one-sentence summary of the excerpt. Then, using that sentence as a topic sentence, paraphrase the entire excerpt, enclosing in quotation marks any phrases or sentences taken directly from the text.

From *Shooting an Elephant and Other Essays*. New York: Harcourt, Brace, 1950.

Documenting Sources with Parenthetical Citation Format

MLA parenthetical citation format requires that the author's last name (if available) and the page number on which cited information appears be listed any time you incorporate source material into your writing. The author's name may appear either in an introductory tag (e.g., *Stephen L. Carter states; Carter claims; Carter argues that*) or within parentheses immediately after the material appears in your paragraph. When you summarize or paraphrase instead of quoting material directly, it's a good idea to use introductory tags so your reader always knows where the summary or paraphrase begins. Following the paraphrase, readers will also need some signal that you're shifting to your own follow-up of the material. This is why you should place the page documentation right after the close of the cited material, as shown here:

> Stephen Carter argues that those who receive the benefits of affirmative action have a responsibility to put that opportunity to work after graduating (87). But would he expect the same thing from, say, students who receive sports scholarships? Or federal grants?

The page number or numbers are placed within the parentheses that follow the source material. You also have the option of saving the author's name for inclusion in parentheses with the page information, especially if the source is a minor one who only appears once in your paper and doesn't need a full introduction by name and credentials.

> One author argues that those who receive the benefits of affirmative action have a responsibility to put that opportunity to work after graduating (Carter 87).

Notice that you don't place a comma between the name and page, nor should you use any abbreviations for "page" or "pages" between the two.

Summarizing Longer Excerpts

While it's relatively easy to paraphrase a short excerpt without looking at the original, it's much more difficult to summarize a longer excerpt without doing so. This is why, in doing research reading, it helps to take notes on your sources before starting to write. But taking notes isn't the same thing as highlighting, where you're not actually producing any text yourself. Using a highlighter helps you to refer to the marked sections later, but writing a summary from highlighted material carries the same danger as writing one from the original because the text is open in front of you. If you take notes as a record of your own understanding of a source, and if you write them *after* you understand that source, the danger of plagiarism decreases.

For example, notes on the entire excerpt from Carter could look like this:

- proper goal of AA—opportunity for those who don't have it
  – justifies *some* racial preference in college and prof. school
    - responsibility to not waste opportunity
- "affirmative action pyramid"—"preference narrows as one moves upward"
  – some preference in college, less in prof. school, none in employment
    - job promotion s/b based on talent and preparation, not skin color

When you make notes, be careful to put quotation marks around any original terms or phrases that you might include in the summary. This will remind you to use quotation marks around those exact words in your summary.

The following is a non-plagiarized summary of Carter's excerpt:

Stephen L. Carter, in discussing the merits of racial preferences, proposes an "affirmative action pyramid" in which "preference narrows as one moves upward." By this he means that affirmative action is justified in college and less justified in professional school. But by employment, all preference should be eliminated, and all promotion in the workforce should be based on talent and preparation rather than skin color (87).

Documenting Direct Quotations

Whenever you quote an author's *exact* words in a paper, you have to present those words inside quotation marks. Full and partial quotes (even single words, if they're unique to or are particularly identified with the author) can appear in your paper when paraphrase or summary aren't sufficient. You don't, however, want to make the mistake of over-quoting—using long quotations or too many quotations from an original source where a summary or paraphrase would work better. Too much quotation interferes with the steady flow of the argument and can rob a paper of the author's voice.

Research writers follow a number of conventions when using direct quotation effectively. The following excerpt from Thomas Nagel's "A Defense of Affirmative Action" (p. 70) is used to illustrate some of the most common conventions for using direct quotation.

MLA Conventions for Direct Quotation

A direct quotation can be formatted the following ways:

Formal Quotation:

```
In discussing Affirmative Action, Thomas Nagel states, "It
is strong affirmative action—the policy of preference—that
arouses controversy" (71).
```

(Note: With a formal quotation, place a comma after the introductory tag [i.e., *Nagel states, Nagel believes, Nagel asserts*] and the period *after* the parenthetical citation.)

Informal Quotation: You can quote the same material using a more informal style:

```
Thomas Nagel believes that it is only "strong affirmative
action—the policy of preference—that arouses controversy"
(71).
```

(Note: When introducing an informal direct quotation with the word "that," don't use a comma.)

Quotation Without Author's Name in Tag: You could also quote the same material without mentioning the author's name in an introductory tag. In this case, place the author's last name within the parenthetical citation.

```
"It is strong affirmative action—the policy of preference—
that arouses controversy" (Nagel 71).
```

(Note: Don't place a comma or the letters *p.* or *pp.* between the author's name and the page number in the parenthetical citation.)

While you need to quote the author's exact words in a direct quotation, you must also reflect the author's true *meaning* as well. It's easy to distort an author's meaning by lifting just enough words out of a quotation to fit your own counterargument—but it is unethical to do so. Authors whose meanings have been distorted in such a way often charge that their words have been *taken out of context*.

For example, a writer who quoted Nagel in the following manner would be true to the author's words, but definitely not to his context:

Quotation Out of Context:

```
Nagel opposes affirmative action, arguing that "there are
serious arguments against it" (71).
```

In the above quotation, Nagel's words are used to indicate that Nagel opposes affirmative action, which a reading of the entire article will clearly establish is not the case.

Ellipsis and Interpolation

While the author's exact words must be used in a direct quotation, there will be times when you don't wish to use all of an author's words within a particular quotation, will need to insert clarifying information within the quotation, or will need to make minor adjustments in direct quotations to fit your own sentence structure.

Ellipses (three spaced dots) are used to signify that something even as minor as a single letter has been omitted from within a quotation:

```
"It is strong affirmative action . . . that arouses
controversy" (Nagel 71).
```

```
Thomas Nagel believes that the meaning of affirmative action
"has changed . . . since it was first introduced" (71).
```

If the information being removed from the quotation comprises more than one sentence, use four spaced dots:

```
"More recently the term has come to refer also to some
degree of definite preference. . . . It is strong
affirmative action–the policy of preference–that arouses
controversy" (71).
```

Interpolation: Occasionally you'll need to insert explanatory information within a direct quotation. Interpolated information is always enclosed in [brackets]—never (parentheses) or {braces}:

```
"More recently the term [affirmative action] has come to
refer also to some degree of definite preference" (Nagel
71).
```

(Note: By inserting an explanation for what "the term" *is,* you clarify for readers what Nagel is referring to.)
Interpolation can also be used to identify whether emphasis (italics) appears in the original text, or if you have added it when quoting the material:

```
"The term affirmative action has changed in meaning since
it was first introduced [emphasis in original]" (Nagle
71).

Nagel believes that it is only "strong affirmative action–
the policy of preference–that arouses controversy
[emphasis added]" (71).
```

Occasionally both ellipsis and interpolation are used together to conform to the grammatical structure of the writer:

```
Nagel defines affirmative action as "originally
refer[ring] . . . only to special efforts to ensure equal
opportunity for members of groups that had been subject to
discrimination" (71).
```

(Note: One commonly seen interpolation is [sic], which signifies that a mistake (in spelling, grammar or the factuality of information that appeared in the original has been faithfully reproduced in the direct quotation.)
Quotation Within Quotation: When material you're quoting already contains quotation marks inside it, those quotation marks are replaced by single quotes within the double:

> Nagel writes, "Let me call the first sort of policy 'weak affirmative action' and the second 'strong affirmative action'" (71).

Block (Extended) Quotation: When a quote from a source will take up more than four full lines of your paragraph, you'll need to present that material in a block quote format. When you use block quotes, a number of added conventions also apply:

> Thomas Nagel does not support all types of affirmative action:
>
> > It is strong affirmative action—the policy of preference—that causes controversy. Most people would agree that weak or precautionary affirmative action is a good thing, and worth its time in cost and energy. But this does not imply that strong affirmative action is also justified. (71)

Note that with a block quote, you don't use quotation marks. Instead, just indent the left margin (only) by ten spaces (two presses of the tab key on most computers). In addition, block quotes are often introduced by a complete sentence followed by a colon, but if your lead-in to the quote isn't a complete sentence, then use no punctuation before the direct quotation. Use interpolation, via brackets, to adjust the quote to fit if necessary:

> Thomas Nagel explains that
>
> > [i]t is strong affirmative action—the policy of preference—that causes controversy. Most people would agree that weak or precautionary affirmative action is a good thing, and worth its time in cost and energy. . . . But this does not imply that strong affirmative action is also justified. (71)

Finally, note that with a block quote, the period appears before the parenthetical citation. This is a reversal of the period placement used in all other sections of your paper where you use shorter quotes, paraphrases or summaries.

Incorporating Tables, Graphs, and Other Visuals

Because tables, graphs, pie charts, and other visuals can be produced pretty easily using various graphics software (e.g., Excel, Access, FileMaker, AppleWorks), many instructors have raised their expectations of students who have access to campus computer labs. Today, it's not uncommon for you to be asked to include visual representations of facts and statistics in your research paper.

Introducing and Interpreting Visuals

Often writers, even professionals, make the mistake of incorporating visuals into text without introducing or interpreting them—a situation that's very frustrating for readers. Because the purpose of your visuals is to help illustrate the points you're making, always introduce and interpret every visual you incorporate in your writing.

Note how Steve, one of our students, both introduces ("Figure 1.1 shows the three highest and three lowest average salaries . . . ") and interprets ("Michigan's salaries are second only to California's") his bar graph on teachers' salaries:

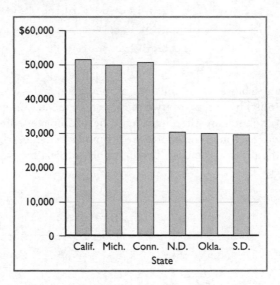

Figure 1.1   Highest and Lowest Average Wage for Teachers
Figure 1.1 shows the three highest and three lowest average salaries for teachers with master's degrees. Michigan is second only to California's $55,020 per year, while South Dakota has the lowest average salary at $32,240 per year.

Other points to remember when incorporating a visual such as a table or graph into text include the following:

- Title your visual. Be sure the title clearly expresses the major information being illustrated. "Figure 1" tells readers nothing, but "Figure 1: Glucose Interaction in the Bloodstream" does.
- Title both the vertical and horizontal axes (if applicable).

- Use a legend to clearly label your lines, bars or segments.
- Label all tables with consecutive table numbers (Table 1, Table 2) and all other visuals with consecutive figure numbers (Figure 1, Figure 2). Use the table number or figure number in all references in your text that you make to the visual:
  "Figure 1 illustrates . . . "
  Not: "The pie chart on the bottom of the next page illustrates . . . "
- Include source information directly under the visual, and remember to include a full citation of the source on your Works Cited page.

The MLA Works Cited Page

Parenthetical citations should indicate which sources you are citing in a specific passage, but you also need a complete citation for every source used in your paper. The Works Cited page, which appears at the end of your paper, gives your readers enough information to enable them to find the sources you used.

Complete MLA guidelines for citing sources can be found in the *MLA Handbook for Writers of Research Papers, 6th ed.* (New York: Modern Language Association, 2003) and on the Internet. Following are citation formats for the sources most commonly used in student papers.

General Guidelines for the Works Cited Page. Begin your Works Cited list on a new page: start with the words *Works Cited* centered on the first line of that page.

Alphabetize your list by authors' last names. Sources that do not list authors' names are alphabetized by the first word of the title (omitting "The," "A," or "An"). Double-space all entries and don't put an extra space between entries. Begin the first line of each entry on the left margin; indent each subsequent line five spaces. (This is the reverse of standard paragraphing.) End each entry (even for entries ending with Internet addresses) with a period.

Sample MLA Book Citations

1. Book by One Author.

   Chomsky, Noam. *Hegemony or Survival: America's Quest for Global Dominance.* New York: Holt, 2003.

   [Note: Place a colon between the book's title and subtitle, even if one doesn't appear on the title page. Italicize or underline book titles. Abbreviate publishers' names by omitting first names (*Holt* instead of *Henry Holt*) as well as words such as *Company* or *Incorporated. U* stands for *University; P* stands for *Press.*]

2. Book by Two or Three Authors.

   McCrum, Robert, William Cran, and Robert MacNeil. *The Story of English.* New York: Viking, 1986.

3. Book by More Than Three Authors.

Belenky, Mary Field, et al. *Women's Ways of Knowing*. New York:
    Basic, 1973.

4. A Book With No Author Listed.

American Heritage Dictionary. 3rd ed. Boston: Houghton, 1994.

[Note: Place the edition number of a book directly after the title.]

5. Two or More Works by the Same Author.

Burke, Kenneth. *A Grammar of Motives*. Berkeley, CA: U of
    California P, 1969.

---. *Language As Symbolic Action: Essays on Life, Literature,
    and Method*. Berkeley, CA: U of California P, 1966.

[Note: Use three hyphens in place of the name for second and subsequent entries
by the same author.]

6. Selection from an Anthology.

Morales, Aurora Levins. "Puertoricanness." *Literature Across
    Cultures*. Eds. Sheena Gillespie, Terezinha Fonseca, and
    Carol Sanger. Boston: Allyn and Bacon, 1994. 677-79.

[Note: Place titles of selections that are within larger works inside quotation
marks. Include page numbers for the selection at the end of the citation. Don't
repeat the first digit of page numbers in the hundreds.]

7. Book by a Corporate Author.

California Commission on Teacher Credentialing. *California
    Teacher Preparation for Instruction in Critical Thinking:
    Research Findings and Policy Recommendations*. Sacramento,
    CA: State of California, 1997.

[Note: Include the state abbreviation for any place of publication for which the
state is not automatically known; i.e., Chicago: *but* Springfield, IL:]

8. Signed Article in a Reference Book.

Reill, Peter Hanns, and Ellen Judy Wilson. "Marat, John Paul."
    Encyclopedia of the Enlightenment. Rev. ed. New York:
    Facts On File, 2004.

9. Unsigned Article in a Reference Book.

"Energy." *The New American Roget's College Thesaurus in
    Dictionary Form*. Ed. Philip D. Morehead. New York:
    Signet, 1985.

10. Government Document.

> United States. Bureau of the Census. *Statistical Abstract of*
>   *the United States.* Washington: GPO, 2000.

[Note: Begin citations for government documents with the level of government (i.e., *State of Michigan, City of Chicago.* United States government documents are generally printed by the Government Printing Office, which is abbreviated *GPO*).]

Sample Periodicals Citations

11. Magazine Article.

> Gregory, Sean. "Golf's Great Divide." *Time* 11 Apr. 2005:
>   46-48.

[Note: Volume dates are presented day/month/year.]

12. Journal Article (paginated continuously from first through last issue of the year).

> Schudson, Michael. "The Informed Citizen in Historical
>   Context." *Research in the Teaching of English* 30.3
>   (1996): 361-69.

[Note: Include the volume and issue numbers where given (30.3 in example).]

13. Journal Article (paginated with each issue).

> Nord, Warren A. "Science, Religion and Education." *Phi Delta*
>   *Kappan* 81.1 (1999): 28-33.

14. Newspaper Article.

> Gray, Madison J. "Redefining His Legacy." *The Grand Rapids*
>   *Press* 27 Feb. 2005, sec. c: C1+.

[Note: Include section number if all sections of the newspaper are not paginated consecutively. The + symbol signifies that the article continues on nonconsecutive pages.]

15. Editorial.

> "Paid Leave for Parents. Editorial. *New York Times* 1 Dec.
>   1999: 31.

Other Sources

16. Corporate or Organizational Web Site.

> *Mustang.* July 2003. Ford Motor Company. 14 November 2004.
>   <http://www.fordvehicles.com/cars/mustang/>.

[Note: The first date is the copyright or "last updated" date, and the second is the date the site was accessed. Note also that you will often need to break the

URL (Web address) manually to maintain evenness of the line spacing in your entries. To break the URL, simply insert the cursor and type a space; you may need to experiment until the sections line up appropriately.]

17. Personal Web Site.

Smith, Joan. Home page. Michigan State University. 14 November 2004. <http://www.mywebspacemsu.edu/students/jsmith254.htm>.

18. Online Book.

Huxley, Aldous. *Brave New World.* New York: Harper, 1932. *The Literature Network.* 2004. JALIC. 14 November 2004. <http://www.online-literature.com/aldous_huxley/brave_new_world/>.

19. Online Poem or Story.

cummings, e.e. "Buffalo Bill's." *Poetry Exhibits.* <http://www.poets.org/poems>.

20. Online Database Entry.

"Rocket Fuel." *Britannica Online* Vers. 99.3.1. April 1999. Encyclopedia Britannica. 17 Oct. 2001. <http://www.britannica.com>.

21. Online Journal (Article or Essay).

Smith, Judith. "How We Learn." *Cognition Quarterly* 27.3 (March 2002). 14 Nov. 2004 <http://www.uid.edu/cognition/273/learn.htm>.

22. Online Magazine Article.

Klare, Michael. "Oil, Geopolitics, and the Coming War with Iran." *Mother Jones* 11 April 2005. 9 July 2005. <http://www.motherjones.com/news/dailymojo/2005/04/blood_oil_iran.html>.

23. Music & Video/Film.

- Amos, Tori. "Me and a Gun." *Little Earthquakes.* Atlantic, 1992.
- *The Terminator.* Dir. James Cameron. With Arnold Schwarzenegger, Linda Hamilton. Carolco, 1984.
- "Peruvian History." *Travels in South America.* Prod. Joan Secrest. NPR. WFLB, Middleton. 16 August 2001.

24. Interviews—Published—Transcript.

Hetfield, James. "Monsters Live." Interview. By Helen Poletti. *Metal Musician* Dec. 2003: 12-18.

25. Interview—Self-Conducted.

> Russo, Lilly. Telephone Interview. 16 May 2001.

[Note: The interview may also be a *personal* or *e-mail* designation in place of "telephone" in the sample.]

Research Basics Review Quiz

1. Research writers can use [brackets] to change the following items:
   a. lower case letters from a source to [C]apitals in the researcher's paper
   b. unclear things [pronouns and references] to specific ones
   c. parenthetical citation information
   d. all of these
   e. A and B only

2. Research writers should use a *blocked quote* when
   a. the quote comes from a government source
   b. the quote will take up more than four lines of the researcher's paragraph
   c. the quote will be used more than one time in the researcher's paper
   d. all of these

3. Which of these is the correct pattern for formatting source titles?
   a. major work = CAPITALS/minor work = **boldface**
   b. major work = lowercase/minor work = *lowercase italics*
   c. major work = *Italics*/minor work = "Quotation Marks"
   d. titles may be formatted in any way that fits the researcher's creativity

4. Which of these page-citation entries is the correct one for MLA format?
   a. "The program is terrible," former police sergeant Jane Smith argues in her book. (Smith 27).
   b. "The program is terrible," former police sergeant Jane Smith argues in her book (pg. 27).
   c. "The program is terrible," former police sergeant Jane Smith argues in her book. (27)
   d. "The program is terrible," former police sergeant Jane Smith argues in her book (27).

5. The following is a typical quote from a professional athlete announcing retirement. Notice that, while there are many *words* in the quote, the *idea* behind them is fairly simple. Please present that idea in a *paraphrase* (your own words):

> "I've had a satisfying career, and I've accomplished what I set out to do when I came to the pros from college. And since I can't run like I used to, I'd rather retire now, when people still remember me at my best, than to play another year or two and be remembered for not stepping out when I should have" (42).

Complete this paraphrase: *The athlete explains that she*

TECHNIQUES FOR WRITERS 7-e
Research Paper—Argument

Write an eight-to-ten–page research paper, using either the inductive or mediated argumentation patterns discussed in Chapters 3 and 4. Your teacher may assign a topic for your paper. If not, choose a topic from the selection in Section 4 or another argumentative topic. Be sure that the topic you choose is argumentative (that is, that it is a topic that reasonable people can, and do, disagree about). Write an argumentative proposition for your topic.

Before beginning your research, utilize several invention techniques (freewriting, mapping, pro-con grids, stasis theory, dialogue) to explore your own feelings and beliefs on your topic.

Select five to eight sources, choosing sources that meet the standards of quality (currency, variety, consistency, reliability) discussed earlier in this chapter. Follow MLA format for page layout and documentation; include in your citations both summaries/paraphrases and direct quotation. Aim for approximately two to three citations per page. Prepare your Works Cited page following MLA guidelines as well.

Concentrate on solid argumentation, good integrated use of source materials, competence in grammar and mechanics, and style that fits the demands of the content and audience.

Peer Revision Questions—Research Paper

1. What is the purpose (argument, proposal, etc.) of the research paper?
2. Comment on the effectiveness of the introduction.
3. Comment on the author's selection of research.
4. Has the author presented sufficient support for whatever positions or recommendations are given? What other information do you believe is needed?
5. Has the author correctly cited his/her sources in the text?
6. Is the Works Cited page included? Is it correctly done? What needs to be changed?
7. What grammatical/mechanical errors need correcting?
8. Any other comments?

Student Writing: Research Paper/
MLA Documentation Format

Smaltz 1

Sandra Smaltz

Professor Stolarek

English 150

6 May 2005

Affirmative Action in College
and University Admissions:
Necessary or Not?

I have long suppressed this truth, insisting
instead that I got where I am the same way
everybody else did. Today I am a professor at the
Yale Law School. I like to think that I am a good
one, but I am hardly the most objective judge.
What I am fairly sure of, and can now say without
trepidation, is that were my skin not the color
that it is, I would not have had the chance to
try. (Carter, "Racial Preferences," 87-88)

Stephen L. Carter's experience illustrates the
intended outcome of affirmative action policies in
university admissions; however, the nature of the policies
themselves is increasingly under scrutiny in the United
States. Regardless of which side is arguing, the arguments
themselves are vehement and compelling. What makes the
affirmative action debate so contentious? The debate in
and of itself is multifaceted, starting with what actually
constitutes affirmative action versus preferential
treatment.

In reality, there is no set definition of
"affirmative action." Thomas Nagel notes that the original

Smaltz 2

definition "referred only to special efforts to ensure
equal opportunity for members of groups that had been
subject to discrimination. . . . More recently, the term has
come to refer also to some degree of definite preference
for members of these groups" (71). The more recent of the
definitions, while being more prone to controversy, still
does not articulately define the nature of the policies
themselves. Affirmative action policy specifics are
largely hodgepodge, a set of various policies versus a
coherent ideology. Author William G. Tierney offers that
"one of the central problems for affirmative action has
been [an] inability to develop a cohesive, analytical
framework" ("The Parameters," 169). While legal
definitions abound, the ideas and controversies
surrounding affirmative action policies are far easier to
articulate. Affirmative action policies in college and
university admissions often take the form of preferential
admissions. Preference is given to minority students as
one of the factors weighed when applications are
evaluated. The preference can take the form of extra
points, additional merit, or other such preferential
considerations. By law, schools cannot have formal
admission quotas for minorities unless past practices of
discrimination warrant intervention by a court.

   Before addressing the controversies themselves, the
difference between affirmative action and equal
opportunity needs to be established. The two ideas are not
the same thing, although the terms have occasionally been
used interchangeably. Equal opportunity in higher
education simply refers to one having an equal chance to
enroll in an institution of higher learning. Affirmative
action, by contrast, allows the university to weigh

Smaltz 3

applications differently based on set criteria, including race. The following example illustrates:

> A high school student applies to an institution, and we assume that the candidate's race or gender is irrelevant. The individual has excellent test scores, good grades, and strong letters of recommendation. A second individual has similar but slightly lower test scores, equivalent grades, and equally strong letters of recommendation. An equal opportunity plan might well choose the first student. An affirmative action plan might choose the second student if we were to discover that that student is Native American, lives on a reservation, has parents who never attended college, and attended high school where few students go on to college, whereas the initial candidate comes from a college-educated family and a high school in which the college-going rate is over 90%. (Tierney, "The Parameters," 173)

Having defined, to an extent, what affirmative action is and is not, the focus of this paper will revolve around the controversies, both for and against, affirmative action, tenets espoused by both sides, and possible solutions for the future.

Proponents of affirmative action policies offer three main arguments for affirmative action and its continued necessity: compensation, correction, and diversity (Tierney, "Affirmative Action," 123). Compensation, according to Tierney, refers to redress for past injury ("The Parameters," 171). In other words, with the country's history of slavery and subsequent oppression of

blacks, reparations for past injustices are in order.
Thomas Nagel concurs that affirmative action policies
should "reduce egregious racial stratification" (74).
Opponents of compensatory affirmative action policies cite
first, and foremost, that the "compensatory advantage [of
affirmative action] goes to persons who resemble past
victims of discrimination or oppression, in skin color or
minority status, but are not themselves identified as
victims of discrimination" (van den Haag 78). Essentially,
if what we are seeking is to right the wrongs of the past,
we are not compensating the direct victims, rather those
who look like them. Compensation, if it were to be used as
an effective argument in the affirmative action debate,
would better concentrate on the current status of
minorities and discriminatory practices that necessitate
its use. The Supreme Court has, however, struck down the
basic premise of compensation as a rationale for
affirmative action policies.

A second argument put forth by affirmative action
proponents centers around the issue of correction.
Correction tends to focus on efforts made to put present
wrongs to right. According to Tierney, correction involves
the definition of everyday problems and the determination
of their solutions ("The Parameters," 171). The
controversy with correction surrounds the solutions
themselves and that, when seeking to correct for one
individual wrong, another can be created. One argument for
correction is that slavery created an atmosphere and
legacy of black inferiority in U. S. culture:

> The visceral feelings of black inferiority
> and untouchability that this system expressed were
> deeply ingrained in the members of both races, and

Smaltz 5

they continue, not surprisingly, to have their

effect. Blacks still form, to a considerable

extent, a hereditary social and economic community

characterized by widespread poverty, unemployment,

and social alienation. (Nagel 73)

Affirmative action policies seek to correct the results of

this injustice. While quotas and other such numerical

restrictions are illegal, the Supreme Court has said that

companies may pursue targets, goals, and ranges (Fish 80).

One method of pursuing these ideals is through preferential

admission policies. Opponents of affirmative action ask,

since these ideals have numerical data attached to them,

could they too be classified as quotas? Essentially, no,

they cannot. Stanley Fish notes that, "the objection [to

quotas] fails to distinguish between quotas imposed to keep

people out . . . and quotas designed to let previously

excluded persons in" (81). In essence, the dividing line

between affirmative action policies and mandatory quotas is

in the intent of the policy itself. Quotas can be used,

however, when it has been legally determined that specific

discriminatory practices have been committed and specific

guidelines need to be enforced.

The most successful legal argument put forth by

affirmative action proponents is the use of affirmative

action policies to increase the diversity of college

campuses. Studies have outlined the benefits of having a

diverse student body. Since one goal of affirmative action

policies in college and university admissions is to educate

more minority students so they, in turn, can become role

models for their community, "a college or university is not

fulfilling its educational missions if it fails to take a

hard look at the applicant pool to be sure that it is not

Smaltz 6

missing highly motivated students—some of them people of
color, some of them not—who might not be 'sure things'"
(Carter, "Racial Justice," 81). One reason the Supreme
Court is partial to this argument centers around the
reasoning that with more blacks entering institutions of
higher learning, more will graduate, and the numbers of
black professionals will increase as well. The criteria for
diversity are hard to pin down, however, and the
determination of what comprises appropriate levels of
minority representation harkens back to the dreaded quotas.
Additionally, critics are concerned that, with colleges and
universities seeking minority applicants, they would need
to alter their numbers continually based on population
shifts; "affirmative action undertaken to achieve diversity
must be never-ending, since the racial and ethnic mix of
our society is constantly changing" (Eastland).

Proponents of affirmative action seek, through
policy, to address the injustices still perpetrated upon
minorities, but also recognize that

> Social policies are not magic potions. They
> are remedies that, when applied with other policies
> in an interlocking relationship, are conceived and
> put forth in hopes of resolving a particular
> problem. Thus, social change is most often a
> cumulative response to multiple circumstances
> rather than the result of one policy. Affirmative
> action is but one variable among many in a
> constantly fluctuating social policy landscape.
> (Tierney, "Affirmative Action," 125)

Blacks, in particular, have suffered prolonged
effects of oppression because of the prejudice that
pervaded the mindset of whites. This mindset is what

Smaltz 7

brought about the necessity for affirmative action
policies in the first place and, unfortunately,
necessitates its continuation also.

Opponents of affirmative action do not agree with the
idea of weighted admission policies, or virtually any
other affirmative action measure. They maintain that
affirmative action policies create an environment likely
to foster reverse discrimination, perpetuation of minority
stereotypes, and diminished standards. But affirmative
action policies were never intended to discriminate
against whites. Some will undoubtedly pay that price,
although the number of white students who will feel the
effects of reverse discrimination is marginal in the
overall scheme of college admissions. The policy's
effectiveness in raising the number of minority students
far outweighs the perception of discrimination of whites.

Additionally, white students tend to apply to far
more colleges and universities than do black students and
are, therefore, more likely to be accepted at more than
one school. Opponents maintain that, "if it was wrong for
Jim Crow laws to penalize people just for being black,
then it is equally wrong to give preference to some people
just for being black. It's reverse racism" (Fish 80).
Those seeking to end affirmative action preferences in
college admissions would lament the idea of whether or not
the preferences were "fair." Blacks are perceived as using
their minority status to gain an advantage at the expense
of others and to be placed above personal qualifications.

Another objection to affirmative action policies is
the idea that they go against the American ideal of
fairness and open market competition and thus, perpetuate
negative stereotypes of minorities. Opponents feel that

individuals should be judged solely on merit; race should
not be a factor in admission policies for any reason.
While this line of reasoning would work well in an ideal
world where all were treated equally all of the time, it
brings to question how other students perceive a
successful minority applicant upon admission. Opponents of
affirmative action often view minority students with a
degree of suspicion, as if their admission was somehow
tainted and they are unworthy of their placement. Reginald
Wilson points out that "the contention that affirmative
action creates a negative stereotype in the minds of
whites implies naively that whites had no negative
stereotypes of minorities in their minds before" (Tierney,
"The Parameters," 188). Whether correct or not, the
implication is that, "no one in an affirmative action
category who . . . is admitted to a selective university can
be sure he or she has not benefited from the policy. Even
those who would have made it anyway fall under suspicion,
from themselves and from others" (Nagel 73). Stephen L.
Carter, whose experience was reflected at the beginning of
this paper, admits that the existence of racial
preferences will always bring into question blacks'
success ("Racial Preferences," 88). Carter also points out
that, "when a person admitted because of membership in a
special category does not succeed, that lack of success is
often attributed to others in the same category" ("Racial
Justice," 82); therefore, if one black student fails, then
none of them are seen as being capable of succeeding, no
matter what it is they are attempting, a patent fallacy.

Opponents also maintain that affirmative action
policies dilute admission standards in order for colleges
and universities to admit more minority students. Terry

Smaltz 9

Eastland notes, "The main generalization is that 'minority' plus 'affirmative action' equals 'low standards,' and the inference drawn is that whatever success is achieved by members of a minority is traceable to the workings of that equation" (Eastland). One example often cited is that minority students do not perform as well on standardized tests as do their white counterparts. However affirmative action supporters question, " if we know that research consistently demonstrates that different populations respond differently to standardized tests, then why would we use such tests as indicators of merit?" (Tierney, "The Parameters," 192).

Precedent has been set for adjusting academic standards with regards to college admissions:

> In response to the furor raised by
> affirmative action critics over what they perceive
> as an unjustifiable deflating of academic
> standards at public colleges and universities in
> order to allow more minority students to attend,
> the circumstances surrounding the GI Bill should
> be considered, among others. After WWII, this
> initiative provided financial assistance to
> countless numbers of men and women, former members
> of the armed services, who otherwise would not
> have been able to afford college. As has been
> shown, many colleges and universities waived or
> lowered their entrance requirements in order to
> accept students qualifying for GI Bill aid.
> (Tierney, "Affirmative Action," 130)

Those who benefited most from the GI Bill were non-blacks who would not have met college entrance criteria without adjustment/preference. Further, author Robert Bruce Slater

contends that "without the highly targeted push of
affirmative action it appears that two thirds of the
approximately 3,000 African-American freshmen now enrolled
each year at the nation's 25 highest-ranked universities
would be denied admission to these schools" (57).
Regardless of test scores, standard adjustments, or
admission preferences, one fact remains irrefutable, that
all students, regardless of race, must meet the same
graduation requirements. Therefore, those students who
were admitted to college via affirmative action
preferences and graduated are just as qualified as
everyone else in their profession.

Opponents seek to end affirmative action, regardless
of its benefits to society and to blacks, in particular.
The basic premise of all of their arguments hinges on what
is "fair." The question remains, is affirmative action
unfair or fairness too long denied?

Regardless of all of the arguments for or against
affirmative action, there are some basic tenets that both
sides can agree upon. First, both proponents and opponents
would like the necessity for affirmative action policies to
evaporate. The question is how to go about creating an
environment where the need for affirmative action no longer
exists. Ideally, for those who champion the idea of
affirmative action, the need for the policies should
diminish as one enters the workforce; advancement would
shift to a merit-based system (Carter, "Racial Justice,"
84). Second, when one segment of a society is bettered, the
society as a whole also benefits. An educational system
that works is paramount as an instrument of societal
change. Changing the environment, in this case, the
educational disparities between minorities and whites,

Smaltz 11

changes attitudes. The more successful that students are
early on, the more they will be educationally competitive
when it comes time to enter a college or university. Some
colleges and universities are taking the unprecedented step
of "tutor[ing] college-bound black high school students to
help them meet admissions standards and to benefit from a
college education" (van den Haag 80). Third, both sides
want what is "fair" for them. The question is what is
"fairness" and who determines its distribution? In the
ideal world, everyone would have the same chance to achieve
the American dream, regardless of race. This dream can take
the form of job opportunities, home ownership, or
enrollment in an institution of higher education. Each of
these tenets is something to be ascribed to by all citizens
of this society as being the "right thing to do."

While the tenets are noteworthy in their idealism,
the bottom line is finding a solution that is logistically
feasible. Three such solutions are educational
improvements, socioeconomic-based affirmative action, and
a meritocracy. The reasoning for affirmative action
policies in college and university admissions becomes
apparent when one examines the disparity in educational
quality afforded black students versus that of white
students. Although the idea of "separate but equal" has
long gone by the wayside, schools are seeing a resurgence
in segregation simply because of exurban development.
White families are moving out of the city towards the
suburbs and beyond (exurbia). The schools set up in these
outlying areas are predominantly white, leaving the inner-
city schools to become predominantly black (de facto
segregation). Black families, usually of a lower
socioeconomic status, tend not to have the means to make

Smaltz 12

the same move and are thus subject to their circumstances. What is the difference in educational opportunities? Schools in the inner city often have a harder time attracting quality educators; many teachers simply do not want to assume the additional personal risk associated with working in an inner-city environment. Oftentimes, the school has to settle for who will take the job as opposed to who is best for the job. Another factor that comes into play is economics. With exurban development, the tax base for desperately needed funds is gradually eroding, leaving schools with less funding to adequately confront the education needs of inner-city students.

What is needed to combat the educational disparity is public input and money. Public investment in educational programs such as Head Start, literacy initiatives, job training, parenting classes, and student loans will have a direct effect on a student's future success. This investment, combined with the one that some colleges are making by tutoring college-bound black students, ensures that the educational playing field will be leveled much faster than by denying the problem exists.

Another solution that affirmative action opponents have offered up is a shift from a race-based affirmative action plan to one that is based on socioeconomic status. Affirmative action opponents contend that "because blacks are more likely to be poor than whites, blacks would be much more likely than whites to benefit from what they call race-blind socioeconomic affirmative action" (Slater 57). On the surface, this sounds reasonable; however, when one digs deeper, the flaws reveal themselves. Were a strict socioeconomic affirmative action program enacted at colleges and universities, most of the available slots

Smaltz 13

would be taken by non-blacks (Slater 57). The fact remains
that "in the United States, whites outnumber blacks eight
to one and white poor outnumber black poor by 2.5 to 1"
(Slater 58). Unfortunately, this type of policy would also
exacerbate some of the arguments that opponents of
affirmative action currently cite. A socioeconomic
affirmative action policy could also cause reverse
discrimination against the wealthy while stigmatizing and
stereotyping the poor. In order to avoid this situation,
standards may also have to be adjusted to encourage
admissions (Tierney, "The Parameters," 189). While on the
surface a socioeconomic-based affirmative action program
might seem more "fair," the reality is much different and
just as problematic as the current program.

The, seemingly, most equitable solution is doing away
with affirmative action altogether and shifting to a
meritocracy, or merit-based system of evaluating college
applicants. In a controversial move in 1995, the University
of California did just that. The Regents decided to
eliminate their affirmative action policy and go to a
strictly merit-based system. The result was a quick and
sharp drop in the number of black students enrolling in the
university. While a merit-based approach seems fair by
eliminating the "victim" status on both sides of the
argument, is it really? With the educational disparities
between blacks and whites, the differences in test scores,
and the differences in economic ability to pay for a
college education, the answer is a resounding "NO;" at
least, it is until such time as each of the disparities
addressed above is dealt with at a societal level.

Throughout the research for this paper, one thing was
endemic: the desire for change. Simply defining the

argument does not eliminate the controversy. Likewise, the
question exists of what change would best suit the society
as well as the needs of the individual. As the saying
goes, "one size does *not* fit all." No matter how much "the
system" is tweaked, not everyone will be satisfied, even
if a colorless, classless, totally egalitarian society
prevailed. American society was founded on rebellion and
the ability to be an individual amongst peers. Therefore,
not everyone will be equal all the time in every way.
However, as Harlon Dalton maintains, pervasive attitudes
amongst whites about black inferiority still plague us
from the years spent enslaving blacks:

> Slavery continues to shape our lives more
> than a century after abolition because of the
> link it forged between Blackness and inferiority.
> Blackness and subservience, slavery's enduring
> legacy is that our 'subhumanity' has been deeply
> imprinted in the American psyche. It does not
> matter that contemporary black folk were not
> personally enslaved so long as we carry the
> stigmata of those who were—dark skin. (Tierney,
> "The Parameters," 191)

Those attitudes are what need focus and change. While each
of us would like to see the need for affirmative action
vanish, we have to realize that, until such time as that
revolution of thought and attitude comes about,
affirmative action policies are necessary to ensure
equitable treatment of all as laid forth in the
Constitution.

Smaltz 15

Works Cited

Carter, Stephen L. "Racial Preferences? So What?"
    Classical Techniques and Contemporary Arguments.
    Elizabeth A. Stolarek and Larry R. Juchartz. New
    York: Longman, 87-99.

---. "Racial Justice on the Cheap." *Classical Techniques
    and Contemporary Arguments.* Elizabeth A. Stolarek and
    Larry R. Juchartz. New York: Longman, 80-84.

Eastland, Terry. "Is Affirmative Action on the Way Out?
    Should It Be? A Symposium." *Commentary.* (1998). 25
    Apr. 2005.

Fish, Stanley. "The Nifty Nine Arguments Against Affirmative
    Action in Higher Education." *The Journal of Blacks in
    Higher Education.* 27 (Spring 2000): 79-81.

Nagel, Thomas. "A Defense of Affirmative Action."
    Classical Techniques and Contemporary Arguments.
    Elizabeth A. Stolarek and Larry R. Juchartz. New
    York: Longman, 70-75.

Slater, Robert Bruce. "Why Socioeconomic Affirmative
    Action in College Admissions Works Against African
    Americans." *The Journal of Blacks in Higher
    Education.* 8. (Summer 1995). 57-59.

Tierney, William G. "Affirmative Action in California:
    Looking Back, Looking Forward in Public Academe." *The
    Journal of Negro Education.* 65.2 (Spring 1996): 122-132.

---. "The Parameters of Affirmative Action: Equity and
    Excellence in the Academy." *Review of Educational
    Research.* 67.2 (Summer 1997): 165-196.

van den Haag, Ernest. "Affirmative Action and Campus
    Racism." 223-226. *Classical Techniques and
    Contemporary Arguments.* Elizabeth A. Stolarek and
    Larry R. Juchartz. New York: Longman, 79-80.

APA Documentation Format: Description and Examples

You can find complete information on the APA (American Psychological Association) documentation format in the *Publication Manual of the American Psychological Association,* 5th ed. (Washington, DC: APA, 2001) or on the Internet. APA documentation format includes the same basic information as MLA, but it is arranged in significantly different ways.

In APA documentation format, parenthetical citations include the author's last name and the date of publication. For direct quotations, the page number is placed immediately after the quotation:

```
Nagel (1986) believes that it is only "strong affirmative
action—the policy of preference—that arouses controversy"
(p. 71).
```

As in MLA documentation format, you may instead include the author's last name within the parenthetical citation:

```
One author believes that it is only "strong affirmative
action—the policy of preference—that arouses controversy"
(Nagel, 1986, p. 71).
```

One difference between MLA and APA formats is that APA doesn't require the inclusion of a parenthetical citation for summaries in which the author's first name and the date published appear:

```
In a 1986 essay, Thomas Nagel illustrated the differences
between affirmative action policies that met controversy
and those that did not.
```

The APA References Page

Parenthetical citations indicate which source you are citing, but a complete citation must also appear for every source used in your paper. The References page, which appears at the end of your paper, gives your readers enough information to enable them to find the sources you used.

General Guidelines for the References Page. Begin your references on a new page: start with the title, *References,* centered on the first line of that page.

Alphabetize your list by authors' last names. Sources that do not list authors' names are alphabetized by the first word of the title (omitting "The," "A," or "An").

Double-space all entries, and don't put an extra space between entries. Begin the first line of each entry on the left margin; indent each subsequent line five spaces. (This is the opposite of standard paragraphing.) End each entry (with the exception of entries that end with internet addresses) with a period.

Sample APA Book Citations

1. Book by One Author.

Chomsky, N. (2003). *Hegemony or survival: America's quest for global dominance*. New York: Holt, 2003.

[Note: Place a colon between the book's title and subtitle, even if one does not appear on the title page. Italicize book titles. Abbreviate publishers' names by omitting first names (*Holt* instead of *Henry Holt*) as well as words such as *Company* or *Incorporated*. Spell out *University* and *Press*. Don't list authors' first names. Capitalize only the first word of the title and subtitle and any proper names.]

2. Book by Two or More Authors.

McCrum, R., Cran, W., & MacNeil, R. (1986). *The story of English*. New York: Viking.

3. Book With No Author Listed.

American heritage dictionary. (3rd ed.). Boston: Houghton, 1994.

[Note: Place the edition number of a book within parentheses directly after the title.]

4. Selection from an Anthology.

Morales, A. L. Puertoricanness. In S. Gillespie, T. Fonseca, & C. Sanger (Eds.), *Literature across cultures* (pp. 677–679). Boston: Allyn and Bacon, 1994.

[Note: Don't place titles of selections that are within larger works inside quotation marks. Place inclusive numbers for the article between the book title and the publishing information.]

5. Book by a Corporate Author.

California Commission on Teacher Credentialing. (1997). *California teacher preparation for instruction in critical thinking: Research findings and policy recommendations*. Sacramento, CA: State of California.

[Note: Include the state abbreviation for any place of publication for which the state is not automatically known.]

6. Signed Article in a Reference Book.

> Reill, P. H, & Wilson, E. J. (2004). "Marat, John Paul." In
> *Encyclopedia of the enlightenment.* (Rev. ed.) New York:
> Facts On File.

7. Unsigned Article in a Reference Book.

> Energy. (1985). In P. D. Morehead (Ed.), *The new American*
> *Roget's college thesaurus in dictionary form.* New York:
> Signet.

8. Government Documents.

> U.S. Census Bureau. (2000). *Statistical abstract of the United*
> *States.* Washington, DC: Author.

Sample Periodicals Citations

9. Magazine Article.

> Gregory, S. (2005, April 11). Golf's great divide. *Time,*
> 46-48.

[Note: Capitalize all major words of periodical titles, and italicize periodical titles.]

10. Journal Article (paginated continuously from first through last issue of the year).

> Schudson, M. (1996). The informed citizen in historical
> context. *Research in the Teaching of English,* 30 (3),
> 361-369.

[Note: Include the volume and issue numbers where given: 30 (3) in example.]

11. Journal Article (paginated with each issue).

> Nord, W. A. (1999). Science, religion and education. *Phi Delta*
> *Kappan,* 81, 28-33.

12. Newspaper Article.

> Gray, M. J. (2005, February 27). Redefining his legacy. *The*
> *Grand Rapids Press,* pp. C-1, C-4.

Other Sources

The APA system for citing electronic sources requires at least a document title (or description), a date—either copyright/update or date of access), and a URL. Identify authors of online materials as well. The general template for APA citation entries for online materials is:

Author(s), I. (Date*). Title of work. (Online), Date Retrieved. *Name of Database or Internet address of the specific document.* URL

[Note: Use "n.d." (without " ") if no date is posted.]

13. Corporate or Organizational Web Site.

> Ford Motor Company (July 2003). Mustang. (Online), 14 November
>   2004. http://www.fordvehicles.com/cars/mustang/

[Note: You'll often need to break the URL (Web address) manually to maintain evenness of the line spacing in your entries. To break the URL, simply insert the cursor and type a space; you may need to experiment until the sections line up appropriately.]

14. Personal Web Site.

> Smith, J. (2005). Home page. (Online), 14 November 2004.
>   http://www.mywebspacemsu.edu/students/jsmith254.htm

15. Online Book.

> Huxley, A. (1932). *Brave new world*. (Online), *The Literature*
>   *network*. New York: Harper, 1932. JALIC, 2004. 14 November
>   2004. http://www.online-literature.com/aldous_huxley/
>   brave_new_world/

16. Online Poem or Story.

> cummings, e.e. (n.d.). Buffalo Bill's. (Online), *Poetry*
>   *Exhibits*. http://www.poets.org/poems

17. Online Database Entry.

> Rocket fuel. (1999). *Britannica Online* 99.3.1. 17 Oct. 2001.
>   Encyclopedia Britannica. http://www.britannica.com

18. Online Journal (Article or Essay).

> Smith, J. (Mar. 2002). How we learn. (Online), *Cognition*
>   *Quarterly* 27.3. 14 Nov. 2004 http://www.uid.edu/
>   cognition/273/learn.htm

19. Online Magazine Article.

> Klare, M. (April 11, 2005). Oil, geopolitics, and the coming
>   war with Iran." (Online), *Mother Jones*. 9 July 2005.
>   http://www.motherjones.com/news/dailymojo/2005/04/
>   blood_oil_iran.html>

20. Music & Video/Film.

> • Amos, T. (1992). Me and a gun. *Little earthquakes*. Atlantic.
> • Thomas, E. (Producer), & Webster, T. (Director). (1956).
>   *When does the train leave?* [Motion picture]. Burbank, CA:
>   Warner Brothers.

- Secrest, J. (Executive Producer). (2001, August 16).
  Peruvian history. *Travels in South America.* [Television broadcast.] Middleton: NPR.

21. Interview——Published—Transcript.

Poletti, H. (Dec. 2003). "Monsters live." Interview with James Hetfield. *Metal Musician* pp. 12-18.

22. Interview—Self-Conducted.
[Note: Self-conducted interviews are mentioned fully in the text of the paper but are not listed on the References page.]

Student Writing: Research Paper/ APA Documentation Format

Affirmative Action   1

Affirmative Action in College
and University Admissions:
Necessary or Not?

Sandra Smaltz

Ferris State University

Affirmative Action   2

Abstract

Stephen L. Carter's experience illustrates the intended outcome of affirmative action policies in university admissions; however, the nature of the policies themselves is increasingly under scrutiny in the United States. Regardless of which side is

Affirmative Action   3

arguing, the arguments themselves are vehement and
compelling. What makes the affirmative action
debate so contentious? The debate in and of itself
is multifaceted, starting with what actually
constitutes affirmative action versus preferential
treatment.

> I have long suppressed this truth,
> insisting instead that I got where I am the
> same way everybody else did. Today I am a
> professor at the Yale Law School. I like to
> think that I am a good one, but I am hardly
> the most objective judge. What I am fairly
> sure of, and can now say without trepidation,
> is that were my skin not the color that it is,
> I would not have had the chance to try.
> (Carter, 2005a, p. 87-88)

In reality, there is no set definition of
"affirmative action." Thomas Nagel (2005) notes
that the original definition "referred only to
special efforts to ensure equal opportunity for
members of groups that had been subject to
discrimination . . . . More recently, the term has
come to refer also to some degree of definite
preference for members of these groups" (p. 70-71).
The more recent of the definitions, while being
more prone to controversy, still does not
articulately define the nature of the policies
themselves. Affirmative action policy specifics are
largely hodgepodge, a set of various policies

Affirmative Action   4

versus a coherent ideology. Author William G.
Tierney (1997b) offers that "one of the central
problems for affirmative action has been [an]
inability to develop a cohesive, analytical
framework" (p. 169). While legal definitions
abound, the ideas and controversies surrounding
affirmative action policies are far easier to
articulate. Affirmative action policies in college
and university admissions often take the form of
preferential admissions. Preference is given to
minority students as one of the factors weighed
when applications are evaluated. The preference can
take the form of extra points, additional merit, or
other such preferential considerations. By law,
schools cannot have formal admission quotas for
minorities unless past practices of discrimination
warrant intervention by a court.

Before addressing the controversies
themselves, the difference between affirmative
action and equal opportunity needs to be
established. The two ideas are not the same thing,
although the terms have occasionally been used
interchangeably. Equal opportunity in higher
education simply refers to one having an equal
chance to enroll in an institution of higher
learning. Affirmative action, by contrast, allows
the university to weigh applications differently
based on set criteria, including race. The
following example illustrates:

A high school student applies to an
institution, and we assume that the

Affirmative Action   5

candidate's race or gender is irrelevant. The
individual has excellent test scores, good
grades, and strong letters of recommendation.
A second individual has similar but slightly
lower test scores, equivalent grades, and
equally strong letters of recommendation. An
equal opportunity plan might well choose the
first student. An affirmative action plan
might choose the second student if we were to
discover that that student is Native American,
lives on a reservation, has parents who never
attended college, and attended high school
where few students go on to college, whereas
the initial candidate comes from a college-
educated family and a high school in which the
college-going rate is over 90%. (Tierney,
1997b, p. 173)

Having defined, to an extent, what affirmative
action is and is not, the focus of this paper will
revolve around the controversies, both for and
against, affirmative action, tenets espoused by
both sides, and possible solutions for the future.

Proponents of affirmative action policies
offer three main arguments for affirmative action
and its continued necessity: compensation,
correction, and diversity (Tierney, 1996a, p.123).
Compensation, according to Tierney (1997b), refers
to redress for past injury (p. 171). In other
words, with the country's history of slavery and
subsequent oppression of blacks, reparations for
past injustices are in order. Thomas Nagel (2005)
concurs that affirmative action policies should
"reduce egregious racial stratification" (p. 74).
Opponents of compensatory affirmative action
policies cite first, and foremost, that the

Affirmative Action   6

"compensatory advantage [of affirmative action]
goes to persons who resemble past victims of
discrimination or oppression, in skin color or
minority status, but are not themselves identified
as victims of discrimination" (van den Haag, 2005,
p. 78). Essentially, if what we are seeking is to
right the wrongs of the past, we are not
compensating the direct victims, rather those who
look like them. Compensation, if it were to be used
as an effective argument in the affirmative action
debate, would better concentrate on the current
status of minorities and discriminatory practices
that necessitate its use. The Supreme Court has,
however, struck down the basic premise of
compensation as a rationale for affirmative action
policies. . . .

The most successful legal argument put forth
by affirmative action proponents is the use of
affirmative action policies to increase the
diversity of college campuses. Studies have
outlined the benefits of having a diverse student
body. Since one goal of affirmative action policies
in college and university admissions is to educate
more minority students so they, in turn, can become
role models for their community, "a college or
university is not fulfilling its educational
missions if it fails to take a hard look at the
applicant pool to be sure that it is not missing
highly motivated students—some of them people of
color, some of them not—who might not be 'sure
things'" (Carter, 2005a, p. 81). One reason the

Affirmative Action   7

Supreme Court is partial to this argument centers
around the reasoning that with more blacks entering
institutions of higher learning, more will
graduate, and the numbers of black professionals
will increase as well. The criteria for diversity
are hard to pin down, however, and the
determination of what comprises appropriate levels
of minority representation harkens back to the
dreaded quotas. Additionally, critics are concerned
that, with colleges and universities seeking
minority applicants, they would need to alter their
numbers continually based on population shifts;
"affirmative action undertaken to achieve diversity
must be never-ending, since the racial and ethnic
mix of our society is constantly changing"
(Eastland, 1998). . . .

    Opponents of affirmative action do not agree
with the idea of weighted admission policies, or
virtually any other affirmative action measure. They
maintain that affirmative action policies create an
environment likely to foster reverse discrimination,
perpetuation of minority stereotypes, and diminished
standards. But affirmative action policies were
never intended to discriminate against whites. Some
will undoubtedly pay that price, although the number
of white students who will feel the effects of
reverse discrimination is marginal in the overall
scheme of college admissions. The policy's
effectiveness in raising the number of minority
students far outweighs the perception of
discrimination of whites.

Affirmative Action   8

Additionally, white students tend to apply to far more colleges and universities than do black students and are, therefore, more likely to be accepted at more than one school. Opponents maintain that, "if it was wrong for Jim Crow laws to penalize people just for being black, then it is equally wrong to give preference to some people just for being black. It's reverse racism" (Fish, 2000, p. 80). Those seeking to end affirmative action preferences in college admissions would lament the idea of whether or not the preferences were "fair." Blacks are perceived as using their minority status to gain an advantage at the expense of others and to be placed above personal qualifications. . . .

Opponents also maintain that affirmative action policies dilute admission standards in order for colleges and universities to admit more minority students. Terry Eastland (1998) notes, "The main generalization is that 'minority' plus 'affirmative action' equals 'low standards,' and the inference drawn is that whatever success is achieved by members of a minority is traceable to the workings of that equation." One example often cited is that minority students do not perform as well on standardized tests as do their white counterparts. However affirmative action supporters question, " if we know that research consistently demonstrates that different populations respond differently to standardized tests, then why would

Affirmative Action   9

we use such tests as indicators of merit?"
(Tierney, 1997b, p. 192).

Precedent has been set for adjusting academic standards with regards to college admissions:

> In response to the furor raised by
> affirmative action critics over what they
> perceive as an unjustifiable deflating of
> academic standards at public colleges and
> universities in order to allow more minority
> students to attend, the circumstances
> surrounding the GI Bill should be considered,
> among others. After WWII, this initiative
> provided financial assistance to countless
> numbers of men and women, former members of
> the armed services, who otherwise would not
> have been able to afford college. As has been
> shown, many colleges and universities waived
> or lowered their entrance requirements in
> order to accept students qualifying for GI
> Bill aid. (Tierney, 1996a, p.130)

Those who benefited most from the GI Bill were non-
blacks who would not have met college entrance
criteria without adjustment/preference. Further,
author Robert Bruce Slater (1995) contends that
"without the highly targeted push of affirmative
action it appears that two thirds of the
approximately 3,000 African-American freshmen now
enrolled each year at the nation's 25 highest-
ranked universities would be denied admission to
these schools" (p. 57). Regardless of test scores,
standard adjustments, or admission preferences, one
fact remains irrefutable, that all students,
regardless of race, must meet the same graduation
requirements. Therefore, those students who were

Affirmative Action   10

admitted to college via affirmative action
preferences and graduated are just as qualified as
everyone else in their profession.

Opponents seek to end affirmative action,
regardless of its benefits to society and to
blacks, in particular. The basic premise of all of
their arguments hinges on what is "fair." The
question remains, is affirmative action unfair or
fairness too long denied?

Regardless of all of the arguments for or
against affirmative action, there are some basic
tenets that both sides can agree upon. First, both
proponents and opponents would like the necessity
for affirmative action policies to evaporate. The
question is how to go about creating an environment
where the need for affirmative action no longer
exists. Ideally, for those who champion the idea of
affirmative action, the need for the policies
should diminish as one enters the workforce;
advancement would shift to a merit-based system
(Carter, 2005b, p. 84). Second, when one segment of
a society is bettered, the society as a whole also
benefits. An educational system that works is
paramount as an instrument of societal change.
Changing the environment, in this case, the
educational disparities between minorities and
whites, changes attitudes. The more successful that
students are early on, the more they will be
educationally competitive when it comes time to
enter a college or university. Some colleges and
universities are taking the unprecedented step of

"tutor[ing] college-bound black high school students to help them meet admissions standards and to benefit from a college education" (van den Haag, 2005, p. 80). Third, both sides want what is "fair" for them. The question is what is "fairness" and who determines its distribution? In the ideal world, everyone would have the same chance to achieve the American dream, regardless of race. This dream can take the form of job opportunities, home ownership, or enrollment in an institution of higher education. Each of these tenets is something to be ascribed to by all citizens of this society as being the "right thing to do."

While the tenets are noteworthy in their idealism, the bottom line is finding a solution that is logistically feasible. Three such solutions are educational improvements, socioeconomic-based affirmative action, and a meritocracy. The reasoning for affirmative action policies in college and university admissions becomes apparent when one examines the disparity in educational quality afforded black students versus that of white students. Although the idea of "separate but equal" has long gone by the wayside, schools are seeing a resurgence in segregation simply because of exurban development. White families are moving out of the city towards the suburbs and beyond (exurbia). The schools set up in these outlying areas are predominantly white, leaving the inner-city schools to become predominantly black (de facto segregation). Black families, usually of a

Affirmative Action   12

lower socioeconomic status, tend not to have the means to make the same move and are thus subject to their circumstances. What is the difference in educational opportunities? Schools in the inner city often have a harder time attracting quality educators; many teachers simply do not want to assume the additional personal risk associated with working in an inner-city environment. Oftentimes, the school has to settle for who will take the job as opposed to who is best for the job. Another factor that comes into play is economics. With exurban development, the tax base for desperately needed funds is gradually eroding, leaving schools with less funding to adequately confront the education needs of inner-city students.

What is needed to combat the educational disparity is public input and money. Public investment in educational programs such as Head Start, literacy initiatives, job training, parenting classes, and student loans will have a direct effect on a student's future success. This investment, combined with the one that some colleges are making by tutoring college-bound black students, ensures that the educational playing field will be leveled much faster than by denying the problem exists.

Another solution that affirmative action opponents have offered up is a shift from a race-based affirmative action plan to one that is based

Affirmative Action   13

on socioeconomic status. Affirmative action
opponents contend that "because blacks are more
likely to be poor than whites, blacks would be much
more likely than whites to benefit from what they
call race-blind socioeconomic affirmative action"
(Slater, 1995, p. 57). On the surface, this sounds
reasonable; however, when one digs deeper, the
flaws reveal themselves. Were a strict
socioeconomic affirmative action program enacted at
colleges and universities, most of the available
slots would be taken by non-blacks (Slater, 1995,
p. 57). The fact remains that "in the United
States, whites outnumber blacks eight to one and
white poor outnumber black poor by 2.5 to 1"
(Slater, 1995, p. 58). Unfortunately, this type of
policy would also exacerbate some of the arguments
that opponents of affirmative action currently
cite. A socioeconomic affirmative action policy
could also cause reverse discrimination against the
wealthy while stigmatizing and stereotyping the
poor. In order to avoid this situation, standards
may also have to be adjusted to encourage
admissions (Tierney, 1997b, p. 189). While on the
surface a socioeconomic-based affirmative action
program might seem more "fair," the reality is much
different and just as problematic as the current
program.

The, seemingly, most equitable solution is
doing away with affirmative action altogether and
shifting to a meritocracy, or merit-based system of

evaluating college applicants. In a controversial move in 1995, the University of California did just that. The Regents decided to eliminate their affirmative action policy and go to a strictly merit-based system. The result was a quick and sharp drop in the number of black students enrolling in the university. While a merit-based approach seems fair by eliminating the "victim" status on both sides of the argument, is it really? With the educational disparities between blacks and whites, the differences in test scores, and the differences in economic ability to pay for a college education, the answer is a resounding "NO;" at least, it is until such time as each of the disparities addressed above is dealt with at a societal level.

Throughout the research for this paper, one thing was endemic: the desire for change. Simply defining the argument does not eliminate the controversy. Likewise, the question exists of what change would best suit the society as well as the needs of the individual. As the saying goes, "one size does *not* fit all." No matter how much "the system" is tweaked, not everyone will be satisfied, even if a colorless, classless, totally egalitarian society prevailed. American society was founded on rebellion and the ability to be an individual amongst peers. Therefore, not everyone will be equal all the time in every way. However, as Harlon Dalton maintains, pervasive attitudes amongst

whites about black inferiority still plague us from
the years spent enslaving blacks:

> Slavery continues to shape our lives more
> than a century after abolition because of the
> link it forged between Blackness and
> inferiority. Blackness and subservience,
> slavery's enduring legacy is that our
> 'subhumanity' has been deeply imprinted in the
> American psyche. It does not matter that
> contemporary black folk were not personally
> enslaved so long as we carry the stigmata of
> those who were—dark skin. (Tierney, 1997b,
> p. 191)

Those attitudes are what need focus and change. While each
of us would like to see the need for affirmative action
vanish, we have to realize that, until such time as that
revolution of thought and attitude comes about,
affirmative action policies are necessary to ensure
equitable treatment of all as laid forth in the
Constitution.

Affirmative Action   16

References

Carter, S. L. (2007a). Racial preferences? So what? In E.
A. Stolarek & L. R. Juchartz, *Classical techniques and
contemporary arguments* (pp. 87-89). New York: Longman.

Carter, S. L. (2007b). Racial justice on the cheap. In E.
A. Stolarek & L. R. Juchartz, *Classical techniques
and contemporary arguments* (pp. 80-84). New York:
Longman.

Eastland, T. (1998). Is affirmative action on the way out?
Should it be? A symposium. *Commentary.* April 25, 2005.

Fish, S. (2000, Spring). The nifty nine arguments against
affirmative action in higher education. *The Journal
of Blacks in Higher Education,* 27, 79-81.

Nagel, T. (2007). A defense of affirmative action. In E. A.
Stolarek & L. R. Juchartz, *Classical techniques and
contemporary arguments* (pp. 70-75). New York: Longman.

Slater, R. B. (1995, Summer). Why socioeconomic
affirmative action in college admissions works
against African Americans. *The Journal of Blacks in
Higher Education,* 8, 57-59.

Tierney, W. G. (1996a, Spring). Affirmative action in
California: Looking back, looking forward in public
academe. *The Journal of Negro Education,* 65 (2),
122-132.

Tierney, W. G. (1997b, Summer). The parameters of
affirmative action: Equity and excellence in the
academy. *Review of Educational Research.* 67 (2),
165-196.

van den Haag, E. (2007). Affirmative action and campus
racism. In E. A. Stolarek & L. R. Juchartz, *Classical
techniques and contemporary arguments* (pp. 77-80).
New York: Longman.

Alternative Strategies for Arguments

CHAPTER 8

Recognizing and Creating Deductive Arguments

Induction and Deduction: A Comparison

In Chapter 3, you were introduced to induction, a system of thinking that depends on evidence in the form of facts, statistics, and testimony. You use inductive reasoning every day in decision making and problem solving. It's the system most representative of contemporary Western thought in many formal argumentative situations (e.g., legislative debates, school debates, and courts of law).

While induction is central to Western rhetoric, another form of thought, **deduction,** is used every day as well. Deduction, or deductive reasoning, is based on **principle**: that is, on statements considered to be basic truths. To understand the differences between induction and deduction, it's necessary to understand the basic assumptions that underlie each system. To do this, let's return to the works and the worlds of two men: Plato and Aristotle.

Defining Rhetoric

Deduction: a process of reasoning that is based on principle. Deductive reasoning follows the pattern of the syllogism.

Principle: a basic truth or law.

The thinking system most associated with Aristotle, induction, presupposes a world in which the major decisions a person or a society must make have multiple solutions. Chapter 3 introduced you to the argumentative proposition, a statement with which reasonable people can and do disagree. Your job as a thoughtful person in a society that recognizes multiple solutions to problems, according to inductive reasoning, is to examine the evidence presented to determine which of those solutions is most appropriate for the given proposition.

Aristotle's system of thinking is central to rhetoric. To Aristotle, the major purpose of reasoning was to determine the best possible means of persuasion, in an effort to turn people's thoughts and actions toward one's own position. Plato, on the other hand, distrusted rhetoric and instead promoted dialectic, a system that differs both in its world view and its application.

Seeing the World Through Plato's Eyes

One of the most striking differences between Plato's and Aristotle's worldviews is that, while Aristotle recognized multiple answers to society's important questions, Plato believed that in every situation and for every argument there was only one truly good and correct answer. Plato believed in the *Ideal:* that such things as ideal beauty, ideal good, ideal truth, and ideal justice existed, but that humans were incapable of ascertaining what was ideal on their own. The best way for a man (women were not educated in such things as rhetoric in Athens during Plato's time) to begin to comprehend the ideal was through thorough discussion, or dialectic, on the topic. Only then could he form the principles that were the basis of deductive reasoning.

Plato's purpose in dialectic also differed markedly from Aristotle's purpose in rhetoric. Rather than seeking persuasive arguments, Plato was seeking the truth—the *Ideal Truth* in any situation. (Plato, however, was not completely adverse to using dialectic to persuade; he says in the *Phaedrus* that "when a man sets out to deceive someone else without being taken in himself, he must accurately grasp the similarity and dissimilarity of the facts.") Plato saw the most dangerous form of deception to be self-deception, or self-delusion, the danger of convincing oneself of what was false.

Formulating Syllogisms

The basic form of the deductive argument is the **syllogism**. A syllogism is a three-statement argument, in which the first statement, the *major premise (MP)*, is the principle, which is considered truthful by reasonable people. The second statement, the *minor premise (mp)*, presents a particular case that is a specific example of the major premise. The third statement, the *conclusion* (▲), logically follows from the relationship between the major premise and the minor premise.

─Defining Rhetoric

Syllogism: the basic form of the deductive argument. A syllogism contains three parts: the major premise, or principle; the minor premise, or specific example; and the conclusion.

A classic example of the syllogism follows:

> MP: All men are mortal.
>
> mp: Socrates is a man.
>
> ▲   Socrates is mortal.

All reasonable people accept the major premise: that is, that all men are mortal, that they all will die. If you also accept the minor premise, that Socrates is a man, then it follows that Socrates, like all men, is mortal and therefore will die. The previous example, then, is an acceptable syllogism.

In order for a syllogism to be acceptable, both the major premise and the minor premise must be accepted as truth. In addition, the conclusion must be valid—it must follow directly from the premises. Are the next four examples acceptable syllogisms?

> **Example 1**
>
> MP: All men are bald.
>
> mp: Joe is a man.
>
> ▲   Joe is bald.

In Example 1, the major premise is obviously false. All men aren't bald. Because no reasonable person would accept the truth of the major premise, Example 1 isn't a true syllogism.

> **Example 2**
>
> MP: All men are mortal.
>
> mp: Superman is a man.
>
> ▲   Superman is mortal.

Despite the possibility of any number of hypothetical arguments (many containing such words as "kryptonite") between comic book or action movie fans, Superman isn't a man—he's a fictional character. Because the minor premise isn't true, the conclusion is called into question. But what about the following example?

> **Example 3**
>
> MP: All men are mortal.
>
> mp: Jennifer Aniston is a man.
>
> ▲   Jennifer Aniston is mortal.

The conclusion in Example 3 is correct. Does that make the syllogism a true one? No, because even though the conclusion is correct, the minor premise is false, so the conclusion couldn't have followed from the relationship between the major and minor premises.

> **Example 4**
>
>   MP: All men are mortal.
>
>   mp: Fido is a dog.
>
>   ▲   Fido is not mortal.

In Example 4, both the major and minor premises are true. All men are mortal, and Fido could be proved to be a dog. But the conclusion does not follow logically from the interaction of the major and minor premises. While the major premise states that all men are mortal, it doesn't state that *only* men are mortal: cows are mortal, butterflies are mortal, redwoods are mortal. All living creatures will eventually die. The major and minor premises do not exclude the possibility of Fido the dog being mortal.

Finding Syllogisms in Text

While example syllogisms like the ones presented above may seem rather silly or elementary, it's a much more difficult, though absolutely necessary, skill to discover syllogisms hidden in arguments. For example, you may at some time have heard someone say something like this:

> I don't understand all this garbage about Miranda rights—"you have the right to remain silent," etc. The police have a difficult enough time catching criminals; they shouldn't have to worry about what they're saying when arresting these scumbags. And if they don't get the wording exactly right, some lawyer will get the thug out and pretty soon he'll be out harassing innocent victims again. It seems that criminals have more rights these days than law-abiding people.

The logic in this statement may seem perfectly sound, but problems with the reasoning are readily apparent once the argument is placed into a syllogism:

>   MP: Criminals should lose the rights that law-abiding citizens enjoy.
>
>   mp: Persons who are arrested are criminals.
>
>   ▲   Persons who are arrested should lose their rights.

While all reasonable people would agree that breaking the law and getting caught at it can result in a loss of rights, it's easy to see that the syllogism falls apart at the level of the minor premise. Not all arrested persons are guilty. Some are cleared during the course of investigation and others are found not guilty during their trials. Because in our system of government those charged with crimes are assumed innocent until proven guilty, they maintain all of their rights as citizens, with the exception of reasonable measures taken to assure their availability for court proceedings.

TECHNIQUES FOR WRITERS 8-a
Developing Syllogisms

Write three syllogisms that you believe to be both true and valid. Compare your syllogisms with three syllogisms written by a classmate. If you're unsure about the truth or validity of any of your syllogisms, discuss them with your teacher or the class. (Hint: In creating your syllogisms, think of *defining characteristics*—those qualities or features that set something apart. For example, you might consider "All birds have wings" as a Major Premise, if you believe that wings are a defining characteristic of birds.)

TECHNIQUES FOR WRITERS 8-b
Recognizing and Analyzing Syllogisms in Text

Compose the syllogism that is the basis of each of these scenarios. Determine whether the syllogism is true and valid.

1. *Beer commercial:* A beautiful young woman is enjoying a drink at a sports bar. An attractive young man, holding a beer, tries to engage her in conversation. She's not interested. Another, less attractive young man, holding a beer made by the ad's sponsor, tries to engage her in conversation and is successful in doing so. He buys her a beer made by the ad's sponsor.

2. A mother, worried about the effect that playing violent video games may have on her young children, is organizing a campaign to ban the sale of excessively violent video games in her community.

3. A college student is amassing a large collection of music CDs he has downloaded from his computer. When asked whether he believes that it's fair to do this, he argues that recording artists can make money doing tours and that the music he wants is too expensive for him to buy.

4. *Clothing commercial:* Set on a cruise ship, this commercial features a number of young, attractive people, all obviously having fun: playing games, swimming, and sunning on deck. They're all wearing clothing made by a particular manufacturer. The name and logo of the manufacturer appear at the end of the commercial.

TECHNIQUES FOR WRITERS 8-c
Critical Analysis

Choose a scenario from Techniques for Writers 8-b and write a two-to-three–page critical analysis of the logic behind the scenario, using syllogism as the tool of inquiry. What line of reasoning makes the argument false or invalid?

Revisualizing the Declaration of Independence as a Syllogism

Much longer texts than the arguments listed in Exercise 8-b can be based on syllogistic thinking. The Declaration of Independence, one of the most famous and powerful documents ever written, is based on a syllogism. Thomas Jefferson, as a scholar of both classical Greek and Latin, would have been very familiar with the works of Plato and Aristotle. Seen as an idealist by both his contemporaries and current historians, Jefferson chose deductive argument to construct a document that has had far-reaching effects on both the United States and the world.

As you read The Declaration of Independence, try to determine what syllogism was the basis of Jefferson's argument. A rhetorical analysis of the text follows.

The Declaration of Independence

A Transcription
In Congress, July 4, 1776.

The unanimous Declaration of the thirteen united States of America,

When in the Course of human events, it becomes necessary for one people to dissolve the political bands which have connected them with another, and to assume among the powers of the earth, the separate and equal station to which the Laws of Nature and of Nature's God entitle them, a decent respect to the opinions of mankind requires that they should declare the causes which impel them to the separation.

We hold these truths to be self-evident, that all men are created equal, that they are endowed by their Creator with certain unalienable Rights, that among these are Life, Liberty and the pursuit of Happiness. —That to secure these rights, Governments are instituted among Men, deriving their just powers from the consent of the governed, —That whenever any Form of Government becomes destructive of these ends, it is the Right of the People to alter or to abolish it, and to institute new Government laying its foundation on such principles and organizing its powers in such form, as to them shall seem most likely to effect their Safety and Happiness. Prudence, indeed, will dictate that Governments long established should not be changed for light and transient causes; and accordingly all experience hath shewn, that mankind are more disposed to suffer, while evils are sufferable, than to right themselves by abolishing the forms to which they are accustomed. But when a long train of abuses and usurpations, pursuing invariably the same Object evinces a design to reduce them under absolute Despotism, it is their right, it is their duty, to throw off such Government, and to provide new Guards for their future security. —Such has been the patient sufferance of these Colonies; and such is now the necessity which constrains them to alter their former Systems of Government. The history of the present King of Great Britain is a history of repeated injuries and usurpations, all having in direct object the establishment of an absolute Tyranny over these States. To prove this, let Facts be submitted to a candid world.

5   He has refused his Assent to Laws, the most wholesome and necessary for the public good.

He has forbidden his Governors to pass Laws of immediate and pressing importance, unless suspended in their operation till his Assent should be obtained; and when so suspended, he has utterly neglected to attend to them.

He has refused to pass other Laws for the accommodation of large districts of people, unless those people would relinquish the right of Representation in the Legislature, a right inestimable to them and formidable to tyrants only.

He has called together legislative bodies at places unusual, uncomfortable, and distant from the depository of their public Records, for the sole purpose of fatiguing them into compliance with his measures.

He has dissolved Representative Houses repeatedly, for opposing with manly firmness his invasions on the rights of the people.

10   He has refused for a long time, after such dissolutions, to cause others to be elected; whereby the Legislative powers, incapable of Annihilation, have returned to the People at large for their exercise; the State remaining in the mean time exposed to all the dangers of invasion from without, and convulsions within.

He has endeavoured to prevent the population of these States; for that purpose obstructing the Laws for Naturalization of Foreigners; refusing to pass others to encourage their migrations hither, and raising the conditions of new Appropriations of Lands.

He has obstructed the Administration of Justice, by refusing his Assent to Laws for establishing Judiciary powers.

He has made Judges dependent on his Will alone, for the tenure of their offices, and the amount and payment of their salaries.

He has erected a multitude of New Offices, and sent hither swarms of Officers to harrass our people, and eat out their substance.

15   He has kept among us, in times of peace, Standing Armies without the Consent of our legislatures.

He has affected to render the Military independent of and superior to the Civil power.

He has combined with others to subject us to a jurisdiction foreign to our constitution, and unacknowledged by our laws; giving his Assent to their Acts of pretended Legislation:

For Quartering large bodies of armed troops among us:

For protecting them, by a mock Trial, from punishment for any Murders which they should commit on the Inhabitants of these States:

20   For cutting off our Trade with all parts of the world:

For imposing Taxes on us without our Consent:

For depriving us in many cases, of the benefits of Trial by Jury:

For transporting us beyond Seas to be tried for pretended offences

For abolishing the free System of English Laws in a neighbouring Province, establishing therein an Arbitrary government, and enlarging its Boundaries so as to render it at once an example and fit instrument for introducing the same absolute rule into these Colonies:

25   For taking away our Charters, abolishing our most valuable Laws, and altering fundamentally the Forms of our Governments:

For suspending our own Legislatures, and declaring themselves invested with power to legislate for us in all cases whatsoever.

He has abdicated Government here, by declaring us out of his Protection and waging War against us.

He has plundered our seas, ravaged our Coasts, burnt our towns, and destroyed the lives of our people.

He is at this time transporting large Armies of foreign Mercenaries to compleat the works of death, desolation and tyranny, already begun with circumstances of Cruelty & perfidy scarcely paralleled in the most barbarous ages, and totally unworthy the Head of a civilized nation.

30   He has constrained our fellow Citizens taken Captive on the high Seas to bear Arms against their Country, to become the executioners of their friends and Brethren, or to fall themselves by their Hands.

He has excited domestic insurrections amongst us, and has endeavoured to bring on the inhabitants of our frontiers, the merciless Indian Savages, whose known rule of warfare, is an undistinguished destruction of all ages, sexes and conditions.

In every stage of these Oppressions We have Petitioned for Redress in the most humble terms: Our repeated Petitions have been answered only by repeated injury. A Prince whose character is thus marked by every act which may define a Tyrant, is unfit to be the ruler of a free people.

Nor have We been wanting in attentions to our British brethren. We have warned them from time to time of attempts by their legislature to extend an unwarrantable jurisdiction over us. We have reminded them of the circumstances of our emigration and settlement here. We have appealed to their native justice and magnanimity, and we have conjured them by the ties of our common kindred to disavow these usurpations, which, would inevitably interrupt our connections and correspondence. They too have been deaf to the voice of justice and of consanguinity. We must, therefore, acquiesce in the necessity, which denounces our Separation, and hold them, as we hold the rest of mankind, Enemies in War, in Peace Friends.

We, therefore, the Representatives of the united States of America, in General Congress, Assembled, appealing to the Supreme Judge of the world for the rectitude of our intentions, do, in the Name, and by Authority of the good People of these Colonies, solemnly publish and declare, That these United Colonies are, and of Right ought to be Free and Independent States; that they are Absolved from all Allegiance to the British Crown, and that all political connection between them and the State of Great Britain, is and ought to be totally dissolved; and that as Free and Independent States, they have full Power to levy War, conclude Peace, contract Alliances, establish Commerce, and to do all other Acts and Things which Independent States may of right do. And for the support of this Declaration, with a firm reliance on the protection of divine Providence, we mutually pledge to each other our Lives, our Fortunes and our sacred Honor.

Critical Reading Questions

1. Who is the audience for The Declaration of Independence? Look particularly at the first and last paragraphs to answer this question.

2. Jefferson states that "all men are created equal, that they are endowed by their Creator with certain unalienable Rights, that among these are Life, Liberty and the pursuit of Happiness." What kind of equality is he speaking of? "Life" and "Liberty" seem pretty straightforward, but what might the meaning of "pursuit of Happiness" be? What would that phrase mean to you?

3. According to the Declaration, what is the purpose of government? What is the responsibility of the people if their government does not meet their needs? Why do you suppose that this issue is still being argued today?

4. The delegates to the Continental Congress had been governed by a constitutional monarchy in which, although the governed held certain rights, the king's power was transferred through inheritance. How would you expect King George III and his loyal subjects to respond to the Declaration?

5. What are some of the grievances Jefferson holds against King George III? Would you agree with his statement that the king's actions have labeled him a tyrant?

6. In the final sentence, the delegates "pledge to each other our lives, our Fortunes and our sacred Honor." How does this pledge establish their credibility (their ethos)? In what other ways does Jefferson establish the credibility of the signers of the document?

While The Declaration of Independence is perhaps the best-known example of American political prose (you probably studied it in a high school civics or American history course), let's look at it from a fresh perspective, in light of what we know about deductive argument.

Jefferson states his intention of using principle early in The Declaration: "We hold these truths to be self-evident, that all men are created equal, that they are endowed by their Creator with certain unalienable Rights, that among these are Life, Liberty and the pursuit of Happiness." While Jefferson asserts the "truths" he lists to be self-evident, the concept of the equality of men was far from accepted by most of the people of the late eighteenth century. Most European governments were monarchies—and it is highly unlikely that King George III or any of the British nobility would have believed Thomas Jefferson to be their equal.

Jefferson further asserts that governments derive their "powers from the consent of the governed" and that "whenever any Form of Government becomes destructive of these ends [the people's right to life, liberty and the pursuit of happiness]…it is the Right of the People to…institute new Government." These sentiments would have been foreign to most people living in the eighteenth century as well. So the "principles" upon which Jefferson made his arguments were anything but universally accepted during his time. His "self-evident" truths are actually bold, revolutionary statements, and it is upon these statements that he builds the major premise that's the basis of his syllogism:

> **MP:** It is the right of the people to abolish any government that denies them their rights to life, liberty, and the pursuit of happiness, and to establish a new government.

Having asserted this statement as a principle, Jefferson must then go on to state a specific instance that exemplifies the principle:

> **mp:** The government of King George III has denied the people of the American colonies their rights to life, liberty, and the pursuit of happiness.

Jefferson asserts "The history of the present King of Great Britain is a history of repeated injuries and usurpations." But he realizes that it will not be enough to simply make this statement because his audience, which includes not only the king and the people of Great Britain, but also the American colonists and the inhabitants of (primarily) Western Europe, will need some proof. After all, many of the American colonists didn't support the American Revolution; their loyalty was to King George. And the monarchies and populations of Western Europe, whose support Jefferson hoped to win, would have some understandable bias against the idea of forcibly overthrowing a government.

Jefferson, then, must show the ways in which King George III has usurped the freedoms of the American colonists, and the largest part of The Declaration of Independence does just that. Jefferson accuses the king of everything from forbidding the passage of laws to imposing taxes without the colonists' consent to creating a huge bureaucracy of government workers who "harrass [sic] our people, and eat out their substance." It's only after presenting this list of complaints against the king that Jefferson can complete his syllogism:

> **MP:** It is the right of the people to abolish any government that denies them their rights to life, liberty, and the pursuit of happiness, and to establish a new government.
>
> **mp:** The government of King George III has denied the people of the American colonies their rights to life, liberty, and the pursuit of happiness.
>
> ▲ It is the right of the American colonists to abolish their current government and to establish a new one.

In words of simplicity and eloquence, Jefferson in his last paragraph declares the independence of the former colonies and the establishment of the United States of America (the first time "The United States of America" appears in print) and pledges, on behalf of all of the Declaration's signers, "our Lives, our Fortunes and our sacred Honor."

Of course, King George III, upon reading this document, didn't immediately grant the American colonies their freedom. The Americans had to fight a long and bloody war to actually gain the freedoms they had claimed. But the king wasn't Jefferson's primary audience. Jefferson's powerful deductive argument helped to persuade not only many of the reluctant American colonists, but also many possible allies in Europe, that the United States of America was a legitimate entity that deserved the support of its citizens and the world.

Jefferson and Plato: Two Viewpoints on the Individual and Society

In The Declaration of Independence, Jefferson's topic—the responsibilities owed by governments to their citizens and by citizens to their governments—is one that has appeared innumerable times in print. In the more than 200-year history of the United States, its citizens and lawmakers have tried to determine, through such venues as the courts and the media, what the scope and the limits of these duties are. In Chapter 3, you encountered the same topic addressed by a different author in a very different time, when Plato, in the *Crito,* wrestled with the same argument, coming to a very different conclusion.

You may remember that the *Crito* is set in Socrates' jail cell, where Socrates' good friend, Crito, is urging him to escape Athens before he is executed. Socrates gives Crito his reasons for remaining in Athens and accepting death. The syllogism at the base of his argument can be stated this way:

> **MP:** Citizens who enjoy the benefits of citizenship in a government owe allegiance and obedience to that government.
>
> **mp:** Socrates has enjoyed the benefits of Athens.
>
> ▲ Socrates owes Athens allegiance and obedience.

How did Jefferson and Socrates come to such different conclusions about such an important issue? Both were political thinkers, and each was devoted to his country. But all syllogisms rest ultimately on the strength of their major premises: if the major premise isn't accepted as a principle, the syllogism won't be accepted. In a pluralistic society such as that of the United States, finding complete agreement among its many citizens on virtually any principle is unlikely.

This doesn't mean that deductive reasoning is less valid or useful than inductive reasoning, because we use both forms of reasoning every day. It would be impossible to function in society without deductive reasoning because subjecting every choice we make in a day's activities to the scrutiny of induction would immobilize our thinking.

For example, most people accept "Stealing is wrong" as a principle. This is probably a principle your parents worked hard to establish in you from a very early age. And by doing so, they did you a great favor: can you imagine how difficult your life would be if everywhere you went—from a store, to a library, to a friend's house—you needed to run through all the various inductive arguments for and against stealing, every time you saw something you liked? The thinking that gives our lives structure, that makes us capable of functioning in society, is often deductive reasoning.

But deductive reasoning can lead to the irrational thinking represented by stereotypes. And you've seen how falsehood in either of the premises or an invalid relationship between them can lead to poor thinking. An awareness of deductive reasoning can help you to determine the strengths and weaknesses of both your own and others' arguments.

Imitating Jefferson: Stanton and Douglass

The Declaration of Independence, one of the most powerful political statements of all time, has served since its creation as a model for many who wished to bring various injustices to light. Both the "Women's Declaration of Citizenship" by Elizabeth Cady Stanton and the "Independence Day Speech at Rochester" by Frederick Douglass owe much to The Declaration of Independence for their structure, style, and message. In reading these two pieces, try to determine the syllogism that is the basis for each of the author's positions.

Elizabeth Cady Stanton (1815–1902) was an early feminist leader who joined with Susan B. Anthony and Anna Howard Shaw to form the National Women's Suffrage Group, which sought to obtain equality for women in such areas as voting privileges and property ownership. The *Women's Declaration of Citizenship* was issued at the first women's rights convention, which was held in Seneca Falls, New York, in 1848.

Women's Declaration of Citizenship
Elizabeth Cady Stanton

When, in the course of human events, it becomes necessary for one portion of the family of man to assume among the people of the earth a position different from that which they have hitherto occupied, but one to which the laws of nature and of nature's God entitle them, a decent respect to the opinions of mankind requires that they should declare the causes that impel them to such a course.

We hold these truths to be self-evident: that all men and women are created equal; that they are endowed by their Creator with certain inalienable rights; that among these are life, liberty and the pursuit of happiness; that to secure these rights governments are instituted, deriving their just powers from the consent of the governed. Whenever any form of government becomes destructive of these ends, it is the right of those who suffer from it to refuse allegiance to it, and to insist upon the institution of a new government, laying its foundation on such principles, and organizing its powers in such form, as to them shall seem most likely to effect their safety and happiness. Prudence, indeed, will dictate that governments long established should not be changed for light and transient causes; and accordingly all experience hath shown that mankind are more disposed to suffer, while evils are sufferable, than to right themselves by abolishing the forms to which they were accustomed. But when a long train of abuses and usurpations, pursuing invariably the same object, evinces a design to reduce them under absolute despotism, it is their duty to throw off such government, and to provide new guards for their future security. Such has been the patient sufferance of the women under this government, and such is now the necessity which constrains them to demand the equal station to which they are entitled.

From *History of Woman Suffrage*, ed. Elizabeth Cady Stanton et al., Vol. I. New York, 1881, pp. 70–73.

The history of mankind is a history of repeated injuries and usurpations on the part of man toward woman, having in direct object the establishment of an absolute tyranny over her. To prove this, let facts be submitted to a candid world.

He has never permitted her to exercise her inalienable right to the elective franchise.

5   He has compelled her to submit to laws, in the formation of which she had no voice.

He has withheld from her rights which are given to the most ignorant and degraded men—both natives and foreigners.

Having deprived her of this first right of a citizen, the elective franchise, thereby leaving her without representation in the halls of legislation, he has oppressed her on all sides.

He has made her, if married, in the eye of the law, civilly dead.

He has taken from her all right in property, even to the wages she earns.

10 He has made her, morally, an irresponsible being, as she can commit many crimes with impunity, provided they be done in the presence of her husband. In the covenant of marriage, she is compelled to promise obedience to her husband, he becoming to all intents and purposes, her master—the law giving him power to deprive her of her liberty, and to administer chastisement.

He has so framed the laws of divorce, as to what shall be the proper causes, and in case of separation, to whom the guardianship of the children shall be given, as to be wholly regardless of the happiness of women—the law, in all cases, going upon a false supposition of the supremacy of man, and giving all power into his hands.

After depriving her of all rights as a married woman, if single, and the owner of property, he has taxed her to support a government which recognizes her only when her property can be made profitable to it.

He has monopolized nearly all the profitable employments, and from those she is permitted to follow, she receives but a scanty remuneration. He closes against her all the avenues to wealth and distinction which he considers most honorable to himself. As a teacher of theology, medicine, or law, she is not known.

He has denied her the facilities for obtaining a thorough education, all colleges being closed against her.

15 He allows her in Church, as well as State, but a subordinate position, claiming Apostolic authority for her exclusion from the ministry, and, with some exceptions, from any public participation in the affairs of the Church.

He has created a false public sentiment by giving to the world a different code of morals for men and women, by which moral delinquencies which exclude women from society, are not only tolerated, but deemed of little account in man.

He has usurped the prerogative of Jehovah himself, claiming it as his right to assign for her a sphere of action, when that belongs to her conscience and to her God.

He has endeavored, in every way that he could, to destroy her confidence in her own powers, to lessen her self-respect, and to make her willing to lead a dependent and abject life.

Now, in view of this entire disfranchisement of one-half the people of this country, their social and religious degradation—in view of the unjust laws above mentioned, and because women do feel themselves aggrieved, oppressed, and fraudulently deprived of their most sacred rights, we insist that they have immediate admission to all the rights and privileges which belong to them as citizens of the United States.

20   In entering upon the great work before us, we anticipate no small amount of misconception, misrepresentation, and ridicule; but we shall use every instrumentality within our power to effect our object. We shall employ agents, circulate tracts, petition the State and National legislatures, and endeavor to enlist the pulpit and the press in our behalf. We hope this Convention will be followed by a series of Conventions embracing every part of the country.

[The following resolutions were discussed by Lucretia Mott, Thomas and Mary Ann McClintock, Amy Post, Catharine A. F. Stebbins, and others, and were adopted:]

Whereas, The great precept of nature is conceded to be, that "man shall pursue his own true and substantial happiness." Blackstone in his Commentaries remarks, that this law of Nature being coeval with mankind, and dictated by God himself, is of course superior in obligation to any other. It is binding over all the globe, in all countries, and at all times; no human laws are of any validity if contrary to this, and such of them as are valid, derive all their force, and all their validity, and all their authority, mediately and immediately, from this original; therefore,

Resolved, That such laws as conflict, in any way, with the true and substantial happiness of woman, are contrary to the great precept of nature and of no validity, for this is "superior in obligation to any other."

Resolved, That all laws which prevent woman from occupying such a station in society as her conscience shall dictate, or which place her in a position inferior to that of man, are contrary to the great precept of nature, and therefore of no force or authority.

Resolved, That woman is man's equal—was intended to be so by the Creator, and the highest good of the race demands that she should be recognized as such.

25   *Resolved,* That the women of this country ought to be enlightened in regard to the laws under which they live, that they may no longer publish their degradation by declaring themselves satisfied with their present position, nor their ignorance, by asserting that they have all the rights they want.

Resolved, That inasmuch as man, while claiming for himself intellectual superiority, does accord to woman moral superiority, it is preeminently his duty to encourage her to speak and teach, as she has an opportunity, in all religious assemblies.

Resolved, That the same amount of virtue, delicacy, and refinement of behavior that is required of woman in the social state, should also be required of man, and the same transgressions should be visited with equal severity on both man and woman.

Resolved, That the objection of indelicacy and impropriety, which is so often brought against woman when she addresses a public audience, comes with a very ill-grace from those who encourage, by their attendance, her appearance on the stage, in the concert, or in feats of the circus.

Resolved, That woman has too long rested satisfied in the circumscribed limits which corrupt customs and a perverted application of the Scriptures have marked out for her, and that it is time she should move in the enlarged sphere which her great Creator has assigned her.

30   *Resolved,* That it is the duty of the women of this country to secure to themselves their sacred right to the elective franchise.

Resolved, That the equality of human rights results necessarily from the fact of the identity of the race in capabilities and responsibilities.

Resolved, therefore, That, being invested by the Creator with the same capabilities, and the same consciousness of responsibility for their exercise, it is demonstrably the right and duty of woman, equally with man, to promote every righteous cause by every righteous means; and especially in regard to the great subjects of morals and religion, it is self-evidently her right to participate with her brother in teaching them, both in private and in public, by writing and by speaking, by any instrumentalities proper to be used, and in any assemblies proper to be held; and this being a self-evident truth growing out of the divinely implanted principles of human nature, any custom or authority adverse to it, whether modern or wearing the hoary sanction of antiquity, is to be regarded as a self-evident falsehood, and at war with mankind.

[At the last session Lucretia Mott offered and spoke to the following resolution:]

Resolved, That the speedy success of our cause depends upon the zealous and untiring efforts of both men and women, for the overthrow of the monopoly of the pulpit, and for the securing to woman an equal participation with men in the various trades, professions, and commerce.

Critical Reading Questions

1. The *Women's Declaration of Citizenship* is a very close model of The Declaration of Independence. Compare the first paragraph of the

Women's Declaration of Citizenship to the first paragraph of The Declaration of Independence. What is the significance of the differences in the two?

2. Note in paragraph 2 of the *Women's Declaration of Citizenship* where Stanton paraphrases perhaps the most famous words of The Declaration of Independence to read, "We hold these truths to be self-evident: that all men *and women* are created equal [emphasis added]." What is the effect of her addition of these two words?

3. Like Jefferson, Stanton lists a number of grievances to prove her argument. What are some of the most significant grievances? Which, if any, surprised you?

4. Jefferson demanded independence for the thirteen colonies. What does Stanton demand for women?

5. State the syllogism which is the basis for the *Women's Declaration of Citizenship*.

TECHNIQUES FOR WRITERS 8-d
Modeling a Deductive Argument

Consider an injustice, a gripe, or some law or policy that you believe should be changed. Write a two-to-three–page deductive argument, using as your model the Declaration of Independence (as Elizabeth Cady Stanton and Frederick Douglass, beginning on the next page, did).

Before you begin writing, place your argument into a syllogism. This will give you the structure you need to produce an argument that's truly deductive.

Frederick Douglass (1817–95) was born a slave but escaped to Massachusetts in 1838, where he became an eloquent speaker for the abolitionist cause and a supporter of the Underground Railroad, an organization that provided shelter for runaway slaves fleeing north. During the Civil War he helped the anti-slavery movement by assisting in raising two regiments of black soldiers, and after the war his arguments in support of the thirteenth, fourteenth, and fifteenth amendments aided in their enactment. The following is the text of a speech Douglass gave to the citizens of Rochester, New York, on the Fourth of July, 1852. Unlike most such speeches, which uncritically acclaimed the accomplishments of this country, this speech looks at its failure to eliminate the disgrace of slavery.

Independence Day Speech at Rochester 1852
Frederick Douglass

Fellow citizens, pardon me, allow me to ask, why am I called upon to speak here today? What have I, or those I represent, to do with your national independence? Are the great principles of political freedom and of natural justice, embodied in that Declaration of Independence, extended to us? and am I, therefore, called upon to bring our humble offering to the national altar, and to confess the benefits and express devout gratitude for the blessings resulting from your independence to us?

Would to God, both for your sakes and ours, that an affirmative answer could be truthfully returned to these questions! Then would my task be light, and my burden easy and delightful. For who is there so cold that a nation's sympathy could not warm him? Who so obdurate and dead to the claims of gratitude that would not thankfully acknowledge such priceless benefits? Who so stolid and selfish that would not give his voice to swell the hallelujahs of a nation's jubilee, when the chains of servitude had been torn from his limbs? I am not that man. In a case like that the dumb might eloquently speak and the "lame man leap as an hart."

But such is not the state of the case. I say it with a sad sense of the disparity between us. I am not included within the pale of this glorious anniversary! Your high independence only reveals the immeasurable distance between us. The blessings in which you, this day, rejoice are not enjoyed in common. The rich inheritance of justice, liberty, prosperity, and independence bequeathed by your fathers is shared by you, not by me. The sunlight that brought light and healing to you has brought stripes and death to me. This Fourth of July is yours, not mine. You may rejoice, I must mourn. To drag a man in fetters into the grand illuminated temple of liberty, and call upon him to join you in joyous anthems, were inhuman mockery and sacrilegious irony. Do you mean, citizens, to mock me by asking me to speak today? If so, there is a parallel to your conduct. And let me warn you that it is dangerous to copy the example of a nation whose crimes, towering up to heaven, were thrown down by the breath of the Almighty, burying that nation in irrevocable ruin! I can today take up the plaintive lament of a peeled and woe-smitten people!

"By the rivers of Babylon, there we sat down. Yea! we wept when we remembered Zion. We hanged our harps upon the willows in the midst thereof. For there, they that carried us away captive, required of us a song; and they who wasted us required of us mirth, saying, Sing us one of the songs of Zion. How can we sing the Lord's song in a strange land? If I forget thee, O Jerusalem, let my right hand forget her cunning. If I do not remember thee, let my tongue cleave to the roof of my mouth."

5   Fellow citizens, above your national, tumultuous joy, I hear the mournful wail of millions! whose chains, heavy and grievous yesterday, are, today, rendered more intolerable by the jubilee shouts that reach them. If I do forget, if I do not faithfully remember those bleeding children of sorrow this day, "may my right hand forget her cunning, and may my tongue cleave to the roof of my mouth"! To forget them, to pass lightly over their wrongs, and to chime in with the popular theme would be treason most scandalous and shocking, and would make me a reproach before God and the world. My subject, then, fellow citizens, is *American slavery*. I shall see this day and its popular characteristics from the slave's point of view. Standing there identified with the American bondman, making his wrongs mine. I do not hesitate to declare with all my soul that the character and conduct of this nation never looked blacker to me than on this Fourth of July! Whether we turn to the declarations of the past or to the professions of the present, the conduct of the nation seems equally hideous and revolting. America is false to the past, false to the present, and solemnly binds herself to be false to the future. Standing with God and the crushed and bleeding slave on this occasion, I will, in the name of humanity which is outraged, in the name of liberty which is fettered, in the name of the Constitution and the Bible which are disregarded and trampled upon, dare to call in question and to denounce, with all the emphasis I can command, everything that serves to perpetuate slavery—the great sin and shame of America! "I will not equivocate, I will not excuse;" I will use the severest language I can command; and yet not one word shall escape me that any man, whose judgment is not blinded by prejudice, or who is not at heart a slaveholder, shall not confess to be right and just.

   But I fancy I hear someone of my audience say, "It is just in this circumstance that you and your brother abolitionists fail to make a favorable impression on the public mind. Would you argue more and denounce less, would you persuade more and rebuke less, your cause would be much more likely to succeed." But, I submit, where all is plain, there is nothing to be argued. What point in the antislavery creed would you have me argue? On what branch of the subject do the people of this country need light? Must I undertake to prove that the slave is a man? That point is conceded already. Nobody doubts it. The slaveholders themselves acknowledge it in the enactment of laws for their government. They acknowledge it when they punish disobedience on the part of the slave. There are seventy-two crimes in the state of Virginia which, if committed by a black man (no matter how ignorant he be), subject him to the punishment of death; while only two of the same crimes will subject a white man to the like punishment. What is this but the acknowledgment that the slave is a moral, intellectual, and responsible being? The manhood of the slave is conceded. It is admitted in the fact that the Southern statute books are covered with enactments forbidding, under severe fines and penalties, the teaching of the slave to read or to write. When you can point to any such laws in reference to the beasts of the field, then I may consent to argue the manhood of the slave. When the dogs in your streets, when the fowls of the air, when the cattle on your hills, when the fish of the sea and the reptiles that crawl shall be unable to distinguish the slave from a brute, then will I argue with you that the slave is a man!

For the present, it is enough to affirm the equal manhood of the Negro race. Is it not astonishing that, while we are plowing, planting, and reaping, using all kinds of mechanical tools, erecting houses, constructing bridges, building ships, working in metals of brass, iron, copper, silver, and gold; that, while we are reading, writing, and ciphering, acting as clerks, merchants, and secretaries, having among us lawyers, doctors, ministers, poets, authors, editors, orators, and teachers; that, while we are engaged in all manner of enterprises common to other men, digging gold in California, capturing the whale in the Pacific, feeding sheep and cattle on the hillside, living, moving, acting, thinking, planning, living in families as husbands, wives, and children, and, above all, confessing and worshiping the Christian's God, and looking hopefully for life and immortality beyond the grave, we are called upon to prove that we are men!

Would you have me argue that man is entitled to liberty? That he is the rightful owner of his own body? You have already declared it. Must I argue the wrongfulness of slavery? Is that a question for republicans? Is it to be settled by the rules of logic and argumentation, as a matter beset with great difficulty, involving a doubtful application of the principle of justice, hard to be understood? How should I look today, in the presence of Americans, dividing and subdividing a discourse, to show that men have a natural right to freedom? speaking of it relatively and positively, negatively and affirmatively? To do so would be to make myself ridiculous and to offer an insult to your understanding. There is not a man beneath the canopy of heaven that does not know that slavery is wrong for him.

What, am I to argue that it is wrong to make men brutes, to rob them of their liberty, to work them without wages, to keep them ignorant of their relations to their fellow men, to beat them with sticks, to flay their flesh with the lash, to load their limbs with irons, to hunt them with dogs, to sell them at auction, to sunder their families, to knock out their teeth, to burn their flesh, to starve them into obedience and submission to their masters? Must I argue that a system thus marked with blood, and stained with pollution, is wrong? No! I will not. I have better employment for my time and strength than such arguments would imply.

10   What, then, remains to be argued? Is it that slavery is not divine; that God did not establish it; that our doctors of divinity are mistaken? There is

blasphemy in the thought. That which is inhuman cannot be divine! Who can reason on such a proposition? They that can may; I cannot. The time for such argument is past.

At a time like this, scorching iron, not convincing argument, is needed. O! had I the ability, and could I reach the nation's ear, I would today pour out a fiery stream of biting ridicule, blasting reproach, withering sarcasm, and stern rebuke. For it is not light that is needed, but fire; it is not the gentle shower, but thunder. We need the storm, the whirlwind, and the earthquake. The feeling of the nation must be quickened; the conscience of the nation must be roused; the propriety of the nation must be startled; the hypocrisy of the nation must be exposed; and its crimes against God and man must be proclaimed and denounced.

What, to the American slave, is your Fourth of July? I answer: a day that reveals to him, more than all other days in the year, the gross injustice and cruelty to which he is the constant victim. To him, your celebration is a sham; your boasted liberty, an unholy license; your national greatness, swelling vanity; your sounds of rejoicing are empty and heartless; your denunciation of tyrants, brass-fronted impudence; your shouts of liberty and equality, hollow mockery; your prayers and hymns, your sermons and thanksgivings, with all your religious parade and solemnity, are, to Him, mere bombast, fraud, deception, impiety, and hypocrisy—a thin veil to cover up crimes which would disgrace a nation of savages. There is not a nation of savages. There is not a nation on the earth guilty of practices more shocking and bloody than are the people of the United States at this very hour.

Go where you may, search where you will, roam through all the monarchies and despotisms of the Old World, travel through South America, search out every abuse, and when you have found the last, lay your facts by the side of the everyday practices of this nation, and you will say with me that, for revolting barbarity and shameless hypocrisy, America reigns without a rival.

Critical Reading Questions

1. Imagine this scene. It's a beautiful Fourth of July in 1852. You've just finished your picnic lunch with your family and are gathered with your friends and neighbors to hear the afternoon's speaker. You've become used to Fourth of July speeches that patriotically focus on the country's accomplishments. You hear that today's speaker, the freed slave Frederick Douglass, is a powerful orator and are looking forward to hearing him. What might your response be to his speech?

2. Douglass establishes his ethos early in his speech. What does he mean when he says, "What have I, or those I represent, to do with your national independence?"

3. How does he respond to those in his audience who might respond that he should "argue more and denounce less...persuade more and rebuke less"?

4. Why does Douglass feel that "it is not light that is needed, but fire; it is not the gentle shower, but thunder. We need the storm, the whirlwind, and the earthquake"?

5. What arguments does he offer to prove that a slave is a man?

6. How do you suppose Douglass's audience responded to his closing line, "for revolting barbarity and shameless hypocrisy, America reigns without a rival."

7. Look for particularly powerful statements in Douglass's speech. Are they persuasive? Why or why not?

8. To what extent does Douglass model The Declaration of Independence?

9. State the syllogism that is the basis for the "Independence Day Speech."

CHAPTER 9

Recognizing and Creating Narrative Arguments

Aesop's Fables: "The Wind and the Sun"

A dispute once arose between the wind and the sun over which was the stronger of the two. There seemed to be no way of settling the issue. But suddenly they saw a traveler coming down the road.

"This is our chance," said the sun, "to prove who is right. Whichever of us can make that man take off his coat shall be the stronger. And just to show you how sure I am, I'll let you have the first chance."

So the sun hid behind a cloud, and the wind blew an icy blast. But the harder he blew the more closely did the traveler wrap his coat around him. At last the wind had to give up in disgust. Then the sun came out from behind the cloud and began to shine down upon the traveler with all his power.

The traveler felt the sun's genial warmth, and as he grew warmer and warmer he began to loosen his coat. Finally he was forced to take it off altogether and to sit down in the shade of a tree and fan himself. So the sun was right, after all!

Application: Persuasion is better than force.

This is a favorite fable for many parents, one told countless times when their children become angry or frustrated over trying to make a point with a friend, or more likely, a sibling. The "Application" of the story, that "persuasion is better than force," is a clear rhetorical message in itself.

"The Wind and the Sun" from *Aesop's Fables*. New York: Grosset & Dunlap, 1963, pp. 229–230.

But this fable also illustrates another major principle of rhetoric: that an audience is often more easily persuaded through a well-told story than through a formal argument. This principle is the basis for the **narrative argument.**

Defining Rhetoric

Narrative argument: an argument that is made through the telling or writing of a story.

In a narrative argument, you make your point not through a detailed presentation of evidence (as in an inductive argument) or through a carefully constructed syllogism (as in a deductive argument), but through the story itself. *Aesop's Fables,* which date to classical Greece, and the parables of the New Testament are only two examples of narrative arguments from more than 2000 years ago. Cultures as diverse as early American Plains Indian tribes and nineteenth-century German householders (*Grimm's Fairy Tales*) also used stories to direct both children and adults toward the kinds of behavior that were expected within those cultures.

Seeing the Story as Argument

Parables and fables generally are written *explicitly:* the *moral* (the "Application" in these examples) of the parable or fable is stated, often at the end of the story. In the following fable from Aesop, look for connections between the story and its moral: does the moral clearly summarize the point the fable seems to be making?

Aesop's Fables: "The Fox and the Grapes"

Mister Fox was just about famished, and thirsty too, when he stole into a vineyard where the sun-ripened grapes were hanging up on a trellis in a tempting show, but too high for him to reach. He took a run and a jump, snapping at the nearest bunch, but missed, Again and again he jumped, only to miss the luscious prize. At last, worn out with his efforts, he retreated, muttering: "Well, I never really wanted those grapes anyway. I am sure they are sour, and perhaps wormy in the bargain."

Application: Any fool can despise what he cannot get.

"The Fox and the Grapes" from *Aesop's Fables.* New York: Grosset & Dunlap, 1963, p. 17.

The power of *Aesop's Fables* in illustrating human nature and directing people toward certain behavioral patterns can be seen in expressions commonly used today, such as "sour grapes," which originated with this fable.

TECHNIQUES FOR WRITERS 9-a
Writing a Fable

Write a short fable (three to five paragraphs) using as your model the *Aesop's Fables* presented in the chapter. Because fables are explicit narrative arguments, be sure to include the moral, or application, of your fable.

Finding the Elements of Argument in Narrative

Not all narrative arguments, however, are made explicitly. In an *implicit* narrative argument, the "moral of the story" isn't stated: it's the job of the reader to determine the point or points the author seems to be making. Often the author's point is ambiguous; readers, all of whom come to stories with different attitudes and experiences, can disagree about the point the author is trying to make, or whether the author is, in fact, trying to make any point at all. But carefully examining the rhetorical elements of a text can help a reader decide to what extent the author is attempting to persuade an audience through narrative argument.

As you read this excerpt from the autobiography of poet Langston Hughes, look for clues in the details and the language of the story that direct you to Hughes's attitudes toward religion, peer influence, and conventional parental practices in religious training.

Salvation
Langston Hughes

I was saved from sin when I was going on thirteen. But not really saved. It happened like this. There was a big revival at my Auntie Reed's church. Every night for weeks there had been much preaching, singing, praying, and shouting, and some very hardened sinners had been brought to Christ, and the membership of the church had grown by leaps and bounds. Then just before the revival ended, they held a special meeting for children, "to bring the young lambs to the fold." My aunt spoke of it for days ahead. That night I was escorted to the front row and placed on the mourners' bench with all the other young sinners, who had not yet been brought to Jesus.

My aunt told me that when you were saved you saw a light, and something happened to you inside! And Jesus came into your life! And God was with you from then on! She said you could see and hear and feel Jesus in your soul. I believed her. I had heard a great many old people say the same thing and it seemed to me they ought to know. So I sat there calmly in the hot, crowded church, waiting for Jesus to come to me.

The preacher preached a wonderful rhythmical sermon, all moans and shouts and lonely cries and dire pictures of hell, and then he sang a song about the ninety and nine safe in the fold, but one little lamb was left out in the cold. Then he said: "Won't you come? Won't you come to Jesus? Young lambs, won't you come?" And he held out his arms to all us young sinners there on the mourners' bench. And the little girls cried. And some of them jumped up and went to Jesus right away. But most of us just sat there.

A great many old people came and knelt around us and prayed, old women with jet-black faces and braided hair, old men with work-gnarled hands. And the church sang a song about the lower lights are burning, some poor sinners to be saved. And the whole building rocked with prayer and song.

5   Still I kept waiting to *see* Jesus.

Finally all the young people had gone to the altar and were saved, but one boy and me. He was a rounder's son named Westley. Westley and I were surrounded by sisters and deacons praying. It was very hot in the church, and getting late now. Finally Westley said to me in a whisper: "God damn! I'm tired o' sitting here. Let's get up and be saved." So he got up and was saved.

Then I was left all alone on the mourners' bench. My aunt came and knelt at my knees and cried, while prayers and songs swirled all around me in the little church. The whole congregation prayed for me alone, in a mighty wail of moans and voices. And I kept waiting serenely for Jesus, waiting, waiting—but he didn't come. I wanted to see him, but nothing happened to me. Nothing! I wanted something to happen to me, but nothing happened.

I heard the songs and the minister saying: "Why don't you come? My dear child, why don't you come to Jesus? Jesus is waiting for you. He wants you. Why don't you come? Sister Reed, what is this child's name?"

"Langston," my aunt sobbed.

10   "Langston, why don't you come? Why don't you come and be saved? Oh, Lamb of God! Why don't you come?"

Now it was really getting late. I began to be ashamed of myself, holding everything up so long. I began to wonder what God thought about Westley, who certainly hadn't seen Jesus either, but who was now sitting proudly on the platform, swinging his knickerbockered legs and grinning down at me, surrounded by deacons and old women on their knees praying. God had not struck Westley dead for taking his name in vain or for lying in the temple. So I decided that maybe to save further trouble, I'd better lie, too, and say that Jesus had come, and get up and be saved.

So I got up.

Suddenly the whole room broke into a sea of shouting, as they saw me rise. Waves of rejoicing swept the place. Women leaped in the air. My aunt threw her arms around me. The minister took me by the hand and led me to the platform.

When things quieted down, in a hushed silence, punctuated by a few ecstatic "Amens," all the new young lambs were blessed in the name of God. Then joyous singing filled the room.

15   That night, for the last time in my life but one—for I was a big boy twelve years old—I cried. I cried, in bed alone, and couldn't stop. I buried my head under the quilts, but my aunt heard me. She woke up and told my uncle I was crying because the Holy Ghost had come into my life, and because I had seen Jesus. But I was really crying because I couldn't bear to tell her that I had lied, that I had deceived everybody in the church, that I hadn't seen Jesus, and that now I didn't believe there was a Jesus any more, since he didn't come to help me.

Analyzing "Salvation" as Narrative Argument

Every narrative argument is different, of course, but many of them share various components. To be able to understand the persuasive force of narrative arguments and to write them yourself, it's necessary to look carefully at some of the components that writers use in creating narrative arguments.

For a narrative argument to be effective, the writer must place the reader into the situation. For this reason, narrative arguments often begin much as play scripts begin, with a paragraph establishing the *setting*, the time and place in which the action recounted in the narrative takes place.

Many of Hughes's audience members, both his contemporaries and later readers, would be familiar with the situation of the Southern religious revival, but many would not. The details he uses in his introductory paragraph and later throughout the narrative encourage remembrance in those readers familiar with revivals while at the same time informing readers unfamiliar with them.

Accordingly, in his first paragraph, Hughes lists the activities of the revival ("preaching, singing, praying, and shouting") and its purpose ("some very hardened sinners had been brought to Christ"), while also letting us know that this revival was an event in the community, something that was highly anticipated. The exclamation points at the ends of the first three sentences in paragraph two reinforce his aunt's excitement at the upcoming activities. But as early as the second sentence of the first paragraph, Hughes indicates trouble ahead: "I was saved from sin when I was going on thirteen. *But not really saved* [emphasis added]."

Details throughout the story also serve to situate the reader. Hughes describes the revival participants carefully: "old women with jet-black faces and braided hair, old men with work-gnarled hands"; Westley "swinging his knickerbockered legs and grinning down." But Hughes uses more than visual imagery to set his reader into the heart of the action. Aural images abound: "all moans and shouts and lonely cries"; "a mighty wail of moans and voices"; "a hushed silence, punctuated by a few ecstatic 'Amens.'" Hughes realized that it was as important for his readers to "hear" the revival as to "see" it.

Perhaps Hughes's most powerful sense images are his tactile ones—the images that actually cause us to *feel* the church and the situation. He tells us "the whole building rocked with prayer and song," and "prayers and songs swirled all around me in the little church." We get the sense of young Langston's feelings: pressured by those around him, he seems caught in a vortex, swirled into a situation over which, ultimately, he loses control.

Other details foreshadow the coming *climax*. In paragraphs three and four, Hughes mentions two particular hymns that were sung, one "about the ninety and nine safe in the fold, but one little lamb . . . left out in the cold" and the other "about the lower lights . . . burning, some poor sinners to be saved." In the weeks of the revival, surely dozens of hymns had been sung, but Hughes focuses on just these two. And Westley's whispered comment to Langston, "'God damn! I'm tired o' sitting here,'" reinforces the falseness of Westley's actions and their outcome.

Even the paragraphing contributes to the rhetorical impact. Short, one-sentence paragraphs are unusual in narrative writing; writers generally use them only for emphasis or as transitional elements. The paragraphs "Still I kept waiting to *see* Jesus" and "So I got up" do both. They reinforce major elements of the story (waiting, the decision) while moving us from one action sequence to the next.

In the final sentence of the narrative, we learn the *irony* that is the basis of the story: that young Langston lost his faith in the process of "being saved." Because the argument is implicit, we can't know for certain what message Hughes wished his readers to take from the story, or even if he consciously attempted to give his readers a message at all. But the last paragraph certainly leads the reader to think about the dangers of coercing someone (even with the best intentions) in matters of faith and of following the crowd into action that goes against one's beliefs or principles. Elements he uses throughout the story, such as foreshadowing, use of detail, and structure, turn a simple story about a childhood event into a narrative argument.

Avoiding Common Narrative Pitfalls: Tense and Person Shifts

Two common mistakes in student narratives are tense shifts and person shifts. Either of these problems can distract the reader from the story you're telling and the point you wish to make.

Tense Shifts

Tense refers to the time in which some action takes place. English has various ways of forming the present (*go, am going*), past (*went, has gone, has been going*), and future (*will go, will have gone*) tenses.

Every narrative has a controlling tense—the sense of time in which the story is structured. Most narratives are set in past tense, and the controlling tense of the narrative can usually be determined with the first sentence: "I *was saved* from sin when I *was going* on thirteen" (Hughes, "Salvation") or "He *went* out on patrol with the others the night of the ambush at exactly eight o'clock" (Kovic, "On Patrol").

Occasionally an author will choose to write a narrative in present tense: "It *is* very seldom that mere ordinary people like John and myself *secure* ancestral halls for the summer" (Charlotte Perkins Gilman, "The Yellow Wallpaper"). Placing a narrative in present tense gives the story a sense of timeliness or urgency. But generally, narratives are written in the past tense, probably because of our sense of the narrative as a retelling of a past event.

Whether the narrative is written in the past or present tense, it's important to maintain that controlling tense throughout the story. This rule doesn't apply to dialogue within the story: "And now the lieutenant turned and looked at him. 'Sergeant,' he said, 'Molina and I *are going* to get a look up ahead'" (Kovic, "On Patrol"). And past tenses need to be modified to signify that the author is stepping even further back into time: "He remembered how difficult it *had been* when he *had* first *come* to the war to tell the villagers from the enemy and sometimes it *had seemed* easier to hate all of them, but he *had* always *tried* very hard not to" (Kovic, "On Patrol").

But problems arise when tenses are switched within the controlling structure of the story. Note how confusing tense switches would have made the following paragraph from Kovic:

> One by one the scouts *moved* slowly past the thick barbed ware and *begin* to walk along the bank of the river, heading toward the graveyard where the ambush *will be* set up. They *are moving* north exactly as planned, a line of shadows tightly bunched in the rain. Sometimes it *stopped* raining and they *spread* out somewhat more, but mostly they *continue* to bunch up together, as if they *were* afraid of losing their way.

TECHNIQUES FOR WRITERS 9-b

Past to Present

One good way to develop an awareness of tense within narration is to rewrite text in a different tense. Rewrite the following paragraph from "On Patrol," which is written in past tense, to the present tense. How does switching to present tense change the effect of the paragraph?

> They were on a rice dike that bordered the graveyard. The voices from the huts nearby seemed quite loud. He looked up ahead to where the lieutenant who had come along with them that night was standing. The lieutenant had sent one of the men, Molina, on across the rice dikes almost to the edge of the village. The cold rain was still coming down very hard and the men behind him were standing like a line of statues waiting for the next command.

Person Shifts

Narratives are generally written in first person (*I, me*), when the author chooses to place himself or herself *within* the story, or third person (*he, she, they, the woman, Mike Green*) when the author chooses to step *outside* the story. As with tense, person can usually be determined with the first sentence of any narrative:

> First Person: "*I* was saved from sin when *I* was going on thirteen." (Hughes, "Salvation")
> Third Person: "*He* went out on patrol with the others the night of the ambush at exactly eight o'clock, loading a round into the chamber of *his* weapon before *he* walked outside the tent and into the dark and rain." (Kovic, "On Patrol")

Most students don't confuse first with third person when writing narratives, but as teachers, we frequently see second person (*you*) appearing in places where either the first or the third person should have been used. The only appropriate uses for second person in narrative writing are within dialogue and when the writer actually means *you, the reader,* as in this example from the first paragraph of Mark Twain's *The Adventures of Huckleberry Finn:*

> You don't know about me without you have read a book by the name of *The Adventures of Tom Sawyer;* but that ain't no matter. That book was made by Mr. Mark Twain, and he told the truth, mainly. There was things which he stretched, but mainly he told the truth. . . .

But inserting a second person pronoun where a first or third person should have appeared interrupts the even flow of the narrative. For example, notice how changing "he" to "you" in this excerpt from Kovic misdirects readers:

> There was a rice paddy on the edge of the graveyard. No one said a word as they walked through it and he thought he could hear voices from the village. *You* could smell the familiar smoke from the fires in the huts and he knew that the people who went out fishing each day must have come home. They were the people *you could see* every morning moving quietly in their small boats down toward the mouth of the river, heading out to the sea.

TECHNIQUES FOR WRITERS 9-c
First and Third

Rewrite the first paragraph of "Salvation," changing all first-person references to third person. Then rewrite the first three paragraphs of "On Patrol," changing all third-person references to first person. How does switching person change the tone of each narrative?

Narrative Arguments: Models

The following stories illustrate some of the ways narrative arguments can be constructed. The first, Ron Kovic's "On Patrol," recounts the author's actual experience. The second, an excerpt from Virginia Woolf's *A Room of One's Own*, combines elements of more traditional argumentative forms with a narrative that introduces a hypothetical character. The third story, Ursula Le Guin's "The Ones Who Walk Away from Omelas," is a narrative argument written in the science fiction mode.

Questions for Thinking and Writing

As you read each narrative, try to determine the point the author seems to be making. Is the author's point expressed implicitly or explicitly? Which sentence or sentences best express the point? Which rhetorical elements throughout the story led you to determine the author's point?

On Patrol

Ron Kovic

He went out on patrol with the others the night of the ambush at exactly eight o'clock, loading a round into the chamber of his weapon before he walked outside the tent and into the dark and rain. As usual he had made all the men put on camouflage from head to toe, made sure they had all blackened their faces, and attached twigs and branches to their arms and legs with rubber bands.

One by one the scouts moved slowly past the thick barbed wire and began to walk along the bank of the river, heading toward the graveyard where the ambush would be set up. They were moving north exactly as planned, a line of shadows tightly bunched in the rain. Sometimes it would stop raining and they would spread out somewhat more, but mostly they continued to bunch up together, as if they were afraid of losing their way.

There was a rice paddy on the edge of the graveyard. No one said a word as they walked through it and he thought he could hear voices from the village. He could smell the familiar smoke from the fires in the huts and he knew that the people who went out fishing each day must have come home. They were the people he watched every morning moving quietly in their small boats down toward the mouth of the river, heading out to the sea. Some of the older men reminded him of his father, going to work each morning and coming back home every night to sit by their fires with their children cooking their fish. They must talk about us sometimes, he thought. He wondered a lot what it was they thought about him and the men.

He remembered how difficult it had been when he had first come to the war to tell the villagers from the enemy and sometimes it had seemed easier to hate all of them, but he had always tried very hard not to. He wished he could be sure they understood that he and the men were there because they were trying to help all of them save their country from the communists.

5   They were on a rice dike that bordered the graveyard. The voices from the huts nearby seemed quite loud. He looked up ahead to where the lieutenant who had come along with them that night was standing. The lieutenant had sent one of the men, Molina, on across the rice dikes almost to the edge of the village. The cold rain was still coming down very hard and the men behind him were standing like a line of statues waiting for the next command.

But now something was wrong up ahead. He could see Molina waving his hands excitedly trying to tell the lieutenant something. Stumbling over the dikes, almost crawling, Molina came back toward the lieutenant. He saw him whisper something in his ear. And now the lieutenant turned and looked at him. "Sergeant," he said, "Molina and I are going to get a look up ahead. Stay here with the team."

Balancing on the dike, he turned around slowly after the lieutenant had gone, motioning with his rifle for all of the men in back of him to get down. Each one, carefully, one after the other, squatted along the dike on one knee, waiting in the rain to move out again. They were all shivering from the cold.

They waited for what seemed a long time and then the lieutenant and Molina appeared suddenly through the darkness. He could tell from their faces that they had seen something. They had seen something up ahead, he was sure, and they were going to tell him what they had just seen. He stood up, too excited to stay kneeling down on the dike.

"What is it?" he cried.

10   "Be quiet," whispered the lieutenant sharply, grabbing his arm, almost throwing him into the paddy. He began talking very quickly and much louder than he should have. "I think we found them. I think we found them," he repeated, almost shouting.

He didn't know what the lieutenant meant. "What?" he said.

"The sappers, the sappers! Let's go!" The lieutenant was taking over now. He seemed very sure of himself, he was acting very confident. "Let's go, goddamn it!"

He clicked his rifle off safety and got his men up quickly, urging them forward, following the lieutenant and Molina toward the edge of the village. They ran through the paddy, splashing like a family of ducks. This time he hoped and prayed it would be the real enemy. He would be ready for them this time. Here was another chance, he thought. He was so excited he ran straight into the lieutenant, bouncing clumsily off his chest.

"I'm sorry, sir," he said.

15   "Quiet! They're out there," the lieutenant whispered to him, motioning to the rest of the men to get down on their hands and knees now. They crawled to the tree line, then along the back of the rice paddy through almost a foot of water, until the whole team lay in a long line pressed up against the dike, facing the village.

He saw a light, a fire he thought, flickering in the distance off to the right of the village, with little dark figures that seemed to be moving behind it. He could not tell how far away they were from there. It was very hard to tell distance in the dark.

The lieutenant moved next to him. "You see?" he whispered. "Look," he said, very keyed up now. "They've got rifles. Can you see the rifles? Can you see them?" the lieutenant asked him.

He looked very hard through the rain.

"Can you see them?"

20   "Yes, I see them. I see them," he said. He was very sure.

The lieutenant put his arm around him and whispered in his ear. "Tell them down at the end to give me an illumination. I want this whole place lit up like a fucking Christmas tree."

Turning quickly to the man on his right, he told him what the lieutenant had said. He told him to pass the instructions all the way to the end of the line, where a flare would be fired just above the small fire near the village.

Lying there in the mud behind the dike, he stared at the fire that still flickered in the rain. He could still see the little figures moving back and forth against it like small shadows on a screen. He felt the whole line tense, then heard the WOOOORSHH of the flare cracking overhead in a tremendous ball of sputtering light turning night into day, arching over their heads toward the small fire that he now saw was burning inside an open hut.

Suddenly someone was firing from the end with his rifle, and now the whole line opened up, roaring their weapons like thunder, pulling their triggers again and again without even thinking, emptying everything they had into the hut in a tremendous stream of bright orange tracers that criss-crossed each other in the night.

25   The flare arched its last sputtering bits into the village and it became dark, and all he could see were the bright orange embers from the fire that had gone out.

And he could hear them.

There were voices screaming.

"What happened? Goddamn it, what happened?" yelled the lieutenant.

The voices were screaming from inside the hut.

30   "Who gave the order to fire? I wanna know who gave the order to fire."

The lieutenant was standing up now, looking up and down the line of men still lying in the rain.

He found that he was shaking. It had all happened so quickly.

"We better get a killer team out there," he heard Molina say.

"All right, all right. Sergeant," the lieutenant said to him, "get out there with Molina and tell me how many we got."

35   He got to his feet and quickly got five of the men together, leading them over the dike and through the water to the hut from where the screams were still coming. It was much closer than he had first thought. Now he could see very clearly the smoldering embers of the fire that had been blown out by the terrific blast of their rifles.

Molina turned the beam of his flashlight into the hut. "Oh God," he said. "Oh Jesus Christ." He started to cry. "We just shot up a bunch of kids!"

The floor of the small hut was covered with them, screaming and thrashing their arms back and forth, lying in pools of blood, crying wildly, screaming again and again. They were shot in the face, in the chest, in the legs, moaning and crying.

"Oh Jesus!" he cried.

He could hear the lieutenant shouting at them, wanting to know how many they had killed.

40   There was an old man in the corner with his head blown off from his eyes up, his brains hanging out of his head like jelly. He kept looking at the strange sight, he had never seen anything like it before. A small boy next to the old man was still alive, although he had been shot many times. He was crying softly, lying in a large pool of blood. His small foot had been shot almost completely off and seemed to be hanging by a thread.

"What's happening? What's going on up there?" The lieutenant was getting very impatient now.

Molina shouted for the lieutenant to come quickly. "You better get up here. There's a lot of wounded people up here."

He heard a small girl moaning now. She was shot through the stomach and bleeding out of the rear end. All he could see now was blood everywhere and he heard their screams with his heart racing like it had never raced before. He felt crazy and weak as he stood there staring at them with the rest of the men, staring down onto the floor like it was a nightmare, like it was some kind of dream and it really wasn't happening.

And then he could no longer stand watching. They were people, he thought, children and old men, people, people like himself, and he had to do something, he had to move, he had to help, do something. He jerked the green medical bag off his back, ripping it open and grabbing for bandages, yelling at Molina to please come and help him. He knelt down in the middle of the screaming bodies and began bandaging them, trying to cover the holes where the blood was still spurting out. "It's gonna be okay. It's gonna be okay," he tried to say, but he was crying now, crying and still trying to bandage them all up. He moved from body to body searching in the dark with his fingers for the holes the bullets had made, bandaging each one as quickly as he could, his shaking hands wet with the blood. It was raining into the hut and a cold wind swept his face as he moved in the dark.

45   The lieutenant had just come up with the others.

"Help me!" he screamed. "Somebody help!"

"Well goddamn it sergeant! What's the matter? How many did we kill?"

"They're children!" he screamed at the lieutenant.

"Children and old men!" cried Molina.

50   "Where are their rifles?" the lieutenant asked.

"There aren't any rifles," he said.

"Well, help him then!" screamed the lieutenant to the rest of the men. The men stood in the entrance of the hut, but they would not move. "Help him, help him. I'm ordering you to help him!"

The men were not moving and some of them were crying now, dropping their rifles and sitting down on the wet ground. They were weeping now with their hands against their faces. "Oh Jesus, oh God, forgive us."

"Forgive us for what we've done!" he heard Molina cry.

55   "Get up," screamed the lieutenant. "What do you think this is? I'm ordering you all to get up."

Some of the men began slowly crawling over the bodies, grabbing for the bandages that were still left.

By now some of the villagers had gathered outside the hut. He could hear them shouting angrily. He knew they must be cursing them.

"You better get a fucking chopper in here," someone was yelling.

"Where's the radio man? Get the radio man!"

60   "Hello Cactus Red. This is Red Light Two. Ahhh this is Red Light Two. We need an emergency evac. We got a lot of wounded . . . ahh . . . friendly wounded. A lot of friendly wounded out here." He could hear the lieutenant on the radio, trying to tell the helicopters where to come.

The men in the hut were just sitting there crying. They could not move, and they did not listen to the lieutenant's orders. They just sat with the rain pouring down on them through the roof, crying and not moving.

"You men! You men have got to start listening to me. You gotta stop crying like babies and start acting like marines!" The lieutenant who was off the radio now was shoving the men, pleading with them to move. "You're men, not babies. It's all a mistake. It wasn't your fault. They got in the way. Don't you people understand—they got in the goddamn way!"

When the medivac chopper came, he picked up the little boy who was lying next to the old man. His foot came off and he grabbed it up quickly and bandaged it against the bottom stump of the boy's leg. He held him looking into his frightened eyes and carried him up to the open door of the helicopter. The boy was still crying softly when he handed him to the gunner.

And when it was all over and all the wounded had been loaded aboard, he helped the lieutenant move the men back on patrol. They walked away from the hut in the rain. And now he felt his body go numb and heavy, feeling awful and sick inside like the night the corporal had died, as they moved along in the dark and the rain behind the lieutenant toward the graveyard.

If Shakespeare Had Had a Sister
Virginia Woolf

It is a perennial puzzle why no woman wrote a word of that extraordinary [Elizabethan] literature when every other man, it seemed, was capable of song or sonnet. What were the conditions in which women lived, I

Virginia Woolf, excerpts from *A Room of One's Own* by Virginia Woolf, copyright 1929 by Harcourt, Inc. and renewed 1957 by Leonard Woolf, reprinted by permission of the publisher.

asked myself; for fiction, imaginative work that is, is not dropped like a pebble upon the ground, as science may be; fiction is like a spider's web, attached ever so lightly perhaps, but still attached to life at all four corners. Often the attachment is scarcely perceptible; Shakespeare's plays, for instance, seem to hang there complete by themselves. But when the web is pulled askew, hooked up at the edge, torn in the middle, one remembers that these webs are not spun in mid-air by incorporeal creatures, but are the work of suffering human beings, and are attached to grossly material things, like health and money and the house we live in.

But what I find . . . is that nothing is known about women before the eighteenth century. I have no model in my mind to turn about this way and that. Here am I asking why women did not write poetry in the Elizabethan age, and I am not sure how they were educated; whether they were taught to write; whether they had sitting-rooms to themselves; how many women had children before they were twenty-one; what, in short, they did from eight in the morning till eight at night. They had no money evidently; according to Professor Trevelyan they were married whether they liked it or not before they were out of the nursery, at fifteen or sixteen very likely. It would have been extremely odd, even upon this showing, had one of them suddenly written the plays of Shakespeare, I concluded, and I thought of that old gentleman, who is dead now, but was a bishop, I think, who declared that it was impossible for any woman, past, present, or to come, to have the genius of Shakespeare. He wrote to the papers about it. He also told a lady who applied to him for information that cats do not as a matter of fact go to heaven, though they have, he added, souls of a sort. How much thinking those old gentlemen used to save one! How the borders of ignorance shrank back at their approach! Cats do not go to heaven. Women cannot write the plays of Shakespeare.

Be that as it may, I could not help thinking, as I looked at the works of Shakespeare on the shelf, that the bishop was right at least in this; it would have been impossible, completely and entirely, for any woman to have written the plays of Shakespeare in the age of Shakespeare. Let me imagine, since facts are so hard to come by, what would have happened had Shakespeare had a wonderfully gifted sister, called Judith, let us say. Shakespeare himself went, very probably—his mother was an heiress—to the grammar school, where he may have learnt Latin—Ovid, Virgil and Horace—and the elements of grammar and logic. He was, it is well known, a wild boy who poached rabbits, perhaps shot a deer, and had, rather sooner than he should have done, to marry a woman in the neighbourhood, who bore him a child rather quicker than was right. That escapade sent him to seek his fortune in London. He had, it seemed, a taste for the theatre; he began by holding horses at the stage door. Very soon he got work in the theatre, became a successful actor, and lived at the hub of the universe, meeting everybody, knowing everybody, practising his art on the boards, exercising his wits in the streets, and even getting access to the palace of the queen. Meanwhile his extraordinarily gifted sister, let us suppose, remained at home. She was as adventurous, as imaginative, as agog to see the world as he was. But she was not sent to school. She had no chance of learning grammar and logic, let alone of reading Horace and Virgil. She picked up a book now and then, one of her brother's perhaps, and read a few pages. But then her parents came in and told her to mend the stockings or mind the stew and not moon about with books and papers. They would have spoken sharply but kindly, for they were substantial people who knew the conditions of life for a woman and loved their daughter—indeed, more likely than not she was the apple of her father's eye. Perhaps she scribbled some pages up in an apple loft on the sly, but was careful to hide them or set fire to them. Soon, however, before she was out of her teens, she was to be betrothed to the son of a neighbouring wool-stapler. She cried out that marriage was hateful to her, and for that she was severely beaten by her father. Then he ceased to scold her. He begged her instead not to hurt him, not to shame him in this matter of her marriage. He would give her a chain of beads or a fine petticoat, he said; and there were tears in his eyes. How could she disobey him? How could she break his heart? The force of her own gift alone drove her to it. She made up a small parcel of her belongings, let herself down by a rope one summer's night and took the road to London. She was not seventeen. The birds that sang in the hedge were not more musical than she was. She had the quickest fancy, a gift like her brother's, for the tune of words. Like him, she had a taste for the theatre. She stood at the stage door; she wanted to act, she said. Men laughed in her face. The manager—a fat, loose-lipped man—guffawed. He bellowed something about poodles dancing and women acting—no woman, he said, could possibly be an actress. He hinted—you can imagine what. She could get no training in her craft. Could she even seek her dinner in a tavern or roam the streets at midnight? Yet her genius was for fiction and lusted to feed abundantly upon the lives of men and women and the study of their ways. At last—for she was very young, oddly like Shakespeare the poet in her face, with the same grey eyes and rounded brows—at last Nick Greene the actor-manager took pity on her; she found herself with child by that gentleman and so—who shall measure the heat and violence of the poet's heart when caught and tangled in a woman's body?—killed herself one winter's night and lies buried at some cross-roads where the omnibuses now stop outside the Elephant and Castle.

That, more or less, is how the story would run, I think, if a woman in Shakespeare's day had had Shakespeare's genius. But for my part, I agree with the deceased bishop, if such he was—it is unthinkable that any woman in Shakespeare's day should have had Shakespeare's genius. For genius like Shakespeare's is not born among labouring, uneducated, servile people. It was not born in England among the Saxons and the Britons. It is not born today among the working classes. How, then, could it have been born among women whose work began, according to Professor Trevelyan, almost before they were out of the nursery, who were forced to it by their parents and held to it by all the power of law and custom?

The Ones Who Walk Away from Omelas
Ursula Le Guin

With a clamor of bells that set the swallows soaring, the Festival of Summer came to the city Omelas, bright-towered by the sea. The rigging of the boats in harbor sparkled with flags. In the streets between houses with red roofs and painted walls, between old moss-grown gardens and under avenues of trees, past great parks and public buildings, processions moved. Some were decorous: old people in long stiff robes of mauve and grey, grave master workmen, quiet, merry women carrying their babies, and chatting as they walked. In other streets the music beat faster, a shimmering of gong and tambourine, and the people went dancing, the procession was a dance. Children dodged in and out, their high calls rising like the swallows' crossing flights over the music and the singing. All the processions wound towards the north side of the city, where on the great water-meadow called the Green Fields boys and girls, naked in the bright air, with mud-stained feet and ankles and long, lithe arms, exercised their restive horses before the race. The horses wore no gear at all but a halter without bit. Their manes were braided with streamers of silver, gold, and green. They flared their nostrils and pranced and boasted to one another; they were vastly excited, the horse being the only animal who has adopted our ceremonies as his own. Far off to the north and west the mountains stood up half encircling Omelas on her bay. The air of morning was so clear that the snow still crowning the Eighteen Peaks burned with white-gold fire across the miles of sunlit air, under the dark blue of the sky. There was just enough wind to make the banners that marked the racecourse snap and flutter now and then. In the silence of the broad green meadows one could hear the music winding through the city streets, farther and nearer and ever approaching, a cheerful faint sweetness of the air that from time to time trembled and gathered together and broke out into the great joyous clanging of the bells.

Joyous! How is one to tell about joy? How describe the citizens of Omelas?

They were not simple folk, you see, though they were happy. But we do not say the words of cheer much any more. All smiles have become archaic.

Given a description such as this one tends to make certain assumptions. Given a description such as this one tends to look next for the King, mounted on a splendid stallion and surrounded by his noble knights, or perhaps in a golden litter borne by great-muscled slaves. But there was no king. They did not use swords, or keep slaves. They were not barbarians. I do not know the rules and laws of their society, but I suspect that they were singularly few. As they did without monarchy and slavery, so they also get on without the stock exchange, the advertisement, the secret police, and the bomb. Yet I repeat that these were not simple folk, not dulcet shepherds, noble savages, bland utopians. They were not less complex than us. The trouble is that we have a bad habit, encouraged by pedants and sophisticates, of considering happiness as something rather stupid. Only pain is intellectual, only evil interesting. This is the treason of the artist: a refusal to admit the banality of evil and the terrible boredom of pain. If you can't lick 'em join 'em. If it hurts, repeat it. But to praise despair is to condemn delight, to embrace violence is to lose hold of everything else. We have almost lost hold; we can no longer describe a happy man, nor make any celebration of joy. How can I tell you about the people of Omelas? They were not naive and happy children—though their children were, in fact, happy. They were mature, intelligent, passionate adults whose lives were not wretched. O miracle! but I wish I could describe it better. I wish I could convince you. Omelas sounds in my words like a city in a fairy tale, long ago and far away, once upon a time. Perhaps it would be best if you imagined it as your own fancy bids, assuming it will rise to the occasion, for certainly I cannot suit you all. For instance, how about technology? I think that there would be no cars or helicopters in and above the streets; this follows from the fact that the people of Omelas are happy people. Happiness is based on a just discrimination of what is necessary, what is neither necessary nor destructive, and what is destructive. In the middle category, however—that of the unnecessary but undestructive, that of comfort, luxury, exuberance, etc.—they could perfectly well have central heating, subway trains, washing machines, and all kinds of marvelous devices not yet invented here, floating light-sources, fuelless power, a cure for the common cold. Or they could have none of that: it doesn't matter. As you like it. I incline to think that people from towns up and down the coast have been coming in to Omelas during the last days before the Festival on very fast little trains and double-decked trams, and that the train station of Omelas is actually the handsomest building in town, though plainer than the magnificent Farmers' Market. But even granted trains, I fear that Omelas so far strikes some of you as goody-goody. Smiles, bells, parades, horses, bleh. If so, please add an orgy. If an orgy would help, don't hesitate. Let us not, however, have temples from which issue beautiful nude priests and priestesses already half in ecstasy and ready to copulate with any man or woman, lover or stranger, who desires union with the deep godhead of the blood, although that was my first idea. But really it would be better not to have any temples in Omelas—at least, not manned temples. Religion yes, clergy no. Surely the beautiful nudes can just wander about, offering themselves like divine souffles to the hunger of the needy and the rapture of the flesh. Let them join the processions. Let tambourines be struck above the copulations, and the glory of desire be proclaimed upon the gongs, and (a not unimportant point) let the offspring of these delightful rituals be beloved and looked after by all. One thing I know there is none of in Omelas is guilt. But what else should there be? I thought at first there were no drugs, but that is puritanical. For those who like it, the faint insistent sweetness of *drooz* may perfume the ways of the city, *drooz* which first brings a great lightness and brilliance to the mind and limbs, and then after some hours a dreamy languor, and wonderful visions at last of the very arcana and inmost secrets of the Universe, as well as exciting the pleasure of sex beyond all belief; and it is not habit-forming. For more modest tastes I think there ought to be beer. What else, what else belongs in the joyous city? The sense of victory, surely, the celebration of courage. But as we did without clergy, let us do without soldiers. The joy built upon successful slaughter is not the right kind of joy; it will not do; it is fearful and it is trivial. A boundless and generous contentment, a magnanimous triumph felt not against some outer enemy but in communion with the finest and fairest in the souls of all men everywhere and the splendor of the world's summer: this is what swells the hearts of the people of Omelas, and the victory they celebrate is that of life. I really don't think many of them need to take *drooz*.

Most of the processions have reached the Green Fields by now. A marvelous smell of cooking goes forth from the red and blue tents of the provisioners. The faces of small children are amiably sticky; in the benign grey beard of a man a couple of crumbs of rich pastry are entangled. The youths and girls have mounted their horses and are beginning to group around the starting line of the course. An old woman, small, fat and laughing, is passing out flowers from a basket, and tall young men wear her flowers in their shining hair. A child of nine or ten sits at the edge of the crowd alone, playing on a wooden flute. People pause to listen, and they smile, but they do not speak to him, for he never ceases playing and never sees them, his dark eyes wholly rapt in the sweet, thin magic of the tune.

5   He finishes, and slowly lowers his hands holding the wooden flute.

As if that little private silence were the signal, all at once a trumpet sounds from the pavilion near the starting line: imperious, melancholy, piercing. The horses rear on their slender legs, and some of them neigh in answer. Soberfaced, the young riders stroke the horses' necks and soothe them, whispering, "Quiet, quiet, there my beauty, my hope. . . . " They begin to form in rank along the starting line. The crowds along the racecourse are like a field of grass and flowers in the wind. The Festival of Summer has begun.

Do you believe? Do you accept the festival, the city, the joy? No? Then let me describe one more thing.

In a basement under one of the beautiful public buildings of Omelas, or perhaps in the cellar of one of its spacious private homes, there is a room. It has one locked door, and no window. A little light seeps in dustily between cracks in the boards, secondhand from a cobwebbed window somewhere across the cellar. In one corner of the little room a couple of mops, with stiff, clotted, foul-smelling heads, stand near a rusty bucket. The floor is dirt, a little damp to the touch, as cellar dirt usually is. The room is about three paces long and two wide: a mere broom closet or disused tool room. In the room a child is sitting. It could be a boy or a girl. It looks about six, but actually is nearly ten. It is feeble-minded. Perhaps it was born defective, or perhaps it has become imbecile through fear, malnutrition, and neglect. It picks its nose and occasionally fumbles vaguely with its toes or genitals, as it sits hunched in the corner farthest from the bucket and the two mops. It is afraid of the mops. It finds them horrible. It shuts its eyes, but it knows the mops are still standing there; and the door is locked; and nobody will come. The door is always locked; and nobody ever comes, except that sometimes— the child has no understanding of time or interval—sometimes the door rattles terribly and opens, and a person, or several people, are there. One of them may come in and kick the child to make it stand up. The others never come close, but peer in at it with frightened, disgusted eyes. The food bowl and the water jug are hastily filled, the door is locked, the eyes disappear. The people at the door never say anything, but the child, who has not always lived in the tool room, and can remember sunlight and its mother's voice, sometimes speaks. "I will be good," it says. "Please let me out. I will be good!" They never answer. The child used to scream for help at night, and cry a good deal, but now it only makes a kind of whining, "eh-haa, eh-haa," and it speaks less and less often. It is so thin there are no calves to its legs; its belly protrudes; it lives on a half-bowl of corn meal and grease a day. It is naked. Its buttocks and thighs a mass of festered sores, as it sits in its own excrement continually.

They all know it is there, all the people of Omelas. Some of them have come to see it, others are content merely to know it is there. They all know that it has to be there. Some of them understand why, and some do not, but they all understand that their happiness, the beauty of their city, the tenderness of their friendships, the health of their children, the wisdom of their scholars, the skill of their makers, even the abundance of their harvest and the kindly weathers of their skies, depends wholly on this child's abominable misery.

10   This is usually explained to children when they are between eight and twelve, whenever they seem capable of understanding; and most of those who come to see the child are young people, though often enough an adult comes, or comes back, to see the child. No matter how well the matter has been explained to them, these young spectators are always shocked and sickened at the sight. They feel disgust, which they had thought themselves superior to. They feel anger, outrage, impotence, despite all the explanations. They would like to do something for the child. But there is nothing they can do. If the child were brought up into the sunlight out of that vile place, it if

were cleaned and fed and comforted, that would be a good thing, indeed; but if it were done, in that day and hour all the prosperity and beauty and delight of Omelas would wither and be destroyed. Those are the terms. To exchange all the goodness and grace of every life in Omelas for that single, small improvement: to throw away the happiness of thousands for the chance of the happiness of one: that would be to let guilt within the walls indeed.

The terms are strict and absolute; there may not even be a kind word spoken to the child.

Often the young people go home in tears, or in a tearless rage, when they have seen the child and faced this terrible paradox. They may brood over it for weeks or years. But as time goes on they begin to realize that even if the child could be released, it would not get much good of its freedom: a little vague pleasure of warmth and food, no doubt, but little more. It is too degraded and imbecile to know any real joy. It has been afraid too long even to be free of fear. Its habits are too uncouth for it to respond to humane treatment. Indeed, after so long it would probably be wretched without walls about it to protect it, and darkness for its eyes, and its own excrement to sit in. Their tears at the bitter injustice dry when they begin to perceive the terrible justice of reality, and to accept it. Yet it is their tears and anger, the trying of their generosity and the acceptance of their helplessness, which are perhaps the true source of the splendor of their lives. Theirs is no vapid, irresponsible happiness. They know that they, like the child, are not free. They know compassion. It is the existence of the child, and their knowledge of its existence, that makes possible the nobility of their architecture, and poignancy of their music, the profundity of their science. It is because of the child that they are so gentle with children. They know that if the wretched one were not there snivelling in the dark, the other one, the flute-player, could make no joyful music as the young riders line up in their beauty for the race in the sunlight of the first morning of summer.

Now do you believe in them? Are they not more credible? But there is one more thing to tell, and this is quite incredible.

At times one of the adolescent girls or boys who go to see the child does not go home to weep or rage, does not, in fact, go home at all. Sometimes also a man or woman much older falls silent for a day or two, and then leaves home. These people go out into the street, and walk down the street alone. They keep walking, and walk straight out of the city of Omelas, through the beautiful gates. They keep walking across the farmlands of Omelas. Each one goes alone, youth or girl, man or woman. Night falls; the traveler must pass down village streets, between the houses with yellow-lit windows, and on out into the darkness of the fields. Each alone, they go west or north, towards the mountains. They go on. They leave Omelas, they walk ahead into the darkness, and they do not come back. The place they go towards is a place even less imaginable to most of us than the city of happiness. I cannot describe it at all. It is possible that it does not exist. But they seem to know where they are going, the ones who walk away from Omelas.

TECHNIQUES FOR WRITERS 9-d

The Narrative Argument

Write a three-to-five–page narrative argument detailing some meaningful event in your life. "Meaningful" should also extend to your audience: the student narratives in this chapter hinge on themes of betrayal by adult caretakers, sudden awareness of class divides, and shame overcome by self-forgiveness. Because these topics affect nearly all readers' lives at some point, they engage audience interest in a way that "my trip to Disneyland" (big fun) or "my prom dress" (big price tag) won't because they're so specialized. However, coming to some kind of *awareness* at Disneyland or spending so much money on a one-time dress may work well.

Moreover, *focus* is everything in writing an argumentative narrative. If your main point is that you had fun at Disneyland, readers can't engage by saying *No, you didn't.* Nor can they argue that the dress cost a lot and you looked nice in it. So, you have to focus the topic in a way that readers could feasibly argue against your point.

When drafting your own narrative argument, focus only on details that make your point meaningful: i.e., if you are discussing the way in which your first river rafting adventure changed your life, you won't need to begin your essay with making plane reservations, packing, eating the food on the plane, or other mundane details. And try, in your writing, to place the reader into the event as it is happening. Your descriptions of the time, place, impact, and other aspects of the event should be so vivid and convincing that the reader almost experiences the event—and as a result, can supply the thesis if you want to leave the main "moral of the story" implied rather than stated. (You can make your point either implicitly or explicitly.)

Beware of these four problematic areas common in narrative writing:

- **Use of direct quotation**. Be sure to follow punctuation standards.
- **Tense switches**. Begin your essay in either present or past tense, and switch tense only when the time element of your narrative requires it.
- **Chronology.** Flashbacks (going back to an earlier time) in a narrative are very common and can be very effective. If you use flashbacks in your narrative, or if you jump ahead to a later time in the story, be sure to use transitional elements that will make this time-switch clear to your reader.
- **Second person.** Unless you are referring to the reader specifically or are using dialogue, the use of "you" is probably not applicable.

For those who prefer a creative approach, you may consider writing in *persona;* that is, writing about the event through the voice of someone else in the story other than yourself. For instance, if a narrative were to describe the death of a loved one, the piece could be written through the voice of the deceased, rather than through the voice of the surviving writer. A narrative about an abusive husband/boyfriend could be written through the perspective and persona of the abuser rather than his victim. Possibilities with persona-based writing are almost limitless.

Peer Revision Questions—Narrative Arguments

1. What point do you believe the author is trying to make? How effective is he or she in making that point?
2. How effective is the author's title?
3. How effective is the author's introduction? Does it make you want to read further?
4. Is the chronology of the essay easy to follow?
5. What is the controlling tense of the narrative (past, present, future)? Are tense changes appropriate?
6. Is anything unclear in the paper? What, if anything, needs to be clarified?
7. What grammatical/mechanical errors need to be cleared up?
8. What other helpful comments would you give this author?

Student Writing: Rhetorical Narratives

The following three essays are student models of rhetorical narratives. As you read them, try to discern the point the author is making and whether that point is explicit or implicit. Also, notice how the authors use details—visual, aural, tactile—to bring you into the story.

Twinkle, Twinkle, Little Star

Brian Larson

As a little kid in Sunday school, I got to play a part in each year's Christmas pageant at church. But they were crummy parts: a sheep, a donkey, a cow, maybe a camel. That's how things worked in the Sunday school pecking order. As long as you were under the age of eight, you had to play one of the animals at the Nativity.

Every year, dressed in my silly critter costume, I'd look around at the older kids wearing their beautiful shepherd robes and angel gowns, and I'd feel embarrassed all over again, and I'd do math in my head: *Last January I turned five, add the year that's followed, now I'm almost six. Add another year, and I'll be even closer . . . closer. . . .*

Finally, it came—a real part. I was eight years old. I was going to be a *person*. But not just a person. Oh, no. I was going to play one of the wise men, the one who brought the gold to the stable. And I would play my part in fine style, too, because as soon as I found out I had the role, my mother went out to the sewing store and bought the most expensive wise-man fabric they had. While she spent the next two weeks carefully stitching my robe together, my dad and I worked on the star that would hover over my head, the star that would lead me to the stable. We cut out a pattern from quarter-inch plywood, then spray-painted it silver, but that wasn't shiny enough. So we covered the wood with aluminum foil, being careful to keep the metal perfectly smooth, shiny side out, then stapled a black coat hanger to it to attach it to my robe and keep it hanging over my head. When we finished, the star was perfect.

On Christmas Eve, all of the kids gathered in the church basement, and one of the teachers came by to ask for my star. I thought he would just keep it in a safe place for me while I got into my costume, so I gave it to him without question. My dad helped me put on my robe, then the white headgear my mom had made of silk, and I completed the outfit by taking off my tennis shoes and putting on sandals. Then, with a great deal of pride, I stood at the back of the room and smiled as my mom and some of the other church ladies took my picture and told me I looked as if I'd stepped out of a Christmas card—my costume was that good.

My little sister, who had just turned three that year, was dressed in my old sheep outfit, and she was proud of me, too. She and the other little kids looked at me in admiration as I passed them and went upstairs—just as I'd admired the kids who were older than me for all those years.

Now that all of the players in the pageant were dressed, we reassembled in the lobby at the back of the church and waited for our cue from the minister to come up the aisle. About a minute before the cue came, the teacher who'd taken my star came around to pass out our props—shepherd's staffs, angel's halos, and stars. But there was a problem with the stars, because it wasn't just the wise men who had them. The angels had them, too, and a couple of the shepherds, and the teacher couldn't remember who had brought which star, so he just reached into his box and gave them out as he grabbed them. I watched with alarm as he came to me and pulled out a bent and wrinkled thing with uneven sides and the dull side of the foil turned out.

"This isn't mine," I said. I looked around the lobby, but I couldn't see my star.

"Someone else has mine," I said.

"No time for that now," the teacher said, and he shrugged in apology.

The minister gave us his cue.

"This isn't my star," I told my mother, but she repeated what the teacher had said and turned me around so she could hook the bent piece of wire to my robe. Then it was attached, and she gave me a little push toward the door. The other two wise men were already halfway to the altar.

"Go up now," she said. "Hurry."

So I went up, but slowly, shuffling my feet, staring down at the floor, and then I was at the altar, and I went up the steps. The three wise men stood at the base of the manger. One of them had frankincense for the baby Jesus; the other had myrrh.

The third had only a mangled and misshapen star, hunkering above him like floating garbage, and he stood with his head down, his back to the congregation, a bitter taste in his throat and hatred in his heart. After all those years of embarrassment, his big night had finally arrived.

* * *

Them

Ron Prush

The difference between me and them becomes apparent as soon as I step inside the building. My tickets are glossy white with silver print. Accordingly, the gate attendants won't let me pass through the turnstiles; instead, they point me to a separate room where a young blond woman in a black tuxedo smiles graciously and leads me to a private elevator.

"Tonight's going to be exciting," she says as the car lifts us, quickly and gently, to the second floor. "One more win and we've got the division title."

I want to respond, but the ride is short; the elevator doors open and the attendant motions with a white-gloved hand that I should step out. "Enjoy the game, sir," she says, then disappears as the doors close.

Sir. My high-tops and black leather jacket are both scuffed, but my tickets are glossy white with silver print. Noting this, an usher in a maroon sports coat quickly steps forward to escort me to the suite. He leads me through the concourse, through the crowds of well-dressed suburban couples quickly filling it, past the pizza stands and nacho stands and hot dog stands and beer stands, and he never stops to ask if I might want to buy something from these vendors. He knows better. The stands in the concourse are for *them,* and I am not one of them. Their tickets are plain. My tickets are glossy white with silver print.

The usher leads me down a brightly lit passageway, then stops at a door on the left. He turns and smiles. "Enjoy the game, sir."

Sir. Again. I thank him and open the door, and the noise from the concourse disappears when the door closes automatically behind me. *They* are out *there.* I am in *here,* with my fancy tickets.

I look around. On the oak coffee table, in the center of the room, sits a platter piled high with rippled potato chips, and on the oak buffet against the wall are bowl after bowl of fresh fruits, vegetables, cookies and pastries. On the white Formica counter, next to the sink, a warming pan full of breaded chicken breasts—boneless—sits above a refrigerator stocked full with beer and soda. I open a Diet Coke and pour it into a crystal glass from the cupboard. When I put down the empty can, another blond attendant wearing white gloves steps into the room to take the can away. Seeing the surprised look on my face, she laughs and tells me her perfect timing is just a coincidence.

When she leaves, I sit on the gray leather couch, put my feet up on the gray leather ottoman, and look at my glossy white tickets. The price at the bottom, embossed in silver, seems unreal. It constitutes many things: a third of my biweekly paycheck, my whole family's weekly grocery bill, the quarterly insurance payment on my car. All of these cost the same as my ticket. And if I multiply that price by eight hundred, I could lease this room, and this couch, and the color TV up in the corner, for a year.

Or, with the same amount of money, I could buy my parents *and* myself houses in an older neighborhood. Or twelve cars. Or fifteen years worth of groceries. Or an Ivy-league education for my kids when I have them. Or even a scholarship fund for someone *else's* kids.

"Eddie," I said when my host arrives, "I— "

But he has ten other people in tow behind him, and so I shut up and shake hands with all of them as he introduces me. Two women in the entourage head straight for the platter of cookies as their husbands stand at the closet to hang up their coats and begin talking, in Wall Street-ese, about corporate mergers and stock splits. The men speak of dollars with great adoration.

"Eddie," I say, wiping their greed from my hands against my blue jeans, "I don't fit in here. These aren't my people. Give me a floor ticket instead."

He looks at me, surprised.

"You want to sit out there with *them?*"

"Yeah."

The two women, their mouths full of cookies, open the sliding door leading out to the arena and begin to mumble to each other through the crumbs. Other people crack open beers. I wait for the white-gloved attendant to step in and take the empty cans before they can touch the countertop.

Eddie gives me a floor ticket. He gets four of them with every game. It's part of the package when anyone leases a suite at the arena. "Enjoy the game," he says. "Stop back up at halftime."

I give him my silver-gloss tickets and take the plain ones. "Okay," I tell him. "I'll stop back up."

I go out into the hallway, where the usher in the maroon
sports coat waits. He begins to walk toward me, but when he sees
the plain ticket in my hand, he stops. I go into the arena alone.

When I find my row, I see that my seat is in the middle of
the row, and the people who have to stand up to let me pass get
yelled at by the people behind them who can't see the court. In
my hurry to stop causing trouble, I step on a woman's foot, but
she doesn't say anything. She can't; she has a mouthful of
nachos.

"PHILLY!" shouts a bellowing voice behind me when I sit
down, so loudly that a sharp pain goes through my left ear, "YOU
AIN'T NUTHIN' BUT A BUNCHA CRYBABIES!"

"GODDAM THUGS!" the loud man yells, as the Philadelphia
players come trotting toward their bench and the court quickly
clears for the game. I turn around so I can get a glimpse of this
refined gentleman. He's fiftyish, with a gray beard, wearing a
black T-shirt with the Chevrolet logo on the front. His
overweight belly bulges through the shirt like a basketball.

I turn and face the court again. The woman next to me smiles
and says, "Wait until the game actually starts. Then he'll *really*
get going."

Out on the floor, Detroit gets the tip-off and scores a
quick two.

"You know the guy?" I ask the woman.

She looks horrified at the suggestion. "No, no, not
personally," she says. "But he has season tickets, and we've all
gotten to know him well. We call him 'Leatherlungs.' He's so—"

"WHATCHA GONNA DO ABOUT *THAT*, PUNKS?" the man explodes just
then. The refs have just called Philadelphia for an early foul,
and their coach is upset. "HAVE A LITTLE *CRY* LIKE THE *BABIES* YOU
ARE?"

The people around me smile. I look over toward the suite and
see Eddie sitting out on his plush red chair with his group.
Eddie has changed a lot over the past few years. He was the guy
who turned me on to *Brave New World* and *This Perfect Day* and *1984*
when we were in high school together, the guy who always warned
me about the dangers of conformity, and now he's sitting up there

in the ultimate symbol of corporate life, sipping a Heineken, snug in his button-down collar and pleated Banana Republic khakis and calfskin docksiders and yuppie values, but locked safely away from guys like the bearded bullhorn behind me.

As if on cue, the woman next to me suddenly knocks her giant cup of Coca-Cola off her lap, drenching her leg—and mine—in brown syrup.

I get up and step on her feet on my way down the row, then go out to the concourse where legions of blond, white-gloved attendants pass me, pushing silver carts with re-filled platters of fresh fruits and vegetables to the suites. Other carts are full of empty beer and soda cans. When I get back up to the suite, the usher in the maroon sports coat won't let me in. He knows perfectly well that I had a glossy white ticket earlier, but now I don't, so he treats me accordingly. He makes me stand aside while he knocks, and he makes Eddie come to the door and give him a personal assurance that I'm okay to enter.

"Sure," Eddie tells him, smiling. "This is one of my people."

And I go inside.

                              Purgastory
                           Michael -----

The nights in New Orleans during Mardi Gras bled into days and everything seemed distorted. Social Niceties of civilized people fell away and became perverse mockeries themselves. Mardi Gras was a funhouse mirror, and every day in that mirror I saw things in myself that I'd never seen before. Before boarding the airplane to New Orleans I'd been thinking, "This will be fun." But the trip became a surreal journey through the reeking sewers of one of America's most notorious cities, and it provided me with a major crisis of conscience. My time in the city simultaneously brought me to, and delivered me from, some of the darkest moments in my life.

Reprinted by permission of Michael.

The Christian soldiers marched through the crowd two by two, down Bourbon Street and into the heart of the French Quarter. They were marching as to war, carrying various banners, many of which proclaimed that God hated everyone but them. No wonder the crowd spit on them. I saw this mutual intolerance as a reflection of how it must have been on the road to Christ's crucifixion, because even with all of the anger around them, the "soldiers" ministered to anyone who wanted to listen, praying with those who knelt in the gutter. I wondered, drunkenly, if any of them had ever seen the devil. What would they do if he walked up right now and joined the parade?

A raggedy man looked like a blend between ancient condemned Jesus and a modern homeless person. He touched his bloody scalp, then turned a red-soaked hand toward the man who had struck him with a bottle. "I've got AIDS, man, I'll kill you with my blood!" I felt I should do something, but instead I just moved away, not really caring about the homeless Jesus. But a moment later, my apathy turned into a hot guilt that punched me viciously in the stomach.

What could I do? People like the raggedy man chose their own fates, didn't they? Besides, I had my own problems—plenty of them. I walked on, with the puree of beer, vodka, vomit, urine, and assorted bodily fluids soaking in my shoes. I walked past the stinking six-foot piles of garbage on every corner. I thought that God should burn this place to ashes.

Dante's *Divine Comedy* contains the classic line, "Abandon hope, all ye who enter here." The message is written above the entrance to Hell. In this place, New Orleans, "The Big Easy," among the bottom-feeders and the degenerates, the topless women and bottomless men, the losers and the lost, that line seemed terribly appropriate. I belonged here.

Back home, my real life—and what I'd done to it—waited for my return. I had charged over ten thousand dollars to my credit cards, buying lap dances from strippers. The interest alone was crushing me. I struggled just to make a $200 minimum payment sixty days past its due date. Creditors were calling every day. And my parents didn't know, and I couldn't keep it a secret much longer. I was morally, spiritually, and financially bankrupt. I looked around at the French Quarter, seeing the place where I had come, on impulse, to escape my actions. My soul screamed.

Why had I done this to myself? Why did I know the right things to do, yet lack the will to do them? I looked up, past the rooftops, to the sky. The sun still shined, even through the haze. All my life, I had strived to be one thing: a servant of justice and goodness. I wanted to be a police officer, or a soldier. I wanted to be one of the good guys. I wanted to be the hero. I wanted to save the world. Now, crippled by my lust, I had killed all of the honor within me. But had I? Seeing the sun, I knew that I could wallow here in my self-pity and fear, or I could take responsibility, humble myself by asking for help, and try to carry on.

Walk past the garbage. Walk past the filth. It was all in the past.

CHAPTER 10

Recognizing and Creating Oral and Visual Arguments

"I write the way I talk."

We hear this frequently from students, especially those who have had limited writing experience. Although writing and speaking may share the same words and sentence structures, writers and speakers face different challenges and have access to different tools when they set out to communicate. And in an age when the term "post-literate" has been coined to reflect a cultural emphasis on images in place of words, a third form of communication—*visual*—presents still more techniques and strategies to challenge both writers and readers. In this chapter, you'll have an opportunity to consider the sounds and sights of argument.

Most speakers, including those who present formal speeches, communicate through gestures and facial expressions (frequently called **body language**), as well as changes in volume, rhythm, and tone of voice. While punctuation can take the place of some of these tools in writing—a comma or period to mark phrases and sentences, italics to signify rising volume—it really can't duplicate the physical force and effect of a well-presented speech. This is why written transcripts of speeches may appear flat and unpersuasive in printed form, and why reading a speech aloud to yourself or others can bring out elements of the message that might otherwise seem unremarkable.

Defining Rhetoric

Body language: gestures and facial expressions that express meaning. Many people are unaware of their body language, but orators and others use their own body language as a tool for persuasion.

Speakers have another advantage over writers in the physical proximity of their audiences. While effective speakers use body language to persuade, they also have an opportunity to observe the reactions of their listeners. A skilled speaker can respond quickly to gestures or facial expressions that suggest confusion, anger, or loss of interest, while a writer essentially has one chance to convey a message. (This is one of the most important things to consider while you're in a college English course where peer-critique groups provide a chance to "test drive" your writing before a live audience—a benefit not so readily available after college.)

Writers, on the other hand, have an advantage over speakers because a writer's audience can re-read passages or change the reading pace when trying to comprehend basic, complex, difficult, or even confusing information. Because listeners can't do this, effective speakers must choose vocabulary, arrange ideas, and structure sentences carefully to give the audience maximum opportunity for comprehension. Speakers also use devices such as repetition, rhyme, and meter rhyme to hold the attention of their listeners. But most significantly, nearly all speakers *compose* their messages—mentally or through writing—before delivering them to an audience.

Finding the Roots of Classical Rhetoric in Oral Argument

The earliest rhetoricians concentrated on oral, rather than written, persuasion. Plato disdained writing, asserting that "no discourse worth serious attention has ever been written in verse or prose" (*Phaedrus*). Three hundred years later, in the *Institutio Oratoria*, the Roman rhetorician Quintilian established the educational sequence and procedures considered proper for the time, focusing on *oratory*, not written rhetoric. Young Greek and Roman men of that era needed oral communication skills in order to function well in their societies; writing was seen as a minor skill relegated to secretaries and scribes. The oral tradition is central to rhetoric's roots.

In Chapter 4 you learned about two of the Canons of rhetoric that Aristotle considered crucial to developing effective arguments: *invention,* or idea generation, and *dispositio,* or arrangement. Appendix 2 of this book focuses on a third Canon, *elocutio,* or style, but here we need to look at the Canons of *memoria* and *pronuntiatio* because they deal specifically with concerns that are central to oral argument.

In the early days of rhetoric, *memoria,* or memory, offered techniques for committing a speech to memory. Classical rhetoricians perceived the human mind as a sort of warehouse holding images that were gradually committed to memory over time. They believed a speaker could effectively memorize even a very long speech by associating the ideas and points he wished to make with the images held in his memory. (At the time, rhetoric and public oratory were almost exclusively reserved for men.) For example, Cicero, in *De Oratore,* suggested that speakers memorize the points they wished to make by associating those points with the rooms of a house. As the speakers mentally walked through each room, they could then call to mind the points they had previously associated with the images from the room. (You may have learned similar association techniques, called *mnemonics,* in elementary school if you memorized the names of the Great Lakes by associating them with the word "HOMES"—Huron, Ontario, Michigan, Erie, Superior—or read music by memorizing the notes, E-G-B-D-F, as the sentence, "Every good boy does fine.")

Pronuntiatio, or delivery, focused on techniques for using the voice and body effectively while speaking. While Aristotle, Cicero, and Quintilian all mentioned delivery, this Canon did not gain its greatest prominence until the eighteenth and nineteenth centuries, when rhetoricians such as Thomas Sheridan and Gilbert Austin discussed specific techniques for improving elocutionary skills. So seriously did they take the matter that Austin even developed a system including descriptions and illustrations of effective positions for speakers.

It's doubtful that a contemporary speaker would be concerned about specific gestures to the extent that Austin suggested. Even so, intuition and prior experience confirm the ways that gestures, facial expressions, and vocal modulations affect the reactions of audiences.

But what happens when an argument is purely auditory, with no accompanying visual cues? A 2004 series of public service announcements (PSAs) by Project

From Gilbert Austin, *Chironmia.*

Safe Neighborhoods and the Ad Council took a three-pronged approach to promoting awareness of gun violence, using print ads, TV commercials, and radio spots to reach a unique audience. One radio spot featured a few seconds of random street sounds—car horns, exhausts, faint shouting—followed by the voice of a very young boy, perhaps kindergarten age, saying, "On June 4, my big brother was sentenced to seven years in prison for a gun crime. That day, he sentenced me to seven years without my best friend." After ten more seconds of street sounds, an adult voiceover added the tag line: "When you commit a gun crime, your family pays the price."

In this example of oral argument, the entire appeal lies not only in the tragic message of loss and harm to innocents, but also in the power of the two voices. The boy, so young that the simple word "sentenced" is pronounced as two distinct syllables—*sen-tensed*—conveys heartbreak and despair, while the adult announcer adds gravitas to the message with his basic, direct equation: *you + gun = family as victim.*

The message is simple, powerful, and effective—but who is its audience? According to John A. Calhoun, President and CEO of the National Crime Prevention Council, his organization wanted these radio spots to "reiterate the hurt and pain, or 'sentence' that innocent family members experience." Thus the NCPC's goal was

> to spur family members to act to prevent a potential offender from carrying an illegal gun or using a gun illegally. It could be as much as having a full-blown conversation with a brother or son who might carry a gun illegally or as little as reminding that person how much it will hurt if they are not around as part of the family.

Because these spots were intended for an audience not likely to respond easily to emotional appeals, the ad agency's creative director knew that "they wouldn't listen to anything fake. So this work is real, no fancy editing, no music . . . just a harsh dose of reality."

Questions for Thinking and Writing

1. What would be the effect of the voices switching roles in this oral argument? If the adult narrator described the little boy's loss and the boy supplied the tag line, how would the argument's appeals be affected?
2. What role do the street sounds play in this argument—and why do they go on for such a relatively long time without narration?

In the twenty-first century, as messages are clipped into shorter and shorter sound bites, such harshness and directness seems commonplace. But oral argument, like every other kind, offers those who use it a wide range of choices for the delivery of their messages, in large part determined by the audience that will be receiving them. And as you'll see in the next section, one of the most famous oral arguments of our time was anything but harsh, direct, or plain.

Situating Context in Oral Argument: Martin Luther King, Jr.'s "I Have a Dream"

Considered to be among the most powerful public speakers of the twentieth century, Dr. Martin Luther King, Jr., received a broad education in classical rhetoric as part of his theological training. Combining rhetorical strategies for arrangement and style with the already-compelling Southern Baptist sermonic form, many of King's writings and speeches have become essential parts of American civil rights history. One speech, King's "I Have a Dream" message given on August 28, 1963, on the steps of the Lincoln Memorial in Washington, D.C., has become a centerpiece of American oratory. While many African Americans rightly complain that this is often the *only* speech by a black orator that children learn in school, it continues to be anthologized in countless textbooks, collections, and Web sites, and excerpts of the speech appear frequently in documentaries and newscasts during Black History Month. If only through excerpts and sound bites, most Americans have encountered the speech at some point in their lives.

Certainly the *context* of the speech—delivered in the nation's capital before a quarter of a million people at a time when the need for civil rights was just beginning to be recognized by many Americans, by a gifted and controversial speaker who would be assassinated only five years later—contributes to its lasting influence. And Dr. King's gestures and inflections, delivered in the Southern Baptist preaching style, powerfully affected all who heard him that day. But because *Classical Techniques and Contemporary Arguments* is a guide to *writing*, it's important to look at particular aspects of the speech that can be adapted to a written argument.

"I Have a Dream"
Martin Luther King, Jr.

I am happy to join with you today in what will go down in history as the greatest demonstration for freedom in the history of our nation.

Fivescore years ago, a great American, in whose symbolic shadow we stand today, signed the Emancipation Proclamation. This momentous decree came as a great beacon light of hope to millions of Negro slaves who had been seared in the flames of withering injustice. It came as a joyous daybreak to end the long night of their captivity.

But one hundred years later, the Negro still is not free; one hundred years later, the life of the Negro is still sadly crippled by the manacles of segregation and the chains of discrimination; one hundred years later, the Negro lives on a lonely island of poverty in the midst of a vast ocean of material prosperity; one hundred years later, the Negro is still languishing in the corners of American society and finds himself in exile in his own land.

So we've come here today to dramatize a shameful condition. In a sense we've come to our nation's capital to cash a check. When the architects of our republic wrote the magnificent words of the Constitution and the Declaration of Independence, they were signing a promissory note to which every American was to fall heir. This note was the promise that all men, yes, black men as well as white men, would be guaranteed the unalienable rights of life, liberty, and the pursuit of happiness.

5   It is obvious today that America has defaulted on this promissory note in so far as her citizens of color are concerned. Instead of honoring this sacred obligation, America has given the Negro people a bad check; a check which has come back marked "insufficient funds." We refuse to believe that there are insufficient funds in the great vaults of opportunity of this nation. And so we've come to cash this check, a check that will give us upon demand the riches of freedom and the security of justice.

We have also come to this hallowed spot to remind America of the fierce urgency of now. This is no time to engage in the luxury of cooling off or to take the tranquilizing drug of gradualism. Now is the time to make real the promises of democracy; now is the time to rise from the dark and desolate valley of segregation to the sunlit path of racial justice; now is the time to lift our nation from the quicksands of racial injustice to the solid rock of brotherhood; now is the time to make justice a reality for all God's children. It would be fatal for the nation to overlook the urgency of the moment. This sweltering summer of the Negro's legitimate discontent will not pass until there is an invigorating autumn of freedom and equality.

Nineteen sixty-three is not an end, but a beginning. And those who hope that the Negro needed to blow off steam and will now be content, will have a rude awakening if the nation returns to business as usual.

There will be neither rest nor tranquility in America until the Negro is granted his citizenship rights. The whirlwinds of revolt will continue to shake the foundations of our nation until the bright day of justice emerges.

But there is something that I must say to my people who stand on the warm threshold which leads into the palace of justice. In the process of gaining our rightful place we must not be guilty of wrongful deeds.

10   Let us not seek to satisfy our thirst for freedom by drinking from the cup of bitterness and hatred. We must forever conduct our struggle on the high plane of dignity and discipline. We must not allow our creative protest to degenerate into physical violence. Again and again we must rise to the majestic heights of meeting physical force with soul force.

The marvelous new militancy which has engulfed the Negro community must not lead us to a distrust of all white people, for many of our white brothers, as evidenced by their presence here today, have come to realize that their destiny is tied up with our destiny and they have come to realize that their freedom is inextricably bound to our freedom. This offense we share mounted to storm the battlements of injustice must be carried forth by a biracial army. We cannot walk alone.

And as we walk, we must make the pledge that we shall always march ahead. We cannot turn back. There are those who are asking the devotees of civil rights, "When will you be satisfied?" We can never be satisfied as long as the Negro is the victim of the unspeakable horrors of police brutality.

We can never be satisfied as long as our bodies, heavy with fatigue of travel, cannot gain lodging in the motels of the highways and the hotels of the cities. We cannot be satisfied as long as the Negro's basic mobility is from a smaller ghetto to a larger one.

We can never be satisfied as long as our children are stripped of their selfhood and robbed of their dignity by signs stating "for whites only." We cannot be satisfied as long as a Negro in Mississippi cannot vote and a Negro in New York believes he has nothing for which to vote. No, we are not satisfied, and we will not be satisfied until justice rolls down like waters and righteousness like a mighty stream.

15   I am not unmindful that some of you have come here out of excessive trials and tribulation. Some of you have come fresh from narrow jail cells. Some of you have come from areas where your quest for freedom left you battered by the storms of persecution and staggered by the winds of police brutality. You have been the veterans of creative suffering. Continue to work with the faith that unearned suffering is redemptive.

Go back to Mississippi; go back to Alabama; go back to South Carolina; go back to Georgia; go back to Louisiana; go back to the slums and ghettos of the northern cities, knowing that somehow this situation can, and will be changed. Let us not wallow in the valley of despair.

So I say to you, my friends, that even though we must face the difficulties of today and tomorrow, I still have a dream. It is a dream deeply rooted in the American dream that one day this nation will rise up and live out the true meaning of its creed—we hold these truths to be self-evident, that all men are created equal.

I have a dream that one day on the red hills of Georgia, sons of former slaves and sons of former slave-owners will be able to sit down together at the table of brotherhood.

I have a dream that one day, even the state of Mississippi, a state sweltering with the heat of injustice, sweltering with the heat of oppression, will be transformed into an oasis of freedom and justice.

20   I have a dream my four little children will one day live in a nation where they will not be judged by the color of their skin but by content of their character. I have a dream today!

I have a dream that one day, down in Alabama, with its vicious racists, with its governor having his lips dripping with the words of interposition and nullification, that one day, right there in Alabama, little black boys and black girls will be able to join hands with little white boys and white girls as sisters and brothers. I have a dream today!

I have a dream that one day every valley shall be exalted, every hill and mountain shall be made low, the rough places shall be made plain, and the crooked places shall be made straight and the glory of the Lord will be revealed and all flesh shall see it together.

This is our hope. This is the faith that I go back to the South with.

With this faith we will be able to hear out of the mountain of despair a stone of hope. With this faith we will be able to transform the jangling discords of our nation into a beautiful symphony of brotherhood.

25   With this faith we will be able to work together, to pray together, to struggle together, to go to jail together, to stand up for freedom together, knowing that we will be free one day. This will be the day when all of God's children will be able to sing with new meaning—"my country 'tis of thee; sweet land of liberty; of thee I sing; land where my fathers died, land of the pilgrim's pride; from every mountain side, let freedom ring"—and if America is to be a great nation, this must become true.

So let freedom ring from the prodigious hilltops of New Hampshire.

Let freedom ring from the mighty mountains of New York.

Let freedom ring from the heightening Alleghenies of Pennsylvania.

Let freedom ring from the snow-capped Rockies of Colorado.

30   Let freedom ring from the curvaceous slopes of California.

But not only that.

Let freedom ring from Stone Mountain of Georgia.

Let freedom ring from Lookout Mountain of Tennessee.

Let freedom ring from every hill and molehill of Mississippi, from every mountainside, let freedom ring.

35   And when we allow freedom to ring, when we let it ring from every village and hamlet, from every state and city, we will be able to speed up that day when all of God's children—black men and white men, Jews and Gentiles, Catholics and Protestants—will be able to join hands and to sing in the words of the old Negro spiritual, "Free at last, free at last; thank God Almighty, we are free at last."

"I Have a Dream" (reproduced here in print, but easily available on the Internet in audio or video versions) was only one of many speeches presented that day in Washington, D.C., yet it alone remains a model of American thought and expression. What makes it both memorable and still relevant more than forty years after it was given has much to do with the way it was structured. Utilizing language both biblical ("the glory of the Lord shall be revealed") and patriotic ("My country 'tis of thee, sweet land of liberty") the content of the message is still familiar to all who hear or read it today. King's use of repetition throughout the speech is also a main feature; from "one hundred years later" to "let freedom ring," he repeats phrases that evoke particular themes, making the speech easier to comprehend and remember. And his repetition of the phrase, "I have a dream," not only gives the speech its popular title, but also sets forth the goals and hopes—literally, the dream—of both Dr. King and his assembled listeners.

Dr. King uses comparison to contrast what *is* from what *can be:* the "dark and desolate valley of segregation" becomes "the sunlit path of racial justice," and "quicksands of racial injustice" become "the solid rock of brotherhood." He has faith that "this sweltering summer of the Negro's legitimate discontent" will transform into "an invigorating autumn of freedom and equality," and that a "mountain of despair" will provide "a stone of hope." In addition to these metaphors, King employs more imagery throughout the speech to solidify his ideas for the audience:

"flames of withering justice"

"lonely island of poverty"

"vast ocean of material prosperity"

"whirlwinds of revolt"

"winds of police brutality"

"oasis of freedom and justice"

"curvaceous peaks of California"

In almost every paragraph of the speech's written transcript, "I Have a Dream" gives its audience solid imagery to anchor their imaginations.

In the time since Dr. King's assassination, troubling facts have come to light about his failure to attribute sources in some of his own college work (see Chapter 7 here for a discussion of plagiarism). And while the "Dream" speech itself has been attacked for sharing some features with a sermon that had been given years earlier by a fellow clergyman and colleague of King's, this criticism ignores the fact that the other pastor was flattered by the tribute, and that it was customary for clergy to adapt parts of successful sermons delivered by other ministers. No matter what charges may be leveled against King, they do not take away from the fact that the power of his words, both spoken and written, were due to his careful attention to rhetorical structure, or *dispositio.* (See also "Letter from Birmingham Jail" in Chapter 4.) What's more, because it also reflects skill in both memory (*memoria*) and delivery (*pronuntiatio*), his style (*elocutio*) contributes significantly to the impact of his ideas. Ultimately, Martin Luther King, Jr., remains one of America's foremost speakers and writers because he was a master at the art of rhetoric.

A Final Note

Still, when it comes to oral arguments, the moment a famous speech appears as a written transcription in print, it isn't a speech anymore. It's writing.

Questions for Group Discussion

■ What other oral arguments and/or speakers can you think of that share a prominent place in history? What current speakers or oral arguments do you think might be remembered in the future in the same ways that Martin Luther King, Jr., and "I Have a Dream" are remembered now?

■ In what ways do "conscious rap" and "political rock" use rhetorical strategies described in the previous section on Dr. King's speech? How much does the *performance* (delivery) of the message count toward its impact? What happens to the message when its words are merely written on an Internet lyric database or a CD liner note?

■ If your instructor requires you to read drafts aloud in peer groups, why is it important to read with measured inflection and emphasis, rather than in a racing or flat monotone? How does reading aloud help you—the writer—to identify areas for revision?

TECHNIQUES FOR WRITERS 10-a
Analyzing Oral Argument

Following are excerpts from the 2004 acceptance speeches of George W. Bush and John Kerry. In a two-to-three–page paper, compare the speeches as examples of oral argument. Be sure to look at such elements as use of emotive language, repetition, structure, use of examples, and imagery. Which of the speeches do you find most effective? Why?

President Bush's Acceptance Speech to the Republican National Convention

Mr. Chairman, delegates, fellow citizens, I'm honored by your support, and I accept your nomination for president of the United States.

When I said those words four years ago, none of us could have envisioned what these years would bring. In the heart of this great city, we saw tragedy arrive on a quiet morning. We saw the bravery of rescuers grow with danger. We learned of passengers on a doomed plane who died with a courage that frightened their killers.

We have seen a shaken economy rise to its feet. And we have seen Americans in uniform storming mountain strongholds and charging through sandstorms and liberating millions with acts of valor that would make the men of Normandy proud.

Since 2001, Americans have been given hills to climb and found the strength to climb them. Now, because we have made the hard journey, we can see the valley below. Now, because we have faced challenges with resolve, we have historic goals within our reach and greatness in our future.

5   We will build a safer world and a more hopeful America, and nothing will hold us back.

In the work we have done and the work we will do, I am fortunate to have a superb vice president.

I have counted on Dick Cheney's calm and steady judgment in difficult days, and I'm honored to have him at my side.

I am grateful to share my walk in life with Laura Bush.

Americans have come to see the goodness and kindness and strength I first saw 26 years ago, and we love our first lady.

10   I'm a fortunate father of two spirited, intelligent and lovely young women.

I'm blessed with a sister and brothers who are my closest friends.

And I will always be the proud and grateful son of George and Barbara Bush.

My father served eight years at the side of another great American, Ronald Reagan.

His spirit of optimism and good will and decency are in this hall and are in our hearts and will always define our party.

15   Two months from today, voters will make a choice based on the records we have built, the convictions we hold and the vision that guides us forward.

A presidential election is a contest for the future. Tonight I will tell you where I stand, what I believe, and where I will lead this country in the next four years.

I believe every child can learn and every school must teach, so we passed the most important federal education reform in history. Because we acted, children are making sustained progress in reading and math, America's schools are getting better, and nothing will hold us back.

I believe we have a moral responsibility to honor America's seniors, so I brought Republicans and Democrats together to strengthen Medicare. Now seniors are getting immediate help buying medicine. Soon every senior will be able to get prescription drug coverage, and nothing will hold us back.

I believe in the energy and innovative spirit of America's workers, entrepreneurs, farmers and ranchers, so we unleashed that energy with the largest tax relief in a generation.

20 Because we acted, our economy is growing again and creating jobs, and nothing will hold us back.

I believe the most solemn duty of the American president is to protect the American people.

If America shows uncertainty or weakness in this decade, the world will drift toward tragedy.

This will not happen on my watch.

I am running for president with a clear and positive plan to build a safer world and a more hopeful America. I am running with a compassionate conservative philosophy: that government should help people improve their lives, not try to run their lives.

25 I believe this nation wants steady, consistent, principled leadership. And that is why, with your help, we will win this election.

The story of America is the story of expanding liberty, an ever-widening circle, constantly growing to reach further and include more.

Our nation's founding commitment is still our deepest commitment: In our world, and here at home, we will extend the frontiers of freedom.

The times in which we work and live are changing dramatically. The workers of our parents' generation typically had one job, one skill, one career, often with one company that provided health care and a pension. And most of those workers were men.

Today, workers change jobs, even careers, many times during their lives. And in one of the most dramatic shifts our society has seen, two-thirds of all moms also work outside the home.

30 This changed world can be a time of great opportunity for all Americans to earn a better living, support your family, and have a rewarding career. And government must take your side.

Many of our most fundamental systems—the tax code, health coverage, pension plans, worker training—were created for the world of yesterday, not tomorrow. We will transform these systems so that all citizens are equipped, prepared, and thus truly free to make your own choices and pursue your own dreams.

My plan begins with providing the security and opportunity of a growing economy. We now compete in a global market that provides new buyers for our goods, but new competition for our workers. To create more jobs in America, America must be the best place in the world to do business.

To create jobs, my plan will encourage investment and expansion by restraining federal spending, reducing regulation and making the tax relief permanent.

To create jobs, we will make our country less dependent on foreign sources of energy.

35   To create jobs, we will expand trade and level the playing field to sell American goods and services across the globe.

And we must protect small-business owners and workers from the explosion of frivolous lawsuits that threaten jobs across our country.

Another drag on our economy is the current tax code, which is a complicated mess, filled with special interest loopholes, saddling our people with more than 6 billion hours of paperwork and headache every year. The American people deserve—and our economic future demands—a simpler, fairer, pro-growth system.

In a new term, I will lead a bipartisan effort to reform and simplify the federal tax code.

Another priority in a new term will be to help workers take advantage of the expanding economy to find better and higher-paying jobs. In this time of change, many workers want to go back to school to learn different or higher-level skills. So we will double the number of people served by our principal job training program and increase funding for community colleges.

40   I know that with the right skills, American workers can compete with anyone, anywhere in the world.

In this time of change, opportunity in some communities is more distant than in others. To stand with workers in poor communities and those that have lost manufacturing, textile, and other jobs, we will create American opportunity zones.

In these areas, we'll provide tax relief and other incentives to attract new business and improve housing and job training to bring hope and work throughout all of America.

As I've traveled the country, I've met many workers and small-business owners who have told me that they are worried they cannot afford health care. More than half of the uninsured are small-business employees and their families.

In a new term, we must allow small firms to join together to purchase insurance at the discounts available to big companies.

45   We will offer a tax credit to encourage small businesses and their employees to set up health savings accounts and provide direct help for low-income Americans to purchase them. These accounts give workers the security of insurance against major illness, the opportunity to save tax-free for routine health expenses, and the freedom of knowing you can take your account with you whenever you change jobs.

We will provide low-income Americans with better access to health care. In a new term, I will ensure every poor county in America has a community or rural health center.

As I have traveled our country, I've met too many good doctors, especially OB/GYNs, who are being forced out of practice because of the high cost of lawsuits.

To make health care more affordable and accessible, we must pass medical liability reform now.

And in all we do to improve health care in America, we will make sure that health decisions are made by doctors and patients, not by bureaucrats in Washington, D.C.

50   In this time of change, government must take the side of working families.

In a new term we will change outdated labor laws to offer comp-time and flex-time. Our laws should never stand in the way of a more family-friendly workplace.

Another priority for a new term is to build an ownership society, because ownership brings security and dignity and independence.

Thanks to our policies, home ownership in America is at an all-time high.

Tonight we set a new goal: 7 million more affordable homes in the next 10 years, so more American families will be able to open the door and say, "Welcome to my home."

55   In an ownership society, more people will own their health plans and have the confidence of owning a piece of their retirement.

We'll always keep the promise of Social Security for our older workers.

With the huge baby boom generation approaching retirement, many of our children and grandchildren understandably worry whether Social Security will be there when they need it.

We must strengthen Social Security by allowing younger workers to save some of their taxes in a personal account, a nest egg you can call your own and government can never take away.

In all these proposals, we seek to provide not just a government program, but a path, a path to greater opportunity, more freedom and more control over your own life.

60   And the path begins with our youngest Americans.

To build a more hopeful America, we must help our children reach as far as their vision and character can take them.

Tonight, I remind every parent and every teacher, I say to every child: No matter what your circumstance, no matter where you live, your school will be the path to promise of America.

We are transforming our schools by raising standards and focusing on results. We are insisting on accountability, empowering parents and teachers, and making sure that local people are in charge of their schools.

By testing every child, we are identifying those who need help, and we're providing a record level of funding to get them that help.

65   In northeast Georgia, Gainesville Elementary School is mostly Hispanic and 90 percent poor. And this year, 90 percent of its students passed state tests in reading and math.

The principal—the principal expresses the philosophy of his school this way: "We don't focus on what we can't do at this school; we focus on what we can do. And we do whatever it takes to get kids across the finish line."

See, this principal is challenging the soft bigotry of low expectations.

And that is the spirit of our education reform and the commitment of our country: *No dejaremos a ningun nino atras.* We will leave no child behind.

We are making progress. We are making progress. And there is more to do. . . .

70   I believe in the transformational power of liberty. The wisest use of American strength is to advance freedom.

As the citizens of Afghanistan and Iraq seize the moment, their example will send a message of hope throughout a vital region.

Palestinians will hear the message that democracy and reform are within their reach and so is peace with our good friend, Israel.

Young women across the Middle East will hear the message that their day of equality and justice is coming. Young men will hear the message that national progress and dignity are found in liberty, not tyranny and terror.

75   Reformers and political prisoners and exiles will hear the message that their dream of freedom cannot be denied forever. And as freedom advances, heart by heart, and nation by nation, America will be more secure and the world more peaceful.

America has done this kind of work before, and there have always been doubters. In 1946, 18 months after the fall of Berlin to allied forces, a journalist wrote [*sic*] in the *New York Times* wrote this: "Germany is a land in an acute stage of economic, political and moral crisis. European capitals are frightened. In every military headquarters, one meets alarmed officials doing their utmost to deal with the consequences of the occupation policy that they admit has failed," end quote.

Maybe that same person is still around, writing editorials.

Fortunately, we had a resolute president named Truman who, with the American people, persevered, knowing that a new democracy at the center of Europe would lead to stability and peace. And because that generation of Americans held firm in the cause of liberty, we live in a better and safer world today.

The progress we and our friends and allies seek in the broader Middle East will not come easily or all at once.

80   Yet Americans, of all people, should never be surprised by the power of liberty to transform lives and nations. That power brought settlers on perilous journeys, inspired colonies to rebellion, ended the sin of slavery, and set our nation against the tyrannies of the 20th century.

We were honored to aid the rise of democracy in Germany and Japan, Nicaragua and Central Europe and the Baltics, and that noble story goes on.

I believe that America is called to lead the cause of freedom in a new century. I believe that millions in the Middle East plead in silence for their liberty. I believe that given the chance, they will embrace the most honorable form of government ever devised by man.

I believe all these things because freedom is not America's gift to the world; it is the almighty God's gift to every man and woman in this world.

This moment in the life of our country will be remembered. Generations will know if we kept our faith and kept our word. Generations will know if we seized this moment and used it to build a future of safety and peace. The freedom of many and the future security of our nation now depend on us.

85   And tonight, my fellow Americans, I ask you to stand with me.

In the last four years—in the last four years, you and I have come to know each other. Even when we don't agree, at least you know what I believe and where I stand.

You may have noticed I have a few flaws, too. People sometimes have to correct my English.

I knew I had a problem when Arnold Schwarzenegger started doing it.

Some folks look at me and see a certain swagger, which in Texas is called "walking."

90   Now and then I come across as a little too blunt, and for that we can all thank the white-haired lady sitting right up there.

One thing I have learned about the presidency is that whatever shortcomings you have, people are going to notice them; and whatever strengths you have, you're going to need them.

These four years have brought moments I could not foresee and will not forget. I've tried to comfort Americans who lost the most on September the 11th: people who showed me a picture or told me a story so I would know how much was taken from them.

I have learned first-hand that ordering Americans into battle is the hardest decision even when it is right. I have returned the salute of wounded soldiers, some with a very tough road ahead, who say they were just doing their job. I've held the children of the fallen who are told their dad or mom is a hero, but would rather just have their dad or mom.

I've met with parents and wives and husbands who have received a folded flag and said a final goodbye to a soldier they loved. I am awed that so many have used those meetings to say that I am in their prayers and to offer encouragement to me.

95   Where does that [*sic*] strength like that come from? How can people so burdened with sorrow also feel such pride? It is because they know their loved one was last seen doing good because they know that liberty was precious to the one they lost.

And in those military families, I have seen the character of a great nation: decent and idealistic and strong.

The world saw that spirit three miles from here, when the people of this city faced peril together and lifted a flag over the ruins and defied the enemy with their courage.

My fellow Americans, for as long as our country stands, people will look to the resurrection of New York City and they will say: Here buildings fell, and here a nation rose.

We see America's character in our military, which finds a way or makes one. We see it in our veterans, who are supporting military families in their days of worry. We see it in our young people, who have found heroes once again.

100   We see that character in workers and entrepreneurs, who are renewing our economy with their effort and optimism.

And all of this has confirmed one belief beyond doubt: Having come this far, our tested and confident nation can achieve anything.

To everything we know there is a season—a time for sadness, a time for struggle, a time for rebuilding.

And now we have reached a time for hope. This young century will be liberty's century.

By promoting liberty abroad, we will build a safer world. By encouraging liberty at home, we will build a more hopeful America.

105   Like generations before us, we have a calling from beyond the stars to stand for freedom. This is the everlasting dream of America. And tonight, in this place, that dream is renewed.

Now we go forward, grateful for our freedom, faithful to our cause, and confident in the future of the greatest nation on Earth.

May God bless you, and may God continue to bless our great country.

John Kerry's Acceptance Speech at the Democratic National Convention

Sen. John Kerry's speech accepting the presidential nomination of the Democratic Party at the Democratic National Convention at the FleetCenter in Boston, Mass.

I'm John Kerry, and I'm reporting for duty.

We are here tonight because we love our country. We're proud of what America is and what it can become.

My fellow Americans, we're here tonight united in one purpose: to make America stronger at home and respected in the world.

A great American novelist wrote that you can't go home again. He could not have imagined this evening. Tonight, I am home—home where my public life began and those who made it possible live; home where our nation's history was written in blood, idealism and hope; home where my parents showed me the values of family, faith and country.

5   Thank you, all of you, for a welcome home I will never forget.

I wish my parents could share this moment. They went to their rest in the last few years.

But their example, their inspiration, their gift of open eyes—open eyes and open mind and endless heart and world that doesn't have an end are bigger and more lasting than any words at all.

I was born, as some of you saw in the film, in Fitzsimmons Army Hospital in Colorado when my dad was a pilot in World War II. Now, I am not one to read into things, but guess which wing of the hospital the maternity ward was in?

10   I'm not kidding. I was born in the West Wing.

My mother was the rock of our family, as so many mothers are. She stayed up late to help me with my homework. She sat by my bed when I was sick. She answered the questions of a child who, like all children, found the world full of wonders and mysteries.

She was my den mother when I was a Cub Scout, and she was so proud of her 50-year pin as a Girl Scout leader.

She gave me her passion for the environment. She taught me to see trees as the cathedrals of nature. And by the power of her example, she showed me that we can and must complete the march toward full equality for all women in the United States of America.

15   My dad did the things that a boy remembers. My dad did the things that a boy remembers. He gave me my first model airplane, my first baseball mitt, my first bicycle.

He also taught me that we are here for something bigger than ourselves. He lived out the responsibilities and the sacrifices of the greatest generation to whom we owe so much.

And when I was a young man, he was in the State Department, stationed in Berlin when it and the world were divided between democracy and communism.

I have unforgettable memories of being a kid mesmerized by the British, French and American troops, each of them guarding their own part of the city, and Russians standing guard on that stark line separating East from West.

On one occasion, I rode my bike into Soviet East Berlin, and when I proudly told my dad, he promptly grounded me.

20   But what I learned has stayed with me for a lifetime. I saw how different life was on different sides of the same city. I saw the fear in the eyes of people who were not free. I saw the gratitude of people toward the United States for all that we had done. I felt goosebumps as I got off a military train and heard the Army band strike up "Stars and Stripes Forever."

I learned what it meant to be America at our best. I learned the pride of our freedom. And I am determined now to restore that pride to all who look to America.

Mine were Greatest Generation parents. And as I thank them, we all join together to thank a whole generation for making America strong, for winning World War II, winning the Cold War and for the great gift of service which brought America 50 years of peace and prosperity.

My parents inspired me to serve, and when I was in high school, a junior, John Kennedy called my generation to service. It was the beginning of a great journey, a time to march for civil rights, for voting rights, for the environment, for women, for peace.

We believed we could change the world. And you know what? We did.

25   But we're not finished. But we're not finished.

The journey isn't complete; the march isn't over; the promise isn't perfected.

Tonight, we're setting out again. And together, we're going to write the next great chapter of America's story.

We have it in our power to change the world, but only if we're true to our ideals. And that starts by telling the truth to the American people.

As president, that is my first pledge to you tonight: As president, I will restore trust and credibility to the White House.

30   I ask you, I ask you to judge me by my record. As a young prosecutor, I fought for victims' rights and made prosecuting violence against women a priority.

When I came to the Senate, I broke with many in my own party to vote for a balanced budget, because I thought it was the right thing to do. I fought to put 100,000 police officers on the streets of America.

And then I reached out across the aisle with John McCain to work to find the truth about our POWs and missing in action and to finally make peace in Vietnam.

I will be a commander in chief who will never mislead us into war.

I will have a vice president who will not conduct secret meetings with polluters to rewrite our environmental laws.

35   I will have a secretary of defense who will listen to the best advice of the military leaders.

And I will appoint an attorney general who will uphold the Constitution of the United States.

My fellow Americans, this is the most important election of our lifetime. The stakes are high. We are a nation at war: a global war on terror against an enemy unlike we've ever known before.

And here at home, wages are falling, health-care costs are rising, and our great middle class is shrinking. People are working weekends—two jobs, three jobs—and they're still not getting ahead.

We're told that outsourcing jobs is good for America. We're told that jobs that pay $9,000 less than the jobs that have been lost is the best that we can do. They say this is the best economy that we've ever had. And they say anyone who thinks otherwise is a pessimist.

40   Well, here is our answer: There is nothing more pessimistic than saying that America can't do better.

We can do better, and we will.

We're the optimists. For us, this is a country of the future. We're the can-do people.

And let's not forget what we did in the 1990s: We balanced the budget. We paid down the debt. We created 23 million new jobs. We lifted millions out of poverty. And we lifted the standard of living for the middle class.

We just need to believe in ourselves and we can do it again.

45   So tonight, in the city where America's freedom began, only a few blocks from where the sons and daughters of liberty gave birth to our nation, here tonight, on behalf of a new birth of freedom, on behalf of the middle class who deserve a champion, and those struggling to join it who deserve a fair shot, for the brave men and women in uniform who risk their lives every day and the families who pray for their return, for all those who believe our best days are ahead of us, with great faith in the American people, I accept your nomination for president of the United States. . . .

My fellow Americans, the world tonight is very different from the world of four years ago. But I believe the American people are more than equal to the challenge.

Remember the hours after September 11 when we came together as one to answer the attack against our homeland. We drew strength when our firefighters ran up stairs and risked their lives so that others might live; when rescuers rushed into smoke and fire at the Pentagon; when the men and women of Flight 93 sacrificed themselves to save our nation's Capitol; when flags were hanging from front porches all across America, and strangers became friends. It was the worst day we have ever seen, but it brought out the best in all of us.

I am proud that after September 11 all our people rallied to President Bush's call for unity to meet the danger.

There were no Democrats. There were no Republicans. There were only Americans. And how we wish it had stayed that way.

50   Now, I know there that are those who criticize me for seeing complexities—and I do—because some issues just aren't all that simple. Saying there are weapons of mass destruction in Iraq doesn't make it so. Saying we can fight a war on the cheap doesn't make it so. And proclaiming "Mission accomplished" certainly doesn't make it so.

As president, I will ask the hard questions and demand hard evidence. I will immediately reform the intelligence system, so policy is guided by facts and facts are never distorted by politics.

And as president, I will bring back this nation's time-honored tradition: The United States of America never goes to war because we want to; we only go to war because we have to. That is the standard of our nation . . .

I know what kids go through when they're carrying an M-16 in a dangerous place, and they can't tell friend from foe. I know what they go through when they're out on patrol at night and they don't know what's coming around the next bend. I know what it's like to write letters home telling your family that everything's all right, when you're not sure that that's true.

55   As president, I will wage this war with the lessons I learned in war. Before you go to battle, you have to be able to look a parent in the eye and truthfully say, "I tried everything possible to avoid sending your son or daughter into harm's way, but we had no choice, we had to protect the American people, fundamental American values against a threat that was real and imminent."

So, lesson number one, this is the only justification for going to war.

And on my first day in office, I will send a message to every man and woman in our armed forces: You will never be asked to fight a war without a plan to win the peace. . . .

We believe in the value of doing what's right for everyone in the American family. And that's the choice in this election.

60   We believe that what matters most is not narrow appeals masquerading as values, but the shared values that show the true face of America; not narrow values that divide us, but the shared values that unite us: family, faith, hard work, opportunity and responsibility for all, so that every child, every adult, every parent, every worker in America has an equal shot at living up

to their God-given potential. That is the American dream and the American value.

What does it mean in America today when Dave McCune, a steelworker that I met in Canton, Ohio, saw his job sent overseas and the equipment in his factory was literally unbolted, crated up and shipped thousands of miles away, along with that job?

What does it mean when workers I've met have had to train their foreign replacements?

America can do better. And tonight we say: Help is on the way.

What does it mean when Mary Ann Knowles, a woman with breast cancer I met in New Hampshire, had to keep working day after day, right through her chemotherapy, no matter how sick she felt, because she was terrified of losing her family's health insurance?

65   America can do better, and help is on the way.

What does it mean when Deborah Kromins from Philadelphia, Pennsylvania, works and she saves all her life, and finds out that her pension has disappeared into thin air and the executive who looted it has bailed out on a golden parachute?

America can do better, and help is on the way.

What does it mean when 25 percent of the children in Harlem have asthma because of air pollution?

We can do better, America can do better, and help is on the way.

70   What does it mean when people are huddled in blankets in the cold, sleeping in Lafayette Park, on the doorstep of the White House itself, and the number of families living in poverty has risen by 3 million in the last four years?

America can do better, and help is on the way.

So tonight we come here tonight [*sic*] to ask: Where is the conscience of our country?

I'll tell you where it is.

I'll tell you where it is. It's in rural and small-town America; it's in urban neighborhoods and the suburban main streets; it's alive in the people that I've met in every single part of this land. It's bursting in the hearts of Americans who are determined to give our values and our truth back to our country. . . .

75   My friends, the high road may be harder, but it leads to a better place.

And that's why Republicans and Democrats must make this election a contest of big ideas, not small-minded attacks.

This is our time to reject the kind of politics calculated to divide race from race, region from region, group from group.

Maybe some just see us divided into those red states and blue states, but I see us as one America: red, white and blue.

And when I am president, the government I lead will enlist people of talent, Republicans as well as Democrats, to find the common ground, so that no one who has something to contribute to our nation will be left on the sidelines.

80   And let me say it plainly: In that cause, and in this campaign, we welcome people of faith. America is not us and them.

I think of what Ron Reagan said of his father a few weeks ago, and I want to say this to you tonight: I don't wear my religion on my sleeve, but faith has given me values and hope to live by, from Vietnam to this day, from Sunday to Sunday.

I don't want to claim that God is on our side.

As Abraham Lincoln told us, I want to pray humbly that we are on God's side.

And whatever our faith—whatever our faith, one belief should bind us all: The measure of our character is our willingness to give of ourselves for others and for our country.

85   These aren't Democratic values. These aren't Republican values. They're American values. We believe in them. They're who we are. And if we honor them, if we believe in ourselves, we can build an America that is stronger at home and respected in the world.

So much promise stretches before us. Americans have always reached for the impossible, looked to the next horizon and asked, "What if?"

Two young bicycle mechanics from Dayton asked, "What if this airplane could take off at Kitty Hawk?" It did that, and it changed the world forever.

A young president asked, "What if we could go to the moon in 10 years?" And now we're exploring the stars and the solar systems themselves.

A young generation of entrepreneurs asked, "What if we could take all the information in a library and put it on a chip the size of a fingernail?" We did, and that, too, changed the world.

90   And now it's our time to ask, "What if?"

What if we find a breakthrough to cure Parkinson's, diabetes, Alzheimer's and AIDS?

What if we have a president who believes in science, so we can unleash the wonders of discovery like stem-cell research and treat illness for millions of lives?

What if we do what adults should do, and make sure that all of our children are safe in the afternoons after school? What if we have a leadership that's as good as the American dream, so that bigotry and hatred never again steal the hope or future of any American?

I learned a lot about these values on that gunboat patrolling the Mekong Delta with Americans—you saw them—who come from places as different as Iowa and Oregon, Arkansas, Florida, California.

95   No one cared where we went to school. No one cared about our race or our backgrounds. We were literally all in the same boat. We looked out, one for the other, and we still do.

That is the kind of America that I will lead as president: an America where we are all in the same boat.

Never has there been a moment more urgent for Americans to step up and define ourselves. I will work my heart out. But, my fellow citizens, the outcome is in your hands more than mine.

It is time to reach for the next dream. It is time to look to the next horizon. For America, the hope is there. The sun is rising. Our best days are still to come.

Thank you. Good night. God bless you, and God bless the United States of America.

Discovering Contemporary Rhetoric in Visual Argument

As you've seen, what makes an oral argument powerful is also what makes it memorable. But a great deal of what makes a speech memorable goes beyond words to include its *visual* context. Martin Luther King on the top step of the Lincoln Memorial, with the Reflecting Pool before him and the Washington Monument in the distance, enjoyed the benefit of a powerful and stirringly patriotic setting to coincide with his appeals for freedom and justice. Presidents are sworn into office on the steps of the U.S. Capitol, high above the crowds who gather in the January cold to revel in the ceremony. In countries around the world, leaders watch from prominent viewing stands as rows of military troops, convoys of weapons, and national banners pass by in a display of national strength and pride.

These are all examples of oral argument accompanied by visually powerful backdrops. But by leaving the speech behind and focusing solely on the backdrop itself, modern rhetoricians employ **visual literacy,** or an ability to read visual symbols, to explain how yet another argument is taking place. Here, for instance, is film critic Ken Kelman examining the rhetorical setting surrounding one of Adolf Hitler's messianic speeches in the 1930s, captured by filmmaker Leni Riefenstahl:

> [The] motifs are ancient things (buildings, statues, icons); the sky; clouds (or smoke); fire; the swastika; marching; the masses; Hitler. The central theme which they develop is that Hitler has come from the sky to kindle ancient Nuremberg with primal Teutonic fire, to liberate the energy and spirit of the German people through a dynamic new movement . . .

A key definition of visual literacy hinges on treating **visual symbology** as a language all its own, and this is what Kelman does in his concise reading of the rhetorical backdrop. But notice how his reading differs from a somewhat breathless physical description by one of Hitler's generals, who wrote of the same scene after WWII had ended:

> The speaker's platform, atop thirty granite steps, rose up like a warship. It stood out against a background of bright light. . . . Hitler had even invented an entirely new form of architecture that was made not of stone but of light. He'd had hundreds of air defense beacons installed on the four sides of the giant site. Their beams of light rose up very high and very straight in the night like the pillars of an unreal cathedral. . . .

Defining Rhetoric

Visual literacy: the ability to read visual symbols for their rhetorical intent.

Visual symbology: the use of symbols to promote desired associations with ideas, emotions, etc. Visual symbology is often used to persuade.

It's important, when talking about visual argument, to distinguish between basic *description* (even if it's laced with hyperbole) and more specific *interpretation*. Explaining how something *looks* is very different from explaining what it *says*. With that in mind, see what readings you can supply for the following visual arguments:

- The rusty 1987 Taurus parked next to your car in the student lot
- The shiny new H2 Hummer parked next to your car in the student lot
- The shiny new Porsche parked in the faculty lot
- The American flags on either side of the senator as she speaks
- The large marijuana-leaf tattoo on the hand of the young woman interviewing for a position as a bank teller
- The 1960s-era rock star, with waist-length gray hair and a full gray beard, on stage and singing about a sixteen-year-old groupie
- A television commercial:
  Scene 1: A teacher, alone in an office. Looks at clock, then shakes her head and packs up her briefcase to leave.
  Scene 2: A student, checking her watch while hurrying across campus with a worried look.
  Scene 3: The teacher, turning off the office light and locking the door, turns to see the student approaching and looking apologetic. The teacher appears annoyed at first, then begins to smile and nods her head. She reopens her office door and the two step inside, smiling at one another. Fade to a local college's familiar logo and a slogan: *Our Attitude Makes All the Difference.*

Using Experience in Reading Visual Arguments

How did you read each of those messages? What did each one say to you, although it contained few or no words? Did you find the rusty Taurus sympathetic, the H2 and Porsche offensive? Or were the latter two symbols enviable as marks of hard-earned success, while the Taurus was embarrassing? As the rock star approaches his mid-60s, does his age make the lyrics to "Sweet Little Sixteen" inappropriate for him to perform? Is the teacher in the TV ad being too tolerant by letting the student have a conference past the assigned time, or can you identify with the student's lateness as something that happens sometimes and should be understood? When you see the twin flags, do they stir emotional responses, do you see them as standard political decorations—or do you not really notice them at all?

Now ask yourself this: *To what degree does my personal experience shape my answers to those questions?* Consider the H2 Hummer, for example; if you were raised in a family that enjoyed backpacking vacations, participated in park or river cleanups, and emphasized responsible energy use by always buying fuel-efficient cars, you may read the Hummer quite negatively. That is, if you *share* your family's values. If, on the other hand, you found those values unnecessarily restrictive, you may see the vehicle as a symbol of power and freedom—which of course is exactly the way that its manufacturer would prefer you to see it. And these are only a couple of possible variables, because hunters may see the H2 as a means to get further back into otherwise inaccessible areas. With visual arguments all around us, and in increasing numbers as our culture moves into new forms of literacy and communication, you'll probably find that experience plays a significant role in the ways that we respond—or fail to respond—to those arguments. Just as a written argument's goal is not to *win* a point, but to *establish* it in the audience's mind, visual arguments, no matter how carefully and deliberately crafted, can still be countered. But first they have to be read.

Determining the Roles of Ideology and Values in Reading Visual Arguments

Visual arguments take place all around us in the forms of videos, clothing, architecture, the makeup of TV/film casts, architecture, print layouts (fonts, colors, sizes, alignments), and, of course, in advertising—everywhere from the T-shirt you may be wearing right now to the urinal screen in a public restroom. These are only a handful of examples, however, as a listing of specific, different visual argument forms would take up a whole book in itself. And as you've just figured out by answering the questions about the personal experience that you bring to the reading process for these kinds of arguments, a great deal of *how* they mean to you—beyond the basic *what* they mean—depends upon you, the reader, and the core **ideologies** and **values** to which you subscribe.

Defining Rhetoric

Ideology: a culturally enforced idea so embedded that it's assumed to be true, evident, common sense.

Values: principles or standards that are considered to have inherent worth.

But you're probably aware of this because you're a college student and you're taking a specialized course in rhetoric and argument where your brain is constantly on the lookout for deeper, more critical insights into just about everything. What about average citizens and consumers who, when schooling has finished, fall out of practice with what you're doing now? Do they, for instance, notice the differences in the visual arguments made by these two online dating services?

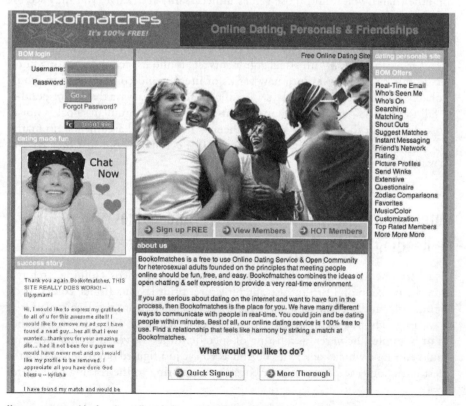

Home page graphic for the online dating service BookofMatches.com
Copyright 2002–2005, Internet Initiative Partners, LLC. Reprinted with permission.

Home page graphic for the online dating service Lavalife.com
© Lavalife Corp. 2005. Reprinted with permission.

Clearly, important differences exist between the arguments made by each of these companies through their visual representations, both online and in print media. And critiquing those differences—identifying, explaining, and questioning the significance of both *what* a visual argument says and *how* it says it—relies a great deal on your ability to identify values and ideologies.

In its simplest form, ideology can be defined as a culturally enforced idea so strongly embedded that it's just assumed to be true, self-evident, common sense. For example, at one time in our cultural history, a children's rhyme held that little girls were made of "sugar, and spice, and everything nice" while little boys were made of "snakes, and snails,

TECHNIQUES FOR WRITERS 10-b

30-Second Ideology Primer: Diamonds

How much should a diamond cost? What should you look for when purchasing a diamond? Can you complete these phrases?

- Diamonds are _____.
- Diamonds are a girl's _____.
- This Christmas, give her the gift of _____.

If you could answer all of these questions correctly, then you realize how powerful and persuasive cultural ideologies can be. In truth, the diamond is a common gem, found in abundant supply but artificially controlled on the market by the DeBeers cartel, which created consumer desire by concocting the catch-phrases and "rules" you just answered. In reality, diamonds are only hard, brilliant rocks—no more, no less. Anything beyond this is the result of a corporate-produced ideology.

and puppy dogs' tails." Still today, many girls are told that certain behaviors "aren't lady-like," while boys exhibiting the same behaviors are excused for "being boys."

Not that many years ago, the ideological rules of dating held that the male extended the invitation, while the female accepted it, and this core ideology still applies to the typical marriage proposal. But today a woman has earned the right to ask a man out, to call him if she likes him, and to arrange the whole first night out if she wishes. Not all men can handle this, because they're still stuck in a previous era's ideology. Nor, for that matter, can all women. For these individuals, the "rules" of dating—which are just socially constructed and perpetuated ideologies—can be pretty oppressive.

Online dating services operate in an ideological system of essentially total equality for everyone involved, because both partners in the eventual date have to sign up, log in, fill out a survey, submit photos, write summaries and descriptions . . . and then wait for the computer to find a good match. Because of this fair system of equal effort and responsibility, the visual arguments made by online dating services can't violate those core values by falling into cultural stereotypes that don't fit. The male can't logically be shown as the aggressor or initiator, but neither can the female; both the search and the eventual date are *mutual* undertakings. Given this, take another look at the two home page graphics shown earlier, and then examine the print ad below.

Print ad for Lavalife.com
Courtesy of Lavalife.

Questions for Thinking and Writing

1. While both the man and the woman are checking each other out equally in the Lavalife.com ad, why are they the only people on the train in full detail? The ad appears in black and white here, but the original print ad uses the color red prominently. What role would the color red play in Lavalife.com's visual argument? How—and why—has red been assigned certain "personality" traits by our culture?

2. Unlike the Lavalife ad which has been reproduced here in black and white, the Bookof-matches.com home page appears in those two colors in its original form as well. In how many ways is the use of black-and-white photography effective in that visual argument? By contrasting that photo with the other elements on the home page, what arguments do you think the company wants to make?

Reading and Critiquing Visual Arguments Beyond "Deceptive Claims"

As our society has moved into its current era of visual literacy, it's become fairly common for writing teachers to assign "ad analysis" papers to students at all levels, from high school through senior year of college, as a way to foster critical investigation of visual symbols and the arguments they present. Some of the best assignments will encourage you to study store window arrangements, billboard placements in community areas, ad clusters during certain kinds of TV broadcasts or networks but not others, and similar investigations that go far beyond a product and its claims.

Not all assignments encourage this kind of depth, however, and sometimes students are almost encouraged to think of advertisement's visual arguments as a series of mere "deceptive claims." Ironically, even this charge can't really hold because the Federal Communications Commission (FCC) strictly monitors the kinds of claims that advertisers can make for their products. What "deceptive claims" most accurately refer to would be the particular *ideologies* being suggested and promoted by an ad's visual argument.

Megan and Jason, two students whose essays appear below, show how asking these kinds of questions about any visual argument, including board games and automotive decorations, can help to identify a number of deeply layered ideologies beneath even the most seemingly simple items. (If you've ever played the game Monopoly and argued over whether your piece would be the race car or the shoe, you many even find out something about yourself and your own core values.) As you read, pay attention to the ways that these two writers structure their critiques from one point to the next, and also follow the techniques and strategies they use to illustrate and develop their observations about the visual argument under consideration.

Reflecting Social Values in the Game of Monopoly

Jason Sharpe

The game Monopoly has been around for decades, and for most of us, it's the first experience we have with managing money, buying and selling, and the process of supply and demand. Hasbro, the manufacturer, should consider changing the name of the game to American Economy 101. Although it may not be used as such, Monopoly is the blueprint for economic success in our society. True, it's mere child's play and one could argue that the outcome of the game happens purely by chance with a shake of the dice. But when it's played for hours on end, the most strategic players gain more money and property, while those less advanced fall by the wayside. This sounds vaguely familiar. Don't American citizens fall into similar roles? The game Monopoly directly reflects our values as a society, and even its name promotes the financially competitive lifestyle of our culture.

Take a look at the game pieces used to represent players' places on the board—the wheelbarrow, the thimble, the shoe, the horseman, the top hat, the dog, the flatiron, the race car, the cannon, and the battleship: ten pieces. None of these were included in the original game. The original designer of the game suggested that players use regular items found around the home, and the cast-iron pieces were eventually added to preserve the heritage of the game. Of all the possible "regular" items around a typical home in the late 1930s to early 40s, why were these ten pieces chosen? Recognizing the importance of these items reveals the importance of social structure.

The wheelbarrow reflects early American agriculture, the foundation for the industrial movement, and the strong work ethic that bind most common American ideologies. The top hat, 1930s roadster, and the dog, all belonging to "the chairman of the board, Mr. Monopoly" represent in one form or another the prestige and high social status gained by someone with the finer things. The shoe, although ragged, represents finer things as well, but with a much different definition. In the early 20th century, it was not uncommon for Americans in the rural south to have no shoes at all, so owning a pair equaled status. Still, the fact that the shoe is ragged gives it character, telling the story of a working class citizen. The cannon and the battleship are symbols of struggle and the "whatever it takes" view that many Americans have toward life.

Collectively, all of the game pieces reflect an idealized "American way," suggesting vast difference in lifestyle and social classes—but also the ability to move freely through them. These "regular" household items, in reality, are never regularly seen in the same household. But in Monopoly, each piece holds a certain prestige and ranking among classes, and everyone has an equal chance at winning, as people from different social classes allegedly have similar chances to become wealthy. Giving players the option to purchase houses and hotels creates even more depth in the levels of wealth and success attainable in the game, thus resembling our social values and the emphasis on ownership in the real American economy.

In addition to introducing players to basic economics and social structures, Monopoly also reveals the presence of a strong and stable government. "Do not pass go, do not collect $200. Go directly to jail." Since this is a "Chance" card and not a punishment for any crime, it establishes an important social value throughout America's history: unquestioning obedience. Establishing and maintaining an effective government is crucial to a free market economy like we have in the United States, so that government must be granted legitimacy by its citizens through their obedience. In Monopoly, that legitimacy is reinforced as players must go to jail, lose a turn, or pay a tax when told. Of these, financial penalty is one of the worst forms of punishment we can receive, as our society's emphasis on possessions makes wealth our ultimate achievement.

Monopoly, the "simple game," is actually a complex reflection of American economics, history, and values. By playing, we gain valuable experience for dealing with the

commercialized "real world," but by *looking at* what we're
playing, we can see that world's most important values and
ideologies at work.

* * *

Support Our Troops—Buy a Magnet

Megan Donahue

In the past year or so, "Support Our Troops" ribbon car
magnets have become increasingly common. Making a short trip down
the highway without spotting at least one magnet is unusual. They
come in different colors and patterns, and cars can be decorated
with one or several of them.

These ribbons reflect popular tastes by visibly reinforcing
the widespread patriotism in 21st century United States society.
Americans care about American soldiers, and the "troops" ribbons
reflect the public's respect for military service. In fact,
ribbons in general provide a whole new way to express our support
for any cause: pink ribbons for breast cancer awareness, red
ribbons for AIDS awareness, and purple ribbons for ending
domestic violence are just a few.

The original meaning intended by the creators of the car
magnets may have been exactly as it sounds: *Support the troops*—
literally, and simply. And for many of us, the sentiment of the
ribbons is still simple: support the troops and be grateful for
their sacrifices. But for others, the meaning has become more
layered now, including supporting the Middle East wars,
supporting the President's foreign policy, supporting the
Republican Party. The troops become just a front for those larger
messages.

Our culture values succinctness (which I privately think of
as "sound-bite-ity"—a new word I have just coined), and this is
well represented in these magnets. The magnets are fairly small,
and the phrases that adorn them are clear and simple. They tell

Reprinted with permission of Megan Donahue.

us to support the troops, but they give no explanation what "support" really means. The range of possible interpretation is wide, and there's no attempt to clarify it. The implication is that we shouldn't *have* to ask, we should already know. The problem here is the subtle suggestion that if your views on an issue are too complicated to fit on a ribbon magnet, they're not worthy of expression.

Another cultural value the magnets represent is the current importance of demonstrating one's righteousness. It is not enough to privately support the troops (whatever *support* means to you); one must make a public show of it. Americans want everyone who drives past our cars to know exactly how patriotic we are. Our love of country isn't legitimate until others recognize and affirm it. At the same time, the magnets also reflect our love of general consumerism. None of us makes our own car magnets, at least not that I've seen: we buy them. The people on the expressway with their magnets didn't think them up, or design them. Creative expression is replaced by conformed consumption— although the ribbon colors do vary, giving us room for at least a tiny amount of personal expression. Even so, the magnets still reflect and reinforce mainstream values. We put them on our cars to identify ourselves as part of the patriotic group, and the magnets end up supporting not so much our troops as our renewed nationalism, making them stronger with very public and visible endorsements.

TECHNIQUES FOR WRITERS 10-c

Rhetoric Online: **Visual Arguments**

Using the essays by Megan Donahue and Jason Sharpe as models, work with one or two classmates in writing a "practice critique" (three to four hand-written pages) for one of the following groupings of visual arguments.

- Hooters, Burger King, and McDonald's Web site home pages
- U.S. Coast Guard and U.S. Army Web site home pages

The BURGER KING® trademarks are used with permission from Burger King Brands, Inc. Activision and Kaboom! are registered trademarks of Activision, Inc. © 1981–82 Activision, Inc. Mott's is a registered trademark of Mott's LLP.

Used with permission from McDonald's Corporation.

TECHNIQUES FOR WRITERS 10-d

Extended Assignment on Visual Arguments

Working individually or as a team/group with classmates, discuss well-known visual arguments from popular culture and choose one for a comprehensive analysis. Examples can include Tickle Me Elmo, *Beavis & Butt-head, South Park,* the Cooper Mini, Apple iPods, *The Sopranos, Desperate Housewives,* baseball caps, tattoos, gauge earrings, the Energizer Bunny, Frank Gehry architecture . . . you literally have thousands to choose from.

First determine how the meaning of the argument is constructed—both by its messengers and by its audience(s). Note that these constructions may be very different.

Next, determine how this item both reflects and shapes popular tastes and desires. What cultural or social values are present in the item? For what audience is the item intended—and has this audience stayed the same as the item has been absorbed into popular culture?

Then carefully examine the item's significant *physical* and *visual* aspects—its color scheme(s), size(s), texture(s), and other physical dimensions that are important in shaping how we interpret it as a *visual argument.* If it were more/less refined, differently colored, larger or smaller, set in a different period, published in a different venue, or altered in any other way, how would the basic message—the argument being posited—change?

Move the discussion along so that your group will have time to report back to the class. Each member of the group should address a specific aspect of the argument analysis your group has performed.

Readings
for Analyzing
and Creating
Contemporary
Arguments

The first three sections of *Classical Techniques and Contemporary Arguments* took you through the process of identifying, developing, and writing arguments, based on techniques and strategies created by classical rhetoricians who lived centuries ago. Section 4 gives you the opportunity to expand your understanding of some of the most contested issues of our time through reading and analyzing articles, poems, and other selections.

Each chapter in Section 4 provides information that addresses and defines the major arguments that make the topic of that chapter controversial. Each chapter's selections offer enough information and commentary to provide the basis of a well-researched short paper, or if supplemented by additional sources, an expanded argument.

As you read the selections from Section 4, be sure to employ the analytical strategies you learned earlier, including but not limiting yourself to the following:

- Identifying the author's *ethos* and *pathos*
- Determining the author's argumentative proposition and position

- Noting the structure of the argument
- Evaluating the author's support of his or her position
- Assessing the effect of the author's style
- Modeling elements of the author's style/structure that you find appealing and relevant to your own writing.

Chapter 11

Recent events, particularly 9/11 and the war in Iraq, have elevated the subject of "Patriotism and Nationalism" to a prominent position in American thought and debate. Chapter 11 addresses such relevant questions as the following: What is the difference between nationalism and patriotism? What are the qualities of a patriot? What responsibilities does a citizen owe his or her country?

Chapter 12

The presidential election of 2004 brought to light very real disparities in American attitudes toward "Gay and Lesbian Rights," particularly in regards to marriage. Chapter 12 examines some of the major arguments used to support and oppose gay rights, focusing in the later selections specifically on marriage.

Chapter 13

Copyright laws have been the subject of much misunderstanding and many lawsuits over time, but the amount of information available and the ease of access to that information through the Internet have given the debate about copyright laws a twist: determining whether copyright laws stifle innovation and need to be revised. "Digital Information and the Ideology of 'Copyright'" examines this new controversy.

Patriotism and Nationalism

Democracy (July 3, 1944)
E. B. White

We received a letter from the Writer's War Board the other day asking for a statement on "The Meaning of Democracy." It presumably is our duty to comply with such a request, and it is certainly our pleasure. Surely the Board knows what democracy is. It is the line that forms on the right. It is the don't in don't shove. It is the hole in the stuffed shirt through which the sawdust slowly trickles; it is the dent in the high hat. Democracy is the recurrent suspicion that more than half of the people are right more than half of the time. It is the feeling of privacy in the voting booths, the feeling of communion in the libraries, the feeling of vitality everywhere. Democracy is a letter to the editor. Democracy is the score at the beginning of the ninth. It is an idea that hasn't been disproved yet, a song the words of which have not gone bad. It is the mustard on the hot dog and the cream in the rationed coffee. Democracy is a request from a War Board, in the middle of the morning in the middle of a war, wanting to know what democracy is.

From *On Civil Disobedience*

Henry David Thoreau

I heartily accept the motto—"That government is best which governs least," and I should like to see it acted up to more rapidly and systematically. Carried out, it finally amounts to this, which also I believe,—"That government is best which governs not at all," and when men are prepared for it, that will be the kind of government which they will have. Government is at best but an expedient; but most governments are usually, and all governments are sometimes, inexpedient. The objections which have been brought against a standing army, and they are many and weighty, and deserve to prevail, may also at last be brought against a standing government. The standing army is only an arm of the standing government. The government itself, which is only the mode which the people have chosen to execute their will, is equally liable to be abused and perverted before the people can act through it. Witness the present Mexican war, the work of comparatively a few individuals using the standing government as their tool; for, in the outset, the people would not have consented to this measure.

This American government,—what is it but a tradition, though a recent one, endeavoring to transmit itself unimpaired to posterity, but each instant losing some of its integrity? It has not the vitality and force of a single living man; for a single man can bend it to his will. It is a sort of wooden gun to the people themselves; and, if ever they should use it in earnest as a real one against each other, it will surely split. But it is not the less necessary for this; for the people must have some complicated machinery or other, and hear its din, to satisfy that idea of government which they have. Governments show thus how successfully men can be imposed on, even impose on themselves, for their own advantage. It is excellent, we must all allow; yet this government never of itself furthered any enterprise, but by the alacrity with which it got out of its way. *It* does not keep the country free. *It* does not settle the West. *It* does not educate. The character inherent in the American people has done all that has been accomplished; and it would have done somewhat more, if the government had not sometimes got in its way. For government is an expedient by which men would fain succeed in letting one another alone; and, as has been said, when it is most expedient, the governed are most let alone by it. Trade and commerce, if they were not made of india rubber, would never manage to bounce over the obstacles which legislators are continually putting in their way; and, if one were to judge these men wholly by the effects of their actions, and not partly by

From Henry David Thoreau, *On Civil Disobedience* (1850).

their intentions, they would deserve to be classed and punished with those mischievous persons who put obstructions on the railroads.

But, to speak practically and as a citizen, unlike those who call themselves no-government men, I ask for, not at once no government, but *at once* a better government. Let every man make known what kind of government would command his respect, and that will be one step toward obtaining it.

After all, the practical reason why, when the power is once in the hands of the people, a majority are permitted, and for a long period continue, to rule, is not because this seems fairest to the minority, but because they are physically the strongest. But a government in which the majority rule in all cases cannot be based on justice, even as far as men understand it. Can there not be a government in which majorities do not virtually decide right and wrong, but conscience?—in which majorities decide only those questions to which the rule of expediency is applicable? Must the citizen ever for a moment, or in the least degree, resign his conscience to the legislator? Why has every man a conscience, then? I think that we should be men first, and subjects afterward. It is not desirable to cultivate a respect for the law, so much as for the right. The only obligation which I have a right to assume, is to do at any time what I think right. . . .

5   How does it become a man to behave toward this American government to-day? I answer that he cannot without disgrace be associated with it. I cannot for an instant recognize that political organization as *my* government which is the *slave's* government also.

All men recognize the right of revolution; that is, the right to refuse allegiance to and to resist the government, when its tyranny or its inefficiency are great and unendurable. But almost all say that such is not the case now. But such was the case, they think, in the Revolution of '75. If one were to tell me that this was a bad government because it taxed certain foreign commodities brought to its ports, it is most probable that I should not make an ado about it, for I can do without them; all machines have their friction; and possibly this does enough good to counterbalance the evil. At any rate, it is a great evil to make a stir about it. But when the friction comes to have its machine, and oppression and robbery are organized, I say, let us not have such a machine any longer. In other words, when a sixth of the population of a nation which has undertaken to be the refuge of liberty are slaves, and a whole country is unjustly overrun and conquered by a foreign army, and subject to military law, I think that it is not too soon for honest men to rebel and revolutionize. What makes this duty the more urgent is the fact, that the country so overrun is not our own, but ours is the invading army. . . .

Practically speaking, the opponents to a reform in Massachusetts are not a hundred thousand politicians at the South, but a hundred thousand merchants and farmers here, who are more interested in commerce and agriculture than they are in humanity, and are not prepared to do justice to the slave and to Mexico, *cost what it may.* I quarrel not with far-off foes, but with those who, near at home, co-operate with, and do the bidding of those far away, and without whom the latter would be harmless. We are accustomed to say, that the mass of men are unprepared; but improvement is slow, because the few are not materially wiser or better than the many. It is not so important that many should be as good as you, as that there be some absolute goodness somewhere; for that will leaven the whole lump. There are thousands who are *in opinion* opposed to slavery and to the war, who yet in effect do nothing to put an end to them; who, esteeming themselves children of Washington and Franklin, sit down with their hands in their pockets, and say that they know not what to do, and do nothing; who even postpone the question of freedom to the question of free-trade, and quietly read the prices-current along with the latest advices from Mexico, after dinner, and, it may be, fall asleep over them both. . . .

The American has dwindled into an Old Fellow,—one who may be known by the development of his organ of gregariousness, and a manifest lack of intellect and cheerful self-reliance; whose first and chief concern, on coming into the world, is to see that the alms-houses are in good repair; and, before yet he has lawfully donned the virile garb, to collect a fund for the support of the widows and orphans that may be; who, in short, ventures to live only by the aid of the mutual insurance company, which has promised to bury him decently. . . .

Unjust laws exist: shall we be content to obey them, or shall we endeavor to amend them, and obey them until we have succeeded, or shall we transgress them at once? Men generally, under such a government as this, think that they ought to wait until they have persuaded the majority to alter them. They think that, if they should resist, the remedy would be worse than the evil. But it is the fault of the government itself that the remedy *is* worse than the evil. *It* makes it worse. Why is it not more apt to anticipate and provide for reform? Why does it not cherish its wise minority? Why does it cry and resist before it is hurt? Why does it not encourage its citizens to be on the alert to point out its faults, and *do* better than it would have them? Why does it always crucify Christ, and excommunicate Copernicus and Luther, and pronounce Washington and Franklin rebels? . . .

10   If the injustice is part of the necessary friction of the machine of government, let it go, let it go: perchance it will wear smooth,—certainly the machine will wear out. If the injustice has a spring, or a pulley, or a rope, or a crank, exclusively for itself, then perhaps you may consider whether the remedy will not be worse than the evil; but if it is of such a nature that it requires you to be the agent of injustice to another, then, I say, break the law. Let your life be a counter friction to stop the machine. What I have to do is to see, at any rate, that I do not lend myself to the wrong which I condemn.

As for adopting the ways which the State has provided for remedying the evil, I know not of such ways. They take too much time, and a man's life will be gone. I have other affairs to attend to. I came into this world, not chiefly to make this a good place to life [*sic*], but to live in it, be it good or bad. A man has not everything to do, but something; and because he cannot do *every thing*, it is not necessary that he should do *something* wrong. It is not my business to be petitioning the governor or the legislature any more than it is theirs to petition me; and if they should not hear my petition, what should I do then? But in this case the State has provided no way: its very Constitution is the evil. This may seem to be harsh and stubborn and un-conciliatory; but it is to treat with the utmost kindness and consideration the only spirit that can appreciate or deserves it. So is all change for the better, like birth and death which convulse the body.

I do not hesitate to say, that those who call themselves abolitionists should at once effectually withdraw their support, both in person and property, from the government of Massachusetts, and not wait till they constitute a majority of one, before they suffer the right to prevail through them, I think that it is enough if they have God on their side, without waiting for that other one. Moreover, any man more right than his neighbors constitutes a majority of one already. . . .

Under a government which imprisons any unjustly, the true place for a just man is also in prison. The proper place to-day, the only place which Massachusetts has provided for her freer and less desponding spirits, is in her prisons, to be put out and locked out of the State by her own act, as they have already put themselves out by their principles. It is there that the fugitive slave, and the Mexican prisoner on parole, and the Indian come to plead the wrongs of his race, should find them; on that separate, but more free and honorable ground, where the State places those who are not *with* her, but *against* her,—the only house in a slave-state in which a free man can abide with honor. If any think that their influence would be lost there, and their voices no longer afflict the ear of the State, that they would not be as an enemy within its walls, they do not know by how much truth is stronger than error, nor how much more eloquently and effectively he can combat injustice who has experienced a little in his own person. Cast your whole vote, not a strip of paper merely, but your whole influence. A minority is powerless while it conforms to the majority; it is not even a minority then; but it is irresistible when it clogs by its whole weight. If the alternative is to keep all just men in prison, or give up war and slavery, the State will not hesitate which to choose. If a thousand men were not to pay their tax-bills this year, that would not be a violent and bloody measure, as it would be to pay them, and enable the State to commit violence and shed innocent blood. This is, in fact, the definition of a peaceable revolution, if any such is possible. If the tax-gatherer, or any other public officer, asks me, as one has done, "But what shall I do?" my answer is, "If you really wish to do anything, resign our office." When the subject has refused allegiance, and the officer has resigned his office, then the revolution is accomplished. But even suppose blood should flow. Is there not a sort of blood shed when the conscience is wounded? Through this wound a man's real manhood and immortality flow out, and he bleeds to an everlasting death. I see this blood flowing now. . . .

I have paid no poll-tax for six years. I was put into a jail once on this account, for one night; and, as I stood considering the walls of solid stone, two or three feet thick, the door of wood and iron, a foot thick, and the iron grating which strained the light, I could not help being struck with the foolishness of that institution which treated me as if I were mere flesh and blood and bones, to be locked up. I wondered that it should have concluded at length that this was the best use it could put me to, and had never thought to avail itself of my services in some way. I saw that, if there was a wall of stone between me and my townsmen, there was a still more difficult one to climb or break through, before they could get to be as free as I was. I did not for a moment feel confined, and the walls seemed a great waste of stone and mortar. I felt as if I alone of all my townsmen had paid my tax. They plainly did not know how to treat me, but behaved like persons who are underbred. In every threat and in every compliment there was a blunder; for they thought that my chief desire was to stand the other side of that stone wall. I could not but smile to see how industriously they locked the door on my meditations, which followed them out again without let or hinderance, and *they* were really all that was dangerous. As they could not reach me, they had resolved to punish my body; just as boys, if they cannot come at some person against whom they have a spite, will abuse his dog. I saw that the State was half-witted, that it was timid as a lone woman with her silver spoons, and that it did not know its friends from its foes, and I lost all my remaining respect for it, and pitied it.

15   Thus the State never intentionally confronts a man's sense, intellectual or moral, but only his body, his senses. It is not armed with superior wit or honesty, but with superior physical strength. I was not born to be forced. I will breathe after my own fashion. Let us see who is the strongest. What force has a multitude? They only can force me who obey a higher law than I. They force me to become like themselves. I do not hear of *men* being *forced* to live this way or that by masses of men. What sort of life were that to live? When I meet a government which says to me, "Your money or your life," why should I be in haste to give it my money? It may be in a great strait, and not know what to do: I cannot help that. It must help itself; do as I do. It is not worth the while to snivel about it. I am not responsible for the successful working of the machinery of society. I am not the son of the engineer. I perceive that, when an acorn and a chestnut fall side by side, the one

does not remain inert to make way for the other, but both obey their own laws, and spring and grow and flourish as best they can, till one, perchance, overshadows and destroys the other. If a plant cannot live according to its nature, it dies; and so a man. . . .

I do not wish to quarrel with any man or nation. I do not wish to split hairs, to make fine distinctions, or set myself up as better than my neighbors. I seek rather, I may say, even an excuse for conforming to the laws of the land. I am but too ready to conform to them. Indeed I have reason to suspect myself on his head; and each year, as the tax-gatherer comes round, I find myself disposed to review the acts and position of the general and state governments, and the spirit of the people, to discover a pretext for conformity. I believe that the State will soon be able to take all my work of this sort out of my hands, and then I shall be no better a patriot than my fellow-countrymen. Seen from a lower point of view, the Constitution, with all its faults, is very good; the law and the courts are very respectable; even this State and this American government are, in many respects, very admirable and rare things, to be thankful for, such as a great many have described them; but seen from a point of view a little higher, they are what I have described them; seen from a higher still, and the highest, who shall say that they are, or that they are worth looking at or thinking of at all?

However, the government does not concern me much, and I shall bestow the fewest possible thoughts on it. It is not many moments that I live under a government, even in this world. If a man is thought-free, fancy-free, imagination-free, that which *is not* never for a long time appearing *to be* to him, unwise rulers or reformers cannot fatally interrupt him. . . .

The authority of government, even such as I am willing to submit to,— for I will cheerfully obey those who know and can do better than I, and in many things even those who neither know nor can do so well,—is still an impure one: to be strictly just, it must have the sanction and consent of the governed. It can have no pure right over my person and property but what I concede to it. The progress from an absolute to a limited monarchy, from a limited monarchy to a democracy, is a progress toward a true respect for the individual. Is a democracy, such as we know it, the last improvement possible in government? Is it not possible to take a step further towards recognizing and organizing the rights of man? There will never be a really free and enlightened State, until the State comes to recognize the individual as a higher and independent power, from which all its own power and authority are derived, and treats him accordingly. I please myself with imagining a State at last which can afford to be just to all men, and to treat the individual with respect as a neighbor, which even would not think it inconsistent with its own repose, if a few were to live aloof from it, not meddling with it, nor embraced by it, who fulfilled all the duties of neighbors and fellowmen. A State which bore this kind of fruit, and suffered it to drop off as fast as it ripened, would prepare the way for a still more perfect and glorious State, which also I have imagined, but not yet anywhere seen.

My Mother, Drunk or Sober?: George Orwell on Nationalism and Patriotism

Joanne Barkan

Like a few million other people, I consider George Orwell one of my favorite political writers, but I don't riffle through his books, looking for wisdom whenever a political crisis comes along. In the aftermath of the 9/11 terrorist attacks, however, I did reach for a volume of his essays, specifically the volume that contains his 1945 "Notes on Nationalism." I hadn't read the essay in years, but I thought the distinction Orwell makes between nationalism and patriotism might be useful in thinking about the "blame-America-first" part of the American left. These leftists see only one major problem in the world: the United States with its unlimited power and imperial arrogance. Their initial response to the terrorist attacks: "We had it coming."

More than a year after 9/11, a greater number and variety of voices on the left admit that blame-America-first failed miserably as a response. First, it relied almost exclusively on "blowback" to explain the atrocities: American imperialism understandably generates so much hate for us around the world that some of the haters inevitably turn to mass terrorism. Everything else is left out: no analysis of the Wahhabi brand of fundamentalist Islam, no consideration of the lack of democracy in Arab Muslim nations or the loss of dignity associated with economic underdevelopment or the role of religious brainwashing. Second, blame-America-first leftists have an ingrained ideological aversion to patriotism. They assume it means either a sheeplike loyalty—"my country, right or wrong"—or an aggressive nationalism. They made their disdain for the outpouring of patriotism after 9/11 clear. Some of us saw the desire to fly American flags everywhere as a sign of solidarity and grief (we saw this even when we ourselves didn't care to fly a flag). They saw only jingoism and vulgar sentimentality.

No one knows what proportion of the U.S. left has this Johnny-one-note politics (where do you draw the borders of the left?). But blame-America-

Joanne Barkan, "My Mother, Drunk or Sober?: George Orwell on Nationalism and Patriotism," *Dissent*, Vol. 50, No. 1 (Winter 2003), pp. 83–87. Reprinted by permission of the publisher.

first often seems to dominate the left's public presence—in the media, on campuses, on the lecture circuit. It also represents the left in the popular imagination, where it wins over few hearts and minds. A politics so deeply alienated from a nation can't attract its citizens. Because the inability to distinguish between nationalism and patriotism is part of that alienation, I decided to reread "Notes on Nationalism."

5   The essay begins with definitions of nationalism and patriotism and Orwell's warning not to confuse the terms "since two different and even opposing ideas are involved":

> By "nationalism" . . . I mean the habit of identifying oneself with a single nation or other unit, placing it beyond good and evil and recognizing no other duty than that of advancing its interests. . . . By "patriotism" I mean devotion to a particular place and a particular way of life, which one believes to be the best in the world but has no wish to force upon other people. Patriotism is of its nature defensive, both militarily and culturally. Nationalism, on the other hand, is inseparable from the desire for power.

Orwell analyzed nationalism by classifying the various attitudes of the English intelligentsia—he considered intellectuals the best source of data: "In them, much more often than in ordinary English people, [nationalism] is unmixed with patriotism and can therefore be studied pure." His idiosyncratic notion of nationalism went far beyond the identification with a particular nation to include zealotry of almost any kind. Communism, political Catholicism, color feeling, class feeling, pacifism, Christendom, Islam, and Jewry (all his terms) qualified as instances of nationalism along with the more conventional Celtic nationalism, Zionism, and neo-Toryism. He also created a subcategory called "negative nationalism" for attachments that "work in a merely negative sense, against something or other and without the need for any positive object of loyalty." Negative identifications counted as "nationalism" because they exhibited two core characteristics: obsessiveness and the ability to ignore inconvenient truths. Orwell put anti-Semitism, Trotskyism, and Anglophobia into this subcategory.

Ironically, today's blame-America-first leftists, who undoubtedly consider themselves too enlightened to stumble into jingoism, think exactly like Orwell's negative nationalists: they are obsessive and undiscriminating in their anti-Americanism, but they no longer wave anyone else's flag. Orwell's description of Anglophobia in the 1940s fits their attitude: "Within the intelligentsia, a derisive and mildly hostile attitude towards Britain is more or less compulsory, but it is an unfaked emotion in many cases. . . . English left-wing intellectuals did not, of course, actually want the Germans or Japanese to win the war, but many of them could not help getting a certain kick out of seeing their own country humiliated . . . "

Although Orwell made his distinction between nationalism and patriotism clear in "Notes," the essay says nothing about the possible forms or content of patriotism; it doesn't provide any insights into the components or style of leftist patriotism. Since Orwell's own politics are so often identified with patriotism, I decided to go back to the story of his ideological transformation.

10   After fighting for six months on the Republican side in the Spanish Civil War, Orwell returned to England in June 1937 embittered by the experience. As he saw it, almost all the political forces on the Republican side—liberals, socialists, and, above all, Moscow-directed communists—conspired to abort a working class uprising; they opened the way for a fascist victory which, in the end, they dreaded less than an authentic but autonomous revolution. Bidding a pox on all their houses, Orwell joined the anti-imperialist/anti-war camp, and for the next two years, he argued that fascism did not differ fundamentally from capitalism, and Hitler was no worse than the British imperialists. He aimed his polemics at the Popular Front, defined by Orwell as "a lineup of capitalist and proletarian for the ostensible purpose of opposing Fascism" or, more succinctly, "an unholy alliance between the robbers and the robbed." He believed that, sooner or later, this alliance would drag England into a war with Germany, a war he opposed. In his own words:

> Fascism after all is only a development of capitalism, and the mildest democracy, so-called, is liable to turn into Fascism when the pinch comes. We like to think of England as a democratic country, but our rule in India, for instance, is just as bad as German Fascism, though outwardly it may be less irritating. I do not see how one can oppose Fascism except by working for the overthrow of capitalism, starting, of course, in one's own country. If one collaborates with a capitalist-imperialist government in a struggle "against Fascism," i.e. against a rival imperialism, one is simply letting Fascism in by the back door. The whole struggle in Spain, on the [Republican] Government side, has turned upon this. (Letter to Geoffrey Gorer, September 15, 1937)

No patriotism here. None of the nice cups of tea, homey suet puddings, or red pillar-boxes that Orwell later relied on to communicate his identification with the English people. Thinking about England in the years just preceding the Second World War meant thinking primarily about the misdeeds of its capitalist-imperialist government.

This was not Orwell's finest hour. Given what was happening in the German Reich and in the Far East, his fascism-equals-capitalism worldview had enough obsessiveness and delusions to qualify as a "negative nationalism." Of course, few people did much better in the late 1930s. What surprises is how long Orwell hung on to this myopic position. He expected England to go fascist, but from within, steered by an alliance of the British right and left. As late as March 1939, he was prodding his comrades to stockpile supplies for an underground resistance to the upcoming British regime. In a letter to the writer Herbert Read:

> So long as the objective, real or pretended, is war with Germany, the greater part of the Left will associate themselves with the fascising [*sic*] process, which will ultimately mean associating themselves with wage-reductions, suppression of free speech, brutalities in the colonies etc. . . . I doubt whether there is much hope of saving England from fascism of one kind or another, but clearly one must put up a fight, and it seems silly to be silenced when one might be making a row merely because one had failed to take a few precautions beforehand. If we laid in printing presses etc in some discreet place we could then cautiously go to work to get together a distributing agency, and we could then feel "Well, if trouble does come we are ready."

15   By Orwell's account, nothing in his thinking changed much until the early morning hours of August 21, 1939. He went to bed with one politics and got up with another. In between there was the transformational dream. Orwell wrote about the experience in "My Country Right or Left" (published in autumn 1940):

> For several years the coming war was a nightmare to me, and at times I even made speeches and wrote pamphlets against it. But the night before the Russo-German pact was announced I dreamed that the war had started. It was one of those dreams which, whatever Freudian inner meaning they may have, do sometimes reveal to you the real state of your feelings. It taught me two things, first, that I should be simply relieved when the long-dreaded war started, secondly, that I was patriotic at heart, would not sabotage or act against my own side, would support the war, would fight in it if possible. I came downstairs to find the newspaper announcing Ribbentrop's flight to Moscow. So war was coming, and the Government, even the Chamberlain Government, was assured of my loyalty.

Some Orwell readers regard the dream as a literary device rather than an actual event. Either way it is an accurate account of what happened to Orwell's thinking: this was an about-face, a real or metaphoric overnight conversion. Why that night? For Orwell, the Hitler-Stalin Pact transformed the balance of force, putting England at tremendous risk. The Nazis overrunning the British Isles suddenly looked feasible. Writing about the near future in the same essay, Orwell chose to qualify his predictions with the words "if only we can keep Hitler out" and "if only we can hang on." Before the pact, the prospect of war with Germany didn't seem to threaten England's survival (although he might have changed his mind if a war had actually started). As soon as Hitler and Stalin made a deal, he could picture the destruction of "English-speaking civilization." In The Lion and the Unicorn

(1940), he wrote, "Two incompatible visions of life are fighting one another," and as a result, there was only one question to answer: "Do you want to see England conquered, or don't you?"

Watching the twin towers collapse and the Pentagon burn on 9/11, most Americans (including part of the left) instinctively felt that their way of life and shared values were threatened. It wasn't the overwhelming and imminent threat of a foreign army poised for the kind of war Europeans knew so well, but within a few hours of the terrorist attacks, everyone had enough information about al-Qaeda cells, suicide manuals, and mass murder as a shortcut to paradise to understand the danger. It seemed natural to feel patriotic—protective as well as proud of the best in our national culture—in much the same way Orwell did. When, instead, some leftists responded primarily with the rhetorical question, "Don't you think we deserved it?" they came across as morally, politically, and intellectually deficient. But something emotional was also askew. People outside the left have called it "lack of patriotism," which is a misleading phrase because it carries overtones of treason. A better description focuses on the rancorous and self-destructive alienation from the rest of the country.

Orwell had much the same thing to say about England's intelligentsia (which he considered almost exclusively left-wing). For example, from The Lion and the Unicorn: "England is perhaps the only great country whose intellectuals are ashamed of their own nationality," and "There is little in [left publications] except the irresponsible carping of people who have never been and never expect to be in a position of power." Or from "Boys' Weeklies": "Failure to understand [the patriotism of ordinary people] is one of the reasons why left-wing political parties are seldom able to produce an acceptable foreign policy." At the same time, Orwell felt obliged to demonstrate that patriotism was not conservative; one could be both a leftist and patriotic. In part he needed to explain his own sudden conversion; in part he had to reconnect two identities that had become separated after the First World War to the point of seeming mutually exclusive. He came up with the following formula in "My Country Right or Left" and reiterated it in The Lion and the Unicorn: "Patriotism has nothing to do with conservatism. It is devotion to something that is changing but is felt to be mystically the same. . . . [W]hen the red militias [of the socialist revolution] are billeted in the Ritz I shall still feel that the England I was taught to love so long ago and for such different reasons is somehow persisting."

20   Who knows if this argument persuaded many leftists in the 1940s? Some leftists today find patriotism repellent not so much because it implies conserving what exists but because, for them, it means endorsing a superpower whose unlimited power and arrogance they detest. The rest of us see no inherent or necessary contradiction between left politics and patriotic feeling; on the contrary, left politics seems especially in tune with America's (yet-to-be-realized) ideals. But does the patriotism of leftists have a distinct form?

For Orwell, patriotism meant fond attachment to what you think is distinctive about your country, its "flavor." His England had greener grass, solid breakfasts, smoky towns, winding roads, red pillar-boxes, respect for the law, and addiction to hobbies. But equally characteristic was the willingness to fight and die when England was "in a serious jam." All this was politically neutral; any English person, left or right, might have drawn up a similar list. But even if Orwell's attachments looked conventional, he never gave up his critical option. Dissent did not conflict with patriotism. Unlike some of his interlocutors during the war, Orwell rejected "My country, right or wrong" as a test of patriotism. He made short shrift of the idea by citing conservative author G. K. Chesterton "who courageously opposed the Boer War, and once remarked that 'My country, right or wrong' was on the same moral level as 'My mother, drunk or sober' " ("As I Please," December 24, 1943). Only critical patriotism was palatable to Orwell, but it could be found among both leftists and conservatives. Similarly, "My country, right or wrong" was neither conservative nor left wing, it was simply mindless.

Orwell's concern with patriotism coincided with the war years. Practically everything he wrote on the subject was written between 1939 and 1945, and he invariably elaborated on three observations: first, although the upper, middle, and working classes had different styles of patriotism, they all rallied to the nation's defense; second, without the resolute patriotism of the English people, England would lose the war; and third, only left intellectuals lacked patriotism. When the war ended, Orwell expected the active patriotism of his fellow citizens to return to a more latent state, and his own emotion changed in the same way. After 1945 he continued to write about nationalism, but the theme of patriotism disappeared from the essays. The organization of "Notes on Nationalism" marks the transition. Written in May 1945 just as the war in Europe ended, "Notes" begins with both patriotism and nationalism, but then patriotism drops out. Orwell moves on to classify examples of nationalism, including the Stalinist communism (a type of "transferred nationalism") that he wrote about until his death in 1950.

I never found what I had started to search for in "Notes"—ideas about a distinctly leftwing patriotism. (Perhaps benign patriotism remains essentially the same wherever it resides on the political spectrum.) But coming across the notion of "negative nationalism" again has been useful for thinking about the blame-America-first leftists with their obsessiveness, resentments, and ability to shut out inconvenient realities. The last paragraph of "Notes" alone makes the essay well worth rereading.

As for the nationalistic loves and hatreds that I have spoken of, they are part of the makeup of most of us, whether we like it or not. Whether it is possible to get rid of them I do not know, but I do believe that it is possible to struggle against them, and that this is essentially a moral effort. It is a question first of all of discovering what one really is, what one's own feelings really are, and then of making allowance for the inevitable bias. If you hate and fear Russia, if you are jealous of the wealth and power of America, if you despise Jews, if you have a sentiment of inferiority towards the British ruling class, you cannot get rid of those feelings simply by taking thought. But you can at least recognize that you have them, and prevent them from contaminating your mental processes. The emotional urges which are inescapable, and are perhaps even necessary to political action, should be able to exist side by side with an acceptance of reality. But this, I repeat, needs a moral effort, and contemporary English literature, so far as it is alive at all to the major issues of our time, shows how few of us are prepared to make it.

25   The paragraph has an authentic ring because Orwell himself made the moral effort, again and again, to discover his own aversions and to keep them from contaminating his thinking. Of course he wasn't completely successful. Who ever is? But his enduring appeal depends just as much on this moral effort and the tough independence it produced as on his famously engaging writing style.

The time is long overdue for an examination of the left's negative nationalism. This need doesn't disappear just because we also need to fight the Bush administration's reckless unilateralism abroad and its assault on liberty and social justice at home. On the contrary, the worse the government in Washington (and the current one is execrable), the more urgent the need for an effective left. Examining your own biases and preventing them from "contaminating your mental processes" are intrinsic to radical thought. The viability of the left depends on these practices because critical thinking and the commitment of activists are our side's most valuable resources; the other side has wealth and power. It takes more mental energy as well as a sense of balance to think critically while acting politically, but that's what makes a decent left.

Wrong Ism
J. B. Priestley

There are three isms that we ought to consider very carefully—regionalism, nationalism, internationalism. Of these three the one there is most fuss about, the one that starts men shouting and marching and shooting, the one that seems to have all the depth and thrust and fire, is of course nationalism. Nine people out of ten, I fancy, would say that of this trio it is the one that really counts, the big boss. Regionalism and internationalism, they would add, are comparatively small, shadowy, rather cranky. And I

J. B. Priestley, "Wrong Ism" from *Essays of Five Decades*. Reprinted by permission of SLL/Sterling Lord Literistic, Inc. Copyright 1968 by J. B. Priestley.

believe all this to be quite wrong. Like many another big boss, nationalism is largely bogus. It is like a bunch of flowers made of plastics.

The real flowers belong to regionalism. The mass of people everywhere may never have used the term. They are probably regionalists without knowing it. Because they have been brought up in a certain part of the world, they have formed perhaps quite unconsciously a deep attachment to its landscape and speech, its traditional customs, its food and drink, its songs and jokes. (There are of course always the rebels, often intellectuals and writers, but they are not the mass of people.) They are rooted in their region. Indeed, without this attachment a man can have no roots.

So much of people's lives, from earliest childhood onwards, is deeply intertwined with the common life of the region, they cannot help feeling strongly about it. A threat to it is a knife pointing at the heart. How can life ever be the same if bullying strangers come to change everything? The form and colour, the very taste and smell of dear familiar things will be different, alien, life-destroying. It would be better to die fighting. And it is precisely this, the nourishing life of the region, for which common men have so often fought and died.

This attachment to the region exists on a level far deeper than that of any political hocus-pocus. When a man says "my country" with real feeling, he is thinking about his region, all that has made up his life, and not about that political entity, the nation. There can be some confusion here simply because some countries are so small—and ours is one of them—and so old, again like ours, that much of what is national is also regional. Down the centuries, the nation, itself, so comparatively small, has been able to attach to itself the feeling really created by the region. (Even so there is something left over, as most people in Yorkshire or Devon, for example, would tell you.) This probably explains the fervent patriotism developed early in small countries. The English were announcing that they were English in the Middle Ages, before nationalism had arrived elsewhere.

5   If we deduct from nationalism all that it has borrowed or stolen from regionalism, what remains is mostly rubbish. The nation, as distinct from the region, is largely the creation of power-men and political manipulators. Almost all nationalist movements are led by ambitious frustrated men determined to hold office. I am not blaming them. I would do the same if I were in their place and wanted power so badly. But nearly always they make use of the rich warm regional feeling, the emotional dynamo of the movement, while being almost untouched by it themselves. This is because they are not as a rule deeply loyal to any region themselves. Ambition and a love of power can eat like acid into the tissues of regional loyalty. It is hard, if not impossible, to retain a natural piety and yet be for ever playing both ends against the middle.

Being itself a power structure, devised by men of power, the nation tends to think and act in terms of power. What would benefit the real life of the region, where men, women and children actually live, is soon sacrificed for the power and prestige of the nation. (And the personal vanity of presidents and ministers themselves, which historians too often disregard.) Among the new nations of our time innumerable peasants and labourers must have found themselves being cut down from five square meals a week to three in order to provide unnecessary airlines, military forces that can only be used against them and nobody else, great conference halls and official yachts and the rest. The last traces of imperialism and colonialism may have to be removed from Asia and Africa, where men can no longer endure being condemned to a permanent inferiority by the colour of their skins; but even so, the modern world, the real world of our time, does not want and would be far better without more and more nations, busy creating for themselves the very paraphernalia that western Europe is now trying to abolish. You are compelled to answer more questions when trying to spend half a day in Cambodia than you are now travelling from the Hook of Holland to Syracuse.

This brings me to internationalism. I dislike this term, which I used only to complete the isms. It suggests financiers and dubious promoters living nowhere but in luxury hotels; a shallow world of entrepreneurs and impresarios. (Was it Sacha Guitry who said that impresarios were men who spoke many languages but all with a foreign accent?) The internationalism I have in mind here is best described as world civilisation. It is life considered on a global scale. Most of our communications and transport already exist on this high wide level. So do many other things from medicine to meteorology. Our astronomers and physicists (except where they have allowed themselves to be hush-hushed) work here. The UN special agencies, about which we hear far too little, have contributed more and more to this world civilisation. All the arts, when they are arts and not chunks of nationalist propaganda, naturally take their place in it. And it grows, widens, deepens, in spite of the fact that for every dollar, ruble, pound or franc spent in explaining and praising it, a thousand are spent by the nations explaining and praising themselves.

This world civilisation and regionalism can get along together, especially if we keep ourselves sharply aware of their quite different but equally important values and rewards. A man can make his contribution to world civilisation and yet remain strongly regional in feeling: I know several men of this sort. There is of course the danger—it is with us now—of the global style flattening out the regional, taking local form, colour, flavour, away for ever, disinheriting future generations, threatening them with sensuous poverty and a huge boredom. But to understand and appreciate regionalism is to be on guard against this danger. And we must therefore make a clear distinction between regionalism and nationalism.

It is nationalism that tries to check the growth of world civilisation. And nationalism, when taken on a global scale, is more aggressive and demanding now than it has ever been before. This in the giant powers is largely disguised by the endless fuss in public about rival ideologies, now a largely unreal quarrel. What is intensely real is the glaring nationalism. Even the desire to police the world is nationalistic in origin. (Only the world can police the world.) Moreover, the nation-states of today are for the most part far narrower in their outlook, far more inclined to allow prejudice against the foreigner to impoverish their own style of living, than the old imperial states were. It should be part of world civilisation that men with particular skills, perhaps the product of the very regionalism they are rebelling against, should be able to move easily from country to country, to exercise those skills, in anything from teaching the violin to running a new type of factory to managing an old hotel. But nationalism, especially of the newer sort, would rather see everything done badly than allow a few non-nationals to get to work. And people face a barrage of passports, visas, immigration controls, labour permits; and in this respect are worse off than they were in 1900. But even so, in spite of all that nationalism can do—so long as it keeps its nuclear bombs to itself—the internationalism I have in mind, slowly creating a world civilisation, cannot be checked.

10   Nevertheless, we are still backing the wrong ism. Almost all our money goes on the middle one, nationalism, the rotten meat between the two healthy slices of bread. We need regionalism to give us roots and that very depth of feeling which nationalism unjustly and greedily claims for itself. We need internationalism to save the world and to broaden and heighten our civilisation. While regional man enriches the lives that international man is already working to keep secure and healthy, national man, drunk with power, demands our loyalty, money and applause, and poisons the very air with his dangerous nonsense.

National Prejudices

Oliver Goldsmith

As I am one of that sauntering tribe of mortals, who spend the greatest part of their time in taverns, coffee-houses, and other places of public resort, I have thereby an opportunity of observing an infinite variety of characters, which, to a person of a contemplative turn, is a much higher entertainment than a view of all the curiosities of art or nature. In one of these, my late rambles, I accidentally fell into the company of half a dozen gentlemen, who were engaged in a warm dispute about some political affair;

Oliver Goldsmith, "National Prejudices" from *The Citizen of the World*. London, 1762.

the decision of which, as they were equally divided it their sentiments, they thought proper to refer to me, which naturally drew me in for a share of the conversation.

Amongst a multiplicity of other topics, we took occasion to talk of the different characters of the several nations of Europe; when one of the gentlemen, cocking his hat, and assuming such an air of importance as if he had possessed all the merit of the English nation in his own person, declared that the Dutch were a parcel of avaricious wretches; the French a set of flattering sycophants; that the Germans were drunken sots, and beastly gluttons; and the Spaniards proud, haughty, and surly tyrants; but that in bravery, generosity, clemency, and in every other virtue, the English excelled all the rest of the world.

This very learned and judicious remark was received with a general smile of approbation by all the company—all, I mean, but your humble servant; who, endeavoring to keep my gravity as well as I could, and reclining my head upon my arm, continued for some time in a posture of affected thoughtfulness, as if I had been musing on something else, and did not seem to attend to the subject of conversation; hoping by these means to avoid the disagreeable necessity of explaining myself, and thereby depriving the gentleman of his imaginary happiness.

But my pseudo-patriot had no mind to let me escape so easily. Not satisfied that his opinion should pass without contradiction, he was determined to have it ratified by the suffrage of everyone in the company; for which purpose addressing himself to me with an air of inexpressible confidence, he asked me if I was not of the same way of thinking. As I am never forward in giving my opinion especially when I have reason to believe that it will not be agreeable; so, when I am obliged to give it, I always hold it for a maxim to speak my real sentiments. I therefore told him that, for my own part, I should not have ventured to talk in such a peremptory strain, unless I had made the tour of Europe, and examined the manners of these several nations with great care and accuracy: that, perhaps, a more impartial judge would not scruple to affirm that the Dutch were more frugal and industrious, the French more temperate and polite, the Germans more hardy and patient of labour and fatigue, and the Spaniards more staid and sedate, than the English; who, though undoubtedly brave and generous, were at the same time rash, headstrong, and impetuous; too apt to be elated with prosperity, and to despond in adversity.

5   I could easily perceive that all the company began to regard me with a jealous eye before I had finished my answer, which I had no sooner done, that the patriotic gentleman observed, with a contemptuous sneer, that he was greatly surprised how some people could have the conscience to live in a country which they did not love, and to enjoy the protection of a government, to which in their hearts they were inveterate enemies. Finding that by this modest declaration of my sentiments I had forfeited the good

opinion of my companions, and given them occasion to call my political principles in question, and well knowing that it was in vain to argue with men who were so very full of themselves, I threw down my reckoning and retired to my own lodgings, reflecting on the absurd and ridiculous nature of national prejudice and prepossession.

Among all the famous sayings of antiquity, there is none that does greater honour to the author, or affords greater pleasure to the reader (at least if he be a person of a generous and benevolent heart) than that of the philosopher, who, being asked what "countryman he was," replied, that he was, "a citizen of the world."—How few and there to be found in modern times who can say the same, or whose conduct is consistent with such a profession!—We are now become so much Englishmen, Frenchmen, Dutchmen, Spaniards, or Germans that we are no longer citizens of the world; so much the natives of one particular spot, or members of one petty society, that we no longer consider ourselves as the general inhabitants of the globe, or members of that grand society which comprehends the whole human kind.

Did these prejudices prevail only among the meanest and lowest of the people, perhaps they might be excused, as they have few, if any, opportunities of correcting them by reading, travelling, or conversing with foreigners; but the misfortune is, that they infect the minds, and influence the conduct, even of our gentlemen; of those, I mean, who have every title to this appellation but an exemption from prejudice, which however, in my opinion, ought to be regarded as the characteristical mark of a gentleman; for let a man's birth be ever so high, his station ever so exalted, or his fortune ever so large, yet if he is not free from national and other prejudices, I should make bold to tell him, that he had a low and vulgar mind, and had no just claim to the character of a gentleman. And in fact, you will always find that those are most apt to boast of national merit, who have little or no merit of their own to depend on; than which, to be sure, nothing is more natural: the slender vine twists around the sturdy oak, for no other reason in the world but because it has not strength sufficient to support itself.

Should it be alleged in defence of national prejudice, that it is the natural and necessary growth of love to our country, and that therefore the former cannot be destroyed without hurting the latter, I answer, that this is a gross fallacy and delusion. That it is the growth of love to our country, I will allow; but that it is the natural and necessary growth of it, I absolutely deny. Superstition and enthusiasm too are the growth of religion; but who ever took it in his head to affirm that they are the necessary growth of this noble principle? They are, if you will, the bastard sprouts of this heavenly plant, but not its natural and genuine branches, and may safely enough be lopped off, without doing any harm to the parent stock: nay perhaps, till once they are lopped off, this goodly tree can never flourish in perfect health and vigour.

Is it not very possible that I may love my own country without hating the natives of other countries? that I may exert the most heroic bravery, the most undaunted resolution, in defending its laws and liberty, without despising all the rest of the world as cowards and poltroons? Most certainly it is; and if it were not—But why need I suppose what is absolutely impossible?— But if it were not, I must own, I should prefer the title of the ancient philosopher, viz. a citizen of the world, to that of an Englishman, a Frenchman, a European, or to any other appellation whatever.

The Nationalism We Need
Robert B. Reich

There are two faces of American nationalism—one negative, one positive. The negative face wants to block trade, deter immigrants, and eschew global responsibilities. The positive one wants to reduce poverty among the nation's children, ensure that everyone within America has decent health care, and otherwise improve the lives of all our people.

Both give priority to "us" inside the borders over "them" out there. Both believe that America should come first. Both depend for their force on a nation's sense of common purpose. But negative nationalism uses that commonality to exclude those who don't share it. Positive nationalism uses it to expand opportunities for those who do.

Negative nationalism assumes that the world is a zero-sum game where our gains come at another nation's expense, and theirs come at ours. Positive nationalism assumes that when our people are better off, they're more willing and better able to add to the world's well-being.

These are America's two real political parties. You'll find both positive and negative nationalists among Republicans as well as among Democrats. George W. Bush's "compassionate conservatism," still conveniently undefined, at least urges Americans to be generous toward other Americans. The Republican right, meanwhile, is determined to turn America's back on the rest of the world. Democratic primary challengers Bill Bradley and Al Gore are engaged in a long-overdue debate about how best to meet the needs of America's poor and near-poor, even as some in the Democratic Party are putting priority on fighting a new round of world trade agreements. There may even be positive nationalists in the

Reform Party unless Pat Buchanan—an unreconstructed negative nationalist—takes control.

5   If you look hard, you might be able to find a few globalists who deny that America should come first. They perceive no moral difference between a flood in North Carolina and one in Bangladesh, a sweatshop in Los Angeles and a sweatshop in Ecuador, hungry kids in Alabama and hungry kids in Burundi. To the pure globalist, all are equally worthy of concern. I admire pure globalists, but I also wonder about them. For most of us, it's easier to empathize with compatriots than with humanity as a whole, and easier to think we can do something to help those within our borders than those outside. Pure globalists have noble values, and many act on their convictions, but I worry that globalists may feel less compelled to act than people whose sentiments are more rooted.

History teaches that one of the two faces of nationalism almost always predominates. A society with a lot of positive nationalism is likely to be tolerant and open toward the rest of the world because its people have learned the habits of good citizenship and social justice. Dictators and demagogues, on the other hand, flourish where social capital is in short supply. People who feel little responsibility toward one another will turn against minorities in their midst and outsiders across their borders, in return for promises of glory or comforting fictions of superiority.

Negative nationalists prey most directly on people who are losing ground economically and socially. The recent resurgence of negative nationalism in Austria, France, and Switzerland is especially evident among blue-collar manufacturing workers and young men who feel the economic ground shifting under them. The ugly violence against ethnic Chinese during Indonesia's currency crisis was also rooted in economic fears. People whose livelihoods are at risk find it reassuring to be given specific targets for their frustrations. Among economic insecurity's first scapegoats are always immigrants, foreigners, and ethnic minorities.

A healthy dose of positive nationalism can ease these sorts of anxieties by softening the burdens of economic change. When they feel especially connected to their compatriots, citizens who gain from change are more willing to support the kinds of strong safety nets, employment programs, and educational systems that help ease the burden on those who otherwise would fall far behind. And the generosity of the winners in turn allows the nation as a whole to better contend with the consequences of free trade, open capital markets, and more liberal immigration. But failure to choose positive nationalism almost surely promotes its negative twin because the losers are left vulnerable.

Nations now busily shredding their safety nets and slashing their social spending may believe they're moving toward free markets, and in a narrow economic sense, they are. But in the process, they risk breaking the bonds of positive nationalism and exposing their people to the very fears and uncertainties upon which negative nationalism feeds. The inadvertent consequence may be a backlash against not only free markets but also political freedom.

10   In short, those who believe that membership in a society obligates the successful to help those who are falling behind should not recoil from appeals to nationalism. The moral force of social benevolence rests, after all, on the pre-existence of strong bonds among a people who share common values and aspirations. Nationalism is not the danger. The real danger comes in allowing the negative nationalists to claim the mantle of patriotism for their own ends.

Dissent Is as American as Apple Pie
Ralph F. Young

There are many people in this country—and in this administration—who claim that anyone opposed to the U.S. invasion of Iraq, as well as America's continued presence there, is unpatriotic (at best) and treasonous (at worst). Indeed, the Patriot Act stipulates penalties for criticism of the government.

Patriotism—at least according to current popular belief—means supporting the decisions of our political leaders. Dissent is considered un-American. Protestors at presidential appearances routinely have been herded into "free speech zones" where their signs and slogans are seen only by the encircling cordon of police. (The Constitution makes no mention of free speech being confined to a zone.) The next thing you know, cars will be sporting the "America: Love It or Leave It!" bumper stickers that were all the rage some 30 years ago.

This attitude, however, only calls attention to one of the nation's most conspicuous failings—pervasive historical illiteracy. We need to recognize that dissent is the American way; that protest is patriotic. It is, in fact, one of the fundamental traits that defines this country. Cold War scholar Vladislav Zubok has pointed out that it was only when the Soviet Union saw American protestors take to the streets demonstrating against the Vietnam War that they finally overcame their distrust of the U.S. and began to believe in democracy.

5   The English colonies in North America were founded on dissent, and almost immediately after religious secessionists arrived in Massachusetts

Bay, voices of protest rose up against the Puritan authorities. Anne Hutchinson and Roger Williams were banished for their views during the first decade of settlement. Remember, too, that patriots fought the American Revolution to establish independence from a government that was not responsive to the needs of its subjects—thus, resulting in the Declaration of Independence and, ultimately, the Constitution. None of this could have been accomplished without a great deal of debate, protest, resistance, and argument. Somehow, though, America did evolve into a country that respected all forms of freedom, especially freedom of speech. Or did it?

Lynch Mobs

Abolitionist William Lloyd Garrison once was rescued from being lynched by a proslavery mob when the mayor of Boston had him thrown into jail. While incarcerated, Garrison wrote on the wall: "Wm. Lloyd Garrison was put into this cell Wednesday afternoon, October 21, 1835, to save him from the violence of a 'respectable and influential' mob, who sought to destroy him for preaching the abominable and dangerous doctrine that 'all men are created equal.' . . . "

Neither persecution nor time diminished Garrison's radicalism. On July 4, 1854, he publicly burned a copy of the Constitution, proclaiming that, because it acquiesced in the institution of slavery, it was "an agreement with death and a covenant with hell."

In 1846, when Mexican forces had fired on U.S. troops that had been sent across the disputed southern border to provoke such an incident, Pres. James Polk asked Congress for a Declaration of War. "American blood," he proclaimed, "had been shed on American soil." A freshman congressman from Illinois sarcastically criticized the President's policy by introducing the so-called "Spot Resolution," which would have required Polk to travel to Mexico to point out the exact spot on "American soil" where this had taken place. The resolution was defeated. Moreover, it seems likely that Polk questioned Rep. Abraham Lincoln's patriotism.

Writer Henry David Thoreau, also in protest over the war with Mexico, refused to pay a poll tax because he could not in good conscience support an imperialistic government that sought to expand the institution of slavery into new territory. After his arrest and subsequent release, he penned On Resistance to Civil Government.

10   When there is an unjust law, Thoreau wrote, such as those legalizing the institution of slavery, then it is the duty of every just man to break that law. No true patriot allows injustice to go unchallenged.

Thoreau's friend, Ralph Waldo Emerson, visited him the night he spent in jail. "Henry," he asked, somewhat scandalized by such outrageous behavior, "what are you doing in there?" To which Thoreau purportedly replied, "Ralph, what are you doing out there?"

Former Civil War officer and Secretary of the Interior Carl Schurz denounced U.S. Imperialism in 1899 after America had taken over the Philippines and Puerto Rico during the Spanish-American War. "Certainly," he said, addressing an audience at the University of Chicago, "every patriotic citizen will always be ready, if need be, to fight and to die under his flag wherever it may wave in justice and for the best interests of the country. But . . . woe to the republic if it should ever be without citizens patriotic and brave enough to defy the demagogues' cry and to haul down the flag wherever it may be raised not in justice and not for the best interests of the country. Such a republic would not last long."

Theodore Roosevelt, never one to shun a military solution to a crisis, was so critical of Pres. Woodrow Wilson's policies during World War I that he attacked those who claimed it was wrong to oppose a president in time of war. "To announce that there must be no criticism of the president," Roosevelt contended, "or that we are to stand by the president, right or wrong, is not only unpatriotic and servile, but is morally treasonable to the American public. Nothing but the truth should be spoken about him or anyone else. But it is even more important to tell the truth, pleasant or unpleasant, about him than about anyone else."

Meanwhile, writer Randolph Bourne was a relentless critic of American policy in general. During times of war, Bourne wrote, a "herd-feeling inevitably arises. There always is a demand for 100 percent Americanism, among 100 percent of the population. The State is a jealous God and will brook no rivals. Its sovereignty must pervade everyone, and all feeling must be run into the stereotyped forms of romantic patriotic militarism which is the traditional expression of the State. . . . War becomes almost a sport between the hunters and the hunted. The pursuit of enemies within outweighs in psychic attractiveness the assault on the enemy without. The whole terrific force of the State is brought to bear against the heretics."

15   Many older Americans remember quite vividly the fervent protests against U.S. policies on racism, feminism, and war expressed by such prominent dissenters as Martin Luther King, Jr., Malcolm X, Stokeley Carmichael, Ella Baker, Fannie Lou Hamer, Tom Hayden, Mario Savio, Angela Davis, Abbie Hoffman, Allen Ginsberg, Gloria Steinem, and countless others. All of these individuals believed they were acting in the American tradition for the American people. They were dedicated fully to the ideals of democracy and resisted all those who strove to limit it. As a consequence, they helped shape the nature of our society. Anti-war activist Carl Oglesby hit the nail squarely on the head when he stated in 1968 that "We've come to the point where 'democracy' is considered a radical idea."

Today, American citizens are torn by an ill-advised war and occupation led by leaders who, in seeking to stifle the sort of healthy debate democracy requires, do not seem to understand, indeed, who seem to shun, our nation's history. Many of those who opposed the war not only wanted to give peace a chance, but take back the Federal government, which appears to have been hijacked by ultra-rightist hawks.

Neoconservatives have taken control of a country that, historically, has prided itself on the values of peace, democracy, equality, and freedom. They systematically are eroding (if not actually demolishing) those ideals. There is nothing "conservative" about them.

A democracy depends on an educated, well-informed citizenry as well as leaders who are deeply connected and committed to cherishing, conserving, and nurturing the ideals which are supposed to set the U.S. apart from the rest of the world. Those in power, today, however, are not caretakers of the American Dream. Will they be judged by history—like the despoilers of the pharaohs' tombs—as looters who have drained all meaning from the treasures of American democracy?

Should we reach the point where—in joining with the sentiments of the international community—Americans view their own nation as a threat to world peace, what hope is there? How will countries that do not even pretend to respect or desire freedom ever evolve into the types of societies that are not weighed down by terror and fear. Someday—perhaps sooner than we think we will look at the rest of the world from our "city upon a hill" and all we will see is our own haunted reflection staring back at us.

Excerpts From *Proud Upon an Alien Shore*
Rose Furuya Hawkins

I. *Issei Men:* The First Generation

Japan, 1921

All that autumn of austerity
We wandered over withered fields
Like lost butterflies,
Feeding on half-bowls of rice,
5   Stealing warmth
From pale cups
of tea.

As leaves warped and fell
We talked of a golden land
10   And late into the night
We huddled over letters

From west across the Pacific.
We sipped our tea and dreamed
Until the paper turned to shreds,
15 The ink smearing, then fading
Under the moon's cold shadow.

What was this unknown force
That stirred our hearts?
What fire? What song?
20 What new adventure?

Far into the season
We burned with fever
Whistling in our tea
With noisy slurps.

25 Finally, before the silent snow
We stole away at dawn,
Silent samurai, heavy with hope,
Watching, waiting, until the rising sun
Swallowed up our God, our emperor,
30 And our most honorable parents.

America! America!
After forty-seven days at sea
We glimpsed the fertile ground
So dark against a yellow sky.
35 And leaving the ship on sea legs
We stood tall—*Issei* men,
Proud upon an alien shore.

VI. *Nisei* Daughter: The Second Generation

When people ask
About my mother
I look away and say,
"Oh, she's been gone
5 A long time now.
I hardly knew her
Anyway."

But I know she was
A renegade. Why else
10 Was she standing on some foreign shore,
Uncomfortable in high-heeled shoes
And black dress with bust darts,

Her cherry blossom kimono
Left far behind?

15 How else did she consent
To trade her rice paper walls
For corrugated tin
And to love, honor, and obey
This crude stranger, *Ito-San*
20 Who sipped Coca-Cola
Through a straw?

Yes, my mother was a renegade.
She braved the future
By swallowing her pride,
25 Her delicate fingers
Shaping paper cranes
After a long day
Of picking cotton
In the Imperial Valley.

30 She sewed dresses
For my doll
Long after her feet
Were too tired to work the treadle
Of her prized Singer.
35 She taught me words:
Mi-mi, ha-na, ku-chi,
Pointing to my ear
My nose, my mouth.
She fed me full
40 Of fat rice balls
And pickled radishes,
Afraid I might ask
For bologna sandwiches.

Mama, forgive me.
45 I guess I knew you well.
I was your miracle child,
Your second generation
Nisei daughter,
Born to you
50 When you were already too old,
Already too torn
By barbed wire fences
And mixed loyalty.

Oh, where have you gone
55 Little moon-faced child,
Who once chased fireflies
For paper lanterns
In old Japan?

VII. *Sansei:* The Third Generation

Early this morning
I woke up heart-heavy,
Dreaming of my grandfather.
I pictured him, the immigrant,
5 Standing tall upon the alien shore
With hope enough
For all who dared
And dreams enough
To feed a nation.

10 I remember him standing
In his victory garden
Body so small,
Hair so white,
Bent against
15 The bright wisteria.
The blossoms were
Scattering, scattering
Like so many monarchs,
Free, at last, in the wind.

From *Born on the Fourth of July*
Ron Kovic

For me it began in 1946 when I was born on the Fourth of July. The whole sky lit up in a tremendous fireworks display and my mother told me the doctor said I was a real firecracker. Every birthday after that was something the whole country celebrated. It was a proud day to be born on.

I hit a home run my first time at bat in the Massapequa Little League, and I can still remember my Mom and Dad and all the rest of the kids going crazy as I rounded the bases on seven errors and slid into home a hero. We lost the game to the Midgets that night, 22 to 7, and I cried all the way home. It was a long time ago, but sometimes I can still hear them shouting out in front of Pete's house on Hamilton Avenue. There was Bobby Zimmer, the tall kid from down the street, Kenny and Pete, little Tommy Law, and my best friend Richie Castiglia, who lived across from us on Lee Place.

When we weren't down at the field or watching the Yankees on TV, we were playing whiffle ball and climbing trees checking out birds' nests, going down to Fly Beach in Mrs. Zimmer's old car that honked the horn every time it turned the corner, diving underwater with our masks, kicking with our rubber frog's feet, then running in and out of our sprinklers when we got home, waiting for our turn in the shower. And during the summer nights we were all over the neighborhood, from Bobby's house to Kenny's, throwing gliders, doing handstands and backflips off fences, riding to the woods at the end of the block on our bikes, making rafts, building tree forts, jumping across the streams with tree branches, walking and balancing along the back fence like Houdini, hopping along the slate path all around the back yard seeing how far we could go on one foot.

And I ran wherever I went. Down to the school, to the candy store, to the deli, buying baseball cards and Bazooka bubblegum that had the little fortunes at the bottom of the cartoons.

5   When the Fourth of July came, there were fireworks going off all over the neighborhood. It was the most exciting time of year for me next to Christmas. Being born on the exact same day as my country I thought was really great. I was so proud. And every Fourth of July, I had a birthday party and all my friends would come over with birthday presents and we'd put on silly hats and blow these horns my Dad brought home from the A&P. We'd eat lots of ice cream and watermelon and I'd open up all the presents and blow out the candles on the big red, white, and blue birthday cake and then we'd all sing "Happy Birthday" and "I'm a Yankee Doodle Dandy." At night everyone would pile into Bobby's mother's old car and we'd go down to the drive-in, where we'd watch the fireworks display. Before the movie started, we'd all get out and sit up on the roof of the car with our blankets wrapped around us watching the rockets and Roman candles going up and exploding into fountains of rainbow colors, and later, after Mrs. Zimmer dropped me off, I'd lie on my bed feeling a little sad that it all had to end so soon. As I closed my eyes I could still hear strings of firecrackers and cherry bombs going off all over the neighborhood.

Every Saturday afternoon we'd all go down to the movies in the shopping center and watch gigantic prehistoric birds breathe fire, and war movies with John Wayne and Audie Murphy. Bobby's mother always packed us a bagful of candy. I'll never forget Audie Murphy in *To Hell and Back*. At the end he jumps on top of a flaming tank that's just about to explode and grabs the machine gun blasting it into the German lines. He was so brave I had chills running up and down my back, wishing it were me up there. There were gasoline flames roaring around his legs, but he just kept firing that machine gun. It was the greatest movie I ever saw in my life.

Castiglia and I saw *The Sands of Iwo Jima* together. The Marine Corp hymn was playing in the background as we sat glued to our seats, humming the hymn together and watching Sergeant Stryker, played by John Wayne charge up the hill and get killed just before he reached the top. And then they showed the men raising the flag on Iwo Jima with the marines' hymn still playing, and Castiglia and I cried in our seats. I loved the song so much, and every time I heard it I would think of John Wayne and the brave men who raised the flag on Iwo Jima that day. I would think of them and cry. Like Mickey Mantle and the fabulous New York Yankees, John Wayne in *The Sands of Iwo Jima* became one of my heroes.

We'd go home and make up movies like the ones we'd just seen or the ones that were on TV night after night. We'd use our Christmas toys—the Matty Mattel machine guns and grenades, the little green plastic soldiers with guns and flamethrowers in their hands. My favorites were the green plastic men with bazookas. They blasted holes through the enemy. They wiped them out at thirty feet just above the coffee table. They dug in on the front lawn and survived countless artillery attacks. They burned with high-propane lighter fluid and a quarter-gallon of gasoline or were thrown into the raging fires of autumn leaves blasting into a million pieces.

On Saturdays after the movies all the guys would go down to Sally's Woods—Pete and Kenny and Bobby and me, with plastic battery-operated machine guns, cap pistols, and sticks. We turned the woods into a battlefield. We set ambushes, then led gallant attacks, storming over the top, bayonetting and shooting any one who got in our way. Then we'd walk out of the woods like the heroes we knew we would become when we were men.

10   The army had a show on Channel 2 called "The Big Picture," and after it was over Castiglia and I crawled all over the back yard playing guns and army, making commando raids all summer into Ackerman's housing project blasting away at the imaginary enemy we had created right before our eyes, throwing dirt bombs and rocks into the windows, making loud explosions like hand grenades with our voices then charging in with our Matty Mattel machine guns blazing. I bandaged up the German who was still alive and had Castiglia question him as I threw a couple more grenades, killing even more Germans. We went on countless missions and patrols together around my back yard, attacking Ackerman's housing project with everything from bazookas to flamethrowers and baseball bats. We studied the Marine Corps Guidebook and Richie brought over some beautiful pamphlets with very sharp-looking marines on the covers. We read them in my basement for hours and just as we dreamed of playing for the Yankees someday, we dreamed of becoming United States Marines and fighting our

first war and we made a solemn promise that year that the day we turned seventeen we were both going down to the marine recruiter at the shopping center in Levittown and sign up for the United States Marine Corps.

We joined the cub scouts and marched in parades on Memorial Day. We made contingency plans for the cold war and built fallout shelters out of milk cartons. We wore spacesuits and space helmets. We made rocket ships out of cardboard boxes. And one Saturday afternoon in the basement Castiglia and I went to Mars on the couch we had turned into a rocket ship. We read books about the moon and Wernher von Braun. And the whole block watched a thing called the space race begin. On a cold October night Dad and I watched the first satellite, called *Sputnik*, moving across the sky above our house like a tiny bright star. I still remember standing out there with Dad looking up in amazement at that thing moving in the sky above Massapequa. It was hard to believe that this thing, this *Sputnik*, was so high up and moving so fast around the world, again and again. Dad put his hand on my shoulder that night and without saying anything I quietly walked back inside and went to my room thinking that the Russians had beaten America into space and wondering why we couldn't even get a rocket off the pad.

That spring before I graduated, my father took me down to the shopping center in Levittown and made me get my first job. It was in a supermarket not far from the Marine recruiting station. I worked stacking shelves and numbing my fingers and hands unloading cases of frozen food from the trucks. Working with Kenny each day after school, all I could think of, day after day, was joining the marines. My legs and my back ached, but I knew that soon I would be signing the papers and leaving home.

I didn't want to be like my Dad, coming home from the A&P every night. He was a strong man, a good man, but it made him so tired, it took all the energy out of him. I didn't want to be like that, working in that stinking A&P, six days a week, twelve hours a day. I wanted to be somebody I wanted to make something out of my life.

I was getting older now, I was seventeen, and I looked at myself in the mirror that hung from the back of the door in my room and saw how tall and strong I had suddenly become. I took a deep breath, flexing my muscles, and stared straight into the mirror, turning to the side and looking a myself for a long time.

15   In the last month of school, the marine recruiters came and spoke to my senior class. They marched, both in perfect step, into the auditorium with their dress blue uniforms and their magnificently shined shoes. It was like all the movies and all the books and all the dreams of becoming a here come true. I watched them and listened as they stood in front of all the young boys, looking almost like statues and not like real men at all. They spoke in loud voices and one of them was tall and the other was short and very strong looking.

"Good afternoon, men," the tall marine said. "We have come today be cause they told us that some of you want to become marines." He told us that the marines took nothing but the best, that if any of us did not think we were good enough, we should not even think of joining. The tall marine spoke in a very beautiful way about the exciting history of the marines and how they had never lost and America had never been defeated.

"The marines have been the first in everything, first to fight and first to uphold the honor of our country. We have served on distant shores and a home, and we have always come when our country has called. There is nothing finer, nothing prouder, than a United States marine."

When they were finished, they efficiently picked up their papers and marched together down the steps of the stage to where a small crowd of boys began to gather. I couldn't wait to run down after them, meet with them and shake their hands. And as I shook their hands and stared up into their eyes, I couldn't help but feel I was shaking hands with John Wayne and Audie Murphy. They told us that day that the Marine Corps built men— body, mind, and spirit. And that we could serve our country like the young president had asked us to do.

We were all going in different directions and we had our whole lives ahead of us, and a million different dreams. I can still remember the last stickball game. I stood at home plate with the sun in my face and looked out at Richie, Pete, and the rest. It was our last summer together and the last stickball game we ever played on Hamilton Avenue.

20   One day that summer I quit my job at the food store and went to the little red, white, and blue shack in Levittown. My father and I went down together. It was September by the time all the paperwork was completed, September 1964. I was going to leave on a train one morning and become a marine.

I stayed up most of the night before I left, watching the late movie. Then "The Star-Spangled Banner" played. I remember standing up and feeling very patriotic chills running up and down my spine. I put my hand over my heart and stood rigid at attention until the screen went blank.

Patriot Games

John Fetto

As the sun sets on the Fourth of July, many of us will gather on park lawns across the country to 'ooh' and 'ah' at fireworks displays. Then we'll fold up the flag and call it a day. For marketers, however, the flag-waving will have only just begun.

John Fetto, "Patriot Games." Reprinted with permission from the July 2000 issue of *American Demographics*. Copyright, Crain Communications Inc. 2000.

The American flag—an image known to evoke an emotional response—is commonly used in advertising. That's because the repeated pairing of a product with a national icon engenders a positive response to the product, much in the same way we respond to the original image. In the coming year, marketers will have even more reason to play on these emotions as we ascend to new heights of patriotism brought on by the Olympics, a national election, and the celebration of the 225th anniversary of the signing of the Declaration of Independence.

In anticipation of such nationalistic events, we attempted to determine exactly where the ardent flag-wavers live. We took 19 measures that marketers suggest are associated with traditional American patriotism—e.g., attendance at religious services, employment in the manufacturing sector, living in the same home for at least a decade—and used Easy Analytical Software, Inc.'s (EASI) database to generate a demographic profile in all U.S. counties. The results are indicated on the accompanying map, which displays the distribution of America's national pride based on the criteria we selected. Counties in deep red are the most patriotic, counties in deep blue are the least so.

EASI's research reveals that nationalism runs deep in many parts of the country year-round. Most obvious is the Midwest's concentration of patriots. As for the South, it appears they're not just whistling Dixie. Many of the "Star-Spangled" are found in states such as Virginia, West Virginia, Tennessee, and North Carolina. And, while areas with greater numbers of foreign-born residents show up as being less patriotic, Katy Micken, associate professor of marketing at Roger Williams University, warns against over-generalizations. Immigrants are often quite eager to adopt the culture of their new home even as they remain strongly nationalistic toward their native land, she says.

5   Still, 69 percent of whites claim to be extremely or very patriotic compared with 40 percent of non-whites, according to a Gallup Poll. National pride also increases with age. As Gallup reports, 77 percent of adults 50 and older have high levels of patriotism, as do 65 percent of those between the ages of 30 and 49. Only 40 percent of adults aged 18 to 29 claim to have a strong sense of national pride. The least likely to wrap themselves in stars and stripes: high school and college-age students.

What should marketers keep in mind when targeting these passionate Americans? For one, they like the status quo. "This leads them to buy things their mothers and even their grandmothers bought," says Keith Schloemer of the market research firm SRI Consulting. "They are the most loyal of U.S. consumers. If you can show a flag flapping in the background, they'll be sucked right in."

Yet, Americans aren't the only ones to reach for their wallets when national pride stirs. There's no better example of patriotic packaging than a marketing campaign north of the border for Molson Canada. This March, the brewer introduced an ad in which an average "Joe" extols the virtues of being Canadian. "I have a Prime Minister, not a President," he says, standing on a stage as a series of Canuck icons are projected behind him. "I speak English and French, not American . . . I can proudly sew my country's flag on my backpack. I believe in peacekeeping, not policing. Diversity, not assimilation. And that the beaver is a truly proud and noble animal . . . Canada is the second-largest landmass, the first nation of hockey, and the best part of North America. My name is Joe and I . . . Am . . . Canadian!"

The ad has become a national rallying cry. Crowded sports bars have been known to fall silent when the commercial airs, and Molson credits the ad for a sales uptick. "With globalization and the Internet, there are no more borders that help to define our territory," says Glen Hunt, group creative director for Bensimon Byrne D'Arcy Toronto, the agency responsible for the beer ad. "As we become less and less definable in our groups we look for something to hold onto and identify ourselves."

That's what Macerich Company, owner/operator of 54 U.S. shopping malls, hopes to resonate with its new marketing campaign. The Santa Monica, California-based company plans a summer-long "Gloryous Celebration" to attract shoppers. Events include barbershop quartets, apple pie eating contests, and citizenship ceremonies. It's no coincidence Macerich chose 2000 for the campaign's debut: A company survey revealed that 37 percent of Americans feel most patriotic during the Olympics and 14 percent during national elections.

10   "We're tapping into that patriotic sense of America in order to bring back to the Baby Boomer the feeling of being a Boy Scout [or Girl Scout] at an ice cream social," says Susan Valentine, the Macerich Company's senior vice president of marketing. "If we can bring that back to them, people will have a renewed spirit." And, so will Macerich executives—if the campaign helps to boost sales.

The Meaning of That Star-Spangled Hard Hat
Brent Staples

The trade center disaster came to my neighborhood as a dark thunderhead of smoke that boiled over the river into Brooklyn, showering the streets with burning papers from the desks of the dead. Charred documents were still falling when the first American flag went up along our street. Within 48 hours this tree-lined block of nineteenth-century brownstones was flying more flags than it ever has. The flags have already created a new subset of petty crime. Like bicycles, they get stolen, leaving their owners to rustle up new ones in the midst of a flag shortage.

My wife is a flag purist. Tattered, ill-kept banners offend her. She tolerates the plastic, paper, and synthetic flags that have blossomed since September, but does not view them as "real." A "real" flag for my wife is made of heavy-gauge cotton, sewn together piece by piece so that the seams are visible between the stripes and the flag furls gracefully. No seams, no authenticity.

I was a teenager during the Vietnam War, when the meaning of the flag was hotly disputed, and never became a flag purist. The flags that speak to me most come in nontraditional, Pop Art designs. They were regarded as desecration when they first appeared in the 1960s but are now viewed simply as flags of another color. In my neighborhood I've seen a flag used as a garland, snaked through the railings of window grates and fire escapes, and a flag improvised from red, white, and blue bandannas. There is a spectacular flag painted across the full width of a house with glossy paint like the moist icing on a cake, with chrome yellow stripes instead of white ones. The composition speaks of patriotism with a postmodern twist.

Since September 11 conservative critics have been saying that the 60s generation has finally come round to a patriotism that it despised in the Vietnam era. But this generation did not reject patriotism. It rejected the notion that there was only one way to be patriotic. The protest era broadened the definition of patriotism and created a new, less formal identity for the American flag.

5   The psychedelic-flag hard hat that was worn by Dick Cheney when he visited the trade center site shows how design liberties with the flag have been embraced by groups that would have reviled them in the past. Hats like the vice president wore would have been unwelcome—and might even have gotten you roughed up—on construction sites during the late 60s. Then, the term "hard hat" referred to the working-class white ethnics who were soon to bolt the Democratic Party for Ronald Reagan. The clashes between hard hats and antiwar demonstrators were particularly nasty in New York, especially during the building of the World Trade Center. The hard hats worn when I was a shipyard worker in high school were buckets, in basic colors. The flag decals that appeared on them later in the decade were in response to criticism of the country's policy in Vietnam. A longhair who was smart went the other way when he saw group of flagheads bunched together.

I never burned a flag, never saw one burned. But as a teenager growing up around the shipyards on the Delaware River, I was threatened with tire irons by angry dockworkers who were incensed by flag clothing, most notably the flag that an eccentric friend made into a sash and wore to a Jimi Hendrix concert.

The art critic Jed Perl of the *New Republic* has described this as partly a fashion issue, arguing that young people wished to see the flag "as camp, as Kitsch, or retro chic." But the thing went deeper than that. When the rock diva Grace Slick was photographed nude, wrapped in a flag, during the Vietnam War she personified a generation's desire to seize ownership of a symbol from which we were profoundly estranged.

As a black teenager with a huge cloud of hair, I would have avoided a flag-draped street like the one I live on now, wanting no trouble with the kind of people who flew the colors from their homes. But cruising the same streets today, I note the funky, psychedelic banners among the "real" ones and understand that what we have now is a spacious, postmodern patriotism.

TECHNIQUES FOR WRITERS 11-a

Rhetoric Online: Patriotic Sentiments in Music

Country singer Lee Greenwood had a number of minor hits during his career, but he is best known for a strongly patriotic song called "God Bless the U.S.A." that, although it was first released in 1984, has become forever attached to the terrorist attacks of September 11, 2001. For this reading, go online and use a service such as Google.com to search for the string, *lee greenwood god bless lyrics*. As you read the lyrics, annotate them to identify words and phrases that you think help to establish strong rational or emotional appeals. In what main ways does Greenwood's argument differ from some of the other ones in this section?

Other songs that reflect differing ideas about patriotism are Woody Guthrie's "This Land Is Your Land," John Fogerty's "Fortunate Son," and Toby Keith's "Courtesy of the Red, White & Blue." Extend your Internet search to find lyrics of these songs. How do the arguments of these artists compare with Greenwood's? With other arguments from this chapter?

CHAPTER 12

Gay and Lesbian Rights

Beyond Oppression
Jonathan Rauch

At 10:30 on a weeknight in the spring of 1991, Glenn Cashmore was walking to his car on San Diego's University Avenue. He had just left the Soho coffee house in Hillcrest, a heavily gay neighborhood. He turned down Fourth Street and paused to look at the display in an optician's window. Someone shouted, "Hey, faggot!" He felt pain in his shoulder and turned in time to see a white Nissan speeding away. Someone had shot him, luckily only with a pellet gun. The pellet tore through the shirt and penetrated the skin. He went home and treated the wound with peroxide.

Later that year, on the night of December 13, a 17-year-old named John Wear and two other boys were headed to the Soho on University Avenue when a pair of young men set upon them, calling them "faggots." One boy escaped, another's face was gashed and Wear (who, his family said, was not gay) was stabbed. Cashmore went to the hospital to see him but, on arriving, was met with the news that Wear was dead.

This is life—not all of life, but an aspect of life—for gay people in today's America. Homosexuals are objects of scorn for teenagers and of sympathy or moral fear or hatred for adults. They grow up in confusion and bewilderment as children, then often pass into denial as young adults and sometimes remain frightened even into old age. They are persecuted by the military, are denied the sanctuary of publicly recognized marriage, occasionally are prosecuted outright for making love. If closeted, they live with fear of

Jonathan Rauch, "Beyond Oppression," *The New Republic*, May 10, 1993. Reprinted by permission of the author. © Jonathan Rauch 1993.

revelation; if open, they must daily negotiate a hundred delicate tactical issues. (Should I bring it up? Tell my boss? My co-workers? Wear a wedding band? Display my lover's picture?)

There is also AIDS and the stigma attached to it, though AIDS is not uniquely a problem of gay people. And there is the violence. One of my high school friends—an honors student at Brophy Prep, a prestigious Catholic high school in Phoenix—used to boast about his late-night exploits with a baseball bat at the "fag Denny's." I'm sure he was lying, but imagine the horror of being spoken to, and about, in that way.

5   If you ask gay people in America today whether homosexuals are oppressed, I think most would say yes. If you ask why, they would point to the sorts of facts that I just mentioned. The facts are not blinkable. Yet the oppression diagnosis is, for the most part, wrong.

Not wrong in the sense that life for American homosexuals is hunky-dory. It is not. But life is not terrible for most gay people, either, and it is becoming less terrible every year. The experience of gayness and the social status of homosexuals have changed rapidly in the last twenty years, largely owing to the courage of thousands who decided that they had had enough abuse and who demanded better. With change has come the time for a reassessment.

The standard political model sees homosexuals as an oppressed minority who must fight for their liberation through political action. But that model's usefulness is drawing to a close. It is ceasing to serve the interests of ordinary gay people, who ought to begin disengaging from it, even drop it. Otherwise, they will misread their position and lose their way, as too many minority groups have done already.

"Oppression" has become every minority's word for practically everything, a one-size-fits-all political designation used by anyone who feels unequal, aggrieved, or even uncomfortable. I propose a start toward restoring meaning to the notion of oppression by insisting on *objective* evidence. A sense of grievance or discomfort, however real, is not enough.

By now, human beings know a thing or two about oppression. Though it may, indeed, take many forms and work in different ways, there are objective signs you can look for. My own list would emphasize five main items. First, direct legal or governmental discrimination. Second, denial of political franchise—specifically, denial of the right to vote, organize, speak, or lobby. Third—and here we move beyond the strictly political—the systematic denial of education. Fourth, impoverishment relative to the non-oppressed population. And, fifth, a pattern of human rights violations, without recourse.

10   Any one or two of those five signposts may appear for reasons other than oppression. There are a lot of reasons why a people may be poor, for instance. But where you see a minority that is legally barred from

businesses and neighborhoods and jobs, that cannot vote, that is poor and poorly educated, and that lives in physical fear, you are looking at, for instance, the blacks of South Africa, or blacks of the American South until the 1960s; the Jews and homosexuals of Nazi Germany and Vichy France; the untouchable castes of India, the Kurds of Iraq, the women of Saudi Arabia, the women of America 100 years ago; for that matter, the entire population of the former Soviet Union and many Arab and African and Asian countries.

And gay people in America today? Criterion one—direct legal or governmental discrimination—is resoundingly met. Homosexual relations are illegal in twenty-three states, at least seven of which specifically single out acts between persons of the same sex. Gay marriage is not legally recognized anywhere. And the government hounds gay people from the military, not for what they do but for what they are.

Criterion two—denial of political franchise—is resoundingly not met. Not only do gay people vote, they are turning themselves into a constituency to be reckoned with and fought for. Otherwise, the Patrick Buchanans of the world would have sounded contemptuous of gay people at the Republican convention last year, rather than panicked by them. If gay votes didn't count, Bill Clinton would not have stuck his neck out on the military issue during the primary season (one of the bravest things any living politician has done).

Criterion three—denial of education—is also resoundingly not met. Overlooked Opinions Inc., a Chicago market-research company, has built a diverse national base of 35,000 gay men and lesbians, two-thirds of whom are either not out of the closet or are only marginally out, and has then randomly sampled them in surveys. It found that homosexuals had an average of 15.7 years of education, as against 12.7 years for the population as a whole. Obviously, the findings may be skewed if college-educated gay people are likelier to take part in surveys (though Overlooked Opinions said that results didn't follow degree of closetedness). Still, any claim that gay people are denied education appears ludicrous.

Criterion four—relative impoverishment—is also not met. In Overlooked Opinions' sample, gay men had an average household income of $51,624 and lesbians $42,755, compared with the national average of $36,800. Again, yuppie homosexuals may be more likely to answer survey questions than blue-collar ones. But, again, to call homosexuals an impoverished class would be silly.

15   Criterion five—human rights violations without recourse—is also, in the end, not met, though here it's worth taking a moment to see why it is not. The number of gay bashings has probably increased in recent years (though it's hard to know, what with reporting vagaries), and, of course, many gay-bashers either aren't caught or aren't jailed. What too many

gay people forget, though, is that these are problems that homosexuals have in common with non-gay Americans. Though many gay-bashers go free, so do many murderers. In the District of Columbia last year, the police identified suspects in fewer than half of all murders, to say nothing of assault cases.

And the fact is that anti-gay violence is just one part of a much broader pattern. Probably not coincidentally, the killing of John Wear happened in the context of a year, 1991, that broke San Diego's all-time homicide record (1992 was runner-up). Since 1965 the homicide rate in America has doubled, the violent crime arrest rate for juveniles has more than tripled; people now kill you to get your car, they kill you to get your shoes or your potato chips, they kill you because they can do it. A particularly ghastly fact is that homicide due to gunshot is now the second leading cause of death in high school-age kids, after car crashes. No surprise, then, that gay people are afraid. So is everyone else.

Chances are, indeed, that gay people's social class makes them safer, on average, than other urban minorities. Certainly their problem is small compared with what blacks face in inner-city Los Angeles or Chicago, where young black males are likelier to be killed than a U.S. soldier was in a tour of duty in Vietnam.

If any problem unites gay people with non-gay people, it is crime. If any issue does not call for special-interest pleading, this is it. Minority advocates, including gay ones, have blundered insensitively by trying to carve out hate-crime statutes and other special-interest crime laws instead of focusing on tougher measures against violence of all kinds. In trying to sensitize people to crimes aimed specifically at minorities, they are inadvertently desensitizing them to the vastly greater threat of crime against everyone. They contribute to the routinization of murder, which has now reached the point where news of a black girl spray-painted white makes the front pages, but news of a black girl murdered runs in a round-up on page D-6 ("Oh, another killing"). Yes, gay-bashing is a problem. But, no, it isn't oppression. It is, rather, an obscenely ordinary feature of the American experience.

Of course, homosexuals face unhappiness, discrimination, and hatred. But for everyone with a horror story to tell, there are others like an academic I know, a tenured professor who is married to his lover of fourteen years in every way but legally, who owns a split-level condo in Los Angeles, drives a Miata, enjoys prestige and success and love that would be the envy of millions of straight Americans. These things did not fall in his lap. He fought personal and professional battles, was passed over for jobs and left the closet when that was much riskier than it is today. Asked if, he is oppressed, he says, "You're damn straight." But a mark of oppression is that most of its victims are not allowed to succeed; they are allowed only to fail. And this man is no mere token. He is one of a growing multitude of openly gay people who have overcome the past and, in doing so, changed the present.

20   "I'm a gay person, so I don't live in a free country," one highly successful gay writer said recently, "and I don't think most straight people really sit down and realize that for gay people this is basically a totalitarian society in which we're barely tolerated." The reason straight people don't realize this is because it obviously isn't true. As more and more homosexuals come out of hiding, the reality of gay economic and political and educational achievement becomes more evident. And as that happens, gay people who insist they are oppressed will increasingly, and not always unfairly, come off as yuppie whiners, "victims" with $50,000 incomes and vacations in Europe. They may feel they are oppressed, but they will have a harder and harder time convincing the public.

They will distort their politics, too, twisting it into strained and impotent shapes. Scouring for oppressions with which to identify, activists are driven further and further afield. They grab fistfuls of random political demands and stuff them in their pockets. The original platform for April's March on Washington[1] called for, among other things, enforced bilingual education, "an end to genocide of all the indigenous peoples and their cultures," defense budget cuts, universal health care, a national needle exchange program, free substance-abuse treatment on demand, safe and affordable abortion, more money for breast cancer "and other cancers particular to women," "unrestricted, safe and affordable alternative insemination," health care for the "differently-abled and physically challenged," and "an end to poverty." Here was the oppression-entitlement mentality gone haywire.

Worst of all, oppression politics distorts the face of gay America itself. It encourages people to forget that homosexuality isn't hell. As the AIDS crisis has so movingly shown, gay people have built the kind of community that evaporated for many non-gay Americans decades ago. You don't see straight volunteers queuing up to change cancer patients' bedpans and deliver their groceries. Gay people—and unmarried people generally—are at a disadvantage in the top echelons of corporate America, but, on the other hand, they have achieved dazzlingly in culture and business and much else. They lead lives of richness and competence and infinite variety, lives that are not miserable or squashed.

The insistence that gay people are oppressed is most damaging, in the end, because it implies that to be gay is to suffer. It affirms what so many straight people, even sympathetic ones, believe in their hearts: that homosexuals are pitiable. That alone is reason to junk the oppression model, preferably sooner instead of later.

---

[1]A major gay rights demonstration was held in Washington, DC, on April 25, 1993.

If the oppression model is failing, what is the right model? Not that of an oppressed people seeking redemption through political action; rather, that of an ostracized people seeking redemption through personal action. What do you do about misguided ostracism? The most important thing is what Glenn Cashmore did. After John Wear's murder, he came out of the closet. He wrote an article in the *Los Angeles Times* denouncing his own years of silence. He stepped into the circle of people who are what used to be called known homosexuals.

25   This makes a difference. *The New York Times* conducted a poll on homosexuals this year and found that people who had a gay family member or close friend "were much more tolerant and accepting." Whereas oppression politics fails because it denies reality, positive personal example works because it demonstrates reality. "We're here, we're queer, get used to it," Queer Nation's chant,[2] is not only a brilliant slogan. It is a strategy. It is, in some ways, *the* strategy. To move away from oppression politics is not to sit quietly. It is often to hold hands in public or take a lover to the company Christmas party, sometimes to stage kiss-ins, always to be unashamed. It is to make of honesty a kind of activism.

Gay Americans should emulate Jewish Americans, who have it about right. Jews recognize that to many Americans we will always seem different (and we are, in some ways, different). We grow up being fed "their" culture in school, in daily life, even in the calendar. It never stops. For a full month of every year, every radio program and shop window reminds you that this is, culturally, a Christian nation (no, not Judeo-Christian). Jews could resent this, but most of us choose not to, because, by way of compensation, we think hard, we work hard, we are cohesive, we are interesting. We recognize that minorities will always face special burdens of adjustment, but we also understand that with those burdens come rewards of community and spirit and struggle. We recognize that there will always be a minority of Americans who hate us, but we also understand that, so long as we stay watchful, this hateful minority is more pathetic than threatening. We watch it; we fight it when it lashes out; but we do not organize our personal and political lives around it.

Gay people's main weapons are ones we already possess. In America, our main enemies are superstition and hate. Superstition is extinguished by public criticism and by the power of moral example. Political activists always underestimate the power of criticism and moral example to change people's minds, and they always overestimate the power of law and force. As for hate, the way to fight it is with love. And that we have in abundance.

---

[2]Queer Nation is a gay political organization—many members of which are in their twenties—that advocates a highly visible gay presence in society.

Gay Marriages: Make Them Legal
Thomas B. Stoddard

"In sickness and in health, 'til death do us part." With those familiar words, millions of people each year are married, a public affirmation of a private bond that both society and the newlyweds hope will endure. Yet for nearly four years, Karen Thompson was denied the company of the one person to whom she had pledged lifelong devotion. Her partner is a woman, Sharon Kowalski, and their home state of Minnesota, like every other jurisdiction in the United States, refuses to permit two individuals of the same sex to marry.

Karen Thompson and Sharon Kowalski are spouses in every respect except the legal. They exchanged vows and rings; they lived together until November 13, 1983—when Ms. Kowalski was severely injured when her car was struck by a drunk driver. She lost the capacity to walk or to speak more than several words at a time, and needed constant care.

Ms. Thompson sought a court ruling granting her guardianship over her partner, but Ms. Kowalski's parents opposed the petition and obtained sole guardianship. They moved Ms. Kowalski to a nursing home three-hundred miles away from Ms. Thompson and forbade all visits between the two women. Last month, as part of a reevaluation of Ms. Kowalski's mental competency, Ms. Thompson was permitted to visit her partner again. But the prolonged injustice and anguish inflicted on both women hold a moral for everyone.

Marriage, the Supreme Court declared in 1967, is "one of the basic civil rights of man" (and, presumably, of woman as well). The freedom to marry, said the Court, is "essential to the orderly pursuit of happiness."

5   Marriage is not just a symbolic state. It can be the key to survival emotional and financial Marriage triggers a universe of rights, privileges, and presumptions. A married person can share in a spouse's estate even when there is no will. She is typically entitled to the group insurance and pension programs offered by the spouse's employer, and she enjoys tax advantages. She cannot be compelled to testify against her spouse in legal proceedings.

The decision whether or not to marry belongs properly to individuals— not the government. Yet at present, all fifty states deny that choice to millions of gay and lesbian Americans. While marriage has historically required a male partner and a female partner, history alone cannot sanctify injustice. If tradition were the only measure, most states would still limit matrimony to partners of the same race.

Thomas B. Stoddard, "Gay Marriages: Make Them Legal," *The New York Times*, March 4, 1989. Reprinted by permission of Walter Rieman, Executor of the Estate of Thomas B. Stoddard.

As recently as 1967, before the Supreme Court declared miscegenation statutes unconstitutional, sixteen states still prohibited marriages between a white person and a black person. When all the excuses were stripped away, it was clear that the only purpose of those laws was, in the words of the Supreme Court, "to maintain white supremacy."

Those who argue against reforming the marriage statutes because they believe that same sex marriage would be "antifamily" overlook the obvious: Marriage creates families and promotes social stability. In an increasingly loveless world, those who wish to commit themselves to a relationship founded upon devotion should be encouraged, not scorned. Government has no legitimate interest in how that love is expressed.

And it can no longer be argued—if it ever could—that marriage is fundamentally a procreative unit. Otherwise, states would forbid marriage between those who, by reason of age or infertility, cannot have children, as well as those who elect not to.

10   As the case of Sharon Kowalski and Karen Thompson demonstrates, sanctimonious illusions lead directly to the suffering of others. Denied the right to marry, these two women are left subject to the whims and prejudices of others, and of the law.

Depriving millions of gay American adults the marriages of their choice, and the rights that flow from marriage, denies equal protection of the law. They, their families and friends, together with fair minded people everywhere, should demand an end to this monstrous injustice.

Gay Marriage: Sidestep on Freedom's Path
Alexander Cockburn

I'm for anything that terrifies Democrats, outrages Republicans, upsets the apple cart. But exultation about the gay marriages cemented in San Francisco, counties in Oregon and New Mexico, and some cities in New York is misplaced.

Why rejoice when state and church extend their grip, which is what marriage is all about? Assimilation is not liberation, and the invocation of "equality" as the great attainment of these gay marriages should be challenged. Peter Tatchell, the British gay leader, put it well a couple of years ago: "Equality is a good start, but it is not sufficient. Equality for queers inevitably means equal rights on straight terms, since they are the ones who dominate and determine the existing legal framework. We conform—albeit equally—with their screwed-up system. That is not liberation. It is capitulation."

Alexander Cockburn, "Gay Marriage: Sidestep on Freedom's Path," *The Nation*, Vol. 278, No. 13 (April 5, 2004). Reprinted by permission of the author.

So the good news, as that excellent paper, *Ultra Violet* (newsletter of LAGAI, Lesbian and Gay Insurrection), recently put it, is not that 400 gay couples are now legally married in San Francisco but that 69,201 in the city (Ultra Violet's number) are still living in sin.

Marriage diverts us from the path of necessary reform. Civil union, today lawful only in Vermont, is what makes sense as a national cause. Unmarried couples, straight or gay, need to be able to secure joint property, make safe wills, have hassle-free hospital visits and so forth. But issues of hospital visits or healthcare should have nothing to do with marriage, and marriage as a rite should have nothing to do with legal rights. "Marriage" should be separated from legal recognition of a bond, of a kinship.

5   There's a fork in the road for progressives. One path is sameness, expanding a troubled institution to same-sexers. But that path detours the real problems of relationships today and their official recognition. As a generation of feminists and the divorce rate attest, marriage is in sore trouble, well beyond powers of recuperation offered in Bush's proposed constitutional amendment, which would be a touching souvenir of a world long gone. Why have prenuptial agreements become common among people of moderate income? Prenups challenge the one-size-fits-all straitjacket of marriage, as do other important arrangements devised in recent years in response to changing anthropological and moral circumstance: co-parent adoptions, adoptions by single people, many varieties of public and private domestic partnerships, civil unions. Expand and strengthen the options. Get religion out of the law.

Civil union across the country would help to level a playing field that's become increasingly uneven. In some corporations gay couples have health benefits that unmarried straight couples don't. Contrary to endless rants about the "marriage penalty" in the federal tax code, a larger number of people enjoy a marriage bonus, as reported by the Congressional Joint Committee on Taxation in 1999.

Unmarried workers may lose hundreds or even thousands of dollars per year in employee benefits compensation. For example, as the Unmarried America website (www.unmarriedamerica.org) points out, "Most states will allow workers to collect unemployment compensation if they quit a job to move to a new area when their spouse is relocated by his or her company. But state laws usually will not give these benefits to a worker who quits to relocate with his or her domestic partner."

There are so many tricky questions, particularly now that morals and the surgeon's knife have deepened their own relationship. What happens when, say, a man who is already receiving domestic-partner benefits at work for his male partner goes through sex reassignment surgery and acquires the physical impedimenta of the opposite sex? Should the couple lose their bennies until they get legally hitched?

None of this should have anything to do with various rites of marriage such as a hippie New Age union celebrated waist deep in a river with solemn invocation of the winds and other natural forces, or a white wedding in a high Episcopal church.

10   "The pursuit of marriage in the name of equality," says Bill Dobbs, radical gay organizer, "shows how the gay imagination is shriveling." Judith Butler, professor at the University of California, Berkeley, exhibited kindred disquiet in a quote she gave the *New York Times* in March. "It's very hard to speak freely right now. But many gay people are uncomfortable with all this, because they feel their sense of an alternative movement is dying. Sexual politics was supposed to be about finding alternatives to marriage."

As Jim Eigo, a writer and activist whose thinking was very influential in the early days of ACT UP, put it a while back, what's the use of being queer if you can't be different? "Why are current mainstream gay organizations working to strike a bargain with straight society that will make some queers less equal than others? Under its terms, gays who are willing to mimic heterosexual relations and enter into a legally-enforced lifetime sexual bond with one other person will be granted special benefits and status to be withheld from those who refuse such domestication. . . . Marriage has no more place in efforts to achieve equality than slavery or the divine right of kings. . . . At this juncture in history, wouldn't it make more sense for us to try to figure out how to relieve heterosexuals of the outdated shackles of matrimony?"

And why marriage, or even civil union, to just one person? Why this endless replication of the Noah's Ark principle? You could have several people involved in some version of a reciprocal-beneficiary legal package.

For me the cheering political lesson is that Mayor Gavin Newsom of San Francisco felt the hot breath of a challenge from his left (in the form of his Green opponent, Matt Gonzalez) and felt impelled to radical action to consolidate his victory. That's good, because it shows the value of independent radical challenges, but that's where my cheers stop. Gay marriage is a step back in the march toward freedom. Civil unions for all!

Walking in the Truth
Douglas L. LeBlanc

Three mainline Protestant denominations—the Episcopal Church, the Presbyterian Church (U.S.A), and the United Methodist Church—faced organized pressure this summer to revise their historic and biblical teachings on marriage. Despite the media-savvy civil disobedience of Mel White's

---

Douglas L. LeBlanc, "Walking in the Truth." This article first appeared in the September 4, 2000 issue of *Christianity Today*. Used by permission of Christianity Today International, Carol Stream, IL 60188.

Soulforce activists at three church conferences, the denominations declined to equate homosexual unions with marriage. *Christianity Today* shares the relief of evangelicals within these large denominations.

Nevertheless, we agree with the *Chicago Tribune*'s Steve Kloehn when he writes that "the controversy is only beginning" . . .

Homosexual people are far more visible and vocal than they were before the protests inspired by the Stonewall Inn raid in 1969. Homosexual men and women will not return to the collective closet, the centuries-old practice of culturally imposed silence. Nor should they. Homosexual activists rightly insist that they not face verbal and physical abuse, threats, or even murders because of their sexual orientation.

Further, we need to resist the notion that any individual vote of a national church conference will send pro-homosexual activists limping away from mainline Protestantism's marketplace of theologies, never again to return. These activists show a remarkable tenacity and an unflinching commitment to their goals. Homosexual people should not fear for their safety, but whether their behavior should enjoy cultural approval is an altogether different question. If Christians are foolish to expect homosexuals to return to their closets, many homosexual activists are naïve to expect that they can achieve cultural affirmation by demanding it frequently and loudly enough.

What Should the Church Bless?

5   Whether homosexual couples should receive the church's blessing is a still more important matter, one which strikes at the heart of God's revealed and unchanging purposes for human sexuality. Leading homosexual activists within churches, such as journalist Andrew Sullivan (a Roman Catholic) and English professor Louie Crew (an Episcopalian), correctly frame the debate as concerning the boundaries of marriage: they ask that the church revise its doctrine of marriage to encompass homosexual couples. These activists are more intellectually rigorous than those who dodge the question of marriage, but they ask that Christian churches do the moral and theological equivalent of squaring a circle. Throughout Scripture, God clearly defines his design for marriage as uniting one man and one woman for a lifetime. Despite the best efforts of such authors as John Boswell, William Countryman, and Robin Scroggs, there is no explaining away the consistent words of Scripture and apostolic tradition that homosexual intercourse strays from God's will.

But quite apart from what homosexual activists dismiss as "the clobber verses," churches must face an increasingly clear reality: the advocates of sexual liberation generally proclaim a gospel at odds with historic Christianity. On such basic questions as the Creation, the Fall, and the Atonement, they are far more likely to invoke Matthew Fox's new-agey notion of Original Blessing and a vaguely defined sense of "God's all-inclusive love."

Just how these competing gospels will continue to coexist in major denominations, or part ways, will remain an important news story for years to come. Given the often close votes of this summer, the story could well take a dramatic turn at the next meeting of Episcopalians or Presbyterians.

Scripture, reason, and tradition support the church's received doctrine of marriage. Still, churches have much work ahead to become places of hospitality and pastoral care for homosexual Christians. Something is deeply wrong if a Christian suffers ostracism after admitting to struggles with same-sex attraction. A willful refusal to repent of sin is one matter; confessing to temptation is entirely another.

We fail both the compassionate ministry of Jesus Christ and our fellow Christians when we avoid homosexual men and women who strive to obey the words of Scripture. We dare not send homosexual Christians back into closets of self-loathing and terror. The answer to temptation is mutual confession, accountability, and Christian community, not shunning.

10   Too often our idea of such community begins and ends with referring people to a chapter of an "ex-gay" ministry like Exodus International and bidding them Godspeed. Evangelicals have much to learn from the Roman Catholic ministry known as Courage, which measures success more by chaste lives than by changed orientations. We affirm that God does heal wounded sexual identities, but we recognize that such healing often involves some of the most difficult psychological work imaginable. In a fallen world, insisting that all homosexual Christians must change their orientation is as reckless as the sexual Left's stubborn denial that anybody can make such changes.

Why are North American churches mired in this debate in this era? Perhaps only eternity will make that fully clear. Still, this historic moment offers churches rich opportunities—not only to make the case for the doctrine of marriage but also to walk in compassion beside Christians who struggle with homosexual desires.

Reserve Marriage for Heterosexuals
Bruce Fein

Authorizing the marriage of homosexuals, like sanctioning polygamy, would be unenlightened social policy. The law should reserve the celebration of marriage vows for monogamous male-female attachments to further

Bruce Fein, "Reserve Marriage for Heterosexuals," *ABA Journal,* January 1990, p. 43. © 1990 The American Bar Association. Reprinted by permission.

the goal of psychologically, emotionally and educationally balanced off-spring.

As Justice Oliver Wendell Holmes noted, the life of the law has not been logic, it has been experience. Experience confirms that child development is skewed, scarred or retarded when either a father or mother is absent in the household.

In the area of adoption, married couples are favored over singles. The recent preferences for joint child-custody decrees in divorce proceedings tacitly acknowledges the desirability of child intimacies with both a mother and father.

As Supreme Court Justice Byron White recognized in *Taylor v. Louisiana* (1975): "[T]he two sexes are not fungible; a community made up exclusively of one is different from a community of both; the subtle interplay of influence one on the other is among the imponderables" (quoting from *Ballard v. United States*).

5   A child receives incalculable benefits in the maturing process by the joint instruction, consolation, oversight and love of a father and mother—benefits that are unavailable in homosexual households. The child enjoys the opportunity to understand and respect both sexes in a uniquely intimate climate. The likelihood of gender prejudice is thus reduced, an exceptionally worthy social objective.

The law should encourage male-female marriage vows over homosexual attachments in the interests of physically, mentally, and psychologically healthy children, the nation's most valuable asset.

Crowning homosexual relationships with the solemnity of legal marriage would wrongly send social cues that male-female marriages are not preferable. And there is no constitutional right to homosexual marriage since homosexual sodomy can be criminalized. (See *Bowers v. Hardwick* (1986).)

The fact that some traditional marriages end in fractious divorce, yield no offspring, or result in families with mistreated children does not discredit limiting marriage to monogamous female-male relationships. Anti-polygamy laws are instructive. They seek to discourage female docility, male autocracy, and intra-family rancor and jealousies that are promoted by polygamous marriages. That some might not exhibit such deplorable characteristics is no reason for their repeal or a finding of constitutional infirmity.

To deny the right of homosexual marriage is not an argument for limiting other rights to gays, because of community animosity or vengeance. These are unacceptable policy motivations if law is to be civilized.

10   Several states and localities protect homosexuals against discrimination in employment or housing. In New York, a state law confers on a homosexual the rent-control benefits of a deceased partner. Other jurisdictions have eschewed special legal rights for homosexuals, and the

military excludes them. Experience will adjudge which of the varied legal approaches to homosexual rights has been the most enlightened.

Sober debate over homosexual rights is in short supply. The subject challenges deep-rooted and passionately held images of manhood, womanhood and parenthood, and evokes sublimated fears of community ostracism or degradation.

Each legal issue regarding homosexuality should be examined discretely with the recognition that time has upset many fighting faiths and with the goal of balancing individual liberty against community interests. With regard to homosexual marriage, that balance is negative.

An Amazing Pass
Midge Decter

One minute, we're talking about tolerance for homosexuals; the next, we're watching them marry.

The final weeks of the presidential campaign are filled with talk of homosexuality, specifically the vice president's daughter. Beyond and behind this, of course, is the recent sight of homosexual couples lining up to receive marriage licenses. How did it ever come to this, while most of the country was hoping not to have to pay attention?

Not so many years have passed between the moment that New Yorkers were both bemused and amused to learn that their city would have an annual softball game between the cops and the homosexuals, and the day when those couples lined up to receive their licenses. Not so many years, that is, for a cultural journey as vast as the one that took American society from the decision not to persecute homosexuals to the point of the enthusiastic embrace of them. The time seems especially brief considering that in the years between these two phenomena we saw the spread of a new— and hideous and fatal—disease that resulted from the corresponding spread of a kind of blind and heedlessly driven homosexual promiscuity.

At first, we may remember, denizens of the high culture, fearing that the new spirit of sexual enlightenment might be dampened by the news of this disease, AIDS, tried to tell us that everyone—homosexual and heterosexual alike—was in danger of being struck by the disease. It became a mark of high civic spirit to demand that the government devote whatever resources would prove to be necessary to finding a cure. When the claim

Midge Decter, "An Amazing Pass," *National Review*, Vol. 56, No. 21 (November 8, 2004), pp. 30–31. Reprinted by permission of the author.

that everyone was at risk turned out to be untrue—virtually the only heterosexuals in danger of contracting AIDS were careless intravenous drug-users (at least in the West)—a public show of deep compassion for—indeed the beatification of—those who were afflicted became the new propriety, if not, indeed, the new piety. AIDS was now to be seen as a cruel fate, like a lightning bolt, rather than the result of who knows how many nights and how many blind encounters in those so-exclusive bars and bathhouses. And to speak a word of truth in the face of all that very real suffering would have been considered insufferably cruel. So AIDS was duly given a place on the good people's list of injustices, where its real meaning could be overlooked.

5   After all, Americans in general are nice people, probably the nicest in the world, afraid of mean-spiritedness in others, and perhaps even more afraid of the accusation of being mean-spirited themselves. Now, it took them a long, long time to get around to dealing with their country's shameful conduct toward black people; and it is as if the shame of those years, indeed those centuries, of living comfortably with the crimes committed against the country's blacks has left them quite disarmed in the face of any and all charges of injustice or bigotry, whatever the merits. So it was, for instance, that the country was all too easily mobilized by a largely meretricious campaign to undo the alleged historic wrongs against women. (Insofar as women could rightly claim to be suffering from special disadvantages, nature itself had decreed them, after all, and it was only an unprecedented degree of national wealth combined with the wonders of medical technology that would make it possible to overcome them.) In any case, just as a group of militant women had piggy-backed their so-called cause onto that of the civil-rights revolution, so the homosexuals were almost inevitably next in line with a movement of their own.

No doubt they were within their rights to demand better manners of certain of their fellow citizens, though an angry protest movement with all the usual trappings was hardly necessary to achieve such a thing. No, something as easy to obtain from an already softened community as less bigoted treatment and greater sensitivity barely counted among the homosexuals' demands. They were loaded for bear.

What the movement wanted—beyond, of course, a cure for AIDS that would allow them once again to take up their formerly carefree lifestyle— was an official and unquestioning acknowledgment that how they comported themselves, sexually speaking, was no less normal a way of living than that engaged in by the "straight" community.

And soon we began to see the results. For instance, a largely compliant community of tender-feeling folk sat by as the Boy Scouts were informed that they could no longer abide by their policy of disallowing homosexuals as scoutmasters. Sex-education curricula in the public schools (usually titled "Introduction to Family Life" or something similar) began to include instruction in the acceptance of homosexual "families" and their special sexual practices. And, traditionally at the forefront of sophisticated attitudes, New York City now boasts in its school system a high school specifically designated for homosexual kids. All, of course, in the name of tolerance for those formerly discriminated against. In some places, homosexuals were permitted—in some even encouraged—to adopt children: After all, is not a good and loving home better for a child than being left in an institution?

Today we have reached the point of debating the question of whether homosexuals may receive official community sanction for marrying. Such a logical outcome could have been predicted but wasn't, at least not by most of the people who had been wishing all these years merely to be kind and who had never imagined that common human decency would require them to bless homosexual marriage. Now they are left wondering what to do.

10   It may be too late to stop the onrushing tide, or it may not. The issue has thus far been placed in the hands of judges, and judges, as we know, have recently been deciding things on the basis not of law or even of what they take to be the public's welfare but only of their own personal feelings about things. On the other hand, new organizations have been formed to fight against the legitimation of "gay" marriage. Christian and Jewish religious leaders who still have faith in their own religious doctrines have declared their opposition. And many others have done so as well, including, of course, the president of the United States.

But the question remains: What of all those nice people who have played so important a role in allowing things to get this far? They have done so partly, as I said, because virtually anything proclaiming itself to be a matter of justice stirs their horror at the thought of being found unjust. But even more important is their reluctance to face up to what homosexuality means in practice. Whether homosexuals are born or made is a question that will not be decided, certainly not in our time and maybe not ever. Thus the idea that their being homosexual is not their fault provides a great temptation simply to have done with the issue altogether. It takes only a bit of turning one's head away to imagine that those pictures of the newly licensed happy couples, embracing and celebrating, are but for a small detail like any other wedding pictures. And in a time when marriages all around seem to be made and dissolved so casually, who is to say that these are not marriages like any others?

What people who are now given to this kind of resignation do not appear to understand is that the campaign to legalize homosexual marriage is not so much about homosexuals as about them. It is, as the kids say, the perfect and ultimate "in your face."

This is, to be sure, not so much the case with the lesbians, who anyway tend to engage in something akin to heterosexual marriage: that is, they tend to settle down, to stay together, and to be monogamous. They are women, and women are by nature monogamous, wishing to be mothers, for instance, and to bring up their children in stable households. But the movement for homosexual marriage is really not about them, though they are now taking part in it. The pleasure they express at the prospect of being "legalized" is merely an extension of the way they for the most part already feel.

The real issue here is with, and about, the men. For men are not by nature monogamous—it is women who make them so. And as the continuing spread of AIDS in such key homosexual centers as San Francisco attests, homosexuals are men whose natural promiscuousness has not been traded away to women in exchange for the comforts of home. There are, of course, homosexual men who have married women and made homes and fathered children with them. But the real sexual hunger in such men continues to be for other men, and is almost always acted upon. There have also been homosexual couples who have famously lived together for years and years, sometimes indeed for life, but what heterosexuals would define as marital loyalty has little or nothing to do with it. Indeed, a recent and scantly noted story in the press said that among the Massachusetts couples who had been granted wedding licenses the women said they intended to get married and most of the men said they didn't.

15   What, then, is the exercise for? It is for knocking the remaining pins out from under an already badly creaking culture, for being able to declare the unnatural natural, and for playing the final malicious joke out of a whole bagful of malicious jokes on all those people who want nothing more than to be able to account themselves compassionate.

Moreover, only the very innocent could imagine that this would be the end of it. For if society can by mere judicial fiat determine to overcome the distinction between heterosexuality and homosexuality, why can it not decide, then, to erase the sexual distinction between adults and children? After all, pedophiles, too, are human beings with human feelings; and who is to say that children who would enjoy their attentions are not entitled to? And after pedophilia, where will be found the truly telling argument against incest—especially since such issues, once left in the hands of God, now seem to have been thrown into the laps of judges? We may tremble at the outcome.

The Wedding March
Alisa Solomon

Gay nuptials combine pomp and protest.

"Get down, get down!" a voice yelled from the back of the crowd at a mid-March wedding in New York City, and a chorus of others soon took up the

Alisa Solomon, "The Wedding March." Reprinted with permission from the July 5, 2004 issue of *The Nation*. For subscription information, call 1-800-333-8536. Portions of each week's *Nation* magazine can be accessed at http://www.thenation.com.

call. These were not the cries of partyers going wild on the dance floor, but the irritated admonitions of some fifty newspaper photographers and TV camera folk trying to get celebrants to duck under the frame of their shots. One cable guy elbowed his ways forward so aggressively that he almost pushed a few wedding guests into Ruth Finkelstein and B. C. Craig's chuppah. Gazing intently into each other's eyes, the two brides didn't seem to notice.

That misty morning, they were one of three same-sex pairs solemnizing their commitments on the steps of City Hall to protest the state's refusal to grant them marriage licenses and express support for the mayor of New Paltz, Jason West, and two Unitarian ministers, who had been charged with misdemeanors in the Hudson Valley town for pronouncing dozens of couples wife-and-wife or husband-and-husband. Reached for comment, Mayor Michael Bloomberg told the press that the demonstrators should have taken their rites to Albany, since state laws were their target. "I think this is more theater than anything else," he said.

Effective mass protest has always employed histrionics, of course, but there are other important—and even radical—ways in which Bloomberg was essentially right. Like other public demonstrations, the astonishing nuptial insurgency that spread across the country this year offered an effective mix of sympathetic characters, engaging narrative, fabulous spectacle and sassy rebuke. No matter what you think about marriage as a political goal, there is no denying that these "wedding marches" produced a stirring display of queer desire and anti-Bush defiance. What's more, pointing at the gap between the symbolic ritual of a wedding and the legal, contractual fact of marriage, the protests exposed the tenuousness of the tie between rites and rights—and the vigorous social and cultural forces called out to defend it.

5   The festive two-by-two queues for licenses in San Francisco, the busloads of betrothed in Phoenix, the exuberant exchanges of vows in Portland, all these proliferating images of the love that once dared not speak is [sic] name refusing to shut up shifted the ground of the gay-marriage debate. Favorable rulings from judges have been won by particular couples bringing lawsuits, but the crowds of wedded wannabes, from long-term lovers to the newly smitten, have taken the issue out of the courthouses and into the streets. Like the first gay pride parades, which made the personal step of coming out political by multiplying and flaunting it, the mass rush to the altar over the past six months has turned the relatively private and intimate act of matrimony into a collective action staged for a mass public. (In contrast to the parades, though, which polymorphously present myriad versions of queerness, the marriage demos constrict gay visibility, excluding those who reject nuclear couplehood.)

Meanwhile, the city officials who rebelled against laws and practices they regard as discriminatory revived a dramatic form of direct-action civil disobedience: Like racially integrated lunch-counter sit-ins, the issuing of the licenses accomplishes the very deed whose outlawing the protests seek to undo. Such stagings of possibility are always compelling. In today's parched political landscape they came like a quenching rain. Even people not particularly invested in gay marriage couldn't help getting caught up when renegade mayors and town clerks boldly asserted local authority and brazenly resisted the crushing narrowness of Right-Wing America. Hundreds of straight folks poured into San Francisco's City Hall to volunteers as witnesses or help hasten the paperwork. Others passed trays of steaming coffee along the line of couples waiting hours in the February rain. Cars driving by honked their congrats. Taxis offered "free rides for newlyweds." All were getting in on the giddying opportunity to stand outside the Republican frame. In this context, even among leftists and feminists suspicious of the marital enterprise, whether one actually wanted a queer marriage license became almost beside the point—about as relevant as whether those lunch-counter protesters really wanted to eat the food at Woolworth's.

The pageantry played in Peoria—and drew all those photographers to New York's City Hall—for another irresistible reason: The story follows an enduring, endearing narrative. For centuries, from ancient Roman comedy to *My Big Fat Greek Wedding*, lovers have been overcoming recalcitrant parents and progressing toward the triumph of a marital finale. Gay men and lesbians seeking to tie the knot in one stubborn county after another re-enact this familiar wedding plot again and again. In turn, the state, blustering about the end of civilization like the swaggering capitano of the commedia dell'arte, plays the villainous authority who thwarts the inamorati. The public is well practiced in whom to root for. At a time when tabloid headlines and reality TV shows make a nightly travesty of eternal devotion and connubial bliss, queer sweethearts have provided the season's most sincere and sentimental romantic comedy. This trope is tricky, though, as it has both radical and depoliticizing potential.

Far from the sex-affirming, multiple-partner kiss-ins ACT UP organized in the early years of the AIDS crisis, today's affinity groups of the affianced place themselves within this recognizable story of amorous fulfillment. Like Shakespearean lovers who have fled to the forest to evade the constraints of the court, where they were not allowed to marry the person of their choosing, they return to city halls all over the country to affirm both their love and their rightful place in the larger community. If the authorities don't give in—as in *Romeo and Juliet*—tragedy results (possibly forcing the rigid parental figures to reassess the rules that denied the lovers in the first place). But in comedy, as Puck might say, "Jill shall have Jill/Nought shall go ill": The dukes and kings reliably relent and all are recuperated within the slightly adjusted yet restored social order.

Laying claim to this narrative, queer spousal supplicants have displaced the once-dominant images of their community as perverts and predators. The dildo-wagging drag queens and leather-clad revelers featured in the

1990s antigay propaganda film *The Gay Agenda* inflamed groups like the Traditional Families Coalition, who warned in their fundraising letters, "They
want your children." But the imagery glowing into living rooms today cannot whip up that particular anxiety. The marriage demonstrators make no
demands, for example, that school curriculums include queer material or
that gay, lesbian, bisexual and transgender teachers be protected from job
discrimination. Rather, they seek public equality in the traditionally private
realm of family.

10   Indeed, what ignites the religious right's wrath today is precisely the
acceptability of these heartwarming scenes. As Massachusetts began issuing
licenses to same-sex couples in May, some backers of a state constitutional
amendment restricting marriage to a man and a woman told the press they
feared that the very sight of gay weddings would make the public more tolerant of homosexuality. Some haven't been able to resist the universal
theme of love themselves. Ray McNulty, a spokesperson for the antigay Massachusetts Family Institute, advised that opponents take their complaints to
lawmakers, not to queer couples. "As far as I'm concerned," he was quoted
saying on May 17, "give those people their happiness for the day."

Some liberals, of course, are more inclined to grant the happiness indef-
initely—as romantic comedies always do—by ending with the wedding and
making no mention of the marriage. Likewise, contemporary pop culture
loves gay weddings but holds its peace when it comes to marriage. Mass
media not only permit, but celebrate, queer nuptials in which two people
declare their status as a couple. But they stop far short of insisting that this
event confer status on the couple in the eyes of the state.

The trope of triumphing lovers is so powerful it trumps politics, bull-
dozing past the inconvenient facts of the law with the sheer force of its
familiar imagery and narrative drive. Even the current, campy Off Broadway show *My Big Gay Italian Wedding* never mentions that queer couplings
are not recognized by the state. It's parents and church that stand in the
way of Anthony and Andrew's union in this slapdash sitcom (plus Andrew's
reputation as "the biggest slut in Bensonhurst"). The fellows get their happy
ending—rings, blessings, drunken guests and all—and the marriage's lack
of legal standing simply doesn't come up. Similarly untroubled images of
gay weddings abound. According to the Gay and Lesbian Alliance Against
Defamation, major newspapers in all but two states in the United States now
include gay and lesbian unions among their wedding announcements. The
Commercial Closet, an organization that chronicles homo sightings in
advertising, lists thirty-nine recent print and broadcast ads that feature gay
wedding scenes. The matter of discrimination stays out of the picture, the
great unmentionable that might spoil the happy day.

It seems paradoxical, then, that most Americans respond to the equal-
rights claims of gay and lesbian couples by favoring civil unions for them

but not marriages. It's the schmaltzy old trope, however, that softens them up and makes queers legible within a familiar romantic realm. Thus, when the issue of inequity is brought forward—as gay wedding protests did all year by making equality under the law the centerpiece of the revels—Americans' sense of fairness can't help but kick in. Love is love, after all. The sentiment goes only so far, though, before bumping into homophobia in the dominion of "sacred" marriage.

Moreover, plugging unreservedly into the wedding plot can close down queer options even as it opens straight hearts. In romantic comedies, cast-out and suspect lovers always have to prove that they merit comic closure—whether by answering riddles, retrieving some symbolic object, making it through an ordeal or by simply growing up—and the protest-spectacles for gay marriage have been no exception. In order to be embraced as ordinary couples, the heroes of these nuptials must tacitly renounce such practices as promiscuity or preferences for communal rather than nuclear household arrangements. Even if domestic normality is exactly what innumerable gay and lesbian couples want, the mass public display of this desire as the primary queer demand excludes those in the movement who don't share that dream. Worse, it accepts the meanspirited neoliberal principle that citizens must show that they are worthy of their rights. Like public assistance that is provided only to the so-called "deserving poor," the recognition that gay marriage bestows goes only to "deserving" queers.

15   Some thirty-three years ago, the Gay Activist Alliance (GAA) took over New York's City Clerk's Office and declared "Gay Day" at the marriage bureau. When heterosexuals applied for licenses, the demonstrators gleefully turned them away.

How thrilling the cheekiness of that zap seems now—as does its openness to the possibility of abolishing marriage altogether. But the GAA—having split off from the Black Panther-supporting, Vietnam War-opposing Gay Liberation Front—helped pave the way down the aisle by narrowing the movement to a single-issue gay rights agenda.

Through spectacle and mass action, this year's protest weddings—and then, the first days of the real ones in Massachusetts—have reasserted the heady possibilities of a queer public sphere even as they have pressed for access to a privatized set of rights. Once married—secure in their protections and recognized as full citizens—will gay and lesbian couples step out into that public space and participate in the contentious work of democracy? Might their contentment renew their sense of solidarity and visions of liberation? Everyone is a sucker for a love story that ends with a wedding. What happens after that joyful finale is ours to invent.

CHAPTER 13

Digital Information and the Ideology of "Copyright"

Electronic Copyright in a Shrinking World
Cristine Martins and Sophia Martins

The electronic age is upon us, and as librarians we need to be aware of the new issues involving copyright in electronic media—both in the U.S. and around the world. We don't mean to imply that every librarian needs to be a copyright policeman, but there have been major changes in the last few years from both U.S. Supreme Court decisions and international copyright conventions and organizations that may impact the free availability of information in electronic form.

Sophia Martins and Cristine Martins, the co-authors of this article, are both librarians and lawyers, although for some reason the librarian role always seems to come first. Sophia is an academic law librarian and former public library director, while Cris is an independent records management consultant who has a great deal of experience in running corporate financial, engineering, and other special libraries. In all of these settings the issue of copyright plays a central role—more now than ever, with the ease of availability of materials via electronic media and the disappearing borders within our "global village."

Mapping Out the Basics of Today's Copyright Laws

In academic, public, and special libraries, users routinely ask for access to materials that the library may not own. Hence, the commonplace concept of interlibrary loan (ILL), where one

Cristine Martins and Sophia Martins, "Electronic Copyright in a Shrinking World," *Computers in Libraries*, Vol. 22, No. 5 (May 2002), pp. 28–31. Reprinted by permission of Cristine Martins.

library that owns the material will loan it to another for a short period of time, so that the first library's user can have access to it without violating copyright laws by making copies. That is the simplest form of ILL. Very often, particularly in a special library situation, contracts with copyright clearinghouses will be employed to account for any copies made for which royalties may need to be paid according to copyright laws.

But that all has to do with paper copies. What about electronic media? How can we account for the possible copyright requirements of information found electronically?

One approach is to assume that any online database provider will be watching out for copyright issues in the materials it provides to its paid users. This approach seems to make sense at first glance, because the user pays a fee—usually a very high fee—to the database provider for access to the materials. The assumption is that the database provider is paying the copyright owner to allow its materials to be accessed by its users, and in most cases, this is absolutely true.

The problem arises when the entity that claims copyright ownership of a particular work—either written, photographic, or in some other medium—is not in fact the true owner of the copyright. By this, we mean cases in which the author has signed over certain rights in relation to his work, but has not given authority for its electronic dissemination. Such was the case in two very notable decisions that have come down through the U.S. court system in the past few years.

U.S. Court Decisions

5   We find ourselves in a pivotal time. Instantaneous electronic access to information from sources around the globe is a new phenomenon to which our old laws will have to either be adjusted or be changed completely. The ease with which copyrighted materials can be obtained over the Internet, and then reproduced in electronic form a nearly infinite number of times, is something that many laws and legal decisions have never before taken into account. Perhaps the first, or at least most well-known, wake-up call was the Napster case, where owners of rights to sound recordings sued to protect their copyrighted recordings from being released free of charge over the Internet—and won. The Napster case is only one of many and subsequent cases that have increased the adaptation of old copyright laws to new forms of information dissemination.

On June 25, 2001, for example, the U.S. Supreme Court issued an opinion that was a major victory for freelance writers. The court ruled that reuse of freelance work in online databases and CD-ROMs without the author's express permission infringes the copyright. In this case a group of authors, led by Jonathan Tasini, president of the National Writers Union, sued The New York Times Co.; Newsday, Inc.; Time, Inc.; LexisNexis; and University Microfilms.

At issue was the fact that freelance writer Jonathan Tasini and others had signed contracts with these companies granting "first North

American serial rights." Such rights allow the newspaper or magazine to publish a freelance story in print one time. The problem arose when these newspapers and magazines republished the freelance materials in online databases and CD-ROMs, without paying any further royalties to the freelance writers.

In a landmark decision, the U.S. Supreme Court upheld the rights of the freelance writers, disagreeing with the newspapers' claims that subsequently published electronic versions of the freelance stories were simply reproductions or digital replicas of the original publication, and were therefore within their previously negotiated rights. The writers' argument, which the Court preferred, was that electronic publication of their stories was not covered under their original contracts and was a new form of publication for which they should receive royalties.

In a similar situation, the Court declined to hear the case of National Geographic v. Greenberg, in which the U.S. Court of Appeals for the 11th Circuit had ruled in favor of a photographer whose photographs were republished in CD-ROM format by National Geographic. Most observers see the decision to let the Court of Appeals decision stand as a further victory for freelance writers and photographers.

What This Means for Us

10   However, cases like these will not be as prevalent in the future, since most freelance contracts in the U.S. now contain clauses specifically addressing the issue of electronic publication and publishers' rights, where online databases, CD-ROMs, and other forms of electronic publishing come into play. Still, the effect of these two cases and others like them on many years' worth of research materials is greatly felt. Many fear that access to a large number of 20th century newspaper and magazine articles will be curtailed by these rulings and by the fact that many freelance writers and photographers may be difficult for publishers to track down in order to secure electronic publishing rights. For one thing, this would incur great cost for publishers on essentially obsolete material, both in royalty payments and in man-hours for employees who must coordinate the effort.

Many librarians fear that this could leave gaping holes in electronic databases, as freelance stories and photos will be pulled from the collections because publishers either cannot or will not track down and secure further copyright permissions from the original authors of the works. From the historical perspective, librarians, archivists, and researchers are justifiably worried that large segments of late 20th century newspaper and magazine articles may become unavailable except through traditional paper-based means. If the digital library is our future—and indeed, our present in many cases—then this could potentially be a very big problem as we cease to have the breadth of access we are used to in online searching.

The European Perspective

Copyright law itself is changing to account for advances in technology and the smaller world we live in as a result. Copyright law in Europe, for example, has almost always included two separate classes of rights: the economic right inherent in the publication of someone's work, and the moral right to the integrity of the work. For a long time, the U.S. did not recognize the so-called droit morale, or moral right, as extensively as did our European neighbors, but much of that is changing now as the distances between countries and continents seem to become ever smaller.

The term for which copyrights are effective has also been standardized to the life of the author plus 70 years. Both U.S. and the European Union recently adopted this change in order to standardize copyright protection across borders. It is important to note that each separate country in the European Union has had to adopt national laws that would conform to the standards set forth in the Berne Convention, which is an international treaty governing copyright and intellectual property. Some have done this already, some are in the process of doing so, and some countries have adopted laws that only partially conform. This is a long and arduous process, requiring lawmakers in each country to draft appropriate legislation, debate it, refine it, and adopt it according to each country's customs.

The move toward standardization of copyright protection has been a long-standing goal of those countries that signed the Berne Convention all the way back in 1886. This convention is a basic agreement on the international protection of literary and artistic works, which has been signed by more than 100 countries and is now being interpreted to apply to international publication in electronic formats. All members of the European Union are current signatories to the Berne Convention, as is the U.S.

15   Article 9 of the Berne Convention provides that member states can allow for copying of artistic and literary works only under certain conditions. Until recently, the steps outlined in this section applied only to traditional media, but they have been expanded to apply to electronic media as well. Article 9 (Section 2) allows for copying in " . . . certain special cases, provided that such reproduction does not conflict with a normal exploitation of the work and does not unreasonably prejudice the legitimate interests of the author."

Currently, efforts are underway to adjust international and national copyright regulations to account specifically for electronic publications. This becomes increasingly important when you consider the ways in which normal library activities could possibly infringe on copyright. Simple activities such as copying by library users; copying for users; copying for internal use; copying of sound and images; public performance of videos, CDs, or DVDs; ILL; creating electronic collections; or electronic document delivery (which is becoming more and more popular) could all be possible avenues of copyright infringement in the strictest interpretation of this international law.

In 1994, the European Copyright User Platform (ECUP) was established to define which electronic library services should be considered exceptions to possible copyright infringement in the digital environment. This project was supported by the European Bureau of Library, Information and Documentation Associations (EBL-IDA), which represents more than 95,000 libraries in Europe. You can find current information on European copyright developments at http://www.eblida.org/ecup, a Web site that is funded by the European Commission.

The World Intellectual Property Organization (WIPO) forged an agreement in December 1996 in Geneva, which complements the Berne Convention. It is the first agreement that specifically applies to electronic materials, and it has been signed by 160 members of the WIPO. The WIPO Copyright Treaty states that the reproduction right set out in Article 9 of the Berne Convention fully applies to digital formats, providing strong guidance for libraries and librarians who until that time had been uncertain how the Berne Convention might apply in the digital age.

It is also interesting to note that similar court cases, addressing the issues raised in Tasini v. The New York Times and National Geographic v. Greenberg, have appeared in European Union countries. Just one example is a case that was tried in the Netherlands, in which a Dutch court ordered Amsterdam's second-largest daily newspaper, De Volkskrant, to pay freelance writers who sued after their articles appeared in CD-ROM format and on the Internet. The newspaper tried to argue that the electronic publication was merely an extension of the print publication rights it had already negotiated with the writers. The Dutch court rejected this argument and found the paper guilty of copyright infringement. Also similar to the Tasini case, the three freelance writers involved in the lawsuit in the Netherlands were backed by the Netherlands Journalists Union, which was pleased by the result.

It's a Small World After All

20   It is indeed a wildly changing world we live in, where international boundaries and vast distances make little difference in the delivery of information. Within mere moments we can now send and receive vast quantities of data anywhere on the globe. Our laws have not always kept pace with the speed of our technology, but international efforts have been made, and are still underway, to bring laws up-to-date. In the meantime, courts all over the world are deciding cases and setting precedents that will help map out the future of copyright in the electronic age ever more clearly. As librarians we will need to watch carefully to see how this new era of information dissemination will ultimately be reconciled with the freedom of access to which we are accustomed.

Stopping Music Piracy Without Breaking the Internet

Consumers' Research Magazine

More than a decade ago, digital technology brought a revolutionary increase in the quality and durability of sound recordings. Last month, hundreds of music lovers around the country learned there might be a flip side to the digital-technology bargain, after all. The Recording Industry Association of America filed 261 separate lawsuits against individuals across the country, accusing each of stealing copyrighted music via Internet file-sharing platforms.

This legal tactic represents but a new phase in the record studios' efforts to combat the growing problem of online music piracy. At stake for consumers in this battle is not only the future of music. All digital media (e.g., movies, software, and even books) can be vulnerable to online piracy. Preserving a vibrant market in these products requires figuring out how to ensure that artists and producers continue to make a profit. That may mean accepting stricter enforcement of copyrights.

Yet, stricter enforcement of copyrights has enormous implications for the future of the Internet. In particular, Internet users have developed expectations of privacy that, at the moment at least, seem to conflict with the requirements of enforcing copyrights. Currently, a fierce public-relations skirmish rages over the power of copyright holders to subpoena Internet service providers for the identities of their customers.

5   In the background of this battle lurks another threat to current expectations about the Internet: Some copyright holders, in particular movie makers, have proposed a government-mandated technological fix to the problem of copyright piracy. In theory, computers and other digital devices could be designed to play only authorized digital content. Such a fix might mitigate the need for lawsuits and for privacy-abridging subpoenas. But enforcing such a system means putting the government in charge of supervising the consumer-electronics market. That might destroy incentives for further technological innovation. An even bigger problem, say critics, is how such a set-up would transform both the Internet and computers. Instead of being a general-purpose tool of communication, the Internet would become merely a distribution system for copyrighted material, and computers, instead of being general-purpose appliances, would simply become the players of authorized media.

"Stopping Music Piracy Without Breaking the Internet," *Consumers' Research Magazine*, Vol. 86, No. 10 (October 2003), pp. 10–15. Reprinted by permission of the publisher.

How Did We Get Here?

Consumers might wonder why copyright infringement is such a big problem now. The answer is this: The technology that brought the improved quality of CDs is also the technology that threatens to reduce the economic value of such creations to their producers to zero.

In the days of cassette tapes, you could wear your music out. You could play a tape until it became so scratchy the songs sounded like your cat was singing them. Sometimes, the songs didn't even last that long because a cheap player would catch a little bit of slack in the tape spool and pull the whole thing out until it was destroyed—eaten by the machine.

In the days of cassettes, you could also get away with making copies of tapes, and many people thought nothing of it. Making a copy for a friend or to have an extra to play while driving was considered normal. Contrary to what many consumers may have believed, however, there was no general right to engage in personal copying; but it was understood that the record studios would pursue legal action against only the most egregious violators. Targeting consumers who did only minimal copying would have made little economic sense.

Today, digital technology allows not only high quality but ample opportunity for copyright piracy, too. The technical perfection of the digital format allows perfect copies to be reproduced by just about anybody; copies of copies, too, can be reproduced, and so on. Such copies can then be stored on computers and transferred to other computer users over the Internet. The perfection of the copying combined with the higher speed of distribution allows digital-media pirates to redistribute perfect substitutes for the legitimate product so quickly that the economic value of a new recording can be reduced to zero almost immediately.

10   The growth of file-sharing networks, says the RIAA, allows music piracy to cut into its profits to the tune of $4.2 billion per year. The growth of piracy also accounts, says RIAA President Cary Sherman, for the huge drop in sales of top-selling albums. In recent testimony before the Senate, he noted that the 10 top-selling albums of 2000 accounted for 60 million sales in the United States while the 10 top-selling albums of 2002 accounted for just 34 million comparable sales. The record industry's total sales have also fallen from $14.6 billion in 1999 to $12.6 billion in 2002.

A Privacy Problem?

Suing individuals was not the record companies' first choice of tactic. They first tried to stem the flow of illicit copies by suing the makers of file-sharing software. The RIAA won a court case against the file-sharing service Napster in 2001, but newer file-sharing platforms have survived legal challenge. In April of this year, a federal judge ruled that StreamCast Networks, the company that sells the file-sharing software, Grokster, was not liable for copyright infringement committed by the users of the software.

Today, Grokster and other file-sharing platforms differ from Napster in that they do not have a centralized server that lists the availability of illicit material, whereas Napster did. The files being shared are distributed throughout the network on individual users' computers. Grokster itself is just the software, the platform from which users share digital files. Ruled U.S. District Court Judge Stephen Wilson: "Grokster and Streamcast are not significantly different from companies that sell home video recorders or copying machines, both of which can be and are used to infringe copyrights." Wilson further noted: "It is undisputed that there are substantial non-infringing uses for the defendant's software."

Thus, the RIAA failed in its legal effort to get courts to require file-sharing software to include filters that prevent the sharing of copyrighted material. This failure may have left the RIAA with few legal options except suing individuals. Public-relations-wise, the decision has proven to be a risky maneuver. The RIAA suits have targeted the significant uploaders of pirated music, the so-called "supernodes" that allow many other online file traders to get music for free. Even so, the RIAA has found itself appearing to be the bully. One defendant was a retired grandmother who apparently had nothing to do with online file-trading. The RIAA dropped the suit against her. Another defendant was the mother of a 12-year-old girl who had developed a habit of downloading songs she liked. The mother, who receives public assistance, settled the suit for $2,000.

At the same time, the RIAA action has brought forth concern that copyright holders have been given too much power to obtain the private information of Internet users. The Digital Millennium Copyright Act (DMCA), which became law in 1996, created a special administrative subpoena procedure that allows copyright holders to obtain the name, address, telephone number, and e-mail address of any Internet account holder suspected of unauthorized trading of copyrighted material.

15   When an Internet user logs on to a peer-to-peer network, like Grokster or KaZaA, he or she is operating in an open, public domain. The record studios and other copyright holders are also able to log on to peer-to-peer networks. They can then monitor the activity on these networks and trace the sharing of illicit copies to individual Web addresses. The DMCA authorizes copyright holders to issue subpoenas to Internet service providers for the identity of the user associated with the suspect Web address. A copyright holder is authorized to receive the information based merely on a pro forma assertion that the Internet user has violated the requester's copyrights.

Last month, Internet service providers told Congress the subpoena procedure is ripe for abuse. In a hearing before the Senate Commerce, Science and Transportation Committee, William Barr, Executive Vice President and General Counsel for Verizon, said the DMCA's subpoena procedure "has and will be used and abused by parties far less responsible than the recording or movie industries. In essence, anyone willing to assert that they have a good faith belief that someone has used their words, pictures or other expression without permission becomes their own roving grand jury. . . . " This, said Barr, "opens the door to your identity to people with inappropriate or even dangerous motives, such as spammers, blackmailers, pornographers, pedophiles, stalkers, harassers, and identity thieves."

James Ellis, Executive Vice President and General Counsel for SBC, testified his company has fought 59 subpoenas issued by a distributor of hardcore gay pornography. "Even associating a person's name with such material," said Ellis, "might have far-reaching affects on the individual's personal and professional life beyond any copyright issues that might exist."

The DMCA does not require a copyright holder to file any lawsuit upon receiving the requested information. One way of addressing the privacy concerns of Internet users would be to require copyright holders to file actual lawsuits before they are allowed to subpoena anybody. Sen. Sam Brownback (R-Kan.) has proposed amending the law along these lines. Under such a proposal, defending a copyright would entail a so-called "John Doe lawsuit," which is basically a copyright infringement suit in which the accused is to be named later upon discovery.

Subpoenas under these circumstances would occur with a greater degree of court supervision. That might eliminate the possibility that phony claimants would use the process for harassment or blackmail, but there are some significant downsides for those actually targeted by a copyright infringement suit.

20   Says Alan Davidson of the Center for Democracy and Technology: "A lot of people are concerned that being the target of a federal lawsuit is not a very consumer-friendly approach either." Davidson notes: "A 'John Doe' lawsuit can actually be much more expensive and much more invasive for consumers than a well-crafted subpoena process."

The John Doe solution would seem to require copyright holders to engage in more of the tactics for which the RIAA has been called a bully. While the RIAA has not promised it won't sue grandmothers and schoolgirls, it did announce that it would notify the accused by letter and give them a chance to settle the charges before filing lawsuits. A spokesman for Sen. Norm Coleman (R-Minn.) cited this decision as a positive result of the Senate hearings. The John Doe idea, however, would seem to eliminate the opportunity for copyright holders to exercise discretion in whom they target for lawsuits. (Interestingly, the RIAA itself denies its letter-writing procedure has anything to do with helping it decide whom to sue.)

Another potential problem is that eliminating the administrative subpoena process might cripple copyright enforcement. Record labels say an expeditious subpoena procedure is needed because illicit copies can spread like a virus across the Internet faster than enforcement efforts can keep up. Hampering copyright enforcement might appeal to those in the hacker culture; however, even most of the RIAA's critics agree that copyright holders should have some legal remedy for defending against digital piracy.

Davidson of the CDT says the solution is simply to keep the administrative procedure but amend the law to provide sanctions against copyright holders who misuse the information they gather and sanctions against people who misrepresent themselves as copyright holders in order to get another person's information for other reasons altogether. Such sanctions, says Davidson, "would be very easy to add, and I actually think that the copyright holders who are good actors here—or not bad actors—shouldn't oppose it."

Jonathan Lamy, a spokesman for the RIAA, says his group is happy to take a look at the CDT proposals. Lamy says the RIAA does support requiring ISPs to notify Internet users when their personal information has been given out.

Designing the Internet?

25   Meanwhile, other proposals offer the possibility of sidestepping the privacy/subpoena issue altogether.

A Technical Fix.

Some hold out hope that a technical solution can be designed that would prevent unauthorized copying. One approach, commonly called Digital Rights Management, is to put special code into digitized media that prevents copying. This approach is in fact used widely by the record labels and other media companies. Currently, however, DRM can be defeated if a technologically savvy copyright pirate figures out how to strip the protective code from the product.

This reality introduces an even bigger danger, for some in the copyright community (though not the recording industry itself) have proposed fixing this problem by requiring that all digital media players be designed to play only media containing DRM code.

Professor Edward Felten of Princeton explained the danger of this approach in his testimony before the Senate: "It is tempting to imagine that we can concoct a regulatory regime that is truly technology-neutral, not favoring one technical approach over others but discriminating among products based only on their effectiveness. In practice, though, any regulation will encode certain assumptions into its definitions, its terminology, and its criteria. Those assumptions might seem innocuous when the regulation is written, but over time they will channel and limit progress."

Felten said entrenching a technical fix now might retard innovation that could eventually lead to a truly effective DRM system that would not require a government mandate.

Mandated Licensing.

30   Still others say that the recording industry should drop the idea of law-suits altogether. But how could they make a profit without protecting their copyrights?

Wayne Russo, President and CEO of StreamCast Networks, the company that distributes the file-sharing software Grokster, says he knows the answer: "I'm often asked: 'How do you keep unauthorized files from floating across peer-to-peer networks?' It's real simple. You authorize them."

Russo says a compulsory public license could authorize copyrighted material to be traded on the networks while providing compensation for the artists and the record labels. "Radio is licensed," he says, "and I think that with every single day that goes by, peer-to-peer networks become more and more like radio."

The compensation under this licensing, he says, would work just like radio licensing: "These payment mechanisms have been in place for years—years and years and years. It's something that's not new. It's something that could be easily done."

The Electronic Frontier Foundation, an online consumer advocacy group, supports the idea of a blanket license scheme. Gwen Hintze, a staff attorney with EFF, suggests that the technology for calculating fair compensation for online distribution of artists' works may already exist. She notes that the record labels already monitor and measure what music files are being traded on peer-to-peer networks. She also suggests that the distribution of payment could be administered by an entity like Sound Exchange, which currently handles distribution of royalties for music webcasting.

35   Where a technological mandate would close up the Internet, a compulsory public license system would be mandated openness. That amounts, say some critics, to privatized profit with socialized marketing and distribution. Says the RIAA's Lamy: "We can't think of anything worse than having the government regulate the Internet or try to determine the value of creative works."

Lamy doubts that such a system really could maintain adequate incentives: "If the argument is that you need a compulsory license because piracy can't be stopped with regard to music, then that philosophy should apply to any work that could be digitized whether it's movies, books, software, or video games." He asks skeptically: "You're going to be able to compensate all of the creative people behind all of these copyrighted works within the context of an added charge on your ISP bill?"

Online Distribution.

In the meantime, the record labels are moving ahead with their own version of online distribution by licensing a number of Web sites to sell some songs. Apple iTunes launched to great fanfare earlier this year. Other sites offering licensed music downloads for a price are Emusic.com, Listen.com, Musicnow.com, Musicmatch.com, and Catsmusic.com. Even the infamous Napster will soon be reborn as a licensed music distributor.

The offerings vary, but most of the sites offer songs for 99 cents each and the songs may be copied onto several formats, including CDs and MP3s. Some sites offer both a pay-as-you-go service and a monthly subscription service. The number of songs available typically runs into the hundreds of thousands. The new Napster service will claim a library of half a million songs.

Russo says these initiatives are "all well and good but these models are a year or two behind the curve. Ultimately, what the public wants—and this is what they are demonstrating—they want unmetered access and they want unencumbered MP3 files. Case closed." He adds: "All these guys [the record labels] are doing is perpetuating a per-track business model. That doesn't make sense."

40   The RIAA acknowledges the timing of the industry's online offerings is no accident. "There's a strong connection," says Lamy, "between the continued development of the legitimate marketplace and the timing of our enforcement measures. . . . The idea is not to eliminate piracy. We're never going to do that. The idea is to bring it down to a level of control where legitimate services can get a foothold in the marketplace and eventually flourish."

The contrary risk for the recording industry, say some, is that file traders will go even further underground by using file-sharing networks that claim to offer users even greater protection of their identities. One of the networks claiming to offer total anonymity to users is Blubster. Noting that a handful of the 261 original defendants were caught using Blubster, Lamy says these claims represent "marketing ploys, not really technologies that actually work."

In the end, says CDT's Davidson, some lawsuits are probably the best way: "Enforcement of copyrights is not an inherently bad thing for consumers. In fact, it may actually be a much better approach to making sure that there is some copyright protection than for example these broad technology mandates which we think would really damage the fundamental functioning of the Internet."

Balancing Rights on the Internet.

Another point worth considering in all this is that privacy on the Internet, though an expectation shared by many if not most Internet users, does not match the technical reality of what cyberspace really is. Regardless of how it is perceived, the Web is in fact a very public forum. That it is public, after all, is what allows for both widespread file sharing and detection of file sharing by copyright holders. The Web may be more like a raucous street corner than a private salon—a street corner, moreover, with plenty of conspicuous signs informing users that they are operating in the public domain.

The metaphor of the street corner implies certain things about the balancing of rights on the Internet. Anonymity may be obtained in a crowd, but walking down a street doesn't obligate others to avert their eyes, either. Discovering the Web identity of suspected traders of illicit files requires no special legal measures. Copyright holders can see the same traffic that file traders see on the networks. The privacy issue arises only because a Web identity can't be held accountable and the real identity must be provided by the Internet service provider.

45   Does the fact that a third party must provide the real identity of a suspected infringer necessarily imply a privacy issue? Consider: An ISP is well within its own rights when it voluntarily shares information on suspected copyright infringers. After all, the ISPs include provisions in their terms of service that clearly inform users the service may not be used for copyright infringement and that such use may result in their personal information being divulged. Further, since ISPs are copyright holders, too, they certainly have every incentive to reciprocate the sharing of information with each other.

In this light, the privacy problem appears as an artifact of an intra-industry dispute over who is obligated to do what on the Internet. The DMCA was supposed to have settled the issue, but it hasn't. The record labels say the procedures in the DMCA were part of a bargain that the ISPs struck in order to win broad immunity from liability for infringement of copyrights. The ISPs claim that the compromise in the DMCA never contemplated the problem of file-sharing networks, which didn't exist in 1996. As things stand, the ISPs do little to enforce their own terms of service with regard to copyright infringement, except as the courts have required them to do. (Verizon is currently appealing a ruling by a federal judge that compels it to divulge user information pursuant to the DMCA administrative subpoena process.)

Would there be a privacy issue if the ISPs did enforce their own terms of service and voluntarily shared information with copyright holders? The right of a business to stipulate the terms of service or sale is routinely accepted by consumers in many other circumstances. Consumers may have the right of free speech in public, but they do not have the right to enter a proprietor's place of business and disturb other customers enjoying the service. Thus, a restaurateur may expel a particularly rowdy patron. The right of a proprietor to enforce a code of conduct adds to the value of the service he offers to all consumers. He is able to enforce a code of conduct because he is the property owner.

Yet, the Internet is not owned by the ISPs or by anyone, and it cannot be divided up into lots without destroying its essential value as an open system of communication. Therein lies the difficulty in navigating the consumer interest on this issue. A raucous street corner may have rules of conduct, but it has fewer rules of conduct than a private proprietor is able to enforce. A street corner, like the Internet, is open to all, but its openness makes it a little harder to do business there.

Still, one doesn't expect privacy on a street corner, and neither does one set up a private salon there. Giving up a little bit on the notion of privacy as an absolute right on the Internet may be the proverbial middle way to preserving other things about which Internet users care—like incentives for innovation and creativity. Amending the administrative subpoena process along the lines suggested by the Center for Democracy and Technology might allow for timely copyright protection while giving consumers some—though not complete—protection of privacy.

50   Would this step amount to sacrificing civil liberties for the sake of business? Not really. Pursuing privacy is always a matter of individual choice, and it is always one choice among many. Individuals have the right to protect their privacy; they also have the right to run for governor. No one can reasonably expect that all possible combinations of choices must produce similar amounts of privacy. That it is hard to make the choice not to use the Internet should perhaps be taken as a sign of the Internet's continued vitality and worth, in spite of all its current troubles.

The Rights Management Trap
Simson Garfinkel

Faust made his deal with the devil. In return for the devil's service and knowledge, Faust agreed to surrender his body and soul after 24 years' time. By the time Faust realized the folly of his decision, it was too late.

Today we are being asked to make a similar bargain not with the devil, but with the entertainment industry. The promise is a future in which we'll download music and movies over the Internet at rock-bottom prices. It's a future where digital content—books, magazines, newspapers, and databases—will be at our fingertips. It's a future where software and information will be rented, and people will pay only for what they use. And it's a

Simson Garfinkel, "The Rights Management Trap," *Technology Review*, Vol. 105, No. 9 (November 2002), p. 37. Copyright 2002 by M I T Technology Review. Reproduced with permission of M I T Technology Review via Copyright Clearance Center.

future in which computers will be inherently secure because they will be unable to run viruses and other hostile programs. It is, in short, a high tech paradise.

But it is a trap.

Every bargain has its price. In this case, the price is "digital rights management"—an industrywide project that has been under way for more than a decade and is likely to accelerate within the coming year. Digital rights management starts with a system for marking the "rights" that consumers are granted when they pay for digital media. For instance, an electronic label might say, "This music may be played on your computer but not shared with a friend." Or, "This magazine article may be viewed twice and printed once, and then it must be deleted." But the flip side of the so-called rights is another r-word: restrictions. Rights management systems will make possible software that will watch your computer and make sure you don't break the rules.

5   One of the great things about computers has been that you can throw away any software that comes with them and install something you like better. Digital rights management software shreds that freedom. Underneath this software is new hardware that will prevent computer users from removing the "rights management system" and installing their own systems that do not respect digital restrictions. That hardware, in turn, relies on the force of legislation. The 1998 Digital Millennium Copyright Act, in particular, makes it a crime to circumvent digital rights management software—or even to distribute information that tells other people how to do so. And proposed legislation, the Consumer Broadband and Digital Television Promotion Act, would require all computers sold in the United States to incorporate federally approved rights management technology. Similar legislation is working its way through Europe.

Essentially, consumers will be giving up their right to control their own computers. Citing the widespread piracy of software, music, and videos, the entertainment industry argues that consumers have abused that right. But managing consumers as children will have the side effect of smothering much of the innovation that made the Internet possible. Digital rights management could quash the computer revolution as we know it, transforming our machines from tools for creation and exploration into appliances that run Microsoft Office, play MP3s, browse the Web, and do little else.

Don't get me wrong. I make my living by creating and selling intellectual property, and I'm sometimes a victim of unauthorized copying. A few years ago one of my publishers started selling my books on CD-ROM. Although each disc is licensed only for personal use, at least once a month I discover that someone in Eastern Europe or Russia has taken that whole disc and put it on the Internet. Usually it's a university or a library that is engaging in such wholesale piracy.

But I would rather live with the piracy than have a computer that runs only the software that has been preapproved and digitally signed. I don't want to have my electronic movements constantly monitored and reported to some Big Brother database on the off-chance that I might be violating somebody's copyright.

This isn't the first time publishers have tried to impose unreasonable restrictions on the public. On the inside cover of one of my wife's childhood books, published in England, this ominous warning appears: "This book shall not, by way of trade or otherwise, be lent, re-sold, hired out or otherwise circulated without the publisher's prior consent." Books don't have such restrictions anymore—if they did, we would laugh at them. A hundred years ago, U.S. publishers put similar restrictions in our books; they were deemed by our courts to be unenforceable violations of "fair use." But digital rights management tools will enable publishers to turn back the clock and write the same kinds of restrictions directly into their software. Digital rights management is already at work. Incompatible coding means that DVDs sold in the United States won't play on European DVD players. This is to prevent Europeans from buying cheap DVDs in the United States.

10 Perhaps even more disturbing, the new protection technologies would necessarily have to block a computer from running Linux or any other open-source operating systems. Otherwise, anyone bent on unauthorized copying could create a version of Linux that didn't incorporate the copyright protection system.

The industry's antipiracy arguments are a smoke screen. Digital rights management is about strengthening monopolies, increasing revenues, and restricting our freedoms. We must not be beguiled as Faust was.

Info With a Ball and Chain
Steven Levy

When Steve Jobs introduced the iTunes music store a few weeks ago, the acclaim was nearly universal. Nonetheless, a small but vocal minority viewed the online emporium as a menace—because the iTunes program somewhat limits a consumer's ability to copy and share songs. Even though Apple had broken ground by getting the record labels to accept fairly liberal terms of use—Apple-oids could listen to purchased songs on three computers and burn CDs—this bunch objected to any restrictions at all. They saw the iTunes store as a sugar-coated inducement for consumers to accept a new reality; some stuff on your computer isn't really under your control. And as far as that goes, the critics are right. Say goodbye to the "Information Wants to Be Free" era. We're entering the age of digital ankle bracelets.

The key to this shift is the technology that protects information from unauthorized or illegal use. It's called digital-rights-management software, or DRM. Like it or not, rights management is increasingly going to be a fact of your life. Not only will music, books and movies be steeped in it, but soon such mundane artifacts as documents, spreadsheet files and e-mail will be joining the domain of restricted information. In fact, the next version of Microsoft Office will enable creators of certain documents to issue restrictions that dictate who, if anyone, can read them, copy them or forward them. In addition, you can specify that the files and mail you send may "sunset" after a specified period of time, evaporating like the little tapes deaddropped to Peter Graves in "Mission: Impossible."

On the one hand, it seems that digital-rights management is a no-brainer. What's wrong with media companies' building in antitheft devices to protect their property? And shouldn't the creator of a document or e-mail be able to determine who can read or copy it? Surely, piracy is to be condemned and privacy to be cherished: DRM can go a long way toward implementing both those sentiments.

But certain critics consider the very concept anathema. "I don't think that DRM is in and of itself evil," says David Weinberger, who recently published an essay in Wired titled "Copy Protection is a Crime Against Humanity." "But in the real world, it *is evil.* There's no user demand for it. It's being forced upon us by people with vested interests."

Edward Felton, a Princeton computer scientist, believes that DRM perverts the basic deal of the Internet: the free flow of information benefits all. "The basic problem is that DRM is trying to turn information into something other than information so you can't pass it on," he says. "People want to control their technology, and the more the technology is eroded, the harder it is to use."

DRM's defenders say that the technology actually empowers users. Without protections, entertainment companies would never release their products in the digital marketplace. Microsoft's Erin Cullen says that DRM software is flexible enough to limit illegal uses (like sharing a song with millions of "friends" on the Net) while allowing consumers to enjoy music and films in ways they always have.

In practice, though, DRM can stifle legal activity, too. For instance, copy protection on DVDs blocks not only illegal copying, but the "fair use" ability to copy a frame or short scene into a home movie or school project. (To do this, you have to break the copy-protection scheme—an act that is specifically outlawed by the anticonsumer Digital Millennium Copyright Act.)

Critics like Weinberger also complain that computers enforcing DRM systems lack "the essential leeway by which ideas circulate." Sure, Microsoft rights management will allow creators to set the rules. But will corporations dictate that every e-mail message and document be fitted with a virtual ball and chain: *no copying . . . no forwarding . . . no amending . . . no archiving?* Whistle-blowers won't be able to do what they do," says Joe Kraus of DigitalConsumer.org.

Even Congress, which has so far ignored consumers and coddled rights holders on copy protection, is waking up. Sen. Sam Brownback, a Kansas Republican, is about to introduce a bill "to ensure that our nation's media producers and distributors do not clamp down on the ways in which [consumers] traditionally and legally use media products."

We do need legislative help in keeping DRM under control. But ultimately, its fate will be determined by our own actions. As we have with the iTunes store, we'll vote with our dollars when we're satisfied that restrictions on our music and movies allow us the access we need. And corporations may well come to understand that it's bad policy to strictly hobble the flow of information. Will we suffer the worst-case DRM scenario: a world so constricted that we can't cut or paste a line from a poem, or forward the latest sick Internet joke to our buddies? I doubt it. But I do think that the files that arrive in our IN boxes and juke-boxes will be on tighter leashes. And while I understand the reasoning for this, the prospect doesn't gladden my heart.

Rewriting the Rules of Copyright: Creative Commons Is New Licensing Scheme
Ariana Eunjung Cha

PALO ALTO, Calif. —When Chuck D and the Fine Arts Militia released their latest single, "No Meaning No," several months ago, they didn't try to stop people from circulating free copies on the Internet. They encouraged it.

They posted the entire 3-minute, 12-second song and its various vocal, drum and guitar components online and invited everyone to view, copy, mix, remix, sample, imitate, parody and even criticize it.

The result has been the creation of a flood of derivative work ranging from classical twists on the hip-hop piece to video interpretations of the song. The musicians reveled in the instant fan base. They were so pleased that they recently decided to publish their next entire album, due later this spring, the same way, becoming the first major artists to do so.

"No Meaning No" was released under an innovative new licensing scheme called Creative Commons that some say may be better suited to the electronic age than the hands-off mind-set that has made copyright such a bad word among the digerati.

5   So far, more than 10 million other creations—ranging from the movie "Outfoxed" and songs by the Beastie Boys to the British Broadcasting Corp.'s news footage and the tech support books published under the O'Reilly label—have been distributed using these licenses. The idea has even won the support of Hilary Rosen, formerly of the Recording Industry Association of America, and Jack Valenti, the past head of the Motion Picture Association of America, who became known for their aggressive pursuit of people who share free, unauthorized copies via the Internet.

Interest in Creative Commons licenses comes as artists, authors and traditional media companies begin to warm to the idea of the Internet as friend instead of foe, and race to capitalize on technologies such as file-sharing and digital copying.

Apple Computer Inc. gave many reason to be optimistic. Music lovers who once spent hours scouring the Internet for free, pirated copies of songs are now showing they are willing to pay for online music; the company says it is selling 1.25 million songs, at 99 cents a track, each day.

Rare is the consumer electronics company or music label that is not experimenting with something similar. Sony BMG, Universal Music Group, EMI and Warner Music Group, for instance, inked deals to distribute songs on a fee-based download service run by Wurld Media, a Saratoga Springs, N.Y., peer-to-peer software company.

At the same time, many of the innovators who touched off the file-sharing revolution are seeking to win corporate support for their work. Shawn Fanning, who as a teen developed Napster, is now working on software that would let copyright holders specify permissions and prices for swapping. Vivendi Universal is a backer.

10   Perhaps the most significant cooperative effort, however, is the set of innovative new licensing schemes under which "No Meaning No" was released.

The licenses are the brainchild of online theorist Lawrence Lessig, a Stanford University law professor.

Lessig argues that the current system of copyright laws provides little flexibility—either you give up all permissions for use of your work or you withhold everything. He proposed a solution: a set of copyright licenses that would allow artists to choose to keep "some rights reserved" rather than "all rights reserved."

They could, for instance, choose to allow their works to be enjoyed and copied by others for any purpose, restrict such activity to non-commercial use or allow use of portions of the work rather than all of it. To that end, Lessig co-founded the nonprofit Creative Commons, whose aim, as he describes it, is to "help artists and authors give others the freedom to build upon their creativity—without calling a lawyer first."

"We Get Our Music Out"

What began as an offbeat legal experiment is now prompting people to reconsider the notion of copyright.

15   "What we're doing is not only good for society but it's good for us and our business because we get our music out," said Brian Hardgroove, 40, the co-founder of Fine Arts Militia and the band's bass player.

The way Lessig sees it, art has always been about stealing, recycling and mixing: Vincent Van Gogh and Paul Gauguin were said to borrow from each other's brushwork. The 1990s hit "Clueless" with Alicia Silverstone was a modern-day adaptation of Jane Austen's "Emma."

Technology has given the world an unprecedented ability to digitize works, copy them, take them apart and put them back together again. But Lessig said he worries that the extension of copyright laws is keeping many works out of the public domain, hampering creativity. When the Constitution was written, copyrights covered 14 years, extendable to 28 years. Now, with the passage of the Sonny Bono Copyright Term Extension Act of 1998, these rights last until an author's death plus 70 years.

Lessig's goal with Creative Commons was to create a body of digital work, which he calls "artifacts of culture," for the public domain, accessible to all.

In the year since the licenses were unveiled, a steady stream of works beyond popular music and videos has joined the Creative Commons public domain archive: material for more than 500 Massachusetts Institute of Technology classes; audio of every U.S. Supreme Court argument since 1950 from the Public Library of Science; the archives for Flickr's photo-sharing site; and Cory Doctorow's futuristic novel "Down and Out in the Magic Kingdom."

20   The book's first hardcover run was a sellout—10,000 copies in all—in bookstores, but the number of free electronic copies distributed was much greater. Half a million copies of the science fiction novel were downloaded.

"There is this weird sense that the Internet is broken because it lets people make easy copies. . . . The Internet is a machine for making copies, and artists need to come to grips with that," Doctorow said.

Doctorow's experiment with his first novel went so well that he released his second one, "Eastern Standard Tribe," under a Creative Commons license and hopes to publish a third this spring the same way.

"At every turn in history we see this new model of distribution that people say is going to destroy art itself," Doctorow said. But, he said, such fears been proven wrong time and time again.

Fritz Attaway, Washington general counsel for the Motion Picture Association of America, said work licensed under Creative Commons licenses and those released under traditional copyright restrictions can coexist.

25   "I think it's helpful to educate consumers that there is a place like Creative Commons where one can access intellectual property that has been freely made available to the general public without compensation and that that should be distinguished from sites that are permitting access to infringing material," he said.

Still, even the most optimistic say that Creative Commons will be only part of the solution to ending the long-running battle over copyright. Attaway said he doubts the major movie studios or record labels would ever license large quantities of their work for distribution using Creative Commons licenses because they make plenty of money off the current system.

Boosting Interest

Hollywood producers Robert Greenwald and Jim Gilliam are among those who are challenging such assumptions. They released their movie "Outfoxed" under a Creative Commons license. Their controversial documentary accused Fox News of being a propaganda machine for the Republican Party. Just weeks after it was released in theaters, the producers posted 48 minutes of original interviews from the work online.

Gilliam credits the Internet with boosting interest in the movie because it reached a wider audience than it could in theaters alone. He said many of those who viewed parts of the work online ended up ordering a $9.95 DVD.

"This isn't necessarily just some altruistic thing," Gilliam said. "You can make money off of this, too."

30   Currently, it is not always easy for consumers to know when a work is protected by a Creative Commons license. If the work does not identify itself as such, online users can go to CreativeCommons.org and search its archives. In a few months, the developers behind the new Mozilla Firefox browser plan to release an update designed to allow people to search the World Wide Web for works of art licensed by Creative Commons.

John Buckman, an entrepreneur from Berkeley, Calif., has used the Creative Commons licenses as the foundation for his new online record label. All artists who sign with his company, Magnatune, must agree to allow free use of their work for non-commercial purposes. The site features 326 albums by 174 artists in six different genres from classical to heavy metal. He said the company makes 50 percent of its money from downloads and 50 percent from licensing fees.

He said his label's songs are attractive because cash-strapped filmmakers can use the songs as they like for free and only have to pay when they start making money. "As much as musicians are having a hard time making a living, filmmakers and other creative people are having a hard time finding music to use in their works," he said.

And the start-up is making money, he said—possibly as much as $2 million this year.

China's Love of Linux Has Roots in Ancient Past
Phil Albert

It is a mistake for Microsoft to assume that its toughest competitor is piracy. Maybe it's not even Linux or open source. Microsoft's challenge in China is how to change a mindset that's been ingrained through thousands of years of a great ancient civilization.

Bill Gates was recently quoted as saying, "You know what my toughest competitor is? It's pirated software. . . . If you really look around, you'll find way more pirated Windows than you'll find open-source software. Way more."

Gates couldn't be more wrong. At least in China, his tough stance against piracy is backfiring. The more the Chinese government cracks down on piracy, the more appealing open source, and in particular, Linux, become.

In a knee-jerk fashion, Microsoft (Nasdaq: MSFT) reacts by cutting creative licensing deals and cutting prices, assuming that the open-source movement in Asia is purely driven by cost. It's true that the cost factor is a significant reason behind China's obsession with Linux, but I wonder whether there is something much deeper going on. Perhaps it has less to do with Microsoft and more to do with Chinese history and culture.

Intellectual Property Counterintuitive

5   In his compelling book, *To Steal a Book is an Elegant Offense*, which examines the development of intellectual property law in Chinese civilization, William P. Alford argues that according to ancient Chinese history and culture, copying is not traditionally seen as a "bad" thing. To copy someone's work is considered a compliment. Therefore, the very idea of copyright is counterintuitive to the Chinese.

According to Alford, even though the Chinese are credited with some of the world's greatest contributions, from paper to ink, they have never been concerned with protecting the ideas that are created by putting ink to paper.

Patents, trademarks and copyrights are Western concepts. He argues that in imperial China, there was no indigenous effort to develop a significant body of intellectual property law, even after they invented printing, until Western influences introduced the concept to China at the turn of the twentieth century. Why? For the answer, we might have to turn to Confucius.

At the core of traditional Chinese culture is the connection to a shared past, and the importance of the family. Relationships between ruler and subject, father and son, and husband and wife are enduring and paramount. Connecting to the past provides insight into moral responsibility in the present.

Imperial Chinese Legal System

Confucius said "Lead the people with governmental measures and regulate them by law and punishments, and they will avoid wrongdoing, but will have no sense of honor and shame. Lead them by virtue and regulate them by the rules of propriety and they will have a sense of shame and, moreover, set themselves right."

10   Alford interprets this to mean that the wisdom of the past should guide the leaders of the present.

The imperial Chinese legal system derived its legitimacy by honoring the morality of the past. In this context, only a ruler with the power of the past can restrict access to or exercise control over someone's ideas. Furthermore, as Confucius said, "I transmit rather than create."

Wise rulers transmit the wisdom of the ages. Sharing that wisdom allows us to transform ourselves in the present. This concept is essential in classic Chinese poetry and literature.

Chinese Artists Honor the Past

Alford argues that Chinese artists demonstrate a lineage similar to the succession of Confucian philosophers handing down his wisdom. He quotes Chinese painter Wu Li as saying "to paint without taking the masters as one's basis is like playing chess on an empty chessboard."

In other words, it is honorable for artists to use the past to shape how they express their own vision. Copying the work of others bears honor to the quality of that work, and helps transform that work into original ideas in the present. So the replication of ideas that are not your own does not have the negative connotation that it does in Western cultures.

15   If understanding that interaction with the past is integral to Chinese culture helps explain why the notion of copyright is counterintuitive, consider also the Confucian attitude toward commerce, which says that true scholars let the world discover their work, and real artists create for higher reasons than mere profit.

Because everything comes from nature, humans can only imitate. How can they exclude others from something that belongs to their common past?

China's Love Affair with Linux

That gets us back to the Chinese love affair with Linux. Anyone doing business in other countries knows the importance of understanding the culture before setting up shop. Remember when GM had trouble selling the Chevy Nova in South America until it realized that "no va" in Spanish means "no go"?

Misunderstandings cause damaged reputations and can poison relationships. When Microsoft appears to be heavy-handed by cracking down on software piracy and demanding protection for its intellectual property, it goes against the traditional cultural values in China.

If Alford is right, the real reason why the Chinese government and software industry are so supportive of Linux could be because Linux is, instinctively, much more in tune with ancient Chinese philosophy. It is a better fit for their historical perspective on intellectual property. It is more culturally relevant. By joining the WTO, China agreed to put an end to software piracy, but enforcement is proving to be very difficult. It runs against the grain.

The Art of Software War

20   The ancient Chinese military strategist, Sun Tzu, in his book *The Art of War,* said "If you know yourself but not the enemy, for every victory gained you will also suffer a defeat."

It is a mistake for Microsoft to assume that its toughest competitor is piracy. Maybe it's not even Linux or open source. Microsoft's challenge in China is how to change a mindset that's been ingrained through thousands of years of a great ancient civilization.

Now that's a tough fight to win.

Pirates of the Internet
Steven Levy

Last month I attended a hearing of the Senate Judiciary Committee with an intriguing title: "The dark side of a bright idea: Could personal and national-security risks compromise the potential of peer-to-peer file-sharing networks?" I certainly was aware that some members of Congress wanted to snuff out the grass-roots phenomena of people's swapping copyrighted songs on the Net. But I assumed that the crime of file-sharing, joyfully committed by an estimated 60 million pirates, was mainly a problem of lost revenues for the music industry. Sen. Dianne Feinstein, giving the opening testimony, argued otherwise, calling file-sharing networks a grave security risk to this nation. In reality, the hearing was nothing but one of several signs of a new hardball offensive against file-sharing for the same old reasons: protecting the business model of the record labels.

What was the alleged national-security issue? Strictly yellowcake. Researchers testified that because of a confusing interface in file-sharing services like Kazaa, a clumsy user could inadvertently expose private files to everyone on the network. In theory, this could even happen to a government worker using Kazaa for personal use on an official computer—thus exposing our deepest secrets. No one was able to cite an instance where a government secret was actually exposed by this method.

By the end of the session, the only committee member in attendance, chairman Orrin Hatch—himself a songwriter who sells CDs on his personal Web site—zeroed in on what really bugged him: people sharing copyrighted songs on the Internet without paying for them. Then he ran an idea by one of the panelists: what if you had a system that could detect whether people were getting songs without paying for them and could warn those infringers that what they were doing was wrong? And then, if they didn't stop, the system would remotely "destroy" their computers.

"No one's interested in destroying people's computers," said the panelist.

5   "Well, *I'm* interested in doing that," said the senator. "Warn them, do it again, and then destroy their machine! There's no excuse for anyone violating our copyright laws."

Fortunately Senator Hatch hasn't yet codified his Dr. Strangelovean no-due-process piracy antidote into upcoming legislation. But in the House, Reps. Howard Berman and John Conyers have introduced a bill that encourages a different approach: jail 'em! Among other provisions, the bill lowers the bar for criminal prosecution to the sharing of a single music file and allocates $15 million to go after copyright offenders. Representative Berman says that he anticipates that prosecutors will go only after someone who, knowing the consequences, uploads massive amounts of music. But the bill says in black and white that if you share so much as a single tune with your pals on the Internet—as millions do every day—you are a felon. Penalty: up to five years in jail. (Better fill up your iPod before you go.)

Meanwhile the Record Industry Association of America, the trade and lobbying arm of the big music labels, last week sent out hundreds of subpoenas to Internet service providers and universities to find the identities of those sharing music so it can drag them into court and sue them for thousands of dollars. Is suing your customers the best way to run an industry?

My guess is that the vast majority of those 60 million file sharers would never steal a physical object from the store. In a mixture of self-interest and rebellion they've taken the measure of the record industry's karma (overpriced CDs, a history of ripping off artists), noted that stealing files isn't like stealing stuff (maybe they'll buy a disc later) and concluded that file-sharing isn't that bad.

Carey Sherman, president of the RIAA, and his buddies in Congress think the time for patience is over. "We've reached a point where we have a legitimate marketplace for downloading music, and we want to give it a chance," says Sherman, referring to the spiffy services like Apple's iTunes Music Store, the new Buy.Com store and subscription services like Rhapsody. But the game is just starting, and the best way to make sure that these services come up with compelling innovations is to match them off against the Kazaas of the world, which are far from perfect (the quality is erratic, they put spyware on your computers, they're loaded with porn). You can compete against free—ever hear of bottled water?

10   Ultimately the Internet is going to be great for music lovers, artists and even the record labels, if they are willing to hang loose while new business models emerge. But right now the RIAA and its congressional water carriers are hitting the wrong notes. It makes no sense to bring thousands of people into the dockets—and maybe the prison system—for turning on a friend to the fuzz tones of the White Stripes or the inspirational melodies of Orrin Hatch without a license. There are better things for prosecutors and the courts to focus on.

Like *real* national security.

The Heavenly Jukebox
Charles C. Mann

A little while ago I heard that the future of music was being decided in a nondescript office suite above a bank in San Mateo, California. I couldn't get there in time, so I asked a friend to check it out. A crowd was milling in front of the entrance when he arrived. My friend parked illegally and called me on his cell phone. There are twenty or thirty television cameras, he said, and a lectern with a dozen microphones. Also lots of police officers. I asked about the loud noise in the background. "That," he explained, "is people smashing compact discs with sledgehammers."

From Charles C. Mann, "The Heavenly Jukebox," *The Atlantic Monthly*, Vol. 286, No. 3 (September 2000), pp. 39–59. Reprinted by permission of the author.

The compact discs contained music by the rock band Metallica. Three weeks earlier Metallica had sued a now-notorious Internet start-up called Napster, which is based on the fourth floor of the bank building. (The name comes from the founder's moniker in adolescence.) Far from being the colossus that its media prominence might lead one to expect, Napster is a surprisingly small outfit: it consists mainly of a Web site, about thirty-five hip, slightly disheveled employees, and a hundred or so of the powerful computers known as servers. By connecting to these computers with special software, Napster members can search one another's hard drives for music files, downloading gratis any songs they discover.

As the furor over Napster suggests, the opportunity to share music quickly and without charge has been greeted with more enthusiasm by listeners than by the music industry. Although the company's music-swapping software has only just been officially released, the service already has about 20 million regular users, and the tally is rising every day. Countless other people use Napster's brethren; the company is but the most prominent of many free-music services on the Internet. The result, in Metallica's opinion, is an outrageous pirate's bacchanalia—millions of pieces of music shuttling around the Net uncontrolled. The group filed suit, according to its drummer, Lars Ulrich, "to put Napster out of business."

I asked my friend to visit Napster's headquarters that day because I knew that Ulrich, Metallica's lawyer, and several burly guys in T-shirts were driving to San Mateo in a black sport-utility vehicle. In the SUV were thirteen boxes full of printouts listing the user names of 335,435 Napsterites who, the band said, had traded Metallica songs during the previous weekend. Ulrich and his entourage planned to dump the boxes in the company's tiny, cluttered foyer. The people with the sledgehammers planned to shout unflattering remarks while this was taking place. Suddenly a compact man with high-tide hair and shades came to the podium: Lars Ulrich. My friend held up his phone a few feet from the drummer's face, but I could barely hear Ulrich. The catcalls were too loud.

5   "You suck, Lars! You sellout!"

"This is not about pounding the fans, this is about Napster ... "

"Then why are you busting them? Have you ever even used Napster, Lars?"

Hooting laughter almost drowned out Ulrich's response. In an online chat with fans the previous day, Ulrich had admitted that he had never actually tried Napster. Indeed, he said later, his experience with the Internet was limited to using America Online "a couple of times to check some hockey scores." Nonetheless, his suspicions, however unfounded on experience, were entirely warranted as a matter of fact.

Within the music industry it is widely believed that much of the physical infrastructure of music—compact discs, automobile cassette-tape players, shopping-mall megastores—is rapidly being replaced by the Internet and a new generation of devices with no moving parts. By 2003, according to the Sanford C. Bernstein & Co. Investment Research Group, listeners will rarely if ever drive to Tower Records for their music. Instead they will tap into a vast cloud of music on the Net. This heavenly juke-box, as it is sometimes called, will hold the contents of every record store in the world, all of it instantly accessible from any desktop. And that will be just the beginning.

10   Edgar Bronfman Jr., the head of Universal, the world's biggest music company, predicted in a speech in May that soon "a few clicks of your mouse will make it possible for you to summon every book ever written in any language, every movie ever made, every television show ever produced, and every piece of music ever recorded." In this vast intellectual commons nothing will ever again be out of print or impossible to find; every scrap of human culture transcribed, no matter how obscure or commercially unsuccessful, will be available to all.

Bronfman detests Napster. His speech likened the company to both slavery and Soviet communism. But its servers constitute the nearest extant approximation of his vision of a boundless sea of digital culture. While Ulrich spoke, I logged on to Napster. More than 100,000 people were on the company's machines, frolicking about in terabytes of music. "True fans of the talent are the ones who respect our rights," the drummer was saying. I typed in search terms: Mahler, Mingus, Method Man, Metallica . . . all were free for the taking. And all were freely being taken—users couldn't put a nickel in the machine even if they wanted to. Little wonder that the thought of such systems spreading to films, videos, books, and magazines has riveted the attention of artists, writers, and producers.

"Down in front! Down in front! . . . Metallica sucks!"

"Hey, Lars!"—a reporter. "Are you able to quantify the revenue lost?"

"It's not about revenue."

15   "Yeah? What's it about, then?"

In the short run the struggle is for control of the heavenly jukebox. Technophiles claim that the major labels, profitable concerns today, will rapidly cease to exist, because the Internet makes copying and distributing recorded music so fast, cheap, and easy that charging for it will effectively become impossible. Adding to the labels' fears, a horde of dot-coms, rising from the bogs of San Francisco like so many stinging insects, is trying to hasten their demise. Through their trade association, the Recording Industry Association of America, the labels are fighting back with every available weapon: litigation, lobbying, public relations, and, behind the trenches, jiggery-pokery with technical standards. Caught in the middle are musicians, Metallica among them, who believe that their livelihoods will soon be menaced by their own audiences.

At stake in the long run is the global agora: the universal library-movie theater-television-concert hall-museum on the Internet. The legal and social precedents set by Metallica v. Napster—and half a dozen other e-music lawsuits—are likely to ramify into film and video as these, too, move online. When true electronic books, e-magazines, and e-newspapers become readily available, their rules of operation may well be shaped by the creation of the heavenly jukebox. Music, according to a National Research Council report released last November, is the "canary in the digital coal mine."

This is unfortunate. Silicon Valley denizens often refer generically to writers, painters, filmmakers, journalists, actors, photographers, designers, and musicians as "content providers," as if there were no important differences among them. Yet the music industry—tangled in packages of rights that exist nowhere else, burdened by the peculiar legacies of earlier conflicts— is not like other culture industries, and digital technology is exerting different forces on it. Compared with writers and filmmakers, musicians are both more imperiled by the Internet and better able to slip past the threat. The music industry seems to have less room to maneuver. In consequence, it has been pushing for decisive judicial and legislative action. The Internet will become a principal arena for the clash of ideas that the Founders believed necessary for democracy. Allowing the travails of a single industry—no matter how legitimate its concerns—to decide the architecture of that arena would be a folly that could take a long time to undo.

"It's not about our bank accounts, it's about the thousands and thousands of artists out there who aren't fortunate enough to have the—"

20   "Radio is free! What about radio?"

"We have the right to control our music!"

"Fuck you, Lars. It's our music too!"

Legislation, Litigation, Leg-breaking

Ulrich, it seemed clear, regarded the widespread dissemination of contraband music as a dangerous new thing, another anxiety-provoking novelty from the electronic age. In fact unauthorized music has been around as long as the music industry itself. Ulrich was not even the first musician to sue a business that he regarded as a cover for intellectual piracy. That honor may belong to Sir Arthur Sullivan, of Gilbert and Sullivan. Indeed, Sullivan's problems were, if anything, worse than Metallica's.

Like the members of Metallica, who are unusually independent of their record label, Sullivan was a careful businessman who forced the music industry to accede to his demands. In the last quarter of the nineteenth century, when Sullivan composed his operas, the phonograph was in its infancy and radio broadcasts did not exist; the chief sources of music were churches, theaters, music halls, and the pianos that were prominently featured in most middle-class parlors. All these had to be fed large quantities of sheet music.

In consequence the music industry was dominated by a group of big sheet-music companies. Sheet music was immensely popular—hit pieces sold hundreds of thousands of copies. And the industry would have been even more profitable, its leaders believed, if it had not faced rampant international piracy. Bootleg Brahms and Beethoven were openly hawked on the streets of every city in Europe and the Americas. As one of Britain's most popular composers, Sullivan was a favorite target for bootleggers; he and his manager spent years fighting copyright infringement in court.

25   Technology, law, and culture seemed to conspire against British composers and music publishers. Improvements in printing and shipping methods had made it cheaper and easier for outlaw printers to manufacture and distribute sheet music. Worse, from the publishers' point of view, courts in many countries ruled that piano rolls (the player piano was another new invention) did not infringe composers' copyrights, because the perforations in the rolls did not look like the notes in the original printed music, and hence could not be copies of them. Building on this precedent, phonograph recordings, too, were deemed not to require licenses or payments to composers. When publishers complained, they encountered a distinct lack of popular sympathy for their plight.

One of the biggest sources of illicit sheet music in London [during the late 1800s] was a limited partnership led by James Frederick Willetts, a.k.a. "the London Pirate King." The partnership was known as James Fisher & Co., although there was no James Fisher; the real principals hesitated to do business in their own names. Fisher & Co. had a simple business plan: it sold the scores for musical compositions without paying copyright holders for the right to do so. If customers ordered 500 or more copies, the partners would prepare them to specification. "Piracy while you wait," one publisher's lawyer growled. . . .

The Musical Copyright Act came into effect on October 1, 1902. That day more than a thousand anti-pirate vigilantes, paid by the Music Publishers' Association, swaggered onto the streets of London, searching for and destroying illegitimate editions of "Stars and Stripes Forever," "Brooklyn Cake Walk," and "Pliny, Come Kiss Yo' Baby!" The goons became violent. Skulls were cracked, doors broken, sheet-music bonfires set. Millions of songs were seized. In addition to vigilantes, the publishers hired lawyers, who sued Fisher & Co. in 1905. Testimony was lopsided. The publishers called more than fifty witnesses, Fisher & Co. zero. Willetts was sentenced to nine months in the clink. The light sentence annoyed the publishers, who had gone to considerable expense to prosecute him. Nonetheless, the trial was successful [because] by showing the teeth in the new copyright law, the publishers "scared off" the great majority of music black-marketeers. The pirate trade quickly collapsed, done in by a determined blend of legislation, litigation, and leg-breaking.

Today's music industry, like yesterday's, initially faced unfavorable laws; like yesterday's industry, it induced the legislature to revamp them and then went after infringers with a legal club. The first attempt to prosecute someone who released copyrighted material on the Internet, in 1994, collapsed embarrassingly when the judge threw out the charges—existing case law said that infringement had to be associated with financial gain, and the material had been given away. The No Electronic Theft Act, passed in 1997, closed this loophole. The Digital Millennium Copyright Act, passed in 1998, further strengthened the industry's hand—it banned attempts to circumvent copy protection. With the help of what Edgar Bronfman, of Universal, recently described as a "Roman legion or two of Wall Street lawyers," the Recording Industry Association of America has for the past two years sued or threatened to sue Web sites that contain copyrighted songs, universities that allow students to trade tunes on their computer networks, consumer-electronics companies that produce digital music players, online-music services that lack proper licenses, and, of course, Napster. A&M Records, et al. v. Napster, an RIAA-backed suit by seventeen record companies, was filed in December, ninety-four years after charges were brought against Fisher & Co. . . . .

Joe Average Becomes Jane Hacker

Arguably, the person most responsible for the present turmoil in the recording industry is an Italian engineer named Leonardo Chiariglione, and he is responsible only by accident. The director of the television research division at Telecom Italia's Centro Studi e Laboratori Telecommunicazioni, the Italian equivalent of the old Bell Labs, Chiariglione led the development of a standard means for converting recorded sound into digital form, which is now called MP3. The tale of the development of MP3 explains both how the music industry stumbled into its current predicament and why technophiles believe that the industry's attempts to control online copying are doomed to failure.

30   The International Organization for Standardization, based in Switzerland, is the world's premier standards body, establishing conventions for everything from the dimensions of letter paper to the size of screw threads. Chiariglione approached the organization—and a sister agency, the International Electrotechnical Commission, also based in Switzerland—about putting together a working group to arrive at standards for digital video and audio, both of which were on the horizon. The Moving Picture Experts Group (MPEG) met for the first time in May of 1988. Twenty-five people attended. Not one of them was from a record company. "Some of them came later, when the group became larger," Chiariglione says. "But at the time—well, nobody knew, you see. Nobody, I promise you, had any idea of what this would mean to music."

Converting pictures and sounds into zeros and ones creates files that are too large for most computers and networks to work with easily: a single second of music from a compact disc takes up 175,000 bytes. Researchers have invented methods of shrinking this information without losing its identifying qualities, much as shorthand shrinks written language while leaving its sense intact. Codecs, as these methods are called, take advantage of quirks in human perception. (Codec stands for "coder-decoder.") Because the ear can discern certain frequencies more clearly than others in particular situations, codecs can slice away the tones people don't perceive, decreasing the size of music files without greatly affecting the sound. "You'd think that people would notice if you pulled out half the sounds in their favorite music, but they don't," says David Weekly, an independent programmer who is writing an online book about digital audio. . . .

To show industries how to use the codec, MPEG cobbled together a free sample program that converted music into MP3 files. The demonstration software created poor-quality sound, and Fraunhofer did not intend that it be used. The software's "source code"—its underlying instructions—was stored on an easily accessible computer at the University of Erlangen, from which it was downloaded by one SoloH, a hacker in the Netherlands (and, one assumes, a Star Wars fan). SoloH revamped the source code to produce software that converted compact-disc tracks into music files of acceptable quality. (The conversion is known as "ripping" a CD.)

This single unexpected act undid the music industry. Other hackers joined in, and the work passed from hand to hand in an ad hoc electronic swap meet, each coder tinkering with the software and passing on the resulting improvements to the rest. Within two years an active digital-music subculture was shoehorning MP3 sites into obscure corners of the Net, all chockablock with songs—copyrighted songs—that had previously been imprisoned on compact discs. . . .

"The sharing may be technically illegal, but there's no way to stop it," says Whitney Broussard, a lawyer at the music-law firm of Selverne, Mandelbaum & Mintz. "Already the entire body of important musical works is in compact-disc format—unencrypted digital copies" that are freely convertible into MP3 files. MP3 itself can't be retrofitted to enforce copyrights, because today's ripping and playing software wouldn't be able to comprehend the add-ons. Similarly, CD players can't readily be changed to make copying impossible; indeed, a trial release in Germany of copy-protected CDs foundered early this year, because some consumers couldn't get them to play. As for halting the spread of MP3s ripped from CDs, Broussard says, "it's too late." . . .

35   [In 2000] Microsoft released a new version of Windows Media Audio, an equivalent to MP3 that the company touted as secure: songs in the format could be restricted to a single personal computer. Within hours of its release

somebody with nothing else to do slammed together a program, archly called "unfuck," that intercepted the decrypted data and stripped away the restrictions. Hours after that the program was available on Web sites around the world, from one of which I recently downloaded it. "If your stuff is on everybody's desktop, people will try to tinker with it," Gene Hoffman says. "You're giving the whole world a chance to crack your cryptography on machines that inherently make that easy to do."

These difficulties are not restricted to music. Contemplating the apparently ineluctable growth of the global network, book publishers and film studios see themselves rushing toward a digital dilemma of their own. Like the record labels, they recognize the overwhelming speed, ease, and cheapness of online distribution. At the same time, they fear—with good reason—that what has happened to the music industry will happen to them. On March 14 Stephen King electronically released a novella, Riding the Bullet, in a format that was readable only by using designated electronic books or special software. Just three days later a plaintext version appeared on a Web site in Switzerland. Remarkably, the crackers troubled themselves to break the code even though Amazon and Barnes & Noble were offering the authorized version at no charge.

Film studios use what is called the Content Scrambling System to encrypt digital video discs. Last year at least two groups of European hackers raced to break the CSS encryption; the better software, DeCSS, was released on the Web in October. It was used by yet another band of hackers to create a new compression scheme, called DivX, that can shrink feature films to 600 megabytes—small enough to be traded, Napster-style, by people with ultra-fast connections. The software, which is distributed from a Web site ostensibly based on a group of islands in the Indian Ocean, is hard to use, unreliable, and popular; a week after the release of Mission: Impossible 2, I found DivX copies on the Net. Meanwhile, the movie industry has been trying to suppress not only the hundreds of Web sites around the world that host unauthorized software but also the much larger group of sites that link to them. Because new DeCSS and DivX sites pop up as rapidly as the old ones are taken down, the studios are facing a grim, unwinnable contest of legal Whack-a-Mole. . . .

They're Paying Our Song

Every year Austin, Texas, hosts South by Southwest, the nation's biggest showcase for independent rock-and-roll. Hundreds of bands play in the city's scores of enjoyably scruffy bars, which are thronged by young people with the slightly dazed expression that is a side effect of shouting over noisy amplifiers. When I attended the festival this spring, I was overwhelmed by the list of bands—almost a thousand in all, most of them little-known hopefuls. I had no idea how to sort through the list for what I would like. Luckily for me, I ran into some professional music critics who allowed me to accompany them, which is how I ended up listening to the Ass Ponys late one night.

Led by a husky singer and guitarist named Chuck Cleaver, the Ponys crunched through a set of songs with whimsical lyrics about robots, astronauts, and rural suicide. At the back of the room, beneath an atmospheric shroud of cigarette smoke, was a card table stacked with copies of their most recent CD, Some Stupid With a Flare Gun. By the bar stood a tight clump of people in sleek black clothing with cell phones the size of credit cards. With their Palm hand-helds they were attempting to beam contact information at one another through the occluded air. They didn't look like local students, so I asked the bartender if he knew who they were. "Dot-commers," he said, setting down my beer with unnecessary force. . . .

40   After the show I asked Cleaver if he was concerned about the fate of the music industry in the Internet age. "You must be kidding," he said. With some resignation he recounted the sneaky methods by which three record labels had ripped off the band or consigned its music to oblivion, a subject to which he has devoted several chapters of an unpublished autobiography he offered to send me. (He had nicer things to say about his current label, Checkered Past.) Later I asked one of the music critics if Cleaver's tales of corporate malfeasance were true. More than true, I was told—they were typical. Not only is the total income from music copyright small, but individual musicians receive even less of the total than one would imagine. "It's relatively mild," Cleaver said later, "the screwing by Napster compared with the regular screwing."

Although many musicians resent it when people download their music free, most of them don't lose much money from the practice, because they earn so little from copyright. "Clearly, copyright can generate a huge amount of money for those people who write songs that become mass sellers," says Simon Frith, a rock scholar in the film-and-media department at the University of Stirling, in Scotland, and the editor of Music and Copyright (1993). But most musicians don't write multimillion-sellers. Last year, according to the survey firm Soundscan, just eighty-eight recordings—only .03 percent of the compact discs on the market—accounted for a quarter of all record sales. For the remaining 99.97 percent, Frith says, "copyright is really just a way of earning less than they would if they received a fee from the record company." Losing copyright would thus have surprisingly little direct financial impact on musicians. Instead, Frith says, the big loser would be the music industry, because today it "is entirely structured around contracts that control intellectual-property rights—control them rather ruthlessly, in fact."

Like book publishers, record labels give artists advances on their sales. And like book publishers, record labels officially lose money on their releases; they make up for the failures with the occasional huge hit and the steady stream of income from back-catalogue recordings. But there the similarity ends. The music industry is strikingly unlike book publishing or, for that matter, any other culture industry. Some Stupid With a Flare Gun, for example, contains twelve songs, all written and performed by the Ass Ponys. From this compact disc the band receives, in theory, royalties from three different sources: sales of the disc as a whole, "performance rights" for performances of each of the twelve songs (on radio or MTV, for instance), and "mechanical rights" for copies of each song made on CD, sheet music, and the like. No real equivalent of this system exists in the print world, but it's almost as if the author of a book of short stories received royalties from sales in bookstores, from reading the stories to audiences, and from printing each story in the book itself. The triple-royalty scheme is "extraordinarily, ridiculously complex," says David Nimmer, the author of the standard textbook Nimmer on Copyright. Attempts to apply the scheme to the digital realm have only further complicated matters.

As a rule, the royalty on the CD itself—typically about $1.30 per disc before various deductions—goes to performers rather than composers. After paying performers an advance against royalties, as book publishers pay writers, record labels, unlike publishers, routinely deduct the costs of production, marketing, and promotion from the performers' royalties. For important releases these costs may amount to a million dollars or more. Performers rarely see a penny of CD royalties. Unheralded session musicians and orchestra members, who are paid flat fees, often do better in the end.

Paying back the record label is even more difficult than it sounds, because contracts are rife with idiosyncratic legal details that effectively reduce royalty rates. As a result, many, perhaps most, musicians on big record labels accumulate a debt that the labels—unlike book publishers—routinely charge against their next projects, should they prove to be successful. According to Whitney Broussard, the music lawyer, musicians who make a major-label pop-music compact disc typically must sell a million copies to receive a royalty check. "A million units is a platinum record," he says. "A platinum record means you've broken even—maybe." Meanwhile, he adds, "the label would have grossed almost eleven million dollars at this point, netting perhaps four million."

45   As a standard practice labels demand that musicians surrender the copyright on the compact disc itself. "When you look at the legal line on a CD, it says 'Copyright 1976 Atlantic Records' or 'Copyright 1996 RCA Records'" the singer Courtney Love explained in a speech to a music convention in May. "When you look at a book, though, it'll say something like 'Copyright 1999 Susan Faludi' or 'David Foster Wallace.' Authors own their books and

license them to publishers. When the contract runs out, writers get their books back. But record companies own our copyrights forever."

Strikingly, the companies own the recordings even if the artists have fully compensated the label for production and sales costs. "It's like you pay off the mortgage and the bank still owns the house," says Timothy White, the editor-in-chief of Billboard. "Everything is charged against the musician— recording expenses, marketing and promotional costs—and then when it's all paid off, they still own the record." Until last November artists could take back their recordings after thirty-five years. But then, without any hearings, Congress passed a bill with an industry-backed amendment that apparently strips away this right. "It's unconscionable," White says. "It's big companies making a naked grab of intellectual property from small companies and individuals."

The other two kinds of royalties—performance and mechanical rights— go to songwriters and composers. (The Ass Ponys receive these because they write their own songs; Frank Sinatra did not, because he sang mostly jazz standards.) Songwriters receive performance-rights payments when their compositions are played in public—executed in concert, beamed over the radio, sprayed over supermarket shoppers from speakers in the ceiling. Individual payments are calculated through a complex formula that weighs audience size, time of day, and length of the composition. In the United States the money is collected primarily by Broadcast Music Incorporated and the American Society for Composers, Authors, and Publishers, known respectively as BMI and ASCAP. Mechanical rights derive in this country from the Copyright Act of 1909, which reversed earlier court rulings that piano rolls and phonograph recordings were not copies of music. Today the recording industry pays composers 7.55 cents for every track on every copy of every CD, prerecorded cassette, and vinyl record stamped out by the manufacturing plants. The fee is collected by the Harry Fox Agency, a division of the National Music Publishers' Association, which represents about 23,000 music publishers. In 1998 performance and mechanical rights totaled about $2.5 billion.

Because U.S. labels, publishers, and collecting societies do not break down their cash flow, it is difficult to establish how much of the $2.5 billion American songwriters actually receive. But in an impressively thorough study Ruth Towse, an economist at Erasmus University, in Rotterdam, ascertained that in Britain from 1989 to 1995 the average annual payment to musicians was $112.50. Musicians in Sweden and Denmark made even less. Although the system in the United States is different, the figures, as Towse drily observed, "do not suggest that performers' right considerably improves performers' earnings."

A few composers—the members of Metallica, for instance, who perform their own songs—do extremely well by copyright. But even some of the country's most noted performers and composers are not in this elect group. Among them was Charles Mingus, who wrote and played such now-classic jazz pieces as "Goodbye Pork Pie Hat" and "Better Git It in Your Soul." According to Sue Mingus, his widow and legatee, "Charles used to joke that he wouldn't have recognized a royalty check if it walked in the door." She meant royalties on record sales; Mingus did receive checks for performance and mechanical rights. But when I asked what Mingus's life would have been like without copyright, she said, "It would have been harder. He took copyright very seriously. But what kept him going financially was that he toured constantly." Few rock performers have this alternative: their equipment is so bulky and expensive that their shows can lose money even if every seat is sold. . . .

50   At present the music industry is dominated by what are called the five majors: Warner, Sony, EMI, BMG, and Universal. (Warner and EMI have announced plans to combine; the joint label will become part of the merged America Online and Time Warner.) The majors control about 85 percent of the market for recorded music in this country. They do this by routinely performing the paradoxical task of discovering and marketing musicians with whom a worldwide body of consumers can form relationships that feel individual and genuine. "You want to fill up stadiums with people who think that Bruce Springsteen, the voice of working-class America, is speaking only to them," says David Sanjek, the archives director at BMI and a co-author, with his late father, of American Popular Music Business in the 20th Century (1991). "The labels are often incredibly good at doing this."

Music critics frequently sneer at the practice of manufacturing pop concoctions like Britney Spears and the Backstreet Boys. But in this way the labels helped to create Elvis, the Beatles, and the Supremes—musicians who embodied entire eras in three-minute tunes. As Moshe Adler, an economist at Columbia University, has argued, even listeners who grumble about the major-label music forced on them are probably better off than if they had to sort through the world's thousands of aspiring musicians on their own. But this benefit to consumers comes at a cost to musicians. Records that are hits around the world inevitably draw listeners' attention from music by local artists that might be equally pleasing. "The money is made by reducing diversity," Adler says. . . .

Fear and Greed

When I was younger, I was briefly in a rock band. Some of its members were not completely devoid of musical talent; alas, I was not one of them. As often occurs in such situations, I was assigned to the drums. Eventually the other members decided that having no ability to keep a beat was even more of a handicap on the drums than on other instruments, and I was replaced by someone who also couldn't play drums but at least had the potential to learn.

   I recently obtained a tape we made in performance. Because I wanted to learn more about digital music, I decided to make a project of converting the songs on the tape into MP3 files. After considerable fussing I was able to listen to my younger self on the tinny little speakers that flank my monitor. The experience failed to provoke regret about the road not taken. In fact, it provoked little thought of any kind until a few days later, when I loaded up Gnutella.

   Gnutella is software that (again!) is being developed by a loose band of young people with a lot of spare time. (The name Gnutella comes from a combination of "Nutella," a thick chocolate-hazelnut spread presumably favored by the program's developers, and the GNU Project, a free-software group.) Like Napster, Gnutella allows people to search one another's hard drives for pieces of music; unlike Napster, Gnutella lets its users swap pictures, movies, and texts.

55   After the Gnutella window came up on my screen, I saw that its users were sharing about a million megabytes' worth of pictures, sounds, programs, and texts. And then, to my shock, I saw that somebody was trying to copy my band's music.

   Because the last thing I wanted was to reveal this stuff to the world, I quickly slammed the program shut. After double-checking to ensure that Gnutella wasn't running, I sat in my chair, somewhat unnerved. I was safe—should I run for public office, my opponent would not be able to use the music to ridicule me in attack ads. But who had tried to copy it, and how had they found it? A few minutes later I figured it out. I had stuck the MP3s in a directory with other MP3s. Because I couldn't remember the names of the songs we played, I had awarded whimsical names to the computer files of those songs. Some of the names were variants on the names of famous rock tunes. A Gnutella user searching for the originals had come across mine and tried to download one of them.

   In this small way I walked in Lars Ulrich's shoes. The impetus for Metallica's legal attack on Napster was the circulation on the service of rough drafts of "I Disappear," a single from the soundtrack of *Mission: Impossible 2*. With the volatile promiscuity of the Internet, unfinished versions had been copied hundreds of times, depriving the group of control over its own work and, possibly, of some sales. When the musicians complained, they were astounded by the angry reaction. Trying to stop what they viewed as the forced publication of private material, Metallica—rebellious rock-and-rollers for twenty years—suddenly found themselves accused of censorship and toadying to corporate America. . . .

   "Why would people pay for music if they get it for free?" [Ulrich] asked outside Napster. "We're very lucky—we have all the money we need. But what about the musicians who are just getting started? How are they going to survive?"

The back and forth exemplifies the "fear and greed" that drive the struggle over online music, according to P. Bernt Hugenholtz, of the Institute for Information Law, at the University of Amsterdam. Publishers of all kinds of material fear the unpredictability of the Internet, he argued at a conference in London last year. Their apprehension leads to campaigns of "aggressive, almost paranoid lobbying for increased copyright protection in the digital environment." In turn, the lobbying scares the digital elite, who fear that "the Internet, once hailed as the ultimate vehicle of democracy and empowerment, will succumb to the evil forces of monopoly and capitalism."

60   For "content industries," fear turns directly to greed with the realization that digital technology provides opportunities to extract money from consumers in ways never before attempted. Consider Stephen King's electronic novella, Riding the Bullet. Not only was it "printed" and distributed for next to nothing, but in theory the book could not be copied from one computer to another—owners of Riding the Bullet could not lend it to their friends. Editors often guess that four or five people read every "hard" copy of most popular books and magazines; digital technology offers the captivating possibility of forcing the freeloaders to pay up.

Users feel greed too. Every person to whom I introduced Napster, Gnutella, Scour, and the other services was tempted to use them. (Because I make my living from copyright, I tried to restrict my downloading to music I already own or that is out of print. Although that is probably illegal, I figured the artists wouldn't mind.) At first I thought that most adults would never put up with the uncertainties of illicit downloads—the bad rips, the cut-off transmissions, and the defects of the MP3 codec itself, which are distinctly audible in sustained pure notes. But according to a survey funded by the Pew Charitable Trusts, more than 40 percent of all music-grabbers are thirty or older. Indeed, it is hard to imagine asking people to forgo the twin pleasures of downloading anything they want without paying and coming up with intellectual justifications for doing it. "Information wants to be free." "The labels are thieves." "Everything's going to the Net anyway."

Seeing itself as under threat, each side lashes out at the other. Record labels, invoking the image of the suffering genius in the garret, speak of the need to protect artists. But the copyrights involved are all too often owned by enormous companies. Users, too, see themselves as powerless victims of corporate over-reaching. But one of the features of the Internet, as the development of MP3 shows, is that small groups of people can greatly disturb large organizations. . . .

Today Internet service providers are shielded from responsibility for the traffic they bear. Just as my telephone company is not legally liable if I make criminal plans on the phone, my Internet service provider is not implicated if I trade unauthorized music on the Net. But if providers were required by law to monitor actively for the use of Gnutella, people would be less likely to use it. "If the police started arresting people and seizing their computers," says Robert Kohn, a co-founder of EMusic.com, "music on the Internet would not seem quite so free." Worried about the future of free speech, a computer activist in London named Ian Clarke is leading an effort to create a network called FreeNet that would guarantee anonymity, no matter what. But it, too, could conceivably be prohibited, and if it comes to anything, surely we will see attempts to do so. The Net, Bronfman promised in July, "will not be able to survive if it becomes a haven for illegal activity. Copyrights must be protected online." . . .

2500 Years of Rhetoric: A Quick Review

Classical Greece: Birthplace of Rhetoric

From your readings in earlier chapters, you have seen that most of the earliest rhetoricians were Greek philosophers, many of whom lived in the city-state of Athens. Fourth-century BCE Greece was no world power: two of the most dominant political systems of this time were the Persian Empire, founded by Alexander the Great, and the Egyptian monarchy of the Ptolemies. Why, then, would a communication system that would have vast influence in the Western world for more than 2500 years develop in such a small, out-of-the-way area?

What differentiated the political system of Athens from other systems of its time was its status as a democracy—although modern thinkers would consider it quite un-democratic. Fourth-century Athenians kept slaves and relegated women to the responsibilities of the home and family, but free Athenian men argued issues and voted in the assembly, giving them a reason to develop their skills as speakers. Rhetoricians such as Socrates, Aristotle, and Gorgias were honored and paid well to teach the young men of Athens how to take their place in the political society of the time. (The particular contributions of Socrates, Plato, and Aristotle are covered in earlier chapters here.)

Roman Influence on Rhetoric

When the Roman Empire enveloped Greece, Romans adopted much of Greek culture, including its art, religion, and poetry. Roman rhetoricians also studied the earlier Greek rhetoricians, whose works they adapted to their own needs.

Chief among the earliest Roman rhetoricians was Marcus Tullius Cicero (106–43 BCE), best known for *De Oratore*. While Cicero's work was based largely on Aristotle, he strongly urged that young rhetors study a wide variety of subjects to give them foundations for their arguments, and Cicero is thus credited for establishing the liberal arts as the basis for education. You can thank Cicero (or not) for the general education ("GenEd") requirements that are probably required by your college or university. Cicero also refined Aristotle's ideas about the arrangement of arguments, and his six-part scheme for designing speeches is covered in Chapter 4 of this text.

Marcus Fabius Quintilianus (c. 35–95), known as Quintilian, wrote the *Institutio Oratoria*, the most complete Latin text on the training of young men of its time. This book can be considered the first textbook on rhetoric—in fact, *Rhetoric Revival*, as well as the many rhetoric texts written in the last 2000 years, owes much to the *Institutio Oratoria*. Quintilian believed that in order to be a good orator, a speaker (at that time, male) must have a strong moral character; therefore, parents, according to Quintilian, needed to train their children in moral behavior and good speech very early in life. The *Institutio Oratoria* established a curriculum for teaching young men from the primary grades through what we would now consider high school, establishing an educational system that was prevalent throughout the Middle Ages and beyond.

The Middle Ages and Beyond: Rhetoric Redefined

The Middle Ages has been defined as the period of time between the fall of the Roman Empire (450 CE) and the beginning of the Renaissance (c. 1400). The emergence of Christianity as the dominant cultural force in Western Europe during this time had a profound effect on rhetoric. All knowledge was believed to be contained in the words of the Bible, so the rhetorical art of invention—the generation of ideas—was pretty much abandoned. The rhetoric of the Middle Ages was based on the teachings of St. Augustine (353–430), who believed that rhetoric should be used primarily to promote a Christian life, and students during the Middle Ages studied rhetoric to learn how to write letters and prepare sermons.

But a revival of interest in the classical Greek and Roman rhetoricians flowered during the Renaissance (c.1400–1650), when artists, writers, and philosophers turned again to the earlier, classical thinkers for inspiration. Desiderius Erasmus (c. 1469–1536) wrote a popular and influential textbook, *On Copia of Words and Ideas,* in which he stressed the importance of writing, grammar, and the imitation of classical texts. His emphasis on free thought challenged the Middle Ages' reliance on Biblical texts and introduced a more humanist concept of education.

The Age of Enlightenment, which occurred during the seventeenth and eighteenth centuries, introduced science and literature into rhetorical thought. Peter Ramus (1515–1572) and Francis Bacon (1561–1626) condensed the study of rhetoric in different ways. Ramus insisted that invention and arrangement belonged to the area of logic, not rhetoric (confining rhetoric to the study of grammar and style), while Bacon argued that reason was more important than imagination—i.e., content was more important than style. Meanwhile, Hugh Blair (1718–1800), in his *Lectures on Rhetoric and Belles-Lettres,* lined rhetoric up with literature and taught that rhetoric should be used to achieve style, taste, and beauty in writing, a combination he termed "the sublime."

Contemporary Rhetoric

The "New Rhetoric," as exemplified by Kenneth Burke (1897–1993), connects rhetoric to such contemporary fields of study as psychology and anthropology. While the "New Rhetoric" recognizes persuasion as its goal, the central idea behind Burke's rhetoric is cooperation based on identification: that is, cooperation achieved through understanding and relating to an opposing position. The mediated argument, discussed in Chapter 4, is based on Burke; it relies on finding common ground and developing a solution that takes into account the values of people on both sides of an argument.

This sense of collaboration and consideration of diverse values was further developed through the work of Helene Cixous (b. 1937) and Julia Kristeva (b. 1941), who asserted that these qualities have always been the hallmark of women's communication styles. Cixous and Kristeva sought to develop a rhetoric that sees women's more passive and cooperative ways of communicating not as a disadvantage, but as a form of rhetoric as potent as the more dominant "male" patterns of communication. Other theorists, as well, have sought to expand the scope of rhetoric, including Henry Louis Gates, Jr. (b. 1950), whose study of Black Vernacular English references its distinctive rhetorical style.

This review of rhetoric would not be complete without a reference to Edward P. J. Corbett (1919–1998), whose *Classical Rhetoric for the Modern Student* has done more to revitalize the study of rhetoric in higher education than perhaps any other book in the twentieth century. Faced with preparing literature and composition courses for his post-World War II students, Corbett found no good methods for analyzing writing, a first step that he recognized was essential in learning how to write. While in the library, he happened upon a copy of Blair's *Lectures on Rhetoric and Belles-Lettres,* which piqued his interest in the classical authors Blair cited.

Classical Rhetoric for the Modern Student was the result. It was followed by a number of later rhetoric-readers written by other writers, all of which aim to give students the practical rhetorical skills they need to become effective communicators in their jobs and their lives. One of those books is in your hands right now—and this is your chance to use rhetoric to make you a better thinker and a more effective writer.

Additional Readings

Bizzelle, Patricia & Bruce Herzberg. *The Rhetorical Tradition: Readings from Classical Times to the Present.* Boston: Bedford Books of St. Martin's Press, 1990.

Corbett, Edward P. J. *Classical Rhetoric for the Modern Student, 3rd. ed.* New York: Oxford University Press, 1990.

Covino, William A. & David A. Jolliffe. *Rhetoric: Concepts, Definitions, Boundaries.* Boston: Allyn and Bacon, 1995.

Crowley, Sharon. *Ancient Rhetorics for Contemporary Students.* Boston: Allyn and Bacon, 1994.

Style

"Why did my paper only get a C? I don't see any errors marked on it. I edited it carefully. I know I followed all the directions on the assignment sheet. I don't understand."

If you have ever had reason to say something like that, and particularly if you have received comments on your papers such as "not college level" or "work on syntax," you may have overlooked a very important aspect of writing—**style.**

Defining Rhetoric

Style: selection and arrangement of words and sentences in a piece of writing.

In earlier chapters, we discussed four of the Canons of Rhetoric: *invention,* or idea generation; *dispositio,* or arrangement; *pronuntiatio,* or delivery; and *memorare,* or memory. Style, or *elocutio,* is the third of the five Canons of Rhetoric. Realizing that in persuasion, how you say something is almost as important as what you say, Aristotle devoted a whole book of the *Rhetoric* to style. A later work, the *Rhetorica ad Herrenium* (attributed by some to Cicero), discussed three levels of style: the plain, for teaching; the middle, for pleasing audiences; and the grand, for moving audiences.

It makes sense that your college instructors expect your writing to reflect a more mature style of writing than your high school teachers may have found acceptable. To help you develop a college-level writing style, Appendix II focuses on vocabulary development, sentence combining, and paragraph arrangement.

Vocabulary Development

Because of England's long history of being conquered and conquering, the English language has developed an enormous *lexicon,* or vocabulary. English gets the bulk of its vocabulary from Old German and Norman French, but it includes many words derived from Latin, Greek, and several other languages. In English, many words have *synonyms,* words that share meaning.

Still, many *linguists* (those who study language) would argue that no words are completely synonymous. For example, you might be flattered if someone referred to you as being *slim, slender,* or *thin.* You would be less flattered if they referred to you as *skinny, bony,* or *gaunt.* And you might be insulted if they called you *emaciated, frail,* or *anorexic.* All words have **denotations,** or literal meanings, which you might think of as their dictionary meanings. But many words also have **connotations**—slight differences in meaning from their synonyms—that could make the difference between a compliment and an insult. Understanding the connotations of words can give your writing a nuanced, mature style.

Defining Rhetoric

Denotation: the literal, or dictionary meaning, of a word.
Connotation: a secondary, shaded meaning of a word.

For example, you might describe a character in a narrative you are writing as "old." But if you described him as "mature," "senior," or "elderly" instead, your readers would have a slightly different understanding of his age. If you wanted his age to connote wisdom or dignity, better synonyms might be "venerable" or "distinguished." And if you saw his advanced age as detrimental or limiting, you might refer to him as "senile" or "decrepit." Any of those synonyms would give a clearer, more nuanced idea of your character to readers than would the word "old." What would be the difference in your readers' perceptions of a character described as "bright" or "cunning"? As "perceptive" or "shrewd"? As "intelligent" or "brainy"?

Synonyms can be found in dictionaries or thesauruses, and you should equip your writing area with some good copies of both, but most of us would not care to carry a dictionary or thesaurus with us every day. Still, developing your vocabulary should be a *daily* process. You can become a better wordsmith simply by becoming more aware of the words you hear or read every day. Think about the words you encounter. Consider them in context. Compare them to their synonyms. Look up any that you do not know or that are unclear. And *use* words that are new to you in your speech and writing—only then will they become part of your working vocabulary.

At the same time, think in terms of "degrees" of words that you use for actions, because these degrees can range from basic (nonspecific) to precise. If you want your writing to be descriptive, detailed, and vivid for readers, move up from "first degree" words to at least second- or third-degree ones instead, as shown in the examples below:

First degree: She came over and told us to leave.

Second degree: She walked over and ordered us to leave.

Third degree: She stormed over and demanded that we leave.

First degree: She made us mad.

Second degree: Her order made us angry.

Third degree: Her demand infuriated us.

REAL RHETORIC APPENDIX II-a
Connotations

In each category of terms below, rank the synonymous words in order of their desirability as personal attributes, using "1" for the most desirable. Then compare your listings with those of a classmate to see whether your connotations agree.

Terms of pride: dignity, insolence, conceit, self-respect, vanity, arrogance

Terms of courage: audacity, bravery, rashness, recklessness, boldness, daring, foolhardiness, nerve, guts, daring

Terms of obedience: loyalty, compliance, acquiescence, servility, devotion, obsequiousness, tractability, submission

REAL RHETORIC APPENDIX II-b
Vocabulary Note

Many English words change their parts of speech by adding or removing suffixes. One way to improve your vocabulary is by developing awareness of this process. All of the words in the **Real Rhetoric, "Connotations,"** box above are nouns. See how many you can change to adjectives by adding, deleting, or changing suffixes. For example, a person who has *obedience* is *obedient*. A person who has *dignity* is *dignified*. (Not sure how one of the nouns can be changed? By looking above and below the word in a dictionary, you will find the possibilities—in fact, sometimes several of them.)

Sentence Combining

One way to elevate your writing style is by combining short, choppy sentences. This not only improves your *syntactic maturity,* or the maturity of your sentence structure, it also helps to eliminate **wordiness,** the addition of excess words that convey no added meaning.

Defining Rhetoric

Wordiness: employing an excessive number of words that convey no added meaning.

The paragraph below uses very short, "one point at a time" sentences that do not connect with each other clearly. As a result, you may find yourself re-reading a few of the sentences just to be sure you understand what they are saying in relation to the one(s) before them.

> The essay I chose to analyze was written by Jennifer. Her essay has a strong emotional appeal to the audience. The opening paragraph is a catchy one. She starts out with the familiar words of a parent, "Jimmy, stop. No, Jimmy. Jimmy, I said *stop*." She did a wonderful job of wording this introduction. This introduction does two things. First, it leaves the reader wondering where she is going with this. Second, it brings reality to the paper because most people have either heard this from a parent, or are guilty of saying the same thing as a parent.

Now take a look as we reverse-engineer the paragraph by simply breaking each of the lines apart into a list. Can you see the need for transitions/connections between ideas more clearly?

- The essay I chose to analyze was written by Jennifer.
- Her essay has a strong emotional appeal to the audience.
- The opening paragraph is a catchy one.
- She starts out with the familiar words of a parent, "Jimmy, stop. No, Jimmy. Jimmy, I said *stop*."
- She did a wonderful job of wording this introduction.
- This introduction does two things.
- First, it leaves the reader wondering where she is going with this.
- Second, it brings reality to the paper because most people have either heard this from a parent, or are guilty of saying the same thing as a parent.

The list lets you see the pattern of fragmentation that comes from such short statements. Now here is an example of how the paragraph might read when it is revised for transitions and connections:

> The essay I chose to analyze, by Jennifer, makes an emotional appeal to the audience by starting with the familiar words of a parent, "Jimmy, stop. No, Jimmy. Jimmy, I said *stop*." This opening technique makes readers wonder where the author is going with this, and it brings reality into the paper because most people have either heard this from a parent or are guilty of saying the same thing as parents themselves.

Clearly, the author's insights about Jennifer's essay and its opening techniques are good ones—they just need to be "unburied" from the graveyard of dead-end sentences. With a clearer, smoother, more integrated style, any writer's ideas are much more effective in showing what that writer knows.

REAL RHETORIC APPENDIX II-c

Sentence Combining

Combine the sentences in this short narrative to raise syntactic complexity and eliminate wordiness. Be creative with your combinations, as more than one way exists to connect many of the passages.

It was a dark and stormy night. Michael was alone in the house. He was playing Resident Evil Outbreak on his Playstation. His character was David, the plumber. Suddenly the lights went out. He was frustrated. He had been about to enter the fifth level for the first time. He knew that the power would come back on shortly. He stretched out on the sofa.

A few minutes later he heard strange noises outside. He got up to investigate. He opened the front door slightly. He felt a hard push from the outside. The push knocked him to the floor. He heard a rush of footsteps. He looked up. Dozens of zombies were rushing through the door. The zombies were enormous. The zombies were ugly.

The zombies started trashing his apartment. They smashed his television and computer to the floor. They tore apart his sofa. They destroyed his Playstation. He wanted to object. Instead he decided to escape. He got up. He tiptoed to the open door. He was nearly outside. One of the zombies saw him and mumbled something to the others. They all started chasing Michael.

Michael ran in the pouring rain. There were many cracks of thunder. He ran fast. He ran for a long time. The zombies were chasing him. He saw a large building far in the distance. He did not recognize the building. He ran to it. It was an Umbrella Corp. research facility. He ran through an open door. He found a flamethrower on the floor. He picked it up. It was broken. He could see zombies just outside the door.

Michael noticed his repair kit. The zombies were rushing through the door. He . . .

(Finish the story in three or four sentences of your own.)

REAL RHETORIC APPENDIX II-d

Combining Your Own Sentences

Check your drafts or returned papers for sentences to combine. Not all sentences should be combined—sometimes a short sentence is needed for emphasis or to break up a too-repetitive rhythm of longer sentences. But if your writing contains short, choppy sentences with excess words that do not convey any additional meaning, use a variety of the sentence combining methods discussed above to revise them.

The following sentence constructions are all good opportunities for sentence combining:

1. Sentences introduced by the expressions "it is," "it was," "there were," and "there are":
    a. It was a beautiful spring morning. I decided to plant some daffodils.
    On a beautiful spring morning, I decided to plant some daffodils.
    b. There are fourteen children in the class. All the children like to solve equations.
    All fourteen children in the class like to solve equations.

2. Sentences in which the object of the first is the subject of the second:
    a. He threw the ball to the child. The child threw it into the river.
    He threw the ball to the child who threw it into the river.

3. Sentences in which subjects or verbs are repeated:
    a. Amy did well on the history test. She also did well on her physics test.
    Amy did well on both her history and physics tests.
    b. A woman lived in the old brick house. Her six children lived in the house with her.
    A woman and her six children lived in the old brick house.
    c. In my junior year, I met a great guy named Dan. Dan not only treated me well, but he treated my father with respect, too.
    In my junior year, I met a great guy named Dan who treated me well and showed my father respect.

4. Sentences that can become modifying phrases:
    a. Juan checked his parachute and headed for the open hatch. He feared for his life.
    Fearing for his life, Juan checked his parachute and headed for the open hatch.

"I Was Delighted . . . "

In *On Copia of Words and Ideas,* Desiderius Erasmus, perhaps the most famous Renaissance rhetorician, demonstrated how a simple sentence like "I was delighted to receive your letter" could be restated in many ways. Erasmus' exercise is a good way to build both a stronger vocabulary and greater syntactic skills. For our examples below, we will make just one small change to reflect a changing culture: the letter becomes an e-mail message.

- You could, for example, restate the sentence by changing only the vocabulary:
    - *I was thrilled to receive your message.*
    - *I was delighted to get your message.*
    - *I was delighted to receive your e-mail.*

REAL RHETORIC APPENDIX II-e
"I Was Delighted to Receive Your Letter"

Using all of the methods listed above, restate the sentence, "I Was Delighted to Receive Your E-mail Message," ten times, without duplicating any of the sample sentences. Then compare your restated sentences against a classmate's—do all of the syntactical changes between the two lists work grammatically? Which ones are the best?

- Or you could restate the sentence by changing the syntax:
  - *Receiving your message delighted me.*
  - *To receive your message was a delight.*
- You could add literary elements, such as similes, to the sentence.
  - *I was as delighted as a child at Christmas to receive e-mail from you.*
- Or you could use two or more of the processes listed above.
  - *Receiving e-mail from you made me feel like a child at Christmas.*

As a class exercise, our students have often produced as many as two hundred ways to restate Erasmus' sentence—much to their amazement. Now it is your turn to try.

Paragraph Arrangement

When you read about arrangement (*dispositio*) in Chapter 4, you considered how the carefully thought-out arrangement of ideas and paragraphs leads to the development of effective arguments. But the arrangement of sentences in paragraphs is also important. Notice how poor sentence arrangement makes this paragraph difficult to read:

> Americans are being encouraged to pursue more healthful lifestyles. Nutritionists promote a daily diet that includes a variety of grains, particularly whole grains, and a number of fruits and vegetables. One of the most important factors in assuring good health is a proper diet. In addition, they provide needed fiber, vitamins, and other nutrients. Eating more whole grains, fruits, and vegetables can lead to a better, more healthful life. These foods do not add saturated fat and cholesterol or processed sugars and salt to the diet.

The paragraph contains *subordinated* ideas, or ideas that elaborate previous ideas. But the ideas are not arranged in a subordinated manner. The following paragraph arranges the sentences in their subordinated sequence:

Americans are being encouraged to pursue more healthful lifestyles.

- One of the most important factors in assuring good health is a proper diet.
  - Nutritionists promote a daily diet that includes a variety of grains, particularly whole grains, and a number of fruits and vegetables.
    - These foods do not add saturated fat and cholesterol or processed sugars and salt to the diet.
    - In addition, they provide needed fiber, vitamins, and other nutrients.
- Eating more whole grains, fruits, and vegetables can lead to a better, more healthful life.

The bullets illustrate the way in which the sentences subordinate. The second sentence elaborates the first (or base) sentence, the third elaborates the second, etc. Sequencing sentences so that subordinated ideas follow their base ideas leads to paragraphs that are more easily understood.

But as you saw in the opening paragraph about Jennifer's essay earlier, not all paragraphs follow subordinate structure. The following paragraph illustrates a *coordinate* structure in which most sentences elaborate the first, or base sentence.

Americans are being encouraged to pursue more healthful lifestyles.

- One of the most important factors in assuring good health is a proper diet.
- Another important factor is engaging in daily physical activity.
- Moderating the intake of alcohol and eliminating nicotine and other drugs are also important steps toward good health.
- And the benefits of plenty of sleep and a reduction in stress cannot be underestimated.

Following these suggestions will lead to better health.

Still other paragraphs combine coordinate and subordinate structure:

Americans are being encouraged to pursue more healthful lifestyles.

- One of the most important factors in assuring good health is a proper diet.
  - Nutritionists promote a daily diet that includes a variety of grains, particularly whole grains, and a number of fruits and vegetables.
- Another important factor is engaging in daily physical activity.
  - Exercise routines should include both aerobics for stamina and anaerobic exercises for flexibility and strength.
- And the benefits of plenty of sleep and a reduction in stress cannot be underestimated.

Following these suggestions will lead to better health.

REAL RHETORIC APPENDIX II-f

Subordinate and Coordinate Structures

Choose one of the following base sentences and write a paragraph of at least six sentences, using both subordinate and coordinate structure. Mark each sentence as being either *coordinate* or *subordinate* to the preceding sentence.

- Succeeding in college is possible, but only if you follow some standard rules.

- Electronic technology has provided us with goods and services unimaginable to earlier generations.

- The election of 2004 has taught us a great deal about the directions we are taking as a society.

Grammatical Components of the First Sentence of "Silence"

While it has been our experience that the majority of students prefer to imitate using *semantic,* or meaning-based cues, some students prefer to base their imitations on grammatical structure. The grammatical structure of the first sentence of "Silence" follows:

On the gravel shore	(prepositional phrase)
of the canal,	(prepositional phrase)
at the far end	(prepositional phrase)
of a vacant lot	(prepositional phrase)
on the southwest side	(prepositional phrase)
of town	(prepositional phrase)
where a cement factory once stood	(dependent clause)
a ten-year-old boy sits	(independent clause)
smoking a Kool	(verbal phrase)
and fishing for steelheads	(verbal phrase/prepositional phrase)
with his dog.	(prepositional phrase)

Index

Page numbers in *italics* indicate illustrations.

K. J. | MITHALS